Professionalization

Prentice-Hall International, Inc., *London*
Prentice-Hall of Australia, Pty., Ltd., *Sydney*
Prentice-Hall of Canada, Ltd., *Toronto*
Prentice-Hall of India (Private) Ltd., *New Delhi*
Prentice-Hall of Japan, Inc., *Tokyo*

PROFESSIONALIZATION

Edited by

Howard M. Vollmer
Stanford Research Institute

and

Donald L. Mills
University of Alberta, Calgary

PRENTICE-HALL, INC., *Englewood Cliffs, New Jersey*

Editors' Introduction

. . . in my own studies I passed from the false question "Is this occupation a profession?" to the more fundamental one, "What are the circumstances in which people in an occupation attempt to turn it into a profession, and themselves into professional people?"—*Everett C. Hughes.*

A man can be many things, depending upon how you look at him. To his wife he is a husband, and to his children, a father. To his physician he is a patient, and is perhaps also a client for some attorney. In the context of the nation-state he is probably a citizen. In a broader religious context, he may be regarded as a child of God. Typically, he may think of himself as all of these things; taken together, they can be considered to define much of the human condition.

Thus man differs from the primates and other higher forms of animal life in that man is a player of many roles. Basic to all of these roles, however, is the fact that man is a worker. Although it may have occurred relatively late in the process of evolution, man, in a degree uncommon to other forms of animal life, became a "drawer of water and a hewer of wood." He does not accept his environment as he finds it; he attempts to change it through his own efforts in directions supposedly more conducive to human happiness. Hence work activities have become fundamental to all aspects of the human condition, and the kind of work that a man does has come to affect all significant aspects of his life and how he views himself. To understand men and their relations with one another, we must seek to understand their work.*

It is obvious to any casual observer that work activities in modern society are quite diversified. The nursery rhyme reminds us that there are doctors, merchants, beggarmen, and thieves. Different kinds of work vary in what it means to those who are involved in these different activities, and they vary in respect accorded by others. Those who have attempted to examine work activities systematically, however, have begun to note what appear to be common elements, themes, or processes which pervade a wide variety of what may seem at first glance to be disparate occupations. Thieves actually do have certain things in common with physicians, even though their work also differs in other important respects. In so far as we are seriously interested in understanding man as a worker, we must seek to identify and analyze

---

* See Talcott Parsons, "The Professions and Social Structure," in *Essays in Sociological Theory* rev. ed. (New York: Free Press of Glencoe, Inc., 1954), p. 34-35.

similarities as well as differences in work activities of people in varied walks of life and in different cultural contexts. The readings provided in this book are intended to stimulate our investigation in this direction.

The "educated layman" may have an interest in understanding more about his own work activities, even though this book itself may contain no specific reference to his particular occupation. (There are 57 different readings in this book which focus attention mainly upon 27 different occupational groups, while the *U.S. Dictionary of Occupational Titles* indicates that there are over 25,000 specific occupations, by title, in our modern industrialized society). Nevertheless in so far as there are certain common elements that extend through a wide variety of work activities, the layman may be able to learn some new things about his own work from reading the writings of individuals who have made careful studies and analyses of other work situations. In many areas of human experience, we find that we cannot see the "big picture" for the many details. Comparative analysis of more distant phenomena can often broaden our understanding of more familiar matters.

This is certainly not intended to be a "how to do it" book for educators or guidance counselors, but the writings on the variety of occupations represented in this book might be expected to indicate a number of basic processes that affect the policies and techniques of modern educators and guidance personnel for the guidance and preparation of youth for careers in the world of work. In addition many of us work in an organization that employs people who are more or less professional in their orientation toward their work, and this may create special management problems in companies, government agencies, and other institutions that employ professionals. There is a need, then, to examine the interaction of professionalized * occupational roles and complex organizations. There is also a need to be concerned with political and legal aspects of professionalization and the interrelation of professionals and the government. To complete the analysis, a book of this kind must also consider internal professional controls, occupational associations and colleague relations, client and public relations, and relations among professional groups.

This is a book with a point of view. Readings have been selected and interpreted in a manner that stresses the dynamics of occupational change, rather than structural differences between occupations. The book focuses attention more specifically upon the characteristics, antecedents, and social consequences of the process of professionalization as it affects a wide variety of occupations in modern society. There is a need for students of occupational dynamics to have access within one volume to a wide variety of papers on various aspects of professionalization which have been published since the time of the original formulations of Professor A. M. Carr-Saunders. Many of these papers first appeared in scattered sources that are not readily available to the student, especially in smaller libraries. Also, some readings included here are original papers not published elsewhere.

* This term has been in use for at least one-half century, as may be seen in Louis D. Brandeis, *Business—A Profession* (Boston: Small, Maynard & Co., 1914).

In selecting and editing the readings for this volume, tables and statistical evidence in support of the author's conclusions have sometimes been de-emphasized or omitted. The main purpose was to present a series of ideas—an intellectual theme and variations, so to speak—along with some illustrative evidence, rather than to present a set of conclusions. In turn, it is hoped that the ideas presented here will suggest further research to elaborate, test, confirm, and modify the ideas about professionalization presented in the readings.

The reading of a few of the selections in this volume will indicate a certain looseness, or even confusion, in the terminology used by the various authors. However, in exploratory investigations into any phenomena, a considerable degree of flexibility in the definition and use of concepts can be advantageous in the building of a science. We use concepts to sensitize us to aspects of phenomena that we might otherwise miss. Our openness to important aspects of these observed phenomena could be inhibited by premature agreement upon precise definitions of concepts. Nevertheless, consideration of the literature on professionalization has now led the editors of this volume to the point that we are prepared to suggest a more precise use of (1) *professionalization,* (2) *professionalism,* (3) *professionals,* (4) *professional groups,* and (5) *professions* in future studies and reports of studies.

In our discussion of the readings, for example, we avoid the use of the term "profession," except as an "ideal type" of occupational organization which does not exist in reality, but which provides the model of the form of occupational organization that would result if any occupational group became completely professionalized. In this way, we wish to avoid discussion of whether or not any particular occupational group is "really a profession," or not. In accord with Hughes' experience, we feel that it is much more fruitful to ask "how professionalized," or more specifically "how professionalized in certain identifiable respects" a given occupation may be at some point in time.

We suggest, therefore, that the concept of "profession" * be applied only to an abstract model of occupational organization, and that the concept of "professionalization" be used to refer to the dynamic *process* ** whereby

---

* Numerous attempts have been made to define profession. Many of these are reviewed by Morris L. Cogan in an article entitled "Toward a Definition of Profession," *Harvard Educational Review,* Vol. 23, Winter, 1953, pp. 33-50. He discerns there are "dictionary and legal definitions," "arbitrary and applied definitions," "definitions expressed in terms of power and prestige," "profession as formal association," and definitions in terms of "techniques of internal regulation." On the basis of his study of the literature he offers the following tentative definition:

> A profession is a vocation whose practice is founded upon an understanding of the theoretical structure of some department of learning or science, and upon the abilities accompanying such understanding. This understanding and these abilities are applied to the vital practical affairs of man. The practices of the profession are modified by knowledge of a generalized nature and by the accumulated wisdom and experience of mankind, which serve to correct the errors of specialism. The profession, serving the vital needs of man, considers its first ethical imperative to be altruistic service to the client. [p. 49]

** See A. M. Carr-Saunders and P. A. Wilson, *The Professions* (Oxford: The Clarendon Press, 1933), pp. 491-92, for an example of the "evolution" of occupations.

many occupations can be observed to change certain crucial characteristics in the direction of a "profession," even though some of these may not move very far in this direction. It follows that these crucial characteristics constitute specifiable criteria of professionalization.

What we have called the process of professionalization here has been frequently referred to as "professionalism," and you will see it so labeled in several of the readings in this book. However, we have similarly been led to the conclusion that it is useful to distinguish between "professionalization" and "professionalism." We would prefer to use "professionalism" to refer to an *ideology* and associated activities that can be found in many and diverse occupational groups where members aspire to professional status.* Professionalism as an ideology may induce members of many occupational groups to strive to become professional, but at the same time we can see that many occupational groups that express the ideology of professionalism in reality may not be very advanced in regard to professionalization. Professionalism may be a necessary constituent of professionalization, but professionalism is not a sufficient cause for the entire professionalization process.

Finally, we suggest that "professional groups" be used to refer to associations of colleagues in an occupational context where we observe that a relatively high degree of professionalization has taken place. "Professionals," then, are those who are considered by their colleagues to be members of professional groups.

Before embarking on the investigation of selections on professionalization, however, it should also be recognized that professionalization is not the only social process that has affected the work activities of modern man. Consequently each of the chapters in this book includes explorations of the interrelationship of professionalization and other basic social processes. For example, the process of *bureaucratization* has certainly affected most work activities significantly in modern society, for as noted earlier, most of us now work as employees of complex bureaucratic enterprises. The process of *socialization* into an occupational group encompasses background education (sometimes called pre-professional) and job-specific training (sometimes called professional) whereby the person comes to take on the skills and values of a particular occupation. The process of *acculturation* is also intimately related to work activities into which members of diverse ethnic groups have been able to move and to associate with each other in more recent times; the demand for talented labor in many of the more specialized occupations in modern society has been the occasion for the blending of individuals of different backgrounds in occupational groups that have become interethnic and indeed international in scope.

Underlying all these occupational changes—including the process of professionalization—is the basic process of *industrialization,* which has had such a great impact upon practically all facets of modern life. The emergence of the factory and associated mass production techniques caused

---

* Strauss delineates four "values" associated with professionalism: "expertise," "autonomy," "commitment," and "responsibility." See George Strauss, "Professionalism and Occupational Associations," *Industrial Relations,* II, No. 3 (May, 1963), 8-9.

the segregation of work activities from other aspects of human life which were more closely integrated with each other in pre-factory society. The rise of the factory also saw the rationalization of work and the differentiation of jobs and occupations to an extent previously unknown. For a century, or so, the shadow of the factory dominated the skyline of the newly emerging urban complex, and Karl Marx and others saw its inevitable consequences in social revolution.

In this second half of the twentieth century, however, new shadows are emerging, and their shape is as yet not clearly defined. Machines are replacing men in factories and also in offices, and what some have called "a second industrial revolution" is taking place. New and rapidly changing technologies are requiring new kinds of occupations and notable changes in old occupations. New organizational arrangements are exerting profound influences on the occupational order. Many of these changes woud appear to enhance the process of professionalization among occupational groups, as several readings in this volume will indicate. The time seems especially appropriate for investigation of "the circumstances in which people in an occupation attempt to turn it into a profession, and themselves into professional people."

H.M.V. and D.L.M.

Preface

There is ample evidence for believing that modern society has a distinctive character which sets it apart from earlier societies. It is massive in scope, highly heterogeneous in composition, endowed with intrinsic pressures toward transformation, and confronted with an ever shifting world to which it has to adjust. It may be viewed quite validly as struggling for structure. One of the most interesting, important, and ill-understood aspects of this structuring process is the growth of professionalization. Professionalization represents an indigenous effort to introduce order into areas of vocational life which are prey to the free-playing and disorganizing tendencies of a vast, mobile, and differentiated society undergoing continuous change. Professionalization seeks to clothe a given area with standards of excellence, to establish rules of conduct, to develop a sense of responsibility, to set criteria for recruitment and training, to ensure a measure of protection for members, to establish collective control over the area, and to elevate it to a position of dignity and social standing in the society.

The pursuit of such complex goals is one of the most notable trends in the shaping of modern life; the movement toward professionalization is expanding in scope and becoming more sophisticated in character. Yet the effort to achieve the goals of professionalization is fraught with difficulties and problems, and the process of professionalization in a changing world turns out to be complicated and challenging to analytical study. Many different scholars from diverse backgrounds have been intrigued with one or another aspect of this process of professionalization and have addressed their concerns with different degrees of penetration and insight. The result is a vast yet scattered literature and a literature of greatly varying merit.

The editors of the present text have done a notably fine job of carefully examining this diverse literature and selecting from it those pieces of study and analysis which lay out and illuminate the more important facets of the process of professionalization. They have added their own incisive observations—observations which have matured over years of close and reflective study of the field. The materials have been brought together in a commendable logical organization which meets nicely the analytical interests of the scholar and the pedagogical needs of the instructor. The reader will find that this volume gives an excellent coverage of the topic, a clear presentation of the knowledge in the field, and an illuminating consideration of its central problems.

HERBERT BLUMER

Acknowledgement

The editors of this volume wish to express special appreciation to Mrs. Klara Evans for many hours of extra effort in checking citations, obtaining permissions, and handling correspondence necessary for this enterprise. We are also very grateful to the authors and publishers who have permitted the use of their material herein.

Research connected with the preparation of this book of readings has been sponsored, in part, by the Behavioral Sciences Division of the Air Force Office of Scientific Research under Contract No. AF 49(638)-1028, Task No. 37707, Project No. 9778, and in part by the University of Alberta, Calgary.

Contents

3

Individuals and Professionalization, 72

4

Professional Controls, 110

5

Professional Associations and Colleague Relations, 153

9

Professionals and the Government, 295

10

Status Differences and Professionalization, 327

I

The Concept of Professionalization

The constituent elements of social life are neither "black" nor "white." Human behavior, however we want to describe it, exhibits varying shades of "gray." Max Weber, the eminent German social scientist, recognized this when he wrote about "ideal types" in the last decade of the nineteenth century and the first decade of the twentieth. He described changes in political organization as movements from "traditional" to "rational-bureaucratic" forms of administration. These he called "ideal types," or what we today might term "models," of administrative behavior. Needless to say, no individual organization is completely bureaucratic or completely traditional in its structure and behavior. The chief use of ideal types or models, then, is to describe and understand administrative behavior; they permit us to locate particular administrative patterns along a *continuum* ranging from traditional forms at one end to rational-bureaucratic patterns at the other. Insofar as the elements in the continuum are unidimensional, we can describe organization X as being more or less bureaucratic in comparison with organization Y. Having made this description, we have then established the basis for making certain predictions about the behavior of these organizational entities and about the individuals within them. Adequate description along meaningful base dimensions is the first task in the social as in the natural sciences.

Those who have studied occupational institutions in recent years have begun to establish the basis for what promises to be a useful classification scheme similar in method to Weber's use of ideal types to describe administrative organization. It focuses in large part upon the way human beings tend to organize their work activities along a career perspective, rather than the way they administer, coordinate, and control collective efforts in a particular organizational context. Individual patterns of work transcend administrative boundaries. In modern industrial society, at least, people tend to move from one job position to another, and from one employer to another. Yet there is often some continuity between

1

one job and the next; people are not randomly assigned from job to job. Whatever skills or knowledge they have acquired in one job, they carry to the next.
When they become self-conscious of this continuity, they begin to speak of a
"career." What is more, human beings tend to develop social and cultural
mechanisms to protect and enhance this continuity. Thus we find a trend
toward more formal occupational associations and more formalized occupational codes of behavior in many diverse lines of work. This we describe as a
movement toward professionalization.

In the terminology that we shall use here, a "profession" is really an ideal
type of occupational institution. The ministry, law, and medicine have been
considered to be the traditional and original professions in Western society.
However, when we look at a diverse sample of occupational groups, we find that
today many are assuming, at least in rudimentary form, some of the characteristics commonly attributed to the traditional professions. Furthermore, we
find that many groups usually considered within the context of the traditional
professions fall short of the professional model in significant respects. Therefore,
it seems more useful to analyze and describe the characteristics of occupational
institutions in terms of the concept of *professionalization,* assuming that many,
if not all, occupations may be placed somewhere on a continuum between the
ideal-type "profession" at one end and completely unorganized occupational
categories, or "non-professions," at the other end. Professionalization is a
process, then, that may affect any occupation to a greater or lesser degree.

But what are the specific attributes of professionalization? To what degree
has professionalization affected different occupations or lines of work? What
are its antecedents and what are its consequences? These are some of the
matters that we wish to explore initially in this chapter.

Professionalization in Historical Perspective

Professor A. M. Carr-Saunders in England was perhaps the first social
scientist to analyze systematically the transition of diverse occupations in terms
of the process of professionalization. In the Herbert Spencer Lecture delivered
at Oxford in 1928, Carr-Saunders discussed the development of what he called
"professionalism" in its historical perspective. (This was five years in advance
of the publication of the famous treatise by Carr-Saunders and P. A. Wilson,
*The Professions.**) In this lecture, reprinted here in part, he points out the
growth of new professions in England, especially during the nineteenth century.
He then begins to define professionalization in terms of specialized skill and
training, minimum fees or salaries, formation of professional associations, and
codes of ethics governing professional practice. He mentions, moreover, that all
special interest associations are not necessarily professional in character; professional associations are distinguished by the degree to which they seek to establish
minimum qualifications for entrance into professional practice or activity, to
enforce appropriate rules and norms of conduct among members of the pro-

* A. M. Carr-Saunders and P. A. Wilson, *The Professions* (Oxford: Clarendon Press,
1933).

fessional group, and to raise the status of the professional group in the larger society. Carr-Saunders concludes by remarking that members of professional groups tend to become very attached to their professional associations and codes of conduct, and that these characteristics of professionalization, in turn, may be expected to have important consequences for many aspects of modern business and industry.

A. M. Carr-Saunders (General)

It is of some of the problems connected with the evolution of new professions and with the changes that have come over the older professions that I wish to speak today. To bring these problems more clearly into light it may be well very briefly to review the course of events during the last two centuries. In 1711 Addison referred to the "three great professions of divinity, law, and physic.' Even at that time the profession of physic was in process of evolution. The apothecaries were assuming some of the functions of the physicians, and persons who, towards the end of the century came to be known as chemists and druggists, were encroaching upon the field of the apothecaries. New professions were arising. In 1665 Pepys recorded of his wife: "she had a fore tooth drawn out to-day which do trouble me." The operator was a barber surgeon and master of his Company. In the following century Beardmore seems to have been what we now call a dentist and to have acted as dentist-in-ordinary to George III. But change was not yet swift. As late as 1838 a writer in *Tait's Magazine* says that "dentistry, as we find it called is growing into a profession." It was not until the nineteenth century was some way advanced that new professions began to achieve recognition in rapid succession. The first half of the century saw the rise of the dentists, veterinary surgeons, engineers, and architects. The Royal College of Veterinary

Reprinted from *Professions: Their Organization and Place in Society* (Oxford: The Clarendon Press, 1928), pp. 3–31. Used by permission of the Clarendon Press, Oxford, England. The original publication of this lecture bore the following author's note: "In this lecture use has been made of material collected by Mr. P. A. Wilson and myself in the course of a study of professional associations that we propose to publish. I am indebted to Mr. Wilson for drawing my attention to some of the facts mentioned in the lecture and to the benefit of discussions with him of many of the problems raised."

Surgeons obtained a charter in 1844 while the Royal Institute of British Architects dates from 1834. The civil engineers, so calling themselves in distinction to military engineers, began to be heard of towards the end of the eighteenth century. The Institution of Civil Engineers was founded in 1818, Thomas Telford being the first president. The Institution of Mechanical Engineers, of which George Stephenson was the first president, dates from 1847. Meanwhile the evolution of the medical profession continued. The Apothecaries' Act was passed in 1815 and John Keats was one of the first persons licensed under that Act. The Apothecaries ultimately became the general practitioners, and the unity of the medical profession was achieved by the Medical Act of 1858.

The Medical Act was one of many acts passed in the second half of the century to regulate the professions. The first Pharmacy Act of 1852 secured important powers for the Pharmaceutical Society which had been founded eleven years previously. Other examples are the Dental Act of 1878 and the Veterinary Surgeons Act of 1881. But the second half of the century did not merely witness legal regulation; it also saw the rise of numerous new professions especially those relating to the land, to teaching, to administration and to the technique of business. As evidence of this the foundation of the Surveyors' Institute in 1868, of the National Union of Teachers in 1870, and of the Institute of Chartered Accountants in 1880 may be mentioned. The process continues to this day, and the legal regulation of the profession of architecture has been discussed in the present Parliament.

In this brief sketch I have employed the word profession in the commonly accepted sense. A little reflection shows that what we now call a profession emerges when a number of persons are found to be practicing a definite technique founded upon a specialized training. A profession may perhaps be defined as an occupation based upon specialized intellectual study and training, the purpose of which is to supply skilled service or advice to others for a definite fee or salary. I say fee or salary. It is sometimes held that the typical professions, or even that the only true professions, are those in which the practitioners are free lance workers and therefore remunerated by fee. It happens that the older professions are mostly free lance professions and this view seems to amount to a refusal to recognize any occupation as a profession unless it is of relative antiquity. But remuneration is only of the essence of the matter insofar as it must be direct and definite. The profession of medicine is not ceasing to be a profession because the mode of remuneration is coming increasingly to be by salary instead of by fee, nor are those newer professions which are arising around the technique of business and of administration any the less professions because from the nature of the case the practitioners were salaried from the beginning.

Official sanction has recently been given to an extension of the use of the word profession. The term "professional fireman" is frequently employed in the Fire Brigades Pensions Act 1925. A "professional fireman" is defined "as any member of a fire brigade maintained by a local authority who is wholly and permanently employed on fire brigade duties and to whom the Police Pensions Act 1921 does not apply." Without in any way wishing to disparage the valuable services of whole time firemen, I suggest that to describe their functions as professional is to misuse a word to which a restricted and definite meaning is commonly attached. Specialized intellectual training is one criterion of a profession and definite remuneration another. It might be urged that there is every degree of specialized intellectual training. This is not exactly the case. Those with specialized training are more clearly marked off than might be expected. In any case such gradation as there is does not greatly matter for

my present purpose because I propose only to consider those professions in which the specialized training is the basis of a particular form of organization and they are easily discovered.

It is not difficult to account in general for the emergence of new professions. Large scale organization has favored specialization. Specialized occupations have arisen round the application of the new scientific knowledge. Chemists and engineers have now long been included within the professional ranks. More interesting is the specialization which is arising round the technique of public administration and of business organization and control. It is in this latter field that the most important developments are now taking place. The story of the evolution of the professions is, however, an unwritten chapter in the social history of the last two centuries. No aspect of the matter has received the attention it deserves. This development of many new forms of specialized occupation has immensely increased the possibility of the use of human capacities which formerly for lack of opportunity remained dormant. Many specialized faculties which enable excellence to be achieved in the performance of some skilled service can now be exercised to the greatly increased satisfaction of their fortunate possessors and to the advantage of their fellows.

It is, nevertheless, to the future rather than to the past that I wish to look. I propose to take note only of certain characteristics of the professions as manifested in the present and in the immediate past which seem to throw light upon the place in society which they may come to hold in the future. The matter cannot be unimportant. Professional men collectively possess the ability to perform all those skilled services upon which the continued functioning of modern society depends. The subject may be said to have an especial reference to universities. In them are to be found the practitioners of tomorrow.

The history of the evolution of the professions brings a significant fact to light. As soon as a profession emerges, the practitioners are moved by the recognition of common interests to attempt to form a professional association. These attempts are by no means always immediately successful. It was long after dentistry had become a recognized profession that the dentists succeeded in forming a strong organization. The engineers have been more fortunate. As the various branches of engineering have segregated out, those who practice them have been able to found what have proved to be enduring organizations. The varying fates of these first attempts would form an interesting subject for inquiry. What concerns us, however, is that these attempts are made in the early days of every profession, and so strong are the motives impelling practitioners to form professional associations, that they continue their efforts until success comes. Moreover, the tendency is towards the dominance of a single professional association in each profession. Some professions have never been troubled by the rivalry of associations. Where rivalry formerly existed, it is generally found either that one association has grown to overshadow all the others, or that amalgamation has taken place, as among the architects, or that associations, once in competition, have settled down to occupy what are in fact true subdivisions within the field of the profession, as is the case among the teachers and the accountants.

What then are the motives common to the members of every profession which lead to the formation of professional associations? I set aside the interest which professional men have in the subject matter of their profession, not because it is not a powerful motive leading towards association, but because it is often satisfied by associations specially established for that purpose. What may be called pure subject associations are numerous. When professional associations attempt to satisfy the subject interest, that object may be regarded as incidental. Professional associations as such came into existence for other reasons. Of these the first is that, as a profession emerges, the better equipped among the practitioners realize that they possess a certain craft. They call themselves engi-

neers, veterinary surgeons, architects, accountants, as the case may be. But the public does not accord them an exclusive right to that description. Not only may the poorly equipped call themselves by these titles and attain public recognition, but so also may those without any equipment whatever. The better equipped desire that they should somehow be distinguishable, and to that end they form associations, membership of which is confined to those possessing certain minimum qualifications. In the *Pharmaceutical Journal for* 1847, that is six years after the foundation of the Pharmaceutical Society, this aspect of the matter is summed up in the following sentence: "The Pharmaceutical Society was designed as a means of raising the qualifications of pharmaceutical chemists and placing between them and unqualified persons a line of demarcation."

Those associations which date from the first half of the last century were in their early days sometimes truly exclusive in the sense that they sought to exclude would-be members for reasons not strictly relevant to professional competence. Various devices were employed. But the exclusiveness of these bodies has been exaggerated. The members, it is true, desired to be recognized as forming the élite among the practitioners, and in general they justified their claim to be so regarded. Later the attitude of the members of these older associations underwent a change. They came to desire that all practitioners should possess at least the minimum qualifications admitting to the association, and that all practitioners should join the association. This has been the aim of the more recently formed associations from the beginning. With a few unimportant exceptions, professional associations can now be said to be exclusive only in the sense that they exclude the unqualified. They do indeed aim at obtaining for their members the exclusive patronage of clients and employers requiring the service of their craft. But with this aim is associated the ideal of including within their ranks all competent practitioners.

The qualified members of a profession are thus moved to form associations and mutually to guarantee their own competence. But this is not the only motive leading to association. Another motive is present from the beginning. Among the original objects of the Royal Institute of British Architects was "the maintenance of a high standard of professional character and honourable practice." The responsible members of a profession in fact desire to see a proper standard of professional conduct set up and maintained. Just as the qualified are not readily distinguished from the unqualified, so the scrupulous are not readily distinguished from the unscrupulous. Thus professional associations define and enforce rules of professional conduct. The members in other words, mutually guarantee not only their competence but also their honor.

Some features of codes of professional ethics are common to all professions. A universal rule is that against advertising. Another universal rule is that which aims at making the fee or salary paid for service rendered the sole remuneration or advantage which a practitioner receives. . . . In addition to such rules, which are found in the ethical codes of all professional associations, there are rules in the code of each profession specially applicable to that profession. Thus the second schedule to the standing orders of the Institute of Journalists contains a list "of acts or proceedings" which "may be deemed to be an act or default discreditable to a journalist." The Council has power to expel or suspend any member proved guilty of any of the offenses described, the first of which is "the supplying of false news or exaggerated reports."

A survey of the history of the professions in modern times thus shows that when a profession becomes clearly defined the competent and responsible practitioners form an association two of the chief objects of which are to bring up the qualifications of all who hold themselves out as practicing the craft to a certain minimum standard and to enforce rules of honorable conduct. It is not easy to assess the part that professional organizations have played in raising the level of professional attainments. It is probably true to say that it is much underrated. The facilities for instruction in technical sub-

jects, such as they are, have in many cases been provided in response to demands by professional organizations. Some organizations have founded their own educational institutions; others have endowed teaching posts in existing institutions. It is by no means true that the interest of the organizations is confined to technical education. A charge of exclusiveness has been brought against them because they demand evidence of a good general education before specialization. But it is not their fault that only a small percentage of the population can fulfill these requirements. Again, it is not correct to say that, so far as they are interested in technical education, they are always interested in making it more narrow. The greater emphasis placed in late years by the accountants upon the study of law is evidence against this view.

It is still less easy to assess the results of their efforts to raise and maintain standards of professional honor. Prejudice and ignorance abound in regard to this matter. The elaborate codes ruling in the legal and medical professions are commonly held to constitute a maze of restrictions which are unnecessary and vexatious where, indeed, they are not designed in the selfish interests of the practitioners. . . . It could be shown that these ethical codes are based upon a few simple rules which should command general approval. The rule against indirect profit should need no defense. I have indicated the reasons for the rule against advertising. If the foundations of the codes were better understood they would not be generally regarded with hostility. It does not follow that the codes as elaborated always represent the inevitable amplification of these rules. . . . . There is a third motive leading to the formation of professional associations. "To raise the status of the teaching profession" is one of the objects of the National Union of Teachers. The National Union of Teachers was founded in 1870. In the case of those associations which were founded earlier somewhat different language was employed. The preamble to the Charter granted to the Royal College of Veterinary Surgeons in 1844 states that it has been represented that incorporation would "contribute to the respectability" of veterinary sugeons. Every profession in its early days has to fight for a proper recognition of its status. Newcomers among the professions are looked down upon by the established professions.... The connection between status and remuneration is close, and in their efforts to improve the status of their members professional associations have been led to pay attention to remuneration. "It is impossible," says the writer of a leading article in the *Proceedings of the Institute of Chemistry,* "to ignore the fact that the status of the professional man must be dependent upon the salary or fees which he receives. Therefore, as the Institute hopes to raise and maintain the status of the chemist, it must take the economic aspect into consideration....[1] [The development of professional associations]...is in harmony with the most outstanding feature of recent social evolution—the growth of organized groups. "There are many to tell us," said Maitland, "that the line of advance is no longer from status to contract but through contract to something that contract cannot explain, for which our best, if an inadequate name, is the personality of the organized group."[2] Groups organized for industrial, commercial, and administrative purposes occupy the most prominent position in the field of view today. There are many reasons why this should be so. There are also reasons for anticipating that groups organized around vocations will come to assume at least equal prominence. Of these the most important is that professional associations are groups organized around the most enduring of men's practical interests. A man's permanent attachment is to his profession. A teacher is a loyal member of the university, school, or college in which he is serving. He can, and frequently does, transfer that loyalty to another institution. And the same is true of the engineer and of other professional men. Moreover, groups organized for practi-

cal ends are more transitory than groups organized around functions. Professions evolve, and in consequence their organizations are modified, but on the whole they change less rapidly than do the institutions in which men practice their crafts. In the world of industry, commerce, and administration groups are always in process of formation for the carrying out of certain specific objects. When those purposes have been achieved, the organizations are superseded or transformed. Those who collaborated to achieve these objects seek for opportunities to practice their craft in other organizations.

Vocational associations are thus likely to claim increasing attention. We need not expect, and far less desire, any radical transformation of social organization such as would be implied by the substitution of vocational for geographical representation. The enhanced prestige of professional associations will tend to bring about a development of those public activities to which reference has been made. We may expect to see them regarded as sources of authoritative information and advice in regard to matters within their own spheres. As problems of legislation and administration become increasingly technical, the Government may turn to them and request not only their advice but also their cooperation.... It is, however, not on possible developments such as these that I wish to dwell. I wish to consider in conclusion the possible influence of the growth of the prestige of professional associations upon the organization of industrial and commercial activities. I have emphasized the fact that a professional man may be remunerated either by fee or salary. From the point of view of the economist, however, there is a distinction between the fee-taker and the salaried man. Further, the position of the fee-taking professional is in some respects analogous to that of the manufacturer or dealer.... There remains, however, the profound distinction that manufacturers and dealers do, whereas professional men do not, buy and sell material goods as an essential feature in the performance of their functions. This

[1] *Proceedings of the Institute of Chemistry,* 1919, part ii.

[2] F. W. Maitland, *Collected Papers,* vol. iii, p. 315.

distinction is so important that, however closely the organization of some professions may come to resemble business organization and however much specialized study and training in relation to these functions may come to be a characteristic of the manufacturer or dealer, there can be no transformation of the one into the other.

It does not follow that, because there must remain a fundamental distinction between the fee-taking professional man and the *entrepreneur,* the growth of professionalism has no bearing upon the organization of industrial and commercial activities. The future is not with the *entrepreneur.* The story is familiar—the rise of corporations, the devolution of the functions of the *entrepreneur,* risk-bearing passing to shareholders and insurance companies, adaptation of new knowledge for industrial purposes to men trained in science, auditing to accountants, supervision to managers. It is not so obvious that the most important of these functions are passing to men who belong to organized professions or to men whose special skill and training are coming to form the basis of new professions. What influence will this growth of organizations based upon function exert upon the further development of corporations which occupy so large a place today and seem likely to increase than to diminish in impor tance?. ...Facing these corporations, however, there are growing up vocational organizations, professional associations, and associations of workpeople, as yet of no imposing stature but with promise of development, in which with all their faults some of the motives are generated necessary for the progress of commercial corporations along the path desired by Mr. Keynes. These corporations may come to be recognized as secondary and composite bodies requiring the services of those trained in many professions and of workpeople with various forms of skill. They may come to be regarded as offering opportunities for the exercise of skill whether the basis be intellectual or manual training. Men may tend to go out from their vocational organizations, to find in industry and commerce the opportunities they desire, to return to

their organizations in times of difficulty such as unemployment, and to look increasingly to them for protection as to their rights and guidance as to their duties.

If development on these lines takes place, professional associations have something to offer towards the solution of certain of the problems which face commercial corporations. Towards the solution of the problem of efficiency they offer the ideal of adequate qualifications being demanded of those who undertake specialized functions. There seems to be no reason why business organization and management should not come to be included among these functions. Laissez faire offered the rough and ready test of financial success but this test was always more rough than generally imagined and the larger the organization the less ready it is. It can hardly be the case that evidence of definite training and experience, as approved by those practioners best qualified to judge, has not its part to play here as elsewhere.

Again, what is there to substitute for private advantage and speculative gain except the conception of the just price? Difficult as it is to translate this conception into figures, it is not unsubstantial. And beneath the tangled and apparently sordid discussions in which professional associations are often engaged respecting fee and salarly, there lies the ideal, or at least something that is capable of being transformed into the ideal, of a fair remuneration. Further, how are we to ensure that the efforts of those who control these bodies are directed to the public good? We may value efforts to arouse a social conscience and yet hesitate to expect great things from them. Out of this difficulty a hopeful way of escape lies in the focusing and letting loose of that energy which is represented by the desire of the good craftsman, be he accountant, engineer, chemist or what not, to see full and efficient use made of his craft. In the long run it is in the public advantage that this desire should be fulfilled and it is increasingly one of the aims of professional associations to arouse and find outlets for this desire.

Professionalism has its problems of organization. It has its weaknesses and its dangers. But taking all in all the growth of professionalism is one of the hopeful features of the time. The approach to problems of social conduct and social policy under the guidance of a professional tradition raises the ethical standard and widens the social outlook. There is thus reason to welcome a development of which the result will be to increase the influence of professional associations upon character, outlook, and conduct. "I hold," said Bacon, "everyman a debtor to his profession from the which as men do of course seek to receive countenance and profit so ought they of duty to endeavour themselves by way of amends to be a help and an ornament thereunto."[3]

[3] Bacon, *Law Tracts,* Preface.

The Elements of Professionalization

The idea of greater or lesser degrees of occupational professionalization is either implicit or explicit in several recent discussions of the "professions." For example, according to Gross:

> As any occupation approaches professional status, there occur important internal structural changes and changes in the relation of the practitioners to society at large. A useful way of discussing these changes is by reference to the criteria of professionalization: the unstandardized product, degree of personality involvement of the professional, wide knowledge of a specialized technique, sense of obligation [to one's art], sense of group identity, and significance of the occupational service to society.*

Greenwood has attempted to identify and describe essential elements in the ideal-type profession. He maintains that professions are distinguishable by possession of (1) a basis of systematic theory,† (2) authority recognized by the clientele of the professional group, (3) broader community sanction and approval of this authority, (4) a code of ethics regulating relations of professional persons with clients and with colleagues, and (5) a professional culture sustained by formal professional associations. Although Greenwood frames his discussion in terms of professions and non-professions, he also points out that there are no clearcut distinctions between them: "We must think of the occupations in society as distributing themselves along a continuum." He concludes by suggesting that the model of a profession, as he has described it, can provide criteria for evaluation of the degree to which an occupation like his own field of social work has become professionalized. He leaves us with the provocative suggestion that the professionalization of social work may be seen as a mixed blessing from certain viewpoints.

* Edward Gross, *Work and Society* (New York: Thomas Y. Crowell Company, 1958), p. 77. Riesman has been somewhat concerned about this growing tendency and has voiced the hope that the "embryonic field of recreation" will not become, in effect, overly professionalized. See David Riesman, "Recreation and the Recreationist," *Marriage and Family Living,* 16, 1954, 21–26. In another quarter, W. R. Rosengren writes about "Status Stress and Role Contradictions: Emergent Professionalization in Psychiatric Hospitals," *Mental Hygiene,* 45, No. 1 (January 1961), 28–39.

† A. M. Carr-Saunders and P. A. Wilson acknowledge the historical importance of this element in their studies; see their book *The Professions,* p. 296.

Ernest Greenwood (Social Work)

The professions occupy a position of great importance on the American scene.[1] In a society such as ours, characterized by minute division of labor based upon technical specialization, many important features of social organizations are dependent upon professional functions. Professional activity is coming to play a predominant role in the life patterns of increasing numbers of individuals of both sexes, occupying much of their waking moments, providing life goals, determining behavior, and shaping personality. It is no wonder, therefore, that the phenomenon of professionalism has become an object of observation by sociologists.[2] The sociological approach to professionalism is one that views a profession as an organized group which is constantly interacting with the society that forms its matrix, which performs its social functions through a network of formal and informal relationships, and which creates its own subculture requiring adjustments to it as a prerequisite for career success.[3]

Within the professional category of its occupational classification the United States Census Bureau includes, among others, the following: accountant, architect, artist, attorney, clergyman, college professor, dentist, engineer, journalist, judge, librarian, natural scientist, optometrist, pharmacist, physician, social scientist,

social worker, surgeon, and teacher.[4] What common attributes do these professional occupations possess which distinguish them from the nonprofessional ones? After a careful canvass of the sociological literature on occupations, this writer has been able to distill five elements, upon which there appears to be consensus among the students of the subject, as constituting the distinguishing attributes of a profession.[5] Succinctly put, all professions seem to possess: (1) systematic theory, (2) authority, (3) community sanction, (4) ethical codes, and (5) a culture. The purpose of this article is to describe fully these attributes.

Before launching into our description, a preliminary word of caution is due. With respect to each of the above attributes, the true difference between a professional and a nonprofessional occupation is not a qualitative but a quantitative one. Strictly speaking, these attributes are not the exclusive monopoly of the professions; nonprofessional occupations also possess them, but to a lesser degree. As is true of most social phenomena, the phenomenon of professionalism cannot be structured in terms of clearcut classes. Rather, we must think of the occupations in a society as distributing themselves along a continuum.[6] At one end of this continuum are bunched the well-recognized and undisputed professions (e.g.,

Reprinted from "Attributes of a Profession," *Social Work*, 2, No. 3 (July 1957), 44–55. Used by permission of the author and publisher. The original publication bore the following note: "The writer is indebted to Dr. William A. Kornhauser, Sociology Department of the university, for his constructive criticisms during the preparation of this paper."

[1] Talcott Persons, "The Professions and Social Structure," *Social Forces*, 17 (May 1939), 457–467.

[2] Theodore Caplow, *The Sociology of Work* (Minneapolis: University of Minnesota Press, 1954).

[3] Oswald Hall, "The Stages of a Medical Career," *The American Journal of Sociology*, 53 (March 1948), 327–336; "Types of Medical Careers," *The American Journal of Sociology*, 55 (November 1949), 243–253; "Sociological Research in the Field of Medicine: Progress and Prospects," *American Sociological Review*, 16 (October 1951), 639–644.

[4] U. S. Bureau of the Census, *1950 Census of Population: Classified Index of Occupations and Industries* (Washington, D. C.: Government Printing Office, 1950).

[5] The writer acknowledges his debt to his former students at the School of Social Welfare, University of California, Berkeley, who, as members of his research seminars, assisted him in identifying and abstracting the sociological literature on occupations. Their conscientious assistance made possible the formulation presented in this paper.

[6] The occupational classification employed by the U. S. Census Bureau is precisely such a continuum. The categories of this classification are: (a) professionals and semiprofessional technical workers; (b) proprietors and managers, both farm and non-farm, and officials; (c) clerical, sales, and kindred workers; (d) craftsmen, skilled workers, and foremen; (e) operatives and semi-skilled workers; and (e) laborers, unskilled, service, and domestic workers. (U. S. Bureau of the Census, *op. cit.*).

physician, attorney, professor, scientist) ; at the opposite end are bunched the least skilled and least attractive occupations (e.g., watchman, truckloader, farm laborer, scrubwoman, bus boy). The remaining occupations, less skilled and less prestigious than the former, but more so than the latter, are distributed between these two poles. The occupations bunched at the professional pole of the continuum possess to a maximum degree the attributes about to be described. As we move away from this pole, the occupations possess these attributes to a decreasing degree. Thus, in the less developed professions, social work among them, these attributes appear in moderate degree. When we reach the mid-region of the continuum, among the clerical, sales, and crafts occupations, they occur in still lesser degree; while at the unskilled end of the continuum the occupations possess these attributes so minimally that they are virtually nonexistent. If the reader keeps this concept of the continuum in mind, the presentation will less likely appear as a distortion of reality.

SYSTEMATIC BODY OF THEORY[7]

It is often contended that the chief difference between a professional and a nonprofessional occupation lies in the element of superior skill. The performance of a professional service presumably involves a series of unusually complicated operations, mastery of which requires lengthy training. The models referred to in this connection are the performances of a surgeon, a concert pianist, or a research physicist. However, some nonprofessional occupations actually involve a higher order of skill than many professional ones. For example, tool-and-die making, diamond-cutting, monument-engraving, or cabinet-making involve more intricate operations than schoolteaching, nursing, or social work. Therefore, to focus on the element of skill per se in describing the professions is to miss the kernel of their uniqueness.

[7] The sequence in which the five attributes are discussed in this paper does not reflect upon their relative importance. The order selected has been dictated by logical considerations.

The crucial distinction is this: the skills that characterize a profession flow from and are supported by a fund of knowledge that has been organized into an internally consistent system, called a *body of theory*. A profession's underlying body of theory is a system of abstract propositions that describe in general terms the classes of phenomena comprising the profession's focus of interest. Theory serves as a base in terms of which the professional rationalizes his operations in concrete situations. Acquisition of the professional skill requires a prior or simultaneous mastery of the theory underlying that skill. Preparation for a profession, therefore, involves considerable preoccupation with systematic theory, a feature virtually absent in the training of the nonprofessional. And so treatises are written on legal theory, musical theory, social work theory, the theory of the drama, and so on; but no books appear on the theory of punch-pressing or pipefitting or bricklaying.

Because understanding of theory is so important to professional skill, preparation for a profession must be an intellectual as well as a practical experience. On-the-job training through apprenticeship, which suffices for a nonprofessional occupation, becomes inadequate for a profession. Orientation in theory can be achieved best through formal education in an academic setting. Hence the appearance of the professional school, more often than not university affiliated, wherein the milieu is a contrast to that of the trade school. Theoretical knowledge is more difficult to master than operational procedures; it is easier to learn to repair an automobile than to learn the principles of the internal combustion engine. There are, of course, a number of free-lance professional pursuits (e.g., acting, painting, writing, composing, and the like) wherein academic preparation is not mandatory. Nevertheless, even in these fields various "schools" and "institutes" are appearing, although they may not be run along traditional academic lines. We can generalize that as an occupation moves toward professional status, apprenticeship training yields to formalized education, because the function of theory as a groundwork for practice acquires increasing importance.

The importance of theory precipitates a form of activity normally not encountered in a nonprofessional occupation, viz., theory construction via systematic research. To generate valid theory that will provide a solid base for professional techniques requires the application of the scientific method to the service-related problems of the profession. Continued employment of the scientific method is nurtured by and in turn reinforces the element of *rationality*.[8] As an orientation, rationality is the antithesis of traditionalism. The spirit of rationality in a profession encourages a critical, as opposed to a reverential, attitude toward the theoretical system. It implies a perpetual readiness to discard any portion of that system, no matter how time-honored it may be, with a formulation demonstrated to be more valid. The spirit of rationality generates group self-criticism and theoretical controversy. Professional members convene regularly in their associations to learn and to evaluate innovations in theory. This produces an intellectually stimulating milieu that is in marked contrast to the milieu of a nonprofessional occupation.

In the evolution of every profession there emerges the researcher-theoretician whose role is that of scientific investigation and theoretical systematization. In technological professions[9] a division of labor thereby evolves, that between the theory-oriented and the practice-oriented person. Witness the physician who prefers to attach himself to a medical research center rather than to enter private practice. This division may also yield to cleavages with repercussions upon intraprofessional relationships. However, if properly integrated, the division of labor produces an accelerated expansion of the body of theory and a sprouting of

8 Parsons, *op. cit.*

9 A technology is a profession whose aim is to achieve controlled changes in natural relationships. Convention makes a distinction between technologists who shape nonhuman materials and those who deal with human beings. The former are called engineers; the latter practitioners.

theoretical branches around which specialties nucleate. The net effect of such developments is to lengthen the preparation deemed desirable for entry into the profession. This accounts for the rise of graduate professional training on top of a basic college education.

PROFESSIONAL AUTHORITY

Extensive education in the systematic theory of his discipline imparts to the professional a type of knowledge that highlights the layman's comparative ignorance. This fact is the basis for the professional's authority, which has some interesting features.

A nonprofessional occupation has customers; a professional occupation has clients. What is the difference? A customer determines what services and/or commodities he wants, and he shops around until he finds them. His freedom of decision rests upon the premise that he has the capacity to appraise his own needs and to judge the potential of the service or of the commodity to satisfy them. The infallibility of his decisions is epitomized in the slogan: "The customer is always right!" In a professional relationship, however, the professional dictates what is good or evil for the client, who has no choice but to accede to professional judgment. Here the premise is that, because he lacks the requisite theoretical background, the client cannot diagnose his own needs or discriminate among the range of possibilities for meeting them. Nor is the client considered able to evaluate the caliber of the professional service he receives. In a nonprofessional occupation the customer can criticize the quality of the commodity he has purchased, and even demand a refund. The client lacks this same prerogative, having surrendered it to professional authority. This element of authority is one, although not the sole, reason why a profession frowns on advertising. If a profession were to advertise, it would, in effect, impute to the potential client the discriminating capacity to select from competing forms of service. The client's subordination to professional authority invests the professional with a monopoly of judgment. When an occupation strives toward professionalization, one of its aspirations is to acquire this monopoly.

The client derives a sense of security from the professional's assumption of authority. The authoritative air of the professional is a principal source of the client's faith that the relationship he is about to enter contains the potentials for meeting his needs. The professional's authority, however, is not limitless; its function is confined to those specific spheres within which the professional has been educated. This quality in professional authority Parsons calls *functional specificity*.[10] Functional specificity carries the following implications for the client-professional relationship.

The professional cannot prescribe guides for facets of the client's life where his theoretical competence does not apply. To venture such prescriptions is to invade a province wherein he himself is a layman, and, hence, to violate the authority of another professional group. The professional must not use his position of authority to exploit the client for purposes of personal gratification. In any association of superordination-subordination, of which the professional-client relationship is a perfect specimen, the subordinate member—here, the client—can be maneuvered into a dependent role. The psychological advantage which thereby accrues to the professional could constitute a temptation for him. The professional must inhibit his impulses to use the professional relationship for the satisfaction of the sexual need, the need to manipulate others, or the need to live vicariously. In the case of the therapeutic professions it is ideally preferred that client-professional intercourse not overflow the professional setting. Extraprofessional intercourse could be used by both client and professional in a manner such as to impair professional authority, with a consequent diminution of the professional's effectiveness.

Thus far we have discussed that phase of professional authority which expresses

itself in the client-professional relationship. Professional authority, however, has professional-community ramifications. To these we now turn.

SANCTION OF THE COMMUNITY

Every profession strives to persuade the community to sanction its authority within certain spheres by conferring upon the profession a series of powers and privileges. Community approval of these powers and privileges may be either informal or formal; formal approval is that reinforced by the community's police power.

Among its powers is the profession's control over its training centers. This is achieved through an accrediting process exercised by one of the associations within the profession. By granting or withholding accreditation, a profession can, ideally, regulate its schools as to their number, location, curriculum content, and caliber of instruction. Comparable control is not to be found in a nonprofessional occupation.[11] The profession also acquires control over admission into the profession. This is achieved via two routes. First, the profession convinces the community that no one should be allowed to wear a professional title who has not been conferred it by an accredited professional school. Anyone can call himself a carpenter, locksmith, or metal-plater if he feels so qualified. But a person who assumes the title of physician or attorney without having earned it conventionally becomes an impostor. Secondly, the profession persuades the community to institute in its behalf a licensing system for screening those qualified to practice the professional skill. A *sine qua non* for the receipt of the license is, of course, a duly granted professional title. Another prerequisite may be an examination before a board of inquiry whose personnel have been drawn from the ranks of the profession. Police power enforces the licensing system;

---

[10] Parsons, *op. cit.*

[11] To set up and run a school for floral decorating requires no approval from the national florists' association, but no school of social work could operate long without approval of the Council on Social Work Education.

persons practicing the professional skill without a license are liable to punishment by public authority.[12]

Among the professional privileges, one of the most important is that of confidentiality. To facilitate efficient performance, the professional encourages the client to volunteer information he otherwise would not divulge. The community regards this as privileged communication, shared solely between client and professional, and protects the latter legally from encroachments upon such confidentiality. To be sure, only a select few of the professions, notably medicine and law, enjoy this immunity. Its very rarity makes it the ultimate in professionalization. Another one of the professional privileges is a relative immunity from community judgment on technical matters. Standards for professional performance are reached by consensus within the profession and are based on the existing body of theory. The lay community is presumed incapable of comprehending these standards and, hence, of using them to identify malpractice. It is generally conceded that a professional's performance can be evaluated only by his peers.

The powers and privileges described above constitute a monopoly granted by the community to the professional group. Therefore, when an occupation strives toward professional status, one of its prime objectives is to acquire this monopoly. But this is difficult to achieve, because counter forces within the community resist strongly the profession's claims to authority. Through its associations the profession wages an organized campaign to persuade the community that it will benefit greatly by granting the monopoly. Specifically the profession seeks to prove: that the performance of the occupational skill requires specialized education; that those who possess this edu-

cation, in contrast to those who do not, deliver a superior service; and that the human need being served is of sufficient social importance to justify the superior performance.

REGULATIVE CODE OF ETHICS

The monopoly enjoyed by a profession vis-à-vis clients and community is fraught with hazards. A monopoly can be abused; powers and privileges can be used to protect vested interests against the public weal.[13] The professional group could peg the price of its services at an unreasonably high level; it could restrict the numbers entering the occupation to create a scarcity of personnel; it could dilute the caliber of its performance without community awareness; and it could frustrate forces within the occupation pushing for socially beneficial changes in practices.[14] Were such abuses to become conspicuous, widespread, and permanent, the community would, of course, revoke the profession's monopoly. This extreme measure is normally unnecessary, because every profession has a built-in regulative code which compels ethical behavior on the part of its members.

The profession's ethical code is part formal and part informal. The formal is the written code to which the professional usually swears upon being admitted to practice; this is best exemplified by the Hippocratic Oath of the medical profession. The informal is the unwritten code, which nonetheless carries the weight of formal prescriptions. Through its ethical code the profession's commitment to the social welfare becomes a matter of public record, thereby insuring for itself the continued confidence of the community. Without such confidence the profession could not retain its monopoly. To be sure, self-regulative

---

[12] Many nonprofessional occupations have also succeeded in obtaining licensing legislation in their behalf. Witness the plumbers, radio operators, and barbers, to mention a few. However, the sanctions applied against a person practicing a nonprofessional occupation are much less severe than is the case when a professional occupation is similarly involved.

[13] Abraham Flexner, "Is Social Work a Profession?" in *Proceedings of the National Conference of Charities and Corrections* (Chicago: 1915), pp. 576–590.

Robert K. Merton, "Bureaucratic Structure and Personality," in Alvin Gouldner (ed.), *Studies in Leadership* (New York: Harper & Row, Publishers, 1950), pp. 67–79.

[14] Merton, *op. cit.*

codes are characteristic of all occupations, nonprofessional as well as professional. However, a professional code is perhaps more explicit, systematic, and binding; it certainly possesses more altruistic overtones and is more public service-oriented.[15] These account for the frequent synonymous use of the terms "professional" and "ethical" when applied to occupational behavior.

While the specifics of their ethical codes vary among the professions, the essentials are uniform. These may be described in terms of client-professional and colleague-colleague relations.

Toward the client the professional must assume an emotional neutrality. He must provide service to whoever requests it, irrespective of the requesting client's age, income, kinship, politics, race, religion, sex, and social status. A nonprofessional may withhold his services on such grounds without, or with minor, censure; a professional cannot. Parsons calls this element in professional conduct *universalism*. In other words, only in his extraoccupational contacts can the professional relate to others on particularistic terms, i.e., as particular individuals with concrete personalities attractive or unattractive to him. In his client contacts particularistic considerations are out of place. Parsons also calls attention to the element of *disinterestedness* in the professional-client relationship.[16] In contrast to the nonprofessional, the professional is motivated less by self-interest and more by the impulse to perform maximally. The behavior corollaries of this service orientation are many. For one, the professional must, under all circumstances, give maximum caliber service. The nonprofessional can dilute the quality of his commodity or service to fit the size of the client's fee; not so the professional. Again, the professional must be prepared to render his services upon request, even at the sacrifice of personal convenience.

The ethics governing colleague relationships demand behavior that is cooperative, equalitarian, and supportive. Members of a profession share technical knowledge with each other. Any advance in theory and practice made by one professional is quickly disseminated to colleagues through the professional associations.[17] The proprietary and quasi-secretive attitudes toward discovery and invention prevalent in the industrial and commercial world are out of place in the professional. Also out of place is the blatant competition for clients which is the norm in so many nonprofessional pursuits. This is not to gainsay the existence of intraprofessional competition; but it is a highly regulated competition, diluted with cooperative ingredients which impart to it its characteristically restrained quality. Colleague relations must be equalitarian; intraprofessional recognition should ideally be based solely upon performance in practice and/or contribution to theory.[18] Here, too, particularistic considerations must not be allowed to operate. Finally, professional colleagues must support each other vis-à-vis clientele and community. The professional must refrain from acts which jeopardize the authority of colleagues and must sustain those whose authority is threatened.[19]

The ways and means whereby a profession enforces the observance of its ethical code constitute a case study in social control. Self-discipline is achieved informally and formally.

Informal discipline consists of the subtle and the not-so-subtle pressures that colleagues exert upon one another. An example in this connection is the phenomenon of consultation and referral.[20] Consultation is the practice of inviting a colleague to participate in the appraisal of the client's need and/or in the planning of the service to be rendered. Referral is the practice of affording colleagues access to a client or an appointment. Thus, one colleague may refer his client to another, because lack of time

---

[15] Flexner, *op. cit.* Parsons, *op. cit.*

[16] Parsons, *op. cit.*

[17] Arlien Johnson, "Professional Standards and How They Are Attained," *Journal of American Dental Association*, **31** (September 1944), 1181–1189.

[18] Flexner, *op. cit.*

[19] This partly explains why physicians do not testify against each other in malpractice suits.

[20] Hall, *op. cit.*

or skill prevents his rendering the needed service; or he may recommend another for appointment by a prospective employer. Since professional ethics precludes aggressive competition and advertising, consultation and referral constitute the principal source of work to a professional. The consultation-referral custom involves professional colleagues in a system of reciprocity which fosters mutual interdependence. Interdependence facilitates social control; chronic violation of professional etiquette arouses colleague resentment, resulting in the cessation of consultation requests and referrals.

A more formal discipline is exercised by the professional associations, which possess the power to criticize or to censure, and in extreme cases to bar recalcitrants. Since membership in good standing in the professional associations is a *sine qua non* of professional success, the prospect of formal disciplinary action operates as a potent force toward conformity.

THE PROFESSIONAL CULTURE

Every profession operates through a network of formal and informal groups. Among the formal groups, first there are the organizations through which the profession performs its services, these provide the institutionalized setting where professional and client meet. Examples of such organizations are hospital, clinic, university, law office, engineering firm, or social agency. Secondly, there are the organizations whose functions are to replenish the profession's supply of talent and to expand its fund of knowledge. These include the educational and the research centers. Third among the formal groups are the organizations which emerge as an expression of the growing consciousness-of-kind on the part of the profession's members, and which promote so-called group interests and aims. These are the professional associations. Within and around these formal organizations extends a filigree of informal groupings: the multitude of small, closely knit clusters of colleagues. Membership in these

cliques is based on a variety of affinities: specialties within the profession; affiliations with select professional societies; residential and work propinquity; family, religious, or ethnic background; and personality attractions.

The interactions of social roles required by these formal and informal groups generate a social configuration unique to the profession, *viz.,* a professional culture. All occupations are characterized by formal and informal groupings; in this respect the professions are not unique. What is unique is the culture thus begotten. If one were to single out the attribute that most effectively differentiates the professions from other occupations, this is it. Thus we can talk of a professional culture as distinct from a nonprofessional culture. Within the professions as a logical class each profession develops its own subculture, a variant of the professional culture; the engineering subculture, for example, differs from the subcultures of medicine and social work. In the subsequent discussion, however, we will treat the culture of the professions as a generic phenomenon. The culture of a profession consists of its *values, norms,* and *symbols.*

The social values of a professional group are its basic and fundamental beliefs, the unquestioned premises upon which its very existence rests. Foremost among these values is the essential worth of the service which the professional group extends to the community. The profession considers that the service is a social good and that community welfare would be immeasurably impaired by its absence. The twin concepts of professional authority and monopoly also possess the force of a group value. Thus, the proposition that in all service-related matters the professional group is infinitely wiser than the laity is regarded as beyond argument. Likewise nonarguable is the proposition that acquisition by the professional group of a service monopoly would inevitably produce social progress. And then there is the value of rationality; that is, the commitment to objectivity in the realm of theory and technique. By virtue of this orientation, nothing of a theoretical or technical nature is regarded as sacred and unchallengeable simply because it has a history of acceptance and use.

The norms of a professional group are the guides to behavior in social situations. Every profession develops an elaborate system of these role definitions. There is a range of appropriate behaviors for seeking admittance into the profession, for gaining entry into its formal and informal groups, and for progressing within the occupation's hierarchy. There are appropriate modes of securing appointments, of conducting referrals, and of handling consultation. There are proper ways of acquiring clients, of receiving and dismissing them, of questioning and treating them, of accepting and rejecting them. There are correct ways of grooming a protégé, of recompensing a sponsor, and of relating to peers, superiors, or subordinates. There are even group-approved ways of challenging an outmoded theory, of introducing a new technique, and of conducting an intraprofessional controversy. In short, there is a behavior norm covering every standard interpersonal situation likely to recur in professional life.

The symbols of a profession are its meaning-laden items. These may include such things as: its insignias, emblems, and distinctive dress; its history, folklore, and argot; its heroes and its villains; and its stereotypes of the professional, the client, and the layman.

Comparatively clear and controlling group values, behavior norms, and symbols, which characterize the professions, are not to be encountered in nonprofessional occupations.

Our discussion of the professional culture would be incomplete without brief mention of one of its central concepts, the *career* concept. The term career is, as a rule, employed only in reference to a professional occupation. Thus, we do not talk about the career of a bricklayer or of a mechanic; but we do talk about the career of an architect or of a clergyman. At the heart of the career concept is a certain attitude toward work which is peculiarly profes-

sional. A career is essentially a *calling,* a life devoted to "good works."[21] Professional work is never viewed solely as a means to an end; it is the end itself. Curing the ill, educating the young, advancing science are values in themselves. The professional performs his services primarily for the psychic satisfactions and secondarily for the monetary compensations.[22] Self-seeking motives feature minimally in the choice of a profession; of maximal importance is affinity for the work. It is this devotion to the work itself which imparts to professional activity the service orientation and the element of disinterestedness. Furthermore, the absorption in the work is not partial, but complete; it results in a total personal involvement. The work life invades the after-work life, and the sharp demarcation between the work hours and the leisure hours disappears. To the professional person his work becomes his life.[23] Hence the act of embarking upon a professional career is similar in some respects to entering a religious order. The same cannot be said of a nonprofessional occupation.

[21] The term *calling* literally means a divine summons to undertake a course of action. Originally, it was employed to refer to religious activity. The Protestant Reformation widened its meaning to include economic activity as well. Henceforth divinely inspired "good works" were to be both secular and sacred in nature. Presumably, then, any occupational choice may be a response to divine summons. In this connection, it is interesting to note that the German word for vocation is *Beruf,* a noun derived from the verb *berufen,* to call.

[22] Johnson, *op. cit.*

[23] The all-pervading influence of work upon the lives of professionals results in interesting by-products. The members of a profession tend to associate with one another outside the work setting (Oswald Hall, "The Stages of a Medical Career," *op. cit.*). Their families mingle socially; leisure time is spent together; "shop talk" permeates social discourse; and a consensus develops. The profession thus becomes a whole social environment, nurturing characteristic social and political attitudes, patterns of consumption and recreation, and decorum and *Weltanschauung.* See Caplow, *op. cit.;* and William H. Form, "Toward an Occupational Social Psychology," *Journal of Social Psychology,* **24** (February 1946), 85–99.

To succeed in his chosen profession, the neophyte must make an effective adjustment to the professional culture.[24] Mastery of the underlying body of theory and acquisition of the technical skills are in themselves insufficient guarantees of professional success. The recruit must also become familiar with and learn to weave his way through the labyrinth of the professional culture. Therefore, the transformation of a neophyte into a professional is essentially an acculturation process wherein he internalizes the social values, the behavior norms, and the symbols of the occupational group.[25] In its frustrations and rewards it is fundamentally no different from the acculturation of an immigrant to a relatively strange culture. Every profession entertains a stereotype of the ideal colleague; and, of course, it is always one who is thoroughly adjusted to the professional culture.[26] The poorly acculturated colleague is a deviant; he is regarded as "peculiar," "unorthodox," "annoying," and in extreme cases a "troublemaker." Whereas the professional group encourages innovation in theory and technique, it tends to discourage deviation from its social values and norms. In this internal contradiction, however, the professional culture is no different from the larger culture of society.

One of the principal functions of the professional schools is to identify and screen individuals who are prospective deviants from the professional culture. That is why the admission of candidates to professional education must be judged on grounds in addition to and other than their academic

qualifications.[27] Psychic factors presaging favorable adjustment to the professional culture are granted an importance equivalent to mental abilities. The professional school provides test situations through initial and graduated exposures of the novice to the professional culture. By his behavior in these social situations involving colleagues, clients, and community, the potential deviant soon reveals himself and is immediately weeded out. Comparable preoccupation with the psychic prerequisites of occupational adjustment is not characteristic of nonprofessional occupations.

IMPLICATIONS FOR SOCIAL WORK

The picture of the professions just unveiled is an ideal type. In the construction of an ideal type some exaggeration of reality is unavoidable, since the intent is to achieve an internally coherent picture. One function of the ideal type is to structure reality in such manner that discrete, disparate, and dissimilar phenomena become organized, thereby bringing order out of apparent disorder. We now possess a model of a profession that is much sharper and clearer than the actuality that confronts us when we observe the occupational scene. What is the utility of this model for social work?

The preoccupation of social workers with professionalization has been a characteristic feature of the social work scene for years. Flexner,[28] Johnson,[29] Hollis and Taylor,[30] and others have written on the subject, proposing criteria which must be met if social work is to acquire professional status. Whenever social workers convene, there is the constant reaffirmation of the urgency to achieve the recognition from the community befitting a profession. The union of the seven separate organizations into the National Association of Social Workers is

---

[24] Oswald Hall, "The Stages of a Medical Career" and "Types of Medical Careers," *op. cit.*

[25] R. Clyde White, " 'Social Workers in Society': Some Further Evidence," *Social Work Journal,* 34 (October 1953), 161–164.

[26] The laity also entertain a stereotypic image of the professional group. Needless to say, the layman's conception and the professional's self-conception diverge widely, because they are fabricated out of very different experiences. The layman's stereotype is frequently a distortion of reality, being either an idealization or a caricature of the professional type.

[27] Oswald Hall, "Sociological Research in the Field of Medicine: Progress and Prospects," *op. cit.*

[28] Flexner, *op. cit.*

[29] Johnson, *op. cit.*

[30] Ernest V. Hollis and Alice L. Taylor, *Social Work Education in the United States* (New York: Columbia University Press, 1951).

generally regarded as an important milestone in social work history, precisely because of its potential stimulus toward professionalization.

In view of all this, it is proper for social workers to possess clear conceptions of that which they so fervently seek. The model of the professions portrayed above should contribute to such clarification; it should illuminate the goal for which social workers are striving. It is often contended that social work is still far from having attained professional status.[31] But this is a misconception. When we hold up social work against the model of the professions presented above, it does not take long to decide whether to classify it within the professional or the nonprofessional occupations. Social work is already a profession; it has too many points of congruence with the model to be classifiable otherwise. Social work is, however, seeking to rise within the professional hierarchy, so that it, too, might enjoy maximum prestige, authority, and monopoly which presently belong to a few top professions.

The model presented above should also serve to sensitize social workers to anticipate some of the problems that continued professionalization must inevitably precipitate. The model indicates that progressive professionalization will involve social workers in novel relationships with clients, colleagues, agency, community, and other professions. In concluding this paper we refer briefly to one such problem. It is no secret that social workers are not all uniformly enthusiastic about the professionalization of social work. Bisno[32] has given verbalization to a prevailing apprehension that social workers might have to scuttle their social-action heritage as a price of achieving the public acceptance accorded a profession. Extrapolation from the sociologists' model of the professions suggests a reality basis for these fears. It suggests that the attainment of professional prestige, authority, and monopoly by social workers will undoubtedly carry disturbing implications for the social action and social reform components of social work philosophy. The anticipated developments will compel social workers to rethink and redefine the societal role of their profession.

These and other dilemmas flowing from professionalization are bound to tax the best minds among social workers for their resolution. In this connection a proper understanding of the attributes of a profession would seem to be indispensable.

---

[31] Flexner considered that the social work of his day was not a profession. Hollis and Taylor regard present-day social work as still in its early adolescence.

[32] Herbert Bisno, "How Social Will Social Work Be?" *Social Work,* 1, No. 2 (April 1956), 12–18.

The Sequence of Professionalization

From the previous reading, we have gained a further understanding of what professionalization includes. If, however, as we stated earlier, professionalization is a *process,* then it is reasonable to ask whether or not there is ordinarily some predictable *sequence* in the way in which occupations assume the attributes of a profession. Theodore Caplow has maintained that there is such a predictable sequence. He bases this claim upon a historical analysis of the development of such professional groups as medical technicians, a group first described in an editorial in the journal *Minnesota Medicine.* Caplow asserts that this sequence may be verified by examination of the process of professionalization as it affects other occupations. The editorial report and Caplow's generalizations based upon this editorial and studies of other occupations are both presented here.

Minnesota Medicine
(Medical Technology)

"A new profession—medical technology—has rather rapidly come into existence.

"Prior to 1928, the qualifications of the laboratory technician were vague. That year the American Society of Clinical Pathologists, under the direction of Dr. Kano Ikeda of Saint Paul, set up a national registry of clinical laboratory technicians and established preschool and training standards for students. At first, high school graduates were admitted to the laboratory schools. Later, one year of college and then two years were required. Today most matriculates are college graduates.

"Likewise, the American Society of Clinical Pathologists undertook the standardization of the training schools. Later, this was done in cooperation with the Council of Medical Education and Hospitals of the American Medical Association, and in 1935 the Council took over entirely.

"The registered technicians organized as the American Society of Clinical Laboratory Technicians at a meeting held in Chicago in June, 1933. The next year the society's first publication, known as *The Bulletin of the American Society of Clinical Laboratory Technicians,* appeared. In 1936 the name was changed to *The American Journal of Medical Technology.*

"With the increase in preschool requirements and better technical training, the term technologist was adopted instead of technician. The national society became the American Society of Medical Technologists. The purpose of the Society is self-betterment and the encouragement of mutual understanding between members and other medical and scientific organizations. Membership is restricted to those registered by the American Society of Clinical Pathologists.

"An attempt was made to obtain the exclusive right to the letters M. T. to designate a medical technologist registered by the American Society of Clinical Pathologists. That having failed, the designation M.T. (ASCP) was adopted.

Reprinted from an editorial in *Minnesota Medicine,* 35, No. 4 (April 1952), 347. Used by permission.

"The standards of the Registry have been approved by the American Medical Association, the American College of Surgeons, and the American Hospital Association. The AMA and the ACS, in their inspection and standardization of hospitals, stress the necessity of having registered (ASCP) laboratory personnel.

"The American Society of Medical Technology is composed of numerous state societies. It holds annual meetings which until 1947 were held in conjunction with the annual ASCP meetings. With the increase in membership (about 5,000 in 1951), the Society has met independently since 1947.

"Many commercial schools for the training of laboratory technicians have been established throughout the country to meet the growing demand. The graduates of these unrecognized schools are not qualified for registration with the American Society of Clinical Pathologists, nor are they eligible for membership in the American Society of Medical Technology."

Theodore Caplow (General)

The steps involved in professionalization are quite definite, and even the sequence is explicit, so that we may illustrate it with equal facility from the example of newspaper reporters (journalists), real estate agents (realtors), undertakers (morticians), junk dealers (salvage consultants), or laboratory technicians (medical technologists).

The first step is the establishment of a professional association, with definite membership criteria designed to keep out the unqualified.

The second step is the change of name, which serves the multiple function of reducing identification with the previous occupational status, asserting a technological monopoly, and providing a title which can be monopolized, the former one being usually in the public domain.

The third step is the development and promulgation of a code of ethics which

Reprinted from *The Sociology of Work* (Minneapolis: University of Minnesota Press, 1954), pp. 139–140. Copyright by the University of Minnesota. Used by permission.

asserts the social utility of the occupation, sets up public welfare rationale, and develops rules which serve as further criteria to eliminate the unqualified and unscrupulous. The adoption of a code of ethics, despite certain hypocrisies, imposes a real and permanent limitation on internal competition.

The fourth step is a prolonged political agitation, whose object it is to obtain the support of the public power for the maintenance of the new occupational barriers. In practice this usually proceeds by stages from the limitation of a specialized title to those who have passed an examination (registered engineer, certified public accountant) to the final stage at which the mere doing of the acts reserved to the profession is a crime.

Concurrently with this activity, which may extend over a very long period of time, goes the development of training facilities directly or indirectly controlled by the professional society, particularly with respect to admission and to final qualification; the establishment through legal action of certain privileges of confidence and inviolability, the elaboration of the rules of decorum found in the code, and the establishment—after conflict—of working relations with related professional groups.

It is difficult to exaggerate the importance of this general phenomenon for the structure of the economy. So powerful are the motives conducing to professionalization that it may be observed under way in occupations once considered entirely commercial (banking, advertising), in occupations which never involve independent work (drafting, photographic processing), and in those which used to be thought of as quite removed from the economic arena (philanthropy and the research sciences). Even pure management is perhaps in the process of being professionalized, and it is not farfetched to suppose that the professional society may eventually be counted among the major social institutions.

Professionalization and Technological Change

Now that we know something about what professionalization is and how it can be found in a wide variety of occupational groups, we can ask the further question, what causes or promotes it? According to Carr-Saunders and Wilson:

> For an explanation we must look primarily to the mechanical revolution and the progress of science which gave rise to engineers, chemists and physicists, and to the consequential social revolution which brought a demand for intellectual specialists to handle the new and complicated machinery, both material and institutional: actuaries, surveyors, realtors, secretaries, patent attorneys and accountants (virtually unknown in Anglo-Saxon countries before the middle of the nineteenth century). Supplementary causes are the throwing off of dependence, as, for instance, by public administrators, who over the greater part of the world have been freed from their dependence upon the patronage of ministers of the suffrages of electors, and the further recession of the church, because of which the teachers have gained a group consciousness. We have therefore the present situation in the Western world where the day to day functioning of society so largely depends upon the professions. . . .*

Certainly one of the factors that promotes professionalization in modern society is technological change, especially the rapid and advanced technological change to which we are subject in this second half of the twentieth century. The importance of technology for professionalization is noted elsewhere by Carr-Saunders and Wilson, who made a conjecture in 1933 which some subsequent studies appear to support:

* A. M. Carr-Saunders and P. A. Wilson, "Professions," *Encyclopaedia of the Social Sciences,* Vol. 12 (New York: The Macmillan Company, 1934), pp. 477–478.

In the long run technical advance implies an increase in the number of those doing more or less specialized intellectual work relative to the number of those who are engaged in manual labor or in unspecialized intellectual routine. It may be that, while the extension of professionalism upwards and outwards will be fairly rapid, its extension downwards, though gradual and almost imperceptible, will be continuous. Thus, taking the long view, the extension of professionalism over the whole field seems in the end not impossible.†

In a notable, albeit somewhat controversial, paper in 1953 Nelson Foote maintained that automation in the automobile manufacturing industry had begun to result in a trend toward professionalization among Detroit auto workers.‡ In 1959 and 1960 the editors of the present volume carried on a further investigation of the effects of a different form of technology, nuclear technology, upon workers associated with its application in American industry. The results of this investigation are presented in the following reading. In the context of this volume, we believe that this study has a dual significance in that it further supports the contention that technological change is an important stimulus for professionalization in modern society and also illustrates the applicability of the concept of professionalization for understanding significant changes in the character of a wide variety of modern occupations. This time we look at journeymen craftsmen in the process of becoming technicians, an illustration of professionalization in its rudimentary stages.

† Carr-Saunders and Wilson, *The Professions* (Oxford: The Clarendon Press), pp. 493–494; also see p. 296.
‡ Nelson N. Foote, "The Professionalization of Labor in Detroit," *The American Journal of Sociology*, **58**, 1953, 371–380.

Howard Vollmer and Donald Mills (Industrial Technology)

Accurate description of the changing character of labor in relation to technological innovations has been a continuous concern of industrial sociologists. For example, Nelson N. Foote has contended that the nature of our current industrial society may be more meaningfully described in terms of more dynamic social processes such as "the professionalization of labor."[1] He claims that manual laboring occupations are in a process of status change, that is, they are increasingly assuming the technological, organizational, and ideological aspects of professionalization. These aspects were described, respectively, as (1) "a specialized technique supported by a body of

[1] Nelson N. Foote, "The Professionalization of Labor in Detroit," *The American Journal of Sociology*, 53 (January, 1953), 371–80.

theory," (2) "a career supported by an association of colleagues," and (3) "a status supported by community recognition."

Although his illustrations were largely based upon automation of the automobile industry in Detroit, Foote suggested that the "professionalization of labor" is a concept describing a general trend in American society associated with the growth of new technologies. The key question remains, then: Does the concept, "professionalization of labor," apply to the response of labor to new technologies other than automation?

In this paper the authors will discuss

Reprinted from "Nuclear Technology and the Professionalization of Labor," *The American Journal of Sociology*, 67, No. 6 (May 1962), 690–696, by permission of The University of Chicago Press. Copyright 1962 by the University of Chicago. The original publication bore the following note: "Adapted from a paper read at the Annual Meetings of the American Sociological Association, New York, 1960. The authors appreciate comments on this paper provided by Otto N. Larsen, R. R. Tarrice, H. V. Kincaid, and David Bushnell."

consequences of nuclear technology for American labor. By "nuclear technology" we mean the application of nuclear fission and nuclear radiation phenomena to industrial processes. Access to information on this subject has been provided by a series of studies conducted by Stanford Research Institute for the Office of Industrial Relations of the United States Atomic Energy Commission. Information gained in these studies has provided support for Foote's thesis. Furthermore, our attention was drawn to certain health and safety considerations associated with nuclear technology which might further support the "professionalization of labor" thesis.

NUCLEAR TECHNOLOGY AND MANPOWER

There are two general aspects of nuclear technology that have considerable impact upon American industry: (1) reactor technology, in which nuclear reactors are being designed for electric power generation, process heat, and various research uses in industry; and (2) radioisotope technology, in which radioisotopes are being used increasingly for radiographic inspection, radiation gauging, tracing, and other industrial application. At present, more than 1,500 industrial organizations located throughout the nation have been licensed to use radioisotopes, and 146 nuclear reactors are being operated, built, or planned for non-military uses in the United States.[2]

The number of workers involved in these and related aspects of nuclear technology has been increasing in recent years. In 1956 there were about 83,000 persons employed in installations owned directly by the United States Atomic Energy Commission and operated by private contractors; over 40,000 of these were manual or hourly rated em-

ployees.[3] In 1961 there were about 130,000 employees in 158 AEC contractor-operated installations, 53,000 of which were manual workers who worked with, or in the vicinity of, radiation sources. Approximately 25,000 of these manual workers are in skilled crafts or trades. In addition, at least 22,000 employees are now employed in other contexts affected by nuclear technology, such as the construction of nuclear facilities, industrial laboratories using radiation sources (not under contract to the AEC), nuclear instrument manufacturing, radioactive waste disposal, and uranium mining.[4] General Electric Company is an example of an industrial organization that employs more than 1,800 persons who work directly with radiation sources and more than 6,400 persons who work in the vicinity of these sources.[5]

Manual or hourly rated job classifications in nuclear power plants typically require operating personnel to serve as reactor operators, turbine operators, generator operators, or maintenance personnel for mechanical maintenance (including general mechanics, welders, machinists, pipefitters, plumbers, and related trades), electrical maintenance, instrumentation, and chemical analysis. Use of radioisotopes in industry involves production workers (using radiation gauges or tracer techniques), radiographic equipment operators, radiological well-logging equipment operators, maintenance repairmen of radiological equipment, industrial laboratory technicians (using radiological techniques), personnel who manufacture radiological equipment, and persons in related occupations. In addition, the new occupation of radiation moni-

2 Atomic Industrial Forum, *The Atomic Industry: 1958* (New York: Atomic Industrial Forum, 1959), p. 12; and United States Atomic Energy Commission, *Major Activities in the Atomic Energy Programs, January–December 1960* (Washington, D.C.: Government Printing Office, 1961), p. 437.

3 James J. Bambrick, Jr., and Albert A. Blum, *Labor Relations in the Atomic Energy Field* ("Studies in Personnel Policy," No. 158 [New York: National Industrial Conference Board, 1957]), pp. 22–25.

4 *Major Activities in the Atomic Energy Programs,* p. 109.

5 W. A. McAdams, "Radiation Protection in the Industrial Use of Radiation" (paper read at the Second United Nations International Conference on the Peaceful Uses of Atomic Energy, 1958).

toring has developed in response to the potential hazards of use of radiation in industry.

Therefore, it would seem that the impact of nuclear technology upon American labor is worthy of notice, both in terms of numbers of personnel and in terms of the variety of occupations involved.

SPECIALIZED TECHNIQUES

That nuclear technology requires the development of specialized techniques supported by a body of general theory for operating and maintenance personnel has been recognized by various authorities in the field.[6] These needs for specialized and more intensive training of workers for applications of nuclear energy have affected the content of industrial training programs. For example, special training programs for journeyman reactor operators, welders, and instrument repairmen at Shippingport Atomic Power Station, Pennsylvania, require 72 to 133 hours of formal classroom training (excluding on-the-job training) in both theoretical and practical aspects of nuclear power-plant work. Based upon an analysis of training needs and training programs, a Stanford Research Institute report has suggested that at least thirty-two hours of training in basic theory be given to workers in preparation for employment in a nuclear power plant. The suggested course outline provides for training in principles

of atomic structure, radiation, nuclear fission and fusion, nuclear fuels, nuclear reactor types and power generation systems, reactor control and instrumentation, and related safety principles and practices.[7] Courses of this type are now being given in adult-education programs in California, Minnesota, Wisconsin, New York, Pennsylvania, and other states.

In connection with radioisotope utilization, various training courses have also recognized the need for formal training in basic nuclear theory. For example, courses conducted by Industrial Nucleonics Corporation, Columbus, Ohio; by the Budd Nuclear Systems Division, Philadelphia; and by the Picker Laboratories, Cleveland (major manufacturers of radiographic equipment); include instruction in nuclear theory and fundamentals. Based upon analysis of such courses, a study for the Atomic Energy Commission has also suggested thirty-two hours of training in basic theory for radioisotope workers. This course outline provides for training in principles of atomic structure and radiation, similar to the content outlined in the previously mentioned nuclear power-plant course, and additional training in special aspects of radioactivity associated with radiography, radiation gauges, and radioactive tracer techniques.[8] A basic course of this type is also being given in adult-education programs in several states and has been distributed by the Atomic Energy Commission to approximately 250 industrial companies for integration into company training programs.

Contractors of the Atomic Energy Commission give their operating and maintenance personnel at installations like those at Hanford, Washington, or Oak Ridge,

[6] See, e.g., John I. Saks, "Labor Implications of Peaceful Uses of Atomic Energy," *Monthly Labor Review*, 80, 1957, 927–28; F. W. Erhard, "Industrial Training Aspects of the Peaceful Uses of Atomic Energy," *Proceedings of the International Conference on the Peaceful Uses of Atomic Energy* (New York: United Nations, 1956), 13, 66; K. K. Campbell, "Maintenance Work in the Field of Nuclear Energy," *Proceedings–1953 Conference on Nuclear Engineering* (Berkeley: University of California Bookstore, 1953), p. G-12; D. Cochran, "Engineering Problems in Nuclear Power Plant Development," United States Congress Joint Committee on Atomic Energy, *Report on Atomic Power and Private Enterprise* (82d Cong., 2d sess. [Washington, D.C.: Government Printing Office, 1952]), p. 306; and D. O. Woodbury, *Atoms for Peace* (New York: Dodd, Mead & Co., 1955), p. 246.

[7] H. M. Vollmer, *Development of Training Programs for Operating and Maintenance Personnel in Nuclear Power Generating Systems* (Washington, D. C.: Government Printing Office, 1961), p. 36.

[8] H. M. Vollmer, L. J. Towle, and B. J. Maynard, *Development of a Training Program for Radioisotope Workers in Industry* (Washington, D.C.: Government Printing Office, 1961), pp. 29–31.

Tennessee, from seventeen to thirty-three hours of formal training in radiation theory, followed by much more on-the-job training. Thus operators and mechanics who are not themselves nuclear specialists are gaining an elementary knowledge of nuclear theory.

Not all management officials in industrial plants affected by nuclear technology are convinced that training workers in the fundamentals of nuclear theory is necessary or desirable. It has been possible, as in the case of reactor operators at the Hanford facility, for workers during World War II to perform prescribed operations with a minimum of knowledge about the fundamental principles that underlie their work.[9] Some managers still maintain that "a little knowledge is a dangerous thing," inclining workers to assume responsibilities that should be retained by physical scientists or engineers. In most experimental prototype reactor facilities, college-trained engineers are present and exercise technical supervisory responsibilities on all shifts. However, as power-reactor facilities and various uses of radioactive materials become more commonplace in industrial operations, the assignment of professional engineers to continual surveillance of these operations becomes increasingly difficult, especially in more isolated locations, where nuclear power plants or other nuclear facilities are often located. As a result, journeymen operators and workers in the vicinity of radioactive materials are necessarily assuming more responsibility for their own safety and public safety. Because radioactive materials are inherently unstable and potentially dangerous despite physical and procedural safeguards, the personnel responsible for handling or working around these materials must understand something about the underlying "why's" of safety procedures in order to take appropriate action in emergencies.

Furthermore, contrary to the initial opinion of some skeptics, ordinary journeymen

workers in skilled operating and maintenance crafts have demonstrated their ability to assimilate considerable information about fundamental principles of nuclear energy. A Stanford Research Institute study of trial presentations of the suggested nuclear power-plant course in two adult-education programs has indicated that journeymen workers learned as much or slightly more about principles of atomic structure and radiation during the course than managerial and "white-collar" participants in the course. A further study indicated that journeymen operating engineers, selected by West Coast locals of the International Union of Operating Engineers, are capable of effectively assimilating such course materials for the purpose of teaching them to other members of their trade.

Such developments as these seem to support the view of most authorities, in other countries as well as in the United States, that nuclear technology, automation, and similar advanced technologies require increased emphasis upon theoretical knowledge relative to manual skills.[10] In this sense nuclear technology, like automation, requires operating and maintenance personnel who are more like technicians and less like manual workers. Their acquisition of abilities to perform specialized techniques supported by theory (nuclear theory in this case) fulfils Foote's first criterion for professionalization.

CAREER ORIENTATIONS

Several items of information may be presented that support Foote's second criterion for the professionalization of labor—namely, workers are oriented toward a career in their work, sustained by an association of colleagues. Trade unions are now acting to facilitate and support the career stability of their membership in relation to nuclear technology. As early as 1954, the late Martin P. Durkin initiated an atomic energy

---

[9] Military security regulations during World War II required that workers at Hanford know as little as possible about the principles of their work.

[10] International Labor Conference, *Report of the Director General*, Part I: *Automation and Other Technological Developments* (Geneva: International Labor Office, 1957), pp. 47–48.

conference with a keynote speech on the "Challenge of the Atomic Age" before representatives of the United Association of Plumbers and Pipefitters.[11] Shortly thereafter a skills-improvement course in "Nuclear Energy and Its Applications to the Pipe Trades Industry" was established by the United Association.[12] As mentioned earlier, the International Union of Operating Engineers, through its Western Conference of Stationary Engineers, has trained its own cadre of instructors and now has several hundred members enrolled in training classes on nuclear technology in various Western states. The Operating Engineers are now planning to expand this program on a nationwide basis. The International Brotherhood of Electrical Workers is developing a similar training program for its members.

One of the union organizations that has taken a very strong interest in nuclear technology has been the International Brotherhood of Boilermakers. A representative of this union began in 1950 to survey available information and to report the expected effects of nuclear technology upon the boilermaker's trade. A desire to avoid the kind of technological unemployment and disruption of career patterns that had previously affected the boilermakers in connection with dieselization of railroads has caused them to assess very carefully the career opportunities of their membership in nuclear work. Consequently, this union has developed special training programs to upgrade the skills of present journeymen as well as to prepare apprentices for nuclear assignments.[13]

Thus it is not only the fact that nuclear technology requires more training in fundamental theory, but also that this training,

in many cases, is being assumed by workmen's associations of colleagues (trade unions) that is indicative of rudimentary professionalization of labor.

It might also be added that unions have taken other steps to facilitate career stability of their membership in nuclear work. This has been exemplified by many union leaders' attitudes, particularly on the national or international level, toward special hazard pay for workers employed in the vicinity of radiation sources. Although these officials are usually quite concerned with the establishment of adequate structural and procedural safeguards for their members' health and safety, they have generally refrained from pressing for special hazard pay, lest this demand result in automated control systems and consequent technological unemployment. Thus management and union officials usually have agreed that hazard pay is warranted only where job classifications explicitly specify special radiation hazards in the work situation.[14]

COMMUNITY-RECOGNIZED STATUS

Community and societal recognition of nuclear work and the status of nuclear technicians has been expressed in several ways. For example, officials of public sponsored technical and industrial training centers and public junior colleges have recently shown increasing desire to include nuclear-technology subjects in their apprentice and journeymen training programs. Basic courses in nuclear power-plant applications, radioisotope utilization, and radiation safety have been given in California and in several other states, as was mentioned previously. State supervisors of industrial and vocational education have requested that these courses be developed and tried out in preparation for use in the near future in similar training programs throughout the United States.

At present, reactor operators in private industrial plants must be licensed by the Atomic Energy Commission, after taking a qualifying examination prepared by AEC

---

[11] Joint Committee on Atomic Energy, Congress of the United States, *Employee Radiation Hazards and Workmen's Compensation* (Washington, D.C.: Government Printing Office, 1959), p. 376.

[12] American Chemical Society, "Atoms and Labor," *Chemical and Engineering News,* **34** (February 20, 1956), 313.

[13] *Employee Radiation Hazards and Workmen's Compensation,* p. 366.

[14] Bambrick and Blum, *op. cit.,* p. 18.

representatives. Licensing procedures for those who use radioisotopes in industry differ somewhat from procedures for those who operate reactors. Ordinarily, an organization may be licensed to use specific radioisotopes for specific purposes; but in the application for the license, the individuals who will "use or directly supervise use of by-product material," along with their experience and training, must be listed in the application.

Among the responsibilities of the Atomic Energy Commission is the special regulation of manpower management and labor relations in industries using nuclear energy, especially in installations operated by private contractors for the Atomic Energy Commission. This includes regulation of wages, hours of work, and general working conditions, as well as the prompt settlement of labor disputes to assure employment continuity.[15] One effect of such government responsibility in labor relations is to weaken the dependence of employees upon their relationship with their employers in the nuclear plants subject to this regulation. Also, because employers in AEC contractor installations do not own their facilities, and may be removed at any time that the AEC decides to close an installation or to change its management, the presumed continuity of operations typical of private industrial establishments is lacking, or at least weakened, in these nuclear plants. Moreover, where an employer operates an AEC installation in connection with defense contracts, he is also subject to influence by the Army, the Navy, or the Air Force in his dealings with his employees. Such intervention and control of employer-employee relations on the part of public bodies thus serves to further public recognition of nuclear work.

It is reasonable to suspect that this situation contributes especially to the professionalization of labor, in that it makes labor more independent of employers and more dependent upon associations of colleagues (i.e., the trade unions with jurisdiction or

interest in nuclear work) for the improvement of working conditions and career continuity. Any substantial change in working conditions, therefore, is not a matter that can easily be settled between the representatives of a local union and plant management—it is a matter of industry-wide concern affecting community interests represented by the Atomic Energy Commission. This has been a principal factor in the establishment of the Atomic Energy Technical Committee of the AFL–CIO.

HEALTH AND SAFETY

So far in this paper, the thesis has been presented that nuclear technology contributes to the professionalization of American labor in ways somewhat similar to those of automation. It should be pointed out, however, that nuclear technology may make an even greater contribution than automation to the professionalization of labor, insofar as nuclear technology attaches special importance to public health and safety.

After intensive study of thirteen automated plants in a variety of industries, James R. Bright has concluded that the effects of the more advanced phases of automation upon labor have been somewhat less dramatic than many authorities on this subject originally expected. For example, he has pointed out that increased automaticity apparently results in unchanged or reduced skill requirements for most operating and maintenance personnel, except for electronics maintenance specialists. At the same time, he has indicated that there is evidence of need for more "over-all machine repairmen" who are familiar with all the control technologies involved in an automated system. Yet Bright has maintained that there is no evidence that the over-all effect of automation can be expected to increase the proportion of the industrial work force in more skilled specialist or maintenance jobs.[16]

In two nuclear power plants studied by

15 Oscar S. Smith, "Obligations of Government as Owner, Financer, and Consumer in Relation to Collective Bargaining," *Labor Law Journal* (November, 1956), pp. 684–85.

16 James R. Bright, *Automation and Management* (Boston: Graduate School of Business Administration, Harvard University, 1956), pp. 160–162, 176–193.

the authors (the station in operation at Shippingport, Pennsylvania, and the station planned for Indian Point, New York) more skilled operating and maintenance personnel are needed than would be required in a conventional electric power generation plant, even after the initial start-up of the plant. Moreover, from 6 to 8 per cent of the employees in nuclear power plants are radiation-protection specialists—an occupation that does not occur in non-nuclear work. Between 1 and 2 per cent of the employees of AEC contractors operating nuclear installations are radiation-protection specialists.[17]

The development of the occupation of radiation-protection specialists indicates the extreme importance of radiation protection in nuclear facilities. Nuclear radiation, in the form of alpha and beta particles and gamma rays, presents a unique health hazard, in that these forms of radiation are ordinarily undetectible by the human senses, exposure effects are cumulative, and damage to the human system may not result in a health impairment until many years after the exposure has taken place. For these reasons, the Atomic Energy Act of 1954 and other federal and state regulations, as well as administrative regulations of the Atomic Energy Commission, the National Committee on Radiation Protection and Measurement, the United States Public Health Service, and other concerned government agencies, have specified physical and personnel safeguards for workers in nuclear facilities and residents in surrounding communities.

Although elaborate physical safeguards are built into nuclear plants and radiation-safety specialists are given responsibility for full-time surveillance of compliance with

[17] John I. Saks, *op. cit.*, p. 923.

safety regulations, the basic responsibility for radiation safety rests on the nuclear worker. Similar training requirements are placed upon those who handle radioisotopes in their work As in the case of nuclear reactors, radioisotopes in industrial applications constitute a source of radiation hazard not only to employees but also to their families and other members of the surrounding community. Thus nuclear workers appear to have a responsibility for public safety that is greater than the responsibility for safety ordinarily placed upon workers in non-nuclear plants.

In a sense, hazards from nuclear technology are perhaps felt by much of the public to be a dimly understood but present danger; consequently, there is an element of awe involved. Such apprehension has, to some extent at least, surrounded the advent of many major technological innovations (e.g., steam, electricity) with an aura of mystery which has served at times to set certain workers (e.g., the railroad engineer, the airline pilot) apart, as occupying statuses in our society worthy of special prestige, inasmuch as they are considered to have the direct safety of many people in their hands. But with nuclear technology the actual complexity and perceived importance of such industrial applications have perhaps made an even larger contribution to the process of professionalization, because the work has been surrounded by a supporting halo of secrecy and a lack of general public understanding of the processes. It is no accident that the expression "professional secrets" is to be found in everyday speech; for surely this factor is an important ingredient in the process of the professionalization of labor taking place in research and manufacturing involving nuclear energy.

Professionalization in Illegitimate Occupations

Our examination of the concept of professionalization would not be complete without some reference, at least, to professional groups that are considered to be illegitimate with regard to their relations to the larger society. In common parlance, prostitution has long been regarded as "the oldest profession." Some would prefer to call such groups that engage in illegitimate activities "pseudo-professional." However, we feel that this would be begging the question. The striking fact about the aspect of human behavior under discussion here is that individuals, even in activities that are generally disapproved by members of the larger society, establish patterns of activity that are indicative of rudimentary professionalization. There is a real difference, for example, between a professional thief and an amateur thief, *and these differences are recognized by both professionals and amateurs in the world of crime*. The eminent criminologist, Edwin H. Sutherland, described these differences in the following reading, noting the degree to which professional thieves assume many of the characteristics of professionalization as they apply to legitimate occupations.* Could it be that professional thieves are in some respects more professionalized in their attitudes and behavior than clergymen? Or businessmen?

* For an illustration of the professionalization of the "legitimate" occupation devoted to coping with "illegitimate" occupations, see August Vollmer, "Police Progress in the Past Twenty-five Years," *Journal of the American Institute of Criminology*, **24**, 1933–34, 161–175.

Edwin H. Sutherland
(Professional Theft)

The essential characteristics of the profession of theft, as described by the professional thief, ... are technical skill, status, consensus, differential association, and organization. Two significant conclusions may be derived from analysis of these characteristics. The first is that the characteristics of the profession of theft are similar to the characteristics of any other permanent group. The second is that certain elements run through these characteristics which differentiate the professional thieves sharply from other groups. The similarities and differences will be indicated in the following elaboration of these characteristics and of the implications which may be derived from them.

THE PROFESSION OF THEFT AS A COMPLEX OF TECHNIQUES

The professional thief has a complex of abilities and skills, just as do physicians, lawyers, or bricklayers. The abilities and

Reprinted from *The Professional Thief* (Chicago: The University of Chicago Press, 1937), pp. 197–206 and 215–217, by permission of The University of Chicago Press. Copyright 1937 by the University of Chicago.

skills of the professional thief are directed to the planning and execution of crimes, the disposal of stolen goods, the fixing of cases in which arrests occur, and the control of other situations which may arise in the course of the occupation. Manual dexterity and physical force are a minor element in these techniques. The principal elements in these techniques are wits, "front," and talking ability. The thieves who lack these general abilities or the specific skills which are based on the general abilities are regarded as amateurs, even though they may steal habitually.[1] Also, burglars, robbers, kidnapers, and others who engage in the "heavy rackets" are generally not regarded as professional thieves, for they depend primarily on manual dexterity or force. A few criminals in the "heavy rackets" use their wits, "front," and talk-

[1] Several statistical studies of habitual thieves, defined in terms of repeated arrests, have been published. Some of these are excellent from the point of view of the problems with which they deal, but they throw little light on professional thieves because they do not differentiate professional thieves from other habitual thieves. See Roland Grassberger, *Gewerbs-und Berufsverbrecherlum in den Vereinigten Staaten von Amerika* (Vienna, 1933); Fritz Berger, *Die rückfälligen Betrüger* (Leipzig, 1929); Alfred John, *Die Rückfallsdiebe* (Leipzig, 1929).

ing ability, and these are regarded by the professional thieves as belonging to the profession.

The division between professional and nonprofessional thieves in regard to this complex of techniques is relatively sharp. This is because these techniques are developed to a high point only by education, and the education can be secured only in association with professional thieves; thieves do not have formal educational institutions for the training of recruits.[2] Also, these techniques generally call for cooperation which can be secured only in association with professional thieves. Finally, this complex of techniques represents a unified preparation for all professional problems in the life of the thief. Certain individuals, as lone wolves, develop to a high point the technique of executing a specific act of theft—e.g., forgery—but are quite unprepared in plans, resources, and connections to deal with emergencies such as arrest.

Because some of the techniques are specific, professional thieves tend to specialize on a relatively small number of rackets that are related to one another. On the other hand, because of the contacts in the underworld with criminals of all kinds and because of the generality of some of the techniques of crime, professional thieves frequently transfer for longer or shorter periods from their specialty to some other racket. In some cases they like the new racket better than the old and remain in the new field. In many cases they dislike the new racket. Hapgood's thief was primarily a pickpocket; he participated occasionally in burglaries but never liked burglary and remained at heart a pickpocket; he wrote regarding burglary: "It is too dangerous, the come-back is too sure, you have to depend too much on the nerve of your pals, the 'bits' [prison sentences] are too long, and it is very difficult to 'square' it."[3]

The evidence is not adequate to determine whether specialization has increased or decreased. Cooper asserts that it has decreased and explains the decrease as due to the war, prohibition, and the depression. He asserts specifically that confidence men, who, a generation ago would have been ashamed to engage in any theft outside of their own specialty, are now engaging in banditry, kidnaping, and other crimes, and he gives a detailed description of a conference of confidence men held in Chicago in which they attempted to formulate a code which would prohibit their colleagues from excursions outside their own field.[4] Byrnes showed in 1886 in his history of professional criminals in America that many thieves participated for longer or shorter times in crimes outside their own special field.[5]

The Profession of Theft as Status

The professional thief, like any other professional man, has status. The status is based upon his technical skill, financial standing, connections, power, dress, manners, and wide knowledge acquired in his migratory life. His status is seen in the attitudes of other criminals, the police, the court officials, newspapers, and others. The term "thief" is regarded as honorific and is used regularly without qualifying adjectives to refer to the professional thief. It is so defined in a recent dictionary of criminal slang: "Thief, *n.* A member of the underworld who steals often and successfully. This term is applied with reserve and only to

---

[2] Stories circulate at intervals regarding schools for pickpockets, confidence men, and other professional thieves. If formal schools of this nature have ever existed, they have probably been ephemeral.

[3] Hutchins Hapgood, *Autobiography of a Thief* (New York, 1903), p. 107.

[4] Courtney R. Cooper, *Ten Thousand Public Enemies* (Boston, 1935), pp. 271–272; "Criminal America," *Saturday Evening Post,* **207** (April 27, 1935), 6. A confidence man, when asked regarding this conference of confidence men in Chicago, said that Cooper's writings regarding it should have been entitled "Mythologies of 1935."

[5] Thomas Byrnes, *Professional Criminals of America* (New York, 1886). Grassberger (*op. cit.*) has several ingenious methods of measuring the extent of specialization, but the conclusions apply to habitual criminals in general rather than to professional thieves, and the habitual criminals in general probably have less tendency to specialize than do the professional thieves.

habitual criminals. It is considered a high compliment."[6]

Professional thieves are contemptuous of amateur thieves and have many epithets which they apply to the amateurs. These epithets include "snatch-and-grab thief," "boot-and-shoe thief," and "best-hold cannon." Professional thieves may use "rawjaw" methods when operating under excellent protection, but they are ashamed of these methods and console themselves with the knowledge that they could do their work in more artistic manner if necessary. They will have no dealings with thieves who are unable to use the correct methods of stealing.

Professional thieves disagree as to the extent of gradations within the profession. Some thieves divide the profession into "big-time" and "small-time" thieves on the basis of the size of the stakes for which they play, on the preparations for a particular stake, and on connections. A confidence man who regarded himself as "big-time" wrote as follows regarding a shoplifter:

While he is undoubtedly a professional thief, I should a few years ago [before he was committed to prison] have been ashamed to be seen on the street with him. I say this not out of a spirit of snobbishness but simply because for business reasons I feel that my reputation would have suffered in the eyes of my friends to be seen in the company of a booster [shoplifter].

On the other hand, the thief who wrote this document insisted that there are no essential gradations within the profession:

I have never considered anyone a small-time thief. If he is a thief, he is a thief—small-time, big-time, middle-time, eastern standard, or Rocky Mountain, it is all the same. Neither have I considered anyone big-time. It all depends on the spot and how it is handled. I recall a heel touch [sneak theft] at ten one morning which showed $21 and three hours later the same troupe took off one for $6,500 in the same place. Were they small-time in the morning and big-time in the afternoon? The confidence men who play against a store [using a fake gambling club or brokerage office] expect to get large

amounts. But there is considerable interchange, some working for a time at short con and then at elaborate con rackets. Those who play against a store know those who engage in short con; if not, they have many mutual friends.

This difference in opinion is quite similar to the difference that would emerge if lawyers or doctors were discussing the gradations within their professions. In any case there is pride in one's own position in the group. This pride may be illustrated by the action of Roger Benton, a forger, who was given a signed blank check to fill out the amount of money he desired; Benton wrote a big "Void" across the face of the check and returned it to the grocer who gave it to him. He explains, "I suppose I had too much professional pride to use it—after all I was a forger who took smart money from smart banks, not a thief who robbed honest grocerymen."[7]

THE PROFESSION OF THEFT AS CONSENSUS

The profession of theft is a complex of common and shared feelings, sentiments, and overt acts. Pickpockets have similar reactions to prospective victims and to the particular situations in which victims are found. This similarity of reactions is due to the common background of experiences and the similarity of points of attention. These reactions are like the "clinical intuitions" which different physicians form of a patient or different lawyers form of a juryman on quick inspection. Thieves can work together without serious diagreements because they have these common and similar attitudes. This consensus extends throughout the activities and lives of the thieves, culminating in similar and common reactions to the law, which is regarded as the common enemy. Out of this consensus, moreover, develop the codes, the attitudes of helpfulness, and the loyalties of the underworld.

The following explanation of the emphasis which thieves place on punctuality

---

6 Noel Ersine, *Underworld and Prison Slang* (Upland, Indiana, 1935).

7 *Where Do I Go from Here?* (New York: Lee Furman, Inc., 1936 [by permission]), p. 62.

is an illustration of the way consensus has developed:

It is a cardinal principle among partners in crime that appointments shall be kept promptly. When you "make a meet" you are there on the dot or you do not expect your partner to wait for you. The reason why is obvious. Always in danger of arrest, the danger to one man is increased by the arrest of the other; and arrest is the only legitimate excuse for failing to keep an appointment. Thus, if the appointment is not kept on time, the other may assume arrest and his best procedure is to get away as quickly as possible and save his own skin.[8]

One of the most heinous offenses that a thief can commit against another thief is to inform, "squeal," or "squawk." This principle is generally respected even when it is occasionally violated. Professional thieves probably violate the principle less frequently than other criminals for the reason that they are more completely immune from punishment, which is the pressure that compels an offender to inform on others. Many thieves will submit to severe punishment rather than inform. Two factors enter into this behavior. One is the injury which would result to himself in the form of loss of prestige, inability to find companions among thieves in the future, and reprisals if he should inform. The other is loyalty and identification of self with other thieves. The spontaneous reactions of offenders who are in no way affected by the behavior of the squealer, as by putting him in coventry, are expressions of genuine disgust, fear, and hatred.[9] Consensus is the basis of both of these reactions, and the two together explain how the rule against informing grows out of the common experiences of the thieves.

Consensus means, also, that thieves have a system of values and an *esprit de corps* which support the individual thief in his criminal career. The distress of the solitary thief who is not a member of the under-world society of criminals is illustrated in the following statement by Roger Benton at the time when he was an habitual but not a professional forger:

I had no home, no place to which I could return for sanctuary, no friend in the world to whom I could talk freely. . . . I was a lone man, my face set away from those of my fellows. But I didn't mind—at least I didn't think I minded. [A little later he became acquainted in St. Louis with Nero's place, which was a rendezvous for theatrical people.] I liked Nero. I liked the crowd that gathered in his place and I wanted my evening entertainment there to continue. And I found that I was hungrier for human companionship than I had known. Here I found it. . . . It was a gay interlude and I enjoyed it thoroughly, and neglected my own work [forgery] while I played and enjoyed the simple, honest friendships of these children of the stage. [Still later.] I could not rid myself of the crying need for the sense of security which social recognition and contact with one's fellows and their approval furnishes. I was lonely and frightened and wanted to be where there was someone who knew me as I had been before I had become a social outcast.[10]

Among the criminal tribes of India the individual was immersed almost completely in a consistent culture and felt no distress in attacking an outsider because this did not make him an enemy in any group which had significance for him. Nowhere in America, probably, is a criminal so completely immersed in a group that he does not feel his position as an enemy of the larger society. Even after Roger Benton became a member of the underworld as a professional forger, he felt lonely and ill at case: "I was sick of the whole furtive business, of the constant need to be a fugitive among my fellows, of the impossibility of settling down and making a home for myself, and of the fear of imprisonment."[11]

The professional thief in America feels that he is a social outcast. This is especially true of the professional thieves who originated in middle-class society, as many of them did. He feels that he is a renegade when he becomes a thief. Chic Conwell

---

[8] *Ibid.,* p. 269 (by permission).

[9] Philip S. Van Cise, *Fighting the Underworld* (Boston, 1936), p. 321; Josiah Flynt Willard, *Tramping with Tramps* (New York, 1899), pp. 23–24, and *My Life* (New York, 1908), pp. 331–340.

[10] *Op. cit.,* pp. 62, 66–67, 80–81 (by permission).

[11] *Ibid.,* p. 242 (by permission).

states that the thief is looking for arguments to ease his conscience and that he blocks off considerations about the effects of his crimes upon the victims and about the ultimate end of his career. When he is alone in prison, he cannot refrain from thought about such things, and then he shudders at the prospect of returning to his professional activities. Once he is back in his group, he assumes the "bravado" attitudes of the other thieves, his shuddering ceases, and everything seems to be all right. Under the circumstances he cannot develop an integrated personality, but the distress is mitigated, his isolation reduced, and his professional life made possible because he has a group of his own in which he carries on a social existence as a thief, with a culture and values held in common by many thieves. In this sense, also, professional theft means consensus.

THEFT AS A PROFESSION

The professional thief who wrote the manuscript in the preceeding part of this book did not make a comparative study of professions as a method of reaching a conclusion that stealing may be a profession. Rather he assumed that it was and merely applied the name "profession" in accordance with the traditional language of his group. It may be worthwhile to consider very briefly whether theft is really a profession.

Carr-Saunders and Wilson list the following as the characteristics of the learned professions: technical skill, formal association as in medical and legal societies, state regulation of the conditions of admission to the profession by examinations and licenses, a degree of monopoly growing out of the formal association and of the regulations by the state, and ethical standards

which minimize the pecuniary motive and emphasize the social welfare motive.[12]

The profession of theft has most of these characteristics. It has technical skill, an exclusive group, immunity from punishment which almost amounts to a license from the state to steal, a degree of monopoly growing out of their exclusive group relationship and of their recognition by the agents of the state. Each of these is less formal than in the other professions. They do not have written constitutions for their groups or licenses which they may hang on their office walls. They do have the informal equivalents of constitutions and licenses.

The one characteristic listed by Carr-Saunders and Wilson which they lack is the ethical standards which minimize the pecuniary motive. When this point was mentioned to this professional thief, he admitted that his profession did not have this characteristic, but he added that the medical and legal professions would have very few members if that were used as a criterion of membership.

The learned professions do have a huge body of knowledge in written form, and a long period of formal training in sciences which are basic to their vocational activities. The profession of theft, also, has a body of knowledge, not nearly so large and not in written form, which has been accumulating over several centuries. It includes articulate formulation of the principles of the different rackets. This body of traditional knowledge is transmitted to the student by apprenticeship methods rather than through a professional school. For this reason professional theft should not be regarded as a learned profession. It is probably more nearly on the level of professional athletics, so far as learning is concerned.

12 A. W. Carr-Saunders and P. A. Wilson, *The Professions* (Oxford, 1933).

" Professions " and " Non-Professions "

The previous readings and our interpretation of the concept of professionalization as illustrated by them do not emphasize distinctions between "professions" and "non-professions"—we have simply stated that "profession" and "non-profession" are "ideal types," and that in reality, any specific occupational group might be placed or ranked along a continuum ranging between these ideal types according to the degree to which the occupational group manifested the elements of professionalization. However, other writers have been concerned with defining and studying elements that distinguish "professions" from "non-professions."* Professor William Goode has this interest, as is shown in the following paper on librarians. He maintains that librarianship is not now a profession in that it lacks (1) prolonged specialized training in a body of abstract knowledge and (2) a collectivity or service orientation, in terms of professionally defined "needs" of the client, rather than what the client simply "wants." Although Goode admits that librarianship is moving along professionalization continuum, he also maintains that this occupational group is not likely to achieve the status of a "profession," because the general public is not likely to permit librarians to attain the degree of collective self-control required of true professional groups (i.e., more professionalized groups).†

Goode's approach is not contradictory to the general approach taken in assembling this book of readings on professionalization. We need to gain more information about factors that distinguish more professionalized from less professionalized occupational groups, as well as about those elements they may have in common.

* At least as early as 1907 arguments for the professional status of an occupation were presented in the social science literature; see J. E. Sterrett, "The Profession of Accountantcy," *Annals of the American Academy of Political and Social Science,* Vol. **28** (July–Dec. 1906), 16–27. In the same journal a few years later F. M. Feiker was speaking of "The Profession of Commerce in the Making," [*The Annals of the American Academy of Political and Social Science,* **101**, No. 190 (May 1922), 203–207] and made explicit mention of "the professionalizing of commerce." It should also be recognized that the professional status of many specialist occupations in business, industry and government is still highly contentious, and the question is still raised: "Is management a profession?" For opposing answers to the question see Edward Meigh, "The Implications of Membership of a Professional Body," *The British Management Review,* **2**, No. 1 126–140, and Ray Lewis and Angus Maude, *Professional People* (London: Phoenix House, 1952).

† In contrast, in writing about the current status of personnel work the Committee on Professional Standards of the Society for Personnel Administration concluded:

There has been considerable evidence in recent years of the professional nature of personnel work. It is not necessary to debate here whether or not it is a fully developed profession. It probably is not. However, it does have a number of characteristics which indicate that it is an emerging profession. . . .

The element most badly needed for the improvement of personnel work is professional competence. Full professional level performance will follow closely in the wake of competence. Although the need of standards for entrance, performance, and ethics in personnel work is evident, the primary need is for educational standards which will result in an adequate supply of competent personnel workers. . . .[*Professional Standards for Personnel Work,* Pamphlet No. 13 (Washington, D.C.: Society for Personnel Administration, 1956), pp. 2 and 8.]

These matters are discussed in connection with this and other occupations in Chapters 2 and 3.

William Goode (Librarianship)

An industrial society has an open class stratification system; it offers some an opportunity to rise, but it offers no guarantee against downward social mobility. Compared to other types of societies, this one demands a wider variety of higher level skills and thus generates much pressure against the forces that in all societies tend to keep the individual in his original caste or class. Much of the resulting mobility is based on a radical change which has taken place in the occupational structure of modern industrial societies, one which neither Marx nor orthodox economists anticipated, an expansion of the demand for professional and technical skills of a high order.[1]

Thus not only are individuals competing with one another in their efforts to rise in the class system, but occupations, too, are engaged in the same competition and may move up or down in power, prestige, or income.

Both systems may be viewed as zero-sum games. The income which one individual receives cannot be claimed by another. If an occupation rises in income level or in prestige ranking, necessarily others will lose. That many have described our job structure as diamond-shaped—a bulge in the middle ranges of occupations—rather than pyramidal does not change these relationships. An expanding economy may yield more real income for nearly all occupations; but at any given time there is only so much income to be distributed, each occupation has a higher or lower average income than others, and those which have risen have done so at the expense of others.

With reference to other class attributes such as power and prestige, the dynamics are perhaps more complex, but essentially similar. In an industrial society far more jobs and people are to be found in the middle ranges of prestige than would be found in the same ranges in peasant societies. However, each occupation that rises does so at the expense of others which it surpasses, and when many occupations are rising, their net gain is low relative to one another. Librarians are among those occupational groups that are seeking the advantages of professional status. Not only do the professionals form a larger part of

the labor force than they did half a century ago—from 859 per 100,000 in 1870 to 4,353 per 100,000 in 1961[2]—but far more of the labor force is engaged in white-collar and technical occupations that strive by various means to emulate the traditional professions.

Spokesmen for almost every recognized white-collar job have asserted that they are professional. Whether we smile at the pretentiousness of such a claim or grudgingly concede it, we see that no matter how many occupations make the claim, map out a program for professionalization, or even take some steps toward professionalism, very likely most will never become professions. Granted that the occupation of librarian has risen in income and prestige over the past twenty years, that an increasing percentage of college and university librarians have faculty status, that librarians have faculty status, that librarians have more formal education—how far can the occupation go? Can it become a profession?[3]

Such a question does not presuppose an easily visible dividing line between the professions and other occupations. Any traits used in the definition of the term "profession" must be conceived as variables, forming a continuum along which a given occupation may move. Instead of the dichotomy of "professional-non professional," we use the variable of "professionalism," and we may ask how far an

---

[1] See Natalie Rogoff, *Occupational Mobility* (Glencoe, Ill.: Free Press, 1953), for a good analysis of the relation between individual job mobility and shifts in the occupational structure.

[2] The April 1961 figure is a survey estimate, calculated from data in U. S. Department of Labor, *Employment and Earnings,* 7, No. 11 (May, 1961), 6, Table 11. Relevant data from the 1960 Census have not been released, but that 1950 ratio of librarians to population shows that librarianship is one of the faster growing occupations.

[3] I have not been able to find any formal surveys in which the prestige of librarians has been compared with prestige of other occupations. For salaries of librarians, see the informative table in D. E. and R. B. Strout, "Higher Salaries, More Vacancies," *Library Journal,* 86 (June 15, 1961), 2267. The table shows that the "cluster range" of salaries of new graduates of twenty-six library schools increased from $3,300–$3,800 in 1954 to $4,800–$5,200 in 1960. The average salaries given in *American Library and Book Trade Annual,* W. E. Wright (ed.) (New York: R. R. Bowker Co., 1960), conform closely. For faculty status, see the later discussion in this article.

occupation has moved in the direction of increased or decreased professionalism. We can ask to what degree the journeyman plumber or the bulldozer operator is professional, even if an evaluation shows the degree to be low.

Such a formulation does not escape the problem of definitions, nor does it wipe out the differences between the professions and the non-professions. Librarians, nurses, and social workers have spent much energy in trying to professionalize their occupations during the past several decades, but nursing will not become a profession, the other two have not yet become professions, and I am doubtful that the librarians will become full-fledged professionals.

Many of us have read much about, and participated in, the continuing discussions concerning the librarians' claim to professional status. For that reason I shall not repeat the definitions of a profession now available in the literature. Though varying, these definitions do not contradict one another.[4]

Any lengthy analysis of the characteristics of a profession will note that it is autonomous, is organized in professional associations, its members receive higher incomes than most workers and occupy a high proportion of the governing posts in our society, and so on. Two traits, conspicuous because they seem to be found in all definitions, are sociologically central, because they are the main determinants of the others. Any program of action which relies on public relations techniques, or organized demands for high salaries, or the formulation of a code of ethics, will fail unless it changes these two characteristics as well. These two are: (1) prolonged specialized training in a body of abstract knowledge, and (2) a collectivity or service orientation. Let us look at both of these more closely, so that we may later assess where the occupation of librarian stands with reference to them.

The knowledge must first of all be organized in abstract principles, and cannot consist in mere details however vast in quantity. These principles must be applicable to concrete problems. The relevant employers or clients must also believe that the principles exist, and that they can be used to solve problems which are believed to be appropriately solved by others.[5] Moreover, the profession must not only possess this knowledge; it must also help to create it. Next, the profession must be the final arbiter in any dispute about what is or is not valid knowledge. Finally, the knowledge is somewhat like the "mystery" of the ancient guilds, in that the profession largely controls access to it through control over school admissions, school curriculums, and examinations, and in that it seems to be beyond the capacity of ordinary men.

"Service orientation" means that the professional decision is not properly to be based on the self-interest of the professional, but on the need of the client.[6] The practitioner defines, of course, what the client "needs"; it may not always be what the client wants. Next, the profession must, at certain points, make real sacrifices. For example, the individual must defer for some years a full adult status with its gratifications in order to train himself adequately; the practitioner may be asked to contribute services to those who cannot pay; in certain crises, members of the profession are asked to risk their lives or reputations—the scientist should publish the truth at the risk of losing his job, the lawyer defend an unpopular cause, the clergyman oppose even the influential sinner.

4 A handful of such definitions is tabulated and analyzed in William J. Goode and Mary Jean Huntington, "Professions in American Society" (unpublished manuscript), Chap. i. The definitions are taken from such well-known sources as A. M. Carr-Saunders and P. A. Wilson, Abraham Flexner, Roscoe Pound, Louis D. Brandeis, Robert D. Leigh, and Carl F. Taeusch. See also my "Encroachment, Charlatanism, and the Emerging Profession: Psychology, Medicine, and Sociology," *American Sociological Review,* 25 (December, 1960), 902.

5 E.g., most people do not believe that marital counselors are *able* to resolve family conflicts or that families *should* bring their private problems to such outsiders.

6 Thus kickbacks are improper in both law and medicine (though an agent's commission is proper in business), because the practitioner might be tempted to recommend a step that would be in his own interest rather than the client's.

Such an orientation is not to be confused with individual "altruism." Professionals seek their own gain as much as any occupational group, and professional associations fight to increase their privileges and advantages. Rather, the professional community must create a set of controls such that its members are more handsomely rewarded for conforming to its code of ethics than for failing to do so. The rules which it imposes are stricter than those the society embodies in its administrative regulations and statutes. The service orientation also means that the profession spends both time and money in seeking superior candidates and giving them better training, even though this increases competition in the field. Only to the extent that the society believes the profession is regulated by this collectivity orientation will it grant the profession much autonomy or freedom from lay supervision and control.

Analyses of other occupations' rise to professional status cannot furnish guidelines for librarians or yield a "typical" process of professionalization. Few adequate histories of any profession are available.[7]

No prior civilization in world history has given such prominence to technical expertise, though of course all major civilizations have used bureaucracies which depended somewhat on technical competence. The tempo of professionalization has increased markedly in the past half-century, compared with the last half of the nineteenth century. Prior to that time, one must search carefully through the centuries to find *any* examples of the process. At best, they are represented by the slow splitting off of medicine, law, and university teaching from the clergy.

There seem to be no examples of professions that lost that status, because their structural position permits them to absorb, dominate, or supplant any relevant knowledge and skills which might threaten their standing. Thus, in medicine, the bonesetter, midwife, and leech have disappeared, while the new fields of anesthesiology and radio-

logy have simply become medical specialties.[8]

The uniqueness of the contemporary epoch, then, prevents us from tabulating the professions which fell and the occupations which rose, inferring thereby a timeless pattern, a clearcut "natural history" or "embryology" of the profession. No obvious steps can be seen through which an occupation *must* pass on its way to professionalization. All those which have been noted in the literature take place more or less simultaneously. Or, phrased differently, the elite members of all high-ranking occupational groups seem to know what to do, and try all the moves they can accomplish: formulating a code of ethics, founding a professional association, promulgating favorable legislation, establishing curricula for professional training (preferably in a university), making appeals to foundations for funds with which to develop new professional knowledge, writing articles to explain the unique contribution of the occupation, making protests against inaccurate stereotypes of the occupation, and so on. Since, however, the efficacy of any one of these is dependent on how much the others realistically reflect the occupation's social position, none is unequivocally required before others. Hundreds of codes of ethics have been written, for instance, but few occupations are sufficiently integrated to compel their members to obey these rules.

Occupations as varied as pharmacy, nursing, chiropracty, funeral direction, and hair dressing have set up formal curricula, and many have succeeded, if only temporarily, in attaching themselves to colleges and universities, but they have not thereby moved far toward professionalization. Such actions may be viewed as "steps," but often may be more profitably viewed as "testing operations"—if they are accepted and supported by the public or the relevant publics, then the occupation has indeed progressed; otherwise not. They may be also useful because

---

[7] Actually, I know of *none*, but perhaps one exists.

[8] See in this connection Beatrice Mongeau, Harvey L. Smith, and Ann C. Meney, "The 'Granny' Midwife: Changing Roles and Functions of a Folk Practitioner," *The American Journal of Sociology*, 66 (March 1961), 497–505.

of their by-products. In making such demands, or steps, the occupation evaluates its own tasks and, because of its new perspective, begins to initiate changes in its base of knowledge or its service orientation, which do improve its competitive position. This process has been especially evident in librarianship in the postwar period.

Ten years ago, Leigh wrote that librarianship was a "skilled occupation on its way to becoming an organized profession," and commented that "like other occupations the librarians have accepted professional status as a goal."[9] It has certainly continued on its way since that time, but an outsider would, I believe, have to reaffirm Leigh's evaluation: Librarianship is still on its way. Can it achieve that goal? I am inclined to give a negative answer.

Any prediction is risky, this one especially so in view of the initial advantages which librarians enjoy in their struggle for full recognition. First, they are thought to be, and in fact are, attached to learning. Identified as they are with knowledge, a prime source of occupational prestige in our society, their claims can not be dismissed lightly.[10] Second, they are service-oriented, rather than self-interested, at least in certain senses. As one researcher put it, "the discontent of librarians with their salaries tends to be tame and genteel."[11] Librarians administer large budgets, but none of the relevant publics even conceives of graft as a possibility. Librarians view as unworthy an intense concern with money. Almost no peripheral work is available to them, as it is to the university scholar, which would bring in additional income but which would carry the stigma of popularization or commercialization. The public believes that the librarians' main task is service to the reader, and

librarians agree, at least with certain qualifications to be noted later.

Third, an increasing number of librarians are trained in professional schools, some of which offer a doctorate and are associated with universities. Much energy is devoted to curriculum development, and a serious attempt has been made to evaluate these schools.[12] Fourth, librarians belong to professional associations, both state and national, and have formulated a code of ethics.[13]

Fifth, unlike several other occupations striving for recognition as professions, such as nursing or pharmacy, librarians are not subordinate to any other group in the same situs or organization.[14]

Finally, the librarian has no competitors, and indeed librarians themselves have a sense that their occupation is unique.[15]

If, with these characteristics, librarians share in the emulation of professional rank that is characteristic of our epoch, the driving forces are not primarily snobbery. They evince, rather, the librarians' wish to improve the quality of their performance and the occupational standards by which they live. Moreover, there are great advantages in making good such a claim. The profession would then enjoy more deference and money and thereby attract abler recruits, who in turn could develop the field further and justify the position already achieved. This is, of course, a bootstrap operation. It is not possible to obtain the status and *then* get the advantages. The increasing advan-

[9] Robert D. Leigh, *The Public Library in the United States* (New York: Columbia University Press, 1960), p. 192.

[10] Note the importance of this complex factor in the prestige ratings made in the study by Cecil C. North and Paul K. Hatt, "Jobs and Occupations: A Popular Evaluation," in Logan Wilson and William L. Kolb (eds.), *Sociological Analysis* (New York: Harcourt, Brace & World, Inc., 1949), pp. 465, 470–471.

[11] Kaspar D. Naegele, "Librarians" (Vancouver, Canada, 1959), p. 131. (Mimeographed.)

[13] The social and technical difficulties of such evaluations must not be underestimated. In this connection see Louis R. Wilson, "Historical Development of Education for Librarianship in the United States" in *Education for Librarianship,* Bernard Berelson (ed.) (Chicago: American Library Association, 1949), p. 48 ff.; and Neil C. Van Deusen, "Professional Education for Librarianship: Summary," in *Education for Librarianship,* p. 187 ff.

[13] The 1939 formulation of the ALA code is discussed and reprinted in Guy R. Lyle *et al., The Administration of the College Library* (3d Ed.; New York: H. W. Wilson Co., 1961), pp. 210 ff.

[14] Paul K. Hatt, "Occupation and Social Stratification," *The American Journal of Sociology,* 55 (May, 1950), 539–543.

[15] Naegele, *op. cit.,* pp. 122–123.

tages must parallel the intrinsic changes toward professionalism, in a virtuous spiral which is nevertheless extremely slow. There are no immediate rewards in imposing higher standards upon students or curriculum. There are only indirect and delayed rewards. The occupation faces a market situation with reference to all that it has to offer or all that it wishes to obtain. "Success" means changing the relations between professional and client, the professional and other professionals, the professional and the general public, and among the colleagues in their professional community. Because these relations constitute a complex network of social payments and counter-payments, a change in any one of them means some change in the rest but equally means that changes are relatively difficult and slow.

THE KNOWLEDGE BASE OF THE LIBRARIAN

Let us take up in more detail the fundamental problem of librarians in this struggle —the knowledge base on which the occupation is built. . . .

The librarian must organize and order the flow of information. He must help others locate it. He must initially select the best material possible and continue to screen it. The library may be viewed as a gigantic memory drum but one which is not automatic. Instead, it requires the programming of the expert librarian to give its answer. The librarian's task is to "reduce the anonymity of books," films, and other materials embodying the thought of our generation as well as prior generations.

Certainly, professional librarians would generally accept this as at least the core occupational task, but several key elements are missing to prevent its knowledge base from being sufficient for full professional status. The central gap is of course the failure to develop a general body of scientific knowledge bearing precisely on this problem, in the way that the medical profession with its auxiliary scientific fields has developed an immense body of knowledge with which to cure human diseases.

While the general knowledge embodied in professional library curriculums is likely to be communications theory, the sociology or psychology of mass communications, or the psychology of learning as it applies to reading, most day-to-day professional work utilizes rather concrete, rule-of-thumb, local regulations and rules, and a major cataloging system.[16] The problems of selection and organization are dealt with on a highly empiricist basis, concretely, with little reference to general scientific principles. Moreover, little if any of the current research in librarianship attempts to develop such general principles.

Second, even if in fact librarians had such a body of knowledge, the public does not know it, but rather views the librarian as a gatekeeper and the custodian of the "stock room." To them, the library is a kind of department store, offering, in small libraries, the entertainment of current fiction and in large libraries a wider selection; but in either case the librarian is an intelligent clerk who can help them find the goods they need. They are not aware of criteria of selection. Indeed, as more than one librarian has complained, the public rarely sees a professional librarian in the flesh, and almost never sees the librarian in action. His work takes place in areas where the public does not ordinarily go, and the public has no way of seeing what he does. The public does not believe he has a real body of knowledge that is specific to his occupation.

In his contact with most professions, the client does not see the most important work going on, either. The lawyer's client does not see the work that goes into a brief, nor does the architect's client see the work that goes into a design. The "on-stage" activities of the professions are different from, and much less important than, the activities that go on "backstage." However, the public does believe that there *is* a backstage, that,

16 Lawrence S. Thompson, "Preparation and Status of Personnel," in *The Status of American College and University Librarians*, Robert B. Downs (ed.) ("ACRL Monograph," No. 22 [Chicago: American Library Association, 1958]), pp. 102–105, states (without always agreeing with) some of the current doubts as to the importance of formal education for librarianship.

in fact, complex intellectual activities go on when he is not there.

A further structural characteristic of the librarian's occupation is shared with other professions. Librarians have complained that the public does not see the difference between the professional librarian and the nonprofessional, or clerk, because in the main the bookseeker has direct contact only with the latter. Perhaps some two-thirds of library work is nonprofessional in character.[17] Most of the significant technical problems of librarianship occur only at a certain size of "flow"—number of incoming books, number of books on the shelves, number of readers, etc. Otherwise, an individual, a corporation, or a small township might simply use an assistant, an aide, or a clerk to "keep things in order." When the library is large, it utilizes a wide range of skills and, as in other technical professions, the dividing line between professional and nonprofessional is obscure.[18] However, the public does not see, and it is doubtful whether librarians themselves can agree, just what is the knowledge mastery which creates that dividing line. The public, and perhaps most librarians as well, is not convinced that the nonprofessional with experience simply cannot do the job the professionals can do, because he does not know the basic science on which the profession rests.

The failure to define adequately the nature of the intellectual problem means that practitioners themselves often fail to see the challenge of developing the field. . . .

A third element in the structural situation of the professional librarian is of importance as it interacts with the knowledge base. Earlier than in other occupations, the librarian begins to assume administrative tasks. The career line in all professions may, of course, include such work. However, this step is more likely to be taken somewhat late in the career, after a modicum of success. In librarianship, the step is inescapably built into the career sequence, as contrasted with law, for example, where the lawyer's colleagues may see the new job as being out of the profession; certainly, the professor views the elevation to a deanship in such a fashion. Nevertheless, much of this administration is not *specific* to librarianship. I would venture to say that a good chief librarian could transfer most of the skills he uses daily to a high-level managerial position in any corporation. That is, most of his work is not either pushing back the frontiers of knowledge in his field or applying the general principles of his field, but simply integrating human beings in a corporate enterprise.[19] Indeed, it is partly for this reason that librarians may be fitted so easily into civil service categories. As one observer has remarked, "Having to be and to do so many things, it does not know in what sense it really is a profession, whether it wants to be one, and what it is willing to change in order to enhance its present situation."[20]

Without such a firm knowledge base and its recognition by the relevant publics, the professional librarian cannot easily claim autonomy. The fully fledged profession can claim the right to be final arbiter in problems under its jurisdiction by referring to its codified knowledge, over which its mastery is greater than that of any other group. If the problem itself is not generally recognized, and the fund of knowledge for its solution not developed, it is hard to know even in what sense or for what, an occupation demands autonomy. Indeed, as we shall note, since part of the librarian's accepted obligation is to please his clients, he abdicates much of that autonomy from the start.

Perhaps one clear index of the failure to

---

[17] Leigh, *op. cit.*, p. 186.

[18] Consider, e.g., the problem of deciding when an individual is a "professional chemist." A high school student who has studied chemistry can carry out some simple qualitative analyses, and with each succeeding year in college the chemistry student is able to perform still more complex tasks. On the other hand, many chemists work at quite routine operations which could be carried out by persons with much less training. One must, as a rule, simply make an arbitrary definition. By contrast, note the "caste line" between the physician and the highly trained laboratory technician.

[19] Ralph Munn argues that this administrative emphasis is properly a central task of the librarian ("Education for Public Librarianship," in Berelson [ed.], *op. cit.*, pp. 122 ff.).

[20] Naegele, *op. cit.*, p. 176.

develop a clearly defined field of knowledge may be seen in the continuing and successful efforts by college and university librarians to obtain faculty status for themselves.[21] By defining much of their task as "teaching," these librarians can make a fair case for their claim to faculty status. On the other hand, if their definition of core professional problems were unique and special to the tasks of a library, they could gain all of the material advantages—which figure so prominently in their argument—of faculty status without demanding the title of another profession. One might indeed ask in this connection whether such professionals would prefer to belong to an association of academics, or an association of librarians.

SERVICE ORIENTATION AND THE CODE

The service orientation of a profession is expressed in its code of ethics, which in the traditional professions identifies the statuses of colleague and client (also charlatan or quack sometimes), and specifies the role obligations of the professional to the public as well as to colleagues and clients. No one but the professional himself is bound by the code, which is enforced primarily by the professional community but in part, and usually as a last resort, by statute and administrative regulations as well. The code embodies the terms of an implicit contract between the professional and the society, by which the professional agrees to prevent its members from exploiting a potentially helpless layman and in return receives many privileges. In the newer technical professions, growing from the application of academic disciplines to practical problems, this traditional form may be followed, but the practice is different.[22] The client or employer is likely to be a corporate agency whose staff can evaluate the excellence of the professional or his advice and thus can prevent exploitation. The professional is not tightly integrated in a professional community, which therefore exerts little control over him. Not much emphasis is put on professional degrees or admission procedure. The code of ethics of science[23] is perhaps more important than the traditional professional code. Service means "dedication to knowledge" rather than to the client.

The almost unique relations of the librarian to his client makes both of these patterns inapplicable, and the librarian's code reflects that fact. Several of the "rules" do no more than recommend run-of-the-mill administrative and personnel policies, which have no proper place in the code—for example, Section I, dealing with the librarian's relation to the governing authority; Section II, suggesting confidentiality, fairness, and wisdom in book acquisitions, and an effort to acquire needed materials and to make them available; Section IV, urging the librarian to encourage good recruits, develop himself, and improve salaries and working conditions; or Section V, recommending that the librarian take part in community affairs and gain esteem for libraries and librarians.

A code reflects the peculiar genius of the profession that writes it. How lacking in this code is any sense of drama, of moral urgency! How absent is a sturdy awareness that the profession has a task, a destiny, a set of issues about which it is concerned![24]

If the librarian feels this way about himself, how can his public not feel similarly? A profession that has not found itself cannot ask others to do so. The public believes libraries, but not librarians, are important. At present, the librarian has little power over his clients. They do not pay individually for his services, and he can at best send them away with the plea that he is too busy. The client has the right to check out and use the materials of the library even if the librarian believes he cannot use them to advantage. The librarian is a gatekeeper who can exclude almost no one; a guardian

---

21 Various aspects of this struggle are dealt with in Downs (ed.), *op. cit.*

22 See Goode, "Encroachment, Charlatanism, and the Emerging Profession: Psychology, Medicine, and Sociology," p. 905 ff.

23 William J. Goode and Paul K. Hatt, "Values and Science," in *Methods in Social Research* (New York: McGraw-Hill Book Co., 1951), chap. iii.

24 The ALA Bill of Rights, it should be noted, though more forthright in its declarations, was not adopted until nine years later and is *not* part of the code.

who can protect primarily against vandals and thieves; a stockroom custodian who must hand over any of his stock even if he is sure the person really wants or needs something else.

Intellectually, the librarian must work within the client's limitations, instead of imposing his professional categories, conceptions, and authority on the client. In other professions, too, the practitioner must understand the client's notions, but only enough to elicit adequate information and co-operation from him. The practitioner can solve the problem even if the client never understands what the professional is doing.

Thus "serving" the reader means "helping" him, learning his wishes and satisfying them. This comes dangerously close to the position taken by a minority of librarians,[25] that their duty is to give the people what they want. In such a conception not only must the librarian—a clerk serving his customers—compete with commercial entertainment, but he yields a central meaning of service, the commitment to run personal risks in order to fulfil a high obligation to the society, to *educate* the reader and the public. This strain between the wishes and the real needs of a clientele is perhaps to be found in all professions, but in established professions more often it is resolved by the professional's decision.

The relationship is most strikingly revealed in the problem of censorship. The code urges fairness and wisdom in book acquisitions, a pale and watery exhortation, but does not assert the simple ethical duty to follow professional principles in this central matter and to ignore lay opinion as irrelevant and incompetent. Few clearcut cases of censorship arise; the librarian avoids the risk. In a high but unknown percentage of instances, the librarian does not buy the books which might arouse local critics.[26] There is a wide discrepancy between values

and practices, and here again librarianship fails to attain the moral stature of a profession, in which the practitioner must risk unpopularity by serving the larger interests of the society.[27]

The librarian may defend his policy as prudent. After all, he is partially identified with the content of the materials which he buys and circulates, some of which contain threatening arguments and facts about sex, politics, and religion. If his constituency rejects him, he cannot turn to another clientele; he is fired.

He is indeed vulnerable, but his fears outrun reality. Having no clear sense of professional identity, the profession is not enough integrated to be able to protect the practitioner who lives by the principles of the profession but is attacked by laymen. Librarians seem to be characterized by a strong obligation to meet the demands of others, an exaggerated sensitivity to requests and complaints.[28] Intensifying this sense of vulnerability is the public's feeling that it has a *right* to complain. The librarian's acquisitions are open to public inspection, and he is viewed as a civil servant, an employee not an indispensable professional, whose materials may corrupt the young and impressionable.[29] From Stouffer's finding

[27] Note that the lawyer's duty to defend the indigent, the Communist, or the integrationist in the South is not primarily a service to the client but is a contribution to the maintenance of the legal system of our society (see Elliott E. Cheatham, *Cases on the Legal Profession* [2d Ed.; Brooklyn, N.Y.: Foundation Press, 1955], pp. 126–139).

[28] Parsons, *op. cit.,* p. 7. See also Benjamin Weintraub, "The Role of the Librarian in a Small Community" (unpublished Master's thesis, University of Chicago, 1953), Chap. iv; and Robert R. Douglass, "The Personality of the Librarian" (unpublished Ph.D. dissertation, University of Chicago, 1957), p. 119 ff. Leigh comments on the lack of unanimity among public librarians about the authority of their professional judgment, and he notes: "Some felt that since the board represents the popular will, the librarian was fully justified in following the board's instruction as part of the democratic process (*op. cit.,* p. 120). In the same place he says also that librarians often take a "middle course."

[29] Even those who oppose the circulation of certain books or films because of their potential harmfulness deny that they themselves would be corrupted by such materials.

[25] Leigh, *op. cit.,* p. 224. But Fiske (*op. cit.,* p. 11) found that two-thirds of her sample accepted this philosophy.

[26] See Fiske, *op. cit.,* pp. 52–71. Nearly two-thirds of her sample who have a voice in decisions reported instances of not buying a book because it was thought to be controversial (p. 64). Members of library associations were more restrictive than others. See the further analyses of these matters in Danton (ed.), *op. cit.*

that a majority of the United States public does not support a wide range of civil liberties, we must deduce that the librarian who follows public opinion will violate his real trust.[30]

The weakness of his situation is not temporary; it is inherent in his position. Any acquisition and circulation policy *must* be guided by values, which in the nature of things can be argued about but not demonstrated to be correct. Epistemologically, the layman has as good a right as the professional to assert his values, and he has ultimate power in his hands as well. In other professions, for example, in architecture and law where the tensions are especially great, the practitioner can usually demonstrate that the values of his profession are in harmony with at least the broader and longer-term values of both client and society.

Thus, the librarian accepts the task of facilitating the implementation or achievement of standards of excellence whose definition and custodianship belong to others.

[30] Samuel A. Stouffer, *Communism, Conformity and Civil Liberties* (Garden City, N.Y.: Doubleday & Co., Inc., 1955).

In the university library, these "others" are the professors; in the public library, the public. Consequently, the familiar appeals to "fairness" or "neutrality" are irrelevant. The Golden Mean, as Max Weber remarked long ago, is not necessarily more correct than either extreme.

Moreover, the public sees no ways by which the librarian might exploit the reader or the organization. The possibility of graft is not considered. There is no notion of a librarian who is a charlatan or quack. But on balance, this apparent strength may be a weakness. That majority of the public and student body that reads primarily for entertainment or because something was assigned believes the librarian can sometimes help, but not hurt. The reader does not feel he can be saved or harmed by the librarian.

Thus, aside from the danger of acquisition and circulation policies, the librarian is thought to be harmless, and that matter is not left for the librarian's decision anyway. If an occupation is not *allowed* to control itself in a central matter, and *need* not be controlled in others, it will not be granted high prestige for its moral stature, nor will it even assert its right to that grant.

Questions for Discussion and Further Research

The readings presented in this and the following chapters leave some questions unanswered and raise some new ones. Consideration of such questions should stimulate the development of new concepts and theories to help us understand the nature of the process of professionalization and how it relates to other social processes. It should also provide directions and guidelines for further research.

A review of the literature on the concept of professionalization leads to the conclusion that we need more empirical (data-based) studies of the elements that are essential to the professionalization process; we must distinguish these *essentials* from other elements that are merely *correlates* of the process under some circumstances. We will recall, for example, that Carr-Saunders defined professionalization as the acquisition of specialized skill and training among members of an occupation, the establishment of minimum fees or salaries, the formation of professional associations, the formulation of professional codes of ethics, and the establishment and enforcement of minimum qualifications for entrance into professional practice; Greenwood used similar elements in his description of the ideal-type profession. But Foote, and later Vollmer and Mills, condensed his description of these same basic elements into three categories:

(1) acquisition of a specialized technique supported by a body of theory;
(2) development of a career supported by an association of colleagues; and
(3) establishment of community recognition of professional status.

Other authors, like Sutherland, have observed that most of these same elements occur in the activities of members of "offbeat" occupations not commonly recognized by outsiders as "professions." At the same time, Sutherland admitted that the basic fund of information and occupational controls of professional thieves are less explicit than those of more commonly accepted professional groups. Thus thievery differs from more professionalized occupations *in degree.* At the same time, it may also be said to differ *in kind,* for Sutherland pointed out that "the one characteristic listed by Carr-Saunders and Wilson which they [thieves] lack is the ethical standards which minimize the pecuniary motive." This raises the question whether ethical standards which minimize profit considerations are indispensable to the basic process of professionalization. Talcott Parsons throws more light on this question in his paper reprinted in the next chapter, which argues that the basic economic motivations of people in both "professions" and "non-professions" actually do not differ much in modern society, though their modes for expressing these motivations (e.g., through advertising) may vary considerably. He concludes, then, that the often acclaimed "service orientation" is not a meaningful characteristic by which to distinguish professional occupations from others.

In the paper by Goode, on the other hand, the argument that librarianship is not likely to achieve the status of a full-fledged profession is based upon consideration of an additional element not considered explicitly in the previous definitions of professionalization—the finding that librarians respond to the expressed *desires* of their clients rather than to client *needs* as defined by the librarians themselves. Goode maintains that a collectivity or service orientation in terms of professionally defined needs is an essential element of professionalization.

Disagreements about what is and what is not professionalized behavior will continue, we believe, until better methods are developed and applied to measure the distinguishable, but interrelated, elements of the professionalization process. Social science sophistication in the measurement of both verbal behavior (opinions and attitudes) and observable actions is now advancing to a stage where we might attempt to determine whether the acquisition of a specialized technique supported by a body of theory is *always* associated with the development of a career supported by an association of colleagues in work behavior, and whether each is also *always* associated with community recognition of professional status. If not always, but only most of the time, under what conditions are any of these elements *not* associated, or possibly negatively associated (an increase in one element associated with a decrease in the other)? A useful model for analysis of the conditions that strengthen or weaken relations of social variables has been described in detail in a notable paper by Patricia Kendall and Paul Lazarsfeld.* Certainly a more careful analysis of the interrelationship of elements in the process of professionalization is neces-

* "Problems of Survey Analysis," in *Continuities in Social Research: Studies in the Scope and Method of "The American Soldier,"* R. K. Merton and P. F. Lazarsfeld (eds.) (Glencoe, Ill.: Free Press, 1950), pp. 133–196.

sary if we are to test and further expand Caplow's generalizations about a predictable order in the sequence of occurrence of such elements in any given occupation.

More precise means to characterize and measure the elements of professionalization also might provide a basis for more precise analyses of the relations between new technologies and various identifiable elements in professionalization. We assume, but we really don't know, that much of professionalization is inevitable in modern society. But to verify our assumptions, we need to look for exceptions to the rule, and we may have to develop new concepts to describe these exceptions. Can we find any situations in which "de-professionalization" may be occurring today, or may be expected to occur in the future? Do we see traces in present developments as to what may be the next outstanding development in our occupational culture and organization? Beyond professionalization, what?

2

The Social Context of Professionalization

Professionalization does not occur in a vacuum. Like other social processes, it cannot be understood without taking into account certain aspects of the larger society in which it takes place. Some writers have pointed out that professional groups can perform essential functions for the larger society and also that professionalization can be both an antecedent and a consequence of significant social changes. For example, in the Carr-Saunders lecture reproduced in the previous chapter, it was shown that professionalization, as we know it today, did not begin to advance rapidly until the nineteenth century as a concomitant of increasing industrialization in the Western world. As William J. Goode has put it, "An industrializing society is a professionalizing society."* An increasing complex division of labor and specialization of occupational function is not only *induced* by industrialization, it also appears to be *required* by it.

The relation between professionalization, on the one hand, and industrialization and associated technological changes, on the other, may be rather complex. For example, rapid professionalization *before* industrialization might actually inhibit economic and social development in newly-developing countries for the following reasons: (1) professionalization may encourage many of the more talented and educated people (especially those educated abroad) to leave a newly-developing country and to migrate to a more highly industrialized society where they feel that professional practice or employment can be more adequately rewarded; (2) in the absence of a significant middle class, professionalization may also widen status discrepancies between members of professional groups, which become elite groups in a newly-developing country, and the mass of illiterate or semi-literate peasantry and proletariat. The more advanced phase of industrialization (automation), in contrast, may even lead to mechanization of some functions formerly performed by professional person-

* "Encroachment, Charlatanism, and the Emerging Profession: Psychology, Sociology, and Medicine," *American Sociological Review,* 25, 1960, 902.

nel—for example, computerized practices in engineering design and "teaching machines" in education. This, in turn, could lead to unemployment, or at least to employment under conditions that do not meet the professional expectations, among a segment of the professional labor force. And as we know, especially from the experience of the Nazi movement in Germany between the two World Wars, the unemployment or mis-employment of sizable sections of professional and other middle class groups can be a factor in political revolution.

We need more study—especially comparative study—of the relation of professionalization to society and to social change. As a background and point of departure for this study, we have the insightful speculations and investigations of such social scientists as Emile Durkheim, Robert MacIver, Talcott Parsons, N. S. Timasheff, and Everett Hughes.

Occupational Groups and Social Order

In all his writings, the eminent French social scientist Emile Durkheim expressed a concern for establishing the significance of group factors in human behavior and for investigating the bases of social order in the larger society. Ideologically, Durkheim was in the conservative tradition, emphasizing the priority of society and what he called "social facts," in contrast to the individualistic emphasis of nineteenth century liberal social contract theorists. In *The Division of Labor in Society,* first written in 1893, Durkheim contrasted what he called "mechanical solidarity" with "organic solidarity." He maintained that the integration of pre-industrial societies was achieved by means of mechanical solidarity, characterized by little, if any, significant differentiation of labor, but also by a high degree of correspondence between individual conscience and social norms and standards. In other words, everybody did essentially the same kinds of things and shared essentially the same values. Durkheim claimed that, in contrast, modern industrial society has lost a general consensus on norms and values, but has instead become integrated in terms of the division of labor. Now people do very different things, and their work has become highly specialized, but at the same time their work has also become interdependent. Social integration has now become more organic. The key element in this organic solidarity, according to Durkheim, is formal occupational associations— which have been translated as "corporations," but which might more appropriately have been translated as "guilds," or even "professional associations," in modern terminology. Formal occupational associations help to relate individuals in their diverse occupational pursuits to the social structure of the broader society and the state.

Durkheim mentioned this in the first edition of this book, but stated more explicitly what he meant by the social functions of occupational "corporations" in the preface to the second edition of *The Division of Labor in Society,* first published in 1902. This preface, entitled "Some Remarks on Occupational Groups," is reprinted here in part. In these remarks Durkheim described what he believed to be the social need for occupational groups to become organized on a national, rather than a local municipality basis, in relation to the characteristics and requirements of national and international markets. He even maintained that these occupational groups might eventually become fundamental political units, perhaps even replacing territorial units, and thereby providing for representation of diverse occupational interests in a democratic state. Durkheim's concern for the place of viable voluntary associations mediating between state control and the broad mass of individual members of a society has influenced the thinking of many social philosophers and social scientists who have analyzed the dangers of monolithic state control over unattached and undifferentiated populations in more recent times.*

* See, for example, William Kornhauser, *The Politics of Mass Society* (Glencoe, Ill.: Free Press, 1959.)

Emile Durkheim (General)

A group is not only a moral authority which dominates the life of its members; it is also a source of life *sui generis*. From it comes a warmth which animates its members, making them intensely human, destroying their egotisms. Thus, in the past, the family was the legislator of law and ethics whose severity went to extremes of violence, at the same time that it was the place where one first learned to enjoy the effusions of sentiment. We have also seen how the corporation, in Rome and in the Middle Ages, awakened these same needs and sought to satisfy them. The corporations of the future will have a complexity of attributes still greater, by reason of their increased growth. Around their proper occupational functions others which come from the communes or private societies will be grouping themselves. The functions of assistance are such that, to be well filled, they demand feelings of solidarity between assistants and assisted, a certain intellectual and moral homogeneity such as the same occupation produces. A great many educational institutions (technical schools, adult education, etc.) equally seem to have to find their natural environment in the corporation. It is the same for aesthetic life, for it appears in the nature of things that this noble form of sport and recreation develops side by side with the serious life which it serves to balance and relieve. In fact, there are even now syndicates which are at the same time societies of mutual aid; others found common houses where there are organized courses, concerts, and dramatic presentations. The corporative activity can thus assume the most varied forms.

There is even reason to suppose that the corporation will become the foundation or one of the essential bases of our political organization. We have seen, indeed, that if it first begins by being outside the social system, it tends to fix itself in it in proportion to the development of economic life. It is, therefore, just to say that if progress continues to be made in this direction, it will have to take a more prominent and more predominant place in society. It was formerly the elementary division of communal organization. Now that the commune, heretofore an autonomous organism, has lost its place in the State, as the municipal market did in the national market, is it not fair to suppose that the corporation also will have to experience a corresponding transformation, becoming the elementary division of the State, the fundamental political unity? Society, instead of remaining what it is today, an aggregate of juxtaposed territorial districts, would become a vast system of national corporations. From various quarters it is asked that elective assemblies be formed by occupations, and not by territorial divisions; and certainly, in this way, political assemblies would more exactly express the diversity of social interests and their relations. They would be a more faithful picture of social life in its entirety. But to say that the nation, in becoming aware of itself, must be ground into occupations—does not this mean that the organized occupation or

Reprinted from *The Division of Labor in Society* by Emile Durkheim, trans. George Simpson (New York: Free Press of Glencoe, Inc.), pp. 26–28 of the preface. With permission of The Free Press of Glencoe. Copyright 1933 by George Simpson.

corporation should be the essential organ of public life?

Thus the great gap in the structure of European societies we elsewhere point to[1] would be filled. It will be seen, indeed, how, as advances are made in history, the organization which has territorial groups as its base (village or city, district, province, etc.) steadily becomes effaced. To be sure, each of us belongs to a commune, or a department, but the bonds attaching us there became daily more fragile and more slack. These geographical divisions are, for the most part, artificial and no longer awaken in us profound sentiments. The provincial spirit has disappeared never to return; the patriotism of the parish has become an archaism that cannot be restored at will. The municipal or departmental affairs affect and agitate us in proportion to their coincidence with our occupational affairs. Our activity is extended quite beyond these groups which are too narrow for it, and, moreover, a good deal of what happens there leaves us indifferent. There is thus produced a spontaneous weakening of the old social structure. Now, it is impossible for this organization to disappear without something replacing it. A society composed of an infinite number of unorganized individuals that a hypertrophied State is forced to oppress and contain constitutes a veritable sociological monstrosity. For collective activity is always too complex to be able to be expressed through the single and unique organ of the State. Moreover, the State is too remote from individuals; its relations with them too external and intermittent to

penetrate deeply into individual consciences and socialize them within. Where the State is the only environment in which men can live communal lives, they inevitably lose contact, become detached, and thus society distintegrates. A nation can be maintained only if, between the State and the individual, there is intercalated a whole series of secondary groups near enough to the individuals to attract them strongly in their sphere of action and drag them, in this way, into the general torrent of social life. We have just shown how occupational groups are suited to fill this role, and that is their destiny. One thus conceives how important it is, especially in the economic order, for them to emerge from that state of inconsistency and disorganization in which they have remained for a century, since these occupations today absorb the major part of our collective forces.[2]

[2] We do not mean that the territorial divisions are destined to disappear entirely, but only that they will become of less importance. The old institutions never vanish before the new without leaving any traces of themselves. They persist, not only through sheer force of survival, but because there still persists something of needs they once answered. The material neighborhood will always constitute a bond between men; consequently, political and social organization with a territorial base will certainly exist. Only, they will not have their present predominance, precisely because this bond has lost its force. Moreover, we have shown above, that even at the base of the corporation, there will always be found geographical divisions. Furthermore, between the diverse corporations of the same locality or region there will necessarily be special relations of solidarity which will, at all times, demand appropriate organization.

[1] See pp. 218–219.

Professional Groups and Cultural Norms

Whereas Durkheim in the preceding reading did not distinguish between the social significance of craft guilds and professional associations, Robert M. MacIver made this distinction in a paper first published in 1922. MacIver maintained that a key characteristic of professional groups was the degree to which they established autonomy and collective self-control over their standards of performance and behavior. In this respect, MacIver pointed to a difference between the professions and business management. Business managers, he implied, are not really professionalized; they have specialized expertise and standards of ethics, but they do not ordinarily have associations that transcend their business enterprises to enforce these standards. It is difficult, if not impossible, for one to serve the interests of two masters, employers and colleagues, in situations where these interests may diverge.

MacIver goes on to say that, whereas all social groups develop ethics, norms, or standards of behavior with regard to other members *within* the groups, it is especially characteristic of professional groups that they develop ethics and standards with regard to relations with individuals *outside* the group. However, MacIver recognizes that these standards have usually developed most clearly with regard to the behavior of *individual* professionals toward clients and other outsiders, rather than with regard to the external behavior of the professional group as a whole. Also he points to the dangers of narrow concerns, "specific group biases," as limiting the social effectiveness of professional groups. In sum, it might be said that MacIver tended to emphasize both the positive functions and potential dysfunctions of professional groups in relation to the larger society, whereas Durkheim had tended to concentrate only upon what he saw as the positive advantages of formal occupational associations.

Robert MacIver (General)

The spirit and method of the craft, banished from industry, finds a more permanent home in the professions. Here still prevail the long apprenticeship, the distinctive training, the small-scale unit of employment and the intrinsic—as distinct from the economic—interest alike in the process and the product of the work. The sweep of economic evolution seems at first sight to have passed the professions by. The doctor, the lawyer, the architect, the minister of religion, remain individual practitioners, or at most enter into partnerships of two or three members. Specialization takes place, but in a different way, for the specialist in the professions does not yield his autonomy. He offers his specialism directly to the public, and only indirectly to his profession. But this very autonomy is the condition under which the social process brings about another and no less significant integration. The limited "corporations" of the business world being thus ruled out, the whole pro-

Reprinted from "The Social Significance of Professional Ethics," *The Annals of the American Academy of Political and Social Science,* 297 (January 1955), 118–124; in turn, reprinted with some changes from *The Annals,* 101 (May 1922), 5–11. Used by permission of the author and publisher.

fession assumes something of the aspect of a corporation. It supplements the advantage or the necessity of the small-scale, often the one-man, unit by concerted action to remove its "natural" disadvantage, that free play of uncontrolled individualism which undermines all essential standards. It achieves an integration not of form but of spirit. Of this spirit nothing is more significant than the ethical code which it creates.

There is in this respect a marked contrast between the world of business and that of the professions. It cannot be said that business has yet attained a specific code of ethics, resting on considerations broader than the sense of self-interest and supplementing the minimal requirements of the law. Such a code may be in the making, but it has not yet established itself, and there are formidable difficulties to be overcome. When we speak of business ethics, we generally mean the principles of fair play and honorable dealing which men *should* observe in business. Sharp dealing, "unfair" competition, the exaction of the pound of flesh, may be reprobated and by the decent majority condemned, but behind such an attitude there is no definite code which businessmen reinforce by their collective sense of its necessity and by their deliberate adoption of it as expressly binding upon themselves. There is no general brotherhood of businessmen from which the offender against these sentiments, who does not at the same time overtly offend against the law of the land, is extruded as unworthy of an honorable calling. There is no effective criticism which sets up a broader standard of judgment than mere success.

If we inquire why this distinction should hold between business and professional standards the social significance of the latter is set in a clearer light. It is not that business, unlike medicine or law for example, lacks those special conditions which call for a code of its own. Take, on the one hand, the matter of competitive methods. It is a vital concern of business, leading to numerous agreements of all sorts, but there are mere *ad hoc* agreements of a particular nature, not as yet deductions from a fully established principle which business, as a self-conscious whole, deliberately and universally accepts. Take, on the other hand, such a problem as that of the duty of the employer to his workpeople. Is not this a subject most apt for the introduction of a special code defining the sense of responsibility involved in that relationship? But where is such a code to be found?

The Ideal of Service

Something more than a common technique and a common occupation is evidently needed in order that an ethical code shall result. We might apply here the significant and much misunderstood comparison which Rousseau drew between the "will of all" and the "general will." In business we have as yet only the "will of all," the activity of businessmen, each in pursuit of his own success, not overridden though doubtless tempered by the "general will," the activity which seeks first the common interest. The latter can be realized only when the ideal of service controls the ideal of profits. We do not mean that businessmen are in fact selfish while professional men are altruistic. We mean simply that the *ideal of the unity of service* which business renders is not yet explicitly recognized and proclaimed by itself. It is otherwise with the professions. They assume an obligation and an oath of service.

"A profession," says the ethical code of the American Medical Association, "has for its prime object the service it can render to humanity; reward or financial gain should be a subordinate consideration," and again it proclaims that the principles laid down for the guidance of the profession "are primarily for the good of the public." Similar statements are contained in the codes of the other distinctively organized professions. "The profession," says the proposed code of the Canadian legal profession, "is a branch of the administration of justice and not a mere money-getting occupation." Such professions as teaching, the ministry, the civil service, and social work by their very nature imply like conceptions of responsibility. They imply that while the profession is of necessity a means of livelihood or of financial reward, the devoted service which it inspires is motivated by other considerations.

In business there is one particular difficulty retarding any like development of unity and responsibility. It may safely be said that so long as within the industrial world the cleavage of interest between capital and labor, employer and employee, retains its present character, business cannot assume the aspect of a profession. This internal strife reveals a fundamental conflict of acquisitive interests within the business world and not only stresses that interest in both parties to the struggle but makes it impossible for the intrinsic "professional" interest to prevail. The professions are in general saved from that confusion. Within the profession there is not, as a rule, the situation where one group habitually employs for gain another group whose function, economic interest, and social position are entirely distinct from its own. The professions have thus been better able to adjust the particular interests of their members to their common interest and so to attain a clearer sense of their relationship to the whole community.

Once that position is attained the problem of occupational conduct takes a new form. It was stated clearly long enough ago by Plato in the *Republic*. Each "art," he pointed out, has a special good or service. "Medicine, for example, gives us health; navigation, safety at sea, and so on...."

Medicine is not the art—or profession—of receiving pay because a man takes fees while he is engaged in healing.... The pay is not derived by the several 'artists' from their respective 'arts.' But the truth is, that while the 'art' of medicine gives health, and the 'art' of the builder builds a house, another 'art' attends them which is the 'art' of pay." The ethical problem of the profession, then, is to reconcile the two "arts," or, more generally, to fulfil as completely as possible the primary service for which it stands while securing the legitimate economic interest of its members. It is the attempt to effect this reconciliation, to find the due place of the intrinsic and of the extrinsic interest, which gives a profound social significance to professional codes of ethics.

STANDARDS COMMON, CODES DISTINCTIVE

The demarcation and integration of the profession is a necessary preliminary to the establishment of the code. Each profession becomes a functional group in a society whose tendency is to organize itself less and less in terms of territory or race or hereditary status, and more and more in terms of function. Each profession thus acquires its distinctive code. It is important to observe that what is distinctive is the code rather than the standard. The different codes of racial or national groups reveal variant ethical standards, but the different codes of professional groups represent rather the deliberate application of a generally accepted social standard to particular spheres of conduct. Medical ethics do not necessarily differ in quality or level from engineering ethics, nor the ethics of law or of statesmanship from those of architecture. The false old notion that there was for that most ancient and still most imperfectly defined profession of statesmanship a peculiar code which liberated it from the ordinary ethical standards has died very hard. In truth there could be no conflict of ethics and politics, for politics could justify itself only by applying to its own peculiar situations and needs the principles which belong equally to every sphere of life.

Ethics cannot be summed up in a series of inviolate rules or commandments which can be applied everywhere and always without regard to circumstances, thought of consequences, or comprehension of the ends to be attained. What is universal is the good in view, and ethical rules are but the generally approved ways of preserving it. The rules may clash with one another, and then the only way out is to look for guidance to the ideal. The physician may have to deceive his patient in order to save his life. The lawyer, the priest, and the physician may have to observe secrecy and keep confidences under conditions where it might be the layman's duty to divulge them, for the conception of the social welfare which should induce the one to speak out may equally in the peculiar professional relationship compel the other to silence. Every profession has its own problems of conduct, in the interpretation within its own province of the common principles of ethical conduct. The medical man to whom is entrusted, under conditions which usually admit of no appeal save to his own conscience, the safeguarding of the health of his patient, with due consideration for the health of the whole community, has to depend upon a special code applicable to that situation. So with the legal profession which, for example, has to provide professional service for all litigants, irrespective of the popularity or unpopularity of the cause. So with the architect, who has to determine his responsibilty alike to the client, to the contractor, to the workmen, to the "quantity surveyor," and to the community. So with the university professor, who has to uphold the necessity of academic freedom against the pressure of prejudice and the domination of controlling interests which care less for truth than for their own success. So with the journalist, in his peculiarly difficult situation as the servant of a propagandist press. So with the engineer, the surveyor, the accountant, or the technician generally, who has to maintain standards of service and of efficiency against the bias of profit making. So with the manager, the secretary, or the officer of a corporation—for here business assumes most nearly the aspect of a profession—who has to reconcile the trust imposed on him by his employers with the duty he owes to himself and to those whose services he in turn controls. Out of such situations develop the written and the unwritten codes of professional ethics.

RESPONSIBILITY TO THE WIDER COMMUNITY

We need not assume that these codes originate from altruistic motives, nor yet condemn them because they protect the interest of the profession itself as well as the various interests which it serves. To do so would be to misunderstand the nature of any code. An ethical code is something more than the prescription of the duty of an individual towards others; in that very act it prescribes their duty towards him and makes his welfare too its aim, refuting the false disassociation of the individual and the social. But the general ethical code prescribes simply the duties of the members of a community towards one another. What gives the professional code its peculiar significance is that it prescribes also the duties of the members of a whole group towards those outside the group. It is just here that in the past ethical theory and practice alike have shown the greatest weakness. The group code has narrowed the sense of responsibility by refusing to admit the application of its principles beyond the group. Thereby it has weakened its own logic and its sanction, most notably in the case of national groups, which have refused to apply or even to relate their internal codes to the international world. The attempt of professional groups to coordinate their responsibilities, relating at once the individual to the group and the group itself to the wider community, marks thus an important advance.

We must, however, admit that it is in this matter, in the relation of the profession *as a whole* to the community, that professional codes are still weakest and professional ethics least effectively developed. The service to the community they clearly envisage is the service rendered by individual members of the profession to members of the public. The possibility that there may still be an inclusive professional interest—generally but not always an economic one—that at significant points is not harmonized

with the community interest is nowhere adequately recognized.

The problem of professional ethics, viewed as the task of coordinating responsibilities, of finding, as it were, a common center for the various circles of interest, wider and narrower, is full of difficulty and far from being completely solved. The magnitude and the social significance of this task appear if we analyze on the one hand the character of the professional interest and on the other the relation of that interest to the general welfare.

CHARACTER OF THE PROFESSIONAL INTEREST

The professional interest combines a number of elements. It includes what we may term the extrinsic interest, that devoted to the economic and social status, the reputation, authority, success, and emoluments attaching to the profession as a body. It includes also the technical interest directed to the art and craft of the profession, to the maintenance and improvement of its standards of efficiency, to the quest for new and better methods and processes, and to the definition and promotion of the training considered requisite for the practice of the profession. It may also include a third interest which can be classed as cultural. To illustrate, in the profession of teaching the technical interest in the system of imparting knowledge is one thing, and the cultural interest in the knowledge imparted quite another. Even more obvious is the case of the minister of religion, whose technique of ministration is as a rule very simple and whose main interest lies in the significance of the doctrine. The distinction is clear also in the spheres of the sciences and of the fine arts where the interest in truth or beauty may be discerned from the interest in the modes of investigation or of expression. In other professions it may be harder to identify the cultural as distinct from the technical interest, but if we interpret the term "culture" widely enough to include, for example, such objects as health and the beauty of workmanship, it may be maintained that the cultural interest belongs to every profession and is in fact one of the criteria by which to determine whether or not a given occupation is to be classed as a profession.

Now these three strands of interest are usually interwoven in the general professional interest, but sometimes they are separated and subject to the pull of opposite forces. Thus while the technical and economic interests usually go together and while, for example, the maintenance of standards usually works towards the economic advantage of the profession, these may be unfortunately disjoined. Better technique may at points be antagonistic to professional gain. The lawyer may, to take one instance, lose a source of profits by the introduction of a simpler and more efficient system of conveyancing. The architect, working on a percentage basis, may find his pecuniary advantage at variance with his professional duty to secure the best service for the least cost. Likewise, opposition may arise between the economic and the cultural interest. The teacher and the preacher may suffer loss from a wholehearted devotion to the spirit of truth as they conceive it. The artist, the playwright, the author, may have to choose between the ideals of their art and the more lucrative devices of popularity. Finally, the technical and the cultural interest may work apart. Routine methods and processes may dominate the professional mind to the obscuration of the ends which they should serve. A notable statement of this opposition is given in the valuable investigation into professional organization in England which was published in two supplements of the *New Statesman*.[1] The investigation points to "the undisguised contempt in which both solicitors and barristers, notably those who have attained success in their profession and control its organization, hold, and have always held, not only all scholarship or academic learning of a professional kind, but also any theoretic or philosophical or scientific treatment of law."

Here, therefore, in the structure of the general professional interest we find a rich mine of ethical problems, still for the most part unworked but into which the growing ethical codes of the professions are commencing to delve. A still greater wealth of

[1] April 21, and 28, 1917.

the material for ethical reflection is revealed when we turn next to analyze the relation of the professional interest as a whole to that of the community.

PROFESSIONAL INTEREST AND GENERAL WELFARE

Every organized profession avows itself to be an association existing primarily to fulfill a definite service within the community. Some codes distinguish elaborately between the various types of obligation incumbent on the members of the profession. The lawyer, for example, is declared to have specific duties to his client, to the public, to the court or to the law, to his professional brethren, and to himself. It would occupy too much space to consider the interactions, harmonies, and potential conflicts of such various duties. Perhaps the least satisfactory reconciliation is that relating the interest of the client to the interest of the public, not merely in the consideration of the particular cases as they arise but still more in the adaptation of the service to the needs of the public as a whole as distinct from those of the individual clients. Thus the medical profession has incurred to many minds a serious liability, in spite of the devotion of its service to actual patients, by its failure for so long to apply the preventive side of medicine, in particular to suggest ways and means for the prevention of the needless loss of life and health and happiness caused by the general medical ignorance and helplessness of the poor.

In addition it must suffice to show that the conception of communal service is apt to be obscured alike by the general and by the specific bias of the profession. It is to the general bias that we should attribute such attempts to maintain a vested interest as may be found in the undue restriction of entrants to the profession—undue when determined by such professionally irrelevant considerations as high fees and expensive licenses; in the resistance to specialization, whether of tasks or of men, the former corresponding to the resistance to "dilution" in the trade union field; in the insistence on a too narrow orthodoxy, which would debar from professional practice men trained in a different school; in the unnecessary multiplication of tasks, of which a flagrant example is the English serverance of barrister and solicitor. Another aspect of the general bias is found in the shuffling of responsibility under the cloak of the code. This is most marked in the public services, particularly the civil service and the army and navy— and incidentally it may be noted that the problem of professional ethics is aggravated when the profession as a whole is in the employ of the state. "An official," says Emile Faguet in one of his ruthless criticisms of officialdom,[2] "is a man whose first and almost only duty is to have no will of his own."

DANGER OF SPECIFIC GROUP BIAS

This last case brings us near to what we have called the specific bias of the profession. Each profession has a limited field, a special environment, a group psychology. Each profession tends to leave its distinctive stamp upon a man, so that it is easier in general to distinguish, say, the doctor and the priest, the teacher and the judge, the writer and the man of science, than it is to discern, outside their work, the electrician from the railwayman or the plumber from the machinist. The group environment creates a group bias. The man of law develops his respect for property at the risk of his respect for personal rights. The teacher is apt to make his teaching an overnarrow discipline. The priest is apt to underestimate the costs of the maintenance of sanctity. The diplo-

[2] *The Dread of Responsibility* (New York: G. P. Putnam's Sons, 1914).

mat may overvalue good form and neglect the penalty of exclusiveness. The civil servant may make a fetish of the principle of seniority, and the soldier may interpret morality as mere *esprit de corps*.

All this, however, is merely to say that group ethics will not by themselves suffice for the guidance of the group unless they are always related to the ethical standards of the whole community. This fact has a bearing on the question of the limits of professional self-government, though we cannot discuss that here. Professional group codes are, as a matter of fact, never isolated, and thus they are saved from the narrowness and egotism characteristic of racial group ethics. Their dangers are far more easily controlled, and their services to society, the motive underlying all codes, vastly outweigh what risks they bring. They provide a support for ethical conduct less diffused than that inspired by nationality, less exclusive than that derived from the sense of class, and less instinctive than that begotten of the family. As they grow they witness to the differentiation of community. Their growth is part of the movement by which the fulfillment of function is substituted as a social force for the tradition of birth or race, by which the activity of service supersedes the passivity of station. For all their present imperfections these codes breathe the inspiration of service instead of the inspiration of mere myth or memory. As traditional and authoritative ethics weaken in the social process, the ethics formulated in the light of function bring to the general standard of the community a continuous and creative reinforcement.

Professional Groups and Social Structure

Talcott Parsons, in a paper first published in 1939, took an even broader look at the social significance of professional groups. Parsons emphasized both the intrinsic importance of professions to modern society and the degree to which characteristics that are normally considered to be "professional" in nature actually permeate much of "the common institutional pattern of the occupational sphere" in modern society. Whereas MacIver emphasized certain distinctions between business and professional activities, Parsons stresses their similarities. Both are "rational," "functionally specific in their authority," and "universalistic in behavior criteria." Actually it is practically impossible to distinguish between business and professional activities in terms of "egoistic" and "altruistic" motivation. Certain characteristics pervade our entire occupational structure. These characteristics, in turn, are generated by the larger social system in which the occupational structure is functionally imbedded.

Before turning to an excerpt from Parson's paper, however, it may be appropriate to comment upon the controversy that has raged for many years about whether or not business management is "really a profession." After reading both MacIver's and Parson's discussion, we believe that you will come to agree with the conclusion that business management appears to be professionalized in some respects, but not in others. We need more study of the respects in which each occupational group is presently professionalized, and the direction in which each group is likely to change in the future.

Talcott Parsons (Professions and Business Management)

The fact that the central focus of the professional role lies in a technical competence gives a very great importance to universalism in the institutional pattern governing it. Science is essentially universalistic—*who* states a proposition is as such irrelevant to the question of its scientific value. The same is true of all applied science. But the role of universalism is by no means confined to the professions. It is equally important to the patterns governing contractual relationships, for instance in the standards of common honesty, and to administrative office.

It is one of the most striking features of our occupational system that status in it is to a high degree independent of status in kinship groups, the neighborhood and the like, in short from what are sometimes called primary group relationships. It may be suggested that one of the main reasons for this lies in the dominant importance of universalistic criteria in the judgment of achievement in the occupational field. Where technical competence, the technical impartiality of administration of an office and the like are of primary functional importance, it is essential that particularistic considerations should not enter into the bases of judgment too much. The institutional insulation from social structures

Reprinted from "The Professions and Social Structure," *Social Forces,* 17, No. 4 (May 1939), 457–467, by permission of University of North Carolina Press.

where particularism is dominant is one way in which this can be accomplished.

While there is a variety of reasons why disinterestedness is of great functional significance to the modern professions, there is equally impressive evidence for the role of rationality, functional specificity and universalism, as well as, perhaps, other elements which have not been taken up here. In both respects the importance of the professions as a peculiar social structure within the wider society calls attention to the importance of elements other than the enlightened self-interest of economic and utilitarian theory. On the one hand, it does so in that the institutional pattern governing professional activity does not, in the same sense, sanction the pursuit of self-interest as the corresponding one does in the case of business. On the other hand, the very fact that in spite of this difference the professions have all three of these other elements in common with the business pattern, and with other parts of our occupational structure, such as government and other administration, calls attention to the possibility that the dominant importance of the problem of self-interest itself has been exaggerated. This impression is greatly strengthened by the results of extensive comparative study of the relations of our own institutional structure to that of widely different societies which, unfortunately, it is impossible to report on in this paper.

Returning to the professions, however, study of the relation of social structure to individual action in this field can, as it was suggested earlier, by comparison throw light on certain other theoretically crucial aspects of the problem of the role of self-interest itself. In the economic and related utilitarian traditions of thought the difference between business and the professions in this respect has strongly tended to be interpreted as mainly a difference in the typical motives of persons acting in the respective occupations. The dominance of a business economy has seemed to justify the view that ours was an "acquisitive society" in which every one was an "economic man" who cared little for the interests of others. Professional men, on the other hand, have been thought of as standing above these sordid considerations, devoting their lives to "service" of their fellow men.

There is no doubt that there are important concrete differences. Businessmen are, for instance, expected to push their financial interests by such aggressive measures as advertising. They are not expected to sell to customers regardless of the probability of their being paid, as doctors are expected to treat patients. In each immediate instance in one sense the doctor could, if he did these things according to the business pattern, gain financial advantages which conformity with his own professional pattern denies him. Is it not then obvious that he is "sacrificing" his self-interest for the benefit of others?

The situation does not appear to be so simple. It is seldom, even in business, that the immediate financial advantage to be derived from a particular transaction is decisive in motivation. Orientation is rather to a total comprehensive situation extending over a considerable period of time. Seen in these terms the difference may lie rather in the "definitions of the situation" than in the typical motives of actors as such.

Perhaps the best single approach to the distinction of these two elements is in the question, in what do the goals of ambition consist? There is a sense in which, in both cases, the dominant goal may be said to be the same, "success." To this there would appear to be two main aspects. One is a satisfactory modicum of attainment of the technical goals of the respective activities, such as increasing the size and improving the portion of the business firm for which the individual is in whole or in part responsible, or attaining a good proportion of cures or substantial improvement in the condition of patients. The other aspect is the attainment of high standing in one's occupational group, "recognition" in Thomas' term. In business this will involve official position in the firm, income, and that rather intangible but nonetheless important thing, "reputation," as well as perhaps particular "honors" such as election to clubs and the like. In medicine it will similarly involve size and character of practice, income, hospital and possibly medical school appointments, honors, and again reputation. The essential goals in the two cases would appear to be substantially the same, objective achievement and recognition: the difference lies in the different paths to the similar goals, which are in turn determined by the differences in the respective occupational situations.

There are two particularly important empirical qualifications to what has been said. In the first place certain things are important not only as symbols of recognition, but in other contexts as well. This is notably true of money. Money is significant for what it can buy, as well as in the role of a direct symbol of recognition. Hence insofar as ways of earning money present themselves in the situation which are not strictly in the line of institutionally approved achievement, there may be strong pressure to resort to them so long as the risk of loss of occupational status is not too great.

This leads to the second consideration. The above sketch applies literally only to a well-integrated situation. Insofar as the actual state of affairs deviates from this type, the two main elements of success, objective achievement which is institutionally valued, and acquisition of the various recognition-symbols, may not be well articulated. Actual achievement may fail to bring recognition in due proportion, and vice versa achievements either of low quality or in unapproved lines may bring disproportionate recognition. Such lack of integration inevitably places great strains on the individual placed in such a situation, and behavior deviant from the institutional pattern results on a large scale. It would seem that, seen in this perspective, so-called "commercialism" in medicine and "dishonest" and "shady" practices in business have much in common as reactions to these strains.

Even in these cases, however, it is dubious whether such practices result primarily from egoistic motivation in the simple sense of utilitarian theory. The following seems a more adequate account of the matter: "normally," i.e. in an integrated situation, the "interests" in self-fulfillment and realization of goals, are integrated and fused with the normative patterns current in the society, inculcated by current attitudes of approval and disapproval and their various manifestations. The normal individual feels satisfaction in effectively carrying out approved patterns and shame and disappointment in failure. For instance courage in facing physical danger is often far from "useful" to the individual in any ordinary egoistic sense. But most normal boys and men feel intense satisfaction in performing courageous acts, and equally intense shame if they have been afraid. Correlatively they are approved and applauded for courageous behavior and severely criticized for cowardice. The smooth functioning of the mechanisms of such behavior which integrates individual satisfactions and social expectations is dependent upon the close correspondence of objective achievement and the bases and symbols of recognition. Where this correspondence is seriously disturbed the individual is placed in a conflict situation and is hence insecure. If he sticks to the approved objective achievements his desires for recognition are frustrated; if on the other hand he sacrifices this to acquisition of the recognition symbols, he has guilt-feelings and risks disapproval in some important quarters. Commercialism and dishonesty are to a large extent the reactions of normal people to this kind of conflict situation. The conflict is not generally a simple one between the actor's self-interest and his altruistic regard for others or for ideals, but between different components of the normally unified goal of "success," each of which contains both interested and disinterested motivation elements.

If this general analysis of the relation of motivation to institutional patterns is correct, two important correlative conclusions follow. On the one hand the typical motivation of professional men is not in the usual sense "altruistic," nor is that of businessmen typically "egoistic." Indeed there is little basis for maintaining that there is any important broad difference of typical motivation in the two cases, or at least any of sufficient importance to account for the broad differences of socially expected behavior. On the other hand there is a clearcut and definite difference on the institutional level. The institutional patterns governing the two fields of action are radically different in this respect. Not only are they different; it can be shown conclusively that this difference has very important functional bases. But it is a difference in definition of the situation. Doctors are not altruists, and the famous "acquisitiveness" of a business economy is not the product of "enlightened self-interest." The opinion may be hazarded that one of the principal reasons why economic thought has failed to see this fundamentally important fact is that it has confined its empirical attention to the action of the market place and has neglected to study its relations to other types of action. Only by such comparative study, the sociological equivalent of experimentation, is the isolation of variables possible.

Professional Groups and Political Structure

In the following paper, N. S. Timasheff uses the previous reading by Parsons as a point of departure to discuss business and professional organization and activity in nations organized under liberal, fascist, and communist forms of political structure. He finds in 1940 that, in contrast to conditions in fascist and communist societies, professional groups tend to be more decentralized in liberal societies, and consequently tend to become more differentiated in these latter contexts. Timasheff's discussion thus demonstrates one important way in which social context—or more specifically the political structure of the larger society—affects professionalization.

N. S. Timasheff (Professions and Business Management)

There is great divergence in the ideas concerning the correlation of business and the professions in the modern Western world. Whereas there exists a tendency to think that the businessman egoistically pursues his own interests regardless of interests of others, and that the professional man altruistically serves the interests of others, there are scholars who would almost completely assimilate the professions and business. For instance, Henry E. Sigerist, of Johns Hopkins University, says that medicine in the modern Western world has gradually become a trade, that medical service is purchased by the patient and sold by the physician under a competitive system, and that the physicians today are in business, without having lost a high moral standard.[1]

In a well-thought out paper Talcott Parsons[2] expresses the intermediary opinion that, in modern Western society, business and the professions have much more in common than is generally assumed and especially that they cannot be differentiated on the basis of pursuit of self-interest versus disinterestedness.

Professor Parsons does not identify business and the professions, and he ascribes to each of them, in modern Western society, a well-differentiated pattern. He believes, however, that they have some elements in common and that these are rationality, functional specialization, and universalism. But, of course, the most important element

they have in common is structural decentralization as opposed to the centralization of public services.[3] Decentralization means that a certain function is carried out by an indefinite number of independent, although interacting, agencies. The decentralization of business and the professions reveals the "liberal" character of modern society and is consistent with its general structure as manifested in the organization of the state and in the state-church relationships.

It is noteworthy that to minor variations within modern Western society there are fairly corresponding parallel variations in business and the professions; thus, for instance, there is no doubt that the Anglo-American variety of modern Western society gave rise to the highest "rugged individualism" in business and to the greatest freedom of professions.[4] The parallelism of fluctuations certainly forms an additional argument for the basic proposition of Parsons.

Validity can be ascribed to a generalization based on empirical study only within the scope of the material studied. But it is worthwhile to scrutinize whether the proposition that the structure of business and of the professions is parallel and can be related to the general structure of society is valid also outside of the modern Western world. A comparison with the newly created types of modern society—the fascist and the communist—seems to be a conclusive test.

It is characteristic for fascist society to direct business toward public service. Busi-

Reprinted from "Business and the Professions in Liberal, Fascist, and Communist Society," *The American Journal of Sociology*, 45, No. 6, 1940, 863–869, by permission of The University of Chicago Press. Copyright 1940 by the University of Chicago.

[1] *Socialized Medicine in the Soviet Union* (New York, 1937), p. 83.

[2] "The Professions and Social Structure," *Social Forces*, 17 1939, 457–467.

[3] In this paper the term "public service" will be used in a broad sense, including the administrative machinery.

[4] It must be noted that in English the term "profession" can mean free occupation in a certain field, whereas in all other European languages the addition of the word "liberal" or "free" is necessary to express the same conception. Language is merely a symbol, but the use of different symbols is sometimes a very good indication of differences in the actual phenomena they manifest.

ness continues to be based on private ownership of enterprises and on individual profit; but the activity of the owners ceases to be a "free" activity, becomes more and more managed by state agencies, and has to comply more and more with public interest as interpreted by these agencies.[5] The new structure seems contradictory, for we are used to the idea that public service is carried out by men selected in accordance with their particular ability for a specified function and with the special training which they have received; whereas, in fascist society, the shift of the economic function into the number of public services has not been accompanied by a departure from the structural principle of business in liberal society, according to which the economic function is carried out by individuals determined by the accident of their birth in a certain family or by success obtained in profit-making. This is not, however, entirely without historical precedent. In feudal society the exercise of public functions was combined with landownership. Moreover, in fascist society there appears a tendency to require from owners and managers the technical knowledge necessary for the particular situation, under the threat of replacement by others.[6] This is an additional symptom of the evolution of business toward public service.

A parallel evolution takes place in fascist society in regard to professions. The following fact is significant. In Italy the same law of April 3, 1926, which created semicompulsory associations, federations, and confederations of employers and employees, provides also for the organization of the professional classes according to the same pattern—that of semicompulsory associations. Professional men are grouped into seventeen national federations and one con-

federation, which exactly corresponds to the four confederations of employers, i.e., of businessmen. The associations, federations, and confederations are managed by the ruling party. What this means can be shown in the example of journalism.[7] All journalists have been divided into categories depending on their loyalty to the regime, and by means of a purge the members of the lower categories have been expelled and thus prevented from continuing their professional activity. According to Gaetano Salvemini, journalism under the fascist regime has ceased to be a free profession; journalists have become public officials controlled by the Fascist party.[8] This is possibly an exaggerated statement, but the trend of evolution is in that direction. In Germany, the creation on September 12, 1933, of the national chamber of culture had similar effects. Later laws introduced "authors' leaders" whose fuction is to "co-ordinate" the activity of journalists and of authors.[9] These are only examples, but, in general, in fascist countries professions are no longer decentralized activities.

The parallelism in the development in fascist society is obvious. Society has been given a new pattern manifested first of all by the new structure of the state. Both business and the professions have been affected and have been forced into patterns which, from the standpoint of modern Western society, are somewhat in between public service and professions. An interesting corollary can be drawn here: Fascist society is structurally less differentiated than is modern Western society, the three patterns of business, professions, and public service merging into one.

In regard to communist society, there is no need to stress that business is almost completely abolished and replaced by public service. One of the corollaries is that the positions in economic activity depend, officially, exclusively on knowledge, skill, and

---

[5] The best presentation for Italy is W. G. Welk, *Fascist Economic Policy* (Cambridge, Mass., 1938); for Germany, see F. Ermath, *The New Germany* (Washington, 1936).

[6] Both in Italy and in Germany this idea is actualized mainly in the field of agriculture and in some adjacent fields of economic activity. Thus, for instance, the German decrees of October 1, 1936, and January 25, 1937, demand special knowledge on the part of the managers of dairies and of enterprises trading in cattle.

[7] Professor Parsons never mentions this profession, but in Continental Europe it is considered as one of the most representative.

[8] *Under the Axe of Fascism* (New York, 1936), p. 81.

[9] Cf. R. A. Brady, *The Spirit and Structure of German Fascism* (New York, 1937).

efficiency, actually also on what could be called the clique pattern.

A parallel development has taken place in the organization of those social functions which, in modern Western society, are carried out by professional men. Liberal education does not exist in communist society; there is only state education completely subjected to approved programs.[10] Medical service has become public service; all medical men are state officers and must apply their knowledge without any remuneration from patients. Private practice has never been officially prohibited, and, although it has existed up to the present, its importance is rapidly decreasing.[11] Lawyers have been subjected to a regimentation manifesting considerable variety in detail. The general trend is that of transforming the activity of counsels into a public service parallel to that of the prosecution.[12] Journalists are considered an important part of the governmental machinery for propaganda. All teachers, lawyers, medical men, journalists, etc., are organized into trade-unions. (The idea of compulsory trade-unions has been imported to fascist Italy from communist Russia.) The Russian organization presents the peculiarity that the distribution of persons among unions depends not on the personal function but on the function of the institution, so that a counsel of a textile factory belongs to the union of textile workers and that the union of medical men includes the janitors of the hospitals, etc. This is an additional symptom of far-reaching changes in the conception of activities, which men of European culture consider as belonging to the inviolable domain of professions.

Communist society presents another opportunity for testing the validity of many generalizations gained by the observation of modern Western society. In contradistinction to fascism, the advance of which was almost straightforward, communist society was built up by disconnected efforts punctuated by retreats. In regard to the subject which especially interests us, the changes in the standing of the legal profession are significant. During the period of war communism the legal profession was abolished and replaced by a public service simultaneously with the abolition of private business; the remuneration of counsels was equalized with that of judge. During the period of the New Economic Policy, when business was partly restored, some autonomy was given to the lawyers. Everybody possessing the required (very modest) training could apply for admission to the collegium of defenders; the presidium of the collegium and the local soviet could reject the application. The fees were scheduled according to the client's ability to pay and to the complexity of the case. With the shift from the New Economic Policy to the policy of the Five Year plans, private business and autonomy of lawyers again vanished. With the mitigation of communist methods in economics during the past few years, a slight improvement in the situation of counsels has been manifested, first of all, by drastic denunciations of the counterrevolutionary activities of those who, during the previous period, had not given counsels the necessary freedom.[13]

Summing up, it can be said that as regards communist society, a general parallel fluctuation of business and professional

---

[10] N. Hans and S. Hessen, *Educational Policy in Soviet Russia* (London, 1930). In regard to higher educational institutions see also N. S. Timasheff, "Die Hochshule," in a symposium *Die Welt vor dem Abgrunde,* ed. I. Iljin (Berlin, 1931), pp. 519–33.

[11] Sigerist, *op. cit.,* pp. 122–23 and 137. Ground for this change had been prepared by the fact that in Imperial Russia medical service in rural districts was already organized according to the pattern of public service under the direction of the agencies of local self-government. Professor Sigerist calls it the first attempt to organize medicine as a public service on a large scale (*ibid.,* pp. 70–77).

[12] Cf. M. S. Calcott, *Russian Justice* (New York, 1935), pp. 140–58.

[13] It is characteristic for the period of Five Year plans that drastic changes in societal regulation were not expressed in written law which frequently remained unchanged (cf. N. S. Timasheff, "L'Evoluzione del diritto penale sovietico," *Rivisha italiana del diritto penale,* 4, 1932, 174–89). Many important facts belonging to that period can be studied only at the present time when they are denounced as leftist or other "deviations." Very important for clarifying the position of lawyers are the statements in *Sovetskaia Iustitsiia,* No. 22, 1937, pp. 20–22.

organization can be fairly well established, corresponding not only to the general trends but also to minor fluctuations within that society. This is a statement analogous to that made with respect to fascist society. The lack of differentiation established in regard to the latter is still more clearly expressed in communist society, where unification of business, professions, and public service is no longer a trend, as it is in fascist society, but an actuality.

Since in fascist and communist societies busines and the professions tend toward assimilation with each other and with public service, it can be expected that the elements which they already have in common in liberal society—rationality, functional specialization, and universalism—continue to be well expressed in the new types of modern society. This expectation is amply corroborated by facts. In fascist and communist society the element of rationality is obviously stressed in contradistinction to traditionalism. The idea of functional specialization was contested by the fathers of communism,[14] but this has proved to be a highly utopian element in the doctrine, and the pattern of functional specialization had to be restored. The application of the principle of universalism in fascist as well as in communist society experienced a certain curb, in regard both to business and to the professions; neither business, the professions, nor their substitutes could serve racially heterogeneous elements in the first case, or class enemies in the second.[15] But both excep-

tions are of the universalistic type: not persons but classes of persons are excluded, so that they serve to corroborate the principle.

An important background to the unification of business, the professions, and public service is presented by the new theory of motivation. According to the fascist and the communist doctrine, in new society there should be neither egoistic nor altruistic but solidaristic motivation serving the interests not of the actor or other individuals but those of the group considered as a unity. This solidaristic motivation is expected from every citizen in every social situation. Therefore, there can be no different institutional or normative patterns corresponding to the patterns of business, professions, or public service in modern Western society. This is another symptom of the decreasing differentiation in those societies as compared with the latter.

The cursory review of some facts which can be observed in the world surrounding us allows the assumption that the basic proposition which Professor Parsons very cautiously formulated for only modern Western society is valid in a wider field. Freedom in business and freedom in the professions, characteristic for that society, depends on the general type of social organization. With changes in this type parallel variations both in business and in the professions seem to take place. That it is so is probably *a priori*. But it is sometimes worthwhile to verify by facts the validity of common-sense propositions.

14 "Every Cook Should Be Able To Rule the State" was one of the favorite slogans of Lenin.
15 During the past few years restrictions against the members of "hostile classes" have been gradually removed in the Soviet Union; this, of course, manifests a trend toward uni-

versalization. This trend, however, is displayed in a society which is no longer an entirely communist society but presents a compromise between communist and "bourgeois" patterns.

The Social Significance of Professionalization

From the previous readings, we know that the process of professionalization is inextricably linked to the kind of society in which it takes place—to its political form, its cultural norms, and its social structure, as well as its stage of technological development. In a discussion of the "impact of metropolitan conditions" on occupations, Carr-Saunders has gone so far as to maintain that:

Under the impact of metropolitan conditions, the concept of a profession has become transformed. No one speaks any more of the learned professions. Professional men were formerly regarded as possessing a broad culture, a wide special competence, and a general understanding of affairs. Consequently, they were influential members of society. A measure of leadership fell into their hands, and much that we value in our society was evolved under the influence of the older professions.

Today, professional men are regarded by the public as experts—persons with high competence in a restricted sphere. Great deference is paid to them while they act wihin their particular range. Otherwise, they have little prestige. Outside their role, they are thought to have no more claim to be heard than the man in the street.

The change is not so much a transformation as a disintegration of the traditional professional concept...*

It is evident that in the past few decades significant changes in the occupational order have been precipitated by external forces in the larger society. (Of course not everyone would agree that these changes are precisely of the dysfunctional sort described here by Carr-Saunders). Taylor observed this interrelationship in the life insurance occupation, where he found "...a reciprocal relation between the internal structure and the external functions o fthe occupation" such that "the success of planned changes [in the direction of greater professionalization] for an occupational structure is necessarily limited and largely determined by the functions of the occupation for the greater society."† Earlier, in an important essay on occupations, T. H. Marshall recognized that "...the professions today are being weaned from this excessive individualism and are adapting themselves to the new standards of social service. The change has been stimulated by outside pressure, but the professions have made an independent contribution of their own and helped to build up the influences to which they themselves are in turn reacting."‡ But we still may be unclear as to what professionalization actually does for the larger society. What functions do professional groups perform? How do they support or undermine (i.e., change) the social system in which they are so deeply imbedded?

Everett C. Hughes discusses such questions in the following essay and review of significant earlier writings. He points out that professionalization in modern society is not only a mechanism for allowing social mobility of individuals in their working careers, but also for entire *groups* within the larger society—for ethnic groups and for occupational groups. Professionalization is thus an important ingredient in the "open society." Conversely, it can also contribute to intergroup conflicts where ethnic or racial caste barriers restrain career mobility opportunities for certain minority groups.

Furthermore, Hughes points out that, while organizations may be modifying the older concept of the free and independent professional by hiring professionals for salaried positions in increasing numbers, salaried professionals are also doing something to the organizations that are employing them. He hints at the idea that *employing organizations, as well as occupations, can also become more professionalized.*

* A. M. Carr-Saunders, "Metropolitan Conditions and Traditional Professional Relationships," in *The Metropolis in Modern Life,* Robert Moore Fisher (ed.). (New York: Doubleday & Company, Inc., 1955), pp. 286–287.

† M. Lee Taylor, "Professionalization: Its Functions and Dysfunctions for the Life Insurance Occupation," *Social Forces,* 38, No. 2 (December 1959), 110–114.

‡ T. H. Marshall, "The Recent History of Professionalism in Relation to Social Structure and Social Policy," *The Canadian Journal of Economics and Political Science,* 5, 1939, 337–38.

Everett C. Hughes (General)

T. H. Marshall defined professions as, in effect and with some other characteristics, those occupations in which *caveat emptor* cannot be allowed to prevail and which, while they are not pursued for gain, must bring their practitioners income of such a level that they will be respected and such a manner of living that they may pursue the life of the mind.[1] There are certain problems which surround such occupations in all times.

The current changes noted by Marshall are the ever greater dependence of modern society upon professional services, an increase in the variety of such services and in the number of the professions, and the tendency for many practitioners of the older professions and for most or all of some never professions to work in organizations with an employer, rather than to set up a shop to which clients come, one by one, are served, and pay for the service. He also noted that while the community at large is in all times and places concerned with the manner in which professional services are performed, this is especially so in our times; indeed, the community at large is the client of some new professions and, in increasing measure, of older ones.

Marshall was, of course, not the first among those called sociologists to have considered the professions as a central feature of society, a key to the understanding of social structure. Auguste Comte had had his say on the subject when he noted (in a passage which I have not lately been able to find) that. the same engineer had kept the waterworks of Paris going before, during, and after the Revolution. Some professions, it seems, not merely survive revolutions, but keep the rivers of blood flowing.

Herbert Spencer considered the elaboration of professions the essential feature of a civilized society. Other institutions arose to defend, sustain, and regulate life. "What further general function is there? There is the augmentation of life; and this function it is which the professions in general subserve."[2] There follows an eloquent passage in which he tells us that the medical man increases the amount of life; the artist elevates the emotions and pleasurable feelings; the historian and the man of letters raise men's mental states; the scientist and the teacher increase mental illumination, all in their own way increasing life. His conception of the professions is catholic; dancers are allowed a place among those who increase life.

Emile Durkheim, having devoted his chief treatise on human society to the division of social labor, could not well avoid discussing the place of professions. When he did so specifically in the Preface to the second edition,[3] he referred not to professions in the English sense, as did Spencer, but to all occupations. What concerned him was the propensity of professional groups to generate social rules and sanctions and to become impermeable to attempts of outsiders to control them. He saw professional groups as organs of society, partly autonomous systems of relations which cannot, however, exist except in contact with the other organs of society. As social advocate, he favored the kind of society in which occupational groups would be the chief organs of control represented as such in government. He did not, so far as I know, deal with the main trends touched upon

Reprinted from "The Professions in Society," *The Canadian Journal of Economics and Political Science,* 26, No. 1 (February 1960), 54–61. Used by permission of the author and publisher.

[1] T. H. Marshall, "The Recent History of Professionalism in Relation to Social Structure and Social Policy," *The Canadian Journal of Economics and Political Science,* 5, No. 3 (August 1939), 325–340.

[2] *The Principles of Sociology* (London, 1896), XI, Chap. 1. Spencer, Comte, Bagehot, and others of the period wrote in two moods: in one they presented pretentious theories of scoial evolution; in the other, they commented sharply and sometimes passionately on the affairs of their day. The work of such men is often completely misunderstood because the notebooks used by graduate students contain the pretentious theories, and those only in brief caricature, but not the more timely discussions and the ideas and theories implicit in them.

[3] *De la division du travail social,* Préface à la deuxième édition (Paris, 1902), "Quelques Remarques sur les groupements professionels."

by Marshall. Nor had any other sociologists done so explicitly.

Tonnies, Park, Max Weber, and Simmel had all written of the multiplication of occupations based on the application of science and reason as a mark of urban society. But none of them had paid special attention to the other trends noted by Marshall. It was Marshall who heralded the upsurge of the new style of professional practice. He did not agree with his colleague Harold Laski, who advocated doing away with all private practice of professions.[4] Nor would he join the tirade of Messrs. Angus and Maude[5] against use of the term "professions" for any but the few occupations which had been so designated in the past, and against any but the style of private practice which they assumed to have been universal in that blessed era.

The merit of Marshall's article is that it did so clearly indicate trends which were to become marked in all of the industrial countries, no matter what political banner floated over them. All have indeed shown a multiplication of professions, as the term is understood in English; and all have shown the same tendency for them to be practiced inside complicated organizations—complicated in the sense that the relation of the professional with the client is part of some larger complex of relations. In none, not even in the Soviet Union, has private professional practice completely disappeared.

In the years since 1939 professional services have become a matter of increasing public concern in all of these countries, arising in part from the growing belief that everyone has a right to education, health, and to those other kinds of increase of life which Spencer had said it was the function of professions to provide. One might say that a characteristic feature of our time has been a great increase in the expected standard of living in those very aspects of life of which Spencer had spoken. It has also become apparent that the distribution of such services in the expected measure to all was not likely to be achieved by selling them over the counter by the parcel to paying customers, nor by the simple method of allowing the professional person to charge on a sliding scale, taking much from those who have much and little or nothing from those who have little or nothing. More and more philanthropic and public agencies, have become involved in the distribution of professional services; more and more of the cost is paid by various risk- and cost-spreading agencies other than the professional practitioner himself. And one must note, as Marshall did, that many services had never been distributed by that simple method.

The public interest in professions and the services they provide has been reflected in the work of social scientists. In Great Britain, Carr-Saunders and Wilson[6] published a book in 1933 in which they described in general terms the process by which occupations took on the characteristics of professions, and gave the history of a number of cases.

In the United States and Canada, work has lately run rather to the place of professions in prestige-scales derived from surveys of opinion; to the manner in which occupations attempt and sometimes succeed in being accorded professional standing; to the processes by which young laymen choose to enter professions and to their education and initiation into them; and to that progress of professional people through the maze of the appropriate organizations, formal and informal, which is a man's career.

As has been said by W. Lloyd Warner, North America is not class-conscious, but class self-conscious. Work on the professions, as on other matters, reflects this; it is in part a study of social advancement (mobility). The advancement is of two kinds. The first is the rise of the individual by getting into an occupation of high prestige, or by achieving special success in his occupation. The second is the collective effort of an organized occupation to improve its place and increase its power, in relation to others. That effort, in middle-class occupations, characteristically is

---

[4] Laski had lately argued this point in *Harper's Magazine,* as Marshall observes.

[5] *Professional People* (London, 1952).

[6] A. M. Carr-Saunders and P. A. Wilson, *The Professions* (Oxford, 1933).

directed to achieving professional status. For whatever else the word "profession" may mean, it is in modern English a symbol of high ranking among occupations.

We North Americans are especially sensitive to all that affects the chances of individuals of various backgrounds and qualities to enter various kinds of occupations and to achieves success in them. The achievement of success within an occupation includes, in some professional occupations, choice of one of its several specialties and one of several styles of career. These secondary choices are often as fateful as choice of the occupation itself. We have thus an ever increasing number of occupations which aspire to the title, prestige, and privileges of professions and a great number of people attempting to improve their lot by gaining the education and other qualifications for entry to professions—and all this is happening in a time when no one can be quite sure that any occupation will maintain its present position for as many years as a man's normal career; or that the sciences and arts which one learns will not have become obsolete before one is ready to be retired, even before one has achieved a well-paid, honored, and secure position.

These changes are all complicated further by the ethnic and racial variety of the two nations of North America, for entry into professions has been a special road to advancement for ethnic groups who first offered themselves for the humbler positions in the labor markets of these two countries; once they have entered professions, their difficulties in following certain specialties or styles of careers become the issues in the battle of discrimination.[7] This is the key to the present phase of racial and ethnic conflict in the United States. As one might expect, this phase is complicated by the fact that, just as certain ethnic and

religious minorities are entering the professions in large numbers, the change from private practice to work in more complicated organizations for salary and under authority has also accelerated; so the problem for, say, a Negro is not merely whether he can gain admission to a medical school, and to medical practice, but whether he can find a place in hospitals and clinics or in informal referral systems; for in such systems not even a Negro client can determine whether he will be attended by a Negro physician. Other authorities enter into the choice; so the question of discrimination is not merely whether a given kind of patient will accept a given kind of doctor but whether colleagues and those with the power to place physicians are either prejudiced against Negro physicians or afraid to act without prejudice for reasons of policy.[8] I suspect that the relations between French and English in Canada may be affected by the change from private practice, with clients' choices prevailing, to more highly organized and bureaucratic forms.

And while one is speaking of minorities, it seems not too far-fetched to say that the present demands of the neo-feminists concern a shifting of the place of what have traditionally been women's professions in the whole complex of professional services, and of that minority of minorities, the married women, in the labor force in general, but especially in the professions, for working women of some education are concentrated in professional occupations much more than men. Some would say that the occupations in which they are concentrated are quasi-professional—nursing, teaching, social work, librarianship. That but emphasizes collective mobility; for such occupations are prominent among those which are attempting to gain for themselves a more secure standing as *professions*. This they do by the usual means of attempting to require more schooling of aspirants to their occupations, by insisting that they themselves, and not some outside authority, shall judge what is their proper

---

[7] Oswald Hall did one of the pioneer studies in this field, "The Organization of Medical Practice in an Eastern City," unpublished Ph.D. dissertation, University of Chicago, 1944. David N. Solomon pursued certain aspects of the same problems in his Ph.D. dissertation, "Career Contingencies of Chicago Physicians," University of Chicago, 1952.

[8] See Dietrich Reitzes, *Negroes in Medicine* (Cambridge, Mass., 1958).

work, by putting their more routine duties on the shoulders of subordinate workers, and by claiming a mandate to define the public interest in matters relating to their work.

Not the least important of the symbolic steps in raising an occupation to more fully professional standing is to go in for research. The object of research may be the occupation itself, or it may be study of the phenomena with which the occupation is concerned—health, education, human personality. In time these may be redefined so as to bring the research closer to that of older and more general branches of human knowledge. Insofar as the people inside the occupation do this research, those who do it tend to become an elite somewhat removed from practice, and to move into professional schools connected with universities or into special agencies, private or public. They tend to have careers quite distinct from those of people primarily in practice. This may indeed be a sign that the occupation has professional status, for this very distinction between careers of practice and careers of research, education, and administration is becoming marked in all of the older professions. Perhaps what distinguishes the new professions from the old is that, in the new, prestige clearly goes to those in the careers removed from practice, whereas in the older ones this is by no means so clearly the case.

I do not mean to suggest that an occupation on the make undertakes research merely to raise its standing, although that may be the result and although those who would elevate an occupation may be quite aware that it will be. A good many of the new occupations are the result of social and technological changes which are not fully understood and whose consequences may affect not merely the way in which some one occupation does it work, and, consequently, the selection and education of the people who are to do it; they may also change the division of labor as among professions and as between them and other occupations in a given field. Thus the division of labor among the specialities of medicine itself is constantly changing; at the same time, the technical division of

labor between physicians, nurses, technicians, other therapists, scientists, social workers, and various administrative specialties is changing very drastically (although perhaps the fundamental role of the physician has been less affected by it all than he fears). This is the feature of professional change that has led to the calling in of social scientists. Sociologists, social psychologists, anthropologists, and economists in great number have been invited into the sacred precincts to study changes in the relations of occupations to each other in the great complexes of institutions which have grown up about the major professional services; it is a continuation of the social scientist's role as student of the division of social and economic labor (which political scientists call "constitutions"). One danger is that the social scientists will become pundits when dealing with newer professions of less prestige than their own, and that they will overidentify themselves with professions of greater prestige than theirs when such deign to ask them in.

Whatever the dangers, the gain can be great. For social scientists now have access to crucial data about our culture not previously available and to organizations which do not fit the rather simple models which students of business, of political bodies, and of the family had developed in the time when each branch of social science had its favorite institution. For the organizations in which professions work show patterns of authority and interaction which, according to earlier theories of organization, could not possibly work. They are, in general, organizations with more staff than line; their special importance for the study of social organization is that they give us new models to work on just when business organizations, which students have been inclined to take as the prototype of rational organization, are themselves becoming so cluttered by staff advisers (of various old and new professions) that the line is scarcely distinguishable, and this is very frustrating. The newer generation of businessmen, instead of proposing that universities, hospitals, and government agencies (in which the efforts of professional people are somewhat coordinated) be run in a business-like fashion, may turn to these mad-houses for ideas on how to organize their own enterprises; for the staff people, insofar as they are really professional, have another loyalty than that to their employers; they belong to professions which have some sense of solidarity and autonomy.

The professional trend is doing something to organizations and enterprises. But work in organizations and enterprises is also doing something to professions, both as concept and as reality. It is here that German word becomes of importance. The concept *freier Beruf* (free or liberal profession) once stood for something like a complete philosophy. A man in such a profession was self-employed, learned, devoted to his work, full of the sense of honor of an historic estate (Stand), courageously indifferent to pressures from outside, politically neutral (yet, on the whole, *Kaisertreu*). But at the same time there was developed in Germany a model and philosophy of the *öffentlichen Beamten* (civil servant). While all civil servants were to do their work competently and loyally, the higher officials were to be —and were—men of learning, of high professional conscience, and of great prestige. But they were, even more than the men in the liberal professions, to be at once politically neutral and loyal to authority. It was a loyalty which sometimes showed itself in a sort of condescension to those ephemeral and erratic creatures who headed governments and made childishly unwise and impractical policies. There were thus, in German culture, two images of the professional man, one *frei* (self-employed) and one *beamtet* (secure in a bureaucratic position).

One of these conceptions has been rudely shaken by the bureaucratizing of the free professions; the other by the pressures on the civil servants accompanying the violent changes of political regime from Empire to Weimar Republic, to totalitarian national-socialism, and from that to equally totalitarian communism in the East and the return to democracy in the West.

The fate of the older conception of the free profession is dealt with in detail by

J. F. Volrad Deneke in *Die freien Berufe*.[9] Herbert Von Borch deals with the second problem, that of the official and his loyalty, in *Obrigkeit und Widerstand: Zur politischen Soziologie des Beamtentums (Authority and Resistance: An Essay on the Sociology of the Civil Servant)*.[10] These two books thus deal with one of the problems highlighted in Marshall's article, that of professional work performed inside agencies rather than independently. Deneke shows, for a number of professions, just how far the reality is from independent practice. In medicine 42.4 per cent were in dependent positions (not in private practice) in Western Germany in 1950, the figure ranging from nearly all under thirty years of age to 14.7 per cent of those between sixty and sixty-five.[11] In the main, Deneke devotes himself not to the figures, but to the problem of maintaining professional autonomy, solidarity, and standards of work under the prevailing condition of working inside organizations and for salary. There is nothing especially striking in his analysis of the problem; the contribution of his book is essentially a statement of the problem and presentation of the current state of things.

Von Borch, in his study of the conflict of loyalties of the civil servant, is dealing with a problem which has not risen in so extreme a degree in the English-speaking countries in recent times as in those countries which have undergone totalitarian revolutions. The conflict of professional and

9 Stuttgart, 1956. *Arbeit und Beruf,* by Theodor Scharmann (Tübingen, 1956) is perhaps the best recent German general book on this whole matter.

10 Tübingen, 1954.

11 *Die freien Berufe,* p. 124. Deneke compiled a series of tables from the 1950 census of occupations in Western Germany. As one would expect, certain specialties in medicine, law, and other occupations are practised independently more often than others. The newer technical professions are predominantly not independent. The age differences in medicine and law may be due to a secular trend which takes effect first in the young, or it may be due in part to the fact that in some professions a young man must work for older men or in agencies for a long time before he is able to get a private practice.

human conscience with the demand of a totalitarian regime that its civil servants not merely carry out all of its orders but that they also become apostles of its doctrines is the problem of the employed professional in its ultimate degree. But the ultimate degree of any problem is very instructive; it brings out the essential features. It does not serve any analytical purpose, however, if used merely as a horrible example. The problem of all professional codes has always been this: Whose agent is the professional? Turned around it is: Who is the client? The extreme ideology of the private practice of professions gives a simple answer. There is but one client, the person who applies for services and accepts them on the conditions dictated by the profession. This obviously cannot be the case when the application does not come in that way. But between that situation and the complete submission of the civil servant in a totalitarian regime there are many degrees. In Russia, the physician must—as agent of the People's Republic which wants everyone at work—take care not to certify too many people as ill enough to stay at home.[12] But the physician and nurse who work for an industry in our part of the world have in some measure the same problem of determining whether the company or the worker-patient is the client. The problem of acquiescence in the demands or pressures from employing agencies is universal, and has always been so. I will not here go into the many means of defense which professional, or other occupational groups, have developed against such pressures. It certainly is demonstrably true that types of organization are being worked out which do allow the maintenance of professional freedom in balance with the controls necessary in large organizations which involve many kinds of positions and many occupations.

As a matter of fact, there are some indications in recent studies of a great paradox. Part of the cherished freedom of a professional worker is not merely to do his work according to his own best judgment and conscience, but also to choose his own style of work and economy of effort. Lawyers who practice alone—at least in a sample of them taken in Chicago[13]—are utter captives and choreboys of their clients. They have no freedom to choose a branch of law and make themselves expert or learned in it. Most of them, in time, do find their practice narrowed to a special line of chores: they have become specialists by default. Likewise there is growing evidence that something like this is true of physicians who practice alone in certain districts of large cities, and perhaps elsewhere. Joe L. Spaeth found a large number of physicians in Chicago, whose practice has gradually narrowed to a rather low form of industrial medicine, repairing small wounds caused by accidents, examining and treating people who get sick at work, and making due reports for insurance and liability purposes.[14] They, too, have become specialists by default. They could not be called *general practitioners*, for the cases they get are not a random selection of what goes wrong with people, and their knowledge is not any sort of general selection of available medical knowledge.

And here we are at a paradox of modern professional freedom. The effective freedom to choose one's special line of work, to have access to the appropriate clients and equipment, to engage in that converse with eager and competent colleagues which will sharpen one's knowledge and skill, to organize one's time and effort so as to gain that end, and even freedom from pressure to conform to the clients' individual or collective customs and opinions seem, in many

[12] See Mark G. Field, *The Soviet Physician* (Cambridge, Mass., 1958). Also his "Structured Strain in the Role of the Soviet Physician," *The American Journal of Sociology*, 58 (March 1953), 493–502.

[13] Jerome E. Carlin, "The Lawyer as Individual Practitioner: A Study in the Professions," unpublished Ph.D. thesis, University of Chicago, 1959. Carlin compared a sample of lawyers in one-man offices with others.

[14] "Industrial Medicine: A Low-Status Branch of a Profession," unpublished Master's thesis, University of Chicago, 1958.

lines of work, to be much greater for those professionals who have employers and work inside complicated and even bureaucratic organizations than for those who, according to the traditional concept, are in inde- pendent practice. Penetrating analysis of this paradox and of the problems related to it is a major task of social science. It will center largely around study of professions, old and new.

Questions for Discussion and Further Research

Beginning with the selection from Durkheim's writings, all the readings in this chapter have suggested ways in which professional groups serve to support and sustain the social structure and values of the larger society. There are instances, however, where this is not necessarily true. MacIver was most explicit in directing our attention to such instances when he wrote about "specific group biases," which may sometimes concentrate the attention of professional groups upon matters of self-interest which divide one professional group from another and which may even serve to undermine certain key values in the larger society. An example of this may have been occurring in the 1964 election within the State of California. The California Real Estate Association endorsed an amend- ment to the California State Constitution ("Proposition 14") that prohibits the enactment of legislation to prevent racial or religious discrimination in certain aspects of housing throughout the state. Many leading religious and legal groups strongly opposed this amendment, calling it a serious moral issue that would lead to subversion of some of the fundamental values of a liberal democratic society. A considerable number of individual realtors and some local real estate associations have taken this same position, in contradistinction to the official position of their state association. How and why do such political alignments occur? We need further research to identify and understand the conditions under which various professional groups are likely to try to support the values of the larger society in comparison to the conditions under which they are likely to undermine them.

A further extension of this question leads us to consider the relations between professional groups and the larger society in different types of societies. Timasheff's paper stressed the homogeneity of fascist and communist societies in the pre-World War II era with the activities of professional groups highly integrated with and controlled by the state. World War II, however, led to the destruction of the fascist governments, perhaps in part because of their lack of the creative scientific and technical strength that may be more charac- teristic of pluralistic societies. And there are indications that the communist society of Soviet Russia which survived the war has become more pluralistic in the post-war period, allowing relatively more freedom to professional groups in the arts, sciences, and legal spheres. Does this suggest that there may be pressure in all modern societies toward professional independence and autonomy associated with the occupational differentiation that Durkheim's writings claimed to be characteristic of modern times? In order to answer such ques- tions, we need further research on the specific kinds of linkages established with professional groups in different forms of modern society. For example, in newly-developing countries, in contrast to older societies, we need to examine in more detail the ways in which professionalization contributes to the social mobility of entire groups of people, as was suggested in the selection from Hughes' writings.

3

Individuals and Professionalization

Every man seeks to make some sense out of the world around him as he moves through it—to find some meaning, some predictability in events as he experiences them. In older, pre-industrial societies, before a high degree of occupational specialization occurred, the individual's work experiences tended to be a part and parcel of his interpretation of the rest of life. There was little, if any, division between the worksite and other areas of individual and family activity. Today, however, work tends to be compartmentalized from other aspects of life, and sociologists speak of "multiple group membership" and different "reference groups" when they describe the social context of modern life. Certainly the work context exercises crucial influences over other facets of life experience, since life today is economically and, in large part, psychologically dependent upon the successes and failures of the breadwinner in his work. Therefore, an understanding of how an individual enters and moves through a career in a more or less professional work context is fundamental to understanding the totality of his life adjustment.

Career patterns can be examined from two perspectives: the perspective of an outside observer and the perspective of an inside participator. Everett C. Hughes wrote in a notable essay that "in a highly and rigidly structured society, a career consists, objectively, of a series of status and clearly defined offices." In modern industrial society, however, Hughes pointed out that "the individual has more latitude for creating his own position or choosing from a number of existing ones...there are more adventures and more failures." From a subjective point of view, he described a career as "the moving perspective in which a person sees his life as a whole and interprets the meaning of his various attributes, actions, and the things which happen to him."* The following selected

* Everett C. Hughes, "Institutional Office and the Person," *The American Journal of Sociology*, **43**, 1937, 404–413; reprinted in Everett C. Hughes, *Men and Their Work* (Glencoe, Ill.: Free Press, 1958), p. 63.

readings touch upon both subjective and objective aspects of career patterns in occupational contexts that are more or less professionalized.

Individual Background and Professional Careers

Entry into different professional careers is not equally easy for all men or women. Ease of entry varies according to the social origins of entrants, as does the way in which they move through various career patterns. For example, a number of studies of occupational mobility have shown that movement into and through professional careers is conditioned by one's family status, which, in turn, is largely a function of the occupation of one's father.* The following study by Albert J. Reiss, Jr., follows the approach of Carr-Saunders and classifies occupations according to the degree of their professionalization, from "established professions" to "marginal professions," and then examines the social origins and mobility patterns of individuals in each professional category. As might be expected, the author found marked differences in social origin associated with different career patterns.

Unlike most of the previous readings presented in this volume, this paper reports data from an empirical study in some detail. It provides a reader who is unfamiliar with the way in which sociologists collect and interpret such data an opportunity to examine one form of sociological analysis. Here we can observe the sociologist establishing his categories of analysis—the types of professionalization and of occupational mobility—and then drawing his conclusions from survey data related to these categories. Although the data reported here are now more than a decade old, the method of analysis used and the conclusions drawn therefrom can stimulate our thinking about whether a similar analysis would still support similar or different conclusions today.

* For a more recent examination and comparison of the occupational "inheritance" patterns of dental and medical students, see D. M. More, "A Note On Occupational Origins of Health Service Personnel," *American Sociological Review*, 25, No. 3 (June 1960), 403–404.

Albert J. Reiss, Jr. (General)

This paper describes patterns of occupational mobility for men in selected professional statuses. The data are for 654 sample cases of white males 25 years old and over in the four cities of Chicago, Los Angeles, Philadelphia and San Francisco in January,

Reprinted from "Occupational Mobility of Professional workers," *American Sociological Review*, 20, No. 6 (December 1955), 693–700. Used by permission of the American Sociological Association. The original publication bore the following note: "Revised version of paper read at the annual meeting of the American Sociological Society, September, 1954."

1951, who held a professional job at some time during the 1940 to 1950 decade, and who worked one month or more in 1950.[1] The 654 sample cases represent an estimated

[1] The data were obtained from the work history schedules of the Occupational Mobility Survey sponsored by the Social Science Research Council and conducted in cooperation with six university centers and the U. S. Bureau of the Census on behalf of the U. S. Department of the Air Force. See Gladys L. Palmer, *Labor Mobility in Six Cities*, New York: Social Science Research Council, 1954, for a description of the study design. All persons coded O in the U. S. Bureau of the Census occupational code are included in the analysis.

240,063 white males in the four cities combined.[2]

The growth of modern cities and states with the industrial revolution has had a profound influence upon the professions. The increase in complexity of the division of labor, in particular, has had its counterpart in the professions. Sir Alexander Morris Carr-Saunders differentiates four major types of professions in modern industrial states.[3] The *old established professions* are founded upon the study of a theoretical structure of a department of learning which is used in the practice of the art founded on it, and the members of the vocation feel bound to follow a certain mode of behavior. Religion, law, medicine, higher education and aesthetics are associated with the old established professions. The *new professions* have their own fundamental studies upon which their art is founded. Chemists, engineers, natural and social scientists are examples of the new professions. By way of contrast, the *semi-professions* replace theoretical study of a field of learning by the acquisition of precise technical skill. Technical practice and knowledge is the basis of such semi-professions as nursing, pharmacy, optometry and social work. There are, also the *would-be-professions,* where members aspire to professional status. Familiarity with modern practices in business and government generally distinguishes this group. Personnel directors, sales engineers, business counselors, funeral directors, and institutional managers are examples of vocations where members aspire to professional status. A fifth group, the *marginal professions,* is included in this study for comparative purposes, although it is not identified by Carr-

Saunders. The category is made up largely of those who perform technical assignments associated with professional assignments, e.g., medical and laboratory technicians, testers, illustrators, draftsmen, interpreters, and inspectors. The mobility of members of each of these groups is compared below.

A basic objective of this study is to describe occupational mobility patterns of men in five professional status groups, and to analyze a few factors associated with these mobility patterns. A number of studies of mobility made during the past decade provide a measure of occupational mobility in the work force based on a longitudinal view of job or work histories.[4] This study employs a similar approach to the study of occupational mobility in that patterns of occupational mobility are defined for work histories during the 1940 to 1950 decade. Occupational mobility is defined as a change in occupational assignment during the decade involving a shift in the level of the assignment in a rank order of occupations. The relative prestige attached to specific occupational assignments was the criterion used to establish the rank order of occupations.[5] Each change in occupational assign-

---

[2] The raw data come from four separate samples. For each city estimates were made separately based on the weights for that city. The proportion of persons who held a professional job at some time during the decade is not the same for each city. The percentage for each city in this study is: Chicago, 24 per cent; Los Angeles, 32 per cent; Philadelphia, 21 per cent; San Francisco, 23 per cent.

[3] See Alexander Morris Carr-Saunders, "Metropolitan Conditions and Traditional Professional Relationships," in *The Metropolis in Modern Life,* Robert M. Fisher (ed.). New York: Doubleday & Company, 1955, pp. 280–281.

[4] For example, see Seymour M. Lipset and Reinhard Bendix, "Social Mobility and Occupational Career Patterns," Parts I and II, *The American Journal of Sociology,* 57 (January 1952), 366–374, and (March 1952), 494–504; H. D. Anderson and P. E. Davidson, *Occupational Mobility in an American Community,* Palo Alto: Stanford University Press, 1937; D. C. Miller and W. H. Form, "Measuring Patterns of Occupational Security," *Sociometry,* 10 (November 1947), 362–375; and D. C. Miller and W. H. Form, "Occupational Career Pattern as a Sociological Instrument," *The American Journal of Sociology,* 54 (January 1949), 317–329.

[5] The prestige rank order of eighty major occupational assignments by North and Hatt was used to define the rank framework. [See Cecil C. North and Paul K. Hatt, "Jobs and Occupations: A Popular Evaluation," *Opinion News* (September 1, 1947), pp. 3–13.] All other occupational assignments were assigned to this rank order on the basis of the skill requirements for the occupational assignment in the *Dictionary of Occupational Titles.* The specific procedure was as follows: The skill level of each job which is not included in the North-Hatt prestige rank order was determined; each job then was assigned to that North-Hatt prestige rank where the occupational assignment had an "equivalent" skill.

ment during the decade was examined to see if it involved a shift in occupational level (mobility) within this rank order of occupations (occupation structure). Seven patterns of occupational mobility are used to describe these shifts in occupational level.[6] A person is *stable,* i.e., without mobility, if he either held the same occupational assignment or made shifts in assignment without a shift in occupational level during the decade. A move to an occupational assignment at a higher rank in the rank order of occupations is described as an upward move. This is either *proximate upward mobility* or *distant upward mobility* depending upon the magnitude of the occupational shift in rank order distance. With few exceptions, a move to self-employment is called *upward to self-employment.* A move to an occupational assignment at a lower rank is a downward move unless it was a move from self-employment. Most shifts out of self-employment are classified separately as a move *downward from self-employment.* Finally, persons who made one or more upward *and* downward shifts in occupational level are said to experience *fluctuations in occupational level.*[7] An additional indicator of occupational mobility is employed, viz., generation occupational mo-

bility. The professional status on the last professional job held by each man is compared with the longest job his father ever held.

The observed differences among professional status categories are not systematically measured in this paper since the weighting of individual cases for each city in the four city aggregate was not undertaken for subgroups. To guard against "unreliable" conclusions, only those differences are discussed where the percentage difference is also observed for age subgroups of the distribution. Data for these age groups are omitted in the accompanying tables. Some reliance also is placed on the interpretation of patterns rather than pairs of differences.

MOBILITY IN PROFESSIONAL STATUSES

Movement in an occupational structure is conditioned by two major types of occupational barriers. These barriers are particularly effective in controlling movement into and within professional work. The qualitative differences in kinds of work, including differences in capacities, skill, and training, create one type of barrier to movement. Professional persons, in this sense, are qualified to enter only those kinds of professional work in which they can use their capacities, skills, and training. Few medical doctors, for example, are able to practice dentistry. Similarly, professionals are quite limited in their access to certain nonprofessional kinds of work. There also are artificially maintained barriers to occupational movement beyond the artificial scarcity created by the nature of the work and training for it. These artificial barriers are of two kinds. There are the artificial barriers to entry into occupations based on such things as numbers accepted into training, social class origins, educational history, and so on. After entry, there are artificial barriers to movement within the occupation. These may include such "organizational facts" as civil service ratings, apprenticeships, certification, and association memberships. The data below on differences in movement among professional status groups suggest these barriers make for differences in the kind and extent of mobility among professional status groups. It

---

This procedure permitted the assignment of jobs for which prestige rankings were not available in the North-Hatt prestige rank order on the assumption that jobs with equivalent skills have equivalent prestige. A few exceptions were made to this practice, when "coder judgment" assigned the prestige level.

[6] A detailed statement of the technique for delineating the mobility patterns is found in Chicago Community Inventory, *Patterns of Occupation Mobility for Workers in Four Cities,* Chicago: University of Chicago, 1953 (hexographed).

[7] To the writer's knowledge, only one previous mobility study has attempted to define a mobility pattern approximating that of "fluctuating status" in this study. Yet almost 13 per cent of the professional persons in this study experienced fluctuations in occupational level during the 1940 to 1950 decade, rather than a clearly upward or downward move. See W. H. Form and D. C. Miller, *op. cit.,* for a related definition. The failure to define a "fluctuating occupational status" may largely be due to the absence of appropriate data for definition, since a chronological history of occupational assignments is necessary to define it.

TABLE 1

PERCENTAGE DISTRIBUTION BY 1940 TO 1950 PATTERN OF OCCUPATIONAL MOBILITY FOR
PROFESSIONAL STATUS CATEGORIES

Professional Status	Number	Stable	Distant Upward	Proxi-mate Upward	Upward to Self-Em-ployment	Fluctu-ating	Down-ward from Self-Em-ployment	Down-ward
Total Professionals*	(650)	52	8	15	5	13	2	5
Established professions	(105)	71	—	11	5	6	1	6
New professions	(249)	54	9	17	5	11	1	3
Semi-professions	(104)	45	8	20	6	15	4	2
Would-be professions	(49)	35	14	16	—	23	4	8
Marginal professions	(143)	48	10	12	5	16	4	5

1940 to 1950 Pattern of Occupation Mobility (spanning header over columns Stable through Downward)

* Excludes four persons with insufficient information to classify mobility.

is not possible from the data to actually identify the source of the barrier nor to demonstrate its effectiveness in controlling movement. This is a matter for other kinds of research.

The 1940 to 1950 patterns of occupational mobility for categories of professional status are presented in Table 1. Men in the established professions have the highest degree of attachment to an occupational level: 71 per cent of these professional men had stable attachments during the decade. There were 54 per cent of the men in the new professions and 45 per cent in the semi-professions with stable attachments during the decade. Only 35 per cent of the men in occupational assignments aspiring to professional status had stable attachments, however. The proportion of marginal professionals with stable attachments (48%) is similar to that for semi-professionals (45%), the group they perhaps most closely resemble. These very large differences in the proportions of males with stable occupational attachments among professional status groups cannot be accounted for by differences in any *single* kind of mobility, i.e., upward, downward or fluctuating status. There are, nonetheless, several very important differences in the mobility of men in professional status categories.

The comparison of occupational mobility patterns of men in the professional status categories, when marginal professionals are excluded, leads to the conclusion that the less established the professional status, the greater the opportunity for persons to enter or move within the status but the greater also the risk of losing that status when changes are made in occupational assignment. This is inferred from the following differences in the occupational mobility of men in the five professional status categories:

1. Some upward mobility was experienced by 16 per cent of all men in the established professions, 31 per cent in the new professions, 34 per cent in the semi-professions, 30 per cent in the would-be professions and 27 per cent in the marginal professions. This finding suggests that the barriers to upward movement into, *or* within, all but the old established professions are reasonably permeable.

2. The would-be professions provide the greatest opportunity for distant upward mobility. This finding suggests the would-be professions have the most permeable barriers to movement into, and within, the status group. The established professions, of course, provided no means for distant upward movement during the decade. The additional inference that upward occupational mobility is less open to established professionals than to other professionals should not be made, however. By definition, established professionals can move upward to, or downward from, self-employment, although somewhat less than half of the established professionals were self-employed. Theoretically, then, only the kind, and not the volume of, occupational mobility is restricted

for men in any professional status category.

3. There is little variation in the proportion of men who moved to self-employment in the several professional status groups, except that men in vocations aspiring to professional status made no moves to self-employment. This is somewhat surprising, given the fact that the opportunity for self-employment in the would-be professions is roughly that for the new professions and marginal professionals (Table 3). Perhaps more of the would-be professionals than of other professionals originally enter self-employment.

4. The combined per cent of men who experienced downward mobility or fluctuations in occupational level is greatest for men who are aspiring to professional status (35%) and smallest for men in the new professions (15%) and the established professions (13%). Semi-professionals with 21 per cent and marginal professionals with 25 per cent have proportions roughly between the established and new professionals, and the would-be professionals. This finding particularly suggests that the risk to existing status involved in mobility is greatest in the would-be professions and least in the established professions.

5. The highest percentages of distant upward mobility, fluctuations in occupational level and downward mobility occur for men in occupational assignments where incumbents aspire to professional status. This finding suggests the would-be-professions provide both the greatest opportunity for increasing status and the greatest risk to existing status of all professional statuses.

6. The semi-professional, marginal professional and the new professional vocations provide considerable opportunity for proximate upward mobility. They tend, also, to insure against a loss in existing status when changes are made in occupational assignment as compared with the would-be professions.

7. There are no important differences among the several professional statuses in the proportion moving upward to self-employment, except that men in the vocations aspiring to professional status were not mobile to self-employment during the decade. There are, of course, sizable barriers to self-employment in all professional status groups. Mobility out of self-employment was greater, however, for men in the less established professional vocations, suggesting there is a greater risk in entering self-employment in these vocations.

GENERATION OCCUPATIONAL MOBILITY

The effect of barriers to movement into and within professional status groups also can be assessed to some extent by examining the generation occupational mobility. The more occupational inheritance experienced by the members of a professional status, the less permeable the barriers to entry into the status. Furthermore, it is expected that the greater the distance a father's occupation is from professional status, the less permeable the entrance barriers to his son. The data on generation occupational mobility are presented in Table 2. As the number of men in some professional status groups is too small for analysis in a detailed occupational distribution, most of the discussion is limited to comparisons of either white-collar or manual occupational origins of men in each professional status category.

It is obvious that the barriers to movement into any professional status group are very small between generations, if professional occupational inheritance is taken as a criterion. There are reasonably strong barriers for entry into all professional status groups, except marginal professionals, however, if only the high status professional, managerial, official and proprietary origins of sons are considered.

The proportions of would-be professionals with professional fathers (25%) is similar to that for men in the established professions (29%). In point of fact, vocations where the incumbents aspire to professional status more often recruit men from the two highest status occupation groups (71 per cent had fathers classified as a professional, manager, official, or proprietor) than do other professional status groups. It would be interesting to know whether these men in the would-be professions are sons who aspire to their father's status, find barriers to achieving that status, and therefore select a vocation where the chances for movement seem

TABLE 2

PERCENTAGE DISTRIBUTION BY OCCUPATION GROUP OF FATHER'S LONGEST JOB FOR
PROFESSIONAL STATUS CATEGORIES

Professional Status	Number	*Total White Collars**	Professionals	Semi-Professionals	Managers, Officials and Proprietors	Clerical and Kindred Workers	Sales Workers	*Craftsmen, Foremen and Kindred Workers*	*Operatives and Kindred Workers*	*Private Household and Service Workers*	*Laborers, Including Farm*
					Occupation Group of Father's Longest Job						
Total Professionals†	(630)	64*	17	3	33	3	8	*18*	*11*	*4*	*3*
Established professions	(97)	77*	29	3	31	4	10	*10*	*8*	*3*	*2*
New professions	(244)	66*	15	5	34	4	8	*18*	*10*	*3*	*3*
Semi-professions	(103)	62*	13	3	35	4	7	*22*	*9*	*4*	*3*
Would-be professions	(48)	75*	25	—	46	—	4	*6*	*11*	*6*	*2*
Marginal professions	(138)	53*	7	7	29	3	7	*22*	*17*	*4*	*4*

* Includes professionals, semi-professionals, managers, etc., clerical, and sales workers occupation groups.

† Excludes twenty-four persons for whom occupation of father's longest job was not reported.

greatest. Or, are these men the "less able" sons of high status persons for whom the would-be professions become a "convenient way out" for their professional aspirations? The new and semi-professions appear to be most accessible to persons of manual worker status, and almost one-half of the marginal professionals have a manual worker origin. There is relatively less training required for these marginal professional jobs and fewer artificial barriers of all kinds to movement.

TYPE OF EMPLOYMENT

There is a tendency to think of the professional person as self-employed or a "free lance." Yet historically most professional men were not self-employed. In the early Middle Ages, for example, the doctor and lawyer as well as the cleric and teacher were most usually in orders.[8] Of the professional men in this study, only 25 per cent were self-employed, 60 per cent had a private employer and 15 per cent were in government work. Table 3 presents data on the class of worker affiliations for the men in the sample on their last professional job during the 1940 to 1950 decade.

[8] A. M. Carr-Saunders and P. A. Wilson, *The Professions,* Oxford: The Clarendon Press, 1933, Part II, pp. 289–294.

There is considerable variation in class of worker attachment for men in different professional statuses. Among professional statuses the established professions provided the greatest opportunity for self-employment with 43 per cent of established professionals self-employed at the close of the decade. The semi-professionals with 29 per cent self-employed provided the second largest opportunity for professionals to enter self-employment. The new professions with 22 per cent self-employed, the would-be professions with 18 per cent and the marginal professions with 17 per cent had the least opportunity for self-employment. Men in the new professions were more likely to be at work for a government employer at the close of the decade than were men in other professional statuses. This is not surprising, since new professionals are found in relatively large numbers in educational services where government is the largest employer and in health and welfare services, and in public administration, where government is a major source of employment. There is little opportunity for employment of would-be professionals in government, however. Private employment is entered into least by men in the established professions. Only 45 per cent were at work for a private employer at the close of the decade. By way of contrast

TABLE 3

PERCENTAGE DISTRIBUTION BY CLASS OF WORKER ON LAST PROFESSIONAL JOB FOR
PROFESSIONAL STATUS CATEGORIES

| Professional Status | Number | Class of Worker | | |
		Private Employer	Government Worker	Self-employed
Total Professionals*	(653)	60	15	25
Established professions	(105)	45	12	43
New professions	(251)	57	21	22
Semi-professions	(104)	57	14	29
Would-be professions	(49)	76	6	18
Marginal professions	(144)	73	10	17

* Excludes one person for whom class of worker data are not available.

TABLE 4

AGE, MARITAL STATUS, FAMILY STATUS, SCHOOLING, AND MIGRANT STATUS
FOR CATEGORIES OF PROFESSIONAL STATUS

| Professional Status | Social Characteristics | | | | | | |
	Number of Professionals	Average Age at Last Birthday	Per Cent Married	Per Cent Never Married	Per Cent Head of Primary Family	Median School Years Completed	Per Cent Migrant*
Total Professionals	(654)	43.5	85	12	83	13.9	32
Established professions	(105)	47.1	84	12	83	16.4	39
New professions	(252)	43.2	86	10	84	14.6	28
Semi-professions	(104)	42.4	85	14	78	13.1	29
Would-be professions	(49)	44.4	88	6	88	13.8	41
Marginal professions	(144)	41.9	82	15	83	10.5	31

* A migrant is a person who lived in the Standard Metropolitan Area of a city less than twelve
years.

about three-fourths of the would-be professionals and marginal professionals were at work for a private employer. The low status professionals, then, have the least opportunity to enter either government work or self-employment while the highest status (established) professionals are least likely to work for a private employer and most likely to be self-employed.

SOCIAL CHARACTERISTICS OF
INCUMBENTS

Table 4 presents summary statistics of age, marital and family status, schooling, and migrant status for men in the several professional statuses. To interpret the statistics it should be remembered these background data are for white males 25 years old and over in January, 1950.

Among professional status groups, the age of men is highest in the established professions and lowest in the marginal professions. These age differences may be explained, in part, by the fact that fewer of the technician vocations than of other vocations were available to men in the older as compared with the younger ages at the time of first entry into the labor force. Differences in the age composition of professional statuses do not explain most of the observed differences in mobility, however.

The per cent of men never married is higher for men in the semi-professional and marginal professional statuses than it is for all professional men. Part of the difference is accounted for by age differences, but the very low percentages of men never married in the would-be professional status cannot be explained on this basis. The per cent of males married and the per cent who are heads of primary families is correlatively high where the per cent never married is low.

The greatest difference in social characteristics of incumbents of professional statuses occurs for median years of school completed. Among professional statuses, the median years of school completed ranges from 16.4 years for men in the established professions to 10.5 years for the marginal professionals. Additional data available on professional, vocational and technical training for these men present evidence on educational barriers to entry into, or movement within, the professional status. Among professional groups, 58 per cent of the men in the established professions attended a professional school as compared with 23 per cent of all new professionals, 32 per cent of all semi-professionals, 14 per cent of all would-be professionals, and 15 per cent of all marginal professionals. Furthermore, only 14 per cent of the marginal professionals ever graduated from college, while 90 per cent of the established professionals graduated from college. Clearly a college and/or professional school training is requisite for entry into the established professions and relatively absent for entry into the marginal professions.[9] Almost one-third of the marginal professionals, in fact, never graduated from high school. Men in the would-be professions, interestingly enough, were most likely to have gone to college without completing their course of study—37 per cent had "some college" education. This suggests that men in the would-be professions are quite likely to be "professionally oriented," lack the training for entry into the old or new professions, but find the would-be professions a convenient outlet for their professional aspirations. It points, too, to a more permeable educational barrier in the would-be professions.

Men in the established and would-be professions show the highest percentages of migrants—about two-fifths changed their place of residence during the twelve year period prior to January 1951. Examination of the migration patterns of men in the established professions shows that almost all of the younger men in these roles migrate early in their career. The nature of their training and early advancement usually requires migration when going to work with a different employer. The young doctor moves for internship, residency, and specialization, or the college professor moves to a different university, for example. It would seem there are fewer such "professional requirements" for the would-be professions. The comparatively high proportion of migrants among would-be professionals suggests, then, that they are more likely to migrate to achieve occupational mobility.

CONCLUSIONS

A number of conclusions are offered for the consideration of students of social stratification. (1) Students of social stratification generally observe that professional persons are more immobile than persons in other major occupational groups. This study suggests that a sizable part of that immobility is contributed by persons in the old established professions only. (2) Stratification studies are often criticized because the major occupation groupings between which mobility is measured are not homogeneous. The professional, technical and kindred worker group often is considered one of the more homogenous. The findings of this study hardly warrant such a contention. The range in the percentage with stable attachments among professional status groups in fact is greater than that observed when the percentage for all professionals is compared with that for any of the eleven major occupation groups in the Occupational Mobility Survey.[10] Omitting the marginal professionals as outside the "core professions," there remains considerable variation in occupational mobility among professional status categories. And, a division into "professions" and "semi-professions" leaves con-

9 If clergymen are excluded from the established professionals, only one established professional did not graduate from college.

10 *Patterns of Occupational Mobility for Workers in Four Cities, op. cit.,* Table 10.

siderable variation in mobility. The categories proposed by Carr-Saunders and used in this study are suggested as useful ones in further explorations in social stratification and the sociology of work when the "professional" category is considered too heterogeneous. (3) The findings of this study point to the need to examine the various kinds of barriers to entry and movement within professional status groups. There appear to be significant barriers which can be related to mobility differentials.

Motivation for a Professional Career

While the previous reading was a report of a study of objective background factors in professional careers, the following report by D. M. More and Nathan Kohn, Jr., describes certain subjective factors that induce individuals into one specific professional career—dentistry.* The authors' findings indicate that, as in other high status but less professionalized occupations, individuals are apparently motivated to enter dentistry in part because of its general social prestige,† its financial rewards,‡ and its opportunities for human service. However, probably in contrast to many less professionalized occupations, individuals are attracted into dentistry by the independence it offers in relation to managerial control. If the individuals studied had not gone into dentistry, their answers indicate that most of them would have preferred to enter some other profession with a high degree of independence, like medicine or college-level teaching. A strong desire for autonomy characterizes the way of life of a wide variety of highly professionalized occupations.

* Another occupational category is analyzed in the article by C. Kirkpatrick and M. DeFleur, "Influence of Professors on the Flow of Talent to the Academic Profession," *Social Forces,* **38**, 1960, 296–302.

† Occupational prestige has long served as a magnet in the recruitment process, as for example with the clearly delineated prestige hierarchy of the 18th-century France. See E. G. Barber, *The Bourgeoisie in 18th-Century France* (Princeton, N. J.: Princeton University Press, 1955), pp. 20–25. A recent exploration of the relevance of occupational prestige in Great Britain may be found in C. J. Adcock and L. B. Brown, "Social Class and the Ranking of Occupations," *British Journal of Sociology,* **8** (January 1957), 26–32.

‡ One occupation euphemistically referred to as "the world's oldest profession" provides a less common example of economic attraction in the recruitment process for some occupational incumbents; see Kingsley Davis, "Prostitution," in R. Merton and R. Nisbett, *Contemporary Social Problems* (New York: Harcourt, Brace & World, 1961), pp. 276–280.

D. M. More and Nathan Kohn, Jr. (Dentistry)

The reasons for choosing a vocation probably are fairly complex. A thorough explanation would require an intensive analysis of each individual's life-history to find not

Reprinted from "Some Motives for Entering Dentistry," *The American Journal of Sociology,* **66**, No. 1 (July 1960), 48–53, by permission of The University of Chicago Press. Copyright 1960 by the University of Chicago.

only the positive forces behind his choices but also why each potential alternative was not selected. In our study of survey data from a large sample of entrants to a vocation such detailed analyses were not possible; necessarily, then, our findings are incomplete and not applicable to every case.

Our alternative approach was to outline some apparent features of the occupation and then ascertain to what degree they attract persons entering it. The data on these points were gathered in a lengthy questionnaire completed by over thirty-five hundred students entering dental training in the fall of 1958.[1] On the basis of past dental-school experience, roughly 95 per cent of this group can be expected to complete training and enter dental practice in the next four or five years.

Dentistry as a profession has some general features which are important in answering the needs of young people attracted to it. There undoubtedly are other vital features, but we limit attention in this report to the following list:

1. *Prestige.* The occupation carries the title "Doctor," and in the community at large it has high status.[2]

2. *Financial earnings.* The dentist in private practice generally enjoys a good income, well above average and only slightly less than that of the most highly rewarded professional man —the physician.[3]

3. *Human service.* Dentistry directs its efforts in large part to the relief of suffering and disfunction.

4. *Autonomy.* As a profession, dentistry permits great independence to members in their own activities. As with most other professions, the dentist's conduct as such is, within the limits of legal licensing, subject only to the jurisdiction of his professional peers. To a very considerable extent, the dentist can establish his own fees and the hours and conditions of his work.

5. *Manual skill.* Dentistry, since it requires a high level of manual skill and dexterity, offers satisfaction to those who have such talents.

Together, these five features of dentistry provide an initial basis for analyzing some attitudes of entering dental students toward their chosen profession. Within this scheme we will also observe how they rank dentistry compared with some other professions.

In the questionnaire a check list of eleven items (with a twelfth write-in space) inquired of respondents "factors influencing your selection of dentistry as a career (check as many as apply)" (Table 1). Five of the checklist items are relevant to our analysis, and the remaining items are grouped under "outside" and "internal" influences as footnoted. We need to take special note here of the phrasing of the first item in the table, because as it stands it does not necessarily imply "human service" and could as easily apply to sales, waiting on table, or any other work involving a great deal of interaction with people. Likewise we must recognize that the desire to be one's own boss is only one aspect of autonomy.[4]

In Table 2 are summarized responses to an open-ended question about what the students would stress in advising a younger person, the assumption being that the respondent actually is revealing his own motives. The idea of satisfying one's own desires is most often mentioned. To a certain extent this is related to being autonomous, a point specifically covered in the sixth category. It is notable, however, that the students seldom give first place to autonomy (2.45 per cent), prestige (2.23 per cent), money (1.89 per cent), or service (1.31 per cent). Having the necessary skills (which, in their thinking, may include manual skills) and possessing the necessary intelligence are both more often given first place.

The influence of prestige was checked as important in determining choice of the dental profession by nearly 80 per cent of our sample (Table 1). For the material reported in Table 3, respondents were asked to rank the six given professions as to "how you feel people in the community value [them]." The exact phrasing here is important because the underlying reasons why a student thinks of others as "valuing" a

[1] This work has been supported by a grant from the American College of Dentistry. The background of the study, the nature of the sample, and the data in the schedule are described in D. M. More, "Social Origins of Future Dentists," *Midwest Sociologist,* 21, No. 2 (July 1959), 69–76.

[2] Cf. C. C. North and P. K. Hatt, "Jobs and Occupations: A Popular Evaluation," *Opinion News,* September, 1947, pp. 3–13.

[3] Median income for dentists seems to be in third rank behind physicians and lawyers (Bureau of the Census, *1950 United States Census of Population,* Bull. P-C1 [Washington, D.C.: Government Printing Office, 1953], Table 129, "Detailed Characteristics," pp. 1–279).

[4] For the definition of autonomy implicit in this study see R. F. Winch and D. M. More, "Does TAT Add Information to Interviews?" *Journal of Clinical Psychology,* 12, No. 4 (1956), 316–321.

TABLE 1

Some Factors Influencing Choice of Dentistry as a Career

REASON INDICATED IN CHECK LIST	CHECKED		NOT CHECKED	
	N*	Per Cent	N*	Per Cent
Desire to work for and with people	3,201	89.5	377	10.5
Desire to be my own boss	2,998	83.8	580	16.2
Prestige of the profession	2,843	79.5	735	20.5
Desire to work with my hands	2,651	74.1	927	25.9
Monetary advantages of the profession	2,647	74.0	931	26.0
Other "outside" influences†	2,192	61.3	1,386	38.7
Other "internal" influences‡	3,146	87.9	432	12.1

* Total $N = 3,578$ in each row.

† Includes respondents to any of three items: (1) discussions of dentistry at a high school career day; (2) aptitude testing and counseling in college; and (3) the booklet, *Careers in Dentistry,* or similar publications.

‡ Includes respondents to any of four items: (1) interest in content of the profession; (2) "because my own teeth were poor"; (3) "better chance of getting into dental school than into school of my first choice"; and (4) other (write in).

TABLE 2

Responses to Item on Counseling*

Category of Response	N	Per Cent
Following one's personal interests, motives, likes, and desires	1,757	48.95
Aptitudes for the work; having the particular abilities it requires	395	11.01
The intelligence needed	321	8.94
Courses and grades needed ..	263	7.33
The need to begin early in life	127	3.54
Independence (autonomy) to do as one wishes in his work	88	2.45
Prestige; status the work confers on one	80	2.23
Financial rewards of the job	68	1.89
Serving others; wanting to work with people	47	1.31
Security (job tenure)	31	0.86
All other responses	269	7.49
Left blank	143	3.98
Total	3,589	99.98

* "If I were counseling a high school senior about choosing the right vocation, I would stress these factors." Space for four comments was provided; only the first response is tabulated here.

particular profession may or may not include the idea of the status or prestige of the occupation. He might see it as being "valued" because of the income it provides, its relative service to mankind, its power to control others, or a variety of other reasons. The assumption is, therefore, only partly justified that the relative rankings given in Table 3 are indicative of perceived relative occupational prestige. On this assumption we would say that the entering dental students see the dentist as having lower status than the physician and higher status than the lawyer. The prestige scores obtained by the National Opinion Research Center study by North and Hatt indicate much the same ordering, except that they found that dentistry and law were equal in prestige in the eyes of the general public.[5]

When the students were asked, "What other professions have you considered?" 38 per cent named medicine; 10 per cent, teaching; 9 per cent, engineering; 4 per cent, law; and less than 0.5 per cent, any field of social science. Similar results were obtained from the question, "If you could choose any career you wanted except dentistry, what would you choose?" Most often mentioned was medicine (39 per cent), second was teaching (7.5 per cent), and farther down the list were engineering (4.6 per cent) and the law (3.2 per cent), but social service was not mentioned. In effect, prestige is important, but the predominant choice is between medicine and dentistry. The other professions mentioned are seen as acceptable alternatives in such small percentages that they probably have

[5] *Op. cit.*

TABLE 3

Ranking of Professions by Entering Dental Students

Rank Assigned	Physician N	Per Cent*	Dentist N	Per Cent	Lawyer N	Per Cent	Engineer N	Per Cent	Teacher N	Per Cent	Social Worker N	Per Cent
1	2,684	91.8	180	6.2	27	0.9	13	0.5	69	2.5	13	0.5
2	193	6.6	2,079	71.2	437	15.2	99	3.5	121	4.3	19	0.7
3	31	1.1	533	18.3	1,472	51.1	459	16.3	399	14.1	45	1.6
4	4	0.1	107	3.7	549	19.1	1,361	48.5	604	21.4	178	6.4
5	3	0.1	16	0.5	231	8.0	617	22.0	1,436	50.9	466	16.7
6	9	0.3	5	0.1	163	5.7	259	9.2	193	6.8	2,072	74.2
Subtotal†	2,924	81.7	2,920	81.6	2,879	80.5	2,808	78.5	2,822	78.9	2,793	78.1
Missing†	654	18.3	658	18.4	699	19.5	770	21.5	756	21.1	785	21.9
Total	3,578	100.0	3,578	100.0	3,578	100.0	3,578	100.0	3,578	100.0	3,578	100.0
Mean rank		1.1		2.2		3.4		4.2		4.3		5.6

* Percentages for ranks (1–6) are calculated from subtotals.
† Percentages for "Subtotal" and "Missing" are calculated from totals.

not been accorded really serious consideration by the majority sampled.

Table 4 reports on the students' conceptions of other goals. They were confronted with three statements:

1. "Dentistry provides opportunity for greater human service."
2. "Dentistry makes it possible to make money more easily."
3. "Dentistry as a profession offers the most independence."

Reading down appropriate columns in Table 4, it is clear that they regard the physician as contributing more and the lawyer and the engineer less to human service than their own profession. As to human service, opinion seems to be split uniformly when the students compare dentistry with teaching and social work. Strictly, they would see themselves in third place and behind teachers by a plurality among the six professions.

As to making money, the subjects clearly regard the physician and the lawyer as being ahead of them and the engineer, social

worker, and teacher below them. The exact phrasing of our question leaves some doubt here, for we did not ask about the relative *amount* of money earned but rather about the relative *ease* of making it. The allied questions of hours worked and effort expended per dollar of potential return may have influenced some respondents.

In relative opportunity to control one's own destiny in his career, the students definitely place dentistry first. Even the physician, who is seen as having higher prestige, making more money, and being of greater service to man, is regarded by nearly half the sample as having less personal autonomy than the dentist. In the interviews supplementing the questionnaire frequent mention was made of the physician's duty to make night calls, to serve in emergencies of all sorts, and to accept responsibilities not placed on the dentist. Many of those interviewed said that their final choice between medicine and dentistry was influenced by the desire to avoid such responsibility. Our data in the questionnaire do not permit us to distinguish the importance of autonomy

TABLE 4

ENTERING DENTAL STUDENTS' COMPARISON OF DENTISTRY
WITH FIVE OTHER PROFESSIONS

PROFESSION COMPARED	DENTISTRY PROVIDES:	RELATIVE OPPORTUNITY FOR:					
		Human Service		Making Money		Autonomy	
		N	Per Cent	N	Per Cent	N	Per Cent
Law	More	2,468	71.9	1,086	31.0	1,986	58.1
	Less	310	9.0	1,861	53.0	658	19.2
	Same	657	19.1	563	16.0	777	22.7
	Subtotal	3,435	100.0	3,510	100.0	3,421	100.0
Teaching	More	995	29.1	2,929	85.5	2,922	83.5
	Less	1,239	36.2	421	12.3	338	11.1
	Same	1,188	34.7	76	2.2	188	5.4
	Subtotal	3,422	100.0	3,426	100.0	3,498	100.0
Social work	More	1,316	38.5	2,913	85.1	2,852	83.3
	Less	1,016	29.7	437	12.8	443	12.9
	Same	1,085	31.8	71	2.1	129	3.8
	Subtotal	3,417	100.0	3,421	100.0	3,424	100.0
Engineering	More	2,684	78.1	1,558	46.0	2,634	76.9
	Less	290	8.4	1,204	35.5	504	14.7
	Same	463	13.5	626	18.5	286	8.4
	Subtotal	3,437	100.0	3,388	100.0	3,424	100.0
Medicine	More	141	4.1	426	12.5	1,689	49.4
	Less	1,507	43.9	2,011	59.0	549	16.1
	Same	1,783	52.0	970	28.5	1,178	34.5
	Subtotal	3,431	100.0	3,407	100.0	3,416	100.0

as compared with avoidance of responsibility.

To the question, "Has previous success in
using your hands in hobbies or mechanical
work helped you to decide to apply for
admission to dental school?" 63 per cent of
the 3,459 who answered this item checked
"Yes." To another item only 6 per cent
indicate among their "fears about studying
dentistry" that they really lack sufficient
mechanical aptitude. Less than 3 per cent
list a lack of the necessary manual skills as
a reason why they think that people do not
apply to enter dentistry.

The five motives here discussed clearly
are not unique to dentistry; moreover, we
have not delved into other, perhaps vitally
important, aspects of the work. We have
not, for example, looked here into compul-
siveness—dentistry's demands for exactness
in detail, care, orderliness, and cleanliness.
Likewise, the intellectual demands in the
study of dentistry surely may have attracted
many students to it. If we were to parcel
out the total "attraction" of dentistry
among its many components, the five elements would in all likelihood account for
an appreciable share, but there would remain without question a considerable
"unexplained" variation.

It is something of a leap to assert that
some overt feature of work motivates a
person to choose a given occupation. This
may not be the case for any individual in
our study sample. A detailed study of the
material summarized in Table 1 is being
undertaken to determine what, if any, predominant patterns of features appear in
the items checked. These in turn are being
checked against students' essays on reasons
for entering dentistry. From the evidence
reported here a predominating pattern can
be deduced.

Although "desire to work for and with
people" is a frequently selected item, its
intensity as a possible desire for altruistic
service is weakened by the extent to which
conflicting motives are selected. However
the apologists of business may argue, the
motive of pure service is at least slightly
incompatible with the acquisitive drive,
with striving for prestige and status, and
with insistence on being to a large extent

independent of many of the usual constraints of occupations. To this degree, then,
we may posit a built-in conflict among the
patterned forces inherent in the requirements of the work. Part of training for
dentistry is the student's resolution of such
conflicts, at least partially. One common
solution, though a debated one within the
profession, has been to maintain a flexible
fee-service system. For example, charging
some patients modest to very high fees is
justified, they believe, if the dentist gives
time to low-cost clinics or accepts some
partly charitable or "research" cases.

In Table 2 by far the largest group
stressed "following one's own desires." This
notion may include any of the other more
sharply specified motives, but in a broad
sense it implies a need to be autonomous
and to become self-directing and self-grati-
fying in one's own actions.

The dental students' expressed unwillingness to follow directions imposed by authority figures, as would typically be required of
company employees, may indicate some degree of inner-directedness. They do present
some features in common with the small,
independent entrepreneur. Mixed with this
is a pronounced conformity in religion,
politics, and memberships but some atypi-
cality in marital pattern. Also the students
and practicing dentists interviewed reveal a
striking unwillingness to participate in aesthetic community activities or social better-
ment to the same extent as physicians and
lawyers. As one respondent put it, "Sure,
I want this status, but I'm not going to
give up my free time to all these organizations that come around." They want to
hunt, fish, and do workshop projects. In
this sense they conform, but they do not
conform to the role of public benefactor
which is often ascribed to those enjoying the
title "Doctor."

We can readily argue that prestige and
financial independence are handmaidens to
the more basic drive for autonomy: behavior alleged to satisfy one need may, in
fact, be satisfying another. Ordinarily, the
covert need will be less acceptable socially
than the overt one masking it. In the
present instance we see the service motive
as the most obviously acceptable one for a

person in a dedicated health profession. However, for the motives of status-striving, independence, and material acquisition, if kept within bounds, we also have strong positive sanctions: in our culture it is "right" to strive to get ahead,[6] to want material possessions,[7] and to seek maturity in outgrowing emotional dependence on others.

What draws the young man into dentistry must be seen as a complex pattern of motives, each of which may be related to a well-defined characteristic of the occupation. (We are not considering here some rather obvious influences, such as parental pressure or vocational counseling in high school and college.) Our main assertion is that, of the five motives considered here, the need

[6] See, e.g., W. Lloyd Warner *et al., Democracy in Jonesville* (New York: Harper & Row, Publishers, 1949), esp. Chaps. 1 and 16.

[7] *Ibid.,* pp. 294–295.

for autonomy is the most decisive. None of the other four motives is unnecessary, but without autonomy they seem insufficient. Our interviews provided repeated evidence that entering dental students would accept a career with less prestige, less money, and less opportunity to serve than the physician's, because dentistry would afford them greater independence.

Any campaign to enlist more applicants to dentistry could ill afford to ignore symbolic or even direct appeals to the possible candidates' desires for social status and occupational prestige, for financial return with concomitant material security, for the opportunity to give genuinely needed service to mankind, and for the chance to make creative use of manual talent. Above all, it seems necessary to point clearly to the potential of dentistry to provide practitioners with great independence in determining their own life-styles.

Stages in a Professional Career

Becoming a professional is a gradual process—it doesn't happen all at once. We may forget this if we concentrate our attention upon problems of "occupational choice," for example.* The gradualness of career decisions appears to be one characteristic of more professionalized occupations in contrast to less professionalized lines of work. You can decide to take a job as a factory worker or an office clerk in one day, perhaps in response to an employment advertisement, assuming of course that you have certain minimal skills that can be acquired relatively rapidly. To become a professional, however, you must generate an ambition that will sustain you through many years of preliminary training. The great importance here of formal education, especially the professional school, in learning the occupational role has been widely recognized.† Even after this preliminary training you will have to pass certain institutional barriers, build a clientele, and establish colleague relationships, all of which are

* See D. L. Mills, "Status, Values and Certainty of Occupational Choice," unpublished doctoral dissertation (Stanford University, 1959).

† For example, the effects of dental school on the development of professionalism may be found in D. M. More, "The Dental Student Approaching Graduation—1962," *Journal of the American College of Dentists,* September, 1962, pp. 183–195; or for a discussion of other aspects of the functions of professional schools in education for work see T. Parsons, "Remarks on Education and the Professions," *Ethics,* **47**, pp. 365–369; S. Hiltner, "The Essentials of Professional Education," *Journal of Higher Education,* 23 (May 1954), pp. 245–262, 286; W. J. Hayes, "The Place of Sociology in Professional Education," *Social Forces,* 26, 292–298; E. C. Hughes, "Stress and Strain in Professional Education," *Harvard Educational Review,* 29, No. 4 (Fall 1959), 319–329.

essential to professional success. Of course it must be recognized that in some professions; for example, pharmacy; there may be markedly conflicting values —money making versus public service, for instance—which must be resolved to the individual's satisfaction during this process.‡ In other words, you will have to go through an extended period of socialization, as sociologists might describe it, until you finally develop a psychological and social commitment to a professional career.

In many occupations this commitment is not sufficient to ensure a pleasant and orderly career development because forces within and without the occupation tend to undermine the expectations of the individual: other people do not find the work as noteworthy as the occupational incumbents, there is really little autonomy, etc.§ Moreover, at many points in the socialization process, many individuals who lack the internal self-direction to continue fall by the wayside. Hence professionals have learned principles of deferred gratification to a high degree. They are typically "inner-directed" in David Reisman's meaning of this concept. Were he alive today, Max Weber might say that they represent the last bastion of the Protestant ethic.

In the following reading, Oswald Hall describes the sequence of entry into a medical career.

‡ T. H. McCormack, "The Druggists' Dilemma: Problems of a Marginal Occupation," *The American Journal of Sociology,* **61** (January 1956), 308–315.
§ This has been documented in the work of D. L. Westby, "The Career Experience of the Symphony Musician," *Social Forces,* **38**, No. 3 (March 1960), 223–230.

Oswald Hall (Medicine)

Medicine, like other professions, is practiced in a network of institutions, formal organizations, and informal relationships. The medical career may be conceived as a set of more or less successful adjustments to these institutions and to the formal and informal organizations. In this paper I trace the stages of the medical career, so conceived, as I observed them in the study of the medical profession in an eastern American city.[1]

For purposes of discussion four stages may be singled out as follows: (1) the generating of an ambition; (2) gaining admittance to the various medical institutions (noting among other things the ethnic,

Reprinted from "The Stages of a Medical Career," *The American Journal of Sociology,* 53, No. 5 (March 1948), 327–336, by permission of The University of Chicago Press. Copyright 1948 by the University of Chicago.

[1] Oswald Hall, "The Informal Organization of Medical Practice in an American City" (unpublished Ph.D. thesis, University of Chicago, 1944).

class, and religious character of such institutions, the points at which various types of recruits enter them, and the steps by which one climbs within or among these institutions) ; (3) acquiring a clientele, retaining and improving it, and perhaps eventually transferring it to a successor; and (4) developing a set of informal relationships with colleagues which facilitate the above in some fashion.

The stages of a career, so conceived, are by no means unique to the medical profession. Presumably one could investigate similar phenomena in the academic field, in law, in the ministry, in engineering, and so forth. Although the content of each of the above differs substantially, for purposes of analysis they are fundamentally alike.

The materials have been drawn from interviews centered around the circumstances involved in success and failure in the practice of medicine. Almost without exception the subjects interviewed were enthusiastically interested in the problems raised and were eager to discuss their hunches and observations with an outsider.

In reporting on them ordinary care has been taken to conceal the identity of the subjects, but this in no way detracts from the relevance of the documents.

GENERATING AN AMBITION

One function of an ambition is to discipline present conduct in the interest of a future goal. An ambition is usually conceived to be a highly subjective matter, generated in private fashion and internalized as a drive. Some careers are presumed to require more of it than others do. The medical career is supposed to require a great deal of ambition of the tough type. The fewer the day-to-day rewards in the early stages of a career and the longer delayed the substantial rewards, the more ambition is needed. The medical career is characterized by long periods of training and probation.

In the case of the doctors studied it appeared that the ambitions were largely social in character. They had their genesis in social groups and were nourished by such groups which in turn provided constant redefinition and redirection of the ambition. In most cases family or friends played a significant role by envisaging the career line and reinforcing the efforts of the recruit. They accomplished the latter by giving encouragement, helping establish the appropriate routines, arranging the necessary privacy, discouraging anomalous behavior, and defining the day-to-day rewards.

From this point of view one can see why doctors tend to be recruited from the families of professional workers. The latter possess the mechanisms for generating and nurturing the medical ambition. Only the member of a profession can translate the public protestations of the profession into the vernacular of useful advice. By contrast, families of nonprofessional background may generate the initial urge or itch in their members but fail to nourish the ambition. Such a family may endow a member with the anxiety to achieve a professional career but fail to provide the means for implementing that ambition. Much of the aggressiveness ascribed to new groups invading the medical field may be attributed

to their individual (and often misguided) efforts to achieve those things which are usually managed by an informal group. Excluded from the subtle nuances of meaning which are involved in communicating the steps in a career, the newcomer and his individual efforts strike the initiated as singularly uncouth.

Excerpts from interviews with two doctors who stand at opposite poles as far as professional success is concerned throw light on the ways in which professional ambitions are generated and nourished. The first is a young general practitioner at a disadvantage because of his Armenian origin. He is an introverted person who seems to suffer from self-consciousness when meeting his patients.

My parents were too poor to help me through medical school. An aunt had promised that if I did well in school she would help. She did until the depression came along, and after that I had to scrape along as best I could.

I had a lot of trouble getting a good internship; of course that is the important thing in success in medicine. I went to a big medical school in Philadelphia, but the large hospital there was very choosy. My roommate was much more brilliant than I, but they turned him down too. So I came back to my home town for an interview and left feeling confident that I would get an appointment. But none came. Finally I had to take one in a small Philadelphia hospital. When I came back here I got a chance at X Hospital, and stayed there for seven months.

The hospital is the place where I really come alive. Every moment there is thrilling. My internships from beginning to end were thoroughly enjoyable. The saddest day of my life was the day I left X Hospital and started practice. One of the other interns lent me a hundred and fifty dollars, and promised to let me have forty or fifty a month.

The medical world is a hard one to start up in. It is a terrific change to come from the medical world to the practice of medicine. I thought that when I graduated my troubles would be over. But this part of medicine was just the opposite of what I had anticipated. I thought that when I opened my office all these sick people needing help would come in. But it isn't so. You wait for days and days and no one comes. Then you become frantic and wonder if you have gotten into the wrong kind of work. Sometimes I stayed in the office for six days and no one came. The first calls were those that no one else would take, ones that came late at night. For a while I stayed up nights, and slept in the daytime, in case I missed any of the night calls. I was sure that I was going to be a doctor—my mother had impressed that on me since I was three years old.

The second of these doctors is a successful specialist. He belongs to the Yankee elite of the community. He has a very substantial practice and does considerable consultant work. His office, which is part of a large structure shared by a group of cooperating specialists, is in the best residential area. He has posts in the most important hospitals of the community. In addition he plays an active part in the administration of the hospitals with which he is connected and he has a leading role in the medical organization of his city and state.

I guess I pretty well took it for granted that I was going to be a doctor. My family was a medical family, and there was always lots of interesting reading matter lying around. At college my teachers in biology were connected with the hospital and they had a way of making me feel that I would go to medical school. They seemed to feel that I should go to Harvard Medical after I finished University.

When I came back from medical school I got an internship in the large hospital here. One of my old college teachers was acting as superintendent of the hospital, and he seemed glad to have me send in an application.

Of course it takes a while to get started in a medical practice. My father bought my instruments for me and paid my office rent for the first couple of years.

When the specialty board was set up in this field, I was invited in as one of fifty charter members. My friends say that if I had had to try the examinations that I would never have passed them. Being a charter member gives a person a real sense of belonging.

The second doctor is conspicuously successful by whatever standards success in medicine is judged. By comparison the first will remain moderately unsuccessful. The initial drive was presumably greater in the first than in the second, but the latter was continuously assisted by groups who had an inside knowledge of the profession. These groups were able to redefine the career at its various stages in such a way that the young doctor made a minimum of false

steps. He was left free to devote his energy to achieving relatively clearcut goals. The other doctor received aid and advice but it lacked a realistic touch.

INCORPORATION INTO THE INSTITUTIONS OF MEDICINE

Medical services in the urban community are mediated through a multiplicity of institutions, such as doctors' offices, hospitals, clinics, laboratories, nursing homes, dispensaries and drugstores, various medical associations, and so forth. Although each institution has significance in the doctor's career, only the hospital is considered here.

The first point for discussion concerns the hierarchical nature of hospitals. The doctors of a given department, the various departments of the hospital, and the range of hospitals in the community form a hierarchy in each case. The doctors in a specific department are arranged in strata, such as intern, extern, staff member, staff association member, and the like. Within these strata there are finer gradations. For example, the staff members (those doctors who have full access to the facilities of the hospital) may be organized into many distinct levels which indicate clearly the prerogatives and prestige of the men concerned. Such a hierarchical pattern provides an exceedingly large number of steps for the new member of the profession. His progress through them symbolizes achievement in his personal career. For the administrator the hospital is a finely articulated status structure; the various positions represent a wide range of rewards to be conferred on the doctors attached to the hospital. The number and variety of these rewards function to keep a large staff reasonably satisfied by providing neat packages of advancement at relatively short intervals.

Within the departments competition goes on among the doctors. This competition is tempered by the established set of authority relations and the code of ethics which discourages individualistic striving for position. Between departments there is practically no competition because of the rigid nature of the specialization concerned. There is, however, a jealous struggle for prestige between different lines of specialization.

The various hospitals of the community studied form a status hierarchy. The Yankee Protestant hospitals have the most adequate facilities, those organized by the Catholics follow, while those organized by the Jewish group or by medical sects are the least adequate. The prestige of identical positions in the various hospitals would vary in the same way. There is very little moving between these institutions. Actually there are serious barriers hindering the doctor who has become associated with one hospital from moving up in another. Hence, the acceptance of an appointment in any of these hospitals represents a crucial point in his career. This is particularly the case with initial appointments. The internship that a doctor has served is a distinctive badge; it is one of the most enduring criteria in the evaluation of his status.

The second point to be borne in mind concerns the linkages between the various medical institutions. Hospitals, for example, are linked with the medical and the preprofessional schools. These provide typical chains in which each institution aids the newcomer to move along to the next level. The religious cleavages in medicine provide the most conspicuous illustrations. The major hospitals are organized along religious lines within which class and ethnic differentiation are discernible. Thus, in the community studied the upper-class Yankee generally goes to an undergraduate school where fees are high, proceeds to Harvard Medical school, interns at the dominant Yankee hospital, and enters the competitive practice of medicine from that vantage point. The Italian lad aspiring to a medical career would find these avenues almost completely blocked. However, there are other chains of institutions (in this case Catholic) which provide an alternative route, and not only open a road to a medical career for him, but also shelter him in some degree from the competition of those whose advantages are indicated above. This second set of institutions was originally organized for the Irish Catholic group, but other Catholics can use them in the manner in-

dicated. It is worth noting that the marginal men in medicine are largely those who have forsaken the shelter of these enabling institutions and are seeking their fortunes in the wider competitive field of medical practice. Such cases lie outside the purview of this paper.

Hospital appointments are crucial for successful medical practice. The more important hospital posts are associated with the highly specialized practices and usually with the most lucrative types. The two form an interrelated system. Success in one's private practice may lead to advancement in the hospital system. Such advancement becomes an outward symbol of achievement and enhances the doctor's status in his own eyes and in the eyes of colleagues. His new position is likely to bring him into a new set of relationships with other doctors and permit him to participate more extensively in the cooperative system in which medicine is practiced. This again may influence his private practice. The linkage is discussed below in connection with gaining a clientele.

The gist of the foregoing is that the successful practice of medicine involves participation in the hospital system. This system is integrated with a series of other institutions. These constitute a sifting device which functions to establish the status of the various doctors in the community. In this sense they influence markedly the careers of medical men.

To illustrate the above points, materials are presented from interviews with key figures in the administrations of the big hospital and the Catholic hospital. Dr. S is Irish Catholic, a specialist, and heads one of the departments in the Catholic hospital.

One of our most important problems here is picking interns. The main qualification as far as I can see is "personality." Now that is an intangible sort of thing. It means partly the ability to mix well, to be humble to older doctors to the correct degree, and to be able to assume the proper degree of superiority toward the patient. Since all medical schools now are Grade A there is no point in holding competitive examinations. So the main problem confronting the selection committee is that of getting interns who will fit well into the pattern of the hospital.

Not all interns can fit in well here. There are trouble makers who just can't help being that way. You know the kind. Just like labor agitators in industry. If they get in they disrupt hospital efficiency no end. Another reason for not holding competitive examinations for internships is that there are a lot of Jews in medicine. Did you know that? Now there is something about the Jew. Of course there is prejudice against him, but there is also something else. He seems to lack a sense of balance. He finds too many things wrong and too many symptoms. He tends to overtreat his patients.

Now for the ideal type of internship the young doctor should come to the city where he intends to practice. This probably means taking a general type of training and getting little of the specialized kinds of things that he wants to do. However, it is more important to get to know the doctors with whom one is going to associate. After he gets established in this fashion, he should go away to a larger hospital for the specialized kind of internship that fits his interests.

In my own case I made the mistake of going to New York to a large hospital and getting to see a large number of the kinds of cases I was interested in. That was a blunder. I received only an alternative appointment at the big hospital so the New York plan was second choice. They had competitive examinations here then. Three other young fellows besides myself tried them. But none of us secured an appointment. One of the others was so disgusted that he omitted interning and went straight off to practice in New Hampshire. The next year he came back and secured a very handsome internship in the very field he was interested in. I asked him if he knew more a year later, and he said that he knew less medicine but more people. All such appointments can be manipulated if one knows powerful friends.

The significance of the above is not the refreshingly frank discussion of the manipulation of appointments; one would expect that personal factors would enter into the selections. The main point is the importance of such appointments—especially initial appointments—for the later careers of the beginners. Moreover, the likelihood of being appointed depends much less on superior technical competence than on one's ac-

ceptability by an established institution with its defined policies.

Dr. R is one of the main administrators of the large hospital in the community. He discussed at length the recruitment of personnel into the hospital.

We have a formal policy here with respect to internships. Applications must be in by a specified date, and then a committee goes to work to judge the applicants. They are judged on a variety of bases with a personal interview in some cases. In the earlier days we had competitive examinations, but we had to discontinue these. The person who did best on an examination might not show up well in the intern situation. He might lack tact; he might not show presence of mind in crises; or he might not be able to take orders. And more than likely the persons who did best on the written examinations would be Jewish.

The externs are usually chosen from the intern group. This is not always the case, but the interns are usually offered the privilege when an opening occurs in the Outpatient Department. Similarly the members of the Outpatient Department are brought back into the house if and when openings occur. There is a continuous selecting process at work; the judgment of the head of the department plays a large part in determining the speed of promotion for a given person.

The biggest change going on here concerns the setting up of the specialty boards in each of the specialized fields. They set examinations to establish membership in the various specialized fields. These tend to raise the standards and they simplify the problems of the hospital administrator. The older doctors on the staff recognize this but are slow at falling in line. Of course it is a bit unfair to expect these older men to go off and write examinations, especially in competition with young fellows. Besides there are good specialists among the older doctors who cannot pass examinations but they still deserve to be protected in their positions in the hospitals.

These things have lengthened the period it takes the person to become a practitioner. The surgeons are the ones most affected. It lengthens the time that the student must be subsidized, and pretty well prohibits the student from working his way through in medicine. In this way it raises the ethics of the profession. It means that the specialists are selected from the old established families in the community, and family and community bonds are pretty important in making a person abide by a code.

The doctors on the active staff here carry a very heavy load of charitable work. This, of course, is part of the code, but at times it gets very arduous. There are a lot of people who never pay their bills and make suckers of every new doctor who comes to town until they get wise. Also there are a lot of low-income people who like to live like the upper group and who contract for better medical services than they can afford. Doctors have had to get better at bookkeeping and better at collecting. Most doctors go into medicine because of their humanitarian impulses and for the love of the game.

From the above statements some generalizations emerge. Appointments are not made on the basis of technical *superiority*. The appointee must be technically *proficient,* but after that level of competence is reached other factors take precedence over sheer proficiency. At this level personal factors play a part in determining who will be accepted. However, the question is not whether the applicant possesses a specific trait, such as dark skin, or is of the wrong sex, but whether these traits can be assimilated by the specific institution. Hence, personal traits are not nearly so important in determining admission as is institutional acceptability. To the extent that hospitals have distinctive policies and unique histories they tend to exclude doctors with specified backgrounds and to encourage others.

Acquiring a Clientele

Acquiring a clientele is an enterprise as far as the doctor is concerned—an enterprise in which he plays the role of promoter. It is not sufficient for the doctor merely to attract patients; he must adopt the type of strategy which will enable him to retain them. Success in medicine also involves improving the practice. The doctor must carry on an intelligent campaign to attract the desired type of patient, and he must discourage those who do not fit well into the pattern of his practice. The practice of medicine goes on in a competitive milieu; freedom of choice for the patient requires the doctor to exercise constant vigilance or see his patients gravitate to competitors with more power of attraction. In this competitive struggle intelligent enterprise may be more important than medical knowledge and skill.

As stated earlier, the good practices of the city are the specialized practices. The statistics on income differentials[2] between specialists and non-specialists and the data on trends toward specialization are equally convincing on this point. The specialists are highly conscious of their superior status and refer to the general practitioners by unflattering terms such as "signposts" and "information booths." In discussing below the ways in which clienteles are acquired, attention has been directed to the specialized practices. In order to provide perspective two facts should be kept in mind. A specialized practice cannot be achieved without the active assistance of a group of colleagues. These must refer cases to the specialist; and he must have some corresponding way of repaying them for their favors. A specialized practice is a hospital practice and requires access to hospital facilities. Moreover, hospital connections facilitate the development of referral relationships between doctors.

As noted earlier such practices are carried on in a competitive milieu. This competition is never of the cutthroat variety. A profession connotes a code of ethics. The code of the medical profession specifically defines the degree of advertising that a doctor may indulge in. However, in a community in which the profession is well organized the code is practically superseded by a set of expectations and understandings deeply imbedded in the personalities of the doctors concerned. These understandings may go so far as to control the entry of new practitioners into the community, allocate them to posts in the various medical institutions, and incorporate them into the established office practices.

The extent to which these expectations control the conduct of the established doc-

[2] M. Leven, *The Incomes of Physicians* Publications of the Committee of the Costs of Medical Care, No. 24 (Chicago: University of Chicago Press, 1932).

tors can be seen in the following comments by an old obstetrician.

A ticklish problem arises when a doctor has left the city for a while and turned his practice over to other doctors temporarily. Recently a young woman came to me whose chosen obstetrician was out of the city. I took care of her confinement and everything went smoothly. The next time she became pregnant she came to me and said that she had been so pleased with her former treatment at my hands that she wanted me to take her on as a patient. I had to tell her that she could go to any other obstetrician in town in preference to her old one, but that she couldn't have me. A person just can't be too meticulous in such cases.

There is another difficult question in dealing with the mother and child. As long as the child gets along satisfactorily in the hospital all is well. But if the child develops some illness, what should the obstetrician do? He has the responsibility for the mother and child while they are in the hospital. Should he refer the matter back to the family doctor who may think that he (the family doctor) can handle the case? Or should he safeguard the interests of the mother and child by calling in a qualified pediatrician? And if he does the latter, how many more patients will that family doctor send him? Doctors are jealous and shortsighted about such things. One must be scrupulously honest about such things or he will get labeled by his colleagues.

One has to be careful at the Maternity Hospital not to antagonize the pediatricians. It would be dangerous to play favorites. I make the patient take the initiative in choosing her own. Of course I may have to help her to remember the names of the pediatricians and help her eliminate some. I just wouldn't feel justified in helping her choose her pediatrician. They are all equally good as far as I am concerned.

This doctor seems to recognize that the hospital pediatricians comprise an established unit and that he should not discriminate among them. However, he would be equally solicitous not to deflect patients to an intruder trying to establish himself.

Dr. P is a surgeon who is well liked by the most influential leaders of the medical community but whose relations with his fellow specialists are far from congenial.

How does one get ahead? There are just two things to keep in mind. First, do good work and your reputation will get around. Second, keep your mouth shut. It does no good to talk about your achievements. Doctors are a jealous group.

In medicine one has to build a practice. And in medicine there is no structural steel. With steel one can go straight up like a skyscraper. Medicine is like building with stones. One has to build on a solid foundation. This goes for the kind of training one gets and the type of clientele he gathers. My practice is largely a personal kind. One person is pleased and he tells another. There is very little referred work. I refuse to give any *quid pro quo* for the cases that other men send me. One or two men do send me a few. My practice would be a lot bigger if I did otherwise. However, I never allow the doctor who sends the patient to act as assistant at the operation (and hence receive the assistant's fee). Operating is teamwork and only my anesthetist and my own assistant can work together satisfactorily.

Although his own is not of that type, this doctor recognizes the existence of practices based on referrals. Some, but not all, of these turn out to be convenient arrangements for sharing fees. Although this doctor protests that surgery is an open competitive field he gives the impression that his surgical colleagues, the older medical men in the community, and the closed hospital system not only control entry to the field but also delay the age at which an accepted entrant can start practicing. Finally, the discussion of these aspects of a career arouses emotion at an early stage of the interview.

The materials which follow are from interviews with one of the prominent heart specialists of the community. His Irish Catholic allegiance is largely nominal, making him acceptable to the Yankee Protestant segment of the community. His comments indicate that in a community there is usually a preeminent hospital, and that the prestige of being associated with that hospital is sufficient recompense for undergoing a long probationary period and assuming onerous duties into the bargain.

The goal of every good doctor here is to get on the staff of X Hospital. I spent twelve years on the outpatient staff and then twelve years on the active staff, working up to be head of that department. When I came here I got an appointment on the staff of a small hospital. At one of the meetings of the local medical society I met one of the doctors on the staff of X Hospital, and he asked me about my training and whether I would like a position over there. I didn't tell him that I would give my eye teeth for a chance, and you can bet I was over there in plenty of time the next day.

Over there a person rises by merit. Of course there may be some personal factors involved. For instance when questions of promotions come up I was always approached privately by the administration and asked who should go ahead. It's true that the Italians and Jews don't seem to catch on there. Many of them get tired of waiting, especially when they see themselves get jumped over in the course of promotions. And in the meantime they are building up private practices and feel that they can no longer spare the time. And some of them try to go ahead too fast. A Jew has just opened up an office across the way with a lot of that ornate furniture. I had him as an intern once. After two days he asked me to let him operate. I told him his chances were pretty slim for a while yet. He complained to the Mother Superior and resigned later on. Do you think the other doctors are going to do much for him?

In the above, one can discern a rigorous system of selection, and a system of prolonged apprenticeship. The participants in the system must be prepared to expect long delays before being rewarded for their loyalty to such a system. The doctor interviewed seemed to think his twelve-year apprenticeship eminently fair. In his eyes a satisfactory clientele is one which he can treat in the best hospital in town. Hence it is selected as to social class and income level. His ability to offer it the desired hospital facilities required a long, intelligent campaign.

Dr. G was ready to volunteer information on how much aid he gives to his colleagues. He is an outstanding physician and heads the department of medicine in the big hospital.

A doctor's career consists of an upgrade, a plateau, and a downgrade. Doctors don't usually discuss the reasons for the downgrade. Partly it is the competition of the young men coming in. Partly it is a matter of patients retiring the doctor. Many doctors end up with a shriveled practice. In a way their colleagues help retire

them. In the old days I sent a lot of surgery to Dr. R. He was one of the big men in surgery —a fifty-thousand-dollar-a-year man. He was the owner of the building as well as being my landlord, so there was an added reason for sending cases to him.

But every doctor has one or two young doctors in whom he is interested and he needs to send them all the work that he can in order to get them launched. Because of this I have had to withdraw almost all my support from Dr. R.

When a person gets up to a position like mine there are a lot of kinds of help you can give your staff. I can always give a good fellow a couple of kicks in the right direction. I can always get an internship for a good boy if I really want to. I did that for M. I met him at a medical banquet while he was a student. I found out that he was a local boy and wanted an internship here. He was a nice sort with a good character. Now I've got him on the staff, and in a year or two I'm going to bring him into this office to share my practice. Then there was young Y. He was a nephew of the mayor. I got him an internship and the position of resident physician. Young D was another fine lad. I helped him the same way but then he was drafted. But I've arranged things so that when he comes back there will be a good position waiting for him.

Dr. B represents still a different type of doctor. He is a heart specialist who had spent some time teaching and then, as a stranger, decided to take up practice in this community. Having a private income, he is willing to break in to the local situation slowly.

One of the ways that a person can start up is to split fees with the person who refers the case. I don't think that is common here. It may occur to some extent in surgery, but I wouldn't know about that. In some newer towns the surgery is practically offered for sale.

I don't need to try anything of that sort. I expect to do sufficiently good work so that my name will get around, and in the meantime I can afford to wait. The first two years I was here my practice was pretty slim. Now I'm going into the forces, but when I come back a lot of the older men here will be through.

Fee-splitting must be a different thing for the young fellow who needs money to feed his family and cover his overhead. In that case the temptation must be almost unbearable. The usual manner in which these things develop is for a general practitioner to send a case to the specialist as a gesture. If the latter reciprocates then an association develops without anything overt being said.

A new man who tries to start in a community like this has to be very good and very careful. The other men watch him like hawks. One error would be too much and would jeopardize his reputation. News spreads fast.

Dr. B lacks completely the several kinds of assistance enjoyed by the doctors who are sponsored by one of the established practitioners. Only a doctor with substantial financial resources could assume the risks involved in trying to build up a practice in this fashion.

Further light on the problems of the unsponsored doctor is supplied by Dr. B who is an outstanding physician and an able administrator.

How would a new specialist get into the setup here? Well, there is a case in point now. A new heart specialist came here, practically unknown. He had very good recommendations from the medical school where he had been teaching. Naturally there is a considerable waiting period. A person may have to wait a couple of years before he finds things coming his way. This man was reputed to be one of the best in his field. Doctors waited to see. Some of them rate his work very high. Others have been a bit disappointed in what he can do. The local medical association had investigated when it heard that he was coming. However, there had been no overt attempts to keep him out.

Of course local conditions differ in such cases. In some cases the local doctors would advise a man not to come in. For example, a man came here very well trained in psychiatry, intending to settle. He met some of the local men in medicine and they advised him not to come. The reason was that the field was pre-empted by a man not nearly as well trained, but who would be hard on the newcomer. He would be tough on him and the new man would have a disagreeable time here, and might never catch on. The man coming had decided to go to another place and was eminently happy there.

THE INNER FRATERNITY

The interviews indicate that as far as recruiting new members, allocating them to positions in the various medical institutions,

and securing clienteles are concerned there exists a set of controls exercised by a central core of the profession. This gives the main clue to the structure of the profession. It comprises four major groups of practitioners. The inner core is made up of the specialists who have access to, and dominate, the main hospital posts. Below these there are a number of recruits at various stages in their careers who will in the future inherit the positions of the central core. Around the core are men who practice medicine in a general fashion (as opposed to specialization) and who are bound to it in the sense that they refer their complicated cases to those specialists. Outside the core are doctors who are attempting by their individual efforts to break into the central core. However, as the core has its own specific mechanisms for recruiting and legitimating its members, the would-be intruders gain admittance only with the greatest difficulty.

The inner core has three distinctive features. In the first place, it represents a technical division of labor. Given the present range of knowledge and techniques in modern medicine, it is impossible for one person to master the whole. The specializations represent the manageable segments of present-day medicine. The inner core represents the integration of these distinctive lines of specialization.

Second, this inner core represents a method of organizing the market. It is a system for seeing that the patient eventually gets to the specialist most likely to be able to help him. This implies that the various specialists have access to the various hospital facilities necessary for carrying on specialized medicine. It also implies that there is a sort of machinery which directs patients from the general practitioner to the specialist and from one specialist to another. In general this involves the localization and concentration of the specialists in a specific part of the community; actually, many of them cluster in the same building to afford a closer integration of their services.

The third point is that the members of the inner core comprise a social group. Because of their technical interdependence, their spatial proximity, and their daily working relationships, they become a fraternity. They have roughly similar educational and social-economic backgrounds. They are tied by common professional bonds and participate in the same specialized professional associations. The group is sufficiently small to become a democracy of first names. Taken together, these factors explain why the group can develop an extremely high level of consensus. Because it shows so many of the characteristics of the primary group and of the secret society it has been labeled here "the inner fraternity."[3]

From this perspective one of the major stages of a medical career involves acceptance by the inner fraternity. The interviews show that there are specific accepted mechanisms for both incorporating the newcomer and repelling the unwanted intruder. The mechanisms operate at all levels, from that of intern to that of practicing specialist. Thus they tend to minimize mobility and control competition in such a way as to stabilize the provision of medical services in a community. The mechanisms include such phenomena as the institutional investigation of the newcomer, informal discussion and advice by high-ranking medical personnel, casual neglect in granting promotion in the hospital system, specific acts of encouragement and reward by the established practitioners, and direct sponsorship of a new recruit by one of the inner fraternity.

On balance the system operates more by rewarding the accepted recruit than by punishing the intruder. By and large, one rejection is sufficient to repel the intruder. On the other hand the sponsored protege must be assisted and vouched for at each step in his career. This involves active intervention in his career by the established practitioner who has sponsored him. In some of the cases studied the encouragement originated long before the person went to medical school, then, later, in the form of aiding him over the crisis of securing a

superior appointment as intern; it continued as the young doctor climbed up in the hierarchy of institutional positions, and was evidenced by the referral of patients by the sponsoring doctor.

If the inner fraternity is the central core of the social organization of the profession, then sponsorship is the major social facet of a medical career. It is the positive means by which the inner fraternity controls its members. The function of the inner fraternity is to organize the provision of medical services. In doing so it appears to control the induction of new recruits, to exclude the intruder, to allocate positions in the hospital system, to control competition, to enforce a set of rules, to reward effort, to distribute patients, and to perpetuate the practices of its members. Because it is a going concern dealing with the day-to-day problems of the profession, and because it is a persisting organization which must recruit new members as old ones drop out, it exercises an extremely pervasive influence on the careers of doctors.

It is worth remarking that sponsorship has very few of the characteristics of nepotism. The protégé must live up to the expectations of his sponsor, he must "deliver the goods." Failure on his part would be more than personal failure—it would involve the prestige of his sponsor. The protégé is bound to go through the institutional apprenticeship. He must necessarily accept the discipline of being a functionary in an institution. Progressively he must accept the responsibilities of leadership. Sponsorship is by no means a one-sided set of favors.

In conclusion, it would appear that specialized medicine is no longer an independent profession—a free-lance occupation. It has become highly interdependent rather than independent, and it is carried on within the framework of elaborate social machinery rather than within a freely competitive milieu. The main contingencies of a medical career hinge on the role which the doctor plays in a very complex, informal organization. Within such a frame of reference there is room for much more research on careers and institutions.

[3] Oswald Hall, "The Informal Organization of the Medical Profession," *Canadian Journal of Economics and Political Science,* **12**, February 1946, pp. 30–44.

Professional Socialization

As indicated previously, an individual typically moves through a rather extensive period of socialization during which he develops a commitment to a professional career. This period of socialization certainly includes his formal training, but the more significant influences in professional socialization may take place *after* graduation from a professional school, as Dan Lortie has shown in the following discussion of a study of law students in the city of Chicago. During this period an individual internalizes a professional image which becomes a very significant aspect of his self-concept.

Dan C. Lortie (Law)

Few of us viewing an adept attorney at work can picture him a nervous, uncertain beginner. Yet all "pros" were once less than paragons of easy skill; the highly socialized member of a profession so plays his roles that they appear inseparable from him. But the beginner has much to learn before his self and his daily round conjoin; he must first perceive the multiple expectations that characterize legal roles, and he must acquire the complex skills needed to match those expectations. He must learn the values of his profession in general and in specific; he must puzzle through many dilemmas before experience results in moral decisiveness. He must act in the presence of others, perceive their evaluations of his performance, and find his assertions of identity confirmed. The development of a professional self-conception involves a complicated chain of perceptions, skills, values, and interactions. In this process, a professional identity is forged which is believable both to the individual and to others.[1] When we ask then, as we do in this section, what part law

school plays in the professional socialization of its students, we seek to estimate its contribution to the transformation of a layman into a self-assured member of the legal "culture." Socialization here has nothing to do with the public control of productive resources—it has to do with the complicated processes involved in making a lawyer.[2]

The conditions and timing of professional socialization have shifted in the last hundred years in American legal education.[3] Office apprenticeship—the law school of an earlier era—introduced the neophyte to the principles of law and the principals-at-law simultaneously. In "reading" law, the apprentice combined theory and implementation in a gradually expanding responsibility. He became a lawyer as he saw and assisted in real cases, in concrete situations, and with specific personalities. Exposed to live models of practicing attorneys and clients, he possessed realistic bases for learning the lawyer role. He coupled this increasing awareness with the gradual assumption of the rights and obligations of a member of the bar. Technical knowledge, prevailing practices, and professional values were articulated one step at a time.

Today what was once concurrent experience is serial. For three years the young

Reprinted from "Laymen to Lawman: Law School, Careers, and Professional Socialization," *Harvard Educational Review*, 29, No. 4 (Fall 1959), 363–367. Used by permission of the author and publisher.

[1] The underlying conception of the self-concept employed here is that stemming from the work of George Herbert Mead and Charles Horton Cooley. See especially G. H. Mead, *Mind, Self, and Society* (Chicago: University of Chicago Press, 1946), and C. H. Cooley, *Human Nature and the Social Order* (New York: C. Scribner's Sons, 1902).

[2] For a clear presentation of the concept of socialization, see R. Merton, G. G. Reader, and P. L. Kendall, *The Student-Physician* (Cambridge, Mass.: Harvard University Press, 1957), Appendix A.

[3] Harno, "Legal Education in the United States," Harvard Law School Library (mimeographed) and J. W. Hurst, *The Growth of American Law* (Boston: Little, Brown & Co., 1950).

attorney, studying in a special school, is isolated from the market place of legal services, and he often graduates without any contact with real legal work. His school environment provides small opportunity to witness the varieties and subtleties of lawyer roles, and although his knowledge of legal principles probably exceeds that of his nine-teenth-century predecessor, he graduates with minimal knowledge of the procedures and institutions of practice. The social skills necessary for successful practice with anx-ious clients and clever rivals is *terra in-cognita* to those who do not supplement their law school program with legal em-ployment.[4] The law school curriculum pro-vides little opportunity for students to learn and wrestle with the values that must be resolved in everyday practice. One of the most striking omissions is the absence of occasions on which students can actually play the role of lawyer. A few moot court performances before fellow students hardly equal the commitment to interaction in the professional role that we find in medical schools, teacher training programs, or schools of social work. No real clients are served and no real cases are handled by law students prior to graduation.

A schooling so removed from everyday realities leads us to question the strength of its impact on the self-conception of students. Two kinds of data—on role perceptions and skill acquisition—are available to deal with this question. First, we have the re-spondents' review of their successive images of law as *work* from their first recollection to the present and the effect of law school on those images. Secondly, respondents ex-pressed their views freely on the proper function of law schools and evaluated their legal training.

Hughes' thesis that professional education involves the replacement of stereotyped images by more subtle, complex and even ambiguous perceptions of the professional role finds support in these data.[5] Analysis of the modal images held of law as work discloses the gradual replacement of an exotic and dramatized image by one which takes account of routine and pedestrian elements. The dominant initial image— "the courtroom version"—is highly theatri-cal. Content analysis reveals the recurrent themes of an advocate contesting in the defense of a man wrongly charged of a serious crime; the scene is one of electric tension, and resolution is through the almost magical powers of a passionate lawyer show-ing his mastery of the sudden switch, the devastating deduction, the moving plea. The image is a prism of potent American values (courage, association with the right, prag-matic brilliance) and human motives (narcissism, messianic duty, masculine ag-gression) of no less power. Perhaps the crucial attribute of the image is its charis-matic rather than routine quality—it is the antithesis of the prosaic.

The overt elements of the image are, as we might expect, somewhat unstable through time; half of those describing the image as their initial view state that it had changed somewhat before entry to law school. The changes that occurred before and during law school are similar—the young lawyer-to-be realizes that there are other than courtroom roles open to lawyers, and that even those who do work in courts do so only part of the time. Changes prior to law school graduation are primarily external, referring to descriptions of the various roles played by lawyers. A subsidiary theme in changes during law school is the gradual realization that law work is both difficult and taxing.

There is, however, a latent content which apparently persists until the young lawyers face the demands of practice. Asked for the principal changes in the image that occurred after law school graduation, the largest percentage stressed that the tasks they do as practitioners are not what they expected upon graduation. The tasks are different primarily in the way they strike

---

[4] Most sample members did not engage in legal work prior to graduation, but those who did, either in civilian or military life, did so apart from the law school program of study. Many mentioned its great value to them in be-ginning practice. One respondent conducted several hundred trial defenses while in service and was able to join a firm of top-level trial specialists on the basis of this experience.

[5] E. C. Hughes, *Men and Their Work* (Glen-coe, Ill.: The Free Press, 1958); see especially Chap. 9.

TABLE 1

DISTRIBUTIONS OF RESPONDENTS' VIEW OF PROPER FUNCTION OF LAW SCHOOL
BY TYPE OF LAW SCHOOL ATTENDED

Respondent View of Proper Function of Law School	*University*		*Catholic*		*Independent*		*Total*	
	N	Per Cent	N	Per Cent	N	Per Cent	N	Per Cent
1. Law School should provide *practical* training	10	42	15	68	21	81	46	64
2. Law School should provide *theoretical training*	12	50	6	27	3	12	21	29
3. Other and no response	2	8	1	5	2	8	5	7
All	24	100	22	100	26	101*	72	100

* The total is more than 100 per cent because of rounding.

the respondents—they are "more routine," "more difficult," and "less intellectually stimulating." Other responses indicate surprise at finding themselves ill-prepared for the "mechanics" of law, their lack of preparation for the problems of establishing a career, and considerable shock is expressed on discovering the ethical and moral practices within the profession. Elements of glamor, facility, and idealism persist in the image until first-hand contact with legal work; it takes contact with actual practice to bring full recognition that law work is mundane, laborious, and not necessarily idealistic. Nor was knowing what to do for a client enough; first one must acquire the client.

The second set of data—the respondents' evaluations of law school functions and performance—points to limited opportunity to acquire the skills basic to the practice of law. Around two-thirds of the men answered an open-ended question on the proper function of law school with definite answers that it should "prepare for practice.[6] Two-thirds urged revision of the curricula of the schools they attended towards more "practical" instruction. Many suggestions for improvement were made, but the dominant theme throughout is a demand for more training in the technical and social skills required in practice. The statement "I wasn't prepared" is made over and over again. Behind this plaintive cry one senses the disorientation and embarrassment experienced by men who were *for-*

6 See Table 1.

mally qualified to practice law, yet forced to reveal inadequacies, ignorance, and confusion before clients, employers, and friends. If we are correct in assuming that the self-concept crystallizes only where role performance is undertaken in a psychologically meaningful context, the law school years provide minimal opportunity for this development. Furthermore, its products complain in large numbers that they lack the skills—technical and social—needed to play even the beginner's role.

The testimony of these young lawyers on what they learned in law school (and what they wished they had learned there) lends weight to the belief that law school had a limited and partial impact on them and their socialization into the realities of the profession. In the main, they left law school with a hazy and incomplete conception of what lawyers' work consists of. Ironically, they were thus ready for a wide variety of possibilities, for they were free from the domination of any one view held dearly and in detail. Since they did not have a grasp of what it took to do law work, they were forced to learn in terms of the positions they found themselves in after graduation—law became, essentially, the tasks they had to do in their first position or positions. They had to learn, as well, under the particularly powerful influence of doing so while earning a living and establishing a career, and lessons learned under those conditions, one suspects, have a peculiar vitality and subsequent hold on the learner. It appears very much as if laymen become lawmen only partially in law school and that the important transformations take place in the hurly-burly of work after graduation.[7]

7 To say that law school is but a beginning of professional socialization is *not* to say that the beginnings made in all law schools are identical. The dominant themes discussed above were general, and statistically predominant, but additional themes were found in one type of school and not in another. Movement from university to law firm appears to be continuous both in terms of role-set and values. The student may relate to senior partners as to his professors, to other associates as to former colleagues and competitors, and may actually do the same library tasks he performed in law school. University men talk of law school as intellectually exciting (on occasion) and as raising their appreciation of law's importance—these themes are consistent with the law firm definition of success as within the core of law and as based largely on professional competence.

The student leaving independent law schools, on the other hand, leaves teachers who were engaged in private practice and a peer culture which apparently stressed learning "the tricks of the trade" and the general usefulness of law in business and government. The consistency again appears in these themes; high valuation of monetary success is aligned with a recognition of the generality of legal training and a fluid approach to the pursuit of one's ambitions for financial gain. We also find that independent school graduates, generally deprived of the law firm man's apprenticeship, are most agreed on the need for more practical law school training. University men are more likely to defend a strictly theoretical curriculum, but this association is reversed where they enter private practice rather than firms. This suggests that career outcome may be an important factor in the graduate's evaluation of law school. The writer suspects that the key variable here is access to or denial of an apprenticeship where older lawyers guide the neophyte.

Professional Identification

Even though there are certain similarities in the process of socialization into a professional group, there are also differences between professions in the effects of this process. More specifically, individuals tend to develop different kinds of commitment to careers in different professional contexts. In the following reading, Howard Becker and James Carper report how physiologists, philosophers, and mechanical engineers differ in the kinds of commitment they develop toward (1) occupational title and associated ideology; (2) work tasks; (3) particular organizations or institutional positions; and (4) the significance of their position in the larger society.

Howard S. Becker and James Carper
(Physiology, Philosophy, and
Mechanical Engineering)

One of the major problems to which social psychologists are now addressing themselves is the process of identification and the nature and functioning of identity

Reprinted from "The Elements of Identification with an Occupation," *American Sociological Review*, 21, No. 3 (June 1956), 341–347. Used by permission of the American Sociological Association. The original publication bore the following note: "The paper is based on work done while the authors were Ford Foundation Postdoctoral Fellows at the University of Illinois. We wish to thank the Committee on the Ford Grant of the University of Illinois which also provided funds for clerical assistance."

in conduct. These concepts are of strategic importance in any theory which attempts to relate the self and its workings to an ongoing social structure. As Foote[1] and Strauss[2] have pointed out, individuals identify themselves—answer the question "Who am I?"—in terms of the names and categories current in the groups in which they participate. By applying these labels to themselves they learn who they are and

1 Nelson N. Foote, "Identification as the Basis for a Theory of Motivation," *American Sociological Review*, 16 (February 1951), 14–22.
2 Anselm Strauss, "Identification," unpublished manuscript.

how they ought to behave, acquire a self and a set of perspectives in terms of which their conduct is shaped.

It appears theoretically useful to break the concept of identification down into its components, both for comparative purposes and in order to provide finer tools for the analysis of specific problems of social structure and personal development. This paper is an attempt to provide such a breakdown for one type of identification, that of a man with his work. Its purpose is to discover, by comparing three groups of persons about to enter the work world, some of the threads from which the fabric of occupational identification is woven.

The data on which this paper is based were gathered in the course of a study of the genesis of identification with an occupation in students doing graduate work in physiology, philosophy, and mechanical engineering. Graduate students were chosen for study not only because they were convenient but, more importantly, because of the central character of graduate school in developing professional identifications. Interviews lasting from one-half to two hours were tape recorded with students ranging from first year in graduate school to those about to receive the Ph.D.[3] While identifications are not so clearly defined in the first year as they become later, the consistency of our findings indicates that the process is already well started at that time.

The interviews were conducted informally. Questions were asked only to clarify

points or to introduce some area in which information was desired that the interviewee had not spontaneously discussed in answer to the initial question: "How did you happen to get into....?"

Comparison of the three groups suggested four major elements of work identification: (1) occupational title, and associated ideology; (2) commitment to task; (3) commitment to particular organizations or institutional positions; and (4) significance for one's position in the larger society. In what follows we present brief discussions of each of these variables and comparisons of the physiologists, philosophers, and mechanical engineers[4] to illustrate their dimensions and analytic utility. Illustrations are also included of the kind of theoretical use to which these concepts might be put.

OCCUPATIONAL TITLE AND IDEOLOGY

Kinds of work tend to be named, to become well-defined occupations, and an important part of a person's work-based identity grows out of his relationship to his occupational title. These names carry a great deal of symbolic meaning, which tends to be incorporated into the identity. In the first place, they specify an area of endeavor belonging to those bearing the name and locate this area in relation to similar kinds of activity in a broader field. Secondly, they imply a great deal about the characteristics of their bearers, and these meanings are often systematized into elaborate ideologies which itemize the qualities, interests, and capabilities of those so identified.[5]

These things implied by the occupational title are evaluated and are reacted to in terms of such evaluations. One may reject the specific work area the title specifies,

---

[3] Only men were interviewed, to avoid the complications introduced by sex differences in career patterns and ambitions. Foreign students were excluded to eliminate the difficulty of interpreting information relating to social systems about which we knew little or nothing. Three philosophy students were excluded because they had no serious intentions of doing work in the field but were simply taking courses as a hobby. With these exceptions, we interviewed all the remaining students in philosophy (eleven) and mechanical engineering (twenty-two), and a randomly selected 50 per cent sample of those in physiology (eighteen), a total of fifty-one. The work was done at a large state university which may recruit from lower levels in the class structure. For this reason there may be important differences between our subjects and those studying in the same fields elsewhere.

[4] Material on the process by which the identifications we describe as characteristic of each of these groups develop is reported in "The Development of Identification with an Occupation," *The American Journal of Sociology,* **61** (January 1956), 289–298.

[5] See, for example, Howard S. Becker, "The Professional Dance Musician in Chicago," *The American Journal of Sociology,* **57** (September 1951), 136–144; and W. Fred Cottrell, *The Railroader* (Palo Alto: Stanford University Press), 1941.

preferring to be identified with some larger field; or he may eagerly claim the specific field, while minimizing the larger area; he may emphasize neither, or both. Similarly, the implicit statements about the person may be proudly claimed, whether these claims are recognized by others or not; or they may be as eagerly avoided, even though others attempt to impute them. The title, with its implications, may thus be an object of attachment or avoidance, and kinds of identification may fruitfully be compared in this regard.

The physiology students[6] feel themselves part of a larger group, devoted to building the edifice of science, and pride themselves on their participation in this endeavor and on the ultimate value of their work to society in the cure and prevention of disease. Nevertheless, they sharply differentiate their work from that of physicians and of other scientists involved in this enterprise. They feel that they make the important scientific discoveries on which medical practice is based, medicine itself being more empirical and superficial; one student put it metaphorically: "We write the music that the doctors play." Another stressed the fact that the scientist is free to pursue questions until he gets a real answer, while the M.D. must of necessity forego following up any particular problem intensively. In contrast to physicians, many saw themselves as men who would devote their lives to meeting the challenge of the unsolved problems of the field. They compare their work with that of other natural scientists—chemists, zoologists, and others—and conclude that theirs is the only science which really studies the problems of the living organism:

Here you have living organisms, and there are certain rules that these organisms will follow. They don't hold fast; two and two isn't

always four. It's up to you to interpret what happens, to be able to meet any emergency which arises. And you're working with something which is living and therefore responds to its environment. Whereas in chemistry, mathematics, there are certain reactions which occur but you yourself are the one that is producing these changes whereas in a living tissue, it itself is changing.... You're working with something which is alive just as you're alive and it changes and you actually can't control it completely, you just have to be able to work with it.

Others make a similar point in saying that physiology is not "cut and dried," as are the other sciences. In short, these men identify themselves as part of a discipline carrying on a peculiarly valuable kind of work, which no other group can do.

The engineers, like the physiologists, take great pride in their occupational title. Although in a few cases they feel equally identified with the titles of "research scientist" or "teacher," they all share the feeling that it is a good thing to be an engineer. Unlike the physiologists, the majority have no attachment to any particular part of their field; their specialty is the broad area of "technical work." They find the field desirable because of the remarkable skills and abilities engineering training is supposed to produce in them, abilities implied in the occupation's name. With few exceptions, these men are agreed that, as one put it:

All our lives and all through our work we are being trained to think logically and to analyze. And if you can do these two, I don't think anything can stop you.

The ideology tells them that anyone called "engineer" has learned to reason so rationally and effectively that, even though this has been learned only with reference to technical problems, it operates in any line of endeavor, so that the engineer is equipped to solve any kind of problem in any area quickly and efficiently.

The philosophers, in marked contrast, have very little attachment to their occupational title, perhaps because of the august company in which it would place them:

(It's all right to call you a philosopher, isn't it?) Well, I don't know. I do refer to myself

---

[6] Of the eighteen physiology students interviewed, eleven were fully committed to the field; two were committed to closely allied fields of biological research; three were determined to become physicians; and two still had hopes of becoming physicians, but were well on the way to accepting physiology as an alternative. This discussion of aspects of identification describes all but the five interested in medicine and applies in large measure to the two undecided cases.

every once in a while as a philosopher but I rather hesitate to because when I think of a philosopher I think of somebody like Plato or Aristotle.

The image they have of themselves is that of the "intellectual" whose interests cover the whole range of artistic, scientific, and cultural pursuits. Viewing their earlier specialization in particular fields as "too confining," they turn to philosophy which "does deal...with all crucial problems in one way or another."

Frankly, I'm taking the viewpoint of a person who wants to know quite a bit about several things and I never want to give up my catholic interest, catholic meaning of course universal in this sense, and to specialize. Yet I realize that to know very much about anything I have to specialize. Philosophy is the best grab-bag for me. To do something in philosophy I don't have to go terribly deeply into a given discipline and stick with it all my life, so I can shift from one discipline to another. But at the same time to overcome the notion of it being grounded in nothing. Frankly, if somebody asked me what I mean by philosophy it would be very difficult for me to tell them what I mean. I'm just sort of in a big intellectual game and pursuit right now. It happens to go under that name and I think under the aegis of philosophy I'm more able to do this.

In short, they have chosen their occupational title simply as the least undesirable one available, since it will place them in the society's division of labor while allowing them to deal with a broad range of interests ordinarily divided between many specialties.

COMMITMENT TO TASK

Occupations may also be compared with reference to the degree to which their members feel identified with some specific kind of work. There may be a feeling that only some sharply limited set of work tasks, carried on in a particular way, is proper, all others being excluded, and that one is, among other things, the kind of person who does this kind of work. The opposite attitude may also exist: that there is no kind of task which is impossible. Again, a person may simply be vague on the matter, not really knowing what his work is or how he ought to go about it. The elements of attachment, or lack of it, to a specific set of tasks and ways of handling them, and of a feeling of capability to engage in such activities, thus also play an important part in identification with one's work.

The physiology students exemplify one extreme, identifying closely with a set of specific research tasks and a particular way of going about them. Although task and method may vary from individual to individual, each one has a fairly clearcut notion of what he is about. They see a limited range of problems to which their professional lives will be devoted, and a set of basic techniques in which they take great pride:

You learn a little more about handling animals, doing regular surgery. After a while, it becomes automatic. I think the first time I did it it took about twenty-five or thirty minutes. Now I can go into the throat of a dog, sew in the glass tube, isolate the artery there, put a glass tube in it and hook it to a pressure machine and have the whole thing recording in about five minutes.

Beyond this, they are committed to the notion of themselves as persons who do work which is precise, which can be reproduced by other investigators, which is theoretically sound and takes cognizance of existing knowledge available in the discipline's literature. There is no vagueness in this conception; they know what their specific problems are and how they will be handled, and they feel that they are qualified, by virtue of their technical training to handle this kind of research successfully. They possess a concrete image of their professional future in terms of day-to-day activities which they will perform.

The engineers lie at the opposite pole, having almost no commitment to task—no kinds of work strictly theirs and beyond which they would neither dare nor care to go. Far from having a narrow conception of the engineer's work, eight of our twenty-two interviewees would be quite happy doing any kind of work our industrial system has to offer, as long as it is "interesting" and "challenging." Seven others stipulated simply that it be something technical, while only five consciously limited their work to a particular technical specialty. They are quite ready to forget the specific kinds of work for which they have been trained and take on any kind of job which the title of engineer can win for them. This attitude is expressed in comments like this:

(Now what did you have in mind, sort of, as a long-term goal in a thing like that?) Well, I think I have the same goal that probably every other kid fresh out of college has, that of going into some type of engineering work. With me, I think it would be production, as I've said. And eventually working up to higher management, I think. That's every young engineer's goal, whether he expresses it or not. (You mean non-engineering. . . .) Eventually ending up, using engineering as just a channel to go into management of some kind.

In addition to this kind of confident assertion that one is able to handle anything that comes up, the lack of commitment to task is found in the somewhat puzzled statements of younger engineers about what their work really is:

I really didn't have a good idea of what an engineer does. And I still can't tell you. People asked me, "Well, what does a mechanical engineer do?" and I could give them examples, that's all. I could go on and on and on in the examples, and that pertains to any engineer. All you have to do is just look at the placement records of engineers, and they go into everything.

(Six of the men interviewed included teaching, in combination with either specialized or general technical tasks, among the possible kinds of work for them.)

The philosophers present a third possibility. Lacking both the specific task attachment of the physiologists and the calm assurance of the engineers that all tasks are suitable for them, these students are not quite sure what they should be doing. Realizing that their future probably lies in the university, they accept teaching as a necessary task which is, however, not peculiarly theirs. The following is a typical answer to the question, "What does a philosopher do?"

I suppose part of a philosopher's job is in telling people how much they don't know: It seems to be so old fashioned now to tell people how much they don't know. I suppose I will be teaching the various branches of philosophy.

I'm interested in talking to students. In helping them with reading. In helping them with philosophical problems that come up. I'm sure that they can help me with some fresh ideas I hadn't considered heretofore. I'm interested in just learning as much as I can in my spare time. I might decide at some time to dabble in another profession. I just don't know. I'll never feel that there's any dearth of things to do. I don't know if I can ever categorize them. My job, my source of income, will involve taking so many hours of classes, teaching.

The clearest image of their work tends to center around the notion of continuing to learn and read in all areas of intellectual activity. Beyond this, they see all kinds of possibilities, ranging from semi-scientific research through journalism and artistic activity to such things as politics.

ORGANIZATION AND INSTITUTIONAL POSITION

An occupational identity tends to specify the kinds of organizations, and positions within them, in which one's future lies, the places in which it is appropriate, desirable, or likely that one will work. A person may see his professional future as tied to one organization, or to a very restricted range of organizations, or he may conceive of himself acting in his occupational role in a great many kinds of institutions. Again, he may feel tied to one particular kind of institutional position, or find it possible to conceive of holding a large variety of work statuses. These, with the further possibility of vagueness as to these matters, constitute continua along which various kinds of work identification may be located.

Participants in work institutions tend to see themselves in relation to those upon whom their success in these institutions depends. Research has demonstrated the importance of building connections with clients, colleagues, and others in the pursuit of success,[7] and identifications vary in the

[7] See, for example, Oswald Hall, "The Stages of a Medical Career," *The American Journal of Sociology,* **53** (March 1948), pp. 237–337; and Everett C. Hughes, *French Canada in Transition,* (Chicago: University of Chicago Press, 1943), pp. 52–53.

degree to which they reflect dependence on informal systems of sponsorship, recommendation, and control.

The physiology students see themselves as potential occupants of a few well-defined slots in a highly organized work world. There are only a few places in which they might do their kind of work: universities, where they would teach and do research; research foundations and pharmaceutical companies, where they would do only research; and government agencies, where they would engage in applied research. They do not consider themselves competent to handle positions of any other kind. They are unable to see beyond this narrow conception even to entertain the notion of becoming chairman of a Department of Physiology; this would mean moving out of the expected slot a little too far for comfort, involving as it would unfamiliar duties and responsibilities.

They expect such jobs to become available to them through the workings of a sponsorship system centered around their graduate-school professors. The initial job (the aspect of the career that looms largest at this stage) will come through the professor's contacts, and his recommendations will be of great importance. They feel quite dependent on this personal kind of sponsorship system and see no other way to get established professionally. They expect to progress through the hierarchy of university, industry, or government through careful research, knowledge of the field, and publication of important research.

In contrast, the engineers feel that their future lies somewhere in the country's industrial system, but do not think of any company (no matter what its specialty) or any position as impossible for them. Twelve of the twenty-two interviewees are prepared to work in any kind of industrial organization, while only six limit their possibilities to companies doing work in their technical specialty. (Three of the men expect to become teachers, and one wants to open his own business.) For the majority, any industrial firm in the country represents a possible employer.

Within this range of organizations they expect to compete for a broad range of positions. Of the eighteen who were considering industry, only one would restrict himself to a position involving only his technical specialty. Nine are able to see themselves in any kind of technical position in industry, while eight are confident that they can compete successfully for any position, technical or managerial. Lacking any firm commitment to a particular task and armed with an ideology that stresses their universal ability, they see their futures in terms such as these:

(What kind of job would that be that you would get into eventually?) It would be difficult to say. (Well, what are the possibilities?) Oh, assistant, for instance, a job that I would like to have. If I get back to *X Co.* I think I have a good chance, which would be a tremendous step forward, would be assistant to the general manager, for instance. While this would take me out of the technical field, it would be—It's a tremendous stepping stone, it's a big step forward as far as getting to the administrative end of it. I do not fancy myself as a research engineer who's just going to bury himself in his little office, content to work all his life compiling a set of tables, should we say, to take an illustrative example. A lot of people have done this. Or to investigate the natural laws. I think there's a—I don't fancy myself as doing this. I'd like to get ahead into a position where you are directing things, formulating policies, formulating the lines of the company. Do you follow me? (Yeah. Yeah. So you could conceivably end up as a general manager?) General manager of the plant, vice president.... (The sky's the limit, in other words.) It is. It really is. A good engineer can go anyplace these days.

Only a few feel that their future is in any way tied in with their "connections" with either prospective employers or with sponsors in the academic world. The majority felt quite independent in getting jobs, assuming that in the normal workings of the labor market in an economy becoming more and more "technical" they would be able to command a satisfactory position. This independence is reflected in the language they use to describe job-hunting: They are not "interviewed for a job," but rather "interview companies about jobs." This may, of course, be a temporary phenomenon associated with the present high demand for engineers.

The philosophers again suggest another dimension, having for the greatest part of their time in graduate school no clear notion of where they will work or what position they might hold. They think of themselves as intellectuals, and the term implies no specific relation to the occupational world. Late in their training they begin to realize that their futures are to be made in universities, and primarily as teachers rather than philosophers. By this time teaching, originally viewed as an important function of the philosopher, has become simply a way of earning a living and subsidizing the continuation of their intellectual pursuits. Since the state of the job market may limit opportunities to get such positions, they are ready to consider positions involving skills or experience acquired elsewhere. Any position which will allow continued intellectual activity, on or off the job, is considered suitable, even though it may have no relation to the professional organization of philosophy. If they do teach, they feel they are as likely to teach some other intellectual specialty as philosophy; anything within their cultural purview becomes a possible teaching subject.

They are vague about the ways in which jobs become available and professional success is achieved. Only two had a clear notion of the workings of academic sponsorship systems, although several believed that their professors might have some effect on their work future. They tend to be concerned about this, if at all, in a quite offhand manner:

Lately I have begun to think that after all, in part philosophy is a business, so in part business ethics must apply to philosophy—and there are certain things you just have to do. (How about thinks like publishing, and so on...?) Oh, that of course would be in your favor. But that again is something that I haven't thought about, haven't thought about writing any articles for journals. It's certainly...when I decided that I should realize that philosophy is partly a business, I also decided that I should think about writing for journals and I should take systematic notes on articles in journals, what kinds of articles are in there, what sort of thing they write about and how they write about it. (But you haven't done much of that yet?) No. It's certainly time to start, I would say.

SOCIAL POSITION

Occupational identities contain an implicit reference to the person's position in the larger society, tending to specify the positions appropriate for a person doing such work or which have become possible for him by virtue of his work. The most frequent reference is, of course, to social-class position and to the opportunities for class mobility opened up or closed off by entrance into the particular occupation. It is also possible for an identification to contain a statement of a particular relation of members of the occupation to the society, quite apart from class considerations.

The physiology students see themselves as achieving a desired move up in the class system. Twelve are men from the lower or lower-middle class who had hoped to become physicians, with the prestige of that profession playing a large role in their choice. This mobility hope has been wrecked on the reef of medical school entrance standards or abandoned during the tedious and trying voyage through "pre-med," and becoming a physiologist represents the salvage. Their parents, desiring to see their sons better themselves, figured importantly in the choice of medicine as a career, and these men remain sensitive to their parents' aspirations for them. Physiology as an occupation will get them some of the prestige and income they desired, although it is second-best; they will never approach the M.D. in these respects.

For four others (in the remaining two cases we did not get sufficient information to make a classification) physiology represents an escape into science from the mobility demands of their well-to-do families. They see physiology as an occupation giving them a respected position without necessitating the competitiveness of medicine or business. They are typically interested in academic positions, while many of the first group favor research positions in the drug industry, which they believe provide larger incomes.

For seventeen of the engineers, success in their profession spells successful social mobility. They are men whose fathers were skilled or unskilled laborers, farmers, or white-collar workers. Having entered engineering in many instances purely out of interest in "mechanical things," they are pleasantly surprised to find that it enables them to rise significantly (in social class terms) above their families and childhood friends. For the other five, a career in engineering is a means of continuing their families' solid middle-class status. They all expect to do well financially. At the least, they look forward to a very comfortable living, and eight expressed the desire to make "big money": "You can get your mansion on the hill." Being an engineer is a ticket to financial success and its accompanying social prestige.

The philosophy students' identification of themselves as "intellectuals" carried with it the implication that they are different in important respects from other members of the society. In every case they either consider themselves deviant or recognize that they are so considered by friends and relatives. Most importantly, these men of predominantly lower and lower-middle class origin have renounced the pursuit of class mobility in favor of the intellectual life. They have no concern with material success and tend to be proud of the meagerness of their financial future. It is expected that parents and others will be unable to understand these views, and they tend to break relations with people who would keep these interests before them. In contrast to the physiologists, parental aspirations play no part in the formation of their professional ambitions.

Questions for Discussion and Further Research

The older view of education held that a man was trained for his occupation when he was young, and that he then was ready to go forth into the world to practice his profession or trade. Such was an appropriate view for a more static society. However, the readings in this chapter begin to suggest that a new perspective is required by a more dynamic society. Occupational socialization—especially in the more professionalized occupations—has become a life-long process. In almost every modern occupation, technological and social changes are occurring so rapidly that one must be constantly prepared to learn new things in order to keep his occupational skills current.

This development, in turn, requires new institutional arrangements. The growth of the adult education movement and its special institutions has been one response to this need; another has been the proliferation of on-the-job training programs in industry. Trade unions have sponsored many courses designed to upgrade the skills of their journeyman members, and it will be recalled that a paper in Chapter 1 suggested that this be considered an aspect of professionalization in some instances. In what Reiss has characterized the "new professions," as well as in the "established professions," there have been increasing demands for "sabbatical leaves" that would permit professional persons to return to universities for postgraduate study or to engage in independent study in order to regenerate, and perhaps reorient, their professional skills. One estimate has indicated that about one in three adult Americans is currently participating in some kind of adult education connected with his work.

These developments suggest several topics for further research. What is the extent of adult socialization and retraining in different professional groups today? What factors are associated with differences in the demand for such adult education among individuals within various professional groups and between different groups? How does this movement for continuing adult education affect the self-images of members of different professional groups? How does it affect the relations of various professional groups to each other? How does it affect the character of traditional institutions and agencies of professional socialization, like the universities? How does the assumption of certain responsibilities for continuing professional training affect industrial organizations and other institutions that employ professionals outside the universities?

Then, of course, there is also need for further research in order to update our knowledge about the social origins of persons who enter various professional categories and the ability of individuals to move freely through the various stages of professional careers. The work of Lipset and Bendix provided an important milestone in our understanding of occupational mobility in industrial society at the time it was published.* We need further research, however, to determine the degree to which social mobility will be sustained or will become more structured and limited under the impact of advanced professionalization.

* S. M. Lipset and R. Bendix, *Social Mobility in Industrial Society* (Berkeley and Los Angeles: University of California Press, 1960).

4

Professional Controls

The behavior of members of an occupation is controlled both through the persons who pursue the occupation and through other persons who come into direct or indirect contact with the occupation. The occupational control process includes the acquisition of the general occupational culture, discussed in the readings on socialization and professional identification in the previous chapter, as well as the learning of more specific behavioral expectations having to do with the occupation itself—i.e., occupational roles. An ability to perform these roles is acquired in activities ranging from informal on-the-job training at work to formal education in the school or university. In highly professionalized occupations much of the conformity to occupational roles is achieved by an especially thorough internalization of occupational expectations among those who pursue the occupation, with great emphasis placed on individual responsibility throughout the process.* In less professionalized occupations, in contrast, occupational conduct may be governed largely by external rather than internal pressures. In the former, the novice learns a great deal by example—by watching what experienced practitioners do and attempting to pattern himself after their actions as much as possible. In a less professionalized occupation, his conduct may have to be controlled continually from an external source; the worker is told what to do by an authority in a superior position.

Much of this book is devoted to discussions of various aspects of occupational control; later chapters deal with the parts played by other important agencies for occupational control—occupational associations, employing organizations, and various agencies of government. In this chapter, however, we are less concerned with control agencies or the learning of an occupational role than we are with the significance of occupational values—ideational factors—as

---

* See D. Rueschmeyer, "Doctors and Lawyers: A Comment on the Theory of the Professions, "The Canadian Review of Sociology and Anthropology, 1, No. 1, 17–30.

seen from both inside and outside the profession.† More specifically, we are interested first in occupational images and norms and how these affect the control of occupational behavior,‡ and secondly whether these images and norms are explicitly set forth in writing or are found in the informal oral traditions of folklore. These kinds of occupational controls include occupational stereotypes, ethical codes, civil laws, and the like.§

Occupational Images and Norms

The importance of ideational factors in occupations has been recognized for many years. For example, the editor of *The Annals of the American Academy of Political and Social Science* pointed out in 1922:

Codes of ethics are important agencies for social control. The complexities and the specializations of modern industrial life leave many individuals unable to judge whether or not a member of any profession has performed his services with due regard to the interests of all, as well as with due regard to the interests of his client. In all but the crassest and most obvious defaults in service standards the work of the physician must be judged by physicians and that of the lawyer, by lawyers. And so with each of the professions. The higher the skill, the greater the need for organized group effort toward maintaining a fine sense of obligations, not primarily to others in the same profession, but chiefly to the general well-being of all.**

At the beginning of this century an early social scientist, Emile Durkheim, discussed occupational controls and noted:

There is no form of social activity which can do without the appropriate moral discipline.... It is this discipline that curbs him, that marks the boundaries, that tells him what his relations with his associates should be, where illicit encroachments begin, and what he must pay in current dues towards the maintenance of the community. Since the precise function of this discipline is to confront the individual with aims that are not his own, that are beyond his grasp and exterior to him, the discipline seems to him—and in some ways is so in reality—as something exterior to himself and also dominating him.††

Similarly, Leake remarked a number of years ago:

Professional men have more specific moral issues confronting them than the mass experience of humanity has evolved rules to cover. This is especially true for the physician, whose daily professional activity may often involve a choice between acting in the ideal interests of humanity, or in the practical interests of self.‡‡

† The importance of ideational factors is reasserted by contemporary practitioners, e.g., see C. Knight Aldrich, M.D., "The Physician's Public Image and His Social Responsibility," *What's New*, No. 220, 1960, pp. 9–10.

‡ An explanation of how this socio-psychological mechanism operates may be found in Douglas M. More, "The Dental Student Approaching Graduation—1962," *Journal of the American College of Dentists*, September 1962, especially Part IV, "Concept of the Dentist in the Community."

§ E. C. Hughes, "Social Attitudes and the Division of Labor," in *Men and Their Work* (Glencoe, Ill.: The Free Press, 1958), pp. 35–36.

** Clyde L. King, "Foreword to the Ethics of the Professions and of Business," *The Annals of the American Academy of Political and Social Science*, 101, No. 190 (May 1922), vii.

†† Emile Durkheim, *Professional Ethics and Civic Morals* (New York: Free Press of Glencoe, 1958), pp. 14–15.

‡‡ Chauncey Leake (ed.). *Percival's Medical Ethics* (Baltimore: The Williams & Wilkins Co., 1927), p. 4.

The error should not be made of assuming that it is really only the healing arts practitioner who is so greatly concerned with the control of occupational conduct. In the instance of the military, Janowitz has stated: "The tasks of managing more complex and more destructive machinery of warfare has led the professional soldier to become more interested in a set of ideological principles as to 'why we fight.' Self-evident objectives no longer suffice."§§ Many occupations that strive to become more professionalized attempt to manipulate ideational factors both within and without the occupation in the attempt to accelerate the professionalization process.***

There are other types of ideational factors which must be considered. The great concern displayed by persons in highly professionalized occupations about appropriate occupational conduct is reinforced in part through what Professor Caplow has referred to as a "mild paranoia."††† They often look upon themselves as having a more important position in life than outsiders are willing to accord them. The failure of clientele and public to recognize this high status is resented. While it is a kind of exaggeration, perceived status differences contribute strongly to a feeling of group identification.

Moreover, this feeling of occupational identification is enhanced by the acquisition of certain mannerisms which are felt to be appropriate to the performance of the occupation. For example, we may note the dentist's stance of professional calm associated with a tooth extraction, or the architect's attitude of aesthetic correctness associated with a plan. And these may pervade areas of life outside the work situation, exhibiting a halo effect which contributes further to the distinctive identification of the occupational group. The several influences that an occupational stereotype may exert on the control of occupational conduct is shown quite clearly in the selection which follows.

§§ Morris Janowitz, *The Professional Soldier* (New York: Free Press of Glencoe, 1960), p. 402. See also the remainder of this discussion about the search for ideology in the military, *ibid.*, pp. 401–414.

*** For example, see F. Barsalou, M. Blumberg, H. Kincaid, D. Mills, and J. R. Lee, *Chiropractic in California* (Los Angeles: The Haynes Foundation, 1960), especially Chapters 1 and 5.

††† Theodore Caplow, *The Sociology of Work* (Minneapolis: University of Minnesota Press, 1954), p. 131.

Theodore Caplow (General)

The description of an occupation is not complete when we have measured it in terms of prestige, remuneration, and mobility, described its internal organization, and examined the ways in which it shapes the behavior of its members. There remains another set of occupational attributes: a sort of subculture composed

of the manners and mores and folkways peculiar to the calling, the legends grown up about it, and the symbols which it displays.

The sheer age of an occupation has important consequences for its stereotype. To be a cook, a philosopher, a sailor, or a carpenter is to be qualitatively different from oil-well gun perforators, group dynamicists, seismic observers, or acid chambermen. The former, being universally recognized, and each having a very long history, are universally credited with certain moral and personal characteristics.

The member of a highly familiar occupation is continuously aware of his definite role as defined by tradition. He can predict with reasonable accuracy the manner in which he will be received in any company, and the status which will be accorded to him. Where the expectations are very definite, he will even be likely to assume the appropriate personality traits. It is probable that professors are more absent-minded, reporters more cynical, chefs more excitable, and policemen more brutal, than an examination of their Rorschach scores would suggest.

There is, in this matter, the usual relationship between behavior and role. The stereotype is based on certain "real" elements in the working situation. Whyte's study of the restaurant kitchen as a working group shows some factors which predispose chefs to emotional excitability.[1] Wilson shows how the professorial job encourages an appearance of impracticality and unworldliness.[2] However, the stereotype is itself the most important agent for the conditioning of roles.

Most occupations today are relatively unfamiliar, which means that communication between the working situation and the general society is seriously hampered. Achievements on the job cannot be easily exchanged for social prestige. The small coinage of daily experience at work has no currency outside the plant, and the individual is continually subjected to misidentifications. Roethlisberger notes that the unfamiliarity of technical jobs at Western Electric left their holders at a disadvantage in the community.[3]

Not only are thousands of modern occupations unfamiliar; but many others are readily confused. Rural postmen, who are independent contractors, resent identification with urban postmen, who are merely employees. Automobile mechanics are often confused with filling-station attendants, power-house engineers with janitors, and accountants with clerks. Pretentiousness in occupational titles (consulting sales engineer, for example) is often a device to prevent misidentification. Indeed, one of the strongest factors making for professionalization is the attempt to escape an unfavorable stereotype by transmuting undertakers into morticians, bill collectors into credit representatives, and reporters into journalists.

Nevertheless, the very distinctness of the professional stereotype raises certain characteristic problems. In the first place, each of the major professions is engaged in a continuous struggle against interlopers who assume its style and titles. Carr-Saunders[4] has described the desperate efforts of professional engineers in Great Britain to prevent locomotive drivers, furnace tenders, blueprinters, caretakers, millwrights, and others from describing themselves as engineers. In the United States, a similar effort has been even less successful, and the title of engineer is lightheartedly claimed by tree surgeons, shoe salesmen, and snow-plow drivers.

A quite different problem is presented by the unfavorable popular stereotypes which have attached for centuries to lawyers, physicians, dentists, teachers, and the clergy. The situation of a professional group is, after all, somewhat vulnerable. Highly visible, moderately privileged, partially isolated, and responsible in the exercise of their authority for some of the major woes of their fellow men, professional men are logical targets for popular aggression. In the case of physicians, an intensive propaganda has somewhat dissipated this sentiment, but no study of professional groups should overlook the fact that they are usually highly aware of the unfavorable stereotypes of shyster, quack, butcher, pedant, sissy, and the like, which, in spite of full-page, full-color ads, keep them slightly on the defensive.

[1] William Foote Whyte, *Human Relations in the Restaurant Industry* (New York: McGraw-Hill Book Company, 1948).

[2] Logan Wilson, *The Academic Man: A Study in the Sociology of a Profession* (New York: Oxford University Press, 1942).

[3] F. J. Roethlisberger, *Management and Morale* (Cambridge, Mass.: Harvard University Press, 1941).

[4] A. M. Carr-Saunders and P. A. Wilson, *The Professions* (Oxford: Clarendon Press, 1933).

Are we then to expect that there is a one-to-one relationship between occupational expectations and what in fact occurs in occupational behavior? Certainly not. Leake refers to a conflict between public and private interest,* and in a discussion of the medical profession, Parsons indicates that a close adherence to scientific and rationalistic conduct ordinarily would be expected, but that such is not the case.† Often there is a reliance upon less rational modes of behavior in an attempt to protect the independence of the occupation from outside interference and control. Parsons states:

> The general tendency is to fall considerably short of living up to the full "logical" implications of the dominant culture pattern in certain crucial respects. It is suggested that this derives from the fact that it is not possible to "apply" the dominant cultural pattern literally and without restriction and not generate strains which, in turn, would produce responses which would be more disruptive than certain "mitigations" of the rigorous applications of the pattern itself. This deviation from the dominant pattern is what we have called an adaptive structure.‡

On certain occasions there is a reluctance by practitioners to make use of the formal control mechanisms within the occupation, because such might prove to be of embarrassment not only to the individuals who have deviated from the occupational role but also to the occupation as a whole. Rather, reliance is more commonly placed on the use of *informal* controls. This is not to say that formal mechanisms, such as codes of ethical conduct, are of no use, as we shall see later in this chapter. The point is that, in many instances, the use of informal means to control occupational behavior can be equally effective. When serious mistakes are made at work, an attempt is made immediately by the individual or individuals to correct the mistakes quietly and efficiently. Lesser mistakes may go "unrecognized";§ the uninitiated will likely never know.

How is it that the "outsiders" gain a set of attitudes about a particular occupation? There are many ways, of course. There is the folklore handed down by word of mouth. There is the cultural accumulation of explicit statements of conduct in various communications media. One example of the latter describes medical practitioners as they are seen in contemporary literature. Stereotypes of the medical doctor have certain unreal aspects about them in the sense that they do not conform entirely to social realities. Yet these kinds of near caricatures can, in fact, influence the reactions of the general public to the members of an occupation. Ronald Bodley Scott, himself a physician, has noted some of the amusing stereotypes associated with the medical practitioner.

* Leake, *op. cit.*, pp. 6–7; 10–11.
† Talcott Parsons, *The Social System* (Glencoe, Ill.: The Free Press, 1950), pp. 469–473; also, Durkheim, *op. cit.*, pp. 5–7.
‡ Parsons, *The Social System, op. cit.*, p. 470. For an example of this in another occupation see William A. Westley, "Secrecy and the Police," *Social Forces,* 34, 1956, 254–257.
§ The importance of analyzing the sociological consequences of mistakes at work has long been recognised by E. C. Hughes, and a selection from his writings on this subject is included at the end of this chapter.

Ronald Bodley Scott (Medicine)

It is commonly said that the esteem in which the public holds the medical profession has fallen. If this be true, the situation is one which should cause us all concern; although we may reflect on the irony of this decline going hand in hand with an increase in our ability to control disease of which our fathers would not have dared to dream. The barometer of public opinion is not easily read; and any information on this subject, however trivial its source, is of value. It was with these thoughts in mind that I embarked upon the investigation which I shall here describe.

Fiction holds up a mirror to life, and it should be possible to see therein a reflection of the doctor as he appears to the contemporary novelist. To obtain a concentration of experience it was convenient to study a form of fiction in which doctors appeared frequently, while it was advisable to avoid works in which a medical man was one of the major characters, because he would then be invested with attributes not necessarily regarded by the author as typical of his calling. The class of novel which most nearly fulfils these requirements is that of detective fiction, and it was to such works that I turned my attention.

The detective novel in its purest form may have passed the zenith of its fashion; but there is still an outpouring of works in which the central themes are murder, violence, and sudden death, and, as episodes of this kind are inevitably followed by the appearance of a doctor, they suit our purpose equally well. I do not propose to deal with the classics of this form of fiction, but the importance of our profession to the detective was established by the creation of Dr. Watson more than fifty years ago. This practitioner, recently described in the *Times Literary Supplement* as a "clot in the arteries of the Royal Colleges of Physicians and Surgeons," first met Sherlock Holmes within the walls of St. Bartholomew's Hospital. Two years ago a plaque was unveiled there to commemorate this event. Filial piety therefore has added its stimulus to my researches.

It is suitable to begin with the general practitioner because he has characteristics which separate him sharply from the class of doctor always known in novels as "specialists." He is usually portrayed as competent and cheerful. A few quotations pro-

Reprinted from "The Doctor in Contemporary Literature," *The Lancet,* 269, No. 6885 (August 13, 1955), 341–343. Used by permission of the author and publisher.

vide a clearcut picture "a big cheerful middle-aged man," "a squarely built eminently practical young man," "such a nice breezy manner," "a quiet square young man with bushy black hair growing low down over his forehead," "a stolid pleasant looking square capable face." In these descriptions you will have been struck by the squareness of the general practitioner; possibly this is symbolic, denoting the solid virtues of dependability and unimaginative competence which the novelist either sees, or wishes to see, in his medical attendant.

It is, however, not every general practitioner who possesses these desirable qualities. Dr. Smith in *More Work for the Undertaker* is tall and stooping with a back like a camel, and although kind and professional is stigmatised as "not as bright as some." Indeed intellectual capacity does not appear to be a feature of the family doctor. Another Dr. Smith is described with the ring of truth as "a thin man with a tired face." Dr. Shaw, in *Death at the Bar,* is a more attractive personality, "dominating the scene with bright vivid blue eyes, gazing through his spectacles" and combining with "a look of serio-comic solemnity," "a certain air of distinction," while young Dr. Fettes, in *Death of a Ghost,* possesses the enviable gift of "looking blank without appearing foolish."

Examples could be multiplied, but these are sufficient to show the impact the general practitioner makes. On the whole he may be said to emerge with credit: he has an appearance of competence; he is stolid; sometimes he is even distinguished. He remains unruffled by the curious situations which the novelists devise for him.

The accounts of his purely professional abilities and the manner in which he conducts consultations are interesting and revealing. Mr. Todhunter, in *Trial and Error* is told brusquely that he has an aortic aneurysm. "Well," says his doctor, "what can you expect? Your blood pressure's been too high for years." He is, in the timeworn phrase, given six months to live, but the blow is softened by the observation that "life on the physical plane is a darned nuisance and the sooner we're out of it the better." The methods of young Dr.

Tom Croxley in *She Died a Lady* were more devious; he would tell the patient "all the imposing medical terms for what was wrong with him," an approach commended by his father, who was his senior partner, as impressing, pleasing, and inspiring confidence from the start.

We must all at some time have been a little envious of the knowledge of medical jurisprudence and toxicology possessed by these fictional general practitioners. The precise time of death is announced with assurance after a cursory glance at the body. A moment's inspection is enough to make the most obscure of country doctors suspect the most obscure of poisons. "He looks to me," says big cheerful middle-aged Dr. Burwick, "like a typical case of oxalic acid poisoning." Not content with mere impressions, he withdraws to his dispensary with the suspect bottle of sherry, carries out the tests necessary to confirm his opinion, and, on adding a reagent, "is unable to repress an exclamation as it throws down a white precipitate." We can only reflect wistfully upon our own copies of *Aids to Forensic Medicine and Toxicology,* lying in the attic beneath the dust of twenty years.

I must turn now to the "specialist," who stands in marked contrast with the selfless family doctor. Many, like Dr. Mawsley in *Death in Harley Street,* are interested only in the amassing of wealth. Dr. Eugene Arnold, of the *Red Window Murders,* is an example: "as fond of money as Marlborough and as mean about it," he had a "damned superior air...as though he always had his bank book in his hand." He even "took on Ralph Bender—the most brilliant student of his year at the Royal—as a dispensary clerk to handle minor cases without fee."

In matters of appearance the specialist does lead, and his manners are usually irreproachable. Dr. William Pelham, although "a bit of a pompous ass," was plump, bland, and kindly, with silver hair and "the manners of a Prime Minister"—an ambiguous description, it is true—"he could squeeze the last drop of politeness out of a conversation." His "only touch of professionalism was a pair of black-ribboned eye glasses." This last is the hallmark of the succesful consultant, for Sir Daniel Davidson, of whom it was said that "if Disraeli had taken to medicine instead of primroses, he would have been just such another," also wore glasses on a wide black ribbon. A second distinguishing feature is "elegant white hair," although its charm in the case of Sir Gordon Woodthorpe, the eminent society physician, must have been offset by his custom of "licking his lips feverishly, a nervous habit that had persisted since childhood."

Perhaps it is natural that psychiatrists should play so many prominent parts in detective fiction. A man who, in the words of *The Lancet's* peripatetic correspondent, goes to the Folies Bergères to watch the audience, has a powerful dramatic appeal; his activities are always mysterious and usually sinister; he is cast by Nature for the role of villain. Dr. Eugene Arnold was of this specialty with "assured success and poise about him and a hard handsome face which could become kindly like the turning on of an electric light." Dr. Nicholson, a very clever Canadian, was another; "behind his strong glasses pale blue eyes glittered reflectively and his manner suggested great reserves of power." It will astonish those who number psychiatrists among their acquaintances to learn that "he said very little," and it will increase their surprise to hear that he "contrived somehow to make every word sound significant."

Surgeons enjoy less popularity with the writers of detective fiction; they lack the machiavellian qualities of the psychiatrist and the polish of the society physician. A striking exception, however, is Sir John Phillips of the *Nursing Home Murders.* His background of Winchester, Cambridge, and St. Thomas's Hospital only just falls short of being irreproachable, and he possessed that "curious quality people call personality" from which, "next to actors, medical men profit most." He can be forgiven losing his temper when he learned that the Home Secretary had been away for the weekend with the theater-sister whom he hoped to marry, and we can sympathize with him when the minister, whose appendix abscess he was called upon to drain, died immediately after the operation. A very different character is Mr. Thomas, his assistant, "fat, scarlet-faced and industriously facetious, his undistinguished but blameless career punctuated by mild scandals about women." Clearly his education at St. Bardolph's, Essex, and Guy's Hospital, had not fitted him for competition with such giants as Sir John.

The narrower forms of specialism receive scant attention, but one instance is Dr. Mawsley, in *Death in Harley Street,* a specialist in "glands." Although noted for his rapacity, he is in part redeemed by his interest in research. His investigations were prosecuted in an experimental laboratory which led out of his consulting-room where he made use of rats provided by the Marylebone Borough ratcatcher at a cost of 5s. a pair. Ironically enough, it was his interest in the effects of coniine on the glands of these animals which led to his untimely death at the hands of his illegitimate son by a probationer at a hospital where he had been a house-physician.

All specialists lead lives of elegance amongst surroundings of opulent good taste. Dr. Pelham "with a Havana between his lips and a glass of sherry at his elbow" is an example of this leisured luxury. Sir Daniel Davidson's consulting-room in St. Luke's Chambers, Harley Street, provides another illustration. It had "apple green walls, an Adam fireplace and silver starred curtains. A beautiful and expensive room, crying in devious tones of the gratitude of wealthy patients."

It is possible in these glimpses to discern a certain hostility to the specialist. His appearance is too distinguished; his manners are too perfect and he is too well-groomed. With his beribboned eyeglasses, his white hair, and his overwhelming urbanity, he recalls an Ambassador in a play by Pinero. This glittering figure fills his patients with feelings of their own inferiority and with apprehension concerning his fees. This fear is often well founded; behind the facade there is callous avarice. Nevertheless all specialists are "brilliant" and many have distinguished themselves in other fields than medicine. Dr. Eugene Arnold was able to win over a sporting peer by his modest confession that he "happened to be a cricket blue of some distinction." In general it may be said that the specialist is remote and olympian; his only concessions to human weakness are his rapacity and his habit of irregular liaisons with members of the nursing staff.

The contrast between general practitioner and specialist revealed in these composite pictures is interesting. Popular notions lag behind reality and some of these features of consultant life have vanished; the beribboned glasses have disappeared and few specialists now live like merchant princes. To most novelists, moreover, the cloistered life of the hospital remains a mystery. A scene in *The Lift and the Drop* provides convincing evidence of ignorance: the night sister at St. Bartholomew's was behind a screen with a recently admitted casualty and the waiting detective heard the sound of a kiss, followed by a whisper of "now rest and get well for me, soon—soon."

There is another role in which the medical practitioner appears in detective fiction; it is that of the murderer. I was surprised to find him playing this part in little less than half the novels I chanced to read. It may be asked why the novelist should so frequently select the doctor for the murderer. It is widely believed that the medical student early acquires a profound knowledge of toxicology and that he has at his command poisons which leave no trace in the victim's body and which baffle the most erudite chemists. In spite of this, however, the medical murderer is commonly recorded as choosing some mundane drug, such as hyoscine or chloral, or a traditional poison like arsenic. In *Death Leaves a Diary,* for instance, Dr. Furness poisons his mother-in-law with arsenic, and in *The Nursing Home Murders* Dr. Roberts makes use of hyoscine which he administers with a syringe ingeniously built into his anæsthetic apparatus. At other times there is resort to simple violence: Dr. Eugene Arnold belies his polished appearance by using a hammer; Sir Daniel Davidson, having rendered his victim unconscious by a blow with his cigarette case, suffocates him by holding his nose and placing his hand over his mouth.

Only rarely are more ingenious methods employed: Dr. Kingston in the *Case of the Late Pig,* balances a stone urn on a balustrade, supporting it with a block of ice, which melts to allow the urn to fall with devastating precision on the head of a man sleeping below in a deck chair.

It might be supposed that opportunity was responsible for these doctors committing murder, but it is rarely their patients whom they kill. Dr. Roberts was an exception to this rule, but he was obsessed and regarded himself as dedicated to purification of the race by eliminating those who were eugenically unsound. In the end he was betrayed by his custom of cutting a notch in the stem of his wooden stethoscope to celebrate each success. In the main their motives are commonplace: Sir Daniel is afraid that his blackmailing activities will be revealed; Dr. Furness is after his mother-in-law's money; and young Dr. Tom Croxley's frantic passion for the wife of an alcoholic professor of mathematics drives him to murder when she surrenders to the charms of a motor car salesman.

In many instances the fact that the murderer is a doctor is irrelevant to the novel's plot and we must seek out some occult reason for the author's choice. It is probable that we should see in it another indication of the hostility with which the public regards our profession. This feeling has deep roots. The medical profession is, in a sense, a priestcraft with its own language, its incomprehensible code of etiquette, and its objective view of matters which engender great emotional heat in the laity. The public feels resentment at its exclusion from this secret society. The doctor again is in a position of enviable superiority; the patient has no choice but to display to him the sordid workings of his psyche as well as the pitiful shortcomings of his body. Finally the malignant blows of fate are seldom acceptable as inevitable or as the fault of the sufferer, and the medical attendant may find himself the scapegoat.

The most gracious and grateful of patients, amongst whom I am sure we may rank these novelists, have feelings towards our profession which are at best ambivalent. It is these emotions which make them unable to resist the temptation to tear away the veil of professional respectability and to reveal the ravening beast it conceals. At the denouement, "the face...of the previously suave Dr. Furness...was shining with sweat, his skin was mottled and his chin thrust out to show his teeth in a humorless grin;" Dr. Edmund Galley became a "frothing screaming homicidal maniac" and in the eyes of Dr. Kingston shone the "blood light." In these phrases the novelists stand more starkly revealed than their characters: they are hitting back at those who have unwittingly slighted them in the past and avenging critical comments on their steadily increasing weight and on their habits of eating, drinking, and smoking to excess.

I have attempted to present a picture of the medical profession as reflected in a small and specialized sample of contemporary literature. The portrait is, of course, outmoded, because the National Health Service has changed the face of medical practice in this country and these changes have not yet influenced the detective novel; possibly the authors of such works earn incomes which enable them to remain private patients. Nevertheless I submit that there are points in this analysis which are instructive. The novelist makes a sharp distinction between the general practitioner and the specialist, a division which has been unhappily accentuated by the rigid framework of the National Health Service replacing the profession's previously elastic structure. In his view, the specialist adopts a cold scientific attitude to his patients; while the general practitioner, although rated as intellectually inferior, is a warm-hearted friendly character. I have already pointed out the twofold nature of the patients' feelings towards the profession of medicine: admiring gratitude for the friend in need going hand in hand with rebellious dislike for the carping authoritarian who sees him in his unguarded moments and denies him his pleasures. By an unjust dichotomy the novelist diverts the first emotion to the general practitioner and the second to the specialist. The popular identification of the specialist with "science" contributes to this schism: the Englishman is properly suspicious of science and dreads the thought of being made the subject of experiment. The old-fashioned family practitioner, he believes, is as ignorant of the first as he would be innocent of the second. In these emotions we may discern an atavistic longing for the medicine of the witch-doctor—a desire to evade responsibility for one's own ill health, to have done with the tedium of rational explanations, and

to surrender to the narcotic charms of incantations, spells, and sacrifices.

From this we are driven to the conclusion that the public's choice of doctor is dictated by the same considerations that inspired a cartoon in *Punch* in 1884, when a now classic phrase was first used:

"What sort of doctor is he?"

"Oh, well, I don't know much about his ability; but he's got a very good bedside manner."

As Dr. Scott noted, there is usually some connection between what goes on within an occupation and what is described in popular literature. There is an awareness of the influence of specialization within occupations and the attractions specializations may hold for persons with differing personalities. Thus all popular statements about occupations should be examined with some care, because often they reinforce what is believed to be true about an occupation; in fact they may even influence the behavior of the persons within the occupation itself who find themselves endeavoring to live up to aspects of the popular stereotype, particularly when they are portrayed in a very estimable light.

The distinction between the real and the ideal may be viewed from another point of view: that of the would-be medical practitioner still undergoing formal training at medical school. How does the medical student reconcile his early idealistic, altruistic notions about the medical profession with the realities of medical school work? Or with the need for scientific objectivity in dealing with the patient? How does anyone in an occupation reconcile the unrealistic expectations often associated with that occupation and what, in fact, is encountered in the day-by-day carrying out of the occupational role? Howard Becker and Blanche Geer discuss this problem and note that one way of maintaining a sense of integrity is for the student to postpone the ultimate application of his idealistic notions until the time when the occupation is actually being practiced. In the meantime, while he is learning about the occupation, the student sets aside some of these nobler notions while he pursues the grubby business of learning how to become a medical practitioner. The future is seen as a time when he will have an opportunity to control his own activities far more fully, when it will be possible to adhere more closely to many occupational expectations than has seemed possible during the formal occupational learning period.

Howard S. Becker and Blanche Geer (Medicine)

It makes some difference in a man's performance of his work whether he believes

Reprinted from "The Fate of Idealism in Medical School," *American Sociological Review*, 23, No. 1 (February 1958), 50–56. Used by permission of the American Sociological Association.

wholeheartedly in what he is doing or feels that in important respects it is a fraud, whether he feels convinced that it is a good thing or believes that it is not really of much use after all. The distinction we are making is the one people have in mind when they refer, for example, to their calling as a "noble profession" on the one hand or a "racket" on the other. In the one case they idealistically proclaim that their work is all that it claims on the surface to be; in the other they cynically concede that it is first and foremost a way of making a living and that its surface pretensions are just that and nothing more. Presumably, different modes of behavior are associated with these perspectives when wholeheartedly embraced. The cynic cuts corners with a feeling of inevitability while the idealist goes down fighting. *The Blackboard Jungle* and *Not as a Stranger* are only the most recent in a long tradition of fictional portrayals of the importance of this aspect of a man's adjustment to his work.

Professional schools often receive a major share of the blame for producing this kind of cynicism—and none more than the medical school. The idealistic young freshman changes into a tough, hardened, unfeeling doctor; or so the popular view has it. Teachers of medicine sometimes rephrase the distinction between the clinical and pre-clinical years into one between the "cynical" and "pre-cynical" years. Psychological research supports this view, presenting attitude surveys which show medical students year by year scoring lower on "idealism" and higher on "cynicism."[1] Typically, this cynicism is seen as developing in response to the shattering of ideals consequent on coming face-to-face with the realities of professional practice.

In this paper, we attempt to describe the kind of idealism that characterizes the medical freshmen and to trace both the development of cynicism and the vicissitudes of that idealism in the course of the four years of medical training. Our main themes are that though they develop cynical feelings in specific situations directly associated with their medical school experience, the medical students never lose their original idealism about the practice of medicine; that the growth of both cynicism and idealism are not simple developments, but are instead complex transformations; and that the very notions "idealism" and "cynicism" need further analysis, and must be seen as situational in their expressions rather than as

stable traits possessed by individuals in greater or lesser degree. Finally, we see the greater portion of these feelings as being collective rather than individual phenomena.

Our discussion is based on a study we are now conducting at a state medical school,[2] in which we have carried on participant observation with students of all four years in all of the courses and clinical work to which they are exposed. We joined the students in their activities in school and after school and watched them at work in labs, on the hospital wards, and in the clinic. Often spending as much as a month with a small group of from five to fifteen students assigned to a particular activity, we came to know them well and were able to gather information in informal interviews and by overhearing the ordinary daily conversation of the group.[3] In the course of

[1] Leonard D. Eron, "Effect of Medical Education on Medical Students," *Journal of Medical Education,* 10 (October 1955), 559–566.

[2] This study is sponsored by Community Studies, Inc., of Kansas City, Missouri, and is being carried on at the University of Kansas Medical School, to whose dean, staff, and students we are indebted for their wholehearted cooperation. Professor Everett C. Hughes of the University of Chicago is director of the project.

[3] The technique of participant observation has not been fully systematized, but some approaches to this have been made. See, for example, Florence R. Kluckhohn, "The Participant Observer Technique in Small Communities," *American Journal of Sociology,* 45 (November 1940), 331–343; Arthur Vidich, "Participant Observation and the Collection and Interpretation of Data," *ibid.,* 60 (January 1955), 354–360; William Foote Whyte, "Observational Field-Work Methods," in Maria Jahoda, Morton Deutsch, and Stuart W. Cook (eds.), *Research Methods in the Social Sciences* (New York: Dryden Press, 1951), II, pp. 393–514; and *Street Corner Society,* Enlarged Edition (Chicago: University of Chicago Press, 1955), pp. 279–358; Rosalie Hankey Wax, "Twelve Years Later: An Analysis of Field Experience," *American Journal of Sociology,* 63 (September 1957), 133–142; Morris S. Schwartz and Charlotte Green Schwartz, "Problems in Participant Observation," *ibid.,* 60 (January 1955), 343–353; and Howard S. Becker and Blanche Geer, "Participant Observation and Interviewing: A Comparison," *Human Organization* (forthcoming). The last item represents the first of a projected series of papers attempting to make explicit the operations involved in this method. For a short description of some techniques used in this study, see Howard S. Becker, "Interviewing Medical Students," *American Journal of Sociology,* 62 (September 1956), 199–201.

our observation and interviewing we have gathered much information on the subject of idealism. Of necessity, we shall have to present the very briefest statement of our findings with little or no supporting evidence.[4] The problem of idealism is, of course, many-faceted and complex and we have dealt with it in a simplified way, describing only some of its grosser features.[5]

THE FRESHMEN

The medical students enter school with what we may think of as the idealistic notion, implicit in lay culture, that the practice of medicine is a wonderful thing and that they are going to devote their lives to service to mankind. They believe that medicine is made up of a great body of well-established facts that they will be taught from the first day on and that these facts will be of immediate practical use to them as physicians. They enter school expecting to work industriously and expecting that if they work hard enough they will be able to master this body of fact and thus become good doctors.

In several ways the first year of medical school does not live up to their expectations. They are disillusioned when they find they will not be near patients at all, that the first year will be just like another year of college. In fact, some feel that it is not even as good as college because their work in certain areas is not as thorough as courses in the same fields in undergraduate school. They come to think that their courses (with the exception of anatomy) are not worth much because, in the first place, the faculty

4 A fuller analysis and presentation of evidence will be contained in a volume on this study now being prepared by the authors in collaboration with Everett C. Hughes and Anselm L. Strauss.

5 Renee Fox has shown how complex one aspect of this whole subject is in her analysis of the way medical students at Cornell become aware of and adjust to both their own failure to master all available knowledge and the gaps in current knowledge in many fields. See her "Training for Uncertainty," in Robert K. Merton, George G. Reader, and Patricia L. Kendall (eds.). *The Student Physician: Introductory Studies in the Sociology of Medical Education* (Cambridge: Harvard University Press, 1957), pp. 207–241.

(being Ph.D.'s) know nothing about the practice of medicine, and, in the second place, the subject matter itself is irrelevant, or as the students say, "ancient history."

The freshmen are further disillusioned when the faculty tells them in a variety of ways that there is more to medicine than they can possibly learn. They realize it may be impossible for them to learn all they need to know in order to practice medicine properly. Their disillusionment becomes more profound when they discover that this statement of the faculty is literally true.[6] Experience in trying to master the details of the anatomy of the extremities convinces them that they cannot do so in the time they have. Their expectation of hard work is not disappointed; they put in an eight-hour day of classes and laboratories, and study four or five hours a night and most of the weekend as well.

Some of the students, the brightest, continue to attempt to learn it all, but succeed only in getting more and more worried about their work. The majority decide that, since they can't learn it all, they must select from among all the facts presented to them those they will attempt to learn. There are two ways of making this selection. On the one hand, the student may decide on the basis of his own uninformed notions about the nature of medical practice that many facts are not important, since they relate to things which seldom come up in the actual practice of medicine; therefore, he reasons, it is useless to learn them. On the other hand, the student can decide that the important thing is to pass his examinations and, therefore, that the important facts are those which are likely to be asked on an examination; he uses this as a basis for selecting both facts to memorize and courses for intensive study. For example, the work in physiology is dismissed on both of these grounds, being considered neither relevant to the facts of medical life nor important in terms of the amount of time the faculty devotes to it and the number of examinations in the subject.

A student may use either or both of

6 Compare Fox' description of student reaction to this problem at Cornell (*op. cit.,* pp. 209–221).

these bases of selection at the beginning of the year, before many tests have been given. But after a few tests have been taken, the student makes "what the faculty wants" the chief basis of his selection of what to learn, for he now has a better idea of what this is and also has become aware that it is possible to fail examinations and that he therefore must learn the expectations of the faculty if he wishes to stay in school. The fact that one group of students, that with the highest prestige in the class, took this view early and did well on examinations was decisive in swinging the whole class around to this position. The students were equally influenced to become "testwise" by the fact that, although they had all been in the upper range in their colleges, the class average on the first examination was frighteningly low.

In becoming test-wise, the students begin to develop systems for discovering the faculty wishes and learning them. These systems are both methods for studying their texts and short-cuts that can be taken in laboratory work. For instance, they begin to select facts for memorization by looking over the files of old examinations maintained in each of the medical fraternity houses. They share tip-offs from the lectures and offhand remarks of the faculty as to what will be on the examinations. In anatomy, they agree not to bother to dissect out subcutaneous nerves, reasoning that it is both difficult and time-consuming and the information can be secured from books with less effort. The interaction involved in the development of such systems and short-cuts helps to create a social group of a class which had previously been only an aggregation of smaller and less organized groups.

In this medical school, the students learn in this way to distinguish between the activities of the first year and their original view that everything that happens to them in medical school will be important. Thus they become cynical about the value of their activities in the first year. They feel that the real thing—learning which will help them to help mankind—has been postponed, perhaps until the second year, or perhaps even farther, at which time they will be able again to act on idealistic premises. They believe that what they do in their later years in school under supervision will be about the same thing they will do, as physicians, on their own; the first year had disappointed this expectation.

There is one matter, however, about which the students are not disappointed during the first year: the so-called trauma of dealing with the cadaver. But this experience, rather than producing cynicism, reinforces the student's attachment to his idealistic view of medicine by making him feel that he is experiencing at least some of the necessary unpleasantness of the doctor's. Such difficulties, however, do not loom as large for the student as those of solving the problem of just what the faculty wants.

On this and other points, a working consensus develops in the new consolidated group about the interpretation of their experience in medical school and its norms of conduct. This consensus, which we call *student culture,*[7] focuses their attention almost completely on their day-to-day activities in school and obscures or sidetracks their earlier idealistic preoccupations. Cynicism, griping, and minor cheating become endemic, but the cynicism is specific to the educational situation, to the first year, and to only parts of it. Thus the students keep their cynicism separate from their idealistic feelings and by postponement protect their belief that medicine is a wonderful thing, that their school is a fine one, and that they will become good doctors.

LATER YEARS

The sophomore year does not differ greatly from the freshman year. Both the work load and anxiety over examinations probably increase. Though they begin some medical activities, as in their attendance at autopsies and particularly in their introductory course in physical diagnosis, most of what they do continues to repeat the pattern of the college science curriculum. Their attention still centers on the problem of getting through school by doing well in examinations.

[7] The concept of student culture is analyzed in some detail in Howard S. Becker and Blanche Geer, "Student Culture in Medical School," *Harvard Educational Review* (forthcoming).

During the third and fourth, or clinical years, teaching takes a new form. In place of lectures and laboratories, the students' work now consists of the study of actual patients admitted to the hospital or seen in the clinic. Each patient who enters the hospital is assigned to a student who interviews him about his illnesses, past and present, and performs a physical examination. He writes this up for the patient's chart, and appends the diagnosis and the treatment that he would use were he allowed actually to treat the patient. During conferences with faculty physicians, often held at the patient's bedside, the student is quizzed about items of his report and called upon to defend them or to explain their significance. Most of the teaching in the clinical years is of this order.

Contact with patients brings a new set of circumstances with which the student must deal. He no longer feels the great pressure created by tests, for he is told by the faculty, and this is confirmed by his daily experience, that examinations are now less important. His problems now become those of coping with a steady stream of patients in a way that will please the staff man under whom he is working, and of handling what is sometimes a tremendous load of clinical work so as to allow himself time for studying diseases and treatments that interest him and for play and family life.

The students earlier have expected that once they reach the clinical years they will be able to realize their idealistic ambitions to help people and to learn those things immediately useful in aiding people who are ill. But they find themselves working to understand cases as medical problems rather than working to help the sick, and memorizing the relevant available facts so that these can be produced immediately for a questioning staff man. When they make ward rounds with a faculty member they are likely to be quizzed about any of the seemingly countless facts possibly related to the condition of the patient for whom they are "caring."

Observers speak of the cynicism that overtakes the student and the lack of concern for his patients as human beings. This change does take place, but it is not produced solely by "the anxiety brought about by the presence of death and suffering."[8] The student becomes preoccupied with the technical aspects of the cases with which he deals because the faculty requires him to do so. He is questioned about so many technical details that he must spend most of his time learning them.

The frustrations created by his position in the teaching hospital further divert the student from idealistic concerns. He finds himself low man in a hierarchy based on clinical experience, so that he is allowed very little of the medical responsibility he would like to assume. Because of his lack of experience, he cannot write orders, and he receives permission to perform medical and surgical procedures (if at all) at a rate he considers far too slow. He usually must content himself with "mere" vicarious participation in the drama of danger, life, and death that he sees as the core of medical practice. The student culture accents these difficulties so that events (and especially those involving patients) are interpreted and reacted to as they push him toward or hold him back from further participation in this drama. He does not think in terms the layman might use.

As a result of the increasingly technical emphasis of his thinking the student appears cynical to the non-medical outsider, though from his own point of view he is simply seeing what is "really important." Instead of reacting with the layman's horror and sympathy for the patient to the sight of a cancerous organ that has been surgically removed, the student is more likely to regret that he was not allowed to close the incision at the completion of the operation, and to rue the hours that he must spend searching in the fatty flesh for the lymph nodes that will reveal how far the disease has spread. As in other lines of work, he drops lay attitudes for those more relevant to the way the event affects someone in his position.

This is not to say that the students lose

[8] Dana L. Farnsworth, "Some Observations on The Attitudes and Motivations of the Harvard Medical Student," *Harvard Medical Alumni Bulletin,* January, 1956, p. 34.

their original idealism. When issues of idealism are openly raised in a situation they define as appropriate, they respond as they might have when they were freshmen. But the influence of the student culture is such that questions which might bring forth this idealism are not brought up. Students are often assigned patients for examination and follow-up whose conditions might be expected to provoke idealistic crises. Students discuss such patients, however, with reference to the problems they create for the *student*. Patients with terminal diseases who are a long time dying, and patients with chronic diseases who show little change from week to week, are more likely to be viewed as creating extra work without extra compensation in knowledge or the opportunity to practice new skills than as examples of illness which raise questions about euthanasia. Such cases require the student to spend time every day checking on progress which he feels will probably not take place and to write long "progress" notes in the patient's chart although little progress has occurred.

This apparent cynicism is a collective matter. Group activities are built around this kind of workaday perspective, constraining the students in two ways. First, they do not openly express the lay idealistic notions they may hold, for their culture does not sanction such expression; second, they are less likely to have thoughts of this deviant kind when they are engaged in group activity. The collective nature of this "cynicism" is indicated by the fact that students become more openly idealistic whenever they are removed from the influence of student culture—when they are alone with a sociologist as they near the finish of school and sense the approaching end of student life, for example, or when they are isolated from their classmates and therefore are less influenced by this culture.[9]

They still feel, as advanced students, though much less so than before, that school is irrelevant to actual medical practice. Many of their tasks, like running laboratory tests on patients newly admitted

to the hospital or examining surgical specimens in the pathology laboratory, seem to them to have nothing to do with their visions of their future activity as doctors. As in their freshman year, they believe that perhaps they must obtain the knowledge they will need in spite of the school. They still conceive of medicine as a huge body of proven facts, but no longer believe that they will ever be able to master it all. They now say that they are going to try to apply the solution of the practicing M.D. to their own dilemma: learn a few things that they are interested in very well and know enough about other things to pass examinations while in school and, later on in practice, to know to which specialist to send difficult patients.

Their original medical idealism reasserts itself as the end of school approaches. Seniors show more interest than students in earlier years in serious ethical dilemmas of the kind they expect to face in practice. They have become aware of ethical problems laymen often see as crucial for the physician—whether it is right to keep patients with fatal diseases alive as long as possible, or what should be done if an influential patient demands an abortion—and worry about them. As they near graduation and student culture begins to break down as the soon-to-be doctors are about to go their separate ways, these questions are more and more openly discussed.

While in school, they have added to their earlier idealism a new and peculiarly professional idealism. Even though they know that few doctors live up to the standards they have been taught, they intend always to examine their patients thoroughly and to give treatment based on firm diagnosis rather than merely to relieve symptoms. This expansion and transformation of idealism appear most explicitly in their consideration of alternative careers, concerning both specialization and the kind of arrangements to be made for setting up practice. Many of their hypothetical choices aim at making it possible for them to be the kind of doctors their original idealism pictured. Many seniors consider specialty training so that they will be able to work in a limited field in which it will be more nearly pos-

9 See the discussion in Howard S. Becker, "Interviewing Medical Students," *op. cit.*

sible to know all there is to know, thus avoiding the necessity of dealing in a more ignorant way with the wider range of problems general practice would present. In the same manner, they think of schemes to establish partnerships or other arrangements making it easier to avoid a work load which would prevent them from giving each patient the thorough examination and care they now see as ideal.

In other words, as school comes to an end, the cynicism specific to the school situation also comes to an end and their original and more general idealism about medicine comes to the fore again, though within a framework of more realistic alternatives. Their idealism is now more informed although no less selfless.

DISCUSSION

We have used the words "idealism" and "cynicism" loosely in our description of the changeable state of mind of the medical student, playing on ambiguities we can now attempt to clear up. Retaining a core of common meaning, the dictionary definition, in our reference to the person's belief in the worth of his activity and the claims made for it, we have seen that this is not a generalized trait of the students we studied but rather an attitude which varies greatly, depending on the particular activity the worth of which is questioned and the situation in which the attitude is expressed.

This variability of the idealistic attitude suggests that in using such an element of personal perspective in sociological analysis one should not treat it as homogeneous but should make a determined search for subtypes which may arise under different conditions and have differing consequences. Such subtypes presumably can be constructed along many dimensions. There might, for instance, be consistent variations in the medical students' idealism through the four years of school that are related to their social class backgrounds. We have stressed in this report the subtypes that can be constructed according to variations in the object of the idealistic attitude and variations in the audience the person has in mind when he adopts the attitude. The

medical students can be viewed as both idealistic and cynical depending on whether one has in mind their view of their school activities or the future they envision for themselves as doctors. Further, they might take one or another of these positions depending on whether their implied audience is made up of other students, their instructors, or the lay public.

A final complication arises because cynicism and idealism are not merely attributes of the actor, but are as dependent on the person doing the attributing as they are on the qualities of the individual to whom they are attributed.[10] Though the student may see his own disregard of the unique personal troubles of a particular patient as proper scientific objectivity, the layman may view this objectivity as heartless cynicism.[11]

Having made these analytic distinctions, we can now summarize the transformations of these characteristics as we have seen them occurring among medical students. Some of the students' determined idealism at the outset is reaction against the lay notion, of which they are uncomfortably aware, that doctors are money-hungry cynics; they counter this with an idealism of similar lay origin stressing the doctor's devotion to service. But this idealism soon meets a setback, as students find that it will not be relevant for a while, since medical school has, it seems, little relation to the practice of medicine, as they see it. As it has not been refuted, but only shown to be temporarily beside the point, the students "agree" to set this idealism aside in favor of a realistic approach to the problem of getting through school. This approach, which we have labeled as the cynicism specific to the school experience, serves as protection for the earlier grandiose feelings about medicine by postponing their exposure to reality to a distant future. As

[10] See Philip Selznick's related discussion of fanaticism in *TVA and the Grass Roots* (Berkeley: University of California Press, 1953), pp. 205–213.

[11] George Orwell gives the layman's side in his essay, "How the Poor Die" in *Shooting an Elephant and Other Essays* (London: Secker and Warburg, 1950), pp. 18–32.

that future approaches near the end of the four years and its possible mistreatment of their ideals moves closer, the students again worry about maintaining their integrity, this time in actual medical practice. They use some of the knowledge they have gained to plan careers which, it is hoped, can best bring their ideals to realization.

We can put this in propositional form by saying that when a man's ideals are challenged by outsiders and then further strained by reality, he may salvage them by postponing their application to a future time when conditions are expected to be more propitious.

So far, in our discussion of occupational images and norms we have made considerable use of examples from medical occupations, but certainly these forms of professional control are not confined to highly professionalized occupations. All occupations have associated with them certain normative expectations and certain images held by persons within and without the occupations. In the next example, of a somewhat less professionalized occupation—school teaching—we focus on the concept of professionalism; that is, the advocacy of a set of attitudes and behaviors believed to be appropriate to a particular occupation. Professionalism is ordinarily emphasized by occupational associations; certainly the school teachers, in their attempts at professionalization, have become increasingly concerned with the problem of defining the essential ingredients of a professional occupation and of drawing distinctions between what is and what is not professional conduct. In his discussion F. J. C. Seymour notes that, essentially, professionalism does not describe or exhibit what is, but rather what ought to be; it cannot be achieved through external coercion, from whatever source, but only through the teachers' dedicated pursuit of excellence.

F. J. C. Seymour (Teaching)

John Braine in his book, *Room at the Top,* has this interesting passage:

He left us to our own devices; he didn't give a damn how the work was done as long as it was finished when we promised, and he refused to be bothered with details.... We were a team of professionals, not a collection of adding machines.

While the book as a whole is no advertisement for the ethical values of the professional worker, the passage quoted becomes rather significant when we think over the problem of what "professional status" really means.

Any consideration of the problem of professional status among teachers must at the outset take into account the significant changes in the concept of the word "profession" which have developed since theology, law and medicine first laid claim to the title. With the introduction of mass public education, the claim of the professional to an organized and specialized body of knowledge has been challenged by the emergence of the technician who can advance an identical claim. Not only that, but some present-day technicians are probably members of a union which controls standards and membership, sets fees or rates for services, and has a code of ethical relationships with customers, and whose members may or may not be self-employed, and so on.

The point of all this is that the time-honored definition of a professional person may have been good enough when the educated section of society was the very small minority. Now, with the spread of education, the customary criteria for determining

Reprinted from "What is Professionalism?", *The A.T.A. Magazine*, 43, No. 10 (June 1963), 20–23. Used by permission.

professional status have begun to lose their effectiveness.

Anomalies such as this have forced those who would define a profession into looking at the function of a professional person. Perhaps we could say that the professional deals intimately and at first hand with the vital and personal lives of people. Such a definition would include the theologian, the lawyer, the dentist, the doctor and the teacher, but would exclude the engineer, the architect and the electronics technician. In our search for an acceptable definition, also, we will need to examine carefully the time-honored tradition that the professional practices as a single autonomous unit and wonder what this notion does to the doctor who practices in a clinic, the lawyer who practices in a firm, and the teacher who practices in a school. If all of the foregoing does nothing else than to tell us that attempts to define a profession in terms of characteristics can easily become an exercise in semantics, it will have served its purpose.

Within the rationale of a concern for the developing or changing concept of professionalism among teachers, we can set down in a rather naive fashion some simple characteristics of a professional person which may be more sensible than the classical listing we have so far considered.

1. A teacher possesses a body of knowledge and skills related to and essential for the business of teaching.
2. A teacher is prepared to make judgments in his capacity as a teacher and to take appropriate action if necessary.
3. A teacher is responsible for the consequences of his judgments and actions.
4. A teacher places primary emphasis on his function to serve society.
5. A teacher works with his colleagues in developing and enforcing standards which are basic requirements for the continuous improvement of his profession and in his personal practice observes such standards.
6. A teacher engages in a continuing search for new knowledge and skill.
7. A teacher practices his profession on a full-time basis.

To continue our examination of whatever distinction exists between the professional teacher and other workers, we turn next to what appears to be the priceless characteristic of professional practice, that is, the manner in which the teacher accepts and carries out his responsibilities. Within the limits imposed by working as a member of an education team, a teacher must do his own work and make his own decisions. He must see to it that his work is done, that it is done on time, and that it is always done to the best of his ability. It is clear that it is within this framework that a teacher must function if a real and not a fancied profession of teaching is to emerge among occupational groups. Teachers are probably farther away from real professionalism at this time than they would ever care to admit.

It would be interesting to canvass teachers' opinions on a number of questions related to the teaching job, because honest answers might reveal that there is no consensus of opinion among them on some rather significant aspects of the role and responsibility of a professional teacher.

Does a professional teacher require close supervision and direction?

Does a professional teacher accept that he is a fellow-worker on a team of co-workers?

Does a professional teacher regard himself as an employer? Does he ever reach the point at which he will remind his superiors that they as well as he are members of a team and that the line-staff concepts of business and industry are most inappropriate in teaching?

Does the professional teacher believe that he works by the hour? Does he work to "rule"—8:30–4:10—five days a week, 200 days a year?

Does the professional teacher believe that he must accept responsibility? Does he think that he can and ought to pass responsibility along to others in his staff?

Is a professional teacher concerned continuously about the progress of his students, about the methods of instruction he uses and about the total effect on others of his professional practice?

Does a professional teacher constantly seek to improve his practice or does he reach a point at which he can rest on his academic and professional preparation?

This last is one of the most embarrassing of all questions. To answer it the teacher must determine whether he is really ready and anxious to try other methods and other approaches, whether he reads professional literature, whether he is interested, or ought to be interested in such activities as specialist councils, conventions, institutes, seminars, staff meetings. He must wrestle with the problem of how much of his own time and money he is willing to spend on such avenues of professional improvement. He has got to ask himself whether he resists change simply because it is inconvenient; whether he is objective and scientific in approaching the problems which develop in his classroom; whether he is really interested in knowing what educational psychology has to say about the way in which pupils learn. This is a question that is particularly vexing to the teacher who believes that he has taught and that the students have learned when he lectures or reads and admonishes.

Does a professional teacher believe that he ought to contribute to the skill and knowledge of his profession? Does he believe that research is applicable to teaching, or does he think that it is too technical for teachers to attempt? Does he believe that educational research has little to offer by way of improvement in teaching methods? Does he believe that the way in which he was taught and the way in which he teaches cannot be improved?

No consideration of the problem of professional status can be complete without a hard look at what we appear to be in the society in which we flourish. At the best, trying to see ourselves as others see us is a speculative exercise. Do we believe that our public sees us as *The Edmonton Journal* does? Do we think that typical coffee party patter provides a composite picture of teachers and teaching? Closer to home and even more unsettling is what teachers think about other teachers and teaching. If we are honest with ourselves, the pictures others have of us, our public image, is none too flattering.

Regardless of the reasons for this unfortunate situation, we must address ourselves to the problem of correcting what we believe to be a mistaken impression. Let us look to the root of our problem and see what there is to be seen.

John Kenneth Galbraith in his *The Affluent Society* says that these are the days when men of all social disciplines and all political faiths seek the comfortable and the accepted; when men of controversy are disturbing influences; when originality is taken to be a mark of instability. These are all negative thoughts which cannot but strike an uncouth note in the world where positive thinking is and must be without price.

There are many hazards in trying to make our schools all things to all people and maybe there is not too much which we can do about a problem of such magnitude.

But there is one problem about which we can do something and that is the attitude of the teacher to the learner. A reluctant teacher is a dead hand on the living body of education. He is the one who holds a certificate and a contract, but is at odds with the ethics, the objectives, the responsibility, and the nobility of his profession. We must watch this sort of teacher because he or the group to which he belongs can lead us to regard teaching as a job, with tenure, to be performed within stated hours.

This is not to say that a professional person, a good teacher, is not concerned with demands on his time. He should resist and continue to resist regimentation of his services and attempts to reduce his professional service to a piecework basis. Any professional teacher worthy of the name knows and expects that he will often, if not most of the time, work many more hours than his school is open, but he will not tolerate a stated requirement that this is a condition of employment.

We will have failed miserably and utterly to get across to our publics what a teacher is and what a teacher does if we are unable to show people what the nature of the teaching task is. And for this sorry state of affairs we will have ourselves as individuals, school boards, teacher education institutions, and our own professional organization to blame. If we are to right this abominable state, we must do these things.

We must bring home to the public in a completely convincing manner that only the best should be admitted to teaching and that present-day teacher education makes better teachers.

We must convince ourselves that emergency or minimal preparation is not good enough.

We must make it commonly known that teaching is hard and rewarding work.

We must be prepared to evaluate our performance and have the courage to admit that ways must be found to reward superior and excellent performance.

We must learn to police ourselves, to isolate and identify the obvious neurotic and the incompetent itinerant who riddle our ranks.

We must take a fresh and bold look at our obsession with tenure and fringe benefits and our accelerating drive toward professional salaries. We may not longer be able to hold the best from the professional and from the union disciplines.

We must subject our stereotyped concept of teaching, of the school day, and of the school year to the shock of brutal reappraisal so that we cannot be effectively charged with attempt-ing to preserve the status quo in a period of rapid change.

We must be prepared to admit technological assistance and strive to utilize the peculiar talents of teachers as teachers—not as technicians, record keepers, clerks, and supply-doler-outers.

We must learn to strive for excellence—in our performance and in our students' performance. It is this last requirement which means really more than all the rest I have said put together. We need more efficient teaching—based more on psychological principles and less on gimmickry.

Professionalism is a state of mind, not a reality. Neither statute nor regulation, neither code nor shibboleth will make a teacher a professional. If we are to pursue the cult of excellence, we will need a degree of dedication, an expenditure of money and energy and intellect, the like of which we have only the faintest notion at this time.

Codes of Conduct

We turn now to a consideration of quite formal occupational controls. In their most highly developed form these "codes of ethics" touch on what is considered right and wrong within an occupation. Ethical codes, per se, have been more often associated with the most highly professionalized occupations; of late, however, some occupations bent upon upgrading their status have deliberately explored the introduction of formal ethical codes in the belief that such public statements would not only engender greater occupational conformity, but also bring about greater public respect and support. Civil legal codes governing the conduct of occupational affairs are known to have existed at least 4,000 years ago, and professional codes developed by medical practitioners were recorded about 2,500 years ago.[*] The principles expressed in the Oath of Hippocrates deal with many of the same matters as do present-day medical codes.[†] These were, and are, codifications of basic ideals, among them significantly the ideal of devotion to a calling to be of service. According to Jeffery, "One of the marks of a profession is a code of ethics. A profession involves a sense of service and responsibility to the community, and the conduct required of a professional man is above that required of other men."[‡]

[*] Leake, *op. Cit.*, pp. 11 and 18.

[†] *Ibid.*, p. 20.

[‡] C. Ray Jeffery, with the collaboration of E. Eugene Davis and Henry H. Foster, Jr., "The Legal Profession" in E. J. Davis, *et al., Society and The Law* (New York: Free Press of Glencoe, Inc., 1962), p. 345. Chapter 9 in this work contains a useful discussion of legal ethics.

As Carr-Saunders and Wilson have indicated, what is distinguishing historically is

> ...that the observance among them [priests and gentlemen] of certain standards of conduct was largely secured by the mere pressure of opinion and tradition and without the aid of penal sanctions. In the case of the rules of professional conduct, which are largely an adaptation of the standards of the priest and the gentleman to the requirements of certain vocations in present-day life, the same is true.§

Fundamentally, professional codes are group-inspired and sanctioned.** They make explicit the desired kinds of occupational relations between practitioners and clients, among fellow practitioners, and in regard to the public, and they are ostensibly designed to protect all concerned.†† We must also recognize that along with codes go less formal expressions—"understanding," "taboos," "tricks of the trade," etc., which may be equally sacred and compelling.

Interest among the social sciences in formal codes of conduct goes back some time. Durkheim wrote a book about them,‡‡ and in 1922 the American Academy of Political and Social Science devoted most of one issue of *The Annals* to an exposition of ethical problems in 18 occupations.§§ To cite one example, some jurists at that time were raising the question of whether or not codes of conduct ought to be developed for judges. It may be difficult to recall that there was a time when such concerns were expressed about one of the more eminent branches of the legal profession, yet this indicates something about the evolution of an occupation. What are today's accepted occupational standards, may have been, a few decades ago, matters of great controversy. The particular article in question was written by E. A. Harriman, and provided a discussion on the need for standards of ethics for judges.

§ A. M. Carr-Saunders and P. A. Wilson, *The Professions* (Oxford: The Clarendon Press, 1933), p. 421.
** Durkheim, *op. cit.*, pp. 5–10.
†† Caplow, *op. cit.*, p. 114.
‡‡ Durkheim, *op. cit.*
§§ *The Annals of the American Academy of Political and Social Science,* 101, No. 190 (May 1922).

E. A. Harriman (Judiciary)

Is there any need for a code of ethics for judges? The phrase "good behavior" is, of course, extremely vague. It is no vaguer, however, than the phrase in the articles of war by which an officer in the military service of the United States can be tried by court martial for "conduct unbecoming an officer and a gentleman." The vagueness of the phrase is by no means sufficient ground in itself for a more specific state-

Reprinted from "The Need for Standards of Ethics for Judges," *The Annals of the American Academy of Political and Social Science,* 101, No. 190 (May 1922), 30–32. Used by permission of the publisher.

ment of the duties of a judge. It is submitted, however, that a situation has recently arisen which calls for a clearer definition of a judge's duties in some particulars. At the last meeting of the American Bar Association, Mr. Hampton L. Carson, a former president of the Association, presented the following resolution upon the unanimous vote of the executive committee:

Resolved. That the conduct of Kenesaw M. Landis in engaging in private employment and accepting private emolument while holding the position of a Federal Judge and receiving a salary from the Federal Government, meets with our unqualified condemnation, as conduct unworthy of the office of Judge, derogatory to the dignity of the Bench, and undermining public confidence in the independence of the judiciary.

Mr. Carson then read Article IV of the Constitution of the American Bar Association which provides, among other things, that one of the objects of the Association shall be to "uphold the honor of the profession of the law." Of what use was it for the Association to prescribe canons of ethics for the regulation of the conduct of active practitioners, if it knew that a man on whom the judicial ermine had fallen had yielded to the temptations of avarice and private gain? That a Federal judge drawing his salary of $7,500 a year from the Federal Treasury should take $42,500 a year from an allied club of baseball payers was simply to drag the ermine in the mire. Although it must be that impeachment proceedings might not reach him, yet from every bar in this united country there rose up the withering scorn of the profession against the man who had stained its honor. Those who came to deliberate upon that which touches the honor of the profession would go away and hang their heads in shame if they did not rebuke such conduct.

The resolution of Mr. Carson was adopted by the Association. That the Association had a right to express its opinion, is unquestionable. The only body having jurisdiction to inquire into the conduct of that official, is Congress, but any organization is entitled to express its opinion to Congress and to urge any action it may desire. It is for Congress to decide what weight attaches to the different opinions so expressed. Now, as a matter of fact, Congress has had the benefit of the opinion of the American Bar Association, and of the opinion of the National Baseball Association and it has chosen to follow the latter.

It is only fair to assume that the inaction of Congress in the Landis case is due to the fact that the American people as a whole are more in sympathy with the standards of judicial conduct indorsed by the National Baseball Association than with those indorsed by the American Bar Association.

Need for Sovereign Power to Prescribe Standard of Judicial Ethics

Now, while the bar has no jurisdiction over the conduct of the bench, it is undoubtedly a great public misfortune when any judge so conducts himself as to receive the censure of the bar. There is no question as to what the judge in this particular case has done, but the baseball people think that what he has done is right, and the lawyers think that it is wrong. From the fact that Congress follows the opinion of the baseball magnates rather than that of the leaders of the bar, it is clear, either that the judgment of the bar is wrong, or else that its judgment is right but that the people at large have not been sufficiently educated to appreciate the standard of ethics upheld by the bar.

It seems highly desirable, therefore, that the sovereign power, which, in the case of the Federal judges, is the United States, should define more clearly the duties of a judge with reference to the acceptance of employment in other occupations. Whatever resolutions the bar may pass, it is useless to say that Judge Landis has violated any standard of judicial ethics, because no such standard has been prescribed, either by Congress or by the judges themselves, and it is not within the jurisdiction of the bar to prescribe a standard of ethics for the bench. That a proper standard of judicial ethics would prevent a judge from acting as Judge Landis has done is the opinion of most lawyers, but that there is not at the present time any such existing standard is absolutely proved by the action, or rather the inaction, of Congress, which clearly establishes the fact that, in popular opinion, Judge Landis has done nothing to justify his removal from the bench.

The function of the bar, therefore, in the matter of judicial ethics, must be educational, and education is a slow process. It would be unwise to make rules that are too general in regard to the performance by a judge of non-judicial work. The best practical method of dealing with this subject would be provide that a judge shall not engage in any other occupation without the consent of some administrative authority, such as, for example, the Chief Justice of the United States. The freedom of judges from all legislative and executive control is a freedom accompanied with responsibility. In most cases this responsibility is clearly recognized. If a particular judge is more influenced by his personal advantage than by the dignity of his office, some administrative control over that judge is required, and at present no such administrative control exists, while the remedy by impeachment, as the Landis case has shown, is entirely inadequate.

DEGENERATION OF THE IDEA OF SOVEREIGNTY

The Landis case is symptomatic of the degeneration of the idea of sovereignty portrayed by Laski in his theory of the multiple state. Under a monarchy, service of the sovereign is the most important function. Under our American democracy, it is clear that our democratic sovereign regards the management of moving pictures as of more importance than the management of the Treasury or the Post Office Department, and the administration of baseball as of more importance than the administration of justice. Mr. Carson speaks of "dragging the judicial ermine in the mire." As a matter of fact, the judicial ermine is simply used to dust off the home plate; which, to the people at large, seems a more important function than dusting off a law book. This degeneration of the idea of sovereignty is apparent in many ways. The other day a college professor was quoted as saying that any man who had more than 15 per cent of patriotism was a nuisance, asserting that 85 per cent of a citizen's loyalty should be devoted to other organizations than his country. *Panem et circenses* was the motto of the Roman populace when the Twelve Tables had been forgotten. Those who do not share Henry Ford's opinion that history is all bunk, may find an interesting precedent in Roman history as to the effect of a popular belief that amusements are more important than laws.

Today we expect the judiciary to exhibit exemplary behavior, occupational conduct of the very highest order; for example, we rarely concern ourselves with possible linkages between judges and unscrupulous figures in the world of sports. The occupation of judge has clearly undergone change in the direction of greater professionalization. The precise extent to which the explicit statement of ethical standards has done this is not readily ascertainable, but statements like Harriman's must have had their effect.

Turning to another occupation, however, we see a lesser degree of evolution. Writing in the same year and in the same publication, F. H. Newell noted that ideals associated with engineering did exist but did not always find expression in the conduct of engineers. He argued that a general code of ethics for all engineers might correct the situation, at the same time recognizing that some engineers felt such a code was a silly innovation. Newell pointed out that there were groups within engineering which had gone a long way toward the framing of explicit codes of conduct, citing in particular the electrical engineers.

There were, then, diametrically opposed views about the need for such statements within the engineering field, and the great difficulty that had tended to inhibit the adoption of formal codes was the fact that the field had been fragmented into a series of specializations, each with its own historical traditions. There seemed to be no singularly appropriate definitions of an engineer or of engineering. In the words of another engineer, "...a code of ethics becomes necessary not only to assist the mechanical engineer in his conduct, but to acquaint the world with what it may expect from a professional man, thus rendering the profession, as such, stable and recognized by society."*

Newell indicates the process by which one might go about constructing a code. He also makes the case for engineering as a profession (against those who argued engineering was not a profession) and projects the part that group association might take in this development.†

* C. W. Rice, "The Ethics of the Mechanical Engineer," *The Annals of the American Academy of Political and Social Science,* 101, No. 190, 73.

† Durkheim describes the inevitability of codifications arising out of group activity in modern industrialized society; see Durkheim, *op. cit.,* p. 24. For a more recent and detailed discussion of occupational code development see the Committee on Ethical Standards for Psychologists, *Ethical Standards for Psychologists* (Washington, D. C.: The American Psychological Association, 1953), pp. v–xi.

Frederick Haynes Newell (Engineering)

In its ideals the engineering profession is not surpassed by those of any other group of public servants. In practice, however, because these ideals are so altruistic, it has been found difficult to reduce them to a brief statement and to secure general agreement upon such statement. Most attempts to produce a brief code comparable with the Decalogue have resulted in little more than an expansion of the Golden Rule, such, for example, as is the code of ethics adopted by the American Society of Civil Engineers on September 2, 1914.

There has been much discussion by engineers of the need of adopting a comprehensive code in order that the ideals of the profession may be presented clearly to the young engineer. On the one hand, these efforts have been scoffed at; indeed, in the case of one of the national engineering societies, it was "decided that no gentleman needed a code of ethics, and that no code of ethics would make a gentleman out of a crook." At the other extreme, there are elaborate results, such as those of the American Institute of Electrical Engineers and other organizations, quoted by Daniel W. Mead.[1]

Reprinted from "Ethics of the Engineering Profession," *The Annals of the American Academy of Political and Social Science,* 101, No. 190 (May 1922), 76–82. Used by permission of the publisher.

[1] Daniel W. Mead, *Contracts, Specifications, and Engineering Relations* (New York: McGraw Hill Book Company, 1916).

The chief difficulty in agreeing upon and adopting a code of ethics for the entire engineering profession has arisen from the fact that there is little agreement, even among engineers, as to the meaning or limitations of the words "engineer" and "engineering," and of the word "profession" as applied to engineering. In the evolution of the English language, the word "engineer" has come into such common use and has been made to include so many different practices that it is now necessary to use some qualifying adjective in order to have a common understanding as to what is meant when using this term.

GRADATIONS OF THE TERM, ENGINEER

In contrast, there is little relative difference in conception when we speak about an architect. This is a term which applies to a rather limited body of professional men, and, moreover, it has been defined by law. In contrast with this, the word "engineer" as employed by a professional engineer has an entirely different meaning from that understood by the general public or as interpreted by court decision.

In Great Britain the engineer is a mechanic, and, in legal usage, is a man who operates an engine. The organizations of engineers in Great Britain are to a large extent comparable with trade unions in America. In the United States there are possibly a half-million men who, in common usage, are known as engineers, and yet none of whom would be eligible for membership in one of our great engineering societies. The engineer, as the word is popularly used, may be a mechanic, a tradesman, or a professional man. The division between these groups is broad, and it is almost impossible to draw a sharp line.

Some of the best known professional engineers in the United States, prominent in the affairs of technical engineering societies, are themselves business men as well as engineers, managing or controlling directly or indirectly large corporations which construct, build, or sell engineering works, machinery, or power. Many of the leaders have come up through the ranks, and at one time or another have been draftsmen or mechanics, and as such have been eligible for membership in labor unions, even if they have not actually taken out a card. Others, educated in the best engineering schools and for a time serving as professional engineers, have become business men and have gone into contracting or trade relations without losing their standing as professional engineers.

Yet, in spite of these uneven gradations, there is an attempt made at all times to hold before the eyes of the professional engineer certain standards of conduct which differentiate him from the business man, contractor or mechanic. He cannot go so far as the architects in acquiescing to the first rule of their code of ethics, which states that it is unprofessional for an architect "to engage directly or indirectly in any of the building trades." In fact the rigid adoption of such a rule might bring under the ban some of the most prominent members of the engineering profession, owners or partners in engineering corporations, nor has it been found practicable by engineers to follow the architects in their declaration that it is unprofessional to advertise. This drastic rule has been softened by the statement of the civil engineers that it is inconsistent with honorable and dignified bearing "to advertise in self-laudatory language, or in any other manner derogatory to the profession."

The ethical code of the engineer has been founded upon such long experience as has demonstrated that "honesty is the best policy." There may be, and doubtless are, many members of the profession who would prefer to consider that their ethics were purely altruistic and based upon the idealism of Kant, following his stern precepts of absolute devotion to duty and of self-negation. Such men there are in every profession, but the code of ethics has been evolved not by these stern idealists, but rather by the appeal to common sense and fair play, necessitated by the so-called practical conditions that surround the profession. Thus the civil engineers make the prohibition not against advertising but against carrying advertising to the point of self-laudation.

Because of the difficulty, found by the different branches of the engineering profession, in agreeing upon a common code, there has been a tacit agreement upon the point that the only way to perfect a code of engineering ethics is to follow the precedent of the British Institution, namely, to make decision upon specific questions as they arise, the body of decisions thus furnishing a code which it has been found impossible to write out and to agree upon in advance. Such decisions reveal the underlying principles and can be appealed to in other cases until these principles thus become firmly established in the minds of all concerned.

THE CASE METHOD OF CODE BUILDING

This so-called "case" or project method of building up a code has been put into practice by the American Institute of Consulting Engineers and by the American Association of Engineers. In both of these organizations, composed largely of civil engineers, a simple code has been adopted, and then, as specific cases arise which seem to need consideration, each of these has been considered on its merits and a decision published, stating, without giving names, the facts of the case and the conclusion reached by the Practice Committee. As these cases increase in number and cover more and more widely the conditions which occur in actual practice, there must result a better comprehension, not only of the ideals of the profession, but of the way in which these may be put into effect.

There are thus taken up and considered in succession, numerous questions regarding professional conduct as these arise between members or in daily contact with federal, state, or local officials and businessmen. The simpler personal matters are passed over quickly by the Practice Committee, but those involving the application of an important principle of ethics are given full consideration and are ultimately published without name. They thus form the basis for general discussion and become interwoven in the thought of engineers. The decisions result in a body of practice which in effect performs the function of a code of ethics, a code based upon positive or experimental data.

"It is certain that while experience has shown that an authorized and definite code of conduct is generally subversive of moral stamina through its absorption of personal responsibility, still ethics must be made work-a-day to a considerable degree, for they can then, if not slavishly followed, serve as guiding lights, or as points of departure, when a particular situation finds an individual unprepared by his own experience."

Of course, no code can satisfy all conditions. As has been stated, "Engineering, like war, is in practice a far more developed complex than when considered speculatively and coldly as a science. When it enters the world of commerce, it gathers the burdens of human nature. Its problems become those of business as well as those of the laboratory."[2]

ENGINEERING AS A PROFESSION

There has always been, and probably always will be, a wide difference of opinion as to whether or not engineering is a learned profession comparable to law, medicine, and the ministry. There are plenty of examples of devotion to ideals and of a purely professional attitude of mind in engineers comparable to that of any body of men in any one of the older professions. On the other hand, the advocates of the view that engineering is not a profession point to the facts, above noted, that the great body of men who are called engineers are by no means professional men, but are actively engaged

2 *Engineering Record,* March 17, 1917, p. 409.

in the ordinary business of life.

Various organizations of engineers have attempted from time to time to meet this condition, and, as they term it, "to raise the standard" of the profession. Great care is taken in passing upon the credentials offered and in admitting the applicants to full membership, with the idea that in so doing there will be segregated from the great mass of so-called engineers a rather select group who in their professional characteristics will be comparable to an equal number of members of one of the other professions. The principal difficulty, however, arises, as before indicated, in the fact that engineering is entering more and more definitely into the life and business of the ordinary citizen, so that the leaders in the profession often become drawn into executive positions, dealing in a large way with business affairs. Thus arises the anomalous situation in which leaders who may have passed through the professional stage of life have now evolved into businessmen and are conducting great corporate efforts, especially public utilities, along lines which, in the popular mind at least, are not compatible with the code of ethics which should be followed by the younger applicant for admission to the organization.

Engineering is a profession in the same sense that pure mathematics is a science, but the value of engineering to the human race is so great and so dependent upon practical application to everyday life that the profession, and the professional man if successful, becomes immersed in business relations.

GROUP ORGANIZATION AMONG ENGINEERS

The history of the organization of engineers is of interest, as illustrating the continual struggle between idealism on the one hand, which would produce a well-rounded code of ethics and, on the other, the practical considerations which have made such a code impossible of acceptance by all kinds of professional engineers. The first notable attempt at organization was made in the city of Boston and resulted in 1848 in what is now the oldest engineering society in the

United States—the Boston Society of Civil Engineers. This association is carefully guarded in its membership; it attempts to preserve the highest possible professional standards among a type of engineers and of people readily recognized, wherever met in any part of the world, as distinctly "New England." The traditional New England conscience and thoroughness have triumphed through all the decades and have set a model for other engineering organizations, for, on examining the constitutions adopted by nearly every subsequent society, it will be seen that the phraseology of the Boston society has formed the groundwork.

Next in time was the organization in New York in 1852 of the American Society of Civil Engineers, which followed upon the excellent precedents already established. This organization has grown steadily and has adhered largely to its early standards, rigidly holding to these and in effect excluding the great body of practicing engineers. It has thus forced the organization of many other rather specialized national societies, several of which have exceeded it in number of members.

It is to be noted that the Boston Society and that in New York were obliged even at that early date to use the qualifying word "civil" as separating the members not only from the military engineers but from the mechanical engineers, as well as from the engine runners, such as locomotive engineers, who in turn have formed the most powerful trade union of the country.

The tendency to restrict the use of the words "civil engineers" to a rather narrow group of men interested in bridges and other large structures, rivers and harbors, waterworks, sewage and roads, finally forced the rapidly widening groups of engineers who were interested in mechanical lines to form the American Society of Mechanical Engineers; and, because of the fashion thus set, the American Institute of Electrical Engineers then separated themselves from the other engineers. The mining men also found that the requirements for admission to the American Society of Civil Engineers were too restrictive, and they in turn formed the American Institute of Mining Engineers. The requirement for membership in the latter society was so different from that of the older American Society of Civil Engineers that for over a decade the older society refused to come under the same roof, largely because of the feeling that there was not sufficient restriction as regards professional standing in the great body of members of the society of miners.

Thus have been formed many national societies of civil engineers, as distinct from military engineers, divided by somewhat arbitrary technical lines, for the civil engineer frequently has to do with the mechanical and electrical devices or structures of the mechanical and electrical engineers, or vice versa. These divisions have arisen largely from the divergent views as to requirements for admission to the national society. At the same time many state organizations have been formed, largely political in character in the sense that the laws of each state, differing from those of its neighbors, necessitated consideration of engineering matters, such as drainage, road building, water works, and sewage, in their relation to the geographic and political entity of the state. These state societies have necessarily been organizations not of civil engineers alone but of men practicing the profession of engineering. They include in their membership a large proportion of so-called practical men, surveyors and others who have picked up the work and have been educated not in engineering schools but in the "college of hard knocks."

In each of the principal cities of the United States it has also been found desirable to bring together men who practic engineering, in order to increase acquaintance and to discuss engineering problems with particular reference to local conditions. There are also in each city small groups of members of the national societies, either meeting separately or occasionally cooperating with each other and with the local society of engineers, many of whose members are frequently not eligible for membership in the national organizations.

Thus, a list of engineering societies will include a dozen or more national organizations, a score or more of state engineering societies, and a hundred organizations, one or two in each of the principal cities, each with different standards, cooperating occasionally or competing for membership.

The listing of engineering societies is complicated by the fact that there are many organizations, some incorporated, of men who as in the case of the so-called "sanitary engineers" may or may not be engineers according to the definition accepted. Some of the "sanitary engineers" are simply successful plumbers who may or may not have had an education in the theory of engineering, but who are practical business men.

Need for Standards of Engineering Conduct

The reason for the creation of standards is evident from the brief review above given. The older, more conservative societies believe that it is of the highest importance to the public and to the profession that certain standards be set up and carefully observed. Their concern is mainly for creating and preserving a certain prestige and for rigidly excluding the applicants who do not meet this standard. At the same time, internally these older organizations are continually shaken and their growth and influence often reduced by the interminable struggle between the two factions, since the conservatives are continually trying to raise the standard as against the efforts of the progressives who are looking towards the wider influence of the larger society. On the part of these liberals it is urged that every man who is making a living by the practice of engineering should become a member and, as such, be educated and impressed with high standards by contact with men within the society, and not be forced to the alternative of joining a labor union if he desires to do his part toward improving the condition of his fellow engineer.

The reasons for the creation of the "standards" are those which underlie the ideals of the closed shop which, originated by the medical profession, have been adopted in large part by the lawyers and put into still wider effect by the labor unions, who have become most apt pupils in this regard. The engineering profession, as a whole, may be said to alternate between the ideals of an open, competitive business on the one hand, and, on the other, a restricted, licensed, or registered group, such as that of the lawyers and doctors, or the closed shop of the labor unions, each professing to seek the highest service to humanity through raising and maintaining certain group standards.

The kind of intellectual struggle indicated in the last selection needs to be explored further in its historical development. One engineer commented insightfully: "The real measure of progress in ethics is not the number of cases of unethical conduct detected and punished; the real measure is the evolution of clear principles of conduct accepted by a majority of engineers as right and just and worthy of support."* This same engineer, H. A. Wagner, records that the continuing discussion over one-quarter century about ethical standards within the occupation has generated so much interest that all but a small number of practitioners adhere rather closely to the prescriptions.† Nonetheless he does recognize the possibility for unscrupulous practitioners, motivated purely by self-interest, of undertaking professionally unethical activities by exploiting patterns devised to protect ethical standards. Wagner concludes that if we assess what has occurred in balance over the past several decades we are forced to recognize that one set of ethical problems has merely been traded for another—that there appears to be no significant eradication of these kinds of control problems.

* H. A. Wagner, "Principles of Professional Conduct in Engineering," *The Annals of the American Academy of Political and Social Science*, **297** (January 1955), 50.
† For a brief historical summary and bibliography dealing with ethical codes in several occupations see C. F. Taeusch, "Professional Ethics," in the *Encyclopaedia of the Social Sciences*, XII (New York: The Macmillan Company, 1934), 472–476.

H. A. Wagner (Engineering)

When the American Academy of Political and Social Science, in *The Annals* of May 1922, published a symposium on ethical standards of business and the professions, it showed that engineering had made measurable progress in defining professionalism and recognizing its ethical obligations, and also in reducing these first broad concepts to relatively "specific" principles of professional conduct. The symposium also revealed that scant progress had been made in the establishment of agencies to interpret, apply, and enforce these principles. Thirty-two years have elapsed, and the situation is little changed. Then, as now, engineering was hampered by the lack of an inclusive organization, universally recognized as its authorized spokesman, empowered to pass judgment on unethical conduct and punish offenders as the American Medical Association and their contituent state societies deal with unethical practice in their respective fields.[1]

Reprinted from "Principles of Professional Conduct in Engineering," *The Annals of the American Academy of Political and Social Science,* **297** (January 1955), pp. 46–52, *passim.* Used by permission of The American Academy of Political and Social Science and the American Association of Engineers.

[1] Engineers are represented by more than a hundred admirable national societies; preeminent among them are the Founder Societies, each representing one of the four major branches of engineering (civil, electrical, mechanical, mining and metallurgical). Since 1917 they have collaborated in certain types of activities through a series of agencies which they have created. Through some of these agencies, at intervals, other engineering societies have been loosely affiliated with the Founders. None of these agencies has ever been recognized by the public as the equivalent of the American Bar Association or the American Medical Association; consequently, none has ever been able to influence public opinion as do these two organizations, or use this force to discipline offenders against codes of ethics. Engineering's ethical codes, for example, require engineers to discourage the spreading of exaggerated statements regarding engineering, but the societies cannot deal summarily with offenders, as the American Medical Association chastises doctors who publicly endorse or seem to exploit new wonder drugs or therapy not fully tested or not approved by the profession.

CANONS OF ETHICS FOR ENGINEERS

Despite this fact, engineers have reached a certain accord in regard to ethical principles. Many of the national societies and numbers of state and local organizations have officially adopted the Canons of Ethics formulated by the Engineers' Council for Professional Development, an agency created by the Founder Societies in 1932. In 1947, the Council synthesized the major principles found in the ethical codes formulated by many of the leading societies. Many of the original codes were in operation in 1922, and some of these were published in *The Annals,* notably those of the American Institute of Electrical Engineers (which seems to have been the leader of the movement, with a code drafted in 1910 and officially adopted in 1912), the American Society of Civil Engineers, the American Society of Mechanical Engineers, and the American Association of Engineers. Two of these might more properly have been called "creeds" rather than "codes," as they were modeled after the Hippocratic Oath. Others referred to specific practices then too prevalent which were regarded as hurtful to the profession. Through the years the societies extended the coverage of their codes and revised "principles of professional conduct" as changing conditions of practice and new problems required. Nearly all the provisions of these codes could be classified under the headings found in the Canons of Ethics for Engineers adopted by the Engineers' Council for Professional Development, namely, obligations imposed by membership in a profession, and the engineer's relations with the public, with clients and employers, and with other engineers. A copy of the code is appended.

Not all the engineering societies have adopted the ECPD Canons of Ethics, but none of the adopted codes is at variance with the Canons. Some of the societies have found it advisable to retain codes drafted for and by their own members, because these codes deal in greater detail with problems which, if not peculiar to particular segments of the engineering profession, are at least more acute in these fields of practice. In certain branches of engineering, for instance, the ownership of engineering records and data may pose ethical problems of such complexity that a society may find it necessary to incorporate in its code of principles of professional conduct a section devoted to this aspect of ethics more detailed than is necessary in Canons of Ethics drafted for engineering societies in general. Other organizations, especially those composed of engineers engaged in a particular industry (automotive, refrigerating, illuminating, aeronautical engineering, and others), may adopt the Canons officially, or may consider that they have tacitly accepted these rules because most of their members belong to technical societies which have adopted the ECPD Canons of Ethics. Still other technical and industrial groups subscribe to the principles but believe that "moral responsibilities cannot be legislated" and rely upon constitutional provisions for dealing with members who "fail to be honest or live up to the code of any gentleman." It can be said that the societies are in accord with regard to fundamentals, but that there are practices denounced by the societies in their codes which are still defended by large numbers of engineers.

AMERICAN ASSOCIATION OF ENGINEERS

In the invitation to prepare this discussion of ethics in the engineering profession, the author was instructed to detail the work of at least one national and one local group. He has chosen to trace the movement in the American Association of Engineers, first of all because he is most familiar with the procedure in that organization. In the second place, three of the distinguished engineers who contributed to the 1922 symposium were members of this organization and the American Association of Engineers was the agency through which they worked to improve ethical standards.[2] The third rea-

son for choosing the AAE to exemplify the evolution of ethical standards is that two of its original aims, stated in the preamble to its constitution, are basic elements in professional ethics. The AAE announced that it intended to "stimulate public service in the profession" and "to promote unity in the profession." In the first aim the AAE recognized the most distinctive characteristic of a profession—its obligation to serve society. In the second, it recognized an equally important characteristic, the principle that engineers in all stages of professional development are by the very nature of a profession under obligation to deal fairly with each other for the good of the profession and its members. The fourth and most compelling reason for the author's choice of the AAE is the fact that the association's campaign was not fortuitous; it was well planned and carried forward in stages by leaders who were fully aware of the importance of timing.

Engineering's first code

Morris Llewellyn Cooke, well known for his work in later years in the Rural Electrification Administration, was tactician of the movement. It was he, in 1918, who called for a "true-blue and inspiring code of ethics for engineers." He specified that it should be the work of one man, not of a committee, because "committee work is accomplished to a greater or less degree by compromise and we do not want compromise in ethics." At the same time he said:

Until we engineers can place the service of humanity as the significant and dominant plank in our platform, the profession will continue to have the status of the hired servant, and veer here and there as the winds of business and other special interests may dictate....

His suggestion was adopted, and Isham Randolph wrote the code which appeared in the 1922 *Annals,* reprinted in the Appendix of the present article.

Practice Committee codification.

At Mr. Cooke's suggestion the Association created a Practice Committee to which were referred real and hypothetical questions concerning the ethics of specific practices. These questions were considered by the Practice

[2] These three engineers were: Morris Llewellyn Cooke, tactician of the AAE campaign for higher ethical standards; Frederick Haynes Newell (known as Father of the Reclamation Service), President of AAE in 1919–20; H. W. Clausen, in whose memory the Clausen Medal is awarded for "distinguished service for the welfare of engineers."

Committee, and some of them were assigned to state and local chapters of the Association for study and discussion. The decisions of the Practice Committee and reports from the chapters were published in the Association's journal. By every possible means the Association stimulated the interest of its members in questions of ethics. This was in line with the plan made by Mr. Cooke who, in 1920, in an article in *Professional Engineer* (the Association's official publication) said:

Ethical conduct is such as has received more or less general sanction. This means that conduct which at one time or place may receive very generous approval at another time or in a different locality may be generally considered reprehensible.... Higher standards only become the rules for conduct when through education they have become accepted as proper by a sufficiently large or influential element within the constituency....

Mr. Cooke recommended that:

...the Practice Committee should subdivide the cases submitted to it into at least two classes: (a) Those upon which the best sentiment of the profession is now capable of concrete expression, and (b) those which require special analysis and protracted study and discussion in order to develop what is our best thought.

At this time, too, Mr. Cooke warned against any "effort at rigorous discipline." He said that the educational work of the Practice Committee was its most valuable contribution, and that clarifying an engineer's relationship and responsibilities would count more at that time than trials for unprofessional conduct. The questions submitted to the Practice Committee involved many practices detrimental to engineers, to the profession, and to society, but they were accepted or common practices, and presumably in harmony with existing principles of ethics. By provoking discussion of these practices harmful to the profession, the American Association of Engineers led its members to acceptance of higher standards of ethics.

During this period C. F. Taeusch, associate professor of philosophy at Iowa State University, became the adviser of the Practice Committee. Dr. D. B. Steinman, eminent and internationally known bridge engi-

neer of New York, directed the work of codifying Practice Committee decisions for publication in *Professional Engineer* in 1923 (with identifying names of persons or places deleted). In 1927 the Association issued a booklet entitled *The Engineer and His Ethics,* which contained this codification of Practice Committee decisions, the Isham Randolph Code of Ethics, and the Vow of Service, written by Dr. D. B. Steinmann— all reprinted in full in the Appendix. This booklet was distributed to AAE chapters and to engineering schools. Thus the Association followed the advice of Mr. Cooke in clarifying for engineers and future engineers their relationships and responsibilities.

Booklet for the public

Realizing that the public had an important though unrecognized interest in the ethical standards of engineering and a direct influence upon those standards, the Association in 1929 brought out a booklet prepared by its Committee on Services and Fees of Practicing Engineers, entitled *How To Employ and Use the Services of Practicing Engineers.* This booklet struck directly at the unwise practice of engaging engineering services on the basis of competitive bids. In addition to information on legitimate methods of engaging the services of engineers, the booklet contained a typical form of agreement, a schedule of minimum recommended fees, and the Code of Practice of the American Society of Civil Engineers, adopted by that organization in 1927. The Association used the ASCE Code rather than its own 1924 codification of Practice Committee cases "in the interest of uniformity and to avoid duplication of effort."

OTHER NATIONAL SOCIETIES

Since 1927 many of the national societies have developed and published manuals of practice much more comprehensive and detailed than the AAE's booklet on employment and use of the services of practicing engineers. Each society emphasizes problem areas which are of special concern to its members. Every national organization is using its resources to "clarify relationships and obligations" of engineers and to bring about acceptance of principles which prescribe practices beneficial to engineers, the profession, and the public.

Enforcement Practices

Unlike the professions of law and medicine engineering cannot enforce its codes by drastic means, for reasons which were stated in the beginning of this article. Each society must handle violations of its code by its own members. Although a Judiciary Committee was created in 1922 by the American Association of Engineers to serve as a court of appeal from decisions of the Practice Committee and given authority to suspend or expel members who violated the code, it has considered few cases. Other societies have similar agencies, but if they have resorted to rigorous discipline of violators of ethical codes, it has been done with such discretion and dignity that few members of the societies have been aware of the action.

Suspension or expulsion from membership in a major engineering society is a terrific rebuke, but it may have little effect on the individual's future practice of engineering, unless the action is widely publicized. The fear of suspension or expulsion may be a strong deterrent against unethical conduct among members who have joined national organizations for prestige and "contacts." For mercenary reasons they cherish the respect of top-ranking consultants and of engineers eminent in private practice or in industry. Such punishment as can be meted out by the societies is not a strong deterrent against unethical conduct on the part of less sensitive or less ambitious men. The man who is prone to unethical conduct is likely to be callous. He may have a relatively small but satisfactory field of practice in an area where the public generally and most of the businessmen who are potential users of his services know little of the great national engineering organizations. The societies have no disciplinary power over non-members.

Unethical engineers are protected in some degree by the ethical obligation of engineers to refrain from "harming" another member of the profession. Engineers who have seen signs of incompetency or dishonesty are reluctant to initiate action unless the evidence amounts to almost incontrovertible proof, or the element of real and present public danger is so apparent as to compel such action, that is, lay a positive ethical obligation upon the engineer who is aware of the situation.

Major Ethical Issues

Engineering has made giant strides since 1922 and engineers have inherited social problems of staggering importance—responsibilities which their narrow technical training has ill fitted them to assume. The Red Queen in *Through the Looking-Glass* said, "Now here, you see, it takes all the running you can do to stay in the same place. If you want to get somewhere else, you must run at least twice as fast as that!" Engineers, despite their long struggle to raise ethical standards, confronted with unsolved problems, old and new, find themselves in just about the same place they were in 1922. Only a race of supermen could sprint as fast as they must to meet the obligations imposed upon them by the kaleidoscopic changes brought about largely by their own handiwork. They are harassed by petty problems which obscure major ethical issues—on one side by those which deplore "raiding" (the practice of offering irresistible inducements to particularly gifted engineers employed by a competitor) and on the other by those who decry "gentlemen's agreements" between firms (not to hire each other's employees). Perhaps it is fortunate that they find such problems complex and absorbing. Their preoccupation with such details may keep them from facing ethical considerations involved in their responsibility (along with physicists and chemists) for devilish instruments they have devised which may either save our nation from destruction by an aggressor or blast civilization to extinction.

What are the constituents of a code of ethics? Continuing with engineering, the general code considers relations with colleagues, clients, employers, and the general public. These relations the engineering occupation has in common with other occupations where there are explicit codes of conduct; for example, one aspect of colleague relations is designed to further the profession itself—that is, the individual practitioner is asked to set aside certain self-interests, to be concerned with the interests of the profession as a whole. Moreover, he is admonished not to enter into any kind of excessive or unfair competition with fellow engineers. He is encouraged to further educational opportunities and standards within the occupation. As far as relations with clients and employers are concerned, he must not engage in activities which would endanger persons, even those persons who may ultimately be recipients of services from clients and employers. He is instructed in professional contacts; he is urged to avoid conflicts of interest. With regard to public relations, the practitioner is asked to protect the good name of engineering in every possible way and protect the health of the public. He is asked not to exercise professional judgment in public until he has command of the facts.

A similar set of principles may be found in a number of the more professionalized occupations.* Thus the inclusion here of the "Canons of Ethics for Engineers" developed about fifteen years ago by the Engineers' Council for Professional Development may typify what can be found in a number of occupations.

* For example see the "Code of Ethics for the Teaching Profession" in T. M. Stinnett, *The Teacher and Professional Organizations, 1956* (Washington, D.C.: The National Education Association) 1956, pp. 164–166.

Engineers' Council for Professional Development (Engineering)

Canons of Ethics for Engineers[1]

Foreword

Honesty, justice, and courtesy form a moral philosophy which, associated with mutual interest among men, constitutes the foundation of ethics. The engineer should recognize such a standard, not in passive observance, but as a set of dynamic principles guiding his conduct and way of life. It is his duty to practice his profession according to these Canons of Ethics.

As the keystone of professional conduct is integrity, the engineer will discharge his duties with fidelity to the public, his employers, and clients, and with fairness and impartiality to all. It is his duty to interest

Reprinted from "Canons of Ethics for Engineers," *The Annals of the American Academy of Political and Social Science*, 297 (January 1955), 56–58. Used by permission of The American Academy of Political and Social Science.

[1] Adopted by the Engineers' Council for Professional Development, October 25, 1947.

himself in public welfare, and to be ready to apply his special knowledge for the benefit of mankind. He should uphold the honor and dignity of his profession and also avoid association with any enterprise of questionable character. In his dealings with fellow engineers he should be fair and tolerant.

Professional Life

Sec. 1. The engineer will cooperate in extending the effectiveness of the engineering profession by interchanging information and experience with other engineers and students and by contributing to the work of engineering societies, schools, and the scientific and engineering press.

Sec. 2. He will not advertise his work or merit in a self-laudatory manner, and he will avoid all conduct or practice likely to discredit or do injury to the dignity and honor of his profession.

Relations with the Public

Sec. 3. The engineer will endeavor to extend public knowledge of engineering, and will discourage the spreading of untrue, unfair, and exaggerated statements regarding engineering.

Sec. 4. He will have due regard for the safety of life and health of the public and employees who may be affected by the work for which he is responsible.

Sec. 5. He will express an opinion only when it is founded on adequate knowledge and honest conviction while he is serving as a witness before a court, commission, or other tribunal.

Sec. 6. He will not issue ex parte statements, criticisms, or arguments on matters connected with public policy which are inspired or paid for by private interests, unless he indicates on whose behalf he is making the statement.

Sec. 7. He will refrain from expressing publicly an opinion on an engineering subject unless he is informed as to the facts relating thereto.

Relations with Clients and Employers

Sec. 8. The engineer will act in professional matters for each client or employer as a faithful agent or trustee.

Sec. 9. He will act with fairness and justice between his client or employer and the contractor when dealing with contracts.

Sec. 10. He will make his status clear to his client or employer before undertaking an engagement if he may be called upon to decide on the use of inventions, apparatus, or any other thing in which he may have a financial interest.

Sec. 11. He will guard against conditions that are dangerous or threatening to life, limb, or property on work for which he is responsible, or if he is not responsible, will promptly call such conditions to the attention of those who are responsible.

Sec. 12. He will present clearly the consequences to be expected from deviations proposed if his engineering judgment is overruled by nontechnical authority in cases where he is responsible for the technical adequacy of engineering work.

Sec. 13. He will engage, or advise his client or employer to engage, and he will cooperate with other experts and specialists whenever the client's or employer's interests are best served by such service.

Sec. 14. He will disclose no information concerning the business affairs or technical processes of clients or employers without their consent.

Sec. 15. He will not accept compensation, financial or otherwise, from more than one interested party for the same service, or for services pertaining to the same work, without the consent of all interested parties.

Sec. 16. He will not accept commissions or allowances, directly or indirectly from contractors or other parties dealing with his client or employer in connection with work for which he is responsible.

Sec. 17. He will not be financially interested in the bids as or of a contractor on competitive work for which he is employed as an engineer unless he has the consent of his client or employer.

Sec. 18. He will promptly disclose to his client or employer any interest in a business which may compete with or affect the business of his client or employer. He will not allow an interest in any business to affect his decision regarding engineering work for which he is employed, or which he may be called upon to perform.

Relations with Engineers

Sec. 19. The engineer will endeavor to protect the engineering profession collectively and individually from misrepresentation and misunderstanding.

Sec. 20. He will take care that credit for engineering work is given to those to whom credit is properly due.

Sec. 21. He will uphold the principle of appropriate and adequate compensation for those engaged in engineering work, including those in subordinate capacities, as being in the public interest and maintaining the standards of the profession.

Sec. 22. He will endeavor to provide opportunity for the professional development and advancement of engineers in his employ.

Sec. 23. He will not directly or indirectly injure the professional reputation, prospects, or practice of another engineer. However, if he considers that an engineer is guilty of unethical, illegal, or unfair practice, he will present the information to the proper authority for action.

Sec. 24. He will exercise due restraint in

criticizing another engineer's work in public, recognizing the fact that the engineering societies and the engineering press provide the proper forum for technical discussions and criticism.

Sec. 25. He will not try to supplant another engineer in a particular employment after becoming aware that definite steps have been taken toward the other's employment.

Sec. 26. He will not compete with another engineer on the basis of charges for work by underbidding, through reducing his normal fees after having been informed of the charges named by the other.

Sec. 27. He will not use the advantages of a salaried position to compete unfairly with another engineer.

Sec. 28. He will not become associated in responsibility for work with engineers who do not conform to ethical practices.

The Evaluation of Work Performance

In addition to standards or norms of behavior there must be some means by which the quality of work performance can be evaluated in any occupation. But what is it that must be evaluated, and how does this evaluation take place? Who is it that evaluates the quality of work done? With the highly professionalized occupations there is a tendency for the persons *within* each of the occupations to evaluate the quality of performance.* The central question remains, however, by what criteria does the evaluation take place?

It should be fairly evident that the occupational images and norms discussed in earlier portions of this chapter constitute an attitudinal framework by which work activity is judged. "What is evaluated is a kind of skill, but conceived so broadly as to include the practitioner's personality, creativeness, and social contacts."† It may be seen that with highly professionalized occupations, occupational images and norms do not serve as a simple performance yardstick. The individual professional is judged in terms of his behavior both at work and outside. The expectation is that his work performance will display a considerable amount of individuality and uniqueness—the professional person is not expected to provide a carbon copy of some master pattern. Rather he is expected to bring his own creative abilities into the work situation, utilizing the ideal pattern of work norms as a point of departure.

Vagueness in the process of work performance evaluation is related to the rewards associated with highly professionalized occupations. Professional groups have much to say about the kinds and amounts of rewards appropriate to their situation, and community acquiescence or acceptance of the appropriateness of this reward system often follows.‡ Because it is likely that he is not familiar with the specific constituents of work expectations, the layman is in a poor position to delineate an appropriate evaluation and reward system for professional persons.

The evaluation of work performance in our society is related intimately to the concept of success. What determines success at work? With some occupations the determination of success is more easily ascertained than with others,

* Theodore Caplow, *op. cit.*, pp. 110–111.

† *Ibid.*, p. 111.

‡ William J. Goode, "Community Within a Community: The Professions," *American Sociological Review*, **22**, No. 2 (April 1957), 194–200.

and with the highly professionalized occupations it is usually more difficult to ascertain than with the less professionalized. Medicine presents a vivid example of this point: ideally self-regulation and interaction with colleagues play a great role in the control process; as the important research of Freidson and Rhea§ has shown, however, technical performance directly associated with patients receives little scrutiny; in fact, it is only colleague etiquette which is apt to receive colleague control. Who, then, are the truly successful physicians and upon what bases are their reputations established?

To choose a more extreme case in the assessment of success, consider the religious functionary. In writing about religion as an occupation, Joseph H. Fichter has some interesting observations to make. He says that, "unlike other professionals, ... the religious functionary does not represent an equation of income, achievement and desirability." At the same time, Fichter shows that outward manifestations of competency are relevant, as the religious functionary, along with persons in other highly professionalized occupations, is not evaluated by his colleagues alone; he is also evaluated by his superiors and by his clients. Clients are dependent in this instance upon the more obvious readily quantifiable indications of what the religious functionary has done— e.g., size of congregation and magnitude of the church building program. Consequently, from a professional viewpoint the crucial sources of judgment are ultimately the same with the religious occupation as with other highly professionalized occupations—that is, with professional persons themselves.

§ Eliot Freidson and Buford Rhea, "Consensus, Knowledge and Ignorance in Professional Evaluations," a paper presented at the annual meetings of the American Sociological Association at Los Angeles, California, August, 1963.

Joseph H. Fichter (Clergy)

If self-sanctification were the only goal of the religious functionary, the question concerning his success would be a spiritual and psychological one. Insofar as his work is apostolic, involving external activities and other people, the question is sociological. Ordinarily a person is called successful when his work is recognized as competent and praised as such by others. The practical measure of success, however, is not only acclaim and rewards, but the number of people who are buying the product or clamoring for the services.[1]

Reprinted from "What Determines Success?", *Religion as an Occupation, A Study in the Sociology of Professions* (South Bend: The University of Notre Dame Press, 1961), pp. 176–180. Used by permission.

[1] The various ways of defining success are pointed out by Anne Roe, *The Psychology of Occupations* (New York: John Wiley & Sons, Inc., 1956), pp. 280–288; see also the attempt to answer the question, "What is Occupational Success?" *Occupational Psychology*, 24, (London,

In selecting successful Methodist clergymen, whose childhood background he wanted to study, one researcher used the annual salary as the main criterion. He writes that "upward mobility is a consequence of successful face-to-face interaction with laymen and fellow ministers. One's salary is commensurate with his desirability as pastor and preacher, a desirability based upon his reputation and observed performance."[2] In most professions it is probably true, as Brandeis says, that "a large income is the ordinary incident of success; but he who exaggerates the value of the incident is apt to fail of real success."[3] The correlation of income with professional success varies

1950), by J. G. Davies, 7–17; M. B. Stott, 105–112; and J. W. Reeves, 153–159.

[2] Phillip J. Allen, "Childhood Backgrounds of Success in a Profession," *American Sociological Review*, 20, No. 2 (April 1955), 187.

[3] Louis D. Brandeis, *Business—A Profession* (Boston: Small, Maynard, 1925), p. 4.

from one kind of career to another, and it is not likely that a person who seeks great financial success will become a minister or priest or, for that matter, a teacher, nurse or social worker.

In spite of occasional instances of avarice and self-interest, the professions publicly reject size of financial income as the measure of success. The common stereotype of the professional is that of a man who is not interested in money, and who is also supposedly a "poor businessman." He does not work in order to be paid, "he is paid in order that he may work."[4] This notion has a peculiar pertinence in the case of the religious functionary because the example of Christ and the Holy Family, who lived in relative poverty, is frequently held out to him. Furthermore, salary in the diocesan priesthood is nominal and categorized, and not normative and personal. All other Catholic functionaries pronounce the vow of poverty in one form or another.

Unlike other professionals, therefore, the religious functionary does not represent an equation of income, achievement and desirability. Nevertheless, one's desirability in a particularly apostolic function of the Church may be used as a partial criterion of success. Recognition and acceptance by the people he serves constitute one way of judging and measuring his success. Perhaps every large American city contains a few extremely competent confessors who attract large numbers of penitents. Some priests specialize in preaching or in giving missions or retreats, and their services are much in demand. A Sister who is a proficient teacher is praised by the parents of her pupils and sometimes develops a local reputation.[5] Acclaim on occasion comes from the superiors of the religious organization to which the person belongs. The pastor seeks reliable and zealous curates. The superintendent of the hospital asks for competent nurses. Recognition, in this sense a measure success, comes from administrators who direct the work force.

It is characteristic of professions that the most important stamp of approval comes from colleagues in the same profession. The notion here is that ultimately only those who are themselves technically competent in the same field can really judge who are the successful and who the unsuccessful members of the profession. Even the client whose law suit has been won, and the patient whose body has been healed, cannot understand the technical reasons for this success in the way possible for practitioners in the field. Similarly, an administrator who has to appoint or promote a professional, must base his decision on the judgment of those who are fellow professionals.

From what has been said it is clear that success in an occupation can be judged from three different directions. The functionary can be judged by his superiors, his peers and his clients. It is not usual in the so-called free professions that all three sources are heard from by the same individual, but this is precisely the peculiar situation of the religious functionary who is rendering external service in the Catholic Church. The confusing aspect of this triple judgment is that each of the three is using a different criterion of success:[6] the public judges on the vague norms of popularity; colleagues judge on the norms of technical competence; superiors judge on the norms of conformity to institutionalized regulations.

Here again we must take note of the peculiar occupational dichotomy of the professional religious functionary who is also enacting a professional subsidiary role. The determination of success may come from fellow professionals in both areas of activity, but the difficulty arises when one attempts to analyze the norms of success in the religious career as such. Saint John Berchmans was declared an excellent religious and was raised to the altar by canonization, because he kept perfectly the rules of behavior estab-

---

[4] This oft-quoted remark comes from T. H. Marshall, "The Recent History of Professionalism in Relation to Social Structure and Social Policy," *Canadian Journal of Economic and Political Science,* 5, 1939, 325–340.

[5] See the opinions parents had of teachers in author's *Parochial School,* pp. 283–287.

[6] This distinction was suggested by the remarks of Theodore Caplow, *The Sociology of Work* (Minneapolis: University of Minnesota Press, 1954) p. 113.

lished by his organization.[7] In this instance, the regulations set forth by the founder and maintained by professional religious colleagues, were the norms by which success was measured.

When this norm of conformity to rules is employed it allows that a person can be a success in his professional religious work, and at the same time a failure in the apostolic, external work of his organization. Since success is never an absolute, it is possible that a person may be a relative success in one area and a relative failure in the other, and this can easily be the particular case when a person is attempting to pursue two parallel careers. Obviously, something other than sanctity is required for a person who is attempting to enact the role of psychologist, physicist, teacher, or even administrator. Thomas Aquinas hints at this when he says that the holiest person in the community need not be chosen as superior

if there is some less holy person who is a competent administrator.[8]

The religious functionary, by the very nature of his calling, is not seeking acclaim and outward signs of success.[9] Like any other professional, however, he can recognize these indications of success whether they come from colleagues, superiors, or the people he serves. As in other professions, selfless dedication to work carries with it an immeasurable but inescapable satisfaction.[10] The trained professional takes a positive approach to his work, knows when he has done a good job, and takes justifiable satisfaction from it. When this is applied to his whole career, the professional himself becomes the judge of the degree of success he has achieved.

[8] See *Questiones Quodlibetales,* 8, art. 6; and *Summa Theologica,* II–III, q. 185, art. 3.

[9] "One tends to hold suspect the preacher who drives a Cadillac, but considers saintly the one whose clothes are threadbare," says Dubin, *The World of Work* (Englewood Cliffs, N.J.: Prentice-Hall, Inc. 1958), p. 217.

[10] R. Hoppock and his various associates have made numerous reports on research studies of job satisfaction, appearing mainly in *Occupations* from 1936 to 1951.

[7] "It is hardly too much to say that in his canonization, the Rule was canonized." Martin Harney, *The Jesuits in History* (New York: America Press, 1941), p. 171.

In this chapter we have taken the position that in examining the process of professionalization it is essential to give close consideration to the kinds of controls exhibited by the occupation to achieve compliance with its expectations. This point of view has been used by a number of social scientists, and notably by Everett C. Hughes. "Work, I submit, is in all human societies an object of moral rule, of social control in the broadest sense, and it is precisely all the processes involved in the definition and enforcement of moral rule that form the core problems of sociology."* In keeping with this, Hughes has analyzed the evaluation processes from the standpoint of the mistakes and failures associated with work activity.

The question of how mistakes are handled is a much more penetrating one than any question which contains the concept "professional ethics" as ordinarily conceived. For in finding out how mistakes are handled, one must get at the fundamental psychological and social devices by which people are able to carry on through time, to live with others and with themselves. . . .†

Such an analysis is contained in the following selection from the writings of Professor Hughes which employs several examples from the occupational world.

* Everett C. Hughes, "Mistakes at Work," *The Canadian Journal of Economics and Political Science,* 17, No. 3 (August 1951), 327.

† Everett C. Hughes, "Work and Self," *Men and Their Work* (New York: Free Press of Glencoe, Inc., 1958), p. 46.

Everett C. Hughes (General)

...we are faced with...[the problems] ...of defining what a failure or mistake is in any given line of work or in a given work operation. This leads to still another, which turns out to be the significant one for the social drama of work: Who has the right to say what a mistake or a failure is? The findings on this point are fairly clear; a colleague-group (the people who consider themselves subject to the same work risks) will stubbornly defend its own right to define mistakes, and to say in the given case whether one has been made.[1] Howard S. Becker has found that professional jazz musicians will do considerable injury to themselves rather than let any layman, even the one who is paying their wages, say that a musician is playing badly or even that he has struck the wrong note. An orchestra leader who would even relay a layman's complaint to a member of his band would be thought already on the road to becoming a "square," one of those outsiders who do not understand jazz music. Now you may say that jazz music is so lacking in any canons of correctness that there is no such thing as a single false note within the larger noise. It is all a matter of individual opinion. There is no clear and objective standard by which a judgment can be made.

But how clear is it in other lines of work? When one starts comparing occupations in this regard one finds that in most of them it is very difficult to establish criteria of success or failure, and of mistakes as against proper execution of work. The cases where all parties to the work drama would agree are few indeed. In factories which make

Reprinted from "Mistakes at Work," *The Canadian Journal of Economics and Political Science*, 17, No. 3 (August 1951), 322–325. Used by permission of the author and publisher.

1 The colleague-group does not in all cases succeed in getting and keeping this right. Perhaps they do not always want the full responsibility of convicting one another of error and of applying sanctions. It would be more correct to say that a kind of jurisprudence of mistakes is an essential part of the study of any occupation. Professor Norman Ward has suggested that a study of the official *error* in baseball would throw light on the processes involved.

precision parts the criteria are finely measured tolerances, but usually there is an informally agreed upon set of tolerances which are slightly looser than those in the book. Workmen and inspectors are continually at odds over the difference, even when the workmen want the parts they make to be workable. This is a case of the clearest kind of criterion. In medicine the criteria of success and failure are often far from clear. Dr. Bruno Bettelheim recently stated that psychotherapists do not discuss together their successes and failures because there are no standards to go by; that is why, he said, they spend so much time discussing whether their historical reconstructions of the troubles of their patients are correct or not. Health is, after all, a relative matter. Most people are interested in making the old body do as long as possible; this makes medicine quite a different matter from the automobile industry (where the garage man makes his work easier by persuading you the old car isn't worth mending).

Even where the standards may be a little clearer than in medicine and education, the people who work and those who receive the product as goods or services will have quite different degrees and kinds of knowledge of the probabilities and contingencies involved. The colleague-group will consider that it alone fully understands the technical contingencies, and that it should therefore be given the sole right to say when a mistake has been made. The layman, they may contend, cannot even at best fully understand the contingencies. This attitude may be extended to complete silence concerning mistakes of a member of the colleague-group, because the very discussion before a larger audience may imply the right of the layman to make a judgment; and it is the *right* to make the judgment that is most jealously guarded.

In some occupations it is assumed that anyone on the inside will know by subtle gestures when his colleagues believe a mistake has been made. Full membership in the colleague-group is not attained until these gestures and their meaning are known. When they are known, there need not be conscious and overt discussion of certain errors even within the colleague-group. And when some incident makes an alleged failure or mistake a matter of public discussion, it is perhaps the feeling that outsiders will never understand the full context of risk and contingency that makes colleagues so tight-lipped. And if matters have gone to such a point that mistakes and failures are not freely discussed even within the trusted in-group, public discussion may be doubly feared; for in addition to questioning the prerogative of in-group judgment, the outside inquisitor lifts the veil from the group's own hidden anxieties, the things colleagues do not talk about even among themselves. This may be the source of the rather nervous behavior of school teachers when my colleagues and I report to them—at their own request—some of the things we are finding out about them.

One of the differences between lay and professional thinking concerning mistakes is that to the layman the technique of the occupation should be pure instrument, pure means to an end, while to the people who practice it, every occupation tends to become an art. David Riesman,[2] who was once a clerk to Justice Brandeis, and an assistant in the office of the District Attorney of New York, tells of the wonderful briefs which young lawyers draw up for presentation to lower court judges who can scarcely read them, much less judge the law that is in them. The ritual of looking up all the past cases, and the art of arguing out all possibilities are gone through, even when the lawyer knows that the decision will be made upon a much simpler—perhaps also a much sounder—basis. What is more: the ritual and the art are respected, and the men who perform them with brilliance and finesse are admired. The simple client may be dazzled, but at some point he is also likely to think that he is being done by the whole guild of lawyers, including his own, the opposing counsel, and the court. In a sense, the art and cult of the law are being maintained at his expense. The legal profession believes, in some measure, in the cult of the law. The individual case is thought of not merely as something to be decided, but as

part of the stream of observance of the cult of the law.

And here we come to the deeper point of Dr. Bettleheim's remark concerning his own colleagues, the psychotherapists. A part of their art is the reconstruction of the history of the patient's illness. This may have some instrumental value, but the value put upon it by the practitioners is of another order. The psychotherapists, perhaps just because the standards of cure are so uncertain, apparently find reassurance in being adept at their art of reconstruction (no doubt accompanied by faith that skill in the art will bring good to patients in the long run).

Another example of these ways of thinking is to be found in social work. This profession is said to make a distinction between successful and professional handling of a case. The layman thinks of success as getting the person back on his feet, or out of his trouble. The social worker has to think of correct procedure, of law, of precedent, of the case as something which leaves a record. She also appreciates skilful interviewing, and perhaps can chuckle over some case which was handled with subtlety and finish, although the person never got "well" (whatever that would be in social work).

In teaching, where ends are very ill-defined—and consequently mistakes are equally so—where the lay world is quick to criticize and blame, correct handling becomes ritual as much as or even more than an art. If a teacher can prove that he has followed the ritual, the blame is shifted from himself to the miserable child or student; the failure can be and is put upon them.

Ritual is also strongly developed in occupations where there are great unavoidable risks, as in medicine. In such occupations the ritual may, however, be stronger in the second and third ranks of the institutions in which the work is done. Thus, in medicine, the physician, who stands at the top of the hierarchy, takes the great and final risks of decision and action. These risks are delegated to him, and he is given moral and legal protection in taking them. But the pharmacist, who measures out the prescribed doses, and the nurse, who carries out the ordered treatment, are the great observers of ritual in medicine. Pharmacists

2 "Toward an Anthropological Science of Law and the Legal Profession," *The American Journal of Sociology*, **57** (September 1951), 121–135.

are said often to become ritualistic wipers and polishers, flecking infinitely small grains of dust from scales on which they are only going to weigh out two pounds of Paris green. The ritualistic punctiliousness of nurses and pharmacists is a kind of built-in shock-absorber against the possible mistakes of the physician. Indeed, in dramatizing their work, these second-rank professions explicitly emphasize their role as saviors of both patient and physician from the errors of the latter. And here again we get a hint of what may be the deeper function of the art, cult, and ritual of various occupations. They may provide a set of emotional and even organizational checks and balances against both the subjective and the objective risks of the trade.

I suspect that it is a rare occupation whose practitioners develop no criteria of good work, and no concept of mistake or failure other than simply defined successful conclusion of the given case or task. Usually the professional judgment will contain explicit or implicit references to an art, a cult, and a ritual. The function of the art, cult, and ritual is not so much to bring the individual case to an early successful conclusion as to relate it to the on-going occupation itself, and to the social system in which the work is done. In most occupations, a man can be judged as quite wrong by his colleagues for an action which the lay client might consider very successful indeed. The quack, defined functionally and not in evaluative terms, is the man who continues through time to please his customers but not his colleagues. On the contrary, a man may be considered by his colleagues to have done a piece of work properly and without error, even when the client may accuse him of error, mistake, or failure.

Questions for Discussion and Further Research

The selection from Caplow suggests that occupational stereotypes are variously vivid in outline and effectiveness. They are accurate in some respects, inaccurate in others. He argues that it is the highly professionalized occupations which tend to have the clearest and most widely recognized stereotypes—but not always. Thus a complex question with which we are still faced is: by what social and socio-psychological processes do stereotypes of new occupations develop, and how are they altered in already existing occupations? The need for further study in this area has already been acknowledged;[*] Bronislaw Malinowski, in writing about myth in primitive psychology,[†] observed the role that mythology can play in the work activities of nonliterate societies. What we need now is more systematic information on the process by which occupational myths operate in our own contemporary society. This suggests a need for investigation of the related question of how the introduction of accurate factual information may modify existing occupational stereotypes.

Although Bodley Scott's article is primarily humorous, he does call attention to something worthy of note: there are media of entertainment which may shape attitudes about occupations, among both those within an occupation and those looking at it from the outside. In North America it is likely that media of communications other than novels are currently more influential in this shaping process; television in particular appears to be extraordinarily persuasive.

[*] Elvi Whittaker and Virginia Olesen, "The Faces of Florence Nightingale: Functions of the Heroine Legend in an Occupational Subculture," *Human Organization,* 22 (Summer 1964), 123–130.

[†] Bronislaw Malinowski, *Magic, Science and Religion* (New York: Doubleday & Company, Inc., 1948), pp. 101–116.

What we need to know is the precise influence of each of the mass media on the formation and alteration of occupational stereotypes. For example, what are the precise influences of literature and the performing arts? And somewhat further afield, but nonetheless potentially important, what are the influences of children's games and role-playing in the shaping of attitudes about occupations?

The work of Becker and Geer suggests that a major way of coping with a large discrepancy between the real and the ideal pictures of an occupation is to postpone the realization of many occupational expectations until some future, unspecified date. The example that Becker and Geer use to illustrate this process probably represents the most highly professionalized of the occupations, however, and it leaves us with the question of whether or not this process is more typical of highly professionalized occupations than others? If so, then is it, as some have argued, that people entering much less professionalized occupations have no illusions about their work situation and therefore do not find it necessary to pursue this involved and confusing socio-psychological process, instead preoccupying themselves with future goals which are not work-related? If such instances of large discrepancies between the *real* world of work and the *ideal* world of work are very common, is it possible to eliminate all forms of unrealistic idealization of an occupation?

F. J. C. Seymour argues that attitudinal factors are extremely important in bringing about behavioral changes within occupations. It is his conviction that ideals of professionalism, as promoted by professional associations, can be a very positive force in this change process. At the same time, he recognizes that occupational attitudes must become an integral part of the individual's behavioral makeup and must be genuinely felt and genuinely acted upon if they are to be anything other than superficial gestures. The question that remains for serious research consideration is, to what extent can professionalism be promoted consciously and actively and still enhance work performance, or must realistic and useful occupational change be based upon developments which are arrived at without conscious deliberation and plan?

The series of selections on codes of conduct which draw their examples from the judiciary and engineering fields raise the related question of the actual behavioral effectiveness of these particular kinds of formal statements. The contention is made that codes of conduct are effective operational directives. However, little, if any, systematic study has been done to demonstrate the actual changes caused by the introduction of formal codes of occupational conduct. Are these codes mere formalistic window dressings for outsiders which, in actuality, often fail to control behavior to any significant extent? A related aspect of this question is whether or not formal and informal conduct norms tend to coincide more often in the highly professionalized occupations and the extent to which this hypothesized coincidence is a consequence of the existence of formal codes of ethics.

Presumably, the major function of occupational controls is to achieve quality and efficiency in work performance in ways satisfactory both to people who are doing the work and to society at large. This led us, later in the chapter, to discuss evaluation of work performance, using the example drawn from Joseph H. Fichter's writings. One has to take into consideration a wide range of factors which serve as criteria for work performance, and, as Fichter points out, these criteria are by no means restricted to the more obvious activities within the occupation itself. There are widespread and vague external social attitudes which play their part in the evaluation process. But is the adequacy of work performance best judged by the worker, his peers, or his "superiors"? The professional person has long argued that he is the one most competent to judge the quality of the work undertaken. To what extent may this claim for autonomy be used by persons in highly professionalized occupations as a kind of license to avoid the scrutiny of others and cover up incompetence? And there is the corollary question—would industrial society function more effectively and with less social friction if all categories of workers were given considerable voice in the assessment of work performance?

5

Professional Associations
and Colleague Relations

As indicated in Chapter 1, there are a number of ways of looking at professional occupations, and a multiplicity of definitions of the essential elements of any profession. One thing about which most authors writing on the professions would agree, though, is that occupational associations are essential to the process of professionalization. As we have discovered earlier, the antecedents of most highly professionalized occupations go back several centuries, and the process of forming occupational associations has been an integral part of this development; indeed Caplow has maintained that this is the first stage of professionalization.* Thus the importance of examining professional associations in historical perspective.†

The Historical Development of Professional Associations

Occupational associations of one kind or another antedate professional associations per se by a number of centuries. Occupational associations in the form of guilds were well developed in Chaucer's time. Professional associations as such came into being with relatively few functions, particularly in their early stages, ordinarily with the qualifications and integrity of the profession's members the paramount concern. It was not long, however, before they sought to protect their members from undue governmental influences, encroachment of other occupational groups, and interference of the public at large.

* T. H. Caplow, *The Sociology of Work* (Minneapolis: The University of Minnesota Press, 1954), p. 139.
† This is the approach followed by Emile Durkheim in the preface, "Some Notes on Occupational Groups," to the second edition of the *Division of Labor in Society,* trans. by George Simpson (Glencoe, Ill.: The Free Press, 1960), pp. 1–31.

A prominent aspect of these associations throughout their history has been attention to the provision of adequate training. As a corollary, almost everywhere they have been concerned ostensibly with the maintenance and improvement of adequate occupational standards. In an earlier form, occupational associations, as guilds, attempted to maintain monopolistic arrangements to enhance their own gain. This, too, has tended to reassert itself within the highly professionalized occupations—most notably in the instances of medicine, law, and dentistry—to the point where laymen are legally prohibited from practicing the art in question. Just as the guilds were an important part of the government of their day, so the strong professional associations of our day have come to take on quasi-governmental status; that is, some professional associations are empowered by the government to undertake the "public" supervision of their own affairs. Some of these historical trends are outlined in the selection which follows.‡

‡ For discussions of the historical development of occupational associations in the United States for specific occupations, see: T. M. Stinnett, "Beginnings of Teachers' Organizations" in *The Teacher and Professional Organizations, 1956* (Washington, D.C.: The National Education Association, 1956), pp. 81–85; C. R. Jeffery, *et al.*, "The Legal Profession," in E. J. Davis, *et al., Society and the Law* (Glencoe, Ill.: The Free Press, 1962), pp. 343–345; Herbert Harley, "Group Organizations Among Lawyers," *The Annals of the American Academy of Political and Social Science,* 101, No. 190 (May 1922), pp. 33–44; A. D. Whiting, "The Professional Organizations, Training, and Ethical Codes of Physicians, Dentists, Nurses and Pharmacists," *The Annals,* 101, No. 190 (May 1922), pp. 51–67; M. Van Kleeck and G. R. Taylor, "The Professional Organization of Social Work," *The Annals,* 101, No. 190 (May 1922), pp. 158–168.

A. M. Carr-Saunders and P. A. Wilson (General)

Thus far our attention has been concentrated upon the origin of those techniques around which professions are built. But a technique may exist and men may practice it, and yet there may be no profession. Just as a number of families in primitive society do not form a State, so a number of men, though they perform similar functions, do not make a profession if they remain in isolation. A profession can only be said to exist when there are bonds between the practitioners, and these bonds can take but one shape—that of formal association.

When that powerful impulse towards association was manifesting itself in the Middle Ages, those who practiced a particular craft usually came together with ease. The barristers and surgeons formed their own asso-

Reprinted from "The Rise and Aims of Professional Associations," *The Professions* (Oxford: The Clarendon Press, 1933), pp. 298–304. Used by permission of the Clarendon Press, Oxford, England.

ciations, but the other medieval vocations which we have mentioned were not in a position readily to do so. The physicians, for instance, were members of the Church and of the university, and for a long time had no thought of setting up their own association outside these institutions. When a new profession evolves within an existing profession, as at a later time dentistry evolved within medicine, the practitioners of the new craft usually remain for a time in the shelter of their ancient home, and in consequence the segregation of the new profession is delayed. The civil and canon lawyers, the teachers and the civil servants were in a like situation. The two latter professions in addition, as has already been noticed, possess no specialized technique and therefore lack that incentive to association which has proved in the case of other professions to be of such great importance.

In the Middle Ages there were but few techniques around which professions could be built, and association was impeded in some cases by the various obstacles mentioned. When it occurred, it took the shape characteristic of the times. Since it was thought necessary "to curb the audacity of those wicked men who shall profess medicine more for the sake of their avarice than from the assurance of any good conscience"[1] the Royal College of Physicians was incorporated. The college was to "discourage the unskilfulness and temerity of the knavish men mentioned.'[2] The members were given certain privileges and in addition were to have "the oversight and scrutiny, correction and government of all and singular physicians" of London, and "also the oversight and scrutiny of all manner of medicines.'[3] Under an Act of 1540 the four censors of the college were given power to enter apothecaries' houses, to examine drugs, and to destroy them if defective. The college had thus many functions, and it was characteristic of the times that powers and duties of so extensive a nature were granted to vocational associations that they may be regarded as organs of the State.

The new social and economic forces, which began to manifest themselves in the sixteenth century, were antagonistic to the ancient forms of association, and created conditions which, for more than two centuries, were unfavorable to the rise of new forms. The old bonds dissolved, and the medieval associations, for the most part, decayed; no place was found for them in the social and political philosophy of the time. Early in the French Revolution, which gave expression to the views prevalent in the eighteenth century, associations of members of the same trade or profession were forbidden. "Les citoyens de même état ou profession, les ouvriers ou compagnons d'un art quelconque ne pourront lorsqu'ils se trouvent ensemble, se nommer de président, ou secrétaire ou syndic, tener des registres, prendre des arrêtés, former des règlements sur leurs prétendus intérêts communs."[4] The new forces did not attack directly the ancient associations of physicians, lawyers,

surgeons, and apothecaries; they struck with full force at the trading guilds which passed out of the scene, while the former survived though with diminished vitality. In the prevailing atmosphere associations aroused no enthusiasm and little loyalty; they became instruments for the safeguarding of privileges and the enthronement of abuses. The conditions at Oxford and Cambridge in the eighteenth century are familiar, and the Royal College of Physicians and the Inns of Court were in much the same case.

About 1739 a number of attorneys and solicitors founded the Society of Gentlemen Practicers in the Courts of Law and Equity. The Society "took its origin in friendly and convivial meetings"[5] and ultimately gave rise to the Law Society of today. Towards the end of the century the civil engineers, to whom we may attribute a large share in bringing about the industrial revolution, also experienced a desire to meet together periodically, and they formed a dining club. They mingled social activities with informal but serious discussions of their common problems. This was the beginning of a new wave of professional association, entirely spontaneous and aroused by needs that were deeply felt. The importance of the step taken by the attorneys, solicitors, and engineers was apparent neither to them nor to observers outside their group. Opinion was then, and long remained, hostile to professional association as it was then understood. Physicians and barristers were regarded as typical of professional men, and their societies were active only in opposition to movements towards reform.[6] The exclusiveness, selfishness, and slothfulness of their fossilized corporations were the target of reformers for more than half a century after the new wave of association had set in. The critics may not have been in error in their immediate aim, but they went on to generalize from these few examples and con-

---

[1] *The Charter of the Royal College of Physicians of London,* 1518.

[2] *Ibid.*

[3] *Ibid.*

[4] Law of 14th June, 1791. Quoted by Marten Saint-Léon, *Histoire des Corporations et Métiers,* 1897, p. 624.

[5] *The Records of the Society of Gentlemen Practicers in the Courts of Law and Equity,* Edwin Freshfield (ed.), 1897, p. i.

[6] It is worthy of note that the barristers never constituted a caste as did the physicians. "A legal career was open to the ambitions and talents of the poorest, and it led to the very highest positions in society." (E. Halévy, *A History of the English People in 1815,* 1924, p. 19.)

demned all professional associations. They inferred that the abuses then prevalent were inevitable. These hostile criticisms gained a wide popularity owing to the work of satirists such as Dickens; to most men, barristers and public servants recalled Jarndyce and Jarndyce and the Circumlocution Office, and the influence of Dickens may still be traced in the opinion of today.

The new wave of association took some time to gather strength; certain features in the situation were opposed to it. The eighteenth century was the century of patronage, and to patronage civil servants, the early solicitors, and architects were subject. Men who are in that condition of personal subservience do not easily associate with their fellows.[7] Association might seem to indicate a striving towards an independence that would be incompatible with the relation of client to patron. Again, in some cases, contracting had not been divorced from professional duties; the local government servant was part expert adviser and part contractor. So too was the architect. So long as contracting is present, the business outlook dominates over the professional outlook, and the professional functions are not prominent enough to form the basis of association. With the passing away of these obstacles, associations readily sprang up round the new techniques. The immediate motive was the desire for social intercourse with those who were doing the same work and facing the same problems. Association took the shape of dining clubs where "shop" was talked, and it was but a short step to the holding of formal meetings for the reading and discussion of papers. Thus the desire to promote "study" activities was among the first objects of these societies.

Study societies form by far the largest class among the societies to which the new wave of association has given rise, and most of them have originated among those who have in common only the desire to promote the study of some field, historical, archaeological, or whatever it may be. Their objects extend no further than discussion, research, and publication in the chosen field. Pure study societies are not professional associations, and until the dining clubs enlarged their activities they could not be called by this latter term. But members of these clubs had more in common than the study interest. They were applying the same technique in the ordinary business of life; they called themselves civil engineers, architects, and so on. To them these titles indicated men who had attained to a certain degree of competence in their own sphere. But the public accorded these titles to any one who laid claim to them, whether competent or not, and in consequence the skilled practitioners came to desire that the competent should somehow be distinguished and protected. It was hoped to achieve this end by limiting admission to the clubs to those who could show evidence of competence, which in those days meant evidence of experience and accomplishment. In this way prestige would be attached to the members of these clubs or associations. They, and they alone, would be the true civil engineers or architects as the case might be. A passage from the *Pharmaceutical Journal* of 1848, that is only four years after the foundation of the Pharmaceutical Society, when the circumstances leading to that event were fresh in mind, reads as follows: "The Pharmaceutical Society was designed as a means of raising the qualifications of pharmaceutical chemists and placing between them and unqualified persons a line of demarcation."[8] The next step is to raise the standards of competence and to improve the methods of testing them. "It may be," said the President of the Institution of Surveyors early in the history of that body, "a question deserving consideration, with reference to our future, whether the admission of Students to a higher grade should not be accompanied by some sort of examination, so that not only their respectability and character should be secured, but that some degree of guarantee

7 At an earlier date the dependence of solicitors upon patrons stood in the way of their amalgamation with attorneys. At a later date the segregation of land agents was impeded by a similar condition of dependence. At the present day the dependence of secretaries and mine managers, though it is a dependence upon companies and not upon persons, has the result that they adopt much the same attitude to companies as architects used to exhibit towards their patrons.

8 *Pharmaceutical Journal,* **7** 1848, 156.

should be given to the public that they are not unfitted for the work of protecting the interests entrusted to them."[9]

Just as the public may fail to distinguish between competent and incompetent, so it may fail to distinguish between honorable and dishonorable practitioners. Therefore the competent and honorable practitioners are moved mutually to guarantee not only their competence but also their honor. Hence the formulation of ethical codes. It is hoped that the public will come to realize that in giving patronage to members of the association they are assured of honest as well as of competent service. In the earliest surviving entry in the minutes of the Society of Gentlemen Practicers we read that "the Meeting unanimously declared its utmost abhorrence of all male [that is to say, mal] and unfair practice, and that it would do its utmost to detect and discountenance the same."[10] In the preamble to the charter of the Institute of Chartered Accountants granted in 1880 it is stated that

...the petitioners further desire and propose that the Corporation should lay down such rules respecting admission to membership and exclusion therefrom, as would prevent Public Accountants from mixing the pursuit of any other business with the discharge of the higher duties devolving upon them as Public Accountants, and as would put an end to the practice, which has been much objected to, of the division of profits with persons in other professions or callings, in the form of commission and the like.[11]

The members of the first formed of these societies were very conscious that they had no social prestige and that their occupations were not "fit for gentlemen."[12] Their declared objects nearly always included some reference to the raising of status. When application was made for a charter, it was generally submitted that incorpora-

tion in this manner would help to confer the much desired prestige. The petitioners for a charter for the College of Veterinary Surgeons represented that incorporation "would materially contribute to...the respectability of veterinary surgeons," and the charter granted to the College declared that veterinary surgery was a profession.[13] References to status continue to be found among the objects of associations of later date. One of the objects of the National Union of Teachers is "to raise the status of the teaching profession."[14] In time, the emphasis changes from respectability and status to protection of interests. It became obvious that a relatively high level of remuneration implies a public recognition of status, and that the most certain way of attaining the latter is to press for the former. Hence protective activities are added to those already mentioned.

The pursuit of these objects by professional associations inevitably leads them to further activities. Their solicitude for education implies that certain aspects of the educational organization of the country are to them a matter of concern. They are led by slow steps along this and other paths into public activities. Because they are repositories of special knowledge and experience, on the one hand they are approached by public and private bodies for help and advice, and, on the other hand, they are moved to present their views on matters of public policy touching their own special sphere. The later formed associations usually make mention among their objects of such semi-public activities. It is an object of the National Union of Teachers "to afford to His Majesty's Government, the Board of Education, the Local Authorities for education and other organizations—public or private—which have relation to educational affairs, the advice and experience of the associated teachers."[15]

The professional associations, which arose out of study societies in the earlier part of the last century, first took upon themselves

[9] *Institution of Surveyors: Transactions,* **10,** 1877–78, 1, 2.

[10] *The Records of the Society of Gentlemen Practicers,* 1897, p. 1.

[11] *Charter of the Institute of Chartered Accountants,* 1880, preamble.

[12] When attorneys and solicitors began to associate about 1739 it is perhaps significant that they called their society the Society of *Gentlemen* Practicers in the Courts of Law and Equity.

[13] *Charter of the Royal College of Veterinary Surgeons,* 1844.

[14] *Rules of the National Union of Teachers,* 2(*b*).

[15] *Ibid.,* 2 (*e*).

functions relating to the competence and honor of their members, and later included protection of material interests and public activities while retaining study functions. The later formed associations usually set out all these four aims among their original objects, to which they generally, but not always, added study activities. The associations of the eighteenth and early nineteenth centuries were for the most part simple in constitution, consisting of a single grade of members, perhaps adding, as in the case of civil engineers, a group of honorary members. Thus they contrasted strongly with the ancient corporations which were derived from the Middle Ages and had hierarchical constitutions. Those who founded the College of Preceptors, almost alone among the founders of new associations, consciously imitated the ancient model. The new associations also had, if not a single aim, at least closely related aims, in distinction to the multiple functions of the guilds. But as time passed many of the newer associations underwent a curious transformation and assumed something in the nature of the ancient hierarchical constitutions. The addition of new grades in the history of the Institution of Civil Engineers has already been traced, and it was so elsewhere. The associations founded within the last half-century have mostly been endowed with hierarchical constitutions from birth, and thus have a certain resemblance to medieval bodies. Moreover we may perhaps recognize another resemblance in the most recent development of the public activities of professional associations. The medieval associations were organs of the State, and though there is no sign that modern associations will ever undertake the supervisory duties carried out by the former, their pub-

lic activities are sometimes such as to suggest that they also merit the same description.

Looking back on the story of the development of professional techniques and on the rise of professional associations, we have seen that evolution does not always proceed smoothly. Allusion has been made to some of the factors which inhibit evolution or divert its course, but there are features of the story which remain unexplained. The evolution of the legal and medical professions was anything but smooth; and something more than has yet been said is required to account for so tangled a history. On reflection it appears that what happened in both cases was the early segregation of practitioners, advocates, and physicians, whose function at a later date was realized to be specialist. But the associations of these specialists, having attained great power and prestige, attempted to inhibit the development of general practitioners of law and medicine of whose services the public had need.[16] When they could not prevent their appearance, they tried to keep them subservient, and the history of both professions is largely concerned with the problems so brought about. By slow degrees the true place of specialists and general practitioners has come to be understood, and in consequence the evolution of their professions has at last been able to proceed in a clearer and calmer atmosphere. It may be that some of the recent professions will have to face the same troubles unless the proper relations of specialists to general practitioners are understood at the outset.

[16] The term "general practitioner" first came into common use in the decade 1820–30 in relation to the profession of medicine. The term is found in the Public Notaries Act of 1801.

Associational Goals

Why do persons pursuing an occupation come together and, after assessing their occupational situation, come to associate in a professionally meaningful fashion? Obviously they have similar interests, but is their aim simply to protect those interests or to protect their development from encroachment by other occupational groups? Durkheim believed not; he felt their main purpose is

"... just to associate, for the sole pleasure of mixing with their fellows and of no longer feeling lost in the midst of adversaries, as well as for the pleasure of communing together, that is, in short, of being able to lead their lives with the same moral aim."* A sense of professional colleagueship, or what is sometimes called professional consciousness, is partially developed in the formal educational setting of the university and professional school, but professional consciousness is also profoundly influenced and reinforced in later years by members coming together regularly within the occupational associational framework. Professional consciousness develops out of an awareness of the position or status of the occupation in the larger society, and out of an understanding of what social contribution the occcupation is making. And above all, a professional consciousness develops out of a willingness to accept the individual and collective responsibilities of such a status in society.

All occupations are dependent on the individual contributions of those persons who pursue the occupation. But the effectiveness of an occupation is not gauged by individual efforts alone; the total efforts of occupational members working together with some degree of cooperation must also be considered. The public image of an occupation, then, is in part individual and in part collective.

From within an occupation, it is perfectly apparent that there are all sorts of problems facing workers which cannot be solved by individual action. For example, there are what Kinney and Thomas have referred to as common "membership responsibilities" within a highly professionalized occupation.† Moreover, the goals of an occupation are only in a limited sense individual, for the individual responsibility of practitioners and a consciousness of the aims of the occupation are very much a function of collective action. This was recognized some time ago, as is shown in the next selection, which deals with the early development of the employment managers' occupation. In writing about the aim and work of employment managers' associations, Meyer Bloomfield indicated several needs that could be met only through concerted action within the occupation. Bloomfield pointed out how the associating of persons interested in personnel management problems aided their work activities and how they gained greater recognition from management through the device of an occupational association. The benefits gained through the exchange of information among members of an occupational association are noted, along with a concomitant upgrading of personnel management in general. Finally, he noted the importance of the research function in the development of the occupation in question.

---

* Emile Durkheim, *Professional Ethics and Civic Morals* (New York: Free Press of Glencoe, Inc., 1958), p. 25.
† Lucien B. Kinney and Lawrence G. Thomas, *Toward Professional Maturity in Education,* Bulletin No. 5 (San Francisco: California Teachers' Association, 1955), pp. 29–30.

Meyer Bloomfield
(Personnel Management)

The handling of employees is so important a matter that those engaged in it must prepare, and in time will be bound to prepare, as for a profession.

It was in order to bring out the professional ideas involved in this kind of work that those in charge of hiring and supervising employees in a number of Boston establishments were asked to come together four years ago and exchange ideas and experiences. In looking over the then existing associations which might take interest in a program of systematic study of employment management problems, there did not seem to be any which could devote itself in any large degree to such matters. Indeed very few employment managers, or other executives closely related to employing duties, were members of these societies.

There were organizations of credit men, advertising men, accountants, buyers, and many other kinds of trade and business bodies, but never before, so far as the writer is aware, have men in charge of the employing phases of management, the men who pump the life-blood into an establishment, been brought together to consider the nature of the problems their vital work involved.

The fact is, generally speaking, that the employment department has been a much neglected phase of industrial organization, and the person in charge of this kind of work has been rather overlooked in the management scheme.

Several reasons account for this oversight. Employing people and understanding them have not been generally regarded as more than an incident in management. Duties of this nature have been looked upon as unproductive, if not as a necessary evil. In consequence, the men placed in charge of this work were not always the best type procurable nor of the education the work calls for. Notable exceptions in this respect only prove the general rule of practice. Because the department, then, was not seriously considered, and because a petty subordinate was often placed in charge, the heads of a firm could not think of this aspect of the enterprise as of the same importance with other functions, such as finance, production, and sales. When grave problems of industrial relations presented themselves,

Reprinted from "The Aim and Work of Employment Managers' Associations," *The Annals of the American Academy of Political and Social Science*, 65 (May 1916), 76–78. Used by permission of The American Academy of Political and Social Science.

the head of the firm or some other important executive would indeed take deep interest in their solution. Experts, lawyers, and others would be consulted. Perhaps a welfare department, in some cases, would be expected to cope with the issues arising. But the department in the very best possible position to know the facts, the needs of the employees, and the methods best calculated to bring about proper relationship and just treatment, the employment department, has rarely been looked to for help, constructive work, and expert knowledge.

This situation is largely responsible for that great waste known as the labor turnover. It is also responsible for much preventable friction and misunderstanding.

A change for the better has come about since the formation of the first employment managers' association in Boston. The change is not, of course, primarily due to this effort. Other causes have been effectively at work. The movement for employment executives' associations is to some extent a result of wiser methods of management, a more enlightened spirit in industry, the vocational spirit in education, the pressure of employees for better understanding of their needs and desires, and numerous investigations into the social aspects of employment. The formation of employment officers' associations have been, however, a marked influence in the direction of better management methods and a new energy in the study and treatment of personnel problems.

For nearly four years a new type of association, already referred to, dealing with the problems of hiring and developing employees, has been at work in Boston. During 1911, the Vocation Bureau of Boston invited fifty men, who had in charge the hiring of employees in large shops and stores of the city and vicinity, to come together and consider the advisability of meeting regularly. As a result, the Employment Managers' Association was started.

The aims of this association are described as follows in the constitution:

To discuss problems of employees; their training and their efficiency.

To compare experiences which shall throw light on the failures and successes in conducting the employment department.

To invite experts or other persons who have knowledge of the best methods or experiments for ascertaining the qualifications of employees, and providing for their advancement.

It will be seen that the aim of this new association was to provide a professional medium for the exchange of experiences in a field where little interchange of ideas had taken place; to study the human problem in industry on the basis of fair dealing with the employee. In short, there was a conscious effort to make industrial practice square with the dictates of twentieth century enlightenment. . . .

The contributions made by professional associations to professional identity and solidarity, as well as to education and information exchange, are no less important today than they were in Bloomfield's and Durkheim's time.* Indeed, Chapman believes that "the major functions of a professional body are educative in character."† Strauss says "formal programs provide training for younger members. Officers and members learn about human relations, public speaking, and organizational skills. And many members exchange information and tricks of the trade in informal conversation around the bar before and after meetings."‡ The associational aim of maintaining occupational competence is not only promoted through formal education and informal socialization, there is also the process of certification to pursue the occupation; the control of entry through proper credentials and examinations—functions often delegated or partially delegated by the government to professional associations.§

We have already examined in Chapter 4 the intimate relationship between codes of conduct and the occupational associations which generate and promote them. The establishment of an appropriate monetary reward system is another associational goal,** which, in turn, is dependent on the development and enhancement of public confidence and acceptability, carrying the organized occupation into public relations activities.†† Some occupational associations openly operate as direct pressure groups in the formation of public policy. As

---

* George Strauss, "Professionalism and Occupational Associations," *Industrial Relations,* 2, No. 3 (May 1963), 21.

† F. T. Chapman, "The Implications of Membership of a Professional Body: Education," *The British Management Review,* 2, No. 1, 1952, 159.

‡ Strauss, *loc. cit.*

§ J. B. Montague, Jr., "Medicine and the Concept of Professionalism," *Sociological Inquiry* (Winter 1963), p. 46.

** Montague, *op. cit.,* p. 46.

†† Also see M. Janowitz, *The Professional Soldier* (Glencoe, Ill.: The Free Press, 1960), pp. 382–387, where he discusses an extension of this function, making the point that after World War II ". . .each of the services created or transformed one of its professional associations into a general organization, designed to present the service's point of view to the public. In response to the pressure of civilian controls, the services became aware that they could influence the legislative and executive process by influencing public opinion."

Taylor has documented in one instance: "...the objective of organized medicine is to influence government to the extent that the expansion of government-sponsored health programs brings or threatens to bring the services of private medical practitioners within the orbit of public policy."‡‡

Thus we see that the aims of professional associations are many and varied. In speaking about an occupation, some persons are seeking to professionalize more rapidly. Arthur Roberts says of business administration:

> The purposes of our profession may not be a simple bundle of definite ends. We shall almost certainly have to select our ends, partly on intrinsic importance if attained, and partly upon practicability of attainment. We shall cultivate a scientific approach to what, in practice, is an art. As the body of knowledge grows, we shall expect an even closer supervision of standards of individual professional competence, and of professional practice. We shall look to our professional body to provide the community with objective information as to the weight to be attached to individuals, and the freedom of action which may safely be granted....§§

This reliance on the application of scientific procedures to all areas of occupational activity is increasingly discernible in highly professionalized occupations; and research on both external substantive knowledge and internal organization of occupations constitute major goals of occupational associations.***

As an occupational field, management in business and in industry presents interesting problems with respect to the goals of occupational associations. As was pointed out in Chapter 1, many people have asked whether or not management is entitled to be regarded as a profession, arguing that the orientations of the manager ought best to be linked intimately with the particular work organization which employs him as its agent. Other persons have taken the position that a professional association of managers cutting across various specific work organizations is the most promising way of achieving managerial and organizational aims. We are examining here a somewhat controversial area when compared to more highly professionalized occupations where the benefits of associational activity are more obvious. The following selection from the writings of Edward Meigh explores implications connected with looking upon management as a profession, and particularly the goals of such collective action. The specific organization investigated by Meigh is the Institute of Industrial Administration in Great Britain. The benefits accruing to the occupational field are explored. In this he proposes ten criteria of professionalization and examines how they relate to the work of the professional association of managers.

---

‡‡ M. W. Taylor, "The Medical Profession and Public Policy," *The Canadian Journal of Economics and Political Science,* 26, No. 1 (February 1960), 125. This article provides a useful examination of the "private government of the medical profession" in Canada.

§§ Arthur Roberts, "The Implications of Membership of a Professional Body: Sociological and Industrial," *The British Management Review,* 2, No. 1, 1952, 141–142.

*** For an example of the latter, see E. L. Brown, *The Use of Research by Professional Associations in Determining Program and Policy* (New York: Russell Sage Foundation, 1946).

Edward Meigh
(Business Management)

The professional mission of the I.I.A. [Institute of Industrial Administration][1] may be confirmed by considering the objects and requirements of membership of the I.I.A. against the professional attributes, one by one, which have been set out herein.

SPECIALIZED EDUCATION AND TRAINING

All who have been familiar with the educational work of the I.I.A. over the past thirty years will concede that the Institute has built up a specialized course of education for administration, which amply satisfies the professional criterion. Some people, unfamiliar with I.I.A. achievements, belittle management education and others demand that management studies shall be able to test personal qualities and aptitude for

Reprinted from "The Implications of Membership of a Professional Body," *The British Management Review,* 12, No. 3, 1952, 126 and 133-140. Used by permission.

[1] The Institute of Industrial Administration came into being on 27th April, 1920, and one of its objects was "to raise management to the status of an organized profession." Yet after thirty years of persistent and honorable effort how little progress has been made towards realizing this aim. Indeed, how little do many of the Institute's members know of what the Institute signifies, and what professional membership implies, and how less what the Institute could and should become.

Such were the reflections of the special Policy Subcommittee recently set up in response to urgent demands from members of the council, now that the I.I.A. is in fact integrated with the British Institute of Management, that something should be done to augment its membership and to let the world of management know its aims and current activities; and that its facilities are available for raising the general level of management education and practice.

The recommendations of the Policy Subcommittee led to a decision that the first step to be taken should be to urge existing members of the Institute squarely to face their professional responsibilities. It was felt that the established members probably were in need of a new statement of what is involved in the term professional, especially the implied obligations to the professional body.

management, or be regarded as useless. Lewis and Maude, for instance, after quoting from the *Baillieu Report:*

The success of the Institute (B.I.M.) in establishing itself as a professional body will depend on its ability to determine criteria by which individual capacity in management can be assessed. . . .

go on to say,

This the Institute has not been able to do. It has coordinated all the management bodies; it has produced a lot of "management studies" in booklet form; it has, with the help of the Ministry of Education, introduced a common intermediate examination in management studies; it has tried to persuade the universities to pay more attention to business training; but it has not found any method of *certifying that an individual after receiving training in management, can in fact manage.* It may be argued that a man can possess medical degrees without being able to heal, or be called to the Bar only to make a woeful exhibition of himself in Court, but even these two men know more than the mere theory of their art, which is all that a "manager" who has got up the syllabus of the I.I.A. knows of his, and that at a great distance; besides, the doctor and lawyer must have their basic training and degrees to make even a modest success of their professions—but most managers make a success of theirs without the slightest acquaintance with the I.I.A. and all its requirements for general management.[2]

Coming up for breath after this, one might comment that it all depends upon what is meant by "success." If "most managers" are successful they are certainly not successful enough, or British industry would not be in its present condition of backwardness compared with industry in countries having much larger numbers of qualified managers. It may be recalled that many unqualified teachers, unqualified lawyers, unqualified medical practitioners considered that they had made a "success" of their callings before public demand excluded them from practicing until they became qualified. Later in their volume Lewis and Maude write:

[2] Roy Lewis and Angus Maude, M.P., *Professional People* (London: Phoenix House, 1962), p. 271.

Professional bodies such as the I.I.A. would passionately protest that they train only those who have preliminary qualifications and experience, and that these can be in wide fields; but the trouble is that...the present courses are vague and woolly, the concepts unscientific and repulsive to the specialized mind.

They continue:

Administration will become the happy hunting ground of the second-rate mind, which, after taking a pass degree, can readily get through an examination in "management studies."

and later,

There is the I.I.A. teaching the organization of industry, the law affecting employment in factories, and some simple accountancy.

They add that:

These bodies (including the I.I.A.) will indignantly protest that to put the matter like that is to burlesque their impressive syllabuses: but all of them admit that nothing in their syllabus makes, and nothing in their examinations tests, the qualities and character of the sort of man who runs a company, a trade association, a hospital, or a factory with brilliance ...on top of this, more than one nationalized industry professes the profoundest contempt for Chartered Secretaries or Fellows of the I.I.A.[3]

This cheap denigration of the I.I.A. is offered although Messrs. Lewis and Maude had apparently at least looked at the syllabuses of the I.I.A. Evidently, they did not look far enough or with sufficient penetration to realize that the I.I.A. does not do the teaching or the training, that these syllabuses have been adopted almost in their entirety by the Ministry of Education for the certificate and diploma examinations in management studies, and that most of the teaching is carried out in more than one hundred reputable technical institutions. If these gentlemen would take the further trouble to read the examination questions which candidates for I.I.A. examinations are required to answer, or themselves attempt the examinations, they would realize that the "second-rate mind" after acquiring a pass degree or, perhaps, even a first-rate mind with an honors degree, would not so very readily get through the examinations

in management studies. One may reasonably ask why examinations in management studies should be expected to "test the qualities and character of the sort of man who runs a company" any more than the examinations of other professions, teaching, law, or medicine, test the qualities and character of the sort of men who teach, or practice law or medicine? No matter what the profession, the qualities and character of the men must be tested by other means than by written examinations. But apparently Messrs. Lewis and Maude are content that administration shall continue to be the happy hunting ground not merely of second-rate but of the third- and fourth-rate minds, without professional qualifications, who happen to become managers.

A contrary view of management studies appears to be held by J. Munro Fraser who says:

Managers must understand them all (i.e. financial and commercial ventures, technical enterprises, communities of people at work) and their education for this task, if it could be provided at an institution for higher learning, would make many existing courses look trivial.[4]

This view can indeed be confirmed by members of the examinations subcommittee of the I.I.A.

AN INTELLECTUAL TECHNIQUE

The idea that professional men are persons in possession of a special intellectual technique has been present from early days, and can be found for instance in the writings of Bacon. It has been said that the application of intellectual technique to the ordinary business of life acquired as the result of prolonged and specialized training, is the chief distinguishing characteristic of the professions; and where a technique is specialized, the rise of a profession is unescapable.[5] Judged by this standard, industrial administration readily measures up to the professional requirement, for none can

3 *Ibid., pp.* 271, 272.

4 John Munro Fraser, "What I Think of Management," *The Manager,* September 1953, p. 520.

5 A. M. Carr-Saunders and P. A. Wilson, *The Professions* (Oxford: Clarendon Press, 1933), p. 491.

deny that it calls for a highly specialized intellectual technique to deal with the complexities facing the manager in modern industry; and membership of the I.I.A. is for those exercising such a technique.

Desire to study and advance the technique which they share in common, is in fact one reason why professional men associate together.[6]

It would be idle to imagine that the special intellectual techniques possessed by professional men are simply gifts of nature. On the contrary, they are the result of long educational disciplines and strenuous training, and therefore this second professional characteristic is closely bound up with and dependent on the first. The development and improvement of management technique throughout industry is the most urgent present requirement if efficiency and productivity are to be elevated.

Practice and Experience of Their Vocation

Experience is an essential qualification for professional membership and this has always been taken into account by the membership committee of the I.I.A.—experience both before and after examinations. The opponents of the claims of management to be a profession, who are curiously content to believe that a manager may simply evolve by "experience," might well consider a maxim of George Bernard Shaw:

Men are wise in proportion not to their experience, but to their capacity for experience.[7]

Now, capacity for experience depends mainly upon education and training. What is the use of a "born" manager if his experience is to be built up on a defective nucleus of knowledge and an assimilation of errors! It is well known in industry at all levels that those entrants who, instead of being suitably selected, educated, and trained, learn their business by being plunged *in medias res,* are very apt to pick up the bad habits and practices more readily than the good. This seems to justify

the perversity of Oscar Wilde when he declared:

Experience is of no ethical value. It is merely the name men give to their mistakes.[8]

The truth is that although experience of the right kind is one of the essential elements of professional management, it would be very wrong to regard experience as the only, or the most important, element and it would be dangerous to claim it as a reason for dispensing with other qualifications.

Suitable Personal Qualifications

Suitable personality is the foundation of competence and success in every profession, hence the desirability of rigorous selection before training and entry into any profession. As regards management this has long been recognized. The examination handbook of the I.I.A. stresses the value of personality.

Personality is a highly significant factor in management; but training serves to direct and develop personality.[9]

And in the *Urwick Report* there is recognition that

...theoretical study alone cannot make a manager. His success will depend on his innate qualities, his acquired knowledge, his experience under competent guidance and, above all, on the degree to which he combines these elements into a balanced personality.[10]

These affirmations concerning the importance in managers of certain qualities of personality will meet with general acceptance. Good general management is achieved by those able to induce people to work, and work together, to get the best work out of experts, to deal fairly in judging between conflicting alternatives. The presence of such qualities can be assessed by skilled selection but their effectiveness in action can only be tested by results over a long period.

6 *Ibid.*, p. 484.

7 George Bernard Shaw, *Maxims for Revolutionists.*

8 Oscar Wilde, *Lady Windermere's Fan,* Act iii.

9 Examination Handbook of the I.I.A., July 1953, p. 1.

10 Report of a Committee on Education for Management, *Urwick Report,* 1947, p. 6, par. 2(e) (H.M.S.O.).

A Code of Professional Conduct

In all attempts to describe the distinguishing marks of a profession, a high, if not the highest, place is given to standards of professional conduct—the development, within associations of professional people, of special codes of conduct to be observed and if necessary enforced on their members. The building up and recognition of professional ethics has been said to be one of the finest results of professional organization. Some of these codes date back to the early days of the most ancient professions: for example, the Hippocratic Oath administered to candidates for medical degrees, which began:

I do solemnly swear by that which I hold most sacred: That I will be loyal to the profession of Medicine and just and generous to its members: That I will lead my life and practice my art in uprightness and honor.

In many of the professions the codes of conduct are extremely detailed and contain sanctions against their infringement. The desirability of an ethical code for managers has been widely admitted, and a set of principles was put forward by the Professional Standards Committee of the I.I.A. and adopted by the Council in February 1951; and doubtless is being observed by a large proportion of the I.I.A. membership. The six main principles of the code may be restated as:

(1) The attainment of competence as a manager to the degree requisite for the responsibility undertaken.
(2) The maintenance of the honor, integrity, and dignity of the profession.
(3) Service to all sections of the community as a social obligation.
(4) Loyalty to the profession a primary duty, not to be surrendered to expediency but maintained even at the cost of personal position and prospects.
(5) Discipline of continuing personal study of the principles of management and encouragement of colleagues and subordinates to similar study.
(6) Avoidance of the abuse of executive power for personal gain, advantage, or prestige.[11]

When such a code becomes generally observed throughout industry confidence and trust in the profession will be firmly established; and employers will realize that there are certain things they cannot expect managers to do. Managers as a profession will therefore have to face a high challenge to their conduct—so to act that they earn the respect and confidence of their fellow workers and establish in the public mind a right to trusteeship.

Professional Association

Full professional life cannot be achieved in isolation, or in a narrow groove mixing day after day with the same few individuals. A technique may exist and men may practice it and yet there may be no profession. A calling may satisfactorily be pursued by an individual but not so a profession.

A number of men, though they perform similar functions do not make a profession if they remain apart in isolation. A profession can only be said to exist when there are bonds between the practitioners, and the bonds can take but one shape, that of formal association.[12]

And

Professions can only be said to exist where the practitioners come toegther in free association. Desire to associate and ability to do so are the prerequisites of professionalism...when they do not wish to associate for common ends they have no living purposes.[13]

A man may pass his professional examinations and become entitled to letters, he may have good training and experience but unless he associates formally and regularly with the members of his calling he is not a member of a profession. He may try to maintain alone a high standard of management, but as far as profession is concerned, he is merely "beating in the void his luminous wings in vain."[14] This outstanding *sine qua non* of a profession was from the first realized by Elbourne and his co-founders of the I.I.A. Of them it may be said:

11 Report of the Professional Standards Committee of the I.I.A.: *I.I.A. News,* special supplement, April 1951.

12 Carr-Saunders and Wilson, *op. cit.,* p. 298.
13 *Ibid.,* p. 495.
14 Arnold on Shelley.

They met together; they exchanged experiences; they found helpful ideas and were there to exchange them with all who would come and participate. It was neither wholly give nor wholly take but give and take, in person.[15]

Unfortunately this example has not been consistently lived up to by a large proportion of those elected to membership, and this failure to accept responsibility is undoubtedly a cause of the slow progress of the Institute in increasing its numbers, in obtaining the wide recognition it merits, and in fulfilling its mission of raising the quality of management. The advantages of professional association are highly valuable. In addition to providing fellowship and a forum for an exchange of experiences, for person to person contact in outspoken thinking, resulting in cross-fertilization of ideas, studies are undertaken and data are gathered. Thus the common technique is invigorated and developed, and the executive abilities of the member are enhanced. Of course a price has to be paid, not only dues but discipline, precious time, and continued studies.

The attention of the public is called to the existence of a profession through its professional association, and public recognition can hardly be accorded to a group that has not discovered itself.[16]

Other advantages of association are the facilities for combining to express views to government departments, to colleges and official bodies; and maintaining the status of the group and keeping it up to date with information and literature.

A Continuing Discipline of Study, and Assisting in the Technical Advancement of Professional Knowledge

The professions as well as other callings make progress as knowledge increases; many of them are based on the sciences, and necessarily follow them in their forward march for truth. It is therefore es-

sential for all in the ranks of the professions to continue the discipline of study as a life-long practice; otherwise they will trail behind and become decadent, while scientific knowledge advances. Industry cannot afford to be out-distanced in the effort to keep abreast with science, and therefore industrial administrators are especially called upon to continue, by fairly arduous study, their quest for up-to-the-minute information. The I.I.A. has always ministered to this need and by organizing conferences, study-groups, and special series of postgraduate and non-graduate courses, encourages the continuance of serious study by its members and provides facilities for this to be done collectively. It is thus that the technique of the profession advances, and therefore members of a profession should be tireless in their search for technical knowledge.

Willingness to Give Unselfish Service to the Community

It is characteristic of the professions to give what Wickenden calls an "overplus" to the community. Gratuitous service to those in need is often offered by professional men in many ways with impressive generosity, inspired by an ideal of service. Industry has a special obligation to serve the community by supplying goods and services in the quantity required, of the right kind and quality, as economically as possible, and by contributing to a higher standard of living. Industrial managers, therefore, have a prominent part to play in public service and in human well-being, and they cannot play it effectively in isolation; they need the support of intellectual association with their peers.

A Professional Spirit with a Sense of Mission

The true professional is imbued with a profound conviction of the worthiness of his calling, and that conviction guides and dominates his actions. His zeal in the performance of his duty is quickened by a sense of mission—a belief that he and his fellow professionals can uniquely serve their

---

[15] T. M. Linville, *G.E.C. Management Consultant Services, Society for the Advancement of Management Journal,* August 1953.

[16] Carr-Saunders and Wilson, *op. cit.,* p. 295.

day and generation in the exercise of their particular technique. It follows that professional associations exert a stabilizing influence on the community, an influence which grows as the practitioners earn the trust of their fellow men. This they cannot do by resting content merely to demonstrate technical ability. The professional spirit is expressed in practical cooperation in human affairs, and in sustaining the dignities and decencies of life. Professional management, actuated by this spirit is capable of raising industrial morale and ameliorating human relationships in factory and workshop. Professional managers have opportunities greater than those open to almost all the other professions, teaching perhaps being an exception, for they are in daily contact with the men they "manipulate" and may intimately influence them for good or ill.

Implications for Members of the I.I.A.

Here, then, are broadly displayed and analyzed the implications of membership of a professional body, and there can be no reasonable doubt that the I.I.A. is entitled to be classed as such a body with all its grave responsibilities. Every member reflecting on these obligations must face today's challenge, for the idea of responsibility only begins where there is the conception of individual duty. The challenge is to faithful association, to participation in branch activities not as a matter of selfish interest but of resolve to share in the leavening of the vast mass of nonprofessional managers. A real hope, perhaps the best hope, of raising the quality of management in this country may truly be said to reside in the I.I.A. as the professional component of the B.I.M. The reason is clear. "Interest" in management, no matter how attractively fostered

and energetically catered for by the numerous organizations which, today, are busily engaged arranging meetings, courses, conferences and other *ad hoc* activities—with much overlapping and duplication—is useful but is not enough. Interest in management, so aroused, despite the skill and competency of the organizers is apt to be ephemeral; sorely lacking the element of permanence engendered by management undertaken as a profession. Mere interest is easily aroused, it does not invoke responsibility; its transient occasions may stimulate brief thoughts and passing enthusiasms for management problems. But only the confidence based on professional consciousness and professional association with its group activities, fellowship and mutual elevation, can provide the permanent inspiration and abiding sense of mission needed continuously to raise industrial efficiency and to transform industrial relations.

Management is not just a job for a living. Management is a life to be lived, to be lived publicly amongst people who necessarily spend a large part of their lives in conditions dictated by the processes and operations characteristic of the industry they serve. The "management life" may therefore impinge on and involve the happiness of many. The vocation of the professional manager is a high, an onerous and influential, calling.

It is the profound conviction of the writer of this paper that the duties and destinies of the "management life" can be accomplished most worthily by those whose resolve is—expressed by the words of St. Paul in another context—"Let us hold fast our profession."[17]

[17] St. Paul's Epistle to the Hebrews, iv: 14.

Associational Forms

The shape that associations may take is varied in many ways—in complexity, rigidity, hierarchy, and the like. Most professional persons believe that the maintenance of professional freedom is better achieved through the device of professional associations than through another associational form—the labor union.* Is there substance to this contention?

In terms of structure, medical associations have become prototypes for other highly professionalized occupations. The American Medical Association is approximately a century old; some medical associations in other parts of the world date from a considerably earlier period.† In large measure the recognized effectiveness of medicine and the importance accorded medical practitioners is attributable to the structure of their occupational associations. These associations enjoy wide support from practitioners, as they are able to act and react quickly in relatively monolithic fashion when desired. This is true despite the large size of the state and national associations. As the following selection indicates, the way an organization like the American Medical Association is structured allows it to accomplish its aims with efficiency. Playing an integral part in this process is the use of indirect representation and the attendant concentration of immense power in the hands of a relatively small group of physicians.

* It is contended that the professional association is better able to protect the peculiar occupational goals of these persons. The relationship between certain highly professionalized occupations and labor unions is examined later in this chapter. Strauss, *op.cit.*, p. 10, feels that "occupational associations form a continuum, from the learned society (which exists only to advance knowledge) at one extreme, to the economically oriented union at the other."
† For a discussion of the historical antecedents of associational structure see Carr-Saunders and Wilson, *op. cit.*, pp. 326–328.

The Editors of the Yale Law Journal (Medicine)

In its hundred-odd years of existence the American Medical Association has attained a position of undeniable authority and influence over medical affairs. The power of organized medicine affects not only the physician but also everyone who requires the assistance of the healing arts. AMA successes in raising the quality of medical education, practice, and care are beyond question. However, in these endeavors it has acquired such power over both public and practitioner that it can channel the development of American medicine. Dangers inherent in such power are compounded by the layman's ignorance of medical matters and the AMA's monopoly position as spokesman for the profession. Out of this situation arise questions of grave signi-

Reprinted from "The American Medical Association: Power, Purpose, and Politics in Organized Medicine," *The Yale Law Journal*, 63, No. 7 (May 1954), 938–947. Used by permission.

ficance. The AMA is motivated both by obligations to the public and loyalties to its own members. The demands on it from these two points of view underlie all its activities and suggest the possibility of conflict. To what extent does professional self-restraint, combined with present laws and institutions, assure that this conflict will be resolved in favor of the public interest?

THE AMA STRUCTURE

Membership

The American Medical Association consists of 53 state and territorial (constituent) societies and 1987 county (component) societies.[1] Each county society sets its own

[1] AMA, Guide to Services 4 (1952). Each component society serves a separate geographical area, and there can be no more than one county society in such an area. E.g., Va. Med. Soc. By-Laws Art. 3, § 2 (1953). However in some rural areas a local society may cover several counties. E.g., Colo. State Med. Soc. By-Laws c. 11, § 1 (1951–52).

qualifications for membership and its members automatically belong to the state association.[2] Aside from racial barriers in most Southern counties,[3] all "reputable and ethical" licensed M.D.'s are eligible for membership.[4] And in most areas virtually every practicing physician belongs to his local society.[5] Until recently, all members of county and state medical societies were also automatically members of the national association. But in 1950 payment of dues, previously assessed only by the county and state groups, became a prerequisite to AMA membership. Now some physicians belong only to their county and state societies, and are not members of the American Medical Association.[6] On the other hand, since belonging to a county society is a prerequisite to admission at all levels, membership in the AMA depends upon acceptance by the local organization.

Reasons for membership. Many factors contribute to the high percentage of physician membership in organized medicine—a proportion unique among voluntary professional associations.[7] With membership in the society, the doctor receives ready access to the social and professional contacts indispensable to the growth of his practice—contacts which may lead to patient referrals and consultations.[8] Additionally, there is the all-important factor of association with men engaged in his own science, with opportunities for exchange of knowledge and acquisition of professional status. The medical societies disseminate the latest scientific information through professional journals which are available to members either at no cost or at reduced rates, and through lectures, exhibits, and medical libraries which the societies support. In addition to these professional services, the local and state societies aid members by providing group malpractice insurance,[9] and by offering legal advice.[10] Many of the larger societies maintain bill collection agencies.[11] There may also be direct economic benefits incident to membership. Since the societies often contract to furnish medical care to

[2] E.g., *id.* c. 11 § 5. Some county societies in Kansas admit "associate members" although the state society will not recognize them as members. *Reply to Questionnaire,* Kansas Medical Society, Question No. 10. (Hereinafter cited as *Questionnaire* No. ——. A comprehensive questionnaire was sent to the 48 state medical societies and to the Medical Society of the District of Columbia. The following twenty-four fairly representative societies responded in varying degrees of detail to the 83 questions: Alabama, Arkansas, California, Colorado, Connecticut, Florida, Illinois, Iowa, Kansas, Louisiana, Maine, Massachusetts, Missouri, Montana, New Hampshire, New Mexico, Pennsylvania, South Dakota, Texas, Utah, Vermont, Virginia, Washington; and West Virginia. The original answers from each society and a compilation of all the answers given to each question are on file in the Yale Law Library.)

[3] See note 22.

[4] Many county societies impose additional requirements upon applicants for membership: *e.g.,* they must be graduates of an AMA approved medical school, United States citizens, present medical practitioners within the county, and practitioners of nonsectarian medicine. *Questionnaire* No. 9.

[5] *Questionnaire* No. 5. Half of the societies report over 90% membership among active physicians in their states. Only two states —Pennsylvania and Washington—report two-thirds membership or less.

[6] The AMA claims a membership of over 140,000. *Its Your AMA* [1] (1953). Although in one society—New Hampshire—less than 60% of the state society members pay dues to the AMA, more typically 95% to 99% are AMA members. *Questionnaire* No. 8. And in Illinois, the Society's constitution and by-laws require all members to pay AMA dues. Illinois *Questionnaire* No. 8.

[7] "How the Doctors Solved the Coordination Problem," 21 *A.B.A.J.* 221, 223 (1935).

[8] See Group Health Cooperative of Puget Sound *v.* King County Medical Society, 39 Wash. 2d 586, 626, 237 P.2d 737, 759 (1951); Garceau, *The Political Life of the American Medical Association* 103 (1941) (hereinafter cited as Garceau).

[9] A 1950 survey showed 35% of the county societies maintaining group malpractice insurance for their members. AMA, *Activities of County Medical Societies* 6, 7 (1951). Three state societies reporting now offer this insurance to their members and two others formerly did so. *Questionnaire* No. 55.

[10] See, e.g. *You and the Medical Society of New York* 14 (1952) (legal defense provided for members involved in malpractice suits).

[11] Seven per cent of the county societies responding to an AMA questionnaire had collection bureaus for their members. AMA, *Activities of County Medical Societies* 6, 7 (1951).

indigents[12] and veterans,[13] participating physicians have a supplementary source of income from these programs. Membership can also be a conduit to such professional advancements as hospital staff appointments,[14] teaching positions,[15] and specialty ratings.[16]

Beyond the advantages which accrue to the member physicians, there are services which the society renders to the profession as a whole. The AMA has improved curricula and facilities in American medical schools. It gives financial support to research projects and publicizes medical discoveries through its journals and meetings. Moreover, many doctors look to the American Medical Association to protect their interests against encroachment. Thus, the

AMA spearheaded the drive against compulsory health insurance and other governmental inroads into private medical practice. And the Association has worked to rid the profession of quacks, as well as licensed physicians thought guilty of malpractice, and to limit the activities of non-medical practitioners. Since the entire profession profits by these efforts of the AMA, physicians may feel obligated to join and give their material and moral support.[17]

Reasons for non-membership. However, a substantial number of American doctors do not belong to the American Medical Association or its component units.[18] Many of these are retired physicians who let their membership lapse, or young practitioners who have not yet fulfilled the residence requirements for their local society.[19] Doctors who do not conform to the code of medical ethics are not eligible for membership.[20] And many Southern societies exclude Negro physicians.[21] Salaried doctors, such as those

12 In Iowa the county societies conduct indigent patient clinics and in four other societies membership is a prerequisite to physician participation. *Questionnaire* No. 54(c); Iowa State Medical Society, *Handbook for the House of Delegates* 20–44 (1950) (county societies reporting upon relief contracts held with local Boards of Supervisors). See, generally, Stern, *Medical Services by Government* 23–26 (1946).

13 Iowa State Medical Society, *Handbook for the House of Delegates* 55 (1950) (reporting contract with Veterans Administration to furnish medical care in veterans hospitals); *You and the Medical Society of the State of New York* 53 (1952) (reporting fee schedule negotiations with the Veterans Administration for physicians serving veterans).

14 See Group Health Cooperative of Puget Sound *v.* King County Medical Society, 39 Wash. 2d 586, 620, 623–5, 237 P.2d 737, 755–6, 757–8 (1951).

15 E.g., in Illinois, Kansas, and Pennsylvania. *Questionnaire* No. 54(a). *Hearings Before Senate Committee on Education and Labor on S, 1606,* 79th Cong., 2d Sess. 2642 (1946) (non-members of the Chicago Medical Society ineligible for staff membership of teaching or research institutions). But see text note 23.

16 "We [non-society members] cannot be accredited by various specialty boards because membership in the local medical society is a condition of eligibility. This is an increasingly serious handicap, since many hospitals are making certification by a specialty board an absolute condition for practicing within those hospitals." Testimony of Lawrence Jacques, M.D., in *Hearings,* note 16, at 2642. See also Group Health Cooperative of Puget Sound *v.* King County Medical Society, 39 Wash. 2d 286, 626, 237 P.2d 737, 759 (1951).

17 The AMA and the state societies solicit support by emphasizing their contributions to the profession. See, e.g., *It's Your AMA* [1] (1953): "We can take great pride in our AMA. It is the largest, most influential and most active medical association in the world. Even if you are not a member, it is your AMA to a certain extent. The Association began helping you the day you entered medical school and continues to aid your practice and guard your freedom. Though, for one reason or another, you do not share the responsibilities of membership, you benefit daily from the Association's work." See also *You and the Medical Society of the State of New York* 4 (1952) ("The freedom with which you practice and your very livelihood would be seriously jeopardized if the physicians of New York were not organized into a state-wide association.").

18 Of the 215,000 licensed physicians in the United States, *World Almanac* 779 (1954), about 140,000 are AMA members. Note 7. Some non-AMA members belong to local and state societies. Note 5.

19 *Questionnaire* No. 5. Connecticut, for example, has a one-year residence requirement, and reports a corresponding lag in admitting physicians newly arrived in the state.

20 E.g., Tex. Med. Ass'n Const. Art. 1, § 3 (1952).

21 The majority of county medical societies in the Southern states deny membership to Negro physicians. Of those Southern societies responding to the *Questionnaire,* four report no Negro

on the staffs of universities and research institutes, and civil servants often do not join medical societies;[22] here professional advancement is available through channels other than medical society membership. In remote areas, services which the society can render may be so negligible that doctors have little incentive to join.[23] Some phy-sicians may find the dues prohibitive; for example, in parts of California the total of county, state, and national dues runs as high as $190 annually.[24] Undoubtedly some doctors do not join because of apathy,[25] while a small minority of physicians do not choose to belong because they disapprove of the policies of the AMA.[26]

---

members. *Alabama, Louisiana, Texas, Virginia Questionnaire* No. 11 Cf. 140 *Journal of the American Medical Association* 1278 (1949) (hereinafter cited as *JAMA*).

The unsegregated National Medical Association is the organization to which most Negro physicians belong. In 1870 the AMA House of Delegates refused to accredit the NMA as a constituent society. Cobb, *The First Negro Medical Society,* 2 (1939). In rejecting the NMA's then tiny membership the AMA established a policy, since written into the by-laws of many state societies, of one component society only in a given geographical area. E.g., Va. Med. Soc. By-Laws Art 3, § 2 (1953). Members of the colored Medico-Chirurgical Society of the District of Columbia, for example, cannot become AMA members through their present organization since, as the component society for that territory, the District of Columbia Medical Society fills the field.

There have been some signs of progress in the eradication of racial barriers on the local level. Recently, previously exclusionary local societies in the District of Columbia, Florida, and Missouri have admitted Negro members. Cannon, *Why I am a Member of the Physicians Forum,* Physicians Forum Bull., Sept., 1951, p. 10. See also *Arkansas, Florida, Missouri Questionnaire* No. 11 (reporting some Negro members). In 1950, New York sent the first colored member, Dr. Peter Murray, to the AMA House of Delegates. 140 *JAMA* 1278 (1949). Dr. Murray has since been elected to office in the New York County Medical Society. N. Y. Times, May 27, 1952, p. 29, col. 4(Vice-President); *id.,* May 26, 1953, p. 31, col. 8 (President-Elect). And members of the NMA have attended AMA's county, state, and national scientific sessions, and NMA "observers" have been invited to AMA conventions. See, e.g., 140 *JAMA* 1278 (1949).

But the AMA as a national organization has failed to take steps toward a fundamental change in membership policy. Its spokesmen assert their inability to act, pointing out that each county society has absolute control over its own membership qualifications. Cannon, see text at 9; Chicago Tribune, May 19, 1939 (Editorial). However, a group of New York physicians obtained state society approval of a resolution providing that "no constituent association shall exclude from membership any physician for other than professional or ethical reasons." The reso-lutions failed in the AMA House of Delegates. "Medicine: White or Black," 68 *School & Society* 70 (1948). Similarly the Medical Society of North Carolina made an unsuccessful attempt to challenge the one component society geographical rule when it proposed admittance of the colored Old North State Medical Society as a constituent organization. 147 *JAMA* 1241 (1951); 150 *JAMA* 1684 (1952).

The AMA has, however, deemed it politic to court colored non-member doctors for support in its opposition to compulsory health insurance. At the 1950 NMA convention, an AMA representative cited Dr. Murray's election to the House of Delegates as an indication of equality in medicine. Cannon, see text at 9. The NMA, seeking the full benefit of AMA membership for all colored physicians, treated AMA overtures with caution. It avoided the endorsement of either the AMA's or the Truman Administration's position on health insurance, perhaps hoping that its strength of 4000 members might be a bargaining lever to gain full affiliation. *Time,* Aug. 22, 1949, p. 32. But with the compulsory health insurance issue at least temporarily mooted, the southern colored physician will have to look for a change of heart from within the AMA before he can expect full equality with his white colleague.

22. *Questionnaire* No. 5; Garceau 105.

23 Cf. *West Virginia Questionnaire No. 5.*

24 *California Questionnaire* Nos. 12, 13. Several societies mention inability to pay dues as a cause of non-membership. *Questionnaire* No. 5. Other societies mitigate the dues requirement in cases of financial hardships. See, e.g., Colo. State Med. Soc. By-Laws c. 1, § 5a (1951–52); W. Va. State Med. Ass'n By-Laws c 1, § 5 (1952).

The range of county society dues within a state may be wide. E.g., Texas: $1 to $100; California: $5 to $125. *Questionnaire* No. 13. And state society dues vary from $15 to $55 a year; the average is about $25. Questionnaire No. 12.

The AMA assesses its members $25 for annual dues. AMA, *Guide to Services* 10 (1952). However it grants exemptions for the following reasons: financial hardship, retirement from practice or reaching the age of 70, internship or residency within five years of graduation. *Id.* at 17.

25 *Questionnaire* No. 5.

26 See, e.g., *"Dr. J. H. Means resigns from AMA to protest levy to fight Federal Insurance,"* N. Y. *Times,* June 22, 1951, p. 14, col. 4.

Formal structure

The formal structure of the American Medical Association provides for the largest measure of direct democratic control in the county medical societies, and increasingly indirect representation at the state and national levels. Members vote directly for county officials and representatives to the state "legislature," usually known as the House of Delegates.[27] These delegates select their own state officers and elect the state representatives to the national House of Delegates.[28] This body elects the President and other AMA officers and the nine-man Board of Trustees.[29]

In theory, the policy-making function of the American Medical Association is vested in the House of Delegates. However, since the House meets semi-annually, many administrative and policy decisions are necessarily left to the Board of Trustees.[30] Although it is responsible to the House of Delegates, the Board functions with little supervision when the House is not in session. The members of the Board perform the typical role of corporate directors: they approve all AMA expenditures, and generally the Chiefs of the Association's operating bureaus are responsible to them.[31] The Trustees also appoint the Secretary-General Manager[32] and the editor of the *Journal*.[33] The President has little formal power in formulating AMA policy, although he enjoys tremendous prestige as chief spokesman for the organization.[34]

The AMA functions through standing committees or councils elected by the House of Delegates or appointed by the Board of Trustees.[35] Each council directs the activities of the Association in a particular field with the assistance of a full-time staff. The 900 employees of the national organization are supervised by the Secretary-General Manager of the Association, who has chief responsibility for the day-to-day

27 Each county society is entitled to at least one delegate although representation in state Houses is generally proportional to membership in the local society. Apportionment ratios vary among the societies from one delegate for every ten members to one for every hundred; the average representation is one delegate for every twenty-five members. *Questionnaire* No. 19. Densely populated areas tend to be under-represented. E.g., in New York, Schuyler County has one delegate for its eleven members. While New York County (Manhattan) has only 24 delegates representing its 6954 members. Kings County (Brooklyn) also has 24 delegates for 3467 members. *You and the Medical Society of the State of New York* 32 (1952).

28 An AMA delegate's term is two years. State societies are represented by one delegate for every thousand members or fraction thereof. A representative from the Army, Navy, Air Force, Veterans Administration, and U. S. Public Health Service, and twenty representatives from the specialized medical fields within the AMA also serve in the House. AMA By-Laws c. 9, § 1 (B) (1952).

29 The president, president-elect, vice-president, and other AMA officers are elected annually. The president and president-elect serve on the Board of Trustees. The other trustees are chosen for staggered five-year terms and may serve not more than two successive terms. *It's Your AMA* 3 (1953).

30 *Ibid.* The Trustees meet six or eight times a year.

31 AMA By-Laws c. 13, § 4(A) (1952). The powers of the AMA Board of Trustees are duplicated on the state level. E.g., the Texas Board of Trustees serves "as a board of directors, within the meaning of the corporate laws of the state." Tex. Med. Ass'n Const. Art. 4 (1952).

32 AMA By-Laws, c. 13, § 4(D) (1952). After he is appointed General Manager by the Trustees, he is elected secretary by the House of Delegates. Unlike the officers and Trustees, he is a salaried employee. *It's Your AMA* 3 (1953).

33 AMA By-Laws c. 13, § 4(C) (1952). Until recently the editor of the *Journal* was the dominant figure in the Association. Mayer, "The Rise and Fall of Dr. Fishbein," *Harper's*, Nov., 1949, p. 199.

34 The President's official duties consist largely of addressing the House of Delegates and nominating members for various committees, subject to confirmation by the House or Trustees. AMA By-Laws c. 12, § 1 (1952). Prior to his term of office, the president serves as president-elect for one year, during which time he presides over the General Sessions and Council of the Scientific Assembly. AMA Const. Art. 7, § 3; AMA By-Laws c. 12, § 2 (1952). However, the "President's Page" in the *Journal* and his frequent appearances before Congressional Committees increase the president's importance as "chief spokesman for the Association on policy matters." *It's Your AMA* 3 (1953).

35 For a general description of the AMA's operational structure, see *It's Your AMA* 1–6 (1953); *AMA, Guide to Services* 8–9 (1952).

decisions of the organization between meetings of the Board of Trustees.

Real power structure

While democratic procedures exist at the county level,[36] many members do not have sufficient interest in activities to attend meetings.[37] Doctors are extremely busy with their practice and have little time to devote to the problems of organized medicine. In New York, for example, 25% attendance at a business meeting is considered good.[38] Thus, the few doctors who are interested in medical politics can easily wield power and influence out of proportion to their numerical strength.

The nominating process for elections within the American Medical Association allows the officers in power to have the dominant influence in deciding who shall succeed them in office. At the county level, the President appoints a nominating committee which puts up a slate of officers and delegates for the state House of Delegates.[39] The state President functions in the same way in the selection of national delegates.[40] These elections are rarely contested.[41] In at least one state, Alabama, the delegates are appointed by the president.[42] The election of the official slate is made easier by the fact that the state and national organizations forbid electioneering and soliciting votes for office.[43] Even where the official slate offers alternative nominees, basic differences between the candidates are unlikely.[44]

The nominating process, in combination

---

[36] See, however, AMA, "Putting PR to Work," 13 (1st Public Relations Institute, 1952): "You would be surprised how many county societies do not even have a semblance of democracy in their sessions." (Statement of county society official.)

[37] The results of an AMA survey showed that urban county societies had the lowest average attendance at meetings. Sixty of 64 societies with more than 300 members report attendance of under 50%, while only 48 of 581 societies having less than 100 members were in this category. And 111 of the smaller societies report 90–100% attendance. AMA, "Activities of County Medical Societies," 3 (1951). Although the AMA regards these results as indicative of generally good attendance at local meetings, a former AMA President has remarked that "if 10% of the membership [in many areas] attend a meeting it is about average and it is usually the same 10% at each meeting." Bauer, "The Importance of the County Medical Society in the State and National Programs" (address before the Medical Society of the State of New York, January 27, 1947) (copy on file in Yale Law Library).

County societies list as their best attended meetings those featuring speeches on general medical subjects by "well known" and "respected" members of the medical profession. Meetings on socio-economic problems are ranked as poorly attended, "despite the increased interest in...[these] problems by members of the medical profession during the past few years." AMA, "Activities of County Medical Societies," 4 (1951).

[38] Richardson, "Freedom of Speech and Organized Medicine," 4 (undated typewritten manuscript on file with Physicians Forum, 510 Madison Ave., New York City).

[39] E.g., *Pennsylvania Questionnaire* No. 18. In Virginia the county president alone chooses some of the delegates to the State House. *Virginia Questionnaire* No. 18.

[40] E.g., Kans. Med. Soc. By-Laws c. 6, § 1 (1952) (Nominating Committee for the selection of state society officers composed of five former Society Presidents); Colo. State Med. Soc. By-Laws c. 6, § 1 (1951–52) (nominations from the floor permitted); *Connecticut Questionnaire* No. 20 (same).

All state society delegates to the AMA House must meet the AMA constitutional requirements of two years' prior membership in the AMA and its Scientific Assembly. AMA By-Laws c 9, § 1(A) (1952).

[41] *Questionnaire* No. 21 (only four of 24 state societies report competition for position of AMA delegate). Kansas requires Nominating Committees to present two nominees for each delegate position. Kans Med. Soc. By-Laws c 6, § 1 (1952).

[42] *Alabama Questionnaire* No. 20.

[43] E.g., Kans. Med. Soc. By-Laws c 6, § 4 (1952); AMA House of Delegates Standing Rule, adopted June 13, 1902: "Resolved that it is the sense of the House of Delegates of the AMA that the solicitation of votes for office is not in keeping with the dignity of the medical profession, nor in harmony with the spirit of this Association, and that such solicitation shall be considered a disqualification for election to any office in the gift of the Association." Although the Judicial Council has stated that this rule, as phrased, was unenforceable, Fishbein, *A History of the American Medical Association*, 419–20 (1947) (hereinafter cited as Fishbein), it was found to be an "effective moral influence," *ibid.*, and it has never been repealed. *Id.* at 224.

[44] Richardson, *op. cit* note 39, at 3–4.

with the apathy of the average doctor,[45] assures domination by a single faction within the AMA.[46] In New York—one of the few states where an organized opposition has developed—these challengers have had little success.[47] State societies report that reelection of delegates is common,[48] the same names appearing on the ballot year after year. Frequently officers progress steadily from county, to state, to national prominence as they acquire seniority.[49]

[45] The inertia of the majority of AMA members has been attributed to the consuming nature of medicine, the drive toward material success, and an aversion against "politics." Garceau 61–3. Consequently the membership is said to turn to the AMA, thus saving itself from the "awkward predicament of having to think." *Id.* at 101.

[46] Richardson, *op. cit.* note 39, at 4.

[47] The Physicians Forum was organized in 1941 by members of the Medical Society of the County of New York to defeat a proposed amendment to the state society constitution. This amendment provided that members "shall not initiate or participate in any activities outside the structure of the Medical Society of the State of New York, which are contrary to [its] policies. . . . " Chapters have been formed in other cities and the group has promoted health insurance and other measures counter to "official AMA doctrine." 12 N.Y. *Medicine*, Nov. 20, 1952, p. 13 (letter from Ernst P. Boas, M.D., chairman of Physicians Forum). Although the Forum was successful in defeating the amendment and in electing "several liberal minded physicians" to county officerships, its influence was of short duration. Richardson, *op. cit.* note 39, at 16.

[48] Several societies report that all delegates are re-elected while others estimate that between one-third and one-half of the delegates are rechosen. One replied that "receptive delegates" are re-elected and another characterized the tenure of delegates as extending "until they choose to retire." Only three indicated that few or no delegates were "repeaters." *Questionnaire* No. 23.

[49] An example of "devotion to medical society office" is the career of former AMA President Rock Sleyster who served as Secretary of his county society, Secretary, President, Treasurer, and Editor of the Wisconsin Society, Delegate and Vice-Speaker of the AMA House, and member and Chairman of the Board of Trustees. Garceau 59. For further illustrations see *id.* at 58–61.

The "active physician" in the New York Society proceeds from membership in a standing committee to its chairmanship. The second vice-president, who automatically becomes President

One of the major obstacles to the formation of any opposition is the lack of an effective forum for dissident opinion. The *Journal of the American Medical Association,* which is the publication most widely read by members, rarely prints opinions in disagreement with positions taken by the House of Delegates or Board of Trustees.[50] In response to criticism of this policy the American Medical Association asserts that members can present their views initially in their county societies; that if these views win approval, delegates will present them to the state society, and finally the members' opinions will be presented to the national House of Delegates for consideration.[51] In practice, however, because of the indirect system of elections,[52] such a pro-

within a few years, is chosen from such members. Richardson, *op. cit.* note 39, at 3.

[50] Davis, *America Organizes Medicine* 175–176 (1941); Medical Economics, July, 1952, p. 12. Spokesmen have emphasized their desire that organized medicine present a united front. See, e.g., *JAMA* 936 (1938) ("Once the House of Delegates has spoken its actions should be supported by the united voice of American medicine."); 49 N.Y. *State J. of Med.* 2527 (1949); cf. 139 *JAMA* 788 (1949). Perhaps the *Journal's* practice is a result of this attitude. However, this policy has been widely criticized. See 1 N.Y. *Medicine,* Aug. 20, 1945, p. 11 (editorial advising that "some further consideration. . .be given to [the *Journal's*] policy with reference to publication of dissident opinions and views."); 244 *N. Eng. J. of Med.* 307 (1951) (reporting resolution of Mass. Medical Society urging "that the *Journal of the American Medical Association* welcome and provide space for the presentation of considered discussion from varying points of view. . . ."). Cf. N.Y. *Times,* Nov. 30, 1952, p. 54, col. 3 (Editor of *Atlantic Monthly* criticizing *Journal's* refusal to accept paid advertisement of article on compulsory health insurance.)

State society journals have been similarly criticized. Davis, *op. cit.*; Garceau 100; 27 *J. of Pediatrics* 196 (1945). However, there are some exceptions. The *New England Journal of Medicine* maintains that its columns are open to comment critical of the official AMA position and has published divergent viewpoints. 240 *N. Eng. J. of Med.* 397 (1949).

[51] 149 *JAMA* 1227 (1952). But see 5 N.Y. *Medicine,* March 5, 1949, p. 41 (county society member describing his inability to have his views heard); note 37.

[52] See text at note 40 *et seq.*

cedure eliminates any dissident viewpoints above the county level unless they win majority support. And while a member can oppose official policy in his local society, the structure of organized medicine makes it almost impossible for him to effectuate his opinions within this framework.[53]

One study of the American Medical Association has concluded that the physicians who rise to power within the medical societies are predominantly urban practitoners and specialists.[54] Although there is only a slightly larger number of specialists in the United States than general practitioners,[55] usually over 90% of the officers of the AMA are specialists.[56] Specialists, whose incomes are above those of the average practioner,[57] are probably better able to devote time to medical politics. Statistics also reveal that cities contribute a larger proportion of officers than rural areas.[58] And in the AMA House of Delegates those who have served long terms are primarily from urban localities, while the shorter term delegates tend to be from the rural areas.[59]

Although these officers are not "average" American doctors, it would not be accurate to say that their policies are unrepresentative. The support of the membership is clearly shown in the immediate response of most members to a voluntary assessment voted by the House of Delegates.[60] Most members also seem willing to distribute literature and advocate AMA policies. But perhaps the most indicative fact is that groups organized to oppose AMA policies regarding the economic and political aspects of medical practice have never gained widespread support among the doctors. No group of any significance that has been formed to modify or review AMA policy has offered itself as an alternative to the AMA. Doctors are free to join such organizations while retaining their AMA membership but few have enrolled.[61] Even though the actively controlling group within the American Medical Association is a self-perpetuating minority its viewpoint is readily accepted by the passive majority. This acquiescence assists that governing minority in excluding dissident opinion from organized medicine.

53 But cf. 149 *JAMA* 1227 (1952) (example of individual member's securing passage of previously unconsidered resolution concerning physical selection of airplane pilots without prior official support).

54 Garceau 55–58.

55 There were, in 1949, approximately 72,500 physicians exclusively in general practice, 55,000 exclusively practicing a specialty, and 23,000 general practitioners "giving attention" to a specialty. 3 President's Commission on the Health Needs of the Nation, Building America's Health 140 (1952–53) (hereinafter cited as Magnuson Rep.).

56 All but one of the present members of the Board of Trustees and all AMA Presidents, Vice-Presidents, and Speakers since 1947 have been specialists. Compilation on file in Yale Law Library.

57 4 Magnuson Rep. 247.

58 Only seven of 31 recent and present high officers and Trustees of the AMA practice in communities of 25,000 population or less. Compilation on file in Yale Law Library.

59 Garceau 50.

60 Only one state society indicated that less than 50% of its membership paid the 1948 assessment. And 14 societies reported that from 60% to 96% of their members contributed. *Questionnaire* No. 15.

61 Thus, the Committee of Physicians for the Improvement of Medical Care has functioned within the AMA with about 700 members. *Means, Doctors, People, and Government* 147–151 (1953); Davis, *America Organizes Medicine* 298 (1911). The Physicians Forum is open only to members of county societies or the National Medical Association, 12, N.Y. *Medicine,* Nov. 20, 1952, p. 12, and has never drawn much support. See note 48.

Another type of associational form which has been used by some rather highly professionalized occupations is the trade union, and this is particularly true in the field of engineering. We must recognize, however, that the proportion of professional engineers in the labor force who have affiliated themselves with labor unions has, at all times, been small—i.e., less than five per cent. One study of unionism among engineers concludes by saying this:

It appears to be a rather pragmatic adjustment to an immediate situation, consonant with ideological beliefs and attitudes, rather than a function of the social background factors that were tested. . . . Engineering unions will tend to appear where a large number of engineers at a particular site share common problems, where unions of other employees of the company or engineering trade unions have been effective in dealing with similar problems, and where unionism is seen as a method of solving their problems compatible with both their attitudes and their ideals.*

The following selection explores more fully the question of unionization among engineers, and provides information on why unionization, as an associational form, is not expected to make greater inroads among professional engineers. As an extension of this argument, it is probably safe to predict few instances where highly professionalized occupations will utilize the trade union as an associational form. As Dvorak shows, there are certain elements inherent to the highly professionalized occupation which mitigate against the widespread use of this particular associational form.†

* Bernard Goldstein and Bernard P. Indik, "Unionism as a Social Choice: The Engineers' Case," *Monthly Labor Review*, **86**, No. 4 (April 1963), 365–369.
† This was also a point made by Logan Wilson in discussing the American Association of University Professors; he raised the question whether it was a "professional association or a union." This appears in his book *The Academic Man* (New York: Oxford University Press, 1942), 124–126. In addition, Roy Lewis and Angus Maude in their work *The English Middle Classes* (London: Phoenix House, 1949), pp. 150–151, take the position that "trade unions display certain features which are not wholly consistent with the performance of all these [professional] functions" such as "intellectual and political independence," the stimulation of "progress and research in its mystery and—most important of all—must seek always to protect individual clients and the public at large from injury or exploitation."

Eldon J. Dvorak (Engineering)

With the rapid growth of professional and technical workers as a percentage of the labor force, students of the American labor movement have become increasingly interested in this occupational group as a possible source of future growth of unionism in the United States.[1] One of the most rapidly growing occupations has been

Reprinted from "Will Engineers Unionize?", *Industrial Relations*, 2, No. 3 (May 1963), 45–65. Used by permission of the author and publisher. Earlier studies of this topic are to be found in Clarence T. Schock, "The Professional Union—A Contradiction," *The Journal of Engineering Education*, 45, No. 4, (December 1954), 345–357; Bernard Goldstein, "Some Aspects of the Nature of Unionism Among Salaried Professionals in Industry," *American Sociological Review*, 20, No. 2 (April 1955), 199–205; and Strauss, *op. cit.*, pp. 26–29.

[1] The writer is indebted to J. Benton Gillingham, Chairman of the Economics Department, University of Washington, who supervised the Ph.D. dissertation upon which this article is based, and to Dan N. Hendricks, Jr., former president of the Seattle Professional Engineering Employees' Association, who provided considerable information for this analysis.

engineering. By 1950, the number of engineers ranked second only to that of teachers among professional and technical workers. And engineers for some time have been by far the most numerous of the professional and technical workers employed by private industry. Since 1950, the number of engineers has continued to increase more than almost any occupation, including teachers.[2] According to Department of Labor projections for the sixties, "The fastest growth will occur among the professional and technical occupations, especially engineers, scientists and technicians."[3] Consequently, widespread acceptance of

[2] *Historical Statistics of the United States, Colonial Times to 1957*, U. S. Bureau of Census (Washington, D.C.: 1960), p. 75; *United States Census of Population, 1960, United States Summary, General Social and Economic Characteristics*, U. S. Bureau of the Census (Washington, D.C.: 1962), p. 1–216.

[3] *Manpower Challenge of the 1960's*, U. S. Department of Labor (Washington, D.C.: 1960), p. 10.

unionism and collective bargaining in the engineering profession, if it should occur, would have important implications for union growth in general.

This article will be concerned with the experience of engineering unions in the United States in the postwar period, with a view to shedding light on the outlook for unionism in this field.

ORIGIN OF PRESENT-DAY ENGINEERS' UNIONS

The oldest union engaging in collective bargaining in the interests of engineers is the American Federation of Technical Engineers (AFTE), AFL-CIO. Membership in the original organization consisted almost entirely of marine draftsmen. It affiliated with the American Federation of Labor in 1918 under the name International Federation of Draftsmen's Unions; later, the organization used the name International Federation of Technical Engineers, Architects, and Draftsmen's Unions. Subsequently, the name American Federation of Technical Engineers was adopted. Only about a thousand professional engineers are represented by the AFTE. The remainder of the organization's 12,450 members consists of subprofessionals or preprofessionals. Most of its strength has been concentrated in shipyards, government agencies, and public and private construction projects; however, in more recent years some subprofessional membership has been found in other sectors of private industry.[4]

With the exception of the AFTE and the Federation of Architects, Engineers, Chemists, and Technicians (FAECT), collective bargaining organizations representing engi-

neers were almost nonexistent prior to the forties. The FAECT, which was organized during the depression of the thirties and affiliated with the CIO in 1937, merged with the United Office and Professional Workers of America (UOPWA) in 1946. Officers of the UOPWA refused to sign noncommunist affidavits after passage of the Taft-Hartley Act in 1947, and the organization supported Henry Wallace in the 1948 presidential campaign. Subsequently, the UOPWA lost members and contracts, and in 1950 it was expelled from the CIO on charges of Communist domination.[5] Since that time the organization has gone out of existence.

During the forties, a number of independent engineers' unions were organized throughout the country. Most of the existing engineers' unions originated during that period, and by far the greatest portion of the present union membership of engineers is to be found in these independent unions. During that decade, a particular set of circumstances caused significant numbers of engineers, who ordinarily have an apparent aversion to unionism, to accept collective bargaining as a means of influencing their conditions of employment.

A growth in the number of engineers was accompanied by a considerable change, which had begun earlier, in the character of engineering employment. In contrast to earlier times, when most engineers were either self-employed or worked with a few other engineers on a consulting basis, the typical engineer became one of many, in some cases one of several thousand, engineers working for a large firm. Work was increasingly subjected to much closer controls than normally prevail in other professions. In many firms, strict working hours and use of the time clock were required of engineers, as well as production workers. Engineering services apparently began to be considered by management as a variable, rather than a fixed, cost of

[4] *International Federation of Technical Engineers, Architects and Draftsmen's Unions, Silver Anniversary, 1918–1943* (Washington, D.C.: International Federation of Technical Engineers, Architects and Draftsmen's Unions, 1943), pp. 1–9; *Tabulation of Unions Representing Engineering and Technical Employees* (5th ed.: Washington, D.C.: National Society of Professional Engineers, August 1961), pp. 4–8; Interview with H. W. Nelson, Business Manager, Technical Engineers and Architects Association, Local 17, August 28, 29, 1961.

[5] Vera Shlakman, "Unionism and Professional Organizations Among Engineers," *Science and Society,* 14 (Fall, 1950), 323–324; Elinor Waters, "Unionization of Office Employees," *Journal of Business,* 27 (October 1954), 286.

production, and engineering employment tended to fluctuate with fluctuations in product demand, in much the same manner as employment of production workers. During the Great Depression, unemployment among engineers was considerably more widespread than in most other professions.

In addition, the somewhat narrow experience of the typical engineer, which resulted from increased specialization in engineering functions, made him more vulnerable to layoff and less eligible for job opportunities elsewhere if his specialty became obsolete or the demand for his services declined for some other reason. Moreover, since each engineer was usually assigned only one small part of an over-all group effort, he frequently did not know just what he had contributed to solving a broad engineering problem.

The fact that most engineers became employees of business firms also resulted in considerable restriction of research activities. Many other sorts of professional workers were relatively free to choose research subjects and to publish in professional journals. But the engineer's research usually conformed to his firm's objectives and often the results were kept secret for competitive reasons. Also, most firms retained patent rights over inventions of their engineering employees.

Along with changes which tended to lower professional status, engineers suffered a decline in earnings relative to most other workers in the labor force. The widespread unemployment of engineers during the thirties was accompanied by a corresponding drop in earnings.[6] And, according to a study by Blank and Stigler, median salaries of engineers continued to decline relative to those of most other occupations until 1953. The Blank and Stigler study also revealed a compression of the salary structure within the engineering profession, i.e., percentage increases in salary rates tended

to be inversely related to years of experience.[7] This development is also discussed by W. Lee Hansen in another article in this symposium.

Despite the apparent loss of professional status and other problems which prevailed in the engineering profession for some time, few engineers turned to collective bargaining. Apparently most engineers believed that the loss in professional status resulting from joining a union would have been greater than the losses resulting from other factors. It was not until the production unions threatened to include engineers within their jurisdiction, prior to the Taft-Hartley Act, that a substantial number of engineers considered organizing collective bargaining units of their own. In effect, they organized primarily to avoid becoming part of the existing labor movement.

A number of the independent collective bargaining organizations of engineers were organized with the assistance of some of the engineering technical societies, particularly the American Society of Civil Engineers (ASCE). In 1937, the ASCE, in response to pleas from its membership, set up committees to begin studying the problem of unionizing engineers. It was not until after the Sunflower Ordnance Case in 1943, however, that any bargaining units of engineers were formed as a result of the ASCE's efforts. In that case, brought before the War Labor Board, professional engineers protested being represented by a local of the International Federation of Technical Engineers, Architects, and Draftsmen's Unions, AFL, at the Sunflower Ordnance Works, Eudora, Kansas.[8] The ASCE assisted in several appearances before the War Labor Board, but the protest was denied on the grounds that the professional group could not show that they were formally organized to represent a substantial group and that the group could not then

---

[6] *Employment and Earnings in the Engineering Profession, 1929–1934*, U. S. Bureau of Labor Statistics, Bulletin No. 682 (Washington, D.C.: 1941), pp. 3, 7–9, 13, 162.

[7] David M. Blank and George J. Stigler, *The Demand and Supply of Scientific Personnel* (New York: National Bureau of Economic Research, 1957), pp. 25, 127, 131.

[8] "Engineers Protest Affiliation with Subprofessionals," *Civil Engineering,* **13** (July 1943), 337–338.

clearly define "professional engineer" to distinguish its members from the subprofessionals.[9]

Subsequently, the ASCE Board of Direction adopted three proposals for dealing with the situation. First, the Board suggested that local sections of the ASCE amend their constitutions to permit employee-members to form collective bargaining groups. Second, the Society appropriated $50,000 to finance the activities of four field representatives who were to assist and advise the locals. Third, the Board published a lengthy definition of "professional engineering employees" in order to clarify the position of these employees and to assure uniformity in the membership of the employee groups. After a number of bargaining units had been set up with ASCE assistance, the Society's legal counsel advised that such activity might cause the ASCE to be considered a labor organization under New York State legislation. And since the Society's membership included engineers in management positions, its labor-organizing activities were considered to be illegal. The bargaining units were therefore removed from affiliation with the ASCE and became self-administered and self-financed.[10]

Although not all independent engineer bargaining units had the assistance of technical societies, most, if not all, of them were organized as a defense against the traditional labor unions. With only minor exceptions, all the independent units were started in the forties, prior to the Taft-Hartley Act.

In recent years, the International Union of Electrical, Radio, and Machine Workers (IUE), AFL-CIO, and the United Automobile, Aircraft, and Agricultural Implement Workers of America (UAW), AFL-CIO, have established a few locals representing engineers and technical workers. These have considerable autonomy, despite their affiliation with industrial unions.

UNION REPRESENTATION AND MEMBERSHIP

According to data prepared by the National Society of Professional Engineers, independent unions represented a total of 41,538 scientists, engineers, and technicians in August 1961. It seems reasonable to assume that the percentage of the total representation constituted by professionals in all of the independent unions is approximately the same as it is in those for which data are available. Under this assumption, about 87 per cent, or 36,200, of the employees represented by the independent unions are professional scientists or engineers. Applying this same method of estimation to the AFL-CIO affiliated unions, we find that 26 per cent, or 4,900, of the 19,127 workers represented by these AFL-CIO affiliates are professionals. According to these estimates then, a total of roughly 41,100 scientists and engineers are represented by unions.

Using a similar assumption with respect to union membership, about 52 per cent of the 41,538 professional and technical workers represented by the independent unions are probably union members. Assuming further that membership as a per cent of representation is the same for the professionals as it is for all workers represented by these unions, about 52 per cent of the 36,200 engineers and scientists represented, or 18,700 of them, are members of independent unions. Again, the same method of estimation can be applied to the AFL-CIO affiliated unions. Under these assumptions, 91 per cent, or 4,500, of the 4,897 scientists and engineers represented by AFL-CIO affiliates are members of the unions. These rough estimates suggest that total union membership of scientists and engineers is about 23,200.

In 1959, there were 782,800 engineers and 313,400 scientists, a total of 1,096,200, employed in the civilian economy.[11] Thus our estimates suggest that only about 4 per cent of all scientists and engineers employed in the civilian economy are represented by

---

[9] "Sunflower Case Placed Before War Labor Board," *Civil Engineering,* **13** (August 1943), 394.

[10] "Collective Bargaining, A Historical Review," *Civil Engineering,* **14** (July 1944), 311–313.

[11] *The Long-Range Demand for Scientific and Technical Personnel,* U. S. Bureau of Labor Statistics (Washington, D.C.: 1961), p. 49.

unions. Similarly, only about 2 per cent are members of unions. Undoubtedly engineers account for most of the unionism among scientists and engineers. If one assumes that all of the estimated 41,100 professionals represented by these unions and all of the 23,200 professional members are engineers, about 5 per cent of the engineers employed in the civilian economy are represented by unions and 3 per cent are union members. These figures indicate further that less than a half of one per cent of all engineers and scientists in the civilian economy belong to AFL-CIO affiliated unions.

Although the percentage of all white-collar workers who are union members (about 7.7 per cent) is relatively small, the percentage of engineers and scientists belonging to unions apparently is considerably smaller.[12] Moreover, the available evidence, scanty as it is, suggests that both union representation and membership in engineering have been declining in recent years.

First, the relatively complete data for the Seattle Professional Engineering Employees' Association indicate that although representation of this organization has been increasing rapidly, owing to the rapid increase in employment of engineers at the Boeing Company, membership has been growing at a much slower rate, and recently SPEEA membership has actually declined. If SPEEA's experience is typical, union membership of engineers has been dropping steadily as a per cent of representative capacity for some time and recently has declined in absolute terms as well.

Second, some data are available for the bargaining units formerly affiliated with ESA. In 1953, the ESA claimed representation of 40,000 engineers and scientists.[13] A

recent tabulation indicates that total representation—including both professionals and subprofessionals—of the unions formerly affiliated with the ESA was only 38,671 in August 1961. These figures strongly suggest declines in union representation, as well as union membership, among engineers.

Third, with the exception of the unit at Arma (established in 1951), the small unit at Ward Leonard (established in 1954), the Federation of Westinghouse Independent Salaried Unions (started in 1956), and possibly some other small units, no new engineers' unions have been established since the Taft-Hartley Act was passed in 1947. The recent decertification of the Council of Western Electric Professional Employees-National, which represented over six thousand professionals, and the decertification of the Minneapolis Honeywell unit more than offset the additions to union representation provided by the Arma, Ward Leonard, and Westinghouse units. If the Sperry Gyroscope unit fails to regain certification, it may also join the defunct organizations.

Conclusions

Unionism among engineers has never encompassed more than a very small fraction of the total engineering profession; however, it did experience significant growth during the forties and early fifties. This growth was primarily the result of a unique combination of circumstances, which is not likely to be duplicated in the future. The mass employment of engineers had resulted in what appeared to them as a continuing loss in status as professionals. They had suffered considerable unemployment during the depression of the thirties and considerable instability of employment even in later years. For a long period prior to the early fifties, increases in engineers' rates of pay failed to keep pace with those of most other workers in the labor force, and a compression of the salary structure within the profession occurred. Before the passage of the Taft-Hartley Act in 1947, engineers faced the threat of being engulfed by the large bargaining units of production workers.

[12] In 1959, there were 28,447,176 white-collar workers in the experienced civilian labor force. The Bureau of Labor Statistics estimated that approximately 2.2 million, or 7.7 per cent, of all white-collar workers in the civilian labor force were union members in that year. *Employment and Earnings,* 6 (May 1960), 63; *Directory of National and International Labor Unions in the United States, 1959,* U. S. Bureau of Labor Statistics, Bulletin No. 1267 (Washington, D.C.: December, 1959), p. 11.

[13] "ESA Completes First Year," *loc. cit.*

Of these circumstances, the last clearly provided most of the motivation for organizing collective bargaining units of engineers. In the absence of such a threat, it is unlikely that many engineers would have resorted to unionism, despite the other adversities they were experiencing. A brief perusal of the publications of engineers' organizations offers ample evidence that maintainance of an image of professionalism is of primary concern. Engineers consider unionism to be unprofessional, and those who sanctioned collective bargaining organizations of engineers did so primarily in defense against the traditional unions. Section 9 (b) of the Taft-Hartley Act provides that professional employees shall not be represented by a union which includes both professional and nonprofessional employees unless a majority of the professionals vote for such representation. Thus, with the advent of the Taft-Hartley Act in 1947 the principal stimulus to union organization among engineers was largely removed.

The experience of the Seattle Professional Engineering Employees' Association and the Engineers and Scientists of America further exemplifies the conflict between unionism and professionalism among engineers. Such organizations have been faced with a dilemma. If they include subprofessionals and engage in aggressive activities they may gain bargaining strength initially, but lose professional status and consequently lose professional members in the long run. If they include only professionals and use only persuasion, rather than strike threats, in an attempt to attain their objectives, they may maintain professional status but lack effectiveness. And regardless of whom they include, the methods they use, or the name they adopt, these bargaining units are labor unions, certified by the NLRB and consequently somewhat distasteful to most engineers.

Salaries and other conditions of employment in the engineering profession have improved markedly during recent years. However, it is difficult to ascertain the degree of influence which the engineers' unions have exerted in effecting these improvements, particularly in view of the methods employed by the organizations. It seems probable that supply and demand conditions prevailing in the market for engineering services during the past several years would have resulted in comparable improvements in working conditions regardless of the engineers' unions, especially when one considers the relatively small percentage of engineers who are subject to collective bargaining.

Projections suggest that engineers will enjoy continued improvement in their relative economic position for some time to come. The expected shortage of engineers probably will lead to a more efficient utilization of engineering talent and greater stability of employment for the individual engineer. Furthermore, this shortage probably will encourage a greater tendency to treat engineers as professionals. Mass employment and specialization probably will continue to cause dissatisfaction, but it seems unlikely that many engineers believe that unionism can eliminate these remaining sources of discontent.

The engineers' unions no doubt have performed useful functions in disseminating information on salaries and other conditions of employment and in helping to establish formalized management policies pertaining to engineers. However, the recent declines in union representation and membership indicate that most engineers do not consider these functions sufficiently important to warrant their support.

The empirical evidence strongly suggests that unionism among engineers will not gain widespread acceptance but will continue to decline in the foreseeable future.

Associational Activities

By looking at the historical development of professional associations, and associational goals and forms, we have incidentally noted in general terms some broader social functions of occupational associations. It would be useful now to turn to a specific example which would show the range of activities undertaken by a professional association. The following selection outlines the accomplishments over many decades of the organized teaching profession in the United States, reviewing in particular the activities of the National Education Association. These are of interest because they deal with "public acceptance," "a body of scientifically derived knowledge," "salary schedules," "retirement system," "sick leave," "certification," "professional education," "research activities," etc. It is possible to construct from such items a standard list appropriate for comparing the accomplishments of many occupations.

T. M. Stinnett (Teaching)

The accomplishments in any profession result from many and diverse factors. It is not always easy to assign causes. The chief factor, however, in the accomplishments of any profession is the unified, aggressive efforts of its members. Teaching is no exception to the general rule. Although many organizations and individuals have helped to achieve progress in the teaching profession, the impetus for every progressive movement must be ascribed primarily to educational associations. No list of accomplishments of the organized teaching profession could be a complete one. Any such list is suggestive only, and would include objectives only partially achieved. Among the notable accomplishments the following may be listed:

1. General public acceptance of the basic importance of universal free education in a democracy, extending from preschool years through the university.

2. General public acceptance of teaching as a learned profession, requiring high standards of preparation, certification, and service.

3. Development of a body of professional literature and professional content increasing the product of scientific method and research.

4. General public acceptance of the idea of equalization of educational opportunity, regardless of race, color, creed, place of residence, or economic condition, resulting in trends toward minimum foundation programs based upon increased state and federal support.

Reprinted from "Accomplishments of the Organized Teaching Profession," *The Teacher and Professional Organization, 1956* (Washington, D. C.: The National Education Association of the United States, 1956), pp. 147–149. Used by permission.

5. Development of professional salary schedules, cooperatively arrived at, including the single salary principle, based upon preparation and experience, with upper-level salaries reaching to at least twice the beginning salaries within a period not to exceed 15 years.

6. A teacher retirement system or social security for teachers, or both, in each state, Alaska, Hawaii, the District of Columbia, and Puerto Rico.

7. Tenure or continuing contract laws in 45 states, applying to at least some teachers in those states.

8. Minimum salaries mandated by law in 32 states and three territories.

9. Professional salary schedules in most cities over 30,000 population and thousands of local communities.

10. Sick leave mentioned in the laws of 23 states, Alaska, Hawaii, the District of Columbia, Puerto Rico, and in most city school districts.

11. Functioning professional organizations in every state and territory, numbering over 1,000,000 members or about nine of every 10 public school teachers in the United States; local associations in more than 5,000 communities; a national association (NEA) with more than 612,000 members, or about six of every 10 public school teachers in the United States; and many special-interest associations.

12. Health, accident, and disability insurance in many state association programs.

13. Centralization of teacher certification in all chief state education agencies.

14. General acceptance of the principle of minimum professional preparation of four college years for initial teaching service for all teachers in 36 states (including near future) and the principle of five years of college professional preparation for permanent certification in several states.

15. General adoption of professional programs of teacher education by teacher-education institutions.

16. The development of continuous professional growth programs in thousands of local school systems, and particularly in teacher-education institutions.

17. The establishment of UNESCO and WCOTP for international cooperation in education.

18. Collection and dissemination by the U.S. Government of the publications of the NEA and other professions thruout the world.

19. The cultivation of mutual understanding among the teachers of the world through the War and Peace Fund and the Overseas Teacher Relief Fund contributed by the teachers of the United States.

20. Vigorous protection of the rights of teachers through the NEA Commission for the Defense of Democracy Through Education and the Committee on Tenure and Academic Freedom.

The *NEA Handbook for Local, State, and National Associations,* 1955–56 edition, lists the following achievements of the united teaching profession:

World organizations. The establishment of UNESCO and the inauguration of the World Organization of the Teaching Profession (WOTP) are among our greatest achievements.

International services. Publications of the NEA and its departments and its units are being translated by the U.S. Government and used in various parts of the world. Teachers are being brought to the U.S. to study through various private and public programs.

Salaries. Teachers' salaries have been increased from an annual national average of $189 in 1870 to an estimated $4,000 in 1955–56. A minimum salary of $3,600 or more, for professionally prepared teachers, has been established in several states and territories.

Higher standards. The NEA National Commission on Teacher Education and Professional Standards is sponsoring a vigorous campaign to recruit teachers and raise professional standards.

Professional security. All but seven states provide by law some type of job security for all or a large part of their teachers. The NEA Defense Commission and Tenure Committee are constantly protecting and improving employment conditions for teachers.

Retirement provisions.—State-wide retirement or pension systems have been established in 48 states, Alaska, Hawaii, D.C., and Puerto Rico. These plans are being improved.

Sick leave. Twenty-three states, by state law, and Alaska, Hawaii, D.C., and Puerto Rico recognize sick leave. Nearly all city systems provide sick leave with some pay and at least one third of them operate a cumulative sick-leave plan.

Federal aid for education. Aggressive efforts by the NEA and its affiliated associations have substantially increased congressional and public support for federal aid for education.

Teacher participation. Teacher aid in the solution of social, political, economic, and professional problems is growing in practice.

Faith in education. Public appreciation of schools as shown by press, radio, television, and magazine coverage and participation in American Education Week, has reached an all-time high.

Integrated cooperation. Professional unity has been increased by having the chairmen of local and state committees serve as members of corresponding advisory committees of the NEA.

Unified dues. Five states and two territories (Arizona, Idaho, Montana, Nevada, Oregon, Hawaii, and Puerto Rico) and hundreds of local associations have adopted unified dues collected as a single fee by the local association.

Membership growth. The increase in NEA membership to over 612,000 gives added strength to the profession.

George Strauss has found that "Occupational associations promote professionalism: they help protect the occupation's autonomy and raise its status."* At the same time it must be recognized that professionalism may engender unanticipated consequences for the operation of an organization employing professional persons. Management understandably may favor the upgrading of *individual* work performance standards and consequent enhancement of organizational productivity; but there is no avoiding a *collective* expectation by the occupational association of greater freedom of action both on and off the job.†

Examining this from an even wider perspective, Hughes speaks about "license and mandate" in describing the relationship between an occupation and the members of the larger society.‡ What is the extent of "license" to be accorded professional associations? What sort of "mandate" has society conferred on a particular occupation, as compared to the conception of mandate held by the members of the occupation? Montague concludes "...in the case of the medical profession...there has been a widespread questioning about, *not the license and the mandate* which are recognized by all to be of such vital importance to the well-being of the society, *but a questioning of the extent of the license and the interpretation and use of the mandate.*"§

These questions certainly constitute major problem areas with respect to occupational associations.

Professional Associations and the Process of Segmentation

An important aspect of the development of professional associations includes what Bucher and Strauss have referred to as the process of segmentation.** They observed that some forms of occupational associations are developed for specialties or sub-specialties within an occupation. How do these specialties and sub-specialties develop? According to Bucher and Strauss it begins, first of all, by a few persons within the occupation taking a particular position on some aspect or aspects of "professional identity." That is, the persons involved share similar identities, in the form of "circles of colleagueship." Through associational activities, these persons come to organize their work in a manner which sets them apart from other persons in their occupation. Leadership manifests itself, and specific procedures are developed for the conduct of work.

Organizing their activities around an occupational ideology, then, occupational segments develop in ways similar to those we have described earlier in this chapter. An example of this would be those managers in business and industry described in the Meigh selection where managers look upon themselves as professional people and have associated themselves in the Institute of Industrial Administration. Another example of segmentation whose history has been controversy-ridden is that of the medical technologists, where there have been rival occupational associations.††

For Bucher and Strauss, all highly professionalized occupations can be seen as "a loose amalgamation of segments which are in movement." The selection which follows describes the process of segmentation in occupations. Stemming from this analysis, the authors conclude with a series of questions for research.

* Strauss, *op. cit.*, p. 30.
† More is said about this and related topics in Chapter 8, "Professionals and Complex Organizations."
‡ E. C. Hughes, "The Study of Occupations," in R. K. Merton, *et al.*, (eds.) *Sociology Today* (New York: Basic Books, 1959), pp. 442–458.
§ Montague, *op. cit.*, p. 48.
** Rue Bucher and Anselm Strauss, "Professions in Process," *The American Journal of Sociology* (Chicago: The University of Chicago Press), **66**, No. 4 (January 1961), 325–334.
†† For a detailed presentation of this development see: Sister M. Alcuin, O.S.B., "Medical Technology," *Minnesota Medicine*, **35**, (Jan.–Feb. 1952), 331–335, 362.

Rue Bucher and Anselm Strauss (Medicine)

The "process" or "emergent" approach to the study of professions developed in the following pages bears considerable resemblance to a common-sense point of view. It utilizes common language to order the kinds of events that professionals informally discuss among themselves—frequently with great animation. It is even used by sociologists in their less professional moments when they are personally challenged by their own colleagues or by persons from other fields. What is different here is that we shall take the first steps toward developing an explicit scheme of analysis out of these commonplace materials. In addition, it will become apparent that this approach differs from the prevailing "functionalism" because it focuses more pointedly upon conflicting interests and upon change.

Functionalism sees a profession largely as a relatively homogeneous community whose members share identity, values, definitions of role, and interests.[1] There is room in this conception for some variation, some differentiation, some out-of-line members, even some conflict; but, by and large, there is a steadfast core which defines the profession, deviations from which are but temporary dislocations. Socialization of recruits consists of induction into the common core. There are norms, codes, which govern the behavior of the professional to insiders and outsiders. In short, the sociology of professions has largely been focused upon the mechanics of cohesiveness and upon detailing the social structure (and/or social organization) of given professions. Those tasks a structural-functional sociology is prepared to do, and do relatively well.

But this kind of focus and theory tend to lead one to overlook many significant aspects of professions and professional life. Particularly does it bias the observer against appreciating the conflict—or at least difference—of interests within the profession; this leads him to overlook certain of the more subtle features of the profession's "organization" as well as to fail to appreciate how consequential for changes in the profession and its practitioners differential interests may be.

In actuality, the assumption of relative homogeneity within the profession is not entirely useful: there are many identities, many values, and many interests. These amount not merely to differentiation or simple variation. They tend to become patterned and shared; coalitions develop and flourish—and in opposition to some others. We shall call these groupings which emerge within a profession "segments." (Specialties might be thought of as major segments, except that a close look at a specialty betrays its claim to unity, revealing that specialties, too, usually contain segments, and, if they ever did have common definitions along all lines of professional identity, it was probably at a very special, and early, period in their development.) We shall develop the idea of professions as loose amalgamations of segments pursuing different objectives in different manners and more or less delicately held together under a common name at a particular period in history.

Our aim in this paper, then, is to present some initial steps in formulating a "process" model for studying professions. The model can be considered either as a supplement of, or an alternative to, the prevailing functional model. Some readers undoubtedly will prefer to consider the process model as supplementary. If so, then there will be a

Reprinted from "Professions in Process," *The American Journal of Sociology,* 66, No. 4 (January 1961), pp. 325–334, by permission of The University of Chicago Press. Copyright 1961 by the University of Chicago. The original publication bore the following note:

"The intellectual origins of this scheme of analysis are both our own research and various writings of our predecessors and colleagues. Its specific ideas occurred to us when Miss Bucher, several years ago, had occasion to analyze a number of specialty journals and interview a sample of pathologists. Since then we have both been engaged in a study which brings us much information about psychiatrists and psychiatric nurses in Chicago, and we have had available also Everett C. Hughes's interviews with the medical staff at the University of Kansas medical school. The writings to which we are most indebted are those of Everett Hughes on work and professions (cf. *Men and Their Work* [Glencoe, Ill.: Free Press, 1958]) and the symbolic-interaction position in social psychology (cf. George Herbert Mead's *Mind, Self, and Society* [Chicago: University of Chicago Press, 1934]). Because the materials on occupations, work, and professions are well known and readily available, we have not cited all references to pertinent literature; the files of various specialty journals in all the professions are useful to anyone interested in further illustrations."

[1] Cf. William J. Goode, "Community within a Community: The Professions," *American Sociological Review,* **20** (1957), 194–200.

need for a further step, that is, for a transcending model. But we ourselves are concerned here only with sketching the outlines of a process approach, suggesting a few potentially useful concepts, and pointing to certain research problems that flow from our framework and concepts.

"Organized Medicine"

Medicine is usually considered the prototype of the professions, the one upon which current sociological conceptions of professions tend to be based; hence, our illustrative points in this paper will be taken from medicine, but they could just as pertinently have come from some other profession. Of the medical profession as a whole a great deal could be, and has been, said: its institutions (hospitals, schools, clinics); its personnel (physicians and paramedical personnel); its organizations (the American Medical Association, the state and county societies); its recruitment policies; its standards and codes; its political activities; its relations with the public; not to mention the professions' informal mechanisms of sociability and control. All this minimal "structure" certainly exists.

But we should also recognize the great divergency of enterprise and endeavor that mark the profession; the cleavages that exist along with the division of labor; and the intellectual and specialist movements that occur within the broad rubric called "organized medicine." It might seem as if the physicians certainly share common ends, if ever any profession did. When backed to the wall, any physician would probably agree that his long-run objective is better care of the patient. But this is a misrepresentation of the actual values and organization of activity as undertaken by various segments of the profession. Not all the ends shared by all physicians are distinctive to the medical profession or intimately related to what many physicians do, as their work. What is distinctive of medicine belongs to certain segments of it—groupings not necessarily even specialties—and may not actually be shared with other physicians. We turn now to a consideration of some of those values which these segments do *not* share

and about which they may actually be in conflict.

The sense of mission

It is characteristic of the growth of specialties that early in their development they carve out for themselves and proclaim unique missions. They issue a statement of the contribution that the specialty, and it alone, can make in a total scheme of values and, frequently, with it an argument to show why it is peculiarly fitted for this task. The statement of mission tends to take a rhetorical form, probably because it arises in the context of a battle for recognition and institutional status. Thus, when surgical specialties, such as urology and proctology, were struggling to attain identities independent of general surgery, they developed the argument that the particular anatomical areas in which they were interested required special attention and that only physicians with their particular background were competent to give it. Anesthesiologists developed a similar argument. This kind of claim separates a given area out of the general stream of medicine, gives it special emphasis and a new dignity, and, more important for our purposes, separates the specialty group from other physicians. Insofar as they claim an area for themselves, they aim to exclude others from it. It is theirs alone.

While specialties organize around unique missions, as time goes on segmental missions may develop within the fold. In radiology, for example, there are groups of physicians whose work is organized almost completely around diagnosis. But there is a recently burgeoning group of radiologists whose mission is to develop applications of radiation for therapeutic purposes. This difference of mission is so fundamental that it has given rise to demands for quite different residency training programs and to some talk of splitting off from the parent specialty. In pathology—one of the oldest medical specialties, whose traditional mission has been to serve as the basic science of medicine with relatively little emphasis upon clinical applications—lately a whole new breed of pathologists has come to the fore, dedicated to developing pathology as a specialized service to clinical practitioners and threatening those who cling to the traditional mission.

The split between research missions and clinical practice runs clear through medicine and all its specialties. Pediatrics has one of the most rapidly growing fields of practice, but it has also attracted a number of young people, particularly at some centers in the Northeast, specifically for research. They are people who have no conceptions of themselves as family pediatricians at all; they are in this field because of what they can do in the way of research. In the two oldest specialties, surgery and internal medicine, one finds throughout the literature considerable evidence of this kind of split. One finds an old surgeon complaining that the young men are too much interested in research, and in internal medicine there are exhortations that they should be doctors, not scientists. This latter lament is particularly interesting in view of the traditional mission of the internist to exemplify the finest in the "art of medicine": it is a real betrayal when one of them shows too much interest in controlled research.

Work activities

There is great diversity in the tasks performed in the name of the profession. Different definitions may be found between segments of the profession concerning what kinds of work the professional should be doing, how work should be organized, and which tasks have precedence. If, for example, the model physician is taken as one who sees patients and carries out the diagnosis and treatment of illness, then an amazing variety of physicians do not fit this model. This diversity is not wholly congruent with the organization of practice by medical specialties, although there are certain specialties—like pathology, radiology, anesthesiology, and public health—whose practitioners for the most part do not approach the model. Within a core specialty like internal medicine there are many different kinds of practice, ranging from that of a "family doctor" to highly specialized consultation, a service to other doctors. These differences in the weights assigned to elements of practice do not begin to take

into account the further diversity introduced when professionals assign different weights to such activities as research, teaching, and public service.

This point can be made more clearly by considering some of the different organizations of work activities that can be found within single specialties. The people who organize their work life as follows all call themselves "pathologists": (a) time nearly equally divided between research and teaching, with little or no contact with patient care; (b) time divided (ideally) equally between research, teaching, and diagnostic services to other doctors; (c) administration of a hospital service, diagnostic services and consultations with other physicians, and educational activities. (The objects of educational activities are not only medical students and residents but other practitioners of the hospital. These pathologists may also actually examine patients face-to-face and consult on a course of treatment.)

Again, consider the radiologist. There is considerable range in the scope and kind of practice subsumed under radiology. The "country radiologist" tends to function as an all-round diagnostic consultant, evaluating and interpreting findings concerning a broad spectrum of medical conditions. In the large medical center the diagnostic radiologist either does limited consultation concerning findings or else specializes in one area, such as neurological radiology or pediatric radiology. Then there is the radiologist whose work is not primarily diagnostic at all but involves the application of radiation for therapeutic purposes. This man may have his own patients in course of treatment, much like an internist or urologist.

These illustrations suggest that members of a profession not only weigh auxiliary activities differently but have different conceptions of what constitutes the core—*the most characteristic professional act*—of their professional lives. For some radiologists it is attacking tumors with radiation; for others it is interpreting X-ray pictures. For many pathologists it is looking down the barrel of a microscope; for others it is experimental research. A dramatic example of the difference in characteristic professional acts is to be found in psychiatry, which for many of its practitioners means psychotherapy, an intricate set of interactions with a single patient. This is what a psychiatrist does. Yet many practitioners of psychiatry have as little face-to-face interaction with a patient as possible and concentrate upon physical therapies. Still others may spend a good deal of their time administering or directing the activities of other people who actually carry out various therapies.

Not all segments of professions can be said to have this kind of core—a most characteristic activity; many are not so highly identified with a single work activity. But, to the extent that segments develop divergent core activities, they also tend to develop characteristic associated and auxiliary activities, which may introduce further diversity in commitment to major areas, like practice, research, or public health.

Methodology and techniques

One of the most profound divisions among members of a profession is in their methodology and technique. This, again, is not just a division between specialties within a profession. Specialties frequently arise around the exploitation of a new method or technique, like radiology in medicine, but as time goes by they may segmentalize further along methodological perspectives. Methodological differences can cut across specialty—and even professional—lines with specialists sharing techniques with members of other specialties which they do not share with their fellows.

Insofar as these methodological differences reflect bitter disagreements over the reality that the profession is concerned with, the divisions are deep indeed, and communication between the factions is at a minimum. In psychiatry the conflict over the biological versus the psychological basis of mental illness continues to produce men who speak almost totally different languages. In recent years the situation has been further complicated by the rise of social science's perspectives on mental illness. Focusing upon different aspects of reality, psychiatrists of these various persuasions do different kinds of research and carry out various kinds of therapy. They read a variety of journals, too; and the journals a man reads, in any branch of medicine, tend to reflect his methodological as well as his substantive interests.

Social scientists must not suppose that, since psychiatry is closer in subject matter to the social sciences, it is the only branch of medicine marred by bitter methodological disputes (we do not mean to imply that such disputes ought to be avoided). Pathologists are currently grappling with methodological issues which raged in some of the biological sciences, particularly anatomy, some years ago. The central issue has to do with the value of morphology, a more traditional approach which uses microscopic techniques to describe the structure of tissues, as against experimental approaches based upon more dynamic biochemical techniques. While the proponents of the two methodologies appear to understand each other somewhat better than do the psychiatrists, they still do not wholly appreciate each other: the morphologists are disposed to be highly defensive, and the experimentalists a little embarrassed by the continued presence of those purely morphologically inclined. Then, in the primarily clinical specialties, those combining medical and surgical techniques offer their own peculiar possibilities for dispute. Men can differ as to how highly they value and emphasize the medical or surgical approach to treatment; for example, an older urologist complained in a journal article that the younger men in the field are "knife-happy." An analogous refrain can be heard among clinicians who frown upon too great a dependence upon laboratory techniques for diagnosis and accuse many of their colleagues of being unable to carry out a complex physical examination in the grand clinical manner.

Clients

Characteristically, members of professions become involved in sets of relationships that are distinctive to their own segment. Wholly new classes of people may be involved in their work drama whom other segments do not have to take into account. We shall confine ourselves for the moment to considering relationships with clients.

We suspect that sociologists may too easily accept statements glorifying "the doctor-patient relationship" made by segments of the medical profession who have an interest in maintaining a particular relationship to patients. In actuality, the relationships between physicians and patients are highly varied. It does appear that an image of a doctor-patient relationship pervades the entire medical profession, but it is an image which, if it fits any group of physicians in its totality, comes closest to being the model for the general practitioner or his more modern counterpart, the family-practice internist. It seems to set an ideal for other physicians, who may incorporate whatever aspects of it are closest to their own working conditions into an image of the doctor-patient relationship peculiar to their own segment.

Specialties, or segments of specialties, develop images of relationships with patients which distinguish them from other medical groupings. Their own sense of mission and their specialized jobs throw them into new relationships with patients which they eventually formulate and refer to in idealized ways. Moreover, they do not simply define the relationship, but may highly elaborate a relation which this particular kind of doctor, and this kind alone, can have with patients. The pediatricians, for example, have created an image of family practitioner to whom not only the child but the parents and the whole family group surrounding the sick child are patients. According to a spokesman of the pediatricians, the peculiar involvement of parents in the illness of the child creates the conditions under which the pediatrician can evolve his relationship to the family unit. Something similar exists in psychiatry, where it is not the mentally ill patient who may be regarded as the sole or even main client but the family. It is probably in psychiatry, too, that the most highly elaborated doctor-patient relationships exist, since the psychotherapeutic practitioner uses his relationship to patients as a conscious and complex therapeutic tool. The most significant point here is that the young psychiatrist, learning the art of psychotherapy, has to unlearn approaches to the patient that he acquired in medical school.

In addition, there are the physicians who only in a special sense can be said to have patients at all. We are likely to think of pathologists, anesthesiologists, and radiologists as doctors without patients: they may have little or no contact with patients, but they do have a relationship to them. The pathologist practicing in a hospital has a well-developed set of obligations to the patient whom he may never confront, and interest groups among the pathologists are concerned with making the lay public aware of the functions of the pathologist behind the scenes. Practitioners in all three of these specialties appear to be concerned with defining their own relationship to patients.

Colleagueship

Colleagueship may be one of the most sensitive indicators of segmentation within a profession. Whom a man considers to be his colleagues is ultimately linked with his own place within his profession. There is considerable ambiguity among sociologists over the meaning of the term "colleague." Occasionally the word is used to refer to co-workers, and other times simply to indicate formal membership in an occupation—possession of the social signs. Thus, all members of the occupation are colleagues. But sociological theory is also likely to stress colleagueship as a brotherhood. Gross, for example, writes about the colleague group characterized by *esprit de corps* and a sense of "being in the same boat." This deeper colleague relationship, he says, is fostered by such things as control of entry to the occupation, development of a unique mission, shared attitudes toward clients and society, and the formation of informal and formal associations.[2]

This conception of colleagueship stresses occupational unity. Once entry to the occupation is controlled, it is assumed that all members of the occupation can be colleagues; they can rally around common symbols. However, the difficulty is that the very aspects of occupational life which Gross writes about as unifying the profes-

2 Edward Gross, *Work and Society* (New York: Thomas Y. Crowell Co., 1958), pp. 223–235.

sion also break it into segments. What ties
a man more closely to one member of his
profession may alienate him from another:
when his group develops a unique mission,
he may no longer share a mission with
others in the same profession.

Insofar as colleagueship refers to a relationship characterized by a high degree of
shared interests and common symbols, it is
probably rare that all members of a profession are even potentially colleagues. It is
more feasible, instead, to work with a
notion of circles of colleagueship. In the
past, sociologists have recognized such circles of colleagueship, but from the viewpoint of the selective influence of such
social circumstances as class and ethnicity.
The professional identity shared by colleagues, though, contains far more than the
kinds of people they desire as fellows. More
fundamentally, they hold in common
notions concerning the ends served by their
work and attitudes and problems centering
on it. The existence of what we have called
segments thus limits and directs colleagueship.

Identification with segments not only
directs relationships within a profession but
has a great deal to do with relations with
neighboring and allied occupations. We
might use the term "alliances" to distinguish this phenomenon from colleagueship
within a profession. Alliances frequently
dramatize the fact that one branch of a
profession may have more in common with
elements of a neighboring occupation than
with their own fellow professionals. For example, experimentally minded pathologists
consult and collaborate with biochemists
and other basic scientists, while pathologists
oriented toward practice make common
cause with clinicians of various specialties.

Interests and associations

To what extent, and under what conditions,
can we speak of professionals as having
interests in common? (Here we mean
"interests" in the sense of fate, not merely
that they are "interested in" different matters.) Sociologists have been overlooking a
very rich area for research because they
have been too readily assuming unity of
interest among professionals. That interests

do diverge within a profession is clear
enough when the observer looks for it; not
only may interests run along different lines,
but they may be, and frequently are, in
direct conflict.

Pathologists present a particularly striking illustration of conflict of fateful interest
between segments of a specialty. The practitioner pathologists are intent upon promulgating an image of the pathologist that
undermines the identity of the research-
oriented pathologist. The more the practitioners succeed in promoting the notion of
the pathologist as a person who performs
invaluable services to the clinician, and
succeeds in enlarging the area of service,
the more do the pathologists who want to
do research have to ward off demands from
their institutions for more and more service.
Fee-splitting in surgery is an example of
another kind of conflict of interest: many
surgeons can make a living only by engaging in fee-splitting relationships. The more
successful surgeons who dominate the professional associations see the practice as
tarnishing the reputation of the specialty as
a whole and attempt to discredit it in codes
of ethics, but they cannot, and even dare
not, attempt to stamp it out.

Probably the areas in which professionals
come most frequently into conflicts of interest are in gaining a proper foothold in institutions, in recruitment, and in relations
with the outside. Here there are recurrent
problems which segments and emerging
specialties have with their fellow professionals. In order to survive and develop, a
segment must be represented in the training
centers. The medical-school curriculum today is crowded as the medical specialties
compete for the student's time and attention, seeking to recruit or, at least, to socialize the budding professional into the
correct attitudes toward themselves. (Some
specialties regard themselves as having so
little lien on the student's time that they
use that time primarily, in some medical
schools, to impress upon him that only
specialists can safely do certain procedures
—in short, how important and necessary is
the particular specialty of the instructor.)

Then, too, segments require different understandings, even different contractual re-

lations, with clients and institutions. Many a professional association has arisen out of just such conflicts as this. In the 1920's there was a great deal of ferment between the rising specialty of pediatrics and the American Medical Association over governmental ventures into child health legislation, the pediatricians favoring the Shepherd-Towner Act. The pediatricians, recognizing a need for an organization which would represent their own interests independent of the American Medical Association, eventually formed the American Academy of Pediatrics. The big professional associations in the specialty of pathology are all dominated by, and exist for, practitioners in pathology. Therefore, when leading research-oriented pathologists recently became concerned with increasing research potential in the field, and incidentally with capturing some of the funds which the National Institutes of Health were dispensing to pathology, they formed committees especially for this purpose to function as temporary associations. Recently, a Society of Medical Psychiatry has been formed, undoubtedly in response to the growing power of psychoanalytic psychiatry and to the lessening importance, in many academic settings, of somatic psychiatrists.

Looking at professional associations from this perspective, it seems that associations must be regarded in terms of just whose fateful interests within the profession are served. Associations are not everybody's association but represent one segment or a particular alliance of segments. Sociologists may ask of medicine, for example: Who has an interest in thinking of medicine as a whole, and which segments take on the role of spokesmen to the public?

Spurious Unity and Public Relations

There remain to be considered the relations of professions to the lay public and the seeming unity presented by such arrangements as codes of ethics, licensure, and the major professional associations. These products of professional activity are not necessarily evidence of internal homogeneity and consensus but rather of the power of certain groups: established associations become battlegrounds as different emerging seg-

ments compete for control. Considered from this viewpoint, such things as codes of ethics and procedures of certification become the historial deposits of certain powerful segments.

Groups that control the associations can wield various sanctions so as to bring about compliance of the general membership with codes which they have succeeded in enacting. The association concerned with the practice of pathology, for example, has recently stipulated specific contractual relations which the pathologist should enter into with his hospital and is moving toward denying critical services of the association to non-complying members—despite the fact that a goodly proportion of practicing pathologists neither have such contractual relations nor even consider them desirable. But more or less organized opposition to the code-writing of intrenched groups can lead to revision of codes from time to time. Changes occur as the composition of critical committees is altered. Thus, since the clinically oriented pathologists have gained power, they have succeeded in making certification examinations more and more exacting along applied lines, making it steadily more difficult for young pathologists trained for research to achieve certification. Certification procedures thus shift with the relative power of segments, putting a premium on some kinds of training and discriminating against others.

Those who control the professional associations also control the organs of public relations. They take on the role of spokesmen to the public, interpreting the position of the profession, as they see it. They also negotiate with relevant special publics. The outsider coming into contact with the profession tends to encounter the results of the inner group's efforts; he does not necessarily become aware of the inner circle or the power struggles behind the unified front. Thus, in considering the activities of professional associations the observer must continually ask such questions as: Who handles the public and what do they represent? Whose codes of ethics are these? What does the certification stand for? We should also ask, wherever a profession seems to the general public to be relatively unified, why it seems so—for this, too, is a pertinent problem.

SEGMENTS AS SOCIAL MOVEMENTS

Our mode of presentation might lead the reader to think of segments as simple differentiation along many rubrics. On the contrary, the notion of segments refers to organized identities. A position taken on one of the issues of professional identify discussed above entails taking corresponding positions along other dimensions of identity. Segments also involve shared identities, manifested through circles of colleagueship. This allows one to speak of types of pathologist or types of pediatrician —groups of people who organize their professional activity in ways which distinguish them from other members of their profession.

Segments are not fixed, perpetually defined parts of the body professional. They tend to be more or less continually undergoing change. They take form and develop, they are modified, and they disappear. Movement is forced upon them by changes in their conceptual and technical apparatus, in the institutional conditions of work, and in their relationship to other segments and occupations. Each generation engages in spelling out, again, what it is about and where it is going. In this process, boundaries become diffuse as generations overlap, and different loci of professional activity articulate somewhat different definitions of the work situation. Out of this fluidity new groupings may emerge.

If this picture of diversity and movement is a realistic description of what goes on within professions, how can it be analyzed? As a beginning, the movement of segments can fruitfully be analyzed as analogous to social movements. Heretofore, the analysis of social movements has been confined to religious, political, and reform movements, to such problems as the conditions of their origin, recruitment, leadership, the development of organizational apparatus, ideologies, and tactics. The same questions can be asked of movements occurring within professions. Professional identity may be thought of as analogous to the ideology of a

political movement; in this sense, segments have ideology. We have seen that they have missions. They also tend to develop a brotherhood of colleagues, leadership, organizational forms and vehicles, and tactics for implementing their position.

At any one time the segments within a profession are likely to be in different phases of development and engaging in tactics appropriate to their position. In pathology, for example, the clinically oriented segment, which one of its antagonists termed "evangelistic" and which is still expanding, has already created strong organizations, captured many academic departments, promulgated codes of ethics, and is closing in on the battle to secure desirable status for pathologists in hospitals. The more scientifically oriented segment, on the other hand, finds itself in a somewhat defensive position, forced to reaffirm some aspects of its identity and modify others and to engage in tactics to hold its institutional supports. Possibly the acme for some expanding segments is the recognized status of specialty or subspecialty. Certainly, this is the way specialties seem to develop. But the conditions under which segments will become formal specialties is in itself a fascinating research problem. (So also is the whole question of relative development, degree of change, influence and power— matters expressively alluded to when professionals speak of "hot" areas and dead ones.)

We have said that professions consist of a loose amalgamation of segments which are in movement. Further, professions involve a number of social movements in various kinds of relationship to each other. Although the method of analysis developed for studying political and reform movements provides a viewpoint on phenomena of professional life neglected in contemporary research, some differences must be noted between professional movements and the traditional subject matter of analysis. First of all, professional movements occur within institutional arrangements, and a large part of the activity of segments is a power struggle for the possession of them or of some kind of place within them. Second, the fates of segments are closely intertwined: they are possibly more interdependent and responsive to one another than are other kinds of movements. It is probably impossible to study one segment in movement adequately without taking into account what is happening to others. Third, the leaders are men who recognize status within the field, operate from positions of relative institutional power, and command the sources of institutionalized recruitment. Finally, it must be pointed out that not all segments display the character of a social movement. Some lack organized activities, while others are still so inchoate that they appear more as a kind of backwash of the profession than as true segments.

In any case, the existence of segments, and the emergence of new segments, take on new significance when viewed from the perspective of social movements within a profession. Pockets of resistance and embattled minorities may turn out to be the heirs of former generations, digging in along new battle lines. They may spearhead new movements which sweep back into power. What looks like backwash, or just plain deviancy, may be the beginnings of a new segment which will acquire an institutional place and considerable prestige and power. A case in point is that of the progenitors of the clinical pathologists, who today are a threat to the institutional position of research-oriented pathologists but who were considered the failures, or poor cousins, of the specialty thirty years ago.

We have indicated what new kinds of research might originate from the conception of professions that we have presented. However, this perspective has implications for several quite traditional areas of research.

1. *Work situation and institution as arenas.* The work situation and the institution itself are not simply places where people of various occupations and professions come together and enact standard occupational roles, either complimentary or conflicting. These locales constitute the arenas wherein such roles are forged and developed. Work situation and institution must be regarded in the light of the particular professional segments represented there: where the segments are moving and what

effect these arenas have on their further development. Since professions are in movement, work situations and institutions inevitably throw people into new relationships.

2. *Careers.* The kinds of stages and the locales through which a man's career moves must be considered in terms of the segment to which he "belongs." Further, the investigator must be prepared to see changes not only in stages of career but in the ladder itself. The system that the career is moving through can change along the way and take on entirely new directions. The fate of individual careers is closely tied up with the fate of segments, and careers that were possible for one generation rarely are repeatable for the next generation.

3. *Socialization.* An investigator should not focus solely upon how conceptions and techniques are imparted in the study of socialization; he should be equally interested in the clash of opinions among the socializers, where students are among the prizes. Segments are in competition for the allegiance of students: entire schools as well as single departments can be the arena of, and weapons in, this conflict. During their professional training, students pick their way through a maze of conflicting models and make momentous commitments thereby.

4. *Recruitment.* The basic program of recruitment probably tends to be laid down by powerful segments of the profession. Yet different segments require different kinds of raw material to work upon, and their survival depends upon an influx of candidates who are potential successors. Thus, recruitment can be another critical battleground upon which segments choose candidates in their own image or attempt to gain sufficient control over recruitment procedures to do so. Defection by the recruited and recruiters, by the sponsored and the sponsors, is also well worth studying, being one way that new careers take form.

5. *Public Images.* We have seen that images beamed to the public tend to be controlled by particular segments of the profession. However, sometimes segments reject these public images as inappropriate —either to themselves, specifically, or to the profession at large. If only the former, then

they may require that the public acquire specialized images for themselves. In any case, segments from time to time must engage in tactics to project their own images to the public. The situation is more complicated when the whole profession is considered as a public for particular specialties or for segments of specialties. Segments may be at pains to counteract the images which other people in the profession have of them, and attempt to create alternative images.

6. *Relations with other professions.* Different segments of the profession come into contact with different occupations and professions. They might have quite special problems with other occupations which they do not share with other members of their profession. In considering the handling of relations with other professions, it is thus necessary to ask such questions as: Who in the profession is concerned with this problem and what difference does it make to them? Who does the negotiating and in what ways?

7. *Leadership.* Most leadership is associated less with the entire profession than with restricted portions of it. Certainly, it is linked with intellectual movements, and with the fates and fortunes of certain segments. Leadership, strategies, and the fates of segments deserve full focus in our studies of professionalization.

Questions for Discussion and Further Research

According to Carr-Saunders and Wilson, a necessary condition for the existence of a profession is coming together in formal association, a characteristic of professionalization which most writers in the field see as essential to the process. Yet still to be answered is the question of whether or not this is the factor which really contributes most to the professionalization of an occupation. Or is this a highly variable matter among different occupations? The importance of professional associations for professionalization seems quite plausible when we note that many of the other criteria of professionalization intimately involve the activities of occupational colleagues in formal association with each other. It is difficult to conceive of these activities being more effectively sponsored and maintained by other social mechanisms.

In detailing the various functions performed by occupational associations, we have observed the remarks of several authors. For example, Durkheim singled out colleagueship as being the most important of these functions. Others have noted protective and self-corrective functions; the innovative functions, including discovery, and resynthesis; and occupational goal-setting, standards-setting, and rewards-setting. But surely the function which is emphasized most frequently by all authors is the diverse educational contributions of professional associations—both inside the occupation and outside, where educational activities are directed toward clients and the public at large. This was a point made both by Meigh and by Bloomfield in their selections. We need to establish in a more rigorous fashion the rank order and respective contributions of those functions which are most responsible for the professionalization of an occupation. Then there is the related question of whether labor unions, as one type of occupational association, are fundamentally different from those associations more commonly recognized as professional, or whether the differences are merely a matter of degree?

In the material on the American Medical Association prepared by the editors of the Yale Law Review, it is evident that this professional organization is a large, complex social structure, involving several levels of activities with an indirect form of representation in which great amounts of authority are assumed by a relatively small number of persons. Because of this authority, great financial resources, and the prestige of the occupation, officials of the AMA are able to exercise great influence in several major aspects of the nation's life. This suggests the question, does the occupational association which affords broad and direct membership participation in its policy making and policy execution generate more "professional" conduct from members, or are members and the public better served by an association where activities are in the hands of a select—and, presumably, "extra-able"—few? Or does each occupation require a distinctive mode of association for its particular purposes?

When we come to look at the day-to-day activities of occupational associations historically and currently, we are impressed by the mounting multiplicity of their collective concerns. However, as Stinnett shows in his selection, there is increasingly one theme which runs through many of these activities. This is the tendency for associations to encourage, and often impose, the principle of standardization. A research question which needs an adequate answer is, does the concern for uniformity of standards in professional associations militate against creativity, thus retarding occupational innovation and promoting mediocrity? One can argue that what may emerge from such activities is a least-common-denominator effect representing constant pressure toward a minimum level of occupational performance. In turn, this may perpetuate a problem found in many sectors of social life, that of striking a workable balance between freedom and social conformity.

6

Client and Public Relations

In Chapter 4 we noted the importance of individual responsibility in adhering to occupational expectations among members of more highly professionalized occupations. Once again, in discussing client and public relations, it is necessary to examine the concept of individual professional responsibility, for this concept characterizes much of the client-practitioner relationship. Such responsibility is characterized "by a pride in service given,"* often being termed "professional pride," where the primary emphasis is placed both upon the response to a client's needs and the adequacy of professional performance in relation to occupational norms.

What is the relationship between client and public relations? Marshall has maintained that:

> The relationship of trust implies a deep obligation to the client. But an organized profession rightly regards itself as a body placed in charge of an art or science and responsible for directing its use in the interests of society. These two obligations can be reconciled without difficulty if the true interests of society and of the individual are harmonious. A profession proceeds on the assumption that they are. When they seem to be in conflict it is usually because the individual does not know what is good for him. . . .†

Often the client cannot know, in any precise sense what are his actual needs, so he must be informed by the professional person acting as an authority. Moreover, "needs" often go beyond physiological imperatives and hence are socially defined. The social definition upon which the professional can base his statement about client needs may take the obvious form of a civil law, or of a

---

* A. M. Carr-Saunders and P. A. Wilson, *The Professions* (Oxford: The Clarendon Press, 1933), pp. 471–472.

† T. H. Marshall, "The Recent History of Professionalism in Relation to Social Structure and Social Policy," *The Canadian Journal of Economics and Political Science,* 5, 1939, 329–330.

regulation developed by the professional group.‡ But sometimes the practitioner must base his assessment of client needs on his own best judgment and recommend actions which are unpopular with clients and/or the public. There is, then, a basic problem of balancing client and public obligations, and a necessity to keep self-interest out of the assessment process.

It is debatable whether selflessness in response to client needs was more discernible one-third of a century ago when Carr-Saunders and Wilson were writing about this attribute in the relationship between the practitioner, his clients, and his public. Those were less affluent times, and it has been reported commonplace for professional persons to donate services without charge when clients were in no position to pay the regular fees. This is still an expectation associated with many of the more highly professionalized occupations.§ Yet this aspect of responsibility likely is not so pronounced today because of the shift to an economy of greater abundance; hence the need may be reduced. In contrast, another major aspect of responsibility—professional competency—probably receives greater emphasis today.

If these are the primary elements of a general normative orientation for the relationship between the practitioner, the patient, and the public within the more professionalized occupations, what is the specific nature of these relationships? How do the client and the practitioner actually interact?

We have observed that many of the highly professionalized occupations deal with what are often called "vital functions" of society, and many occupational activities cannot be performed adequately without maintaining confidentiality. In the instance of the lawyer, for example, what is discussed by him with his client is largely their affair, since it may include a great many attitudes and actions which, if divulged, would not serve the best interests of the client. Confidentiality is usually explicitly recognized by the public with respect to the most highly professionalized occupations. In other instances the nature of the agreement between the professional and his client may be implicit, and there is a quiet understanding that it is appropriate for certain information to be withheld from free distribution to just anyone who happens to come along.**

Frequently occupational jargon, a special language, is used, presumably both to keep certain information away from the client and to enhance the accuracy of technical communication among practitioners. As a consequence, an aura of mystery comes to be associated with the practice of these occupations which enhances their status. Moreover, in some instances occupational secrecy is used explicitly by practitioners to enlarge status distinctions in comparison with people in other occupations or in other specialties. For this reason, part of the public, or some clients may become highly suspicious of all members of an occupations because the latter are presumed to possess (perhaps needlessly) secret occupational knowledge. Thus the dedicated professional person often tries not to overemphasize the use of secret or privileged information, but rather,

---

‡ *Ibid.*, p. 330.

§ For example medical practitioners may donate services one or two mornings a week at the hospital or lecture without full remuneration at the "med" school; similarly, lawyers are appointed by the court to defend indigent clients.

** E. C. Hughes, "Licence and Mandate," in *Men and Their Work* (New York: Free Press of Glencoe, Inc., 1958), pp. 80–82.

must instil in the client a feeling of confidence, a realization that information may be withheld, but only in the best interests of the client.

The Client and the Practitioner

Continuing our use of the ideal-typical method for studying professionalization, we shall examine the doctor-patient relationship as a notable and extreme form of client-practitioner relationship. The following statement comes from a medical physician who emphasizes the importance of attitudinal preconceptions in the relationship of the practitioner to his client.†† Dr. Henderson's understanding of this relationship is of interest because he appears to be equally sensitive to the proper role behaviors for *both* the client *and* the practitioner, instead of being concerned solely with the expediting of the practitioner's work. This selection is of particular interest because it is, in effect, a doctor's plea to his medical colleagues to increase their understanding of the problems faced by the patient.

†† For examinations of other kinds of practitioner-client relationships see, for example, David Fanchel, "A Study of Caseworkers' Perceptions of Their Clients, "*Social Case Work*, 39, 1958, 543–551; B. D. Soni, "Sociological Analysis of Legal Profession: A Study of Mechanisms in Lawyer-Client Relationship," *The Journal of Social Sciences*, 1, 1958, 63–70.

L. J. Henderson (Medicine)

A patient sitting in your office, facing you, is rarely in a favorable state of mind to appreciate the precise significance of a logical statement, and it is in general not merely difficult but quite impossible for him to perceive the precise meaning of a train of thought. It is also out of the question that the physician should convey what he desires to convey to the patient, if he follows the practice of blurting out just what comes into his mind. The patient is moved by fears and by many other sentiments, and these, together with reason, are being modified by the doctor's words and phrases, by his manner and expression. This generalization appears to me to be as well founded as the generalizations of physical science.

If so far I am right, I think it is fair to set up a precept that follows from all this as a rule of conduct: The physician should see to it that the patient's sentiments do not act upon his sentiments and, above all, do

Reprinted from "Physician and Patient as a Social System," *The New England Journal of Medicine*, 212, No. 18, 1935, 821–823. Used by permission.

not thereby modify his behavior, and he should endeavor to act upon the patient's sentiments according to a well-considered plan. . . .

However, in this case the application of science to practice is peculiarly difficult. If I am to speak about it, I must in the first place beg explicitly to disclaim any skill of my own. . . . Accordingly, what I am now to say to you is, in the main, second-hand knowledge that I have cribbed from others.[1] It represents, so far as I can understand

[1] I owe my information to my colleagues, Professors Elton Mayo, F. J. Roethlisberger, and their associates. The theory and practice of interviewing developed by Mayo were applied and adapted with the advice and collaboration of the Harvard Department of Industrial Research by the Western Electric Company in the course of an elaborate investigation at the Hawthorne Works of the Company. A valuable description of these Western Electric methods of interviewing may be found in Bingham and Moore's *How to Interview*, New York, 1931: Second Edition, 1935. In all this it is possible to discern more than traces of the methods of psychoanalysis, divested however of the usual theoretical and dogmatic accompaniments, and therefore considerably modified.

what I have seen and heard, the soundest judgment, based upon experience, skilful performance and clear analysis in this field. In order to be brief and clear, I shall permit myself the luxury of plain assertion.

In talking with the patient, the doctor must not only appear to be, but must be, really interested in what the patient says. He must not suggest or imply judgments of value or of morals concerning the patient's report to him or concerning the patient's behavior. (To this there is one exception: When the patient successfully presents a difficult objective report of his experiences, it is useful to praise him for doing well what it is necessary that he should do in order to help the physician to help him.) In all those matters that concern the psychological aspects of the patient's experience few questions should be asked and, above all, no leading questions. There should be no argument about the prejudices of the patient, for, at any stage, when you are endeavoring to evoke the subjective aspect of the patient's experience or to modify his sentiments, logic will not avail. In order to modify the sentiments of the patient, your logical analysis must somehow be transformed into the appropriate change of the patient's sentiments. But sentiments are resistant to change. For this reason, you must so far as possible utilize some part of the sentiments that the patient has in order to modify his subjective attitude.

When you talk with the patient, you should listen, first, for what he wants to tell, secondly, for what he does not want to tell, thirdly, for what he cannot tell. He does not want to tell things the telling of which is shameful or painful. He cannot tell you his implicit assumptions that are unknown to him, such as the assumption that all action not perfectly good is bad, such as the assumption that everything that is not perfectly successful is failure, such as the assumption that everything that is not perfectly safe is dangerous. We are all of us subject to errors of this kind, to the assumption that quantitative differences are qualitative. Perhaps the commonest false dichotomy of the hypochondriac is the last of those that I have just mentioned: the assumption that everything not perfectly safe is dangerous.

When you listen for what the patient does not want to tell and for what he cannot tell you must take especial note of his omissions, for it is the things that he fails to say that correspond to what he does not want to say plus what he cannot say. In listening for these omissions, which is a difficult task, you must make use of every aid that is available. Among the available aids are the results of psychoanalysis. Many of them are well established; but if you wish to preserve a scientific point of view, you must beware of psychoanalytical theories. Use these theories, if you must use them, with skepticism, but do not believe them, for they are themselves in no small measure rationalizations built up by an eager group of enthusiastic students who are unquestionably seeking new knowledge, but whose attitude is strangely modified by a quasi-religious enthusiasm, and by a devotion to the corresponding quasi-theological dogmas. As a useful corrective for undue confidence in the importance of such theories, it is well to recall Henri Poincaré's judicious and skeptical remark: "These two propositions, 'the external world exists', or, 'it is more convenient to suppose that it exists', have one and the same meaning." In truth, all theories, but above all others those that refer to the sentiments of men, must be used with care and skepticism.

Therefore, beware of your own arbitrary assumptions. Beware of the expression of your own feelings. In general, both are likely to be harmful, or at least irrelevant, except as they are used to encourage and to cheer the patient. Beware of the expression of moral judgments. Beware of bare statements, of bare truth, or bare logic. Remember especially that the principal effect of a sentence of confinement or of death is an emotional effect, and that the patient will eagerly scrutinize and rationalize what you say, that he will carry it away with him, that he will turn your phrases over and over in his mind, seeking persistently for shades of meaning that you never thought of. Try to remember how as a very young man you have similarly scrutinized for non-existent meaning the casual phrases of those whom you have admired, or respected, or loved.

Above all, remember that it is meaningless to speak of telling the truth, the whole truth, and nothing but the truth, to a patient. It is meaningless because it is impossible—a sheer impossibility. Since this assertion is likely to be subjected to both objective and subjective criticism, it will be well that I should try to explain it. I know of no other way to explain it than by means of an example. Let us scrutinize this example, so far as we may be able, objectively, putting aside all our habits of moralistic thought that we acquired in early years and that arise from the theological and metaphysical traditions of our civilization.

Consider the statement, "This is a carcinoma." Let us assume in the first place that the statement has been made by a skilful and experienced pathologist, that he has found a typical carcinoma—in short, that the diagnosis is as certain as it ever can be. Let us also put aside the consideration that no two carcinomas are alike, that no two patients are alike, and that, at one extreme, death may be rapid and painful or, at another extreme, there may be but a small prospect of death from cancer. In short, let us assume, putting aside all such considerations, that the statement has nearly the same validity as the assertions contained in the nautical almanac. If we now look at things, not from the standpoint of philosophers, moralists, or lawyers, but from the standpoint of biologists, we may regard the statement as a stimulus applied to the patient. This stimulus will produce a response and the response, together with the mechanism that is involved in its production, is an extremely complex one, at least in those cases where a not too vague cognition of the meaning of the four words is involved in the process. For instance, there are likely to be circulatory and respiratory changes accompanying many complex changes in the central and peripheral nervous system. With the cognition there is a correlated fear. There will probably be concern for the economic interests of others, for example, of wife and children. All these

intricate processes constitute the response to the stimulus made up of the four words, "This is a carcinoma," in case the statement is addressed by the physician to the patient, and it is obviously impossible to produce in the patient cognition without the accompanying affective phenomena and without concern for the economic interests. I suggest, in view of these obvious facts, that, if you recognize the duty of telling the truth to the patient, you range yourself outside the class of biologists, with lawyers, and philosophers. The idea that the truth, the whole truth, and nothing but the truth can be conveyed to the patient is an example of false abstraction, of that fallacy called by Whitehead, "the fallacy of misplaced concreteness." It results from neglecting factors that cannot be excluded from the concrete situation and that have an effect that cannot be neglected. Another fallacy also is involved, the belief that it is not too difficult to know the truth; but of this I shall not speak further,

I beg that you will not suppose that I am recommending, for this reason, that you should always lie to your patients. Such a conclusion from what I have said would correspond roughly to a class of fallacies that I have already referred to above. Since telling the truth is impossible, there can be no sharp distinction between what is true and what is false. But surely that does not relieve the physician of his moral responsibility. On the contrary, the difficulties that arise from the immense complexity of the phenomena do not diminish, but rather increase, the moral responsibility of the physician, and one of my objects has been to describe the facts through which the nature of that moral responsibility is determined.

Far older than the precept, "the truth, the whole truth, and nothing but the truth," is another that originates within our profession, that has always been the guide of the best physicians, and, if I may venture a prophecy, will always remain so: So far as possible, do no harm. You can do harm by the process that is quaintly called telling the truth. You can do harm by lying. In your relations with your patients you will inevitably do much harm, and this will be by no means confined to your strictly medical blunders. It will arise also from what you say and what you fail to say. But try to do as little harm as possible, not only in treatment with drugs, or with the knife, but also in treatment with words, with the expression of your sentiments and emotions. Try at all times to act upon the patient so as to modify his sentiments to his own advantage, and remember that, to this end, nothing is more effective than arousing in him the belief that you are concerned whole-heartedly and exclusively for *his* welfare.

What I have said does not conform in my manner of saying it to the rules that I have suggested for your relations with patients. I have tried to talk reason and good sense to you, following, so far as I have been able, the habits of a lecturer upon scientific subjects. With some of you I have surely failed to accomplish my object. To them I suggest that this failure is an excellent illustration of the phenomena that I have been describing, for, unless I am mistaken, if you dislike what I have said, it is chiefly because I have failed to appeal to and make use of your sentiments.

If it is a patient's health or life that is at stake; if it is a legal client's freedom that is at stake; or if it is a client's financial reputation which is at stake, it is understandable that the layman is particularly susceptible to what Talcott Parsons terms "ir- and non-rational beliefs and practices."* Henderson's admonitions in the previous selection would seem to be warranted, and are needed to counteract situations where it is quite possible for the unscrupulous practitioner to exploit individual clients in their moments of weakness. Of course, all truly professional people seek to reassure their clients in such situations, both by the use of the appropriate skills and by the manner of exercising these skills. It is essential that the practitioner develop a balance between being overly sympathetic (to the point where the practitioner loses objectivity and becomes personally involved) at the one extreme, and being coldly uninterested at the other extreme. Appropriately there must be both concern and detachment.

For the medical practitioner, we speak of his "bedside manner," and for other kinds of professional persons we may speak of their behaving in "a professional manner." At the same time, it must be recognized that, on occasion, people in highly professionalized occupations are called upon to do certain things the outcomes of which are clearly not predictable. Sometimes the problem is so unique or the condition so grave that there appears to be no assuredly beneficial mode of conduct. Understandably, this subjects practitioners to strains not likely to be experienced in other occupational situations, and this is why rather exact role expectations develop around such activities to ease strain in the conduct of work.† The keeping of confidences, referred to earlier in this discussion, would be one example of such a role expectation.

No simple description of the practitioner-client relationship meets all of our requirements of comprehensiveness. This is illustrated clearly in a brief article prepared by two psychiatrists who note that there are at least several types of patient and several types of practitioner. Putting these variable constituents together, along with the variations that may take place in a given social situa-

* Talcott Parsons, *The Social System,* (New York: Free Press of Glencoe, Inc., 1951), p. 446.
† Parsons, *op. cit.,* p. 450.

tion, makes for a number of variations in the way any specific doctor-patient relationship may develop. This sometimes amusing description of patient and doctor stereotypes is found in the next selection.

F. W. Hanley and F. Grunberg (Medicine)

Nowadays it has become common to speak of the doctor-patient relationship as reverently as we mention...the instalment buying contract. In a world of rapid and profound change, we are urged to maintain the sanctity of this relationship as diligently as our spiritual forbears guarded the Ark of the Covenant, and somewhat more diligently than we are expected to care for the marriage relationship. But the general concept of the doctor-patient relationship, a phrase which often becomes a shibboleth, requires a little closer scrutiny if it is to have any real meaning in the daily practice of medicine. For, after all, this is a relationship between two people, and hence varies widely according to the personalities of those two individuals, the reasons for their coming together, and the time during which they interact. Many patients and some doctors are human, and the varieties and vagaries of the human personality provide infinite possibilities for interplay—a dynamic interplay that changes with time, like the marital association, and which, like it, may from the start consist of harmony and mutual understanding, of differences leading through conflict to maturity, or of antagonisms eventuating in unhappiness and separation. Whatever course it may take, the doctor-patient relationship is not directed from above by Aesculapius, it is not taught in medical school, and it is not simplified or understood one whit by solemnly referring to it as sacred.

Although no two doctor-patient relationships are alike, we have attempted, with the proclivity of medical men to classify what they cannot treat, to group these relation-

Reprinted from "Reflections on the Doctor-Patient Relationship," *Canadian Medical Association Journal,* 86 (June 2, 1962), 1022–1024. Used by permission. The original publication bore the following note: "Presented at the Western (Prairie) Regional Meeting of the Royal College of Physicians and Surgeons of Canada, November 24, 1961."

ships into some commonly encountered patterns. To do so let us first describe three stereotypes of patients: the hostile, the passive-dependent, and the manipulative-seductive. Let us then delineate three stereotypes of doctors: the omnipotent, the anxious, and the detached. The nine possible combinations of these types produce nine different syndromes that proceed through a characteristic course to a usual outcome. They occur everywhere and in every specialty.

THE THREE STEREOTYPES OF PATIENTS

The *hostile patient* is usually quickly recognized by all of us. He is the man who demands a quick appointment and who may openly express his annoyance if it is not granted. He may be overly familiar with the doctor ("Hello, Doc") or mispronounce his name, and he commonly makes derogatory remarks about other doctors. Any patient who does this already has you on his list for nasty comments. He challenges the doctor with a brief history and then a demand to know the score. During the physical examination he makes further derogatory asides. He is skeptical about further investigation and treatment, making such remarks as "Will it do any good?" or "You're the doctor." He rebels against instructions and follows them poorly, if at all, comes late for his appointments or misses them and complains that he is no better. Finally, he breaks treatment altogether without warning or, if he has a little courtesy, he asks to see another doctor, and he may try to punish the physician by failing to pay his account.

The *passive-dependent patient,* on the other hand, is a model patient when his condition is merely organic. He usually goes to a specialist on referral. He will accept any appointment without protest. He comes early and waits quietly. In the interview he shows little or no spontaneity, and the doctor has to dig information out of him. He remains stoical during the physical examination and obeys instructions to the letter. He loves medication and will often ask if it should be taken a.c. or p.c. In fact, his deference to the wisdom of the physician is so great that he may telephone to ask if it is all right to take an aspirin. Unfortunately, he is liable to a prolonged convalescence with the development of many functional complaints. He is always slightly better indefinitely, but his treatment becomes interminably prolonged. He is very precise at times about trivia but otherwise vague. He never questions any procedures. The marital partner may protest that the patient is not improving, but he never will. He is always most diligent in such details as the payment of his account.

The *manipulative-seductive patient* is usually a woman. She tries to get an early appointment by exaggerating her condition or by coaxing. There is always an incongruity between her appearance and her complaint. She controls the interview, asks questions about the doctor's personal life, gives him her diagnosis and prescribes her own treatment. She is flattering, repetitious, and coy.

This is the type of patient the doctor will spot immediately as "neurotic" and, in fact, for many doctors this is the most commonly encountered type of neurotic patient, being so clearly diagnosable.[1] The psychiatrists call her a hysterical personality. These patients cooperate very well at the beginning of the treatment and give good results, but then shortly deteriorate and begin to telephone and try to manipulate the situation. Sometimes they have their husband or a friend telephone for them, after having worked them up into a suitable panic. They alternate between recovery and disaster. They have a predilection for gynecologists, whose offices they haunt. They will very easily get two or three doctors on the case, who learn too late that they are being played one against the other. Physicians are seduced into an increasing volume of in-

vestigations, for which these patients will often refuse to pay .

The Three Stereotypes of Doctors

One must be more delicate in describing the physician while under his critical gaze, and it will be realized that the following characterizations are greatly overdrawn.

The *omnipotent doctor* was the standard of the old school and, like Model T Fords, there are still a few of them rattling about. This doctor is very conscious of his training and his position in the community and, in fact, is usually very competent and thorough, but overreaches himself to give advice in areas in which he is *not* competent. The advice is always given in a dogmatic matter, e.g. "The thing for you to do, child, [all his patients are children] is to get married," or "Go and have a baby and forget about your troubles" (paradoxically, this advice may be given to a woman whose very functional complaints arise from having too many children to look after already). This doctor expects to be obeyed and tolerates no questions. His work is flawless, and *he* decides if the patient has a pain or not. He controls the interview with the patient entirely, and those patients who fail to respond to his treatment are labelled malingerers or neurotics and after being given some pontifical counselling are cast into outer darkness.

The *anxious doctor* is in many ways the antithesis of the previous type. He goes to meet his patients at the door, he is diffident and very patient, and allows the person who is consulting him to have complete freedom during the interview to the point of control. During his physical examination he is very considerate and over-conscientious, and worries about overlooking things, hence is prone to repeat examinations. He seeks to please the patient and win his approval. This type of doctor tends to hang on to his patients and rarely admits failure or transfers the patient, but often calls in consultants. If the patient breaks treatment he becomes upset, taking the break as a personal criticism.

The *detached physician* is much rarer. He is a bloodhound among the bulldogs

[1] Rose, T. F., *Canad. Med. Ass. J.*, **84**, 1961, 1132.

and cocker spaniels of the species. His main interest is in the intellectual exercise of medicine. He is, in fact, a frustrated detective, a diagnostician rather than a therapist. This is the research-minded physician whose consulting room is his laboratory. He enters into a minimal relationship with his patient, and this is entirely one way. What he can accumulate on the history page is important to him, not what happens in the relationship. The general practitioner who refers patients to him will receive in return long letters of detailed description and infinite instruction.

THE SYNDROMES

By combining these three types of patients with the three types of doctors we have nine possible syndromes:

1. The hostile patient and the omnipotent doctor. This relationship is explosive from the outset. It is a battle between God and Lucifer with Lucifer invariably being cast out. This patient at once thwarts the doctor and immediately brings out his hostility. The patient calls the doctor a big shot, the doctor calls the patient hopeless. The departure of the latter is final and irrevocable, and because the meeting has been so brief no harm is done.

2. The hostile patient and the anxious doctor. The physician struggles desperately to keep the patient within his goodwill. He multiplies his medications and repeats his examinations, but his efforts are doomed to failure. In the end the patient breaks from him anyway, and the doctor is the one who suffers. He feels insecure, he is wondering what he did wrong, while the patient is describing him to his friends as a "slob."

3. The hostile patient and the detached doctor. This is an interesting combination. The patient is at first impressed and bewildered. His hostility is quite futile because there is no response to his provocation, and after a short effort he breaks treatment, muttering that he has been used as a guinea pig.

4. The passive-dependent patient and the omnipotent doctor. In this relationship the patient has found a second father, whereas the doctor feels like a creator, in complete possession of his charge. This is a symbiotic relationship which can persist indefinitely. The doctor may become over-protective of his model patient and aggressive towards relatives, marital partners and work superiors. In fact, he may take over the running of his life. Although physical conditions may be adequately treated, the patient's personality remains at the infantile level which both desire.

5. The passive-dependent patient and the anxious doctor. Here we have a situation of dynamic equilibrium, each trying to please the other. Both go through periods of great insecurity, and there is little or no movement in the relationship. Each feels guilty that he is inconveniencing the other. The situation may finally break up inconclusively by the patient drifting away to find a more authoritarian physician. If this does not happen, the doctor may refer the patient because he becomes frustrated at never knowing whether he is getting better or worse.

6. The passive-dependent patient and the detached doctor. Here the patient is a perfect guinea pig and allows the physician full scope to investigate and diagnose to his heart's content. At the end of this process the physician, well content, sends the disease back to the referring doctor with complete documentation and appropriate references to the literature.

7. The manipulative patient and the omnipotent doctor. The physician immediately falls into the trap of flattery and pseudo-cooperation. There then develop two clearcut stages in the relationship. The patient first uses the doctor to carry out her manipulations, often against marital partner or family members, and the doctor is quite happy to play this role, having found someone who accepts the infallibility of his judgment. However, after a time he begins to feel swindled, realizing that his power has been subverted. Then he makes a desperate bid to regain this power, whereupon the patient becomes rapidly worse and the physician terminates the relationship in anger and disgust. God either condemns his incorrigible and unrepentant to wander in the wilderness, or, with a stroke of lightning, consigns her to the Devil by referring her to a psychiatrist.

8. The manipulative patient and the anxious doctor. Here again we have a symbiotic relationship, that outlined in syndrome no. 4 (the passive-dependent patient and the omnipotent doctor) in reverse. The patient now has complete possession of the doctor, flatters him, protects him against his detractors, and may even send her friends of like personality to the unhappy creature. The relationship is cyclical and interminable, with the patient going through repetitive crises. If the physician ever tries to refer her, she promptly improves.

9. The manipulative patient and the detached doctor. This relationship breaks up quickly because there is nothing to manipulate. Such

a patient often discharges herself in the middle of an investigation and the doctor is left frustrated, clutching the empty air for a disease which has been borne off by a personality with which he was never in touch.

CONCLUSION

References to "the doctor-patient relationship" usually carry the implication that it is as uniform and blissful as the curator-turtle relationship at the zoo, and that it is invariably beneficial to the patient—so much so that he is grateful to pay the fee for service. We have been iconoclastic enough to indicate that it is a human relationship that varies with its components and which may or may not provide the medium through which modern medical science is brought to those who seek its benefits.

Another dimension is introduced into our examination of the practitioner-client relationship when we consider the situation where there are two or more categories of professional persons dealing with a client. The satisfactory accomplishment of the work task is dependent on an understanding of appropriate roles and effective role behavior by persons for each of the three different roles involved. In an article about the present-day nurse, M. M. Johnson and H. W. Martin provide a useful analysis of the nurse as a professional person by relating her (or him) to the medical practitioner and to the patient, that is, the "doctor-nurse-patient social system."

M. M. Johnson and H. W. Martin (Nursing)

The purpose of this paper will be to bring some aspects of sociological theory to bear on the problem of giving a precise though general statement of what the crucial functions of the nurse are. Much has been written about the functions of the nurse, but usually this takes the form of listing in very concrete terms what the nurse's activities include.[1,2,3] Sometimes attempts are made to generalize about the purpose of these activities, but this then leads into vague generalities, such as, "The purpose of the nurse is to meet the total needs of the patient." This paper does not purport to give *the* answer to this problem of the nurse's function, but it attempts to clarify the problem—"what the nurse is basically doing for the patient"—by presenting a frame of reference within which her activities may be analyzed.

The crux of this frame of reference involves not just viewing the nurse as an individual doing certain things in a certain way, but rather involves thinking of the nurse as playing a role in the doctor-nurse-patient social system, and then asking what is the role's specific contribution to this social system.

Reprinted from "A Sociological Analysis of the Nurse Role," *The American Journal of Nursing*, 58, No. 3 (March 1958), 373–377. Used by permission. Original publication bore the following note: "This paper was developed as a part of the investigation supported by a research grant from the National Institute of Mental Health, Public Health Service.

Although theoretical in nature, it is based upon data from four sources. 1) extended individual interviews with the faculty of a 4-year school of nursing, 2) group of interviews with the students of this school, 3) "patient care studies" on medical and surgical patients written by junior and senior nursing students, and 4) hospital and clinical observations.

Other data which lend empirical support to the analysis have been obtained during the course of several years of participation by one of the writers (HWM) in teaching medical students and in sociological research at the clinical level in a large Southern medical teaching center."

[1] Donald S. Stewart and Christine Needham, "Operating Room Nurses' Functions are Studied," *Am. J. Nursing*, 55 (November 1955), 1347–1349.

[2] Claire Mintzer Fagin, *Study of Desirable Functions and Qualifications for Psychiatric Nurses* (New York: National League for Nursing, 1953).

[3] "ANA Statements of Functions, Standards and Qualifications," *Am. J. Nursing*, 56 (July 1956), 898–901.

INSTRUMENTAL AND EXPRESSIVE FUNCTIONS DEFINED

Any social system—that is, two or more people interacting with each other—regardless of its specific size or purpose, has certain functional problems which must be solved if the system is to maintain itself. First, the social system must make progress toward realizing the purpose of the group: it must move toward a goal. Second, the social system must maintain internal equilibrium: relationships between the social system members must be harmonious and integrated and each member must feel good both within himself and toward the other group members.

Thus we may think of any social system as having an external problem, that of moving toward the group goal, and an internal problem, that of maintaining integrated relationships among the members by managing the tensions in individuals in the group. We call actions which are directly related to moving the system toward its goal *instrumental,* and actions which are related to maintaining motivational equilibrium in the individuals composing the group *expressive....* [4]

THE DOCTOR-NURSE-PATIENT SOCIAL SYSTEM

Now, let us turn specifically to an analysis of the doctor-nurse-patient relationship viewed as a social system, but let us not get into the larger social system of the ward or floor with its more complex set of relationships. The instrumental problem in this system is clearly that of "getting the patient well," of utilizing the available knowledge to diagnose and treat the illness, and of securing the cooperation of system members (doctor, nurse, patient) in this effort. The expressive problem of the system is that of managing the tensions of the system members, that are, at least in part, generated by the activities necessary to restore the patient to health.

[4] Talcott Parsons and Robert F. Bales, *Family, Socialization and Interaction Process* (Chicago: Free Press, 1955), p. 47.

The patient, in this triad of doctor-nurse-patient, is in no position to assume leadership in the interaction. If he could "cure" himself he would not be in the hospital. Rather because he is ill he is thought of by society as a person who needs help, who is obligated to seek help, and who cooperates with those qualified to offer it. The patient then cannot be the leader of the interaction, but is a recipient of action on his behalf.

It is our contention, based on extensive interviews and observation in a large medical training center, that these instrumental and expressive system functions are not participated in equally by nurse and doctor, but that there is a clear division of labor in which the nurse assumes the role of expressive specialist and the doctor that of instrumental specialist.

Let us look at some of the activities of nurses and doctors and try to show how, in the last analysis, the nurse's function in the system is primarily expressive. Compared to the activities of the doctor, the nurse's activities are not directly related to the external problem of getting the patient well, but are designed—as it is sometimes put—"to establish a therapeutic environment." This may include a variety of specific behaviors from creating a comfortable, pleasant physical setting to the more directly nurturant activities of explaining, reassuring, understanding, supporting, and accepting the patient.

These acts are mainly meaningful as direct gratifications to the patient which serve to lower his tension level. It is important to recognize that many of the nurse's physical acts of care, although they may involve technical procedures, are primarily significant to the patient as reflections of her attitude toward him. By caring for the patient she shows that she cares about him. By making the patient comfortable, she comforts him. Thus both her physical acts and the attitudes they symbolize are direct gratifications to the patient which serve to maintain his motivational equilibrium.

The doctor's activities in examining, diagnosing, prescribing, and treating, on the other hand, are not directly gratifying to the patient. The patient understands that these activities are necessary as a means to his recovery but in themselves they are often felt by the patient to be embarrassing, painful, and anxiety-provoking. Indeed it is the doctor's instrumental activities which tend to produce the high levels of emotional tension in the patient which the nurse, by her explanations, reassurance, and comforting ministrations, can seek to reduce.

Because of the tension-reducing and hence directly rewarding aspect of her activities, the nurse receives from the patient an emotional response perhaps best described as "appreciation." The nurse tends to judge herself, and her colleagues judge her, in terms of whether the patient likes her and appreciates her. The doctor, in contrast, cannot expect to be "loved" by the patient in the way the nurse is. He has to judge his effectiveness, not in terms of the patient's attitude toward him, but in terms of whether the patient is in fact getting better. Thus, because the nurse plays an expressive role, she gets a reward of "appreciation" from the patient. The doctor gets rewarded less by the patient's attitude than by his own assessment of whether his technical treatment is in fact helping the patient.

Inasmuch as the doctor is primarily responsible for system goal attainment—i.e., getting the patient well—he must be the chief authority in the three-way relationship of doctor-nurse-patient. It is he who must define for the nurse and the patient what must be done in order to get the patient well. This technical-instrumental specialization of the doctor is the basis for the principle that only the doctor has the authority to prescribe medications. The nurse, in contrast, does not have the doctor's authority, but this does not mean that she is without power. She controls the patient, too, but not so much by giving orders as by subtle indirection. This indirect use of power fits with her expressive role. She cannot be the authority figure and at the same time the giver of direct gratifications.

The nurse's role in the three-way relationship is that of system integrator. She serves as a kind of intermediary between the doctor and the patient by interpreting the doctor and his activities to the patient. Thus while the doctor, as instrumental specialist, leads the system, the nurse, as expressive specialist, integrates it.

Now it is quite true that the nurse does perform technical functions, some of them quite complex. It is also true that the doctor performs expressive functions in that he too reassures the patient and shows that he understands. Our point is, however, that if one looks at all the things the doctor does in the doctor-nurse-patient social system the most obvious of them are found to be of an instrumental nature. At the same time, it is found that the nurse does far more for the patient which is of an expressive, immediately gratifying nature than the doctor does.

Functions	Doctor	Nurse
Instrumental	Primary	Secondary
Expressive	Secondary	Primary

In other words, instrumental functions are performed primarily by the doctor and secondarily by the nurse, and the expressive functions are primary for the nurse and secondary for the doctor.

This concept helps the reader to understand how so many radically different statements about nurses can exist. Nurses are aware that some people seem to think of them as "mere technicians" or, even worse, as a sort of "drudge" or "slave." On the other hand, nurses hear that they are wonderful people, "ministering angels." These two grossly contrasting pictures of the nurse exist in the public mind. Which statement best describes her seems to depend on which aspect of the nurse's activities attention is being focused upon. When the public thinks of the nurse as an instrumental specialist, she does not appear to be anything like as important as the doctor because, compared to the technical activities of the doctor, the nurse's technical activities are simply not that complex or crucial.

On the other hand, when the public thinks of the nurse as an expressive specialist because of her kindness, her willingness to listen and understand, her comforting care, she becomes a much more important figure, a "ministering angel." As expressive specialist she is doing something the doctor cannot do as well as she, and is making a unique and important contribution to the doctor-nurse-patient social system.

So far we have been talking about the importance of expressive functions in rather general terms. Let us turn now to a more detailed look at the situation of the ill and hospitalized patient, in order to show specifically what these expressive actions of the nurse are and why they are of such strategic importance in the therapeutic process.

THE THERAPEUTIC FUNCTION OF THE NURSE'S EXPRESSIVE ROLE

The patient, by virtue of being sick, tends to be, to some extent, regressed. He is dependent, egocentric, subject to irrational fears, and in general his capacity for normal self-control is weakened.[5] When he is a patient in the hospital he is taken out of the whole meaningful complex of his ordinary life and isolated from his family and relatives. He is removed from the support his family could give him and placed in a highly impersonal, routine situation where much attention is given to technical instrumental activities. In the hospital the patient is subjected to probing examinations in semi-nude states, he is frequently exposed to technical descriptions of his condition which he does not understand, he may have to undergo painful treatments or operations, the outcome of which is uncertain.

Thus the patient, both by virtue of being ill and by virtue of being in the hospital, needs, more than does the normal adult, reassurance, support, acceptance, understanding, and meaningful explanations. Because of the patient's regressed state of mind and the threatening unfamiliarity of the hospital, if the purely instrumental aspects of restoring him to health are not balanced by tension-reducing expressive mechanism, a great strain is put on the patient's ability to "take it." Indeed, if his tension is built up to intolerable heights his illness may be intensified The nurse, then, in playing an expressive role, serves the important function of maintaining the motivational equilibrium of the patient as he moves from illness to health. . . .

What in essence do all these activities add up to? We are saying that the function of these behaviors is not so much to "cure" the patient as to maintain his motivational balance while he is undergoing the technical procedures necessary to get him well. We are not suggesting that the nurse's technical procedures are unimportant, but rather that their importance lies, not in their instrumental, but in their expressive significance. As we pointed out earlier, her physical acts of care are primarily important as expressions of her attitude toward the patient. By keeping the physical environment pleasant, by caring for the patient, she is expressing an attitude of "caring about" the patient which is so important to his emotional well being. If the nurse does treat the patient as a physical object rather than as a person whom she cares about, much of the therapeutic effect of her activities is lost.

It is our contention that these expressive functions cannot be carried out effectively by the doctor. Although it is important that he be aware of the importance of these expressive functions, it is hardly possible for him to directly implement them in his own role. In large, bureaucratically organized hospitals, which are becoming increasingly typical, the doctor sees the patient for only a few minutes at a time and the patient may have several doctors concerned with different aspects of his illness. The body of medical knowledge is growing at an accelerated rate and with it the technical considerations which the doctor must handle.[6]

Thus, the doctor, while he may certainly be aware of how his instrumental activities are affecting the patient and may attempt to cushion this effect by an attitude of understanding and reassurance, is often not able to give the patient the sustained sup-

[5] Henry D. Lederer, "How the Sick View their World," *J. Social Issues,* **8**, No. 4, 1952, 4–15.

[6] George Rosen, *Specialization of Medicine* (New York: Froben Press, 1944), pp. 73–78.

port he may require. The fact that most nurses are women, who in general play a more expressive role than men, that they are with the patient more constantly than the doctor, that they do not have the doctor's technical competence or authority, makes it particularly appropriate that they assume primary responsibility for expressive functions. Whether or not this expressive function of the nurse is formally recognized and sanctioned by the medical profession, the structure of the situation outlined above makes it almost inevitable that she will take the more expressive role.

So far we have been talking about the nurse-patient relationship and showing what the nurse contributes to the patient. Now let us ask what the nurse contributes to the doctor-nurse-patient relationship as a whole. Here also she has an expressive function, that of integrating the three-way system and making it operate as a harmonious whole. As we pointed out before, she does this by acting as a kind of intermediary between doctor and patient. . . .

It is essential for the best therapeutic results that the doctor-nurse-patient relationship be a harmoniously integrated one. The doctor as team leader is responsible for the major decisions regarding the patient's treatment, but if the patient does not trust the doctor or understand him his treatment may be less effective. It is upon the nurse that primary responsibility rests for establishing and maintaining a harmonious relationship between the two.

LIMITATIONS ON EXPRESSIVENESS

As Parsons and Fox and others have pointed out, there is clearly such a thing as going too far in gratifying and satisfying the patient in his immediate situation.[7] Too much support and tolerance for the patient's dependence and irrationality could be quite dangerous in that it could dispose the patient to become too attached to the sick role. Most nurses are probably familiar with the patient who "loves" the hospital,

[7] Talcott Parsons and Renee Fox, "Illness, Therapy, and the Modern Urban American Family," *J. Social Issues*, 8, No. 4, 1952, 31–44.

who literally dreads to get well. The optimum therapeutic result clearly depends on both expressive gratification and instrumental "discipline." There comes a point when the doctor (and sometimes the nurse) must say in effect to the patient, "You are not trying to get well, and I cannot approve of this kind of behavior or accept it."

The precise nature of the balance between gratification and discipline would depend upon the individual features of the case and the stage of recovery. While it is beyond the scope of this paper to deal in detail with this important problem of how much expressiveness is "too much," we will attempt to show how the possibility of the nurse's becoming overly expressive is reduced and controlled.

The key to this lies in the fact that although the nurse specializes in expressive functions, she also shares with the doctor the common therapeutic goal of getting the patient well. This common goal, which both creates and defines the coalition between nurse and doctor, sets limits on the nurse's expressiveness. It is part of the nurse's role as a member of the therapeutic team to recognize the therapeutic function of her expressive role and correspondingly to recognize that this expressiveness may become therapeutically contraindicated when carried too far.

We also notice that nurses often say, "the nurse must not become *too involved* with the patient." This observation points to the fact that the nurse, although she is expressive and does care about the patient as a person, is also a professional person sharing with the doctor the professional goal of getting the patient well. If she did allow herself to become overly involved with the patient, she could no longer be professionally effective. Obviously the nurse cannot allow herself to be completely crushed by the death of a patient, to fall in love with her patient, or to accept the diffuse obligations of friendship. For instance, if the nurse became too involved with the patient she might be "seduced" into not carrying out the doctor's orders because the procedure might hurt or upset the patient.

From a sociological standpoint, the very essence of "being professional" means that to the professional person (unlike the businessman) the welfare of his client is of primary importance. Because the professional person does have a competence which the client does not have, it is the role obligation of the professional always to act in the interest of his client. When we look specifically at the health professions, the professional role means that the doctor and nurse must do what is best for the patient. If the professional, then, allows himself to become too involved emotionally with the patient, he is no longer in a position to assess objectively what is best for the patient in terms of getting well.

The nurse, then, as a member of the health team, is a professional and is obligated to hold the welfare of the patient as of primary importance. As the expressive specialist on this team, it is her function to lower the tension level of patients and to keep the doctor-nurse-patient relationship harmonious. When she takes her expressiveness too far, by becoming too emotionally involved with the patient and allowing the patient to become too emotionally dependent on her, then this specialized function is no longer fulfilled. In the integrated case, however, her role as professional does not prevent her from being expressive but rather acts to control her expressive function for optimum therapeutic benefit to the patient.

SUMMARY

The nursing profession is seeking to define for itself and for the public the essential functions of the nurse. We have attempted to provide one general answer to this perplexing question. We have stated that the fundamental significance of the nurse's activities in caring for the patient is that these activities serve to give the patient immediate gratifications, and hence tension release, in his stressful situation of being ill and hospitalized. Her activities also serve to keep the relationship between doctor, nurse, and patient harmonious and integrated.

These functions are understood by the sociologist to be expressive functions, fully as important for the social system as the more obvious instrumental or technical functions of the doctor. We have tried to show that "being expressive," far from contradicting "being professional," is the nurse's specialized function as a professional person. We would suggest that, if the nurse is to become an associate of the doctor rather than a handmaiden to him, it will be in her capacity as expressive specialist rather than as a technical expert.

Client-Practitioner Tensions

Tensions sometimes arise between the client and the practitioner; in some instances they may actually be built into the relationship. We can observe circumstances where the social background experiences of the practitioner and his clients are at such variance that this variance tends to influence both the effectiveness of the practitioner in performing the occupational expectations of his colleagues, and the compliance of the client in executing the wishes of the practitioner.

This has been found in the important studies of Hollingshead and Redlich[*] on the effects of social class backgrounds of psychotherapists on patients and therapy programs, and also in the more recent investigations of Kadushin on "the effect of social distance between client and professional on the stability of their interactions."[†] Kadushin studied ministers, physicians, and psycho-

[*] A. B. Hollingshead and F. C. Redlich, *Social Class and Mental Illness; A Community Study* (New York: John Wiley & Sons, Inc., 1958).
[†] Charles Kadushin, "Social Distance Between Client and Professional," *The American Journal of Sociology,* **67**, 1962, 517–531.

therapists in their relations to their clients. "By being socially near its prospective clientele, a profession is more likely to be professionally consulted. This is true of ministers, who are members of the same community as their counsellees."‡ Here "community" connotes shared thought-ways and day-by-day social intercourse. In coping with personal or family problems, however, medical practitioners are viewed as more distant; yet "physicians are able to be somewhat closer to their patients than psychotherapists because they define the medical role in highly functionally specific terms. Most physicians deal almost exclusively with physical symptoms. They are 'too busy,' as patients resentfully report it, to handle other kinds of problems."§ The elevated social class position of the M.D. in combination with the previously described secrets of the occupation effectively serves to create and perpetuate barriers between practitioner and patient. At the same time, because the M.D. largely treats physical symptoms, these barriers are not as formidable as with the psychotherapist. The latter occupation possesses an existence apart from normal life. A different pattern has developed linking psychotherapists to their clientele.

> This device consists of an interstitial "community" to which both patients and therapists belong, but in which they need not interact directly. . . . Knowing others who have had psychiatric treatment, being told by one's friends to go to a psychiatrist, having one's problems noticed by others, and reading works on psychoanalysis are all indicative of belonging to such a community of lay believers and supporters of psychotherapy.**

Thus, what people are and what people do outside of the roles specific to the client-practitioner relationship very profoundly affects what happens when people assume roles of clients or practitioners.

As indicated earlier, an even more extreme form of this phenomenon may be seen where tensions are literally built into the relationship between the worker and the consumers of his services. For example, the dance band musician has a highly developed role component of resentment for his audience. As Howard Becker points out, the audience is almost consistently viewed with hostility, even though the musician performs voluntarily. This attitude is reinforced by the musicians seeing themselves as people apart from the public at large. Dance band musicians maintain a kind of cultural isolation through deliberately devised means—for example, language, dress—which, if they are copied by "outsiders," then the musicians replace by new means of distinction. Emphasis is placed on setting the musician apart from the audience in every way possible because, as Becker describes in the following selection, the client is viewed typically with considerable contempt.

‡ *Ibid.*, 529.
§ *Ibid.*, 530.
** *Loc. cit.*

Howard S. Becker
(Performing Arts—Music)

The service occupations are, in general, distinguished by the fact that the worker in them comes into more or less direct and personal contact with the ultimate consumer of the product of his work, the client for whom he performs the service. Consequently, the client is able to direct or attempt to direct the worker at his task and to apply sanctions of various kinds, ranging from informal pressure to the withdrawal of his patronage and the conferring of it on some other of the many people who perform the service.

This contact brings together a person whose full-time activity is centered around the occupation and whose self is to some degree deeply involved in it and another person whose relation to it is much more casual, and it may be inevitable that the two should have widely varying pictures of the way in which the occupational service should be performed. It seems characteristic of such occupations that their members consider the client unable to judge the proper worth of the service and resent bitterly any attempt on his part to exercise control over the work. A good deal of conflict and hostility arises as a result, and methods of defense against outside interference become a preoccupation of the members.

The present paper outlines the dimensions of such an occupational dilemma as observed among professional dance musicians in a large American city. This occupation presents an extremely favorable situation for studying such phenomena, since in it the problem is, to a greater degree than in many occupations, frankly faced and openly discussed. Musicians feel that the only music worth playing is what they call "jazz," a term which can be defined only as that music which is produced without reference to the demands of outsiders. Yet they must endure unceasing interference with their playing by employer and audience. The most distressing problem in the career of the average musician is the necessity of choosing between conventional success and his "artistic" standards. In order to achieve success he finds it necessary to "go commercial," that is, to play in accord with the wishes of the nonmusicians for whom he works; in so doing he sacrifices

Reprinted from "The Professional Dance Musician and His Audience," *The American Journal of Sociology*, 57, No. 2 (September 1951), 136–144, by permission of The University of Chicago Press. Copyright 1951 by the University of Chicago. The original publication bore the following note:
"I wish to thank Professor E. C. Hughes and Mr. Dan Lortie, who read and commented on a draft of this paper. Thanks are due Professor Hughes, Professor W. Lloyd Warner, and Dr. Harvey L. Smith for their guidance in the prosecution of the original research on which this paper is based."

the respect of other musicians and thus, in most cases, his self-respect. If he remains true to his standards, he is doomed to failure in the larger society. Musicians classify themselves according to the degree to which they give in to outsiders; the continuum ranges from the extreme "jazz" musician to the "commercial" musician.[1]

The discussion will center around the following points: (1) the conceptions which musicians have of themselves and of the nonmusicians for whom they work and the conflict they feel to be inherent in this relation, (2) the basic consensus underlying the reactions of both commercial and jazz musicians to this conflict, and (3) feelings of isolation and the segregating of themselves from audience and community. The analysis is based on materials gathered during eighteen months of interviewing and participant observation. My research was disclosed to few people. In general, I was accepted as just another young piano player by most of the men from whom this material was gathered. The bulk of the material comes from younger men, but enough contact was made with other musicians to permit the analysis of basic occupational problems.

MUSICIAN AND "SQUARE"

The whole system of beliefs about what musicians are and what audiences are is summed up in a word used by musicians to refer to outsiders—"square." It is used as a noun and as an adjective, denoting both a kind of person and a quality of behavior and objects. The term refers to the kind of person who is the opposite of all the musician is, or should be, and a way of thinking, feeling, and behaving (with its expression in material objects) which is the opposite of that valued by musicians.

The musician is conceived of by the professional group as an artist who possesses a mysterious artistic gift setting him apart

[1] A full discussion of this situation may be found in the complete study on which this paper is based: Howard S. Becker, "The Professional Dance Musician in Chicago" (unpublished M.A. thesis, Department of Sociology, University of Chicago, 1949).

from all other people. Possessing this gift, he should be free from control by outsiders who lack it. The gift is something which cannot be acquired through education; the outsider, therefore, can never become a member of the group. A trombone player said, "You can't teach a guy to have a beat. Either he's got one or he hasn't. If he hasn't got it, you can't teach it to him."

The musician feels that under no circumstances should any outsider be allowed to tell him what to play or how to play it. In fact, the strongest element in the colleague code is the prohibition against a musician criticizing or in any other way trying to put pressure on another musician in the actual playing situation "on the job." Where not even a colleague is permitted to influence the work, it is unthinkable that an outsider should be allowed to do so.

This attitude is generalized into a feeling that musicians are completely different from and better than other kinds of people and accordingly ought not to be subject to the control of outsiders in any branch of life, particularly in their artistic activity. The feeling of being a different kind of person who leads a different kind of life is deep-seated, as the following remarks indicate:

I'm telling you, musicians are different than other people. They talk different, they act different, they look different. They're just not like other people, that's all. . . . You know it's hard to get out of the music business because you feel so different from others.

Musicians live an exotic life, like in a jungle or something. They start out, they're just ordinary kids from small towns—but once they get into that life they change. It's like a jungle, except that their jungle is a hot, crowded bus. You live that kind of life long enough, you just get to be completely different.

Being a musician was great, I'll never regret it. I'll understand things that squares never will.

An extreme of this view is the belief that only musicians are sensitive and unconventional enough to be able to give real sexual satisfaction to a woman.

Feeling their difference strongly, musicians likewise believe that beings such as they are under no obligation to follow the conventional behavior of the squares. From the idea that no one can tell a musician

how to play it follows logically that no one can tell a musician how to do anything. Accordingly, behavior which flouts conventional social norms is greatly admired. Stories reveal this admiration for highly individual, spontaneous, "devil-may-care" activities; many of the most noted jazzmen are renowned as "characters," and their exploits are widely recounted. For example, one well-known jazzman is noted for having jumped on a policeman's horse standing in front of the night club in which he worked and ridden it away. . . .

The musician thus views himself and his colleagues as people with a special gift which makes them different from nonmusicians and not subject to their control, either in musical performance or in ordinary social behavior.

The square, on the other hand, lacks this special gift and any understanding of the music or way of life of those who possess it. The square is thought of as an ignorant, intolerant person who is to be feared, since he produces the pressures forcing the musician to play inartistically. The musicians' difficulty lies in the fact that the square is in a position to get his way: if he does not like the kind of music played, he does not pay to hear it a second time.

Not understanding music, the square judges music by standards which are foreign to musicians and not respected by them. . . .

"Squareness" is felt to penetrate every aspect of the square's behavior just as its opposite, "hipness" is evident in everything the musician does. The square seems to do everything wrong and is laughable and ludicrous. Musicians derive a good deal of amusement from sitting in a corner and watching the squares. Everyone has stories to tell about the laughable antics of squares. One man went so far as to suggest that the musicians should change places with the people sitting at the bar of the tavern he worked in; he claimed that they were funnier and more entertaining than he could possibly be. Every item of dress, speech, and behavior which differs from that of the musician is taken as new evidence of the inherent insensitivity and ignorance of the square. Since musicians have an esoteric culture these evidences are many and serve only to fortify their conviction that musicians and squares are two different kinds of people.

But the square is feared as well, since he is thought of as the ultimate source of "commercial" pressure. It is the square's ignorance of music that compels the musician to play what he considers bad music in order to be successful. . . .

Reactions to the Conflict

We will now consider the attitudes of "commercial" and "jazz" musicians toward the audience, noting both the variation in attitude and the basic consensus underlying the two sets of feelings. Two themes run through this conflict: (1) the desire of the musician to live in terms of the creative principle, and (2) the recognition of many forces influencing him to abandon that principle. The jazzman tends to emphasize the first, the commercial musician the second; but both recognize and feel the force of each of these guiding influences. Common to the attitudes of both kinds of musician is an intense contempt for and dislike of the square audience whose fault it is that musicians must "go commercial" in order to succeed.

The commercial musician, though he conceives of the audience as squares, chooses to sacrifice self-respect and the respect of other musicians (the rewards of artistic behavior) for the more substantial rewards of steady work, higher income, and the prestige enjoyed by the man who "goes commercial". . . .

In addition to the pressure to please the audience which emanates from the musician's desire to maximize salary and income, there are more immediate pressures. It is often difficult to maintain an independent attitude. For example:

I worked an Italian wedding on the Southwest Side last night with Johnny Ponzi. We played about half an hour, doing the special arrangements they use, which are pretty uncommercial. Then an old Italian fellow (the father-in-law of the groom, as we later found out) began hollering, "Play some polkas, play some Italian music. Ah, you stink, you're lousy."

Johnny always tries to avoid the inevitable on these wedding jobs, putting off playing the folk music as long as he can. I said, "Man, why don't we play some of that stuff now and get it over with?" Tom said, "I'm afraid if we start doing that we'll be doing it all night." Johnny said, "Look, Howard, the groom is a real great guy. He told us to play anything we want and not to pay any attention to what the people say, so don't worry about it. . . ."

The old fellow kept hollering and pretty soon the groom came up and said, "Listen, fellows. I know you don't want to play any of that s—— and I don't want you to, but that's my father-in-law, see. The only thing is, I don't want to embarrass my wife for him, so play some Dago music to keep him quiet, will yuh?" Johnny looked around at us and made a gesture of resignation.

He said, "All right, let's play the *Beer Barrel Polka*." Tom said, "Oh s——! Here we go." We played it and then we played an Italian dance, the *Tarentelle*.

Sometimes the employer applies pressure which makes even an uncompromising jazzman give in, at least for the duration of the job:

I was playing solo for one night over at the Y—— on ——rd St. What a drag! The second set, I was playing *Sunny Side,* I played the melody for one chorus, then I played a little jazz. All of a sudden the boss leaned over the side of the bar and hollered, "I'll kiss your ass if anybody in this place knows what tune you're playing!" And everybody in the place heard him, too. What a big square! What could I do? I didn't say anything, just kept playing. Sure was a drag.

Somewhat inconsistently, the musician wants to feel that he is reaching the audience and that they are getting some enjoyment from his work, and this leads him to give in to audience demands. One man said:

I enjoy playing more when there's someone to play for. You kind of feel like there isn't much purpose in playing if there's nobody there to hear you. I mean, after all, that's what music's for—for people to hear and get enjoyment from. That's why I don't mind playing corny too much. If anyone enjoys it, then I kind of get a kick out of it. I guess I'm kind of a ham. But I like to make people happy that way.

This statement is somewhat extreme; but

most musicians feel it strongly enough to want to avoid the active dislike of the audience: "That's why I like to work with Tommy. At least when you get off the stand, everybody in the place doesn't hate you. It's a drag to work under conditions like that, where everybody in the place just hates the whole band."

Isolation and Self-Segregation

Musicians are hostile to their audiences, being afraid that they must sacrifice their artistic standards to the squares. They exhibit certain patterns of behavior and belief which may be viewed as adjustments to this situation; they will be referred to here as "isolation" and "self-segregation" and are expressed in the actual playing situation and in participation in the social intercourse of the larger community. The primary function of this behavior is to protect the musician from the interference of the square audience and, by extension, of the conventional society.

The musician is, as a rule, spatially isolated from the audience, being placed on a platform which, being inaccessible to them, provides a physical barrier that prevents any direct interaction. This isolation is welcomed because the audience, being made up of squares, is felt to be potentially dangerous. The musicians fear that direct contact with the audience can lead only to interference with the musical performance. Therefore, it is safer to be isolated and have nothing to do with them. Once, where such physical isolation was not provided, a player commented:

Another thing about weddings, man. You're right down on the floor, right in the middle of the people. You can't get away from them. It's different if you're playing a dance or in a bar. In a dancehall you're up on a stage where they can't get at you. The same thing in a cocktail lounge, you're up behind the bar. But a wedding —man, you're right in the middle of them.

Musicians, lacking the usually provided physical barriers, often improvise their own and effectively segregate themselves from their audience.

I had a Jewish wedding job for Sunday night. ...When I arrived, the rest of the boys were already there. The wedding had taken place late, so that the people were just beginning to eat. We decided, after I had conferred with the groom, to play during dinner. We set up in a far corner of the hall. Jerry pulled the piano around so that it blocked off a small space, which was thus separated from the rest of the people. Tony set up his drums in this space, and Jerry and Johnny stood there while we played. I wanted to move the piano so that the boys could stand out in front of it and be next to the audience, but Jerry said, half-jokingly, "No, man. I have to have some protection from the squares." So we left things as they were....

Jerry had moved around in front of the piano but, again half-humorously, had put two chairs in front of him, which separated him from the audience. When a couple took the chairs to sit on, Jerry set two more in their place. Johnny said, "Man, why don't we sit on those chairs?" Jerry said, "No, man. Just leave them there. That's my barricade to protect me from the squares...."

It may be suggested that similar conflicts are to be found in other service occupations and that research in such areas could profitably focus on such matters as the professional's conception of his client, the manner in which the client impinges on (or, from the professional's point of view, interferes with) his work, the effects of such conflicts on professional organization, with particular reference to the defensive tactics employed by the profession, and the relation of such dilemmas to the individual's participation in the life of the larger society.

The Practitioner and Public Pressure

Much has been said in this volume and elsewhere about the many parts played by public attitudes in shaping occupations and work. Occupational prestige is an outstanding instance of this, and the development of prestige is basically a public process. The following has been said about teaching, but it is equally applicable to other occupations:

From the standpoint of the teacher, professional status may be said to contribute to a feeling of morale, or personal significance. After all, the idea of a profession does convey some notion of prestige in the minds of most people. No matter how devoted the individual may be to his work, there are times when he feels the need for some emotional support—not only that his work is worthwhile, but that other people consider it worthwhile. . . .

At one time teachers in this country had very low professional status, and during that same period teachers took little part in shaping policies on teacher selection and preparation, and organization and development of curricula, the nature of supervision, and academic freedom.

Increasing professional recognition has been accompanied by increasing participation in such matters. This development is a natural one, since the public tends to identify increased professional recognition with increased competence and contribution on the part of the teachers.[*]

Thus high occupational prestige is presumed to bear some positive relationship to the social contribution the public accords an occupation.[†] But practitioner relations with the public are not always so indirect and salutary.

If he is "truly a professional person" governed by his own interpretation of his occupational role, should the practitioner be concerned about what the public thinks? If he develops this concern, how is he to cope with something as intangible as "the public" or "the audience"? Some writers have advocated that special regard be accorded public relations among physicians because it is viewed as an integral part of dealing adequately with patient needs. According to Blum,

Good deeds are the best ammunition for the public relations campaign. Enlightened public relations work neither to hoodwink nor to manipulate the public. Good public relations begins by finding out what is needed to put the medical house in order and to learn what the public justly requires. It must then determine how those requirements can be met by the medical organization in a fashion acceptable to the interests of its members and at the same time in a fashion designed to bring public satisfaction and approval. The public approval can occur only if corrective and constructive actions are, in fact, taken, and then the good deeds widely publicized.

Finally, good public relations for the profession facilitates the management of individual physician-patient relationships: good doctor-patient relations improves medical public relations.[‡]

Such direct efforts to promote "good" public relations are becoming increasingly evident with regard to the highly professionalized occupations.

A further attempt to answer the question of how concerned with the public the practitioner ought to be is examined in the following selection about specialist occupations within the general field of law. The state attorney-general

---

[*] M. H. Willing and J. G. Fowlkes, *et al., Schools and Our Democratic Society* (New York: Harper & Row, Publishers, 1951), pp. 344–345.

[†] The contrary has recently been argued for medicine: see W. A. Gamson and H. Schuman, "Some Undercurrents in the Prestige of Physicians," *The American Journal of Sociology,* **68**, No. 4 (January 1963) 463–470.

[‡] Richard H. Blum, *The Management of the Doctor-Patient Relationship* (New York: McGraw-Hill Book Company, 1960), p. 298. Eric Larrabee, in his article, "Journalism: Toward the Definition of a Profession," *Studies in Public Communication,* No. 3 (Summer 1961), pp. 23–26, discussed some of the factors associated with the professional journalist in relation to his audience.

is contrasted with the federal judge. Both of these categories of workers have had similar kinds of formal legal training, yet the way in which they respond to the demands of their social situations and to the influences of the general public provides an example of dramatically contrasting response patterns. Krislov discusses this in relation to the desegregation problem in the southern United States.

Samuel Krislov (Law)

Why is it that the Southern attorney general has reflected the prejudices, if you will, or the wishes, if you prefer, of his area? Of course he is a Southerner, and a Southern public official. Still this conduct contrasts very sharply with the conduct of others similarly situated. A specific instance seems in order. In June of 1955 a federal district court of three issued an opinion on implementation of the Supreme Court decision that Thurgood Marshall found generally satisfactory.[1] One of the judges was the father of a governor of South Carolina; as a private individual he has denounced the Supreme Court decision and helped force out his pastor for too "broad" an attitude on the race question. Another, during the course of the discussion, sneered at "a foreign communistic anthropologist," an undoubted reference to Gunnar Myrdal, and one reflecting current Southern propaganda.[2] The third judge, whose personal opinions (in all fairness) we don't know too much about, was refused confirmation to the Supreme Court in part due to objections of the NAACP, since in running for office he had once expressed views derogatory of Negroes.[3] The ability of Southern judges on the federal level at least in part

Reprinted from "Constituency Versus Constitutionalism: The Desegregation Issue and Tensions and Aspirations of Southern Attorneys General," *Midwest Journal of Political Science*, 3, No. 1 (February 1959), 80–92, by permission of the Wayne State University Press and author. Copyright 1959 by the Wayne State University.

[1] *Race Relations Law Reporter*, 1, 1955, 73.

[2] *New York Times*, July 26, 1957, p. 7; *Southern School News*, August 1955, pp. 6–9; December 1955, p. 6.

[3] Some definite indications of his views, though, can be found in John J. Parker, "Chief Justice Fred M. Vinson: Meeting the Challenge to Law and Order," *American Bar Association Journal*, 41 (April 1955), 324, especially p. 325.

to set aside their personal opinions and reflect the law as interpreted by the Supreme Court is borne out most clearly by the Southern opposition to the civil rights legislation without jury trial provisions and more positively, by the stand of civil rights adherents in favor of that same provision.

Why is it that on the one hand we have federal judges who can and do put aside their own opinions and ignore the immediate local pressures of public opinion, and on the other hand the Southern attorney general who has reflected his own evaluations of the mores and demands of his area? What is the mechanism that compels the one to be subservient and allows the other to be independent, that makes one responsive to local opinion and the other responsive to national opinion?

It is certainly not enough to speak of the electoral process, for no Southern attorney general has been defeated because of his stand on desegregation. Indeed, none has taken to the hustings in defense of either segregation or desegregation in areas where either course was unpopular. The niceties and irregularities of our democratic government, the evasions that characterize our American system of politics, have prevented the problem of desegregation from being an issue in any but the meagrest number of elections in the United States. We will have to go deeper by looking in more detail at the office of the attorney general.

The position is an historic one dating back to the British sergeant-at-arms. It is certainly a responsible and important office, and it is one that on first sight is fairly obvious in its obligations and duties. The apparent simplicity and obviousness of its responsibilities has in fact made the office largely unknown to observers because there exists virtually no body of investigation or study of what the position entails beyond simple statutory listings or descriptions of statutory requirements in the various states.

But it is a surprisingly complex office. It is curious to see how much of the annual conferences of the attorneys general is devoted to self-conscious discussion of the true nature of the position.[4]

In one sense the attorney general is subservient to federal law. Yet he is at the same time the expounder and defender of state law. Since he is called upon to give legal opinions to the various departments the attorney general basically exercises judicial power. Yet he is not merely a judicial official. More than the independent regulatory commissions he combines the executive, legislative, and judicial functions.

The attorney general is also the chief law enforcement officer for his state, and in the words of a former president of the National Association of Attorneys General, "in many states their powers literally exceed those of the governor in the law enforcement field."[5] Arthur Bromage's description of the attorney general as law enforcer as the head of a "continuous chain of irresponsibility" is no doubt accurate;[6] but his position remains more difficult precisely because of the lack of power given to him to enforce his obligations.

In addition, the attorney general is a policy-making official; as a leading elective official he is called upon and must make decisions beyond the domain of legal processes. At the same time, the attorney general is the trial lawyer—always the appellate trial lawyer and often the lower court trial attorney—for his state. He both advises and represents the administrative units and in many states rules on legal questions expounded by the legislature.

He is also, at least in theory, legal advisor to the governor. But at the same time that he is advisor he is also too often the governor's rival. Both are elective officials and both therefore have a standing with the public largely independent of each other, and often they choose or wish to compete in the future.

The conflicting pressures that are so evident and that bear so strongly upon the attorney general have been rendered particularly irreconcilable by the process of popular election. The anomalies implicit in this arrangement are already reflected in an institutional change—probably the most precise and definite measure of a contradictory governmental arrangement. In practice it is common for the governor to have a legal advisor other than the attorney general, and in many states this is a recognized position with the title of legal advisor or legal counsel to the governor.[7]

Political scientists have usually studied the process of parcelling out the executive power to a number of officials on the state level solely in terms of efficiency. It is also interesting and would be worthwhile to study these officials in terms of irreconcilable and unrealistic multiple pulls and loyalties that are imposed upon the office holder and that make successful carrying out of his office almost impossible. In this process of illogical demands and loyalties no office can hold a candle to the attorney general, for no other office is within the framework of the federal and state law, yet responsible for the enforcement of local law. No other office is elective and yet advisory, policy-making and yet administrative, legal and yet political, creating institutional rivalry with the man he is supposed to work with and advise.

The attorney general, then, is faced with a definite potential in the office. In one sense it would be theoretically possible for him to utilize his position as an important

4 This extends even to the title of the office. A perennial question is what the plural of "attorney general" should be and how to refer to one another. They resolve it by addressing each other as "General" and retaining the older form for the plural.

5 Louis C. Wyman, Attorney General of New Hampshire, communication to writer, May 15, 1957.

6 Bromage, *State Government and Administration in the United States* (New York: Harper & Row, Publishers, 1936), p. 255. For some treatments of the office see John A. Farlie and Donald F. Simpson, "Law Departments and Law Officers in the States," *State Government*, 14, 1941, 237, and G. W. Keeton, "The Office of Attorney General," *Juridical Review*, 58, 1946, 107, 217.

7 Coleman B. Ransone, Jr., *The Office of Governor in the United States* (University of Alabama: University of Alabama Press, 1956).

force in the advancement of a particular program or idea. Yet it is inherent in the multiple stresses and his alternative roles that the attorney general will rather seek to placate all forces and will therefore accommodate himself to these stresses and become a vector rather than a directional force. It is also inherent in the ambiguity of his position, suspended between the importance of the governor and the obscurity of the other state executive officials, that the attorney general will seek to assert some importance and yet will not move decisively and powerfully.

But in his choice between the various roles and in his choice between following the push and pull of particular power relationships or power formations, which will the attorney general choose? In further exploring this problem one suggestion seems appropriate. Interpretive studies have been made of office holders and political pulls and affiliations both in terms of the past and of the present. But students of politics have neglected the future.

Studies of the origins of office holders are common to many schools of thought in political science—Laswellian elite analysis, for example, or Marxist analysis for another. There has also been investigation of present pulls and present affiliations—that is, the study of pressure groups and pressure group activities as well as decision making generally. In doing so political scientists have in part anticipated and in part followed the findings of sociology and social psychology that indicate strongly the extent to which group affiliations and group identifications influence human beings. These findings are summarized under the rubric of "reference group theory" by many sociologists and social psychologists and indicate that people conceive of themselves primarily in terms of identifications and affiliations with some group or groups. Thus faced with pencil and paper and a question, "Who am I?" individuals quickly answer in terms of some objective characteristics which identify them with some external group. Thus "I am a man, a teacher, an American, an Ohioan." All of this would indicate very sharply that individuals, particularly in our society, conceive of themselves in terms of those groups. It is only after exhausting the telling of those external groups that we come to such internal characteristics as "I am happy, I am kind," and the like.

Now in a mobile society, and this is a mobile society, there exists a special type of group which plays a part in our lives. This encompasses those groups that we are not actually members of but that we wish to belong to, not only in a sense of actually knowing and being conscious of our wish, but also in an unconscious sense. "I look up into the hills from whence cometh my promotion." For these groups an appropriate term might be "aspiration groups."[8] From the standpoint of opinion formation, their importance is that they tend to shape and form an individual's opinion often before he is conscious of the fact that he is striving for a change of his group position.

Ultimately the importance of the aspiration group from the viewpoint of the social scientist is that it could provide an addi-

[8] Reference group theory is summarized in the essay by Robert Merton and Alice Kitt Rossi in *Studies in the Scope and Method of the American Soldier* (Glencoe, Illinois: The Free Press, 1954), and reprinted in the revision of Merton's *Social Theory and Social Structure* (Glencoe, Illinois: The Free Press, 1956). Muzafer Sherif has advanced the theory in a number of important statements, particularly in Sherif and Wilson, *Social Psychology at the Crossroads* (Norman, Oklahoma: University of Oklahoma Press, 1953), and Sherif and Sherif, *An Outline of Social Psychology* (New York: Harper & Row, Publishers, 1956). Other important sources include Ralph Turner, "Role Taking, Role Standpoint, and Reference-group Behavior," *The American Journal of Sociology,* 61, 1956, 316, and Shibutani, "Reference Groups as Perspectives," *American Journal of Sociology,* 60, 1955, 562.

"Groups" as used here are shared-attitude groups, not concrete organizations, complex psychological manifestations rather than simple membership units. So far as I know, the use of the term "aspiration group" is a neologism, and linkage with career patterns an innovation. Turner's argument for rejecting the importance of such groups seems an over-zealous application of scientific parsimony, particularly in view of the unconscious element involved in their influence. The present suggestion would allow use of the generic term "reference group" and the subspecies "membership group" and "aspiration group." This is independent of the value versus orientation controversy.

tional tool for analysis. Origin analysis and group pressures tell us what is happening or what has happened, but they do not tell us to any great degree how the individual experiences or interprets either his past experiences or his present pressures. By studying the aspiration group we get in a flash an individual's interpretation of both his past and present, as well as his future. Ideally the aspiration group will provide us with evidence on all of these factors; in practice it will be somewhat less useful as a tool. It is necessary to make the somewhat dangerous assumption that by studying the regular career patterns of a group of individuals we can get a clue as to what these individuals regard as a desirable future and therefore their psychic affiliations for the present. There are many difficulties involved in this approach, as with any other in social science, but perhaps the suggestions here will justify some claims and prove useful.[9]

Career patterns of a group constitute relevant evidence of current thinking in that they are overt manifestations of deeper affiliations not otherwise easily studied. There are several distinguishable patterns of influence that can be assumed to be operative.

An individual in any on-going system will find certain actions generally lead to personal enhancement while other types of activity lead to a loss of effectuality. Thus any system tends to perpetuate within limits a "modal character" (or perhaps several types of personality structures) as a by-product of its own operations. Another force tending toward perpetuation of personality structure and self-identification in any group is to be found in the recruitment pattern. Considerable evidence suggests that social systems recruit individuals who already share attitudes typical of members of the system. Above all, there is a tendency for individuals to adjust their

behavior to conform with that of highly esteemed and prestigious groups and individuals.[10]

So, for example, in *The American Soldier* it was found that enlisted men with attitudes resembling those of officers had a statistically significant greater likelihood of having been promoted when restudied at a later date.[11] It is, of course, difficult to distinguish cause and effect here; the most significant aspect is the recurrence of this type of social behavior rather than the disentanglement of these forces which so often interact. An individual is shaped by what he would like to be; a system tends to recruit and reward individuals who meet important requisites from the standpoint of the system, not only in talents and equipment, but in general outlook and orientation as well.

In line with this reasoning one can consistently assemble data on the career patterns of the attorney general and derive conclusions therefrom. The general pattern that emerges from such data is that primarily the attorney general has been and is a locally oriented official. His aspiration groups are local and his affiliations are local. Those individuals who depart from this pattern tend also to depart from the pattern of politics in their states and thus help confirm the treatment given here.

The data can briefly be set off as follows. First of all, attorneys general do not generally go to Congress. The 1957 Congressional Directory lists only one representative

9 Difficulties include: (1) the fact that career patterns can shift; (2) we are reduced to interpreting individual motivation in terms of mass activity, which of course is not always reliable in the individual case; (3) there may be a striking divergence between aspiration and achievement.

10 See the essay by Alex Inkeles and Daniel Levinson on modal character in Gardner Lindzey, *Handbook of Social Psychology* (Cambridge: Addison-Wesley Pub. Co., 1954) and, *inter alia,* T. M. Newcomb, *Personality and Social Change* (New York: The Dryden Press, 1957), and Elihu Katz and Paul Lazarsfeld, *Personal Influence* (Glencoe, Illinois: The Free Press, 1955). A recent study of the suburban voter seems to indicate that the change in voting behavior precedes the change in residence. This would be in accordance with the position presented here. See John Millet and David Pittman, "The New Suburban Voter: A Case Study in Electoral Behavior," *Southwestern Social Science Quarterly,* 39, 1958, 33.

11 Samuel Stouffer, *et al., The American Soldier* (Princeton: Princeton University Press, 1949), I, 260-264.

TABLE 1

PREVIOUS GOVERNMENTAL SERVICE LISTED
BY MEMBERS OF CONGRESS

List previous service as:	House	Senate
Attorney General	1	4
Governor	2	21
Lieutenant Governor	5	5
Assistant Attorney General	9	1
Highway Commissioner	2	1
State Treasurer	2	2
State Legislature	147	28

Source: *Congressional Directory*, 1957
In the compilation of this and the ensuing data I was aided by Donna Krislov and Donald Slater, now a Fellow, Department of Politics, Princeton University.

TABLE 2

PREVIOUS GOVERNMENTAL SERVICE LISTED
BY MEMBERS OF FEDERAL JUDICIARY

List previous service as:	Court of Appeals	District Court
Attorney General	1	3
Governor	1	6
Governor's Counsel	0	3
Lieutenant Governor	0	1
State or County Judiciary	17	60
House or Senate	4	16
Federal Judicial Experience	20	2

Source: Charles Liebman, ed., *Directory of American Judges*

and four senators with previous experience as attorneys general. This compares with two members of the House and 21 members of the Senate who have been governors. It also compares unfavorably with previous state legislator experience. 28 members of the Senate and 147 members of the House have had such state legislative experience. The attorney general's position is inferior as a stepping stone to the lieutenant governor's position—5 members of the House and 5 members of the Senate have had such experience—and is roughly comparable to that of state treasurers or highway commissioners. We may also say, somewhat surprisingly, that the attorney general does not often move on to federal judiciary, in spite of the rather conspicuous exception at the apex of the federal judiciary. Only one Court of Appeals judge and three district court judges list previous experience as an attorney general in the only authoritative compilation of judicial office holders. Again the governorship was a more likely stepping stone to these positions, while the lieutenant governorship and such other state executive offices as those of the legal counsel to the governor and the state highway commissioner rivaled the attorney general as positions leading to the judicial chair.

What, then, does happen to the attorney general? The answer is that for many his is a terminal position. Particularly in the South the attorney general will often stay on for many years of service. The attorney

general's position may also be terminal in the sense that it is his departure from politics. Many then return to private practice. Another resting place is the state supreme court. Here we have large numbers of former attorneys general. In one-third of the states there is at least one such individual on the bench.

TABLE 3

SUBSEQUENT ACTIVITIES OF OCCUPANTS
OF THE ATTORNEYS GENERAL POSITION

	Occupied office in:	
	1927	1937
Candidate for Governor (defeated)	3	4
Served as Governor	1	3
Died in office	1	1
Remained in office ten years or more	3	4
State Supreme Court	7	6
Other State Judiciary	2	3
Private practice, corporation law, business	9	5
Federal Legislature	0	3

Source: *Who's Who in America*, various years

Above all, many aspire and some succeed in obtaining the gubernatorial position. And those individuals who go on either to federal legislative or judicial positions are those who have succeeded in reaching the governor's chair. This is reflected in the extraordinary attention paid to the fortunes of those who aspire to the governor's post at annual conferences of the attorneys general, and the perennial bad

TABLE 4

PREVIOUS GOVERNMENTAL EXPERIENCE
LISTED BY MEMBERS OF
HIGHEST STATE TRIBUNALS

List previous service as:	Number
Attorney General	20
Governor	3
Lieutenant Governor	3
State or County Judiciary	57
State Legislative Experience	54
U.S. House or Senate	8

Source: As in Table 2

TABLE 5

PREVIOUS GOVERNMENTAL EXPERIENCE
OF GOVERNORS, AUGUST 1957

	Number
Attorney General	5
Lieutenant Governor	10
State Treasurer	2
U.S. House of Representatives	6
U.S. Senate	3
State Legislature	23

Source: *Who's Who in America*, 1956–57;
Current Biography, 1956; *New York Times*,
November 8, 1956, p. 29.

jokes about "demotion" to the executive mansion.[12]

In summary, then, the attorney general normally looks for promotion on the local level. He therefore identifies himself with local groups and derives his opinions from them. This is reinforced by the fact that his contact with the federal government is normally in the position of defender of the state against the national government. The Association, for example, has reflected a surprisingly local point of view. It has opposed the federal government's actions with regard to invalidation of state subversion laws and labor regulations. It has

[12] *Annual Conference of the National Association of Attorneys General*, 1952, pp. 5–6; 1956, p. 60; 1956, p. 25. The National Association of Attorneys General, it should be noted, was organized in 1907, and the Council of State Governments was designated in 1940 as the Secretariat for the Association. It is composed of all Attorneys General of states and territories, as well as the Attorney General of the United States. Annual meetings are held, and the proceedings published. A weekly digest of opinions of the Attorneys General is another major publication.

endorsed the general outline of the Bricker Amendment and was opposed to the Tidelands Oil Decision. It even formally disapproved the action of several states in suing to prevent return of the Tidelands to the states. The most revealing stand was during the war. The Association called for passage of a "Uniform Law to Oppose Federal Encroachments" authorizing the attorneys general to review federal legislation and memorialize both state and federal officials when they found legislation exceeding constitutional bounds. At least one resolution has been reactivated in the current controversy.[13]

The attorney general tends to see himself as a local popular official. This is borne out by the frequent recurrence of the term "politician" in their self-descriptions at the annual conferences. John Ben Sheppard, in his presidential address in 1956, got great applause with his observation that "an attorney general has to have the eye of an Indian scout so he can follow the trail of public opinion, avoid being ambushed along the way, and cover his tracks."[14] Supporting this, in response to a questionnaire, the small number who were willing to commit themselves espoused this view of the office. Of eleven, five thought of themselves as elected policy-making officials, three as executive policy-implementing officials, only one preferred the judicial label, and one insisted upon a combination of the elective judicial tag. On the question of federal versus local orientation, the number who committed themselves to a straight-out preference for state law when in conflict with federal law (which seems an extreme legal doctrine) was about equal to the

[13] *Ibid.*, 1953, pp. 5 and esp. 34–35; 1954, p. 87; 1955, p. 22; 1956, pp. 4, 5 and 76. See also Abram P. Staples, "The Attorneys General and the Preservation of Our System of Government," *State Government*, 16, 1943, 29. *Civil Rights*, Hearings before Subcommittee No. 5 of the Committee on the Judiciary, House of Representatives, 85th Cong., 1st Sess. pp. 1170–1177, contains a copy of the remarkable "uniform law." On the perennially defensive attitude of attorneys general see Walter White, *How Far the Promised Land?* (New York: Viking Press, 1955), pp. 38–40.

[14] *Annual Conference of the National Association of Attorneys General*, 1956, p. 131.

number that were willing to espouse a balance of authority with federal predominance.[15]

[15] The questions and the number selecting each choice were as follows: The following have been suggested as representing different views of the Attorney General's role. Which one would you choose as *most* descriptive:
1. an elective official whose first obligation is to serve the interests of the people of his state.   (5)
2. a judicial official whose first obligation is to carry out the general principles of law.   (1)
3. an executive official whose first obligation is to help maintain and execute the needs of good government.   (3)
4. requiring adherence first of all to your private conscience and conviction   (0)
All of the above (2)   1 and 2 combined (1)
The following have been suggested as representing different views of the obligations of the Attorney General. Which one would you choose as most descriptive?
1. a state official and in case of conflict between the national and state laws bound to obey the state law.   (3)
2. an official of the people of his state and therefore bound in case of conflict to pick that set of laws which is most conducive to the eventual well-being of the state.   (1)
3. bound to carry out the decisions of the federal courts in their full rigor.   (1)
4. bound to carry out the decisions of the federal court, but with modifications due to local conditions.   (4)
1 and combined (1)   None (3)

Here, then, is the situation in a nutshell. The attorney general lives in a universe of local groups and local opinions. The federal judge looks to national groups and the higher judiciary for approval and promotion. It is no coincidence that those who aspire beyond their state borders are to a greater or lesser degree resistant to local opinion. Neither is it coincidence, but necessity, that forces the attorney general with his local attitudes and aspirations to follow the maxim "vox populi vox Dei." It is, in short, in the light of objective sociological data that we can predict and explain some of the social-psychological influences that lie behind overt political actions.

Questionnaires were sent to all 48 states, so the figures are less than conclusive. The pattern of response is of some interest, however. Of the 48, it should be noted, 13 replied to the questionnaire, and two others sent materials from which partial answers could be assumed. Eleven wrote letters indicating various reasons for non-reply. Two Attorneys General from defying states answered the questionnaire, approximately the same proportion as of the total group, but no other response was heard from the other five defying states. Of the complying states in which desegregation was a problem, the proportion of replies to the questionnaire is average—two out of eleven —but two others sent materials, and four sent letters of explanation. Thus virtually every border state Attorney General replied in one way or another.

Questions for Discussion and Further Research

Some of the highly professionalized occupations deal with clients and the general public only indirectly; as a consequence they have few difficulties associated with client-practitioner relationships. Others require very close contact with clients or segments of the public. Some writers are of the opinion that not enough attention has been paid to the possible barriers that may develop in this interaction between the practitioner and non-practitioners, and they point out the need for rapport, trust, and directness in this relationship. Because people in highly professionalized occupations live in complex occupational cultures, particularly with respect to specific work tasks, there may be a tendency to overemphasize the highly technical aspects of the work to the detriment of the human aspects. One question needing further research, then, might be stated somewhat as follows: During the formal education process at professional school, is there a failure in the client-centered professions to provide adequate training in understanding client attitudes because of a preoccupation with the mechanics of the occupation? A corollary question: What is the extent to which the long-accepted expectation of complete client passivity in the client-practitioner relationship is, realistically, to the best interests of the client? The client's attitude of unquestioning acceptance of the practitioner's recommendations signifies a fundamental belief in the highly professionalized occupations: "the practitioner knows best." To what extent has this custom evolved largely for the convenience of the practitioner and to the retardation of the occupational art?

Hanley and Grunberg make the point that there is neither a single type of patient nor a single type of practitioner; every instance of interaction between a practitioner and his client is unique. Yet people continue to act as though there were a standard version of each. This simplistic approach fails to recognize that no standard formula will serve all situations and that there must be an awareness of the importance of differences in personality and circumstance. For example, educational differences may markedly affect the kind of communication between people, and prejudices and biases may structure reactions unrealistically. It would be interesting to know more about how such practitioner prejudices and biases are acquired within the formal educational situation, particularly in professional school. Or, if the prejudices and biases stem from even earlier socialization experiences, we ought to establish how such occupationally deleterious biases and prejudices can be coped with. Moreover, it must be recognized that we are not dealing solely with personality characteristics here, for social status characteristics may profoundly affect what takes place in the client-practitioner relationship. In what sorts of situations are status characteristics as important, or more important, than personality characteristics for the client-practitioner relationship?

In the literature on highly professionalized occupations, much is made of professional detachment, of affective neutrality. But does professional conduct imply, *by definition,* affective neutrality? This question becomes crucial when we examine the doctor-patient-nurse social system, dealt with by Johnson and Martin. They argue that an integral part of the nurse's role is the overt display of supportive feelings requisite for the faster recovery of the patient. If this is true, is nursing permanently precluded from a high degree of professionalization? Following this line of thought further, Johnson and Martin emphasize the possibility that one of the difficulties in the world of work is that too much attention has been paid to occupations in isolation without consideration of the dynamics of their day-to-day relationships with other occupational roles, and client and public roles; only in this way will it be possible to delineate sociologically the relational functions of an occupation.

The interesting work of Howard Becker on the dance band musician notes an instance of considerable hostility in evidence between practitioner and client. On occasions, outright conflict may result. Are such tensions functionally essential in some client or practitioner relationships? Or are dance band musicians unique in the way they have come to view their public? Is innovation—which is at the heart of the activities of the jazz musician—promoted by hostility relationships? In occupations requiring much creativity ought we to expect frequent hostility when the practitioner comes into close contact with the consumers of his services?

Krislov has provided further evidence of the importance of *reference groups* in the behavior of people when he describes attorneys who do not have as their primary reference group the larger context of the legal profession, but rather the concern with public pressures. It would be useful to know whether these perceived pressures from the general public do in fact exist, or whether they are merely contrived by small but vocal pressure groups. What forms do they take, and how do they operate to modify occupational behavior? Are practitioners expected to have any real responsibility to the public at large beyond the adequate servicing of their immediate clients' needs?

7

Relations Among Occupational Groups

It is possible to construct an ideal picture of the relationship among occupations in a harmoniously balanced system, with each occupation making its distinctive and requisite contribution to the world of work. As was pointed out in Chapter 1, however, such an ideal system is not found in the real world. This is not to deny that when an occupation's function is unique and it supplements or complements the work activities of other occupations, problems of interoccupational relationships may be minimal. But where there is duplication or some degree of overlap among occupations, then problems often arise. As has been observed in one occupation, "the effectiveness of the psychologist's contribution, as well as his opportunity to make it, is determined, at least in part, by the sort of relations he establishes with people possessing the interests, competences and methods of other professions."* This indicates the importance of coordinated and harmonious relations among various occupational groups.

Let us view this example more closely. An understanding of relations among occupations is dependent upon having some realization of the aims of the occupations involved. That is, we have to know something about the fundamental values of each occupation, because what occupational members do at work must then be set against these expectations. Psychologists recognized this when the national professional association established basic principles to guide relations of psychology to other professions. In so doing, psychologists delineated some of the following occupational aims. First of all, there is mention of the need for social responsibility. The public has a right to service where there is a genuine need, regardless of ability to pay. There is also an admonition to practitioners to work within the competency provided by training in the field. As a scientific discipline, there is a rejection of final answers to important questions and encouragement for questioning existing knowledge. There is an explicit plea for realistic and cooperative relations with other occupations. There is a

---

* Committee on Relations with Other Professions of the American Psychological Association, *Psychology and Its Relations with other Professions* (Washington, D.C.: American Psychological Association, 1954), p. 1.

recognition that this profession is dependent upon the acquisition of basic knowledge, hence a stressing of balance among research, teaching, and application. Related to this is the expression of a need to sustain adequate communication among what are referred to as "the discoverers," the teachers, and the appliers of knowledge. There is discussion of the significance to be given a code of conduct which primarily protects the client, and is only to a lesser extent concerned with members of the occupation. There is a rejection of overly jealous protectiveness of the occupation, as with a guild; and a rejection of over-exclusiveness in entrance policies into the occupation. Finally, there is a reiteration of the importance of individual autonomy within such a highly professionalized occupation.†

This set of basic occupational values is essentially typical of many highly professionalized occupations. Given an expression of values as guidelines, it is possible for any occupation to examine how its members ought to interact with other occupational groups, that is, as relationship expectations. First we shall concentrate on expectations for an optimal kind of relationship. Later, we shall have something to say about other sorts of relationships which are not so supportive of the operation of the larger society.

Relationship Expectations

Some occupational associations have gone so far as to publish statements which are meant to aid in regularizing interoccupational relations. In other instances, this concern may not have evolved into a statement of principles, but there may have been a recurring discussion at professional meetings on the problems of relationships with other occupations.‡

In the following excerpts from the report mentioned previously which was prepared by the Committee on Relations with Other Professions of the American Psychological Association, the principles, as stated, afford an opportunity to see what they are intended to accomplish, not only within the occupation but also with the public.

† *Ibid.*, pp. 4–8 *passim.*

‡ That there was a need for such concern was recognized some time ago. Charles H. Whitaker, writing on "The Interrelations of the Professions," *The Annals of the American Academy of Political and Social Science,* **101**, No. 190 (May 1922), pp. 12–15, exhorts people in all professions to avoid "commercialism" and "selfish interest" and to pursue a course of professionalism which would create cooperation among the occupations. This was to be essentially an individual matter, however, and not an associational concern.

Committee on Relations with Other Professions of the American Psychological Association (Psychology)

BASIC PRINCIPLES TO GUIDE
THE RELATIONSHIPS BETWEEN
PSYCHOLOGY
AND OTHER PROFESSIONS

The foregoing considerations have led the Committee to the formulation of a series of basic principles which we believe will serve as useful guides to psychology in its relationships with *any* other profession and will also have an important bearing on psychologists' relations with colleagues in other scientific disciplines. Some of the principles have greater relevance to the academic situation, some to the work of the applied psychologist, and still others to the laboratory. Although certain of these principles are implicit in the previous discussion, we believe it useful to state each principle as explicitly as possible. And, because of the several distinctive roles played by psychologists in American society, it seems preferable to formulate certain of the basic principles with respect to these roles, e.g., teacher, researcher, administrator, or practitioner.

Principle 1

Guided primarily by the criterion of social welfare, the American Psychological Association, as the official national organization of psychologists who function as researchers, teachers, practitioners, and administrators, accepts full responsibility for coordinating the development and functioning of the profession of psychology. As members of the Association, psychologists accept: (a) the responsibility for advancing basic knowledge concerning human behavior, (b) the responsibility for training qualified aspirants to professional competence, (c) the responsibility for establishing and maintaining standards of professional competence, and (d) the responsibility of formulating and maintaining high ethical standards.

Principle 2

Psychology is concerned with the application of the methods of science to the problems of human behavior. The profession assumes responsibility for encouraging research and facilitating the communication of research findings. . . .

Principle 3

As teachers, psychologists accept and share the ethics and ideals of the teaching professions. . . .

Principle 4

As administrators of the professional activities of psychologists and/or other professional persons, psychologists accept and share the responsibilities and ethics of persons serving in an administrative capacity. . . .

Reprinted from "Basic Principles to Guide the Relationships Between Psychology and Other Professions," *Psychology and Its Relations with Other Professions*, (Washington, D.C.: American Psychological Association, 1954), pp. 8–14 *passim*. Used by permission.

Principle 5

As appliers of their knowledge, skills, and techniques, psychologists accept and share the responsibilities and ethics of the group of professions which deal with human advancement and welfare. With a primary concern for the welfare of the persons and institutions served, psychologists accept the responsibilities of:

a. developing new knowledge and techniques of practical value;

b. educating new members of the profession, not only in technical competences but also in a profound appreciation of social responsibilities;

c. sharing with related professions its research techniques and findings and its resources for training.

Principle 5.1 The professional services rendered by psychologists vary greatly in their distinctiveness. Some are rarely carried out by nonpsychologists; others are shared with several other professional groups. Public welfare is advanced by the competent performance of socially useful services by a number of professions. Psychology believes it undesirable to attempt to control the practice of all psychological functions by restricting them to members of any single profession *except insofar as it can be clearly demonstrated that such restriction is necessary for the protection of the public*. Psychology, therefore, does not favor narrowly restrictive legislation, which provides that only psychologists (or teachers, or physicians, etc.) may engage in certain applications of psychological knowledge and techniques.

Principle 5.2 In performing its applied functions, either alone or in association with other professions, psychology accepts the responsibility for adopting every feasible means to protect the public from the incompetent or unwise application of psychological knowledge and techniques.

Principle 5.21. Psychology accepts the responsibility for (a) establishing meaningful standards of professional competence, (b) designating to the public those members of the profession who have met these standards, and (c) effectively informing the public concerning the meaning of the established standards of competence.

Principle 5.22. Psychology accepts the responsibility for establishing and certifying standards of professional competence of its own members, and, since some applications of psychology are shared with members of other professions, it believes that these other professions should also accept the responsibility of maintaining standards of professional competence of their own members with respect to the application of psychological knowledge and techniques. Psychology stands ready to cooperate with all other professional groups in devising means of protecting the public from charlatans and quacks in the human relations field.

(Psychology has accepted the responsibility for formulating a code of ethics adequate to protect the public and for enforcing this code among its members.)

Principle 5.23. In the interests of both the public and the client and in accordance with the requirements of good professional practice, the profession of psychology is obligated to seek legal recognition of the privileged nature of confidential communications with clients.

Principle 5.3 In situations in which psychologists share their applied functions with members of other professions, or work in association with them, psychologists accept the obligation:

a. to abide by all applicable legal provisions surrounding the rendering of such professional service;

b. to know and take into account the traditions, mores, and practices of the professional group or groups with whom they work;

c. to collaborate fully with all members of the professional groups with whom a service function is shared.

Principle 5.4 Since society endorses independent private practice of the professions, the profession of psychology regards it as appropriate for its members to choose this mode of practice, provided that they are properly qualified[1]

Principle 5.41. Recognizing that independent private practice, whether in clinical, counseling, or industrial psychology,

[1] See also Principle 6.2.

involves the assumption of grave professional responsibilities[2] requiring both high technical competence and mature judgment, the profession of psychology will support a member's decision to elect this mode of practice only if, in the judgment of his peers, he is qualified by training, experience, maturity, and attitudes to hold himself forth to the public as a qualified psychologist.[3]

Principle 5.42. Since the practice of psychology in institutional settings or under qualified supervision or in team or group practice (whether supported by a community or by private fees) encourages collaborative decisions and provides for certain social controls, such practice may be appropriately engaged in by psychologists who do not yet meet the high qualifications expected of persons for independent practice.

Principle 5.43. Individuals electing to function independently, not as psychologists but in more limited roles where they do not assume the responsibilities for professional decisions, may also appropriately do so with lesser qualifications than are expected of those who hold themselves forth as qualified psychologists. Examples of such persons are those trained as teachers of remedial reading, speech correctionists, or specialists in a particular testing technique. Such

[2] Such as the responsibility for:
a. deciding what kinds of problems and which clients he will accept or reject;
b. deciding on the amount and the nature of his collaboration with other psychologists and other professional persons; and
c. evaluating the quality of his own professional activities.

[3] The most tangible evidence of such endorsement by peers is possession of a diploma issued by the American Board of Examiners in Professional Psychology, a diploma issued only after an intensive evaluation of a psychologist's training, experience, reputation, and professional attitudes in addition to written and oral examinations. Other current symbols of achievement or status (e.g., the possession of an M.A. or Ph.D. degree, membership in the APA or its divisions, previous experience in private practice, and certificate or license of a state) do not guarantee the degree of professional competence deemed necessary for fully independent practice.

Some psychologists not holding an ABEPP diploma may admittedly be fully competent to assume the responsibilities of independent prac-

individuals should confine their professional services to those functions for which they are well qualified by training and experience and refrain from holding themselves forth as psychologists.

Principle 5.44. The profession of psychology approves the practice of psychotherapy by psychologists only if it meets conditions of genuine collaboration with physicians most qualified to deal with the borderline problems which occur (e.g., differential diagnosis, intercurrent organic disease, psychosomatic problems). Such collaboration is not necessarily indicated in remedial teaching or in vocational and educational counseling.[4]

Principle 6

As an autonomous profession, psychology cannot accept limitations upon the freedom of thought and action of its members other

tice. However, psychologists electing to enter independent private practice without a certifying diploma must do so without the assumption that their colleagues or their professional associations will agree with the propriety of their decision.

[4] The substance of this principle was originally adopted by the APA Council of Representatives on September 8, 1949. It is, however, believed desirable that it be included here in the present context. The principle is also included in "Ethical Standards of Psychologists" (Principle 25.1–4, pp. 79–80).

than limitations imposed by its social responsibility and by considerations of public welfare. The profession must resist moves from any source to establish nonfunctional restraints on the behavior of psychologists whether in the role of teacher, researcher, administrator, or practitioner.

Principle 6.1 The profession of psychology will lend every feasible assistance to any responsible member subjected to undue limitations upon his opportunity to function as a responsible teacher, scientific investigator, administrator, or practitioner.

Principle 6.2 Psychology as a profession will resist all attempts at restrictive legislation which promise to limit unduly or to abrogate the psychologist's opportunities to function as an independent professional person. At the same time, through its ethical code, the profession will demand that its members collaborate fully with members of related professions whenever such collaboration appears in the best interests of a client or of society.

Principle 6.3 As a matter of public policy, psychology will cooperate with any responsible professional organization in combatting any unwarranted limitations on the professional functions of the members of that organization.

Analysis of these principles devised for psychologists indicates their obvious relationship to the fundamental values or aims of the occupation discussed earlier in this chapter. The vigor with which these principles are enunciated should not escape notice. (The reason for this will perhaps become somewhat clearer later in this chapter when specific mention is made of the relationship of this occupation to the medical profession.) Similar concern is evident with other highly professionalized occupations existing within complex organizations.* Strauss remarks that professionalism "...complicates the task of developing teamwork *between* occupations. Each profession tends to develop a parochial, specialized point of view. As a result jurisdictional disputes become more common, and the over-all organization starts to break down into a number of semiautonomous departments..."†

In addition, there are complicated, long-standing problems associated with the interrelationship of the so-called "basic" and "applied" occupations, as Cottrell and Sheldon have found in their studies. Consideration of the rela-

* See Chapter 8.
† George Strauss, "Professionalism and Occupational Associations," *Industrial Relations,* 2, No. 3 (May 1963), p. 31.

tionships between basic social science disciplines and what Cottrell and Sheldon have called "the practicing professions" show this, even though most of the practicing professions are dependent in some measure on the fundamental knowledge established by the social science disciplines.‡ They summarized as three-fold the problems confronted in this area: those which are brought about by differences in the occupational cultures, that is, differences bearing on values, goals, ideologies, language, and technologies of these occupations; secondly, problems which arise out of the immediate social situation in which the social scientists work, along with the status backgrounds they bring to the situation; and finally, vagueness and inappropriateness of the expectations for one another held by members of all these occupations.

‡ More effective communication and collaboration among all these occupations has been of great interest to the Russell Sage Foundation for whom Cottrell and Sheldon undertook these studies.

Leonard S. Cottrell Jr. and Eleanor B. Sheldon (Social Sciences)

The Russell Sage Foundation during the past fifteen years has devoted most of its resources to the support of programs directed toward the development of more effective working relations between the behavioral sciences—chiefly sociology, social anthropology, and social psychology—and the various fields of professional practice such as medicine, law, theology, social welfare, and education. The usual pattern in specific undertakings has involved the placement of scientists in professional schools or operating institutional settings with arrangements for them to collaborate with members of the host profession in such things as the planning and conduct of research, development of teaching materials, giving instructions, and preparation of publications. Through its postdoctoral residency program, the Foundation has provided younger social scientists with opportunities to learn how to function as scientists in applied settings.

This paper is an attempt to review our experience to date with respect to the kinds of problems encountered when social scientists and members of a practicing profession seek to define goals of mutual concern and

Reprinted from "Problems of Collaboration between Social Scientists and the Practicing Professions," *The Annals of the American Academy of Political and Social Science*, 346 (March 1963), 127–131. Used by permission of the publisher.

to develop mutually satisfactory working relations in implementing those goals. This is not a report of research in the usual sense. Rather, what we shall present are observations and impressions that have emerged from our experiences in establishing our programs and assisting in the resolution of problems they present, plus extensive comments we have received from our project personnel and postdoctoral residents in response to our requests for information on the kinds of problems of collaboration they encounter and the kinds of resolutions they attempt. This considerable volume of concrete description of problems lends itself rather easily to classification into categories that should certainly not occasion any surprise among social scientists.

CULTURAL DIFFERENCE

The first of these classes of problems can be regarded as cultural or subcultural barriers to communication and collaboration. It takes no great command of anthropology to predict that people of differing cultural backgrounds will have difficulty in communicating and collaborating with one another in any joint endeavor. Much less obvious but just as real and more difficult to deal with because of their low visibility are the subcultural barriers between groups in the same culture. All subgroups of the society tend to develop their own ways of perceiving and conceptualizing the "facts" of their world, their own particular goals and scales of values, their own language, meaningful to them but jargon to the outsider, and their own body of technology with which they operate on the objects of their special concerns.

This painfully trite observation is also painfully real to both social scientists and their practitioner counterparts who have actually confronted the necessities of establishing genuine communication and viable work relations across disciplinary and professional boundaries. In one count we made not long ago, something over a third of all problems mentioned by our project and fellowship personnel fell into this category.

In the health field, for example, the medical practitioner is trained to see his problems in terms of the individual organism or segments of it; the social scientist conceptualizes his problems in terms of interaction among organisms. If the medical man thinks of the environment, it is primarily the physical environment that he considers important. Attempts of the social scientist to analyze the processes of social interaction, the development of roles and their systematic relations in institutional patterns and the relating of these facts to illness and health, are likely to strike the medical man as lacking in reality and relevance. While the social scientist perceives the physician as deplorably narrow and naive about the dynamics of human relations, his own innocence of biological sophistication makes him appear to the latter as unsound and of doubtful competence. The structure of medical institutions is frequently more rigid and authoritarian than the somewhat more informal and much less authoritarian pattern of academic life in which the social scientist is trained. Sometimes the contrasting patterns in this respect are extreme, as in cases where the social scientist finds he is expected to clear all of his papers and public appearances with the medical officer of his institution or department and to list his superior as joint author—sometimes as senior author— of all publications. Indeed, the whole way of life, from basic theoretical orientations to the irksome details such as whether or not to wear a white coat when on duty,

presents the social scientist with the problem of assimilating a strange culture simply to achieve intelligible communication with his new associates.

But the social scientist in the health fields may take some comfort from the knowledge that his colleagues who elect to work with other professions confront problems of subcultural difference, in some cases greater or more difficult to bridge than in the case of the health professions. A lawyer, for example, is not trained to think like a scientist. He is preoccupied with the specific case—not so much to understand it or explain it in any scientific sense but to reach a decision with respect to the issues the case presents. This he does through logical analyses and appeals to established rules and the precedents set by tradition and decisions in previous similar cases. He is extremely dubious of the validity of generalizations arrived at from the analysis of mass data and applicable to populations when these generalizations go counter to his common sense; he questions the value of generalizations so derived that conform to "what he knows already." He is interested primarily in decisions of practical policy and operating issues and in the manipulation of the factors affecting these issues and is much less concerned with the study of social processes simply to "explain" them.

Ironically enough, many lawyers have a firmer grasp of the actual workings of our social system than do many social scientists. This knowledge has come from the necessity to understand the ramifications of issues in specific cases that involve broader problems of the economic and political system. This knowledge is ordinarily not articulated in conceptual systems that can be readily communicated and taught but is gained in the apprenticeship and professional practice. It, therefore, does not emerge as a body of theory from which hypotheses are derived for systematic testing. We cannot here pursue further the interesting subcultural differences of law and social science. Nor can we discuss here the equally fascinating gaps between our fields and others such as social work, education, and theology.

Unfortunately, the participants in these

cross-cultural experiments too often interpret their differences and difficulties in
personal terms. People are judged to be
stupid, stubborn, self-defensive, whereas in
reality they are acting as the products of
their respective occupational subcultures.
The problems at best are not easy to solve,
but, clearly recognized for what they are,
they can be surmounted; misperceived, they
remain obdurate indeed.

Social Structure and Status

A second category of obstacles to effective
communication and collaboration can be
identified as those derived from the nature
of the setting in which the social scientist
works and from the position and status he
occupies in that setting. A rather rigid
bureaucratic, authoritarian, status-conscious
institutional situation is not an easy setting
for a representative of a newly, relatively
unknown, and low-status science to test
and demonstrate the relevance and utility
of his discipline. And yet this is the kind
of situation found in many schools and
operating agencies of the practicing professions. Such conditions make very important, indeed the manner in which the
social scientist is introduced into the situation, where in the system he is located, the
nature of the supervisory and communi-
cative channels defined for him, the ease
and range of contact available to him, and
his status in relation to his associates.

In their zeal to move ahead in achieving
a more effective working relation between
a profession and the social sciences, the
administration of a school or operating
agency may simply employ a social scientist
and literally drop him into the situation.
Introduced in this manner, it should not be
surprising that he finds himself hampered
by attitudes ranging from open hostility to
puzzled friendliness.

Sometimes it appears easier to introduce
the new discipline by way of a relatively
new and low-status department. For example, in medicine, preventive medicine
and psychiatry are regarded as relatively
new and of lower status than the older sectors of the field such as surgery. In a
theological school, practical or pastoral theology does not have the same standing

enjoyed by departments of theology or bibli-
cal studies. Moreover, it is not infrequently
the case that the potential contributions of
social science are more obviously relevant to
some of these newer or lower-status fields.
Entry may be relatively easy, but, unless the
situation is explicitly defined so as to prevent it, the social scientist may find himself
insulated from the other fields of the profession that could make vital use of his
discipline.

Closely related to the problems of a
hampering departmental affiliation are
those occasioned by the bureaucratic com-
pulsion to place the social scientist under
"safe" supervision. Thus, a dean of a
medical school may feel it necessary to insist
that a psychiatrist supervise the work of the
social scientist. Many law schools seem to
think that all research and teaching by a
social scientist should be directed by a lawyer. These conceptions frequently go beyond
those obtaining in the normal relations of
faculty members to their chairmen and
deans. Thus, a psychiatrist or a lawyer or
a social worker who knows little of the
requirements of research will deem it
necessary to pass on choice of problems,
appropriateness of research design, and the
interpretation of the findings. A social
scientist will sometimes find himself becoming a kind of research assistant to
such a supervisor, and, on some occasions
as previously mentioned, he has found that
his writing is expected to be published
either under the sole name of the supervisor
or with him as senior author.

In some instances, the effectiveness of the
social scientist is reduced by a functional
insulation rather than a departmental one.
An example found frequently is that of
defining the role of the social scientist as
that of a technical research methods consultant and making it virtually impossible
for him to participate in other activities,
such as identifying problems for research,
teaching, consulting on the substantive
problems of the professional practice, and
other functions through which he might
further the application of his discipline to
the problems of the profession. Sometimes
this type of functional insulation results not
so much from the structuring of the situation by the host profession as from the

preferences of the social scientist himself or from the sheer limitation of time, energy, and capability.

Another type of hampering insulation results from the fact that frequently the social scientist must function without ready access to other social scientists who "talk his own language." The necessity for interchange of ideas in a sympathetic milieu is so acute that many of our social scientists, who have had to function as the sole representatives of their disciplines, have urged that we never place fewer than two in any situation.

Running throughout the problems that derive from situational structure are the ubiquitous problems of status differentials. Professions like theology, medicine, and law are endowed with the pride of an ancient and honorable past, rich in tradition and lustrous in achievement. Their present positions are weighty and respected. One whose own status is based on a new, relatively untried field is obviously disadvantaged in dealing with members of such professions. This handicap is vastly increased when the social scientist is, as he frequently must be, in a younger age group than those with whom he must deal. Different and somewhat more difficult types of status problems are encountered when dealing with professional groups who themselves occupy somewhat weak or uncertain status positions. Thus, in a professional social work setting, the social scientist is sometimes regarded as a threat to the position of the professional.

ROLE AMBIGUITY AND INCONGRUENT EXPECTATIONS

A third group of problems in collaboration stems from the lack of clarity in and the incongruities of conceptions of self and expectations of others when social scientists and professional practitioners interact. These problems are most acute, of course, in the early phases of collaborative undertakings. Social scientists frequently suffer from the misapprehension that the professions to which they go know nothing about social science, and, consequently, they begin to perform as missionaries and propagandists, with predictable results. In contrast, there is, on the part of some, a tendency to assume too much and thus to

speak at a technical level beyond the audience and so to acquire the reputation of using nothing but jargon. Another type of incongruous self-image occurs when the social scientist loses his identity and begins to act as if he conceived of himself as a practitioner, with resultant loss of his utility. Added to these are the instances of poor taste and blunders that multiply from ignorance and deficiency of empathic sensibility.

The misplacements and misperceptions and obtuseness of the social scientist can be matched on the professional side of the situation. It is interesting that one of the most common errors on the part of the practitioner is that of expecting the social scientist to know more than he does and to have skills and capabilities far beyond not only what he as an individual commands but what his discipline could possibly supply at its present stage of development. Not only with respect to levels of capabilities but in matters of substantive areas of interest and potential contribution, there is usually need for a fairly prolonged period of mutual effort before effective congruent perceptions and expectations are developed. This appears to be necessary even when roles and interests are spelled out in considerable detail in initial plans and agreements. In connection with the problem of incongruent expectations, it is interesting to note that law, which frequently appears to be the most difficult profession for social scientists to work with, has no well-developed model for working with scientists except that of treating them as expert witnesses. The legal profession does not approach its problems within a scientific orientation, and neither the lawyer nor the social scientist has yet developed an appropriate perception of each other's role. Thus far, the Foundation has not hit upon a successful formula for collaboration in this instance.

FREQUENCY OF PROBLEMS

In a recent enumeration of the problems listed by our project personnel and postdoctoral fellows, 36 per cent were classified as problems based on professional subcultural differences in basic orientations, values and goals, language, and levels of research technology; 26 per cent were problems growing out of the structure of the situation and status problems confronting the social scientist in those situations; 36 per cent appeared to be chiefly resultants of lack of clarity and incongruences of self-conceptions and mutual expectations. The remaining 2 per cent were not readily classifiable. The total number of problems identified in this enumeration was 255.

The distributions for the separate professional fields showed some interesting divergence from the over-all distribution. In the health professions, the class of problems growing out of the satisfactory definition of role and the development of congruent expectations bulked the largest. In law, social work, and theology, the problems growing out of rather basic subcultural differences were the largest. It is as if the health professions and the social sciences are closer together in a common scientific subculture and are now at work hammering out a mutually acceptable system of role relations in their collaboration. The other fields are still confronted with the problems of achieving enough of a basic cultural consensus to proceed with the more practical problems of the division of labor and reciprocal interdependence. For example, of the problems listed by those working in the medical and public-health professions, 6 per cent were classified as subcultural differences, and 63 per cent were problems of role ambiguity and incongruent expectations. The comparable figures for law were 59 per cent and 12 per cent. Though these figures are suggestive, they must, of course, be taken with great caution not only because of the vagaries and unreliabilities of interpretations of qualitative material but also because the amount of experience of the Foundation with projects in law is as yet extremely limited.

Concluding their discussion of problems of collaboration between social scientists and the practicing professions, Cottrell and Sheldon summarize the activities which they presumed useful in overcoming the obstacles to collaboration:

(1) Developing optimal initial orientation and level of expectation; (2) maximizing mutual assimilation of professional subcultural values, ideologies, technologies and language; (3) securing an appropriate structural position in the institutional setting for the social scientist; (4) clarification of the roles of the parties to the undertakings; (5) increasing the interpersonal skills of the participants.*

It is quite evident that these suggestions are appropriate to many situations where there are similar difficulties in the relations among occupational groups and where there is a genuine requirement for accommodative or cooperative relations.†

Accommodative Relationships

On the road to closer collaboration among occupational groups, there are some part-way relationships. Some groups are quite far along toward complete

* *Ibid.*, p. 127
† S. Rettig and B. Pasamanick have described parallel problems with psychiatric social workers and have detailed the interrelationship with other occupations in the hospital situation. They conclude by saying, "A rise in the status of the social worker can come about only by improved training, stronger professional organization and, perhaps most of all, better defined job responsibility in those areas in which the social worker has undisputed authority and in which she can make her greatest contribution without having to compete for status with other professions." See "Status, Work Satisfaction and Variables of Work Satisfaction of Psychiatric Social Workers," *Mental Hygiene,* **44,** 1960, pp. 48–54.

collaboration, and others are not nearly so far along, as we shall see momentarily. Some occupations have worked out an accommodation which takes the form of interdependence—for example, physiotherapy in many political jurisdictions is dependent upon the medical practitioners for referral of patients, and most M.D.s rely on this specialist group for the accomplishment of these tasks. With such an arrangement, the physical therapist practices little outside of his relationship with medicine. To a lesser extent, of course, this is true of nursing, especially in the hospital locus where the medical practitioner is in a superordinate position. On the other hand, there are some nurses who practice quasi-independently, as with the public health nurse, or quite autonomously, as a free-lance private nurse.

In the field of engineering, "professional engineers" are interested in establishing this type of relationship with engineering technicians, and to that end, engineering professional associations have been instigating and promoting certification procedures which would link the "professionals" and the technicians more closely, and would also serve to control the latter more effectively. Perhaps this is felt to be one way of upgrading the occupational interests and activities of the engineering technician, and reducing some of the competition as well.‡

A similar, but to date unsuccessful, attempt has been made by some psychiatrists (psychotherapists holding an M.D. degree) to subordinate the clinical psychologist (without M.D. degree) in the diagnosis and treatment of patients with behavior disorders. According to the *Yale Law Journal* the psychiatrist "...regards the psychologist role as ancillary, similar to that of the nurse or X-ray technician."§ Some observers maintain that there was a period when psychiatrists sought to eliminate clinical psychology from a central position in the diagnosis-treatment process by sponsoring legislation designed to limit such practice to psychiatry.** Recently, however, organized psychiatrists seem to be accommodating themselves to a larger and more complementary role for clinical psychology.

The following selection documents the efforts of some occupations to devise relationships leading to increased understanding, and presumably increased toleration and effectiveness at work. This example describes the interrelationship of a number of mental health professions.

‡ M. A. Williamson, "The Certification of Engineering Technicians," *American Engineer* (October 1962), pp. 31–33.
§ The Editors of the *Yale Law Journal,* "The American Medical Association," *Yale Law Journal,* **63**, No. 7, 1954, p. 968.
** *Ibid.,* p. 969.

Alvin Zander, Arthur Cohen, Ezra Statland and Collaborators (Psychiatry, Clinical Psychology, Social Work)

In comparing average attitudes we must keep in mind that the mental health professions comprise a hierarchical society of persons who commonly value close teamwork. Psychiatry is at the top of the triangle while clinical psychology and psychiatric social work occupy the bottom corners. The psychiatrists have the superior position because usually the prescribed working relations are such that they are expected to supervise members of the ancillary professions; the ancillary workers, in turn, are likely to see themselves as subordinated in some manner when working with psychiatrists.

FEELINGS OF PSYCHIATRISTS TOWARD ANCILLARY GROUP MEMBERS

Results reveal that the psychiatrist believes he is admired and liked by those in the assisting groups. He is friendly toward them and willing to work with them, but he is not so interested in winning their favor or good will, nor is he so anxious to have their liking for him increased. He places much higher value on his own profession than he does on theirs.

These attitudes are indications that the average psychiatrist perceives the adjunct persons as facilitative to his own need satisfaction. He reveals no effort either to get them to increase facilitating behavior or to decrease hindering behavior. His feelings demonstrate that he is secure in his relations with the ancillary persons.

Within these averages, however, it is noteworthy that the responses of the psychiatrist toward psychologists are somewhat different from his responses toward social workers. He reveals that he is less comfortable with psychologists and prefers fewer contacts with them. He views psychologists as more challenging than social workers and he tends to value and respect them more. The attitudes of the psychiatrists, then, may be viewed as inclinations to decrease the impact of any potential need frustration in his relations with psychologists. He values and admires their professional contributions yet he seeks to avoid their sphere of influence.

FEELINGS OF ADJUNCT PERSONS TOWARD PSYCHIATRISTS

The typical adjunct person is eager to be liked and respected by psychiatrists, tries to do those things which will gain a favorable impression for himself, and places great value on the profession of psychiatry.

These attitudes, we believe, indicate a desire to increase the need-facilitating be-

Reprinted from "Average Attitudes of One Professional Group Toward Another," *Role Relations in the Mental Health Professions* (Ann Arbor: Research Center for Group Dynamics, Institute for Social Research, 1957), pp. 133–141. Used by permission.

havior of psychiatrists. They represent efforts on the part of the ancillary persons to get psychiatrists to be rewarding and helpful. Such feelings develop because typical members of the adjunct professions must depend in large part upon the good offices of psychiatrists in their attempts to obtain need satisfaction.

FEELINGS OF ANCILLARY GROUPS TOWARD EACH OTHER

The psychologist is eager to be liked and respected by social workers and behaves in a fashion which will promote cordial relationships. He places more value on his own profession than on social work and views the social workers as content in their role as assistants to psychiatrists. His attitudes indicate a desire to win appreciation and support from social workers.

The social worker views psychologists as intent upon winning recognition for their profession. She accepts these aspirations without any uneasiness since, apparently, they represent no threat to her own professional ambitions. At the same time she believes that she is equal to psychologists in ability and influence, and feels that she should remain in that position. The social worker, it appears, feels that psychologists are not highly relevant to her need satisfaction. Because of the low interdependence of her role with that of the psychologist, she perceives psychologists as neither facilitating nor hindering her own need satisfaction.

LOCATION ON INDEPENDENT VARIABLES AND INTERROLE ATTITUDES

We turn to a summary of the interrole attitudes and behaviors reported by persons at different locations in each of the role relationships. In addition, two types of interpretation are offered: (a) why a given location provides high or low probability of need satisfaction, and (b) why a particular type of interrole attitude occurs in association with a given location.

Perceived relative power to influence

In general, we assume that a person who attributes high power to himself in a relationship with those in another role will perceive greater probability of meeting his own professional needs than one who has little power. He can control his own fate and also influence the fate of others. Both of these facts increase the likelihood that events will occur as he might wish.

Results reveal that a psychiatrist with much power perceives that members of the ancillary groups respect and admire him, and seek to win his favor. He is ready to associate with them. These interrole attitudes occur, we believe, because he has sufficient power to do as he wishes, and to maintain that power. As a consequence he views relations with ancillary persons as more need facilitative than hindering. He is willing to work with them because when he does so the contacts gratify rather than threaten his aspirations.

A clinical psychologist or psychiatric social worker who has more than his group's average amount of power (in relation with psychiatrists) wants few contacts with psychiatrists, has little desire to talk to them, is unconcerned with winning their good will, and thinks more highly of his own profession than he does of psychiatry. Apparently the adjunct person perceives himself as able to make autonomous efforts for meeting his own needs without the aid of psychiatrists. He indicates a tendency to avoid psychiatrists because interactions put him in a subordinate role, and thus reduce his possibilities of need satisfaction.

Turning to the persons who attribute low power to themselves, it is evident that a psychiatrist with less power than his group's average believes that members of the ancillary groups do not like him, and that he wishes to avoid associating with them. His attitudes reveal that he is uncomfortable in a low-power position, and that he seeks to reduce the effectiveness of any hindering impact of ancillary persons by avoiding them.

Members of the adjunct professions who are low in power, however, say that they are eager for more frequent contacts with psychiatrists, like to talk with them, seek to win their approval, and value psychiatry more than their own profession. Their professional aspirations, presumably, can best be fulfilled by winning the goodwill and help of their superiors.

High or low power locations have no apparent effect upon the nature of the interrole attitudes and behaviors between clinical psychologists and psychiatric social workers. The members of these two professions apparently do not see one another as either helping or hindering their career aspirations.

Acceptance of power position

It might be expected that most of the members of all three professions would want more power, since power enhances the possibility of fulfilling professional aspirations. Results show, however, that only those who are low in power in each of the three roles feel that they would like to have more. There are several special cases: A social worker with small power, who is also highly satisfied concerning relations with psychiatrists, is not likely to want greater power. In contrast, a psychologist who has little power wants more whether or not he is satisfied in his relations with psychiatrists. The psychologist's professional aspirations make an increase in power more important for him than for the social worker. In fact, the psychologist with high power wants even more if he perceives himself as highly competent.

The psychiatrist who wants more power over psychologists perceives that he is not respected or admired by clinical psychologists, whereas the psychiatrist with little desire to increase his influence over psychologists believes that he is held in high esteem by them. In his relations with social workers, however, a psychiatrist who desires more power is no different from one who is content with his influence. The need for power on the part of the psychiatrist is an indication that he is uncertain about the potentialities of need satisfaction, but only with respect to psychologists. Apparently the stabilized interdependence between his own group as superiors and the social workers as assistants means that a wish for more power over social workers is not an indicator of potential need frustration in that relationship.

The clinical psychologists and the psychiatric social workers who want more power in relations with psychiatrists have strong desires for respect and treatment as equals. Although they are low in power, it is striking that these people show none of the deference and solicitousness toward psychiatrists observed as typical of their groups. Instead, they appear to be intent on decreasing the relative effectiveness of the psychiatrists' influence. Their attitudes reveal the importance they attach to greater power as a means of fulfilling their professional aims.

In the relations between persons in the two ancillary professions, when a member of either is content with his power location, the interrole attitudes are friendly. When he feels that he should have more power over those in the other ancillary profession, he is quite disinterested in maintaining cordial relations with them. Instead, symptoms of competitive relationships appear as well as attempts to resist the influences of the other. In addition, the discontented person becomes uneasy about the nature of the other group's relations with psychiatrists. Though an occupant of either role ordinarily does not see himself as able to help or hinder the other, when he dsires greater power he becomes aware of a non-facilitative interdependence with them which is uncomfortable to him.

Frequency of professional contacts

Professional contacts have a different significance for psychiatrists and for the assisting professions. Psychiatrists in general are ready to work with adjunct persons because, for one good reason, they are helpful to him. The ancillary worker, on the other hand, feels that interactions with psychiatrists place him in a subordinate relationship. Frequent contacts with adjunct workers are a source of need satisfaction for psychiatrists, but often they are just the opposite for the members of the ancillary professions.

The findings reveal that the psychiatrist who has many contacts with members of the assisting professions feels that he is respected and admired by them (though he is more sure that social workers feel this way than that psychologists do), and be-

lieves that they are trying to win his good-will.

The social worker feels accepted and respected by psychiatrists when she shares many professional activities with them. It is the social worker with little power who meets most often with psychiatrists, and it is the psychiatrist with much power who has the most frequent contacts with social workers. Furthermore, the occupants of these two roles are highly interdependent in their task functions. Perhaps, then, the social worker perceives that her abilities are being well used when she collaborates with psychiatrists. She is gratified by the recognition received and by the realization that her services are wanted by them.

The psychologist who has interactions with psychiatrists most often, however, does not feel accepted or admired by them, and freely admits that he seeks to win approval from psychiatrists. His role is not interdependent with that of the psychiatrists. Psychiatrists view the role of clinical psychologists as narrower in function than do psychologists. Close working relations with psychiatrists prevent the psychologist from doing the things he would like to do autonomously. His professional aspirations make it difficult for him to accept this state of dependency and he attempts to increase the facilitative behavior of psychiatrists in order to increase the chances that they will gratify his need.

Finally, frequent contacts between members of the ancillary professions appear to foster friendly relations. A social worker feels that psychologists respect and admire her if she often meets with them. These feelings are reciprocated by the psychologist who frequently associates with social workers. The more contacts he has with social workers, the more he desires their respect.

Professional knowledge and skills

In general, a person who assigns a high degree of professional competence to himself should be more secure in his interactions with others than a person who is less confident. We must keep in mind, however, that the group goals are different among these professions and that the nature of the respective aspirations of each group will be important in determining the quality of individual relationships.

For the psychiatrists the fact that an ancillary worker is highly capable is not a source of need deprivation. His aspirations are such that he welcomes such beneficial assistance. The data indicate that a psychiatrist wishes to have frequent contacts and many communications with members of the adjunct professions when he sees them as able people who are equal, or even superior to himself; and he wishes to avoid association with them if he views them as incompetent. Even when the psychiatrist sees the two assisting groups as capable, he differentiates between them. He is more likely to have high respect and strong positive stereotypes for psychologists than for social workers.

The social worker aspires to obtain increased responsibility so that she can be more useful to psychiatrists. When she has high professional knowledge and skill relative to psychiatrists, she demands from them greater admiration and respect; she wishes to be treated more as an equal. When she perceives herself to be low in ability she is willing to assume a more dependent relationship.

The psychologist aspires to obtain autonomy in some professional areas as well as to make himself more helpful to psychiatrists. Superior professional ability apparently represents for the psychologist a means to obtain improved status. Thus, if he has much professional knowledge and skill he "breaks away" from a dependent relationship with psychiatrists and feels motivated to weaken the effectiveness of psychiatrists' influence. The psychologist who has much respect for his own competence has a strong desire for more power in relation to psychiatrists. He prefers to associate with members of his own profession, and to avoid psychiatrists as much as possible.

In the relations between the two ancillary groups, a social worker who sees herself as highly competent in comparison to psychologists describes them as upward mobile, but she views the psychologists' ambitions objectively without any apparent affect. Since the social worker more regularly turns to the psychiatrist as a major source of support, her awareness of striving by psychologists is of no great concern because she is assured of her stable connections with psychiatrists.

A psychologist who believes that he is very capable in comparison with social workers tends to feel that he is not sufficiently respected and admired by them, and he attempts to win their admiration and respect.

In summary, for the adjunct person a favorable opinion of his own ability seems to stimulate him to move actively toward the gratification of his professional needs. The social worker is willing to meet her needs within her usual role relationship as psychiatric assistant, while the psychologist is more likely to seek autonomy. Low evaluation of himself, however, seems to encourage the perception in the ancillary person that improvements in professional status will come through soliciting the goodwill and facilitative behavior of psychiatrists.

Satisfaction from providing advice for others

When a person provides advice for others he is usually in a position which implies that he is the superior and that the counselees are dependent upon him. An adviser, it is expected, is more likely to feel that he will gratify his professional aspirations, than a person who asks for advice.

The prescribed relations among these roles would have psychiatrists seldom turn to members of the ancillary professions for consultation. Similarly the adjunct groups would anticipate only infrequent solicitation of their advice by a superior. Our data indicate that this prescription still holds: A majority of the psychiatrists state that they give advice more than they ask for it. Only one-fifth of the social workers and psychologists state that psychiatrists seek their advice.

In view of this disparity, it is striking that the large majority in every relationship are highly satisfied with the amount of cross-consultation which occurs. For the ancillary groups this is apparently a case of satisfaction with being asked for counsel even infrequently. Psychiatrists are pleased when they provide advice frequently since presumably they assume advice-giving to be the prerogative of their role.

The psychiatrist who is more than usually gratified because members of the assisting professions ask him for counsel, views them as facilitative to his need satisfaction. He is ready to associate with them and perceives that they admire him. Again he differentiates between the two groups in that he views the psychologists' request for advice as attempts to win approval, but he does not see the social workers' in the same way.

An ancillary worker who is satisfied by the degree to which psychiatrists come to him for advice apparently is confident that he has attained a position in which he is relatively outside the power of psychiatrists. The fact that psychiatrists ask him for help causes him to feel that his professional aspirations will be met. In this situation he begins to act just as a psychiatrist usually does. He is willing to point out the inadequacies of the other group, a prerogative which he does not usually assume. He is also less likely to accuse psychiatrists of attempting to block or restrict the efforts of the adjunct member. He feels that psychiatrists respect and admire him, and he is willing to have frequent and close association with them.

Finally a person in either of the two ancillary professions who is satisfied by the degree of consultation sought by his peers indicates that he intends to be helpful and shows no other types of affective reactions.

Prestige in own profession

A person who has high prestige within his own profession is drawn to closer association with his own group, and wishes to have few contacts with persons in other relevant professions. (There is one exception: The psychiatrist with high prestige feels no closer nor more distant from psychologists than the psychiatrist who has little prestige in his own profession.) Probability of need satisfaction, we believe, is again the crucial variable. A person with much prestige is more secure in his own profession, since his professional aspirations are already gratified there. He may sense that the chances are small that he will derive as much gratification from association with the members of a different profession. Thus, he prefers to remain with his colleagues and to avoid association with the others.

Satisfaction with interrole relations

The degree of satisfaction each respondent reported concerning his relations with those in other roles may be thought of as his evaluation of the locations he has in the prescribed role relationships.

The data reveal that the psychiatrist who describes himself as highly satisfied concerning relations with members of the ancillary groups is ready to associate with them, sees them as admiring and respecting him, regards them as persons who wish to win his good will, makes favorable comments about them, and even feels free to talk to them about the inadequacies of his own profession.

The social worker, who is highly satisfied about her relations with psychiatrists, perceives that psychiatrists are rewarding and supporting persons. She wants frequent professional contacts with them, behaves solicitously toward them, and states a readiness to talk to psychiatrists about any unpleasant behavior on their part.

The psychologist, when satisfied in his relations with psychiatrists, reacts in a way which conforms to what we know about his professional aspirations. The satisfied psychologist is uninhibited in his communications with psychiatrists, feels he is liked and respected by them, wants frequent interaction with them, has positive stereotypes about them, is ready to discuss professional differences of opinion, and feels content that psychiatrists are not trying to block or control his professional activities.

Satisfaction for the two adjunct groups, then, appears to mean something different to each. Social workers are more satisfied when they assume that they are accepted as capable assistants. Psychologists are more satisfied when they are respected as assistants and also are given freedom to develop and use their skills independently. These feelings are clearly in close conformity with the group goals.

Finally, social workers and psychologists

are highly satisfied concerning relations with one another. The social worker is most satisfied when she is low in prestige and psychologists come to her for advice. Psychologists are most satisfied when they have many contacts with social workers, contacts in which social workers often seek their advice. Both groups when satisfied with relations desire more contacts and more communication. In addition, when psychologists are highly satisfied concerning relations with social workers, they perceive that social workers are less intent on winning the approval of psychiatrists (and are more supportive of psychologists).

Avoidance Relationships

From the previous selection, it may be seen that occupations undergoing professionalization are often dependent on more highly professionalized occupations and therefore, tend to be on the defensive. With certain less professionalized occupations where there is an aspiration toward more highly professionalized status, the occupation may perforce engage in a struggle for survival. In this process practitioners may expect at best, to be avoided by related occupations unwilling to recognize their existence, because members of other occupations may feel that the newer work activities impinge on established occupations, or that the calibre of services provided by the new occupation is "not up to standards."

In occupations dealing with gaining fundamental knowledge there is often disdain shown for those who apply this knowledge, and this may even take the form of contempt for those persons particularly concerned with the application of scientific findings. According to Donald Young, sociologists are no less guilty of this than persons in similar occupations. This led him to raise a series of questions about this disregard:

Under what circumstances and to what extent may there be reliance on a policy of laissez faire which assumes that some natural, inevitable process insures the social use of knowledge? Could not the debated questions concerning the service of the individual sociologist in both the research and action roles be analyzed objectively? Why not study the needs of the various practicing professions for sociological data, knowledge and techniques, the resistances to their introduction in specific professions, the means for reducing these resistances, the methods for the development of men and materials better adapted to practitioners' needs? Why are there not more case studies of sociology in application? . . . *

Why were these questions raised? It is evident that a system of genuine colleague relations with "practicing professions" has not developed; instead there is an avoidance relationship. Young suggests that the sociologists have raised largely spurious reasons for their avoidance reactions to the so-called applied occupations: "Difficulties and failures in cooperation with practitioners tend to be attributed to arrogance, narrow-mindedness, trade school education, authoritarianism, professional insecurity, plain stupidity and what not."† The consequences of this attitude held by sociologists (or other scientists) can lead

---

* Donald Young, "Sociology and the Practicing Professions," *American Sociological Review,* **20**, No. 6 (Dec. 1955), 646.
† *Ibid.,* p. 647.

both to unreasonable behavior by "discoverers" and "appliers," and to unfortunate consequences for the clients and the remainder of society.

Another example of avoidance relationships is furnished in the instance of marriage counseling as it relates to the longer established occupations of social work, medicine, law, and religion. Practitioners of these older occupations have been ambivalent about marriage counseling in part because of the aforementioned reasons of potential impingement and possible incompetence.

Richard K. Kerckhoff
(Marriage Counseling)

Sociologists have often observed that the emergence of a new profession is facilitated or retarded by the reactions members of older, established professions have to the newcomer, and that these reactions are usually based on such factors as how these established professionals perceive the functions of the new occupation and how threatened they feel their own interests to be.[1] The assumption derived from these observations has been that professions have characteristics of interest groups or interest categories and that they cannot be expected to relinquish traditional functions to a new profession without some resistance, provided that the functions are based on still-existing interests and that new interests or values do not dictate the transfer of the functions.[2]

Since marriage counseling has recently been assuming many of the characteristics associated with professions[3] and has frequently been referred to by its spokesmen as an "emerging profession," it seems pertinent to determine what reception it is achieving in the ranks of the more established professions and in what ways they are reacting as interest groups.[4]

Data concerning what members of four professions know about marriage counseling, how they react to it both as a task performed by other professions and as a separate profession, and what relationships they see between it and their own profession were collected in a recent study. One hundred and twenty personal interviews and responses to 360 questionnaires have

Reprinted from "Interest Group Reactions to the Profession of Marriage Counseling," *Sociology and Social Research,* 39, No. 3 (January–February 1955), 179–183. Used by permission of the author and publisher.

[1] A. M. Carr-Saunders and P. A. Wilson, *The Professions* (Oxford: Clarendon Press, 1933); Walter I. Wardwell, "A Marginal Professional Role: The Chiropractor," *Social Forces,* 30, 339–348. Also see Everett C. Hughes, "The Sociological Study of Work: An Editorial Foreword," *The American Journal of Sociology,* 57, 423–426; Carlo L. Lastrucci, "The Status and Significance of Occupational Research," *American Sociological Review,* 11, 78–84; and Oswald Hall, "Sociological Research in the Field of Medicine: Progress and Prospects," *American Sociological Review,* 16, 639–644.

[2] "When a number of men unite for the defense, maintenance or enhancement of any more or less enduring position or advantage which they possess alike or in common, the term interest is applied both to the group so united and to the cause which unites them...," R. M. MacIver, "Interests" in the *Encyclopedia of the Social*

Sciences (New York: The Macmillan Company, 1934, Vol. 8), p. 144. Also see MacIver's *Society: Its Structure and Changes* (New York: Ray Long and Richard R. Smith, Inc., 1931); H. E. Barnes, *An Introduction to the History of Sociology* (Chicago: The University of Chicago Press, 1948), and Floyd N. House, *The Development of Sociology* (New York: McGraw-Hill Book Company, 1936), for discussions of the concepts of interest and interest groups and for the contributions to these concepts by Gumplowicz, Ratzenhofer, and Small.

[3] Wayland J. Hayes, "The Place of Sociology in Professional Education," *Social Forces,* 26, 292–298, postulates a natural history of professional growth and uses standard definitions of the term "profession."

[4] The profession of marriage counseling has been described by Ernest W. Burgess, "Marriage Counseling in a Changing Society," *Marriage and Family Living,* 5, 8–10; John F. Cuber, *Marriage Counseling Practice* (New York: Appleton-Century-Crofts, 1948); Ernest R. Groves, "A Decade of Marriage Counseling," *Annals of the American Academy of Political and Social Science,* 212, 72–80; and Emily H. Mudd, *The Practice of Marriage Counseling* (New York: Association Press, 1951).

been obtained from lawyers, social workers, clergymen, and physicians whose names were drawn at random from membership lists of professional organizations in Detroit.[5]

SOME FINDING AND INTERPRETATIONS

The professional people who were interviewed and tested in this study were well acquainted with the concept of marriage counseling, but less well convinced that there is an emerging profession of marriage counseling.

In responses to the questionnaire used in the study, almost all of the 360 respondents said they came into contact with cases of marital difficulties in their professional work; half the social workers and nine tenths of those in the other professional categories said they had done some marriage counseling themselves during the past year, and 23 per cent of the total said they considered themselves marriage counselors. About a third of the respondents—ranging from 10 per cent of the attorneys to almost half of the clergy—said they had made referrals to a marriage counselor at some time, although only 17 per cent of the physicians and attorneys felt they could find a good counselor if they needed one.

In general, the respondents approved of the idea of marriage counseling; they also gave theoretical, but less enthusiastic approval to the idea of a profession devoted to marriage counseling. More than four fifths of the clergy, social workers, and physicians replying to the questionnaire claimed that marriage counseling today is

[5] Questionnaires were returned by 49 per cent of the people receiving them; the data contained in the present article, however, are based on a 36 per cent subsample composed of 120 returns from the social workers and 80 from each of the other three professions drawn from the total returns and subjected to statistical analysis. Reliability and validity checks, percentages and critical ratios, and an estimate of the probable differences between those who returned questionnaires and those who did not are contained in the author's unpublished doctoral dissertation, "The Profession of Marriage Counseling as Viewed by Members of Four Allied Professions: A Study in Sociology of Occupations," The Ohio State University (Department of Sociology), 1952.

either "worthwhile" or "very worthwhile," and two thirds of the attorneys agreed. Less than 10 per cent referred to counseling as quackery or pseudoscience or dangerous.

Forty-two per cent of the questionnaire respondents said that they believed marriage counseling is becoming a profession; to another question 16 per cent replied that it is a profession today, and on a third item 16 per cent said that it would be a mistake to professionalize marriage counseling.

Fifty-eight per cent said they would refer cases to a marriage counselor if a capable one opened a near-by office. However, one should examine some of the concepts upon which members of the sample based their answer to that questionnaire item.

In general, the members of the four professions tended to create a marriage counselor in their own image. On the questionnaire, respondents were asked to check which two professions of nine listed are best prepared to do marriage counseling today. The lawyers, and almost no one else, said the lawyers are; the social workers, and very few others, said the social workers are; the physicians said the physicians are; and the clergymen overwhelmingly said the clergymen are. All four professional categories made "full-time counselors" their second choice.

The ethnocentrism of the members of the four professions is shown again when, from a check list of "academic" subjects thought to be helpful in the training of a marriage counselor, law received few votes except from lawyers, theology was most favored, by far, by clergymen, most of the social worker vote came from social workers, and physicians, with a good second from lawyers, were the chief voters for medicine. "Theory and techniques of counseling" was the second choice of each profession.

In interviews with the professional people it was learned that most of the social workers saw very little chance of making referrals to marriage counselors who were not either caseworkers or psychiatrists. Physicians showed a conservatism concerning the newness of marriage counseling and tended to view marital problems in medical terms. The attorneys were the most outspoken of the four groups against the new profession of marriage counseling. Many seemed to agree with the man who said: "I consider myself a fair hand at counseling. If I were to suggest another person to consult, the matter would certainly drop then and there, and the party would attempt to diagnose his troubles in his own particular way. Besides, counseling is legal work."

The clergymen, although the most enthusiastic concerning the idea of marriage counseling, were the most suspicious of the counseling done by people other than those in their own profession:

I believe pastors are competent to handle these cases. If a minister is intimately acquainted with the lives of his people, he is not likely to refer them to other counselors during times of domestic difficulty—particularly to someone who may not use good Christian principles in his counseling.[6]

Along with holding to the belief that marriage counselors should be of the same profession and training as themselves, the majority of respondents also held the view that counselors should be people with exceptional personal and social characteristics. They felt that it is vital that a counselor have the maximum of education in many fields and that he be mature, open-minded, tolerant, tactful, patient, kind, sympathetic, wise, have common sense, and like people. More than 70 per cent of the clergy thought that counselors should believe in God, be members of a church, and have exceptionally strict moral standards, while about 17 per cent felt that divorcees should be eliminated from counseling, that only people who have exceptionally successful marriages should be marriage counselors, and that people should practice counseling only if they have never violated the sexual code.

A small number of respondents (9 per cent) declared outright that marriage counseling offers a threat to their own professions, and 17 per cent agreed that marriage counselors today are handling many cases that more rightly belong to *some* other profession. When questionnaire items were

6 However, see Andrew L. Wade and Joel V. Berreman, "Are Ministers Qualified for Marriage Counseling? *Sociology and Social Research,* 35, 106–112.

presented which hypothesized the assumption by marriage counselors of functions now performed by other professional people, it became obvious that the professions react as interest groups or interest categories. For instance, the physicians, more than others, would prohibit the nonmedical marriage counselor from giving information about birth control or sexual technique. Also, the physicians were far less convinced than the others that doctors should refer patients to counselors even if the patients' illnesses seemed related to poor marital adjustment. Attorneys, much less than the others, favored nonlawyer marriage counselors being allowed to advise a counselee concerning legal grounds for divorce. And while 58 per cent of the total questionnaire sample—including 85 per cent of the clergy—felt that a lawyer should usually refer a client seeking a divorce to a marriage counselor, if the lawyer is not one himself, only 17 per cent of the attorneys agreed.

There was also a slight relationship between income of respondents and views on marriage counseling. In general, those with higher incomes and those who did marriage counseling themselves as part of their professional work were less friendly to the idea of a separate profession of marriage counselors, although the differences in answers to these items were not satistically significant.

CONCLUSION

Such direct methods as personal interviews and questionnaires were able to provide abundant data concerning knowledge, ignorance, acceptance, and rejection in the views of members of four established professions about a new profession of marriage counseling. In general, the rejection was greatest in those areas which overlapped the functions of the older professions, but there was not a consistent and clearcut interest group reaction toward the new profession. The data show that members of the older professions perceive marriage counseling to be to a great extent a projection of their own beliefs as to what it *should* be, that they feel the profession of marriage counseling is too new and powerless to threaten older professions, and that the aim of marriage counseling—to help people in their marriages—is so related to core values of this society that the profession is difficult to oppose.

The question to be answered by future events is, "Provided marriage counseling proceeds to emerge as a separate profession and provided members of other professions obtain clear perceptions of it and learn that it cannot be all things to all people, will the interest group reaction by members of the older professions become stronger?"[7]

7 See, for instance, "Regulation of Psychological Counseling and Psychotherapy," *Columbia Law Review,* 51: 474–495; and Francis J. Gerty, J. W. Holloway, and R. P. Mackay, "Licensure or Certification of Clinical Psychologists, *The Journal of the American Medical Association,* 148: 271–273, for information on a related situation.

Competitive Relationships

During the early decades of this century, medical practitioners became increasingly interested in the quality of the services they were providing. Through the efforts of their professional associations, influence in legislation, and the improvement of professional education, the occupation underwent marked professionalization. A major focus was on eliminating quackery both within and without the occupation. To control this, licensure prerequisite to practice was established. In the zealous pursuit of upgrading medical standards, the occupation came into frequent contact with other healing arts, particularly chiropractic and osteopathy; and "despite limitations these groups continued to provide the medical profession with active competition."* What has come of these struggles? According to one source, "...although organized medicine's justification for limited licensing for the 'cults' is expressed in terms of protecting the consumer from unqualified practitioners, there may also be present an element of self-protection from this economic encroachment."†

This competition was not a one-way affair. It must be recognized that organized chiropractic and osteopathy have also pursued an active policy of competition with the medical profession. Of late this has sometimes taken the form of exerting political pressure through existing sympathetic pressure groups, like veterans' organizations. In the instance of osteopathy much success has been achieved by gaining direct recognition and support from agencies of government. Because chiropractic has until recently been split organizationally, it was not able to offer unified competition for the American Medical Association, and so had to make greater use of external pressure groups.‡ The feuding between chiropractic and medicine continues unabated, and certain dimensions of the struggle from the chiropractic point of view may be seen in the following selection.

* The Editors of *The Yale Law Journal, op. cit.,* p. 964.
† *Ibid.,* p. 965.
‡ *Ibid.,* pp. 965–966.

W. I. Wardwell (Chiropractic)

The chiropractic ideology of an oppressed minority may be stated as follows:

Although this is nominally a free country, chiropractors do not have real freedom, inasmuch as their constitutional rights to life, liberty, and the pursuit of happiness are being thwarted by a powerful medical monopoly; the AMA and the "drug trusts" care only for their own financial well-being and not for the health of the citizenry; medical doctors prefer to treat symptoms with drugs and opiates or remove diseased tissue by surgery rather than allow chiropractors to remove the *cause* of disease; since the medical monopoly fears that its profits will be cut if chiropractic and natural healing methods become generally available, it raises every possible obstacle to the chiropractors' efforts; it does not hesitate to bribe legislators in order to gain its ends; it enforces a censorship on magazines, newspapers, and radio programs through its power to withhold pharmaceutical advertising; while it keeps people ignorant of chiropractic, it bombards them with free advertising in the form of news releases glorifying medical achievements and the latest wonder drug.

Chiropractors in general believe that the main reason they are persecuted is that their competition threatens the prestige and vested interests of the medical profession. The latter, they reason, is insincere in its protestation that it acts on behalf of the public welfare, since most chiropractic cures have been effected on previous medical failures. They accuse medical leaders of arguing in two directions at the same time: insisting that chiropractic has no scientific validity whatsoever, while at the same time protesting that they have no objection to anyone's practicing chiropractic providing he has first passed the regular medical examination. Thus, when the doctors say that chiropractors could practice under medical prescription, that shows that they either recognize some benefit to chiropractic therapy or that they are scheming thereby to prevent chiropractors from gaining access to patients. Individual physicians are said often to approve of chiropractors and to cooperate with them in aiding the sick, but to be impotent in the face of organized medicine and the drug trusts. Finally, at

the same time that medicine pretends to regard chiropractic as pure quackery, it is incorporating into itself chiropractic principles and techniques, though under such new designations as "physical medicine" and "physiatry," and is "discovering" vertebral impingements and manipulative techniques that have been known to chiropractors for a long time.

This ideology enters into the definition of the chiropractor's situation in the following ways:

1. It accounts for the failure of chiropractic to gain scientific acceptance as a system of therapeutics. The blame is attributed to medically biased research workers. The fact that some physicians have adopted chiropractic and others expound theories nearly identical to it has convinced many chiropractors that it is only the influence of organized medicine and the drug interests that prevents the scientific truth of chiropractic from becoming more generally accepted. Consequently, the chiropractic principle need not be called into question even though scientists in general have not accepted it.

2. It accounts for the present sociolegal status of chiropractors, that is, for the fact that they are not fully accepted as doctors under the law or by society at large. Again the "medical monopoly" is blamed for their plight. And there is just enough basis in fact for the belief that a medical monopoly exists and that organized medicine is principally responsible for the legal restrictions on chiropractors to permit the ideology to function in this way. In the first place, it is organized medicine that actively opposes chiropractic legislation and prods law-enforcement officials to see that the enacted statutes are obeyed. In the second place, organized medicine has accepted cooperative working agreements with related professions (e.g., dentistry, podiatry, optometry) only when these have accepted a limited status subordinate to medicine. Professions which refuse to accept the status of "limited medicine" (osteopathy, chiropractic, naturopathy) are still officially regarded as cults and are excluded from participation in medical activities and in-

Reprinted from "Strain in a Marginal Social Role," *The American Journal of Sociology*, 61, No. 1 (July 1955), 23–25, by permission of The University of Chicago Press. Copyright 1955 by the University of Chicago.

stallations.[1] In the third place, the medical profession has been restrictive in accepting candidates for training and rather reactionary in its general social orientation:

> The medical profession has promoted or permitted itself to be a party to the promotion of intergroup, interracial, and interreligious tensions by setting up quota systems in medical schools, by barring certain races and religions from representation among the employees or even patients of many hospitals, and by being a party to that crowning and unscientific indignity to the American Negro, the Jim-Crowed blood bank and plasma supply.[2]

In the fourth place, drug and pharmaceutical concerns appear to have had some influence on AMA policy.[3] And, in the fifth place, a partial censorship of news unfavorable to medical and drug interests apparently exists.[4] But, true or not, chiropractors firmly believe in a "medical monopoly" and blame it for the present social and legal status of chiropractic.

3. It includes a moral justification of the chiropractors' cause. Chiropractors maintain that it is right that they should continue to practice in spite of the legal and social restrictions simply because chiropractic is the "natural" way of gaining and retaining health and because it eliminates the "cause" of disease. It is also right because it has produced cures in cases where medicine has failed and because it helps suffering humanity without regard for the latter's ability to pay. In contrast, the medical profession's sins of omission and commission and its violations of professional ethics are magnified. This serves to excuse the chiropractors' own failings and to emphasize their moral righteousness.

Medical men, despite their far-flung claims of interest in public health, actually are moti-

vated by the fact that the chiropractic practitioner is taking away patients from them; and taking away patients *means taking away fees.* This economic factor is behind the desire to destroy the science.[5]

Sometimes the chiropractor's rationalization seems to be as simple as this: "I am making a living at chiropractic. That must mean that my patients are satisfied. Therefore I am doing some good for them and hence am morally justified in continuing to practice." There is nothing more reassuring to a doctor than to see his patients get well. Whether it was his doing or not, he ordinarily is given, and takes, credit for the cure. But, whatever their reasoning, most chiropractors, even in states where they are not licensed, feel that they are engaged in a perfectly legitimate undertaking.

4. It defines the situation for future action. It even becomes at times militant and has produced such slogans as "Go to jail for chiropractic!" It is significant that the ideology focuses the chiropractor's attention on the politicolegal sphere rather than on the theory and practice of chiropractic itself, thus projecting the source of difficulty outside the profession. Consequently, the primary effort need not be directed toward self-improvement. The main goal becomes the correction of legal iniquities either by a campaign of public education or by some other program to obtain favorable legislation.

5. It justifies almost any means of combatting medicolegal "oppression." The reasoning is that, when one is being kicked, it is all right to kick back; dirty fighting invites reprisal, and since the medical monopoly resorts to censorship and political deals, chiropractic must do the same if it is to survive.

These, then, are the ways in which the conception of himself as a member of an oppressed minority structures environment for the chiropractor. Holding this set of ideas about his situation greatly facilitates the chiropractor's adjustment to his role. It answers for him, on a small scale, of course,

[1] Cf. "Associating with Osteopaths" (editorial), *Medical Economics,* February 1941, p. 39.

[2] Alfred M. Lee, "The Social Dynamics of the Physician's Status," *Psychiatry,* 7 (1944), 376.

[3] Cf. James Rorty, *American Medicine Mobilizes* (New York: W. W. Norton & Co., Inc., 1939), *passim.*

[4] Cf. George Seldes, *Freedom of the Press* (Indianapolis: Bobbs-Merrill Co., Inc. 1935), Chap. iii, "Bad Medicine"; and Annie Hale, *These Cults* (New York: National Health Foundation, 1926), pp. 193–199.

[5] *ABC of Establishing Chiropractic* (pamphlet) (New York: American Bureau of Chiropractic, 1929), p. 9.

some of life's basic problems: What *is* my relationship to other people? What should be my relationship to the world? How can I account for the discrepancy between what *is* and what *ought* to be? (This is parallel to the problem of evil in theology, for the chiropractor the evil principle being monopolistic medicine.) What goals should a person in my position strive for? And what are the ways by which these goals can be achieved? Throughout, the question of the legitimacy of the chiropractor's role is at stake. Everyone needs a system of ideas that will provide answers to life's basic problems. The cognitive aspect of religion does this for the most important problems of meaning. Similarly, in a more limited way, an ideology does the same thing for participants in a "social movement." The chiropractic "cause" is in many respects a kind of social movement uniting chiropractors and patients working toward reform. American society has seen many social movements, though none just like chiropractic. Each typically has an ideology which performs functions similar to those of the chiropractic ideology—namely, structuring the environment as an action-determinant. This of course is what is meant by the phrase "defining the situation for action." The chiropractic ideology is an accommodative pattern, facilitating adaptation to the chiropractor's role. It is true that this part of the definition of the chiropractor's situation for action partly constitutes his role and may even exert some effect on the objective situation in which chiropractors act, but the ideology as a whole certainly also provides a pattern of adjustment for the chiropractor.

Conflict Relationships

It should be apparent that we are being somewhat arbitrary when we classify the relationship between chiropractic and medicine as competitive. At one extreme on the individual practitioner level, avoidance is most common, but there are numerous examples of accommodative relationships; at the other extreme, conflict has been evident in public areas through the "battles" which have raged on the floors of legislatures and in the nation's courtrooms involving accusations that individual chiropractors are practicing medicine.*

Osteopathy had a history of relationships with medicine akin to that of chiropractic, except that its professionalization has been more rapid, perhaps partly in response to medicine, but mainly through associational and educational activities within the field. The relationships with medicine no longer involve so much conflict, and they are characterized more by accommodation, avoidance, and competition. In California, for example, much of osteopathy is being absorbed by the medical profession, just as homeopathy was decades earlier.

Conflict and other unpleasant forms of relations among occupations are more apt to occur where there are marked status discrepancies between occupations, than where occupations possess nearly equal status. The following selection demonstrates this point clearly, for here the comparison is between so-called "nonprofessional" and so-called "professional" personnel "treating" delinquents in an institutional setting. The dysfunctional consequences of such interoccupational conflict for juvenile offenders is evident.

* F. Barsalou, M. Blumberg, H. Kincaid, J. Lee, and D. Mills, *Chiropractic in California* (Los Angeles: Haynes Foundation, 1960), especially Chapter 1; also, D. Mills, *Chiropractic, Naturopathy and Osteopathy in Canada* (Ottawa: The Queen's Printer, forthcoming), especially Chapters 1 and 6 and Appendix A.

George H. Weber
(Delinquency Treatment)

In an effort to provide better diagnostic and treatment services for juvenile delinquents committed to their care, many institutions, in recent years, have added people from a number of professions to their staffs. These usually include social workers, teachers in special education, psychologists, psychiatrists and recreational therapists. In institutions, these people are frequently known as the "professional staff." They are employed for the study and treatment[1] of delinquents, and the consultation with and guidance of other staff members.

In this latter function, the professionals may be asked by the administration to advise those workers who supervise and manage the everyday living experiences of the delinquents, such as getting up, going to bed, personal hygiene, eating, playing, and working. Within the institutions, these workers are commonly known as the "nonprofessional staff" (as differentiated from the professional staff)[2] and usually include cottage parents, vocational and work supervisors, and maintenance workers.

This division of work, with its theoretical consistency and its apparent applicability, would seem to be acceptable to both groups as it is consistent with the currently accepted principles of delinquency treatment, personnel practice and education. It is a plan which should allow the professionals

an opportunity to increase their practical knowledge of delinquency and to apply the specific skills of their work to the delinquents and the institution. It is a plan which should also give the non-professionals an opportunity to increase their theoretical knowledge of delinquency and to receive some specialized help with some of their difficult problems.

In actual practice, however, this plan may encounter sharp difficulties in acceptance and functioning. Conflicts may emerge when professionals and nonprofessionals attempt to bring their specialties together. Value orientations, statuses and roles and ideas of delinquency causation and treatment, undoubtedly, will differ in each group. Problems are likely to arise from the conceptions that each group has of themselves and each other in each of these different areas.

The material for this paper was secured from two private and three public institutions for delinquents and was gathered over a period of three years. The method of the study was that of participation and observation. The data were gathered by four people, including the writer, who worked in these institutions in either a professional or nonprofessional job. The institutions varied in the number of delinquents in residence from about thirty to nearly four hundred. The proportion of professionals to nonprofessionals varied from two per cent to thirty-seven per cent. With the exception of two institutions, the nonprofessionals preceded the professionals in the setting.

In all institutions studied, conflicts were in evidence. In some, the conflicts were more intense, continuous and dramatic than others. In all the institutions, some cooperation transpired between the professionals and nonprofessionals and the author does not wish to imply that all these conflicts occurred to the same degree in every institution or that they were continuous. However, conflicts were a significant aspect of the relationships existing between the professional and the nonprofessional in all the institutions studied.[3]

Reprinted from "Conflicts between Professional and Nonprofessional Personnel in Institutional Delinquency Treatment," *Journal of Criminal Law, Criminology, and Police Science*, 48, No. 1 (May–June 1957), 26–39. Used by permission. The original publication bore the following note: "I wish to thank Dr. Melville Dalton for his guidance and suggestions in the prosecution of the research on which this paper is based.—G. H. W."

[1] "Treatment," as used in this paper, denotes all the systematic efforts which are carried on within an institutional setting to assist in the rehabilitation of the delinquent. This includes general environmental arrangements, as well as individual and group treatment.

[2] The titles "professional" and "nonprofessional" accentuate the differences between the two groups and appear to facilitate conflict rather than cooperation. It is an unfortunate differentation. For an analysis of the difficulties in defining a profession, see M. I. Cogan, "Toward a Definition of Profession," *Harvard Educ. Rev.*, **23** (Winter 1953), 33–50.

[3] Carl R. Doering describes some similar professional and nonprofessional conflicts in a penal

VALUE ORIENTATIONS

The professionals and nonprofessionals held different values regarding their own and the other's work. The professionals often stressed humanitarianism and service. They thought of themselves as primarily providing a service to the delinquents and they believed that when they went into a particular case or group for study, they should assume full responsibility for it within their specialty. The professionals thought of themselves as cooperative, as sharing and exchanging information and ideas, as respecting the integrity of others and the right of others to express themselves. Keen observations and a reflective and critical approach to problems were held in high regard by them. Formal education and training, as such, were also respected by this group.

The professionals saw the nonprofessionals as holding two sets of values. One view regarded the nonprofessionals as being a hard-working, simple group of people, usually generous and kind to the delinquents in their care, and good-intentioned in their relationships and dealings with the other staff members. They saw them as valuing sincerity, friendliness, courage, simplicity, and industry. The other view regarded the nonprofessionals as strict disciplinarians who demanded hard work and obedience from the delinquents. They thought that they were rigid in their viewpoints, antagonistic toward professionals, and reluctant to take any suggestions concerning their work. Here they regarded the nonprofessionals as valuing formal and restrained behavior, compliance and authoritarianism. In both of these conceptions, the professionals saw the nonprofessionals as having very little importance in working with problems concretely and had little regard for a theoretical approach to these

problems. A psychiatrist alluded to several of these points when he was discussing a cottage mother's management of a boy:

> Mrs. S. wants Bobby punished for his stealing, immediately. She isn't interested in studying it more fully. She says that "if he did it, he should be punished and then he has paid his debt." If anyone expresses any other ideas on it, she feels her position is seriously threatened. If pressed on the matter, she'll take her feelings out on the boy.

On another occasion a psychologist, referring to the uncritical methods of the nonprofessional, said:

> It seems that many of the cottage parents have worked out rather simple schemes for dealing with behavior problems. It apparently makes them more comfortable, even though it may be harmful to the boys. It's difficult to approach them about these things because you are apt to break down whatever relationship you have.

The nonprofessionals emphasized kindness, firmness, the ability to get along with people, and hard work as necessary qualities for work with delinquents. They viewed the immediate, the concrete, the practical, and action—the "getting something done" —as important. Broad experience and intimacy with the problems of working with delinquents were considered indispensable by them. The nonprofessionals considered themselves responsible for the general development and welfare of all the boys.

The nonprofessionals regarded the professionals as generally pseudo-intellectual and theoretical. They also regarded the professionals as valuing material wealth and education. The nonprofessionals often pointed to the higher salaries given to the professionals for work they believed was "easier." They believed that the professionals valued leisure and comfort for themselves above that of the delinquents and that they tended to be authoritarian in their relationships with others. The apparent leisure and comfort of the professionals was referred to by a cottage parent when she said:

> It's fine and easy for you people working up in the administration building to come at eight o'clock, leave at five, and have a half-day off

---

system in Foreword to *A Report on the Development of Penological Treatment at Norfolk Prison Colony in Massachusetts,* Carl R. Doering, (ed.) (New York: Bureau of Social Hygiene, Inc., 1940). For conflicts between psychologists, psychometrists and social workers on the one hand and house officers on the other, see particularly pages 11 and 12.

on Saturday, but we cottage parents are with the boys all the time. If we aren't, one of our helpers is.

Another comment by a vocational supervisor illustrates this situation:

We don't feel they (the professionals) understand or appreciate our job. It's easy enough for them to sit up in the main office in a nice soft chair and behind a fancy desk. They only have to deal with one boy at a time and he is putting his best foot forward most of the time when he is up seeing them. He knows they have a lot to do with the paroles.

The nonprofessionals charged the professionals with confusing "book learning" with workable knowledge, and of ranking such learning above the nonprofessional's practical experience. They contended this theoretical background and professional training, while important to the professional, actually hindered their grasp of the total situation at times.[4] This was being considered by a maintenance worker when he remarked:

That guy who calls himself a psychologist is so busy studying what he calls psychopathology and working in therapy that he doesn't know the rest of the world the kid lives in. The way he is going about things, it doesn't look like he's going to have much chance to learn about it.

A psychologist, reflecting on this point, commented:

The psychologist trained primarily in the psychology of the individual, the social worker trained mainly for case work, and the psychiatrist trained primarily in the diagnosis and treatment of the individual patient are not prepared to deal with the complex problems which the therapeutic management of groups presents. This is no reflection against them, unless they assume they are specialists in something they obviously are not.

Although many nonprofessionals saw the professional as emphasizing a theoretical background and professional training for work with delinquents in practice, the nonprofessionals viewed some as smooth operators without "real know-how," hiding their ineptness and, at times, some hostility behind good manners and the prestige conferred by schooling.[5] They also saw the professionals as placing power and status over democratic practices. A maintenance worker's comment illuminates the nonprofessional's view of some aspects of the professionals' relations to others.

These professional people talk about democratic practices and group processes, and that we have just as much to say about things as they do but I haven't seen it operate that way. Not only do they try to tell us what to do, but the case workers and the others are right next to the superintendent's office and they're telling him what to do. They have been off to school and while they haven't learned much, they have learned how to operate. When you give them a tough kid to deal with, they can't tell you what to do that's of much account—saying nothing about taking the kid on themselves.

Conflicts of values between professionals and nonprofessionals may be further illustrated by an episode in the parole planning for a delinquent. It shows that these conflicts can have a detrimental influence on the adjustment of the delinquents.

Don was a fifteen-year-old boy who had been committed to the "Boys' Training School" for petty stealing. His father had died and his mother had deserted him. While he had been severely deprived of parental love and childhood friendships, his maladjustment was not extreme. His development at the school during his year of residence was excellent. His major activities included study in the academic school where he excelled in the sciences, and work in the school infirmary as an orderly.

Don had been offered two placement plans. One placement was in the home of a dentist and his wife, who were interested in adopting the boy and giving him educational opportunities

---

[4] The specialist's limitations have been described by others: Harold J. Laski, *"The Limitations of the Expert," Harpers,* **162** (December 1930), 102–106; Robert K. Merton, *"The Machine, the Worker and the Engineer," Science,* **105** (January 24, 1947), 79–81; Wilbert E. Moore and Melvin M. Tumin, *"Some Social Functions of Ignorance," American Sociol. Rev.,* **14,** (December 1949), 788–789.

[5] This problem raises several question: (1) Was the professional's education, on which he leaned for support in his work, relevant to and adequate for carrying out his assignments? (2) Were the web of conflicts so complex that the education could not be utilized?

to the limit of his capacity and interest. The other placement was in the home of a farm family, who could offer him a good home but could not give him the education or the material advantages of the dentist's home.

After discussing these possibilities with the social worker, Don also talked about it with his science teacher, cottage mother, and a nurse. The teacher encouraged him to accept placement with the dentist emphasizing the educational opportunities. The nurse encouraged him to do the same. She emphasized the possible material advantages of the dentist's home, the opportunity of making the right kind of friends, as well as the educational opportunities. The cottage mother, however, thought that he should choose the farm family because it was her opinion that they really wanted him and would love him more than the dentist and his wife. She also expressed the opinion that farm life was good and would present fewer temptations than life in the city.

When Don attempted to reconcile these different points of view with his own ambivalence about any type of placement, he became anxious, tense, and restless. He went to see the social worker about his confusion; she accepted his indecision and said it was unfortunate that he had been given so much advice.

After this conference Don talked with some boys who overheard a heated argument between the nurse and his cottage mother. They informed Don that the nurse had flatly informed the cottage mother that her own preference, as well as that of the science teacher, was for his placement in the dentist's home. The boys also told Don several other things: that the nurse insisted that the farm family only wanted to exploit him as a laborer; that the cottage mother had denied this, and pointed out that while he would have to do his share of the work, they had excellent farm machinery and some hired help and that the cottage mother had countered that the dentist only wanted the boy as a show piece to follow in his footsteps.

Don became increasingly uneasy and confused. That night he ran away.

The teacher and nurse, as members of the professional group which valued education and social and economic status favored the dentist's home for Don. The nonprofessional, in this case the cottage mother, attached the values of honesty and independence of rural life and favored the farm placement. This conflict in values, with Don caught in the middle, had damaging results for him.

CONCEPTIONS OF STATUS AND ROLE

The professionals thought of themselves as being primarily responsible for the study of delinquents for diagnostic and planning purposes. While they acknowledged the value of the nonprofessionals' diagnostic observations and opinions for institutional and post-institutional planning, the professionals maintained that this area of responsibility was essentially theirs.

In addition to their diagnostic studies and planning duties, the professionals believed that they should devote a large portion of their time to treatment. For example, they gave suggestions for structuring the delinquent's environment to the nonprofessionals or offered some form of individual or group treatment to the delinquents. If they aided the delinquent by structuring his environment, the professionals usually worked with other professionals and nonprofessionals; if they offered some form of treatment, they worked immediately with the individual delinquent or group of delinquents.

The professionals' conception of their work also included assisting the delinquent to bridge the gap between the institution and outside world by proper orientation upon entry, by communication with relatives and officials during his stay, and follow-up studies with parole agencies after he left.

The professionals thought of the nonprofessionals as primarily guiding and supervising the delinquents. They thought the nonprofessionals were: (1) too restrictive with the delinquents, (2) did not try to understand the delinquents, and (3) resisted the professional's ideas and recommendations. While the professionals recognized that the nonprofessionals had some duties in connection with diagnostic studies and program planning, they regarded such duties as minor. The idea that the nonprofessionals were too restrictive is exemplified by the remark of a social worker.

That's what's the matter with these people, they are too hard on the kids. They want to make them follow a rigid and exact pattern which is their idea of being good. They don't want to hear what we have to say about management of the boys because so often it goes against their whole way of doing their job.

The rejections of the professionals' recommendations by the nonprofessionals was pin-pointed by a psychiatrist when he said:

I have been working with the D's (cottage parents) for approximately a year. I don't believe they have any intention of modifying their cottage management. I don't believe they ever will. We used to get open resistance from them; now it's passive resistance. For example, the strap was used openly, but now you never see a strap around; however, anyone who has anything to do with their cottage knows it's still being used.

A social worker commented further on this problem:

I sincerely believe that we cannot move any faster in creating a good treatment program for the boys than some of the staff (nonprofessionals) are willing and able to move. I also believe in helping them to move forward but after a while, it seems a little foolish to try to help some of these people become good rehabilitative workers.

On the other side of the picture, the nonprofessionals saw themselves as the backbone of the institution. Their constant intimate relationship with the delinquent was believed to be the major part of the delinquent's institutional program and they felt responsible for the boy's total welfare while in the institution. They believed that their duties in this connection were performed in an interested, definite, firm, and consistent manner. A typical attitude was reflected by a cottage parent who said:

We ran this institution well for many years. I'm pretty sure that we did a better job with the boys than is done now with all this high-priced help. We are still doing a good job; if it weren't for us, this place couldn't run.

Whether a staff member is married and/or has reared a family seems to play a role in the staff conflict over the care and treatment of delinquents.[6] A nonprofessional's comment shows this:

6 In one institution where this was a point of conflict, fifty per cent of the professionals were, or had been married, while ninety-seven per cent of the nonprofessionals are, or had been, married. In another institution it was forty-two per

I ought to know something about this. I raised five kids of my own and they are all doing all right. That is more than you can say for some of those young fellows up there in the office who are passing out the word.

On this same point a professional remarked:

The trouble with our cottage parents and vocational supervisors is that they think they can treat these delinquents like they treated their own youngsters. They don't realize that these boys may be quite different. Nor do they recognize that, by thinking of these boys as they thought of their own children, they may get quite personally involved.

Occasionally some nonprofessionals saw themselves as having even broader duties, and they assumed responsibility for the delinquent's welfare outside the institution. This took the form of unofficial parole planning and, at times, unofficial parole supervision. In one institution, after a cottage mother had unofficially written to the relatives of a boy asking them to come and get him, as he was ready for placement, she said:

Social work is fine, I guess, but there is too much red tape to it, or they make it that way. There's no reason to keep a boy waiting six weeks when he is ready to go and his relatives are ready to take him, just to make a lot of agency referrals. These referrals are for the purpose of studying the home to see whether it is all right or not, but what difference does it make? If it is all right, fine. If it isn't, they can seldom find another place for an "adolescent delinquent," as they say. So the boy is ready and waiting. If he doesn't get some satisfaction about placement, he soon will go downhill fast and all the good we have done for him will go, too.

cent of the professionals and eighty-four per cent of the nonprofessionals.

The age differences also appeared to be important in the conflict between the two groups. In one institution the average age of the professionals was thirty years while that of the nonprofessionals was forty-one years. In another institution the average age of the professionals was thirty-four and that of the nonprofessionals was forty-six. Statistically, these are highly significant differences. Together with the other data, they suggest that age differences and experiental disparities in family and parental roles were very important factors in the dissimilar orientations of the two groups toward the delinquents.

There are some similarities in the way in which the professionals view their duties and the way in which nonprofessionals view them. Fcr their part, the nonprofessionals considered the professional's duties as centering around: (1) the delinquent's admission into the institution; (2) initial diagnostic and planning activities; (3) communication with relatives and outside agencies; (4) considerable counseling on situational problems and limited special treatment work with delinquents; (5) some consultation work with staff members; (6) planning with the administration; (7) planning the parole of the boy and (8) liaison work with the parole authorities after the delinquent leaves the institution.

The nonprofessionals formally conceded the diagnostic duties to the professionals, but they believed that diagnosis has only general implications in shaping a boy's program and probably very little significance for them in their areas of work.

A cottage parent's statement makes this clear:

I like to talk with others about the boys and plan for them because there is always a lot one person misses or fails to do. I do not appreciate having some person push an opinion of a boy's character and intelligence on me that they may have formed in a few hour's time. I've worked with some of these boys a long time and I think I know them, too. I've tried different ways with them (professionals), now I just listen and then go ahead and do it my own way.

The necessity of having the professional's diagnosis was questioned by the nonprofessionals. The professionals' means of communication was criticized.

A farmer of an institution had this to say:

I work with boys all day long, every day. I know a boy, what he is like and what he's not like, what he can do and can't do. Just the other day, without me saying a thing, a boy told me all about his home and he cried. I can't put it in the language that those people in the administration building can—that is, put it up so that nobody but them can understand it—but I know this boy. That outfit up at the administration sees a boy for a few hours and they think they know the whole story and then want

to tell us in language we can't understand. And besides the kids come back to us all upset about these tests they give 'em.

The nonprofessionals were reluctant to concede the advisory or consultation role to the professionals. While there was some overt harmony, underlying negative feelings were strong. This underlying resentment was pointed out by a vocational supervisor who said:

I wouldn't mind this long-haired bunch up in the offices who have their education, but when they feel like they have been called on to give it to me too, I don't want it.

The superintendent of one of the institutions of this study who himself was a professional remarked:

The ordinary run-of-the-mill professional clings to his theory too much, and unfortunately, theory is frequently too abstract to be directly applicable to concrete problems. As a result, the cottage parents and others do not have too much confidence or respect for them.

In considering this problem, a social worker talked about professional workers without experience:

People with some professional education bring some valuable knowledge to their job, but they would be better off if they could appreciate themselves a little more realistically. You know, they haven't really learned what is needed to do their job, and all that it implies. Unfortunately, many of them feel compelled to give advice and suggestions. I guess they feel they have to justify their existence on the staff.

The work of the professionals which involved the delinquent's admission into the institution was generally accepted by the nonprofessionals; however, the cottage parents thought that considerable orientation and intake work needed to be done with the delinquents once they reached the cottage. They also accepted the role of the professionals in communicating with relatives and outside agencies, but some difficulties arose in this connection because the cottage parents would give different information to visiting parents than the social workers and other professionals did.

The nonprofessionals were troubled by the part professionals played in planning the institution's treatment program. They felt left out.[7]

The nonprofessionals also felt they were by-passed when it came to parole planning and actual placement. They thought their ideas did not receive adequate consideration. They also complained about delays in placing a boy once he was given parole.

Many conflicts occurred over these divergent ideas of statuses and roles.[8] Those

[7] Status and role conflicts of the professionals are not limited to these institutional settings. Ruth Emerson, writing on *"Standards in Medical Social Work,"* an article in *The Hospital in Modern Society,* a symposium edited by A. C. Bochmeyer (New York: The Commonwealth Fund, 1943) p. 346, says, "That there is too great a diversity of opinion among executives as to the nature of the return to the hospital, which should be expected from the activities of the social service department, seems indubitable. To some, the social worker is a glorified, and yet not altogether satisfactory, bill collector. She is sent on miscellaneous errands and asked to perform various institutional tasks for which there is no provision in the personnel of the hospital budget. Her position in some institutions is to be classed somewhere between that of the cash girl in a department store and the telephone clerk at the information desk."

Further, in this regard, the professional-nonprofessional conflicts of this study bear many similarities to the staff-line conflicts of industrial organizations reported by Melville Dalton in *Conflicts Between Staff and Line Managerial Officers,"* *Amer. Sociol. Rev.* 15 (June 1950), 342–351.

In an unreported research by the author on fifty psychiatric aides, similar status and role conflicts were observed between the aides on the one hand and the physicians and particularly the nurses on the other.

[8] One of the most important components of a healthy and vigorous staff morale is the opportunity the staff has to express their ideas and to contribute suggestions concerning the institutional program, particularly on those matters which involve them. For evidence of the motivational effects of group decision, see Kurt Lewin, *Group Decision and Social Change,"* in T. M. Newcomb and E. L. Hartley (Eds.), *Readings in Social Psychology* (New York: Holt, Rinehart & Winston, Inc., 1947), pp. 330–345; D. McGregor, *"Conditions for Effective Leadership in the Industrial Situation,"* *Jour. of Consult. Psychol.,* 8, (March–April 1945), pp. 55–63, and Robert Tannenbaum and Fred Massarik, *Participation by Subordinates in the Managerial Decision-making Process,"* *Canad. Jour. of Econ. and Pol. Sci.,* 16, (August 1950) 408–418.

stemming from the diagnosis and treatment of the boys were also found to be serious.

John had been in the Training School for approximately two weeks. During this period, his time had been largely taken up by his orientation program and diagnostic studies of him by the staff. The cottage parents had been orienting him to institutional and cottage life and had been observing him in a variety of situations. The psychologist had given him several tests. He had been seen by the psychiatrist, physician, dentist, and social worker.

At the end of these two weeks, a staff meeting was called and each member who had contact with John came with a report of his findings. A professional chaired the meetings and the other professionals consumed the majority of the period with their discussion and recommendations. This was particularly so with the psychologist and psychiatrist, who became involved in a discussion about the nature and extent of the boy's anxiety and the defenses he had available for its control. The social worker raised the point of the historical development of this anxiety and its significance for programming.

After these lengthy discussions, the conference progressed to the point of concrete program planning. John was brought into the group at this time to participate in the planning. While he previously discussed his desires and wishes regarding his institutional program with his social worker, his inclusion here was an effort to have him share more directly in matters concerning his future. John expressed his interests and wishes to the staff. He said he wanted to be assigned to the tailor shop because he wanted to learn the trade.

John left the group and his cottage mother questioned assigning him to Mrs. F. at the tailor shop because she did not believe John was especially interested in tailoring and she knew that the disciplinary control of the boys in the tailor shop was poor. She said she thought he had been attracted to tailoring by reports from the grapevine that this shop allowed more freedom than some others. She acknowledged John's anxiety but emphasized his aggressive behavior in the cottage and urged that he be considered for a work placement that offered more disciplinary control.

The professionals listened to her, respectfully, but no one responded to her ideas. Rather, they discussed other aspects of John's program.

John's case was summarized by the chairman, and his assignment to the tailor shop was included without comment. John's staff conference was finished; everyone returned to his place of work.

Several days later, the woman in charge of the tailor shop reported that John had not reported to the shop as assigned and she wondered what had happened. John's absence was investigated. It appeared that the complete rejection of the cottage mother's proposal and the lack of further discussion of it at the staff meeting had made her angry; she had deliberately sent John to another assignment.

When the cottage mother attempted to participate in the planning for John's program she indicated that she conceived of herself as having responsibilities for planning delinquents' programs. The professionals, reserving this role for themselves, rejected the cottage mother's participation. The cottage mother retaliated by ignoring the job assignment for John that the professionals arranged.

THE CONCEPTS OF DELINQUENCY AND DELINQUENCY TREATMENT

Generally, the professionals viewed delinquency as deviant behavior resulting from the interaction of etiological, predispositional factors with situational variants. They saw this behavior as emerging from the interplay of many elements in which the boy's conscious activity was only one of these involved. They believed that institutional treatment stemming from a constructive institutional milieu, as well as individual and group treatment, provides the boys with rehabilitative experiences and would help them modify their behavior.

The professionals were found to hold the delinquent responsible for his behavior, within a certain framework, but they did not morally evaluate it. Rather, they tried to understand the motivations for this behavior and if some appropriate therapeutic measures were available, they would recommend them. If the professionals thought it was indicated, they would participate in the treatment.

To the nonprofessionals, the professionals seemed inconsistent in their thinking about treatment. The professionals talked about many of the delinquents being activity and action-oriented rather than thoughtful and

verbal in their behavior and thus the major way of treating them was to provide a variety of constructive everyday corrective environmental experiences for them. Yet the professionals continued to see boys in office interview situations. When this was explained to the nonprofessionals on the basis of diagnostic and special treatment work for selected cases, the nonprofessionals countered with: (1) weren't the factors of comfort, easiness, and simplicity entering the professional's decisions, (2) if their (the nonprofessionals') environmental treatment was the most effective approach to the delinquents, why the salary, status and other differentials between themselves and the professionals?

Many nonprofessionals assumed that all similar, surface behavior had the same dynamics or meaning. Thus they were confused when the professionals recommended dissimilar attitudes and activities for what the nonprofessional thought were like delinquents.

The criteria for selecting boys for individual or group therapy seemed confusing to the nonprofessionals, thus such questions as: "If good for some boys, why not for others? I've got a couple over in my shop that need something. I don't see why they weren't included." With little insight as to what the professionals were attempting to accomplish, the nonprofessionals were skeptical, suspicious and at times opposed to therapy.

The majority of the nonprofessionals had not formalized their thinking about delinquency causation; however, many of them believed that delinquent behavior was historically and situationally determined. They believed that present situations and past experiences played an important part in bringing about delinquent behavior, but that once institutionalized, the delinquent would become penitent, see the error of his ways, and of his own free will choose socially constructive goals despite his present obstacles and past experiences.

To the professionals, the nonprofessionals appeared inconsistent and ambiguous in their thinking about treatment. The nonprofessionals talked of past experiences and the current situation as factors in behavior but said that if only the delinquent "would make up his mind, he could do what is right, because after all, he knows right from wrong. If he doesn't know right from wrong, then punish him because a child always learns to leave a hot stove alone after he is burned often enough." At times, they assumed that "if a boy has been mistreated, all you have to do is be nice to him and treat him right and he will be O. K." In this instance, they viewed treatment as being synonymous with kindness. Some of these inconsistencies are apparent in the case of Jim.

Jim was transferred to the "Boys Training School" from the state orphanage because he was "incorrigible." Following the orientation and study period, the staff met to discuss the results of these findings and to plan for his stay at the school. The professionals generally agreed that the boy was suffering from an insidiously developing schizophrenic condition, that his controls over his intense anxiety and hostility were crumbling and that his contact with reality was weak and intermittent. They viewed his judgment as severely impaired and anticipated bizarre hostile behavior from him. Their general recommendations included an environment of acceptance, security and supportive psychotherapy.

The cottage-father listened to these analyses and proposals. He appeared to have difficulty with the terminology but understood it well enough to disagree in principle. He went on to describe several concrete episodes of Jim's behavior in which Jim had torn some plastic tile from the floor of the hall and had collected all the dirty socks he could find and put them in his locker. He further pointed out that when he had confronted Jim with this "nonsense" that he could stop it if he wanted to, especially if there was some penalty attached to such behavior, Jim agreed. The house-father commented that while the medical diagnosis might be "true" he still regarded Jim's behavior as rising from a wish to be "ornery" and that it could be changed "if people would put their foot down on him."

Some bizarre behavior borders on the normal. To the untrained observer, it is frequently difficult to determine where one stops and the other starts. Although Jim's cottage parent could understand the schizophrenic condition of Jim in theory, he could not recognize or accept it as it occurred in Jim's daily living. Perhaps he had known many boys who did some of the very things Jim had done, and they were relatively normal.

He was intimately aware of Jim's actions, but he did not have a diagnostic frame of reference that he could bring to bear on this behavior and thus was unable to understand Jim's condition as being anything else than simple orneriness.

SOME NEGATIVE EFFECTS OF THE CONFLICTS[9]

These conflicts had significant detrimental effects on the system of social relationships as a whole as well as on the groups and individual involved.[10]

In some of the institutions, conflicts between these groups resulted in the system of social relationships becoming so disorganized that constructive interaction among the staff was nearly impossible. For example, some of the institutions required all the professional and nonprofessional people working with a particular delinquent to attend his staff meetings; however, many of the nonprofessionals could not "find time" to attend the meetings even though their work load or schedule of duties had not noticeably increased. In other institutions, the professionals and nonprofessionals avoided meeting each other informally, as in the cafeteria and the staff recreation rooms.

Both professional and nonprofessional groups were disturbed by internal frictions. At times, dissensions pitted the vocational teachers and maintenance workers against the cottage parents and the social workers

[9] This is not to imply that only negative and destructive phenomena are associated with conflict although this is the focus here. For a theoretical discussion of the postive as well as the negative aspects of conflict see, George Simmel, *"The Sociology of Conflict,"* Albion W. Small, (trans.) *Amer. Jour. of Sociol.* 9, 1903–1904, 490–525.

[10] As in society, there were those who took difficulties and conflicts in their stride; however, frustration, anxiety and other reactions were widespread. Some of these problems in society are characterized by Karen Horney, *The Neurotic Personality of our Time* (New York: W. W. Norton and Co. Inc., 1937).

against the psychologists and psychiatrists.

In all of the institutions, a varying number of staff members set up devices to protect themselves and withdrew from some of the normal and expected activities. This, of course, reduced constructive interaction. In one institution the professionals spent much of their time in research although this was not included in the duties of their job. At another institution, the professionals tended to ignore the organizational problems, and discussed instead the theory of their various fields. At several institutions, the professionals carried on exhaustive discussions regarding individual cases of delinquents and the institution's problems, but they rarely advanced beyond diagnosis of a delinquent or criticism of the administration and the nonprofessionals.

The nonprofessionals also had a variety of protective devices. Only one cottage parent would work when both were scheduled to work; the other would be upstairs resting. They would force particularly difficult boys into recreational activities outside the cottage rather than follow the professional's recommendations for providing activities for them at the cottage where the situation at the time was expected to be less complex.

Staff members, in their efforts to work in these situations and adapt to them, may become maladjusted. Anxiety, feelings of discouragement, aggressive and psychosomatic reactions were not uncommon responses among many of the workers in these institutions.

Situationally, these reactions appeared related to the staff conflicts as well as to the nature and intensity of the children's behavior.[11]

Some staff members sought "one sided" solutions outside of the institution by feigning cooperation with the institution's efforts to achieve cooperation. For example, in one institution a group of dissatisfied nonprofessionals appealed directly to the commissioner of the institution's administration concerning their complaints. In several institutions, a powerful cadre of nonprofessionals worked undercover for a change of administration through special interest groups. They wanted to be rid of the present administration and many of the professionals. This group complained about the professionals "meddling with our discipline." In another institution, the professionals, thinking that the administration failed to support their ideas and recommendations, worked secretly to gain a change in the administration.

Further along this web of subterfuge, the "acting out" of certain staff members worked against the institutions' goals. For example, at several schools, the professionals left work early, commenting "What's the use of staying? We can't get any cooperation anyway." Yet they always accepted full-time pay. In another institution, a few of the professionals appropriated books from the library rationalizing that "I might as well get something out of this job," and "You couldn't get anyone around here interested in learning about this."[12] A farmer at one institution was highly critical of administrative laxness concerning intergroup conflicts. He declared vehemently that people should be made to "toe the line or get out." Gradually his criticism waned and he would sarcastically remark, "I'm running my own little playhouse now, I expect others to run theirs. That's the only way a guy can get along here." A short time later he was caught stealing some livestock from the school.

As a result of these staff conflicts, the delinquent is frequently damaged rather than helped. Many delinquents came to these institutions from homes with extremely disturbed family situations where their needs for a secure and stable family life were ignored or where the parents were highly inconsistent. As a result, many delinquents developed devious means of satisfying their needs. They very shrewdly

11 Information was given about these points in a paper entitled, *"The Emotional Reactions of People Working with Emotionally Disturbed and Delinquent Children,"* by Ralph W. Coltharp and George H. Weber, presented at the 1951 Mid-Continent Psychiatric Association, Kansas City, Missouri.

12 For a discussion of this problem on a broader scale, see Lawrence S. Thompson, *Notes on Bibliokleptomania* (New York: The New York Public Library, 1944).

evaluated the social situations about them. They detected weaknesses, and they exploited and manipulated the situation for their personal ends. This behavior-attitude had played a strong role in their delinquency in the first place and was one of the behavioral tendencies that the institution tried to modify. Yet this was quite impossible if the delinquent was exposed to an institutional environment where the surroundings were similar to those which had contributed to his unhealthy condition.

John, a delinquent at a Training School, was denied a holiday pass to his home by his cottage parent because he had persistently been intimidating younger boys and, whenever possible, beating them. Aware that there were differences of opinion regarding treatment methods between the social worker and the cottage parent, John went to see the social worker, complaining that he was restricted from his pass unfairly and that the cottage parent was "down on him" and that "he had just been playing with the other fellows." The social worker was sympathetic and after the boy left, she discussed it with the chief social worker. He took it to the superintendent who, in turn, asked to see the cottage parent. The cottage parent, threatened by this apparent display of power by the professionals, said that "he thought maybe a pass would be the thing to help him." Later, in talking with his associates, the cottage parent bitterly denounced the professionals.

Many delinquents are shrewd and devious in their actions. John was such a boy. By manipulating some staff members, who fell unwittingly into his trap, he got his pass. The conflict of status and role here between the professionals and non-professionals is evident again; a conflict over treatment methods is also indicated. John was aware of these conflicts and cleverly exploited them to his own advantage, and continued his delinquent way of dealing with the world.

Questions for Discussion and Further Research

Statements of basic principles to guide the relationships among various professional groups, such as that delineated in the selection on psychology presented here, are intended to provide for two general types of problems: *encroachment* of other occupations from without, and *confinement* of members to operating within the commonly understood limits of their own occupation. Dealing with encroachment, or possible encroachment, entails establishing boundaries—statements which set forth that with which the occupation is supposed to be concerned. It is not known in a precise and comprehensive way how effective these statements are in interoccupational relations, for in many instances they occur only where there was reason to suspect gross encroachment. What is needed is a study of what occurs between occupations, *before* and after such formal statements are brought into force. Do formal statements concerning relationships with other occupations serve any function other than establishing quasi-legal limits to extremely deviant behavior within an occupation?—do they become operable only when outrageous encroachment from outsiders occurs? And to what extent is encroachment overlooked if the group doing the encroaching is in a more powerful social position? To what extent, if any, do such statements influence the occupational conduct of persons outside the occupation?

As was recognized in the Cottrell and Sheldon selection, friction among occupational groups often arises out of incomplete information, which these authors refer to as vagueness and inappropriateness of expectations. Cottrell and Sheldon also note varieties of occupational differences which may contribute to misunderstandings. They point out that there tend to be attitudes of superiority held by the incumbents of some highly professionalized occupations, particularly those which purport to seek basic discoveries of knowledge. This leads to the question of how we are to account for the hostility of some so-called "basic researchers" for the efforts of those persons in occupations devoted to the application of their research findings? The importance of this question is quite evident when we recognize that the operation of the total society is dependent upon a mutually workable arrangement between "discoverers" and "appliers" of knowledge.

Zander, *et al.,* have described the circumstance which appears to be most typical of the interrelationship of psychiatry, clinical psychology, and psychiatric social work as essentially a relationship of *accommodation,* involving inter-occupational superordination and subordination. Many people willingly conform to this form of interdependence. There is no reason to suppose, however, that the interrelationship among these three occupations will remain one of accommodation because, as other authors have pointed out, there may be inherent difficulties in relations between occupations which define parts of their occupational roles as being highly similar or identical. If it is possible to work out a complimentarity of functions, the friction can be greatly reduced and accommodation becomes effective. The question which arises out of the Zander example is the extent to which interoccupational relations are more fraught with difficulties among the "people-oriented" occupations; or is there just as much difficulty in the working relationship between the structural engineer and the architect, for example?

In illustrating *avoidance* relationships among occupational groups, Kerckhoff makes the observation that this type of relation may develop where the basic social needs of an occupation are of particular importance and are not being met effectively. Even though it is difficult to oppose, people in adjacent occupations may be ambivalent about the development of a "marginal" occupation, fearing the possibility of future encroachment. This naturally leads to other kinds of relationships—competition, and perhaps even conflict; or, in the other direction, accommodation may develop, particularly if the new occupation comes to be viewed as an adjunct to a well-established occupation, the latter exercising some indirect control over standards and boundaries. One research question in this connection is: What is the precise nature of avoidance relationships—are they always transitional, a stage in the development of either accommodative relationships at one extreme, or competitive and conflict relationships at the other? Or is it possible for avoidance relationships to remain relatively stable?

Some people have maintained that competition in social life produces the best sort of social arrangements—a survival of the functionally fit. Utilizing the same occupations that Wardwell discusses as an example of competitive relationships, some people would argue that the fairly recent emergence of physical medicine has been a direct outcome of the long-standing competition between chiropractic and osteopathic medicine, on the one hand, and allopathic medicine, on the other. They would argue that, without such competition, the numerically dominant medical profession would have been slow in exploring and developing certain areas of human diagnosis and therapy.

In another sector of social life, it appears that the business world contains examples of long-standing competition among some rather professionalized occupations. This generates the important research question: Does competition between overlapping occupations contribute to better work performance, or does this represent an uneconomical waste of talent and social effort with everyone suffering—practitioners, clients, and public at large?

In examining conflict relationships among occupations, George H. Weber maintained that such intense forms of interaction are more likely to occur when similar work tasks are performed by people with widely differing training and status. Weber found that the two occupational groups attempting to rehabilitate juvenile offenders did so in radically different ways—ways so discrepant that it was difficult to achieve reconciliation between them. What we need to explore, in some detail, is whether conflict relationships are restricted to instances where such great discrepancies in background experiences exist—with one group referring to the other as "unqualified" and the other responding with the term "inexperienced"—or whether the examples cited in the selection do occur generally—are there any examples of interoccupational conflict involving persons of equivalent occupational status?

8

Professionals and Complex Organizations

The older literature on professionalization focused upon the patterns of behavior of independent professionals, and how this behavior differed from that of bureaucrats or what we might today call "organization men." In the typical pattern, the independent professional was "called" to pursue his trade as a physician, attorney, scientist, etc., in an entrepreneurial role apart from employment in large-scale industrial or governmental bureaucracies. Perhaps he had a few apprentices around to assist in his labors—law clerks and junior partners, laboratory technicians, etc.—but as a full-fledged professional, he was his own master within the ethical and associational framework of a society of professional colleagues.

The recent literature has pointed out that this is no longer an accurate description of the social situation of many modern professionals. Physicians are now affiliated in larger numbers with hospitals and clinics; attorneys with law firms and, in increasing numbers, with industrial corporations;* scientists and engineers also with industry, government, large independent research organizations, and a collection of institutes and departments in academic institutions. Even though the clergy have usually been employed by some kind of church organization, there are indications that sizable aspects of the Christian Church are becoming more bureaucratic in character—a trend that may be supported further by the mergers occurring as part of the ecumenical movement. No profession has escaped the advancing tide of bureaucratization.

The newer salaried professional, therefore, is a different kind of man than the independent professional described so extensively in the past literature. He is a different kind of man because he works under different circumstances. One of the more significant features of these new circumstances is the fact that his

---

* For example, see C. Ray Jeffery, *et al.*, "The Legal Profession," in E. J. Davis, *et al.* (eds.), *Society and the Law* (New York: Free Press of Glencoe, Inc., 1962), pp. 322–327.

work is subject to the evaluation and control of other individuals who are not necessarily members of his professional group. These are managers, whose authority governing the work of *all* employees, including highly professionalized employees, derives from the legitimatizing principles of bureaucratic administration which have been identified and described by Max Weber and those who are associated with the Weberian tradition. In contrast, the professional model of behavior assumes that work is controlled in terms of ethical standards determined by colleagues in a professional association, rather than by managers in an administrative hierarchy. This difference provides the basis for a considerable degree of role conflict when professional individuals become salaried employees in complex organizations†—or conversely, when certain categories of employees in bureaucratized organizations become more professionalized. While many professions are becoming bureaucratized, many bureaucracies are also becoming professionalized.‡

The readings in this chapter provide us with further insights into many kinds of role conflicts that occur when professionals become bureaucratic or when bureaucratic roles become professionalized. As Gross and Herriott have recognized,

> . . . in addition to creating problems for professional staff members, the professional-ism-authority issue in organizations also creates problems for the representatives of the bureaucracy. One such problem is the extent to which executives of professionally staffed organizations should attempt to offer leadership to subordinates whose professional status entitles them to a considerable degree of autonomy in their work.§

We shall also have opportunity to examine some examples of mechanisms that may contribute to the alleviation, or even resolution, of the several types of role conflict existing for professionals working in the bureaucratic setting.

Professionals in Bureaucracies—Areas of Conflict

In the following paper, W. Richard Scott provides a more detailed description of differences between bureaucratic and professional models of organization and four areas of role conflict associated with these differences: (1) the professional's resistance to bureaucratic rules; (2) the professional's rejection of bureaucratic standards; (3) the professional's resistance to bureaucratic supervision; and (4) the professional's conditional loyalty to the bureaucracy.

† J. Ben-David, "The Professional Role of the Physician in Bureaucratized Medicine: A Study in Role Conflict," *Human Relations,* Vol. 11, 1958, 255–274.

‡ A. Etzioni, "Authority Structure and Organizational Effectiveness," *Administrative Science Quarterly,* 4, No. 1 (June 1959), 43–67.

§ Neal Gross and Robert E. Herriott, "Organizational Effects of the Professional Leadership of School Principals," a paper presented at the Annual Meetings of the American Sociological Association, Los Angeles, California, August 29, 1963.

W. Richard Scott (General)

A great deal has been written and a considerable amount of research has been conducted on the problems which result when professional workers are employed in bureaucratic organizations. There are many reasons for studying such organizations, not the least of which is their increasing prevalence and the social significance of the kinds of work carried out within them. However, some sociologists are particularly concerned with these structures because of the light they shed on certain important theoretical problems in the study of organizations. Two such problems may be distinguished. First, professionals participate in two systems—the profession and the organization—and their dual membership places important restrictions on the organization's attempt to deploy them in a rational manner with respect to its own goals. Second, the profession and the bureaucracy rest on fundamentally different principles of organization, and these divergent principles generate conflicts between professionals and their employers in certain specific areas. Both of these problems will be examined although the central focus of this paper will be the latter.

Organization theorists are coming to see more and more clearly that if an organization is to operate as a rational structure it must be relatively insulated from its surrounding institutional environment. Specifically, the organization must have the power to select recruits and control their contributions in such a way as to implement the system goals. This is difficult in cases where organization members participate in more than one system having relevance for the performance of their occupational role. Weber alluded to this problem when he noted the importance of applying technical criteria in the recruitment of officials and when he stipulated that officials should regard their office as their "sole, or at least the primary, occupation."[1] And Udy's studies of the organization of work in pre-industrial societies demonstrate that organizations too closely tied to other institutional systems (e.g., political or kinship) exhibit fewer rational characteristics than those enjoying greater independence from their environment.[2] One important reason for

looking closely at bureaucracies manned by professionals is that such organizations are to a considerable degree "socially involved," to use Udy's phrase. Such organizations are likely to be unable to fully control the criteria by which their professional personnel are to be recruited, since professionals themselves will demand some voice in these matters; and they will have difficulty in controlling the efforts of professionals once recruited insofar as these members retain an identification with their profession and attempt to adhere to its norms and standards. As Kornhauser insists, to examine professionals in bureaucracies is to examine the "relation between two *institutions,* not merely between organizations and individuals."[3]

Two institutions *are* involved in the relation between professionals and bureaucracies. Furthermore, it is important to understand that the two systems are based on fundamentally different principles. In order to better examine the nature of these principles, two simple models—one for each organizational form—will be constructed. These will then be utilized to examine the kinds of conflicts which characterize the relation between professionals and bureaucracies. An attempt at model construction seems necessary for two reasons. First, the terms "profession" and "bureaucracy" are big words in the sense that they encompass many characteristics and their interrelations.[4] It would appear to be worthwhile

"Professionals in Bureaucracies—Areas of Conflict," a previously unpublished paper. The paper was prepared under a grant from the National Science Foundation (G #23990) for a study of "Authority Structures and Evaluation Processes." Participants in the study, in addition to the author, are Joseph Berger, Bernard P. Cohen, Sanford M. Dornbusch and Morris Zelditch, Jr. Used by permission.

1 M. Weber, *The Theory of Social and Economic Organization,* A. M. Henderson and T. Parsons (trans.) and T. Parsons (ed.), (Glencoe, Ill.: The Free Press, 1947), pp. 333–334.

2 S. H. Udy, Jr., "Administration Rationality, Social Setting, and Organizational Development," *The American Journal of Sociology,* 68 (November 1962), 299–308; S. H. Udy, Jr., "Technical and Institutional Factors in Production Organization: A Preliminary Model," *The American Journal of Sociology,* 67 (November 1961), 247–254. See also, S. H. Udy, Jr., *Organization of Work,* (New Haven: HRAF Press, 1959), pp. 55–71.

3 W. Kornhauser, *Scientists in Industry: Conflict and Accommodation,* (Berkeley: University of California Press, 1962), p. 8.

4 Another problem is that the phenomena classified by these labels show great variation; that is, one professional group or bureaucratic

to break these concepts down into simpler components so that the kinds of characteristics involved and the nature of their interrelations can be discerned. Second, an examination of the naturally occurring phenomena reveals that professions and bureaucracies are becoming more and more alike; that is "bureaucrats" are being "professionalized" at the same time that "professionals" are being "bureaucratized." In such circumstances it seems more necessary than ever to shift attention away from the conglomerate concepts to the specific characteristics which comprise them if the essential differences between the two forms are not to be obscured. Once differentiated, these characteristics can aid in the analysis of existing structures, if it is assumed that the particular set of characteristics present as well as their interrelation determines the extent of professionalization (or bureaucratization) of a given organization.

The Two Models

If one has a complicated job to do and a work force at his disposal, two alternative ways of organizing the task immediately suggest themselves. One approach is to instill in each worker all the basic skills required for doing the work together with the norms and standards which will govern his performance. Since each worker possesses the necessary skills, he can perform the entire task independently of the efforts of his colleagues. If each worker has internalized the standards, he will apply them not only to his own work but also to that of his colleagues so that under this system performance is somewhat controlled by external surveillance. The major controls,

organization may differ greatly from another. For general statements on the sets of characteristics which differentiate professions from bureaucracies, see T. Parsons, *Essays in Sociological Theory*, rev. ed., (Glencoe, Ill.: The Free Press, 1954), pp. 34–49; R. G. Francis and R. C. Stone, *Service and Procedure in Bureaucracy: A Case Study* (Minneapolis: University of Minnesota Press, 1956), pp. 153–157; and P. M. Blau and W. R. Scott, *Formal Organizations: A Comparative Approach*, (San Francisco: Chandler Publishing Co., 1962), pp. 60–63.

however, are those which a worker applies to his own performance.

The second alternative is to divide the task into its constituent activities and to train some workers to perform certain of these activities and other workers to perform different ones. Norms and standards are not internalized so that a system of rules which specifies how the work is to be done will be necessary, and some workers must be given the job of interpreting and enforcing the rules. In addition, the rules and the supervisory officials must function to coordinate the efforts of the various workers to assure that the several activities will each contribute to the accomplishment of the assigned task.

The association of complete skills with internalized standards (in the first model) and of partial skills with external controls (in the second model) is not purely arbitrary. On the contrary, these combinations appear to be inherently compatible due to the following considerations. To begin with, external control is difficult to effect when workers possess complete skills. That is, it is harder for someone other than the performer to observe and evaluate a performance involving a broad range of activities—activities which may differ in kind, number, combination, and sequence—than it is for him to evaluate a performance comprised of a narrow set of activities. Then too, a worker who performs the entire task will be more willing and better able to assume responsibility for the control of his performance than will the worker who carries out only a portion of the task and whose performance may in various ways be dependent on the work of others. In addition, the length of training period associated with the two systems has an indirect bearing on the extent to which internalized controls can be established. To train a worker to perform all the basic activities necessary for carrying out a complex task will require more time than to train a worker to perform a subset of these activities. The longer training period furnishes the time which seems to be necessary for the successful inculcation of work-related values and norms. These are the kinds of considerations which suggest that the two skill levels and types of control belong together in the manner indicated.

These simple systems may be expected to generate many additional differences in operation. One of the more important of these is a consequence of the difference in the length of training required for preparing workers to participate in one or the other system. The longer training period required to transmit complete skills creates pressures for the development of training institutions separate from those engaged in practice simply because the practicing agencies usually cannot command resources sufficient to underwrite the prolonged and complicated training required of their workers. Conversely, where only partial skills are to be passed on, few demands are made on the training system and one would expect to more frequently find training and practice carried out within the same organization.

The first model purports to describe some of the features associated with a professional system while the second describes some of the characteristics of the bureaucratic organization. No claim is made that these are the only or even the most important factors distinguishing professions from bureaucracies. They are taken to be factors of some importance, however, and the following discussion attempts to demonstrate their utility for comparing and analyzing the two systems.[5]

The applicability of the models to the empirical phenomena in question should require little explanation or justification. Professionals are usually characterized as persons trained in professional schools, possessing complex skills and special knowledge, and equipped with internalized control mechanisms. And bureaucrats are usually thought of as relatively specialized in function and as operating in a hierarchical structure under a system of formal rules. The one characteristic which may require some justification is the description of professional workers as possessing "all the basic skills required for doing the work," for it is true that many professionals now "specialize" in some subset of activities and in this sense cannot be said to possess "complete" skills. Two considerations argue for the validity of this characteristic so far as the construction of a model is concerned. First, all professionals of a given type are required to master a broad common set of skills and body of knowledge—among physicians, even psychiatrists put in their four years learning anatomy, cell structure, and basic clinical techniques—prior to their specialization. Second, the image after which the professional is modeled is that of a "free" and independent practitioner. Specialization within a particular group of professionals is possible only when practitioners organize, either formally or informally, to dispense their services. Thus, it is argued that the development of a division of labor among professional specialists represents a departure from the professional model in the direction of the bureaucratic form of organization.

The delineation of the two models is meant to emphasize the fact that professional and bureaucratic principles provide *alternative* approaches to the organization of complex tasks.[6] Therefore, it is not surprising to discover that conflicts and problems result whenever these two types of organizational forms are merged into a single structure.

AREAS OF CONFLICT

The models as outlined will provide the framework for a discussion of professional and bureaucratic principles of organization, and, in particular, for an analysis of the

[5] The foregoing discussion of professional and bureaucratic approaches to work implies that there are no differences in the *nature* of the tasks being carried out—only differences in the *way* in which the tasks are organized. Although this is the intended implication, it is true that certain kinds of tasks are more effectively handled by one approach rather than the other. In general, repetitive tasks, the approach to which may be standardized, are more effectively carried out by a bureaucratic type of organization and nonroutine work requiring flexibility, by a professional type. Cf. E. Litwak, "Models of Bureaucracy Which Permit Conflict," *The American Journal of Sociology,* **67** (September 1961), 177–179.

[6] Both Francis and Stone and Stinchcombe have described these organizational forms as alternative ones. See Francis and Stone, *op. cit.;* and A. L. Stinchcombe, "Bureaucratic and Craft Administration of Production: A Comparative Study," *Administrative Science Quarterly,* **4** (September 1959), 168–187.

causes of the types of conflict which are reported to occur whenever professionals are employed by bureaucracies. Conflicts between professionals and their organizational employers are the focus of the discussion both because most studies tend to concentrate on this aspect of the relation and, more importantly, because it is felt that the types of conflicts generated help to illuminate the contrasts between the two systems. Four more or less distinct areas of conflict will be considered: (1) the professional's resistance to bureaucratic rules; (2) the professional's rejection of bureaucratic standards; (3) the professional's resistance to bureaucratic supervision; and (4) the professional's conditional loyalty to the bureaucracy.

Illustrative evidence of the existence of such conflicts will be obtained from an examination of a number of studies of professionals employed in bureaucratic organizations. Most such studies focus on professional workers exclusively, making contrasts *within* this group rather than comparing the behavior of professional with nonprofessional employees. The professionals studied are usually classified according to the extent to which they identify themselves with their professional group as opposed to their employing organization. The existence of professionals with a "bureaucratic orientation" suggests that in practice many professionals accommodate themselves to the demands of the organization by giving up professional commitments. (It is also true, as Kornhauser,[7] has emphasized, that organizations make structural adjustments to mitigate conflicts with professionals.) However, for the purposes of this discussion, the more interesting group are those professionals who are "professionally oriented" since their continuing identification with their profession serves to point up the areas of conflict between the two organizational forms.

THE PROFESSIONAL'S RESISTANCE TO BUREAUCRATIC RULES

The earlier discussion of the two organizational models specified that a set of rules to

control and coordinate performance is essential when tasks are subdivided among workers, as occurs in a bureaucratic organization. Because he performs only a portion of the activities required to complete the task, the individual worker has no basis for making rational judgements concerning the choice of objectives or of means; these are therefore selected for him and assigned to him.[8] Thus, a worker in such a position exercises little discretion; his activities are guided by a set of general rules, and he is expected to follow regularized procedures.[9] Such a worker has no rational basis for flaunting the rules, since he lacks knowledge of the over-all operation and the part he plays within it.[10] In addi-

---

[7] Kornhauser, *op. cit.*

[8] It should be clear that in this and all other discussions the contrast is between bureaucratic and professional *principles* for the organization of work rather than between the types of work actually performed by persons in bureaucratic organizations or professional positions. This discussion, then, in no way conflicts with Blau's notion that many kinds of work in bureaucracies can be "professionalized" by increasing the skills of workers and evaluating their performance more on the basis of results achieved than on conformity to rules. See P. M. Blau, *Bureaucracy in Modern Society,* (New York: Random House, 1956), pp. 62–66.

[9] The same point can be made if organizations are characterized as decision-making structures, following Simon. Within his framework actions are rational if the behavior at the $n - 1$ level serves as a means for attaining ends set at level n and these ends in turn are means from the standpoint of the $n + 1$ level, and so on up the hierarchy. (See H. A. Simon, *Administrative Behavior,* rev. ed., [New York: The Macmillan Company, 1957], pp. 61–78.) In the bureaucratic situation, workers at the lower level have no hand in planning the "means-ends chains" nor do they have any basis for rationally evaluating the effectiveness of the procedures which they are asked to carry out. Effectiveness of means can only be evaluated in relation to the ends served, and only those in the upper levels of the hierarchy are in a position to see the articulation of means with ends.

[10] "Modern bureaucracies function because most of those who fill the organizational posts are usually willing to acknowledge that it is not their business to decide (a) whether the processes prescribed by plan are rational, nor (b) whether the goals implemented by those processes are in proper balance and priority." D. Marvick, *Career Perspectives in a Bureaucratic Setting* (Ann Arbor: Michigan Governmental Studies, No. 27, 1954), p. 9.

tion, this arrangement implies that the worker cannot be held responsible for the choice of goal or for the adequacy of the means chosen to achieve the desired goal, but can only be evaluated on his conformity to or deviation from the rules that control his performance.

The professional, by contrast, has acquired skills which allow him to perform the entire task and has internalized norms which control the application of those skills. Equipped in this manner, he expects to direct his own activities toward the desired ends free from constraining regulations or interference from others. He demands autonomy and at the same time expects to assume responsibility for his decisions and actions. In order to make a sharp contrast with the bureaucratic approach, one would like to say that procedures as viewed by professionals are merely means to an end which when proved ineffective are ignored or discarded. And one would like to say further that the professional's orientation toward the "whole" problem and his corresponding assumption of responsibility make it possible to evaluate his performance entirely on the basis of results achieved rather than on his conformity to specific procedures. But however neat and logical this argument appears, it does not describe the situation accurately. Indeed, many analysts have noted that from the point of view of an impartial observer, the professional often seems more concerned with following correct procedures than with the success or failure of his efforts.[11] Two factors appear to account for this condition. First, a professional's training sensitizes him to the close association between adequacy of means and correctness of conclusions: good results are viewed as a consequence of careful adherence to correct procedures. Second, and more important, in most cases the professional will not be able to control all the circumstances affecting the success

of his performance. For example, the surgeon may "skilfully perform" the operation and yet the patient may die, a victim of forces over which the surgeon has no control; or the geologist may be accurate in all his calculations and yet the drilling team may fail to strike oil.[12] In such cases the professional naturally balks at being evaluated on results, and the only basis for evaluating performance is to ask whether or not he employed appropriate methods in carrying out his work.[13] For these reasons evaluation of the work of a professional is a complex process involving some assessment of procedures employed as well as performance outcomes.

When professionals are employed by organizations, there is a fundamental change in their situation. They must sacrifice some of their autonomy and conform to certain organizational rules for a simple reason: they do not possess all the basic skills for doing the work but are part of a larger and more complex system in which they perform only some of the required activities. Their activities must be regulated to fit in with the over-all organizational purpose as well as coordinated with the activities of others. Here, then, is a potential conflict area. The professional expects to be allowed maximum discretion in the selection of means for achieving desired results, being constrained in his operations only by internalized norms which indicate accepted procedures. The bureaucracy, however, superimposes its own rules on the professional constraining his behavior in various ways and specifically restricting his choice of means.

Professionals object to such limitations but frequently are able to function within them. When, however, the professional feels that adherence to bureaucratic norms will

[11] See, for example, discussions by E. C. Hughes, *Men and Their Work* (Glencoe, Ill.: The Free Press, 1958), pp. 95–98; and A. W. Gouldner, "Organizational Analysis," in R. K. Merton, L. Broom, and L. S. Cottrell, Jr., (eds.) *Sociology Today: Problems and Prospects,* (New York: Basic Books, 1959), p. 414.

[12] For a related discussion, see W. F. Whyte, *Men at Work* (Homewood, Ill.: Dorsey Press and Richard D. Irwin, 1961), pp. 91–92.

[13] In addition to these "rational" factors which predispose the professional to adhere to the procedural norms of his occupational group, his status and self-conception are closely tied in with the exercise of his professional skills and these considerations will sometimes lead him to adhere rigidly to accepted procedures to the detriment of the services he is expected to render.

lead to a violation of the norms of his professional group, he is likely to rebel. In doing so, he may incur the wrath of his bureaucratic superiors but will at the same time gain support from his professional colleagues both within and outside the organization. The bureaucratic employee has no similarly powerful reference group capable of lending a semblance of legitimacy to his "deviant" acts.

Studies of professionals working in bureaucratic organizations indicate that those that are professionally oriented do object and rebel when they feel that their performance is constrained by organizational rules. These data in general do not bear on the reasons for resistance—the problem addressed in the foregoing discussion—but they do confirm its existence in the area indicated. For example, professionally oriented workers in a public welfare agency were more likely than those oriented to the bureaucracy to agree with statements suggesting that agency rules and procedures sometimes interfered with professional performance (providing casework services to clients.)[14] These same workers were also more likely than their bureaucratically oriented counterparts to deviate from certain agency rules.[15] And Marvick, in a study of some 200 professional and administrative personnel in a federal research agency, found that professionally oriented workers were more likely than those oriented to the bureaucracy to express "deprivation" rather than gratification in evaluating a list of task-related job conditions.[16] Another less direct indication of the way in which administrative rules are viewed by professionally oriented workers is provided by Gouldner's study of the faculty of a small liberal arts college. While no information was collected on faculty attitudes toward rules governing their own behavior, Gouldner reports that professionally oriented faculty members were less

willing to resort to formal rules as a means of controlling student behavior.[17]

THE PROFESSIONAL'S REJECTION OF BUREAUCRATIC STANDARDS[18]

A comparison of the two models indicates that one consequence of dealing with workers possessing complete skills is that they are likely to have received their training in institutions other than those by which they are employed. Such training institutions, particularly schools for professionals, supply their students with norms and standards to govern their performance, as well as with certain technical knowledge and skills. Standards advocated by professional training institutions tend to diverge to a greater or lesser extent from those actually utilized to guide the operations of agencies engaged in practice. There are several reasons for this. The most important factor is undoubtedly that there are important differences between advocating a set of ideals and implementing them in a concrete situation. As Selznick states:

Doctrine, being abstract, is judiciously selective and may be qualified at will in discourse, subject only to restrictions of sense and logic. But action is concrete, generating consequences which define a sphere of interest and responsibility, together with a corresponding chain of commitments. Fundamentally, the discrepancy between doctrine and commitment arises from the essential distinction between the interrelation of ideas and the interrelation of phenomena.[19]

The fact that agencies engaged in practice must execute their programs in an arena

14 Blau and Scott, *op. cit.*, p. 73.

15 An analysis of agency records indicated that professionally oriented workers were less likely to visit clients on an agency-devised schedule than were workers oriented to the bureaucracy. *Ibid.*, pp. 73–74.

16 Marvick, *op. cit.*, pp. 77–82

17 A. W. Gouldner, "Cosmopolitans and Locals: Toward an Analysis of Latent Social Roles—I," *Administrative Science Quarterly,* 2 (December 1957), 299.

18 The separation of this area of conflict from the previous one is in many ways arbitrary and hence difficult to maintain. For example, differences in standards of evaluation utilized in the professional and bureaucratic systems have already been alluded to. In general, the distinction attempted is one between means and procedures, discussed in the section above, and goals and objectives, discussed in the present section.

19 P. Selznick, *TVA and the Grass Roots: A Study in the Sociology of Formal Organization,* (Berkeley and Los Angeles: University of California Press, 1949), p. 70.

where they are subject to past commitments and current pressures from both internal and external interest groups severely constrains their capacity to meet the ideals and standards of a particular occupational group. Another consideration is that educators are often engaged in developing and promoting innovations and generally in raising standards, and there is necessarily a time lag between the initiation and testing of new ideas and their acceptance in the programs of practicing agencies.[20]

Whereas professionals are exposed to such standards and attempts are made over a long period by persons significant to the trainees to convince them of their importance, bureaucrats are less likely to come in contact with a set of standards other than those espoused by the organization by which they are employed. The bureaucrat, possessing only partial skills, is much more likely to receive on-the-job training, which will include some indoctrination as to the proper goals and objectives of his activities. He has relatively little basis or social support for questioning the appropriateness of these objectives. The professional employee's case is quite different. He comes equipped with a set of standards shared with many if not most of his colleagues which can be used to evaluate the standards and objectives of his employer. Where the standards conflict he can marshall wide social support to countenance criticisms of or deviations from organizational policy in the directions advocated by professional standards. Such behavior is particularly troublesome for the bureaucracy and requires delicate treatment due to the prestige of professionals both within and outside the structure, the potential power of the organized professional group, and the acknowledged right of such groups to advocate and uphold their occupational standards.

Several studies report that professional workers are likely to perceive a discrepancy between the standards promulgated by their occupational groups and those adhered to by the host organization. Marvick, for example, reports that professionally oriented workers in a research organization did not feel that the agency was "doing its job better today than in the past," nor did they feel that the agency's performance was "likely to improve in the future." Workers oriented to the bureaucracy were neither as critical nor as pessimistic on the two questions.[21] In his study of intellectuals employed by labor unions, Wilensky found that those that were professionally oriented reported that their major problems stemmed from a conflict between the requirements of their job and the standards of their professional groups.[22] A study of social workers employed by a county welfare agency found that professionally oriented workers were more likely to agree with the statement that the agency has a "considerable distance to go before it can claim to be offering a fully adequate, professional welfare program," and they were more likely to believe that there is a "large" discrepancy between "professional standards and social-work theory on the one hand and the actual work performed by this agency on the other."[23] A study of physicians employed by industrial firms indicated conflicts between physicians and administrators over the goals to be served by in-plant medical facilities.[24] And Corwin found in questioning a sample of nurses about both their preferred and actual roles within hospitals that nurses who simultaneously held both strong bureaucratic and strong professional role conceptions expressed greater role discrepancy than those holding other role conceptions, indicating that the two role conceptions "prescribe opposing programs of action."[25] In addition, his data indicate that nurses trained in degree programs were more likely

[20] For another discussion of the factors causing discrepancies between standards advocated by training programs and those current in agencies, see R. G. Corwin, "The Professional Employee: A Study of Conflict in Nursing Roles," *The American Journal of Sociology*, **66** (May 1961), 604–609.

[21] Marvick, *op. cit.*, pp. 100–101.

[22] H. L. Wilensky, *Intellectuals in Labor Unions*, (Glencoe, Ill.: The Free Press, 1956), pp. 129–144.

[23] Blau and Scott, *op. cit.*, pp. 72–73.

[24] B. Goldstein, L. G. Northwood, and R. L. Goldstein, "Medicine in Industry: Problems of Administrators and Practitioners," *Journal of Health and Human Behavior*, **1** (Winter 1960), 263–265.

[25] Corwin, *op. cit.*, 611.

to hold strong professional role conceptions than nurses trained in diploma programs. Since the diploma programs were conducted entirely within hospitals while the degree programs were collegiate in nature and only loosely affiliated with hospitals, this finding points to the important role played by independent training institutions in the transmission of values and norms differing from those found in agencies engaged in practice.

THE PROFESSIONAL'S RESISTANCE TO BUREAUCRATIC SUPERVISION

Authority has very different roots in the two systems which are here being contrasted. In the bureaucratic form, authority is created by fiat: the need for bringing together the various activities which have been separated and for enforcing the rules is met in part by creating new positions which have as their major function coordination and supervision. Workers filling these positions may or may not have had experience in performing the various tasks they supervise. In either case, however, their authority does not stem primarily from their competence in the tasks being supervised but from the fact that they occupy a position which has been allocated certain supervisory rights.

Professionals are unaccustomed to such authority relations. Their own authority vis-à-vis clients or subordinate occupational groups is based on their superior competence, not on their occupancy of a particular organizational position.[26] The fact that they have acquired complete skills and have internalized norms and standards makes unnecessary the existence of workers specialized in supervision. Each worker is expected to function independently and autonomously. Although he may seek out the help of his more competent or experienced colleagues, he receives advice and counsel from them, not orders, makes his own decisions, and faces the consequences.

If the professional resists taking orders from his professional colleagues whom he considers qualified in his area of competence, how much more will he object to the orders received from persons not qualified in his speciality? Yet this is precisely the position in which he finds himself when he becomes an employee of a bureaucratic organization. Professional specialists are subject to the authority of administrators—at least in certain areas—since the latter group assumes responsibility for coordinating the efforts of all groups, adjusting the demands of one group to those of others, and directing all efforts toward the accomplishment of specified goals.

A great many studies indicate that professionals are uncomfortable with bureaucratic authority, at least to the extent of expressing dissatisfaction with supervisory arrangements and complaining about managerial "interference." An early study by Arensberg and Macgregor of an electrical equipment company found that a small group of design engineers were unhappy with supervisory arrangements, the engineers feeling that managers sometimes made decisions which were arbitrary, inconsistent, or interfered with their prerogative to make technical decisions. Managers for their part felt that the design engineers were "temperamental prima donnas" concerned with their own needs and problems and indifferent to the welfare of the company.[27] In a survey of 587 engineers and natural scientists employed in nineteen separate work groups, Moore and Renck found that, compared to the average employee, both engineers and scientists had a low opinion of the technical competence of their supervisors and of the general effectiveness of the administration.[28] Similar dissatisfactions have been found among pro-

---

[26] This widely accepted basis for distinguishing professional from bureaucratic authority was first suggested by T. Parsons, "Introduction," in M. Weber, *op. cit.*, pp. 58–60, fn. 4.

[27] C. M. Arensberg and D. Macgregor, "Determination of Morale in an Industrial Company," *Applied Anthropology*, 1 (January–March 1942), 12–34.

[28] D. G. Moore and R. Renck, "The Professional Employee in Industry," *Journal of Business*, 28 (January 1955), 58–66. Many other studies report conflict between scientists and managers. See, for example, Kornhauser, *op. cit.*, pp. 56–73; and S. Marcson, *The Scientist in American Industry: Some Organizational Determinants in Manpower Utilization* (Princeton: Industrial Relations Section, Princeton University, 1960), pp. 12–20, 73–85, 121–151.

fessionals in non-industrial settings. Becker in a study of public school teachers reports that "conflict arises when the principal ignores his teachers' need for professional independence...."[29] And Ben-David reports that physicians employed by Israeli medical care organizations showed high dissatisfaction, complaining about administrative inefficiency and interference.[30]

While empirical documentation could be extended, the studies which have been cited indicate that when professionals enter bureaucratic organizations conflicts in the area of authority relations are widespread if not ubiquitous.

THE PROFESSIONAL'S CONDITIONAL LOYALTY TO THE BUREAUCRACY

In addition to providing workers with standards and norms independent of those operating within the host organization, prolonged contact with a professional training institution will have consequences for the worker's commitment to any employer. The worker exposed to such a training program often comes to develop a professional self-image in the sense that he values his skills highly and is more concerned with getting and maintaining a reputation among his peers than he is with pleasing his organizational superiors. Such a worker tends to take an instrumental view of the organization to which he is attached: his commitment to it is conditional and depends on his evaluation of the adequacy of the organization's facilities and programs relative to others of which he has knowledge.[31]

The situation of the bureaucrat with respect to commitment to the employing organization is somewhat indeterminant. On the one hand, he is more likely to have been trained by the organization in which he is employed and may for this reason express a relatively high degree of loyalty to that organization. On the other hand, the bureaucrat has relatively few skills and is therefore less likely to be involved in his work or identified with his occupation than the professional worker. He is therefore apt to move from one *type* of work to another more readily than the professionally trained worker. There is, however, another important factor to consider in examining the difference in commitment to the employing organization between the two types of employees. Assuming that most workers wish to improve their position, then quite different mobility routes are available in the two cases. The professional advances by finding more and more desirable work locations—locations which have superior facilities and allow a maximum of freedom for him to pursue his interests. Such advancement comes chiefly by gaining recognition from his professional colleague group, since this is the body which is called upon to evaluate candidates for the various openings. The bureaucrat, however, advances by moving up in the organization's hierarchy to a more responsible position. To thus advance, he must seek to win the approval of his organizational superiors by displaying conforming behavior and by developing appropriate attitudes—including high commitment to the employer. While the professional follows his career line between organizations, the bureaucrat achieves success by moving up within a single organization.

If only professionally trained workers are considered, it is clear that workers oriented to their profession are less likely to exhibit a high degree of loyalty to a particular organization than are those not so oriented. For example, Reissman in a study of forty middle-level civil service workers found that those who were professionally oriented looked on their job as only a temporary place in which to pursue their professional interests.[32] The union intellectuals categorized by Wilensky as

[29] H. S. Becker, "The Teacher in the Authority System of the Public School," *Journal of Educational Sociology,* **27** (November 1953), 137.

[30] J. Ben-David, "The Professional Role of the Physician in Bureaucratized Medicine: A Study in Role Conflict," *Human Relations,* **11** (August 1958) 255–274.

[31] This point is elaborated in Blau and Scott, *op. cit.,* pp. 69–71.

[32] L. Reissman, "A Study of Role Conceptions in Bureaucracy, *Social Forces* 27 (March 1949), 308–309.

"professional-service types" stated that they would willingly change jobs, expressing an interest in moving to those positions where their professional skills would best be utilized. Some indicated that they would even consider company employment![33] Gouldner's study of professors in a small liberal arts college revealed that faculty members who were committed to their specialized professional skills and who were oriented to professional reference groups were more likely than those with opposite characteristics to express low loyalty to the college.[34] And the study of social workers employed by a public agency found that those who were professionally oriented were more likely than other workers to express low loyalty to their employer.[35]

Conclusion

This discussion has rather arbitrarily focused on four areas of conflict which are likely to occur when professional workers are employed by bureaucratic organizations. An attempt has been made to relate these areas of conflict to disparities in the underlying organizational principles, or to differences associated with these principles. It is important to emphasize that these conflicts exist and persist because the professions as groups inculcate their members with certain values and support them in their conflicts with the organization. It is because of these efforts on the part of professional groups that the organization is less of a free agent in dealing with this class of employees: it is in this sense that such organizations may be said to be "socially involved."

This paper has attempted only to identify

33 Wilensky, *op. cit.*, pp. 129–144.
34 Gouldner, *op. cit.*, 292–295.
35 Blau and Scott, *op. cit.*, pp. 68–69.

the areas of potential conflict. An equally important problem is to account for differences in the amount or level of conflict between professionals and their employers. Such differences are probably a complex function of several factors including the relative centrality of the functions performed by the professionals for the organization and the general prestige of the professional group. It appears that the higher the general prestige of the professional group and the more central their skills to the functioning of the organization, the more likely they are to be successful in their attempt to control the conditions under which they work, with the result that there is less actual conflict between professionals and representatives of the bureaucracy. The division of spheres of authority typically found in hospitals, clinics, and universities in which professionals assume relatively complete control over professional matters and submit to representatives of management only in administrative matters is one indication of the extent to which highly prestigious and high centrality professional groups can gain control over the conditions under which they work.[36] In such cases the amount of conflict between professionals and the bureaucracy appears to be relatively low compared to situations where the professional group either has low prestige or does not perform central functions for the organization.

36 For descriptions of such relations see M. E. W. Goss, "Influence and Authority among Physicians in an Outpatient Clinic," *American Sociological Review*, 26 (February 1961), 39–50; and B. R. Clark, "Faculty Authority," *Bulletin of the American Association of University Professors*, 47 (Winter 1961), 293–302. For a related theoretical discussion, see A. Etzioni, *A Comparative Analysis of Complex Organizations* (New York: Free Press of Glencoe, Inc., 1961), pp. 201–232.

Professional Adaptation to Organizations

Although conflicts between professionals and bureaucrats may be frequent, they are not inevitable. Many professionals apparently learn to live in complex organizations. Obviously, one way in which professionals can adapt themselves

to a bureaucratic environment is to become less professional and more bureaucratic over time, and this is what the process of socialization may accomplish
in some organizational settings.* There are other adaptation mechanisms, however, which permit professionals to live in more or less bureaucratic environments *and yet retain their professional integrity and independence.*† What is
described as research entrepreneurship in the next paper is an adaptation
mechanism of this latter type.

* An instance of this may be seen in those ostensibly professional persons who develop
  an intensely "local" orientation (i.e., organizational). This is in contrast to those who
  maintain a "cosmopolitan" orientation (where the profession at large is the reference
  group); see Armond Fields, "Eine Untersuchung über administrative Rollen," *Kölner
  Zeitschrift für Sozialogie und Sozial-psychologie,* 8, No. 1, 1956, pp. 113–123.
  † This possibility was recognized by Carr-Saunders and Wilson; see their book *The
  Professions* (Oxford: The Clarendon Press, 1933), pp. 502–503.

Howard Vollmer (Research)

Professional people are not supposed to
be concerned with money. Professional
norms emphasize the values of service to
society, rather than pecuniary gain. However, as Talcott Parsons has pointed out,
these normative distinctions do not necessarily imply a basic motivation among professionals that is any more "altruistic" than
that of business entrepreneurs.[1] Businessmen sell products or services to customers,
and professionals must sell professional
services to a clientele.[2] The success of business and professional ventures alike depends
upon the degree to which the businessman
or the professional can successfully sell his
services and/or products to a customer or
client who wants to buy them. Thus professional endeavors require *entrepreneur-*

"Entrepreneurship and Professional Productivity among
Research Scientists," a previously unpublished paper.

[1] Robert MacIver stressed differences between
business ethics and professional ethics in "The
Social Significance of Professional Ethics," *Annals of the American Academy of Political and
Social Science,* 101 (May 1922), 5–11. In contrast, Talcott Parsons emphasized similarities in
business and professional normative systems in
"The Professions and Social Structure," *Social
Forces,* 17, 1939, 457–467.

[2] Everett C. Hughes has pointed out that a
key problem in all professional normative systems
is "Who is the client?" or "Whose agent is the
professional?" See "The Professions in Society,"
*Canadian Journal of Economics and Political
Science,* 26 (February 1960), 60.

ship as much as business endeavors. This
is true both in the sense that professional
activities include the *risk of individual
failure* in obtaining client support, and also
in the sense that the "true professional"
or "journeyman-level professional" typically
must assume *individual responsibility* for
seeking out client support.

In some respects, research scientists[3] are
newcomers to the process of professionalization, at least in the United States. What
started out as loosely-organized intellectual
interests on the part of curious and inven-
tive people in various walks of life later
became established as formal scientific disciplines mostly within the somewhat
sheltered environs of academic institutions.
In such contexts, the "general public"
might be considered to constitute the
clientele for scientific outputs. This is a
diffuse clientele, however, and the relation
between scientists and the general public
does not involve requirements for each
scientist to sell a particular client or sponsor
on the value of sponsoring some specific
piece of research. In contrast, as scientists
have moved out from academic departments and have obtained employment in
industrial and governmental institutions (as
well as in university-affiliated research
institutes), there are indications that
scientists have simultaneously developed

[3] The term "scientists," as used in this paper,
includes physical scientists and engineering scientists engaged primarily in research work.

more concern with *professionalization*[4] and with *entrepreneurship*. Robert W. Avery has written in regard to the latter:

It is significant that researchers...talk about the importance of "selling an idea." They use the language of the marketplace and they emphasize that the new graduate must become fluent in two slightly different languages. The enculturated researcher reserves the esoteric vocabulary of his field largely for use with his colleagues. When he seeks to persuade his more business-oriented managers that they should share his enthusiasm for his projected work, he translates his technical abstractions into words that are less exact but more compelling to men who are not immersed, as he is, in the subtle problems of one narrow specialty. Especially, he stresses the economic potential of his idea, however remote it may be.[5]

Other observers of the process of research entrepreneurship among scientists have claimed that this process can be distracting. Thus from a study of social scientists in a university-affiliated research institute, Warren Bennis reported that preoccupations with obtaining continuity in project funding had interfered with the production of professional publications and had restricted the scientists' ability to keep up with new developments in their professional fields.[6] This previous finding has prompted the present examination and reporting of data from a continuing study of adaptations of scientists to different organizational contexts, in order to investigate further the following general questions: (1) What are the various forms that research entrepreneurship may take among scientists? (2) What are the relative frequencies of these various forms? (3) What are the characteristics of participants in research entrepre-

neurship? (4) How does entrepreneurship relate to the process of professionalization among scientists? (5) How does it relate to scientific productivity? and (6) How does it vary in different organizational contexts? The findings on these matters from our sample differ from Bennis' findings.

The study of adaptations of scientists to different organizational contexts, from which these new data are drawn, is a continuing project sponsored by the Behavioral Sciences Division of the Air Force Office of Scientific Research.[7] Space does not permit a complete description of the study design or methodology here,[8] except to point out that data have now been collected by use of standard questionnaire surveys of representative samples of research scientists, supplemented by personal interviews and observations, in the following kinds of research organizations: (1) a research laboratory attached administratively to the department of electrical engineering of a major university; (2) a research division in an aerospace company; (3) a research division of a company operating in the atomic equipment field; (4) an in-house government laboratory in the defense electronics field; and (5) a diversified independent non-profit research organization.

CATEGORIES OF RESEARCH ENTREPRENEURSHIP

We know that social roles involve more or less complementary expectations on the part of individuals who perform these roles and of those who perform significant counter-roles. Following this perspective, we have classified research entrepreneurs into four categories which represent a cross classifica-

[4] Anselm Strauss has written about the increasing concern with professionalization among scientists as they emerge from universities into nonacademic employment, in A. L. Strauss and L. Rainwater, *The Professional Scientist: A Study of American Chemists* (Chicago: Aldine Publishing Company, 1962), Chapter 12.

[5] R. W. Avery, "Enculturation in Industrial Research," *IRE Transactions of the Professional Group on Engineering Management*, **EM-7** (March 1960), 22.

[6] Warren G. Bennis, "The Social Scientist as Research Entrepreneur: A Case Study," *Social Problems*, **3**, 1955, pp. 44–49.

[7] Collaborators in this study include Albert Shapero and William Pedersen of Stanford Research Institute and Todd LaPorte of the School of Public Administration, University of Southern California.

[8] A more complete description of the findings of this study to date is contained in H. M. Vollmer, *A Preliminary Investigation and Analysis of the Role of Scientists in Research Organizations*, and *Adaptations of Scientists in an Independent Research Organization: A Case Study* (Menlo Park, Calif.: Stanford Research Institute, Reports to the Air Force Office of Scientific Research, 1962 and 1963).

tion of the entrepreneurial interests of the research scientists in comparison to the perceived degree to which management has allowed them to express this interest in their present employment context. We have been able to use responses on two standardized questionnaire items to distinguish between these four categories of entrepreneurship, which have been labeled for convenience as follows:

(1) *Satisfied entrepreneurs*—those who reported that "selling research ideas to prospective clients or sponsors" is important to them, and who also reported that they have ample opportunity to sell research ideas in their present context;

(2) *Frustrated entrepreneurs*—those who reported that selling is important to them, but who also said that they do not have adequate opportunity to do it in their present context;

(3) *Reluctant entrepreneurs*—those who said they do have opportunity to sell, but who do not consider it important for themselves;

(4) *Non-entrepreneurs*—those who rated selling as unimportant to them, and who reported that they do not have much opportunity to do it anyway.

(It may be pointed out here that research scientists in the context of the present study may be "selling research ideas to prospective clients or sponsors" who are either located *within* the organizations that employ them, or *outside* these organizations. The entrepreneurial process is similar in both cases.)

In the total sample of 617 non-supervisory research scientists in the five organizations studied to date, 227 could be classified as *satisfied entrepreneurs;* 104 as *frustrated entrepreneurs;* 171 as *reluctant entrepreneurs;* and 115 as *non-entrepreneurs.* Thus, in the total sample, the satisfied entrepreneurs predominate, followed by those who are reluctant, and the non-entrepreneurs are slightly more numerous than the frustrated ones.

This ranking of the relative frequencies of occurrence of the various types was consistent with the rankings of frequencies of types in the university research laboratory, the independent research organization, and the aerospace research division.

These were the same three organizations which interview data also indicated provide the greater amounts of inducement for entrepreneurial activity—that is, research scientists are not as likely to survive in these organizations if they are not successful in individual entrepreneurial efforts. In contrast, in both the atomic equipment research division and the government defense electronics laboratory, scientists are more likely to work on assigned research projects and to have less responsibility (though they still have *some* responsibility) for individually seeking research sponsorship. In the latter contexts, however, satisfied entrepreneurs still constituted the largest category—although frustrated entrepreneurs were second highest in frequency in the atomic research organization, and the proportion of non-entrepreneurs was unusually high in the government laboratory.

At this point in the study we do not have data that can be said to be representative of any defined populations of scientists or research organizations. Nevertheless, our data at least suggest that research entrepreneurship may be common among a large proportion of research scientists, *regardless of whether or not they are employed in an organizational context that places great emphasis upon individual entrepreneurial activity.* Whether officially condoned by organizational policy or not, entrepreneurial activities and interests are facts to be reckoned with in a variety of modern organizational settings.

CHARACTERISTICS OF ENTREPRENEURS

Who are these research enrepreneurs? Where did they come from? What are they doing now, and what do they hope to be doing in the future?

Our data at this point indicate that the *satisfied* and the *reluctant* entrepreneurs are similar to each other in that they are more likely to have higher educational qualifications(doctor's degrees)[9] and high-

[9] In this sample, the highest degrees are about evenly divided between physical science and engineering (mostly electrical engineering) fields, with a very small percentage in other fields (e.g., mathematics, social sciences, and psychology).

er experience qualifications (over five years of service with present employers and over forty years of age) than frustrated entrepreneurs. Satisfied and reluctant entrepreneurs are also more likely to be serving as research project directors and to say they are engaged in basic research (research primarily oriented toward contributing to fundamental knowledge in their research fields).

The *satisfied* and *frustrated* entrepreneurs tend to be similar in certain other characteristics, however, which differentiate these two groups from the reluctant entrepreneurs. The satisfied and frustrated entrepreneurs are more likely to have aspirations for moving into research management positions in the future and to indicate a higher degree of achievement need—i.e., to prefer "getting ahead in a job" to "having a steady job that can be depended upon."

These findings, taken together, suggest that those who are participants in entrepreneurial activities, whether they personally enjoy such activities or not, are more likely to be more highly qualified research scientists in educational and experiential respects. On the other hand, those who are especially *interested* in entrepreneurial activities, whether they are successful at them or not, are more likely to be individually ambitious. Thus, satisfied entrepreneurs tend to differ from those in all other categories by being *both* ambitious *and* highly qualified at the same time.

As might be expected, satisfied entrepreneurs are also most likely to be satisfied with their present jobs in general and are most likely to want to continue at their present place of employment. Interestingly enough, the non-entrepreneurs, although not likely to be especially highly qualified or ambitious, are about equal with the satisfied entrepreneurs in their general job satisfaction and in their intentions to remain with their present employers. This finding could indicate (1) that there are distinguishable functions or roles for both entrepreneurs and non-entrepreneurs to perform in research organizations, (2) that people can get attached to organizations and remain with them either through *suc-*

cess or through *complacency* (and, therefore, may represent an undesirable accretion over time), or (3) that both possibilities may be partly true.

Finally, we may note that, of all the groups examined here, it is the frustrated entrepreneurs who are most likely to be *dissatisfied* with their present jobs in general and to expect to seek employment in other contexts soon. These are the kinds of scientists for whom we would expect the greatest degree of conflict between individual interests and organizational constraints, which William Kornhauser and others have discussed in detail.[10]

ENTREPRENEURSHIP AND
PROFESSIONALIZATION

How does this process of entrepreneurship relate to the process of professionalization among scientists? A clue toward an answer for this question is already contained in the finding that those who say they are presently acting as entrepreneurs (whether satisfied or reluctant about it) are more likely to have more advanced educational qualifications, which is certainly one aspect of professionalization. There is additional evidence from our questionaire data to indicate that satisfied and reluctant entrepreneurs are more likely to say that they have attended professional meetings frequently and have been able to keep up-to-date on new developments in their professional fields.

In contrast, most frustrated entrepreneurs indicate that they would like to have more opportunity to attend professional meetings, but have not been able to do so as much as is desired in their present circumstances.

Thus, these data suggest that satisfied entrepreneurs are like reluctant entrepreneurs in their professional *experiences* and associational attachments, while satisfied entrepreneurs are like frustrated entrepreneurs in their professional *interests*. It is the satisfied entrepreneurs who tend to have *both* professional interests *and* ex-

10 William Kornhauser, *Scientists in Industry: Conflict and Accommodation* (Berkeley and Los Angeles: University of California Press, 1962).

	Satisfied Entrepreneurs (N = 159)	Reluctant Entrepreneurs (N = 92)	Frustrated Entrepreneurs (N = 60)	Non-Entrepreneurs (N = 67)
Professional publications produced in present organizational context				
1 or more	65%	64%	56%	54%
3 or more	44%	39%	33%	28%
5 or more	26%	24%	11%	16%
Papers read at professional meetings while at present organizational context				
1 or more	63%	66%	43%	48%
3 or more	38%	35%	18%	19%
5 or more	16%	18%	15%	7%

periences. In contrast, it is the non-entrepreneurs who appear to be lowest on both the degree to which they have attended professional meetings and the degree to which they say that this is important to them.

Entrepreneurship and Professional Productivity

Our survey data not only indicate that those who are presently acting as entrepreneurs are more likely to attend professional meetings more often, but are also more likely to produce professional publications and papers. This holds for various levels of professional productivity, as may be seen in the data reproduced below for research scientists in four of the five research organizations studied (excluding those in the independent research organization) :[11]

Thus whether scientists are satisfied or reluctant about their participation in entrepreneurial activties, such participation appears to contribute to their professional productivity. *How* entrepreneurship contributes to professional productivity is suggested by the following data showing that these same practicing entrepreneurs (both satisfied and reluctant) are much more like-

ly than frustrated entrepreneurs to say that they have been able to obtain sufficient funds to do the kind of research they want to do, and are also much more likely than *both* frustrated entrepreneurs *and* non-entrepreneurs to say that they have had a large degree of freedom in selecting their research assignments:[12]

Looking at the responses of the non-entrepreneurs on the two questions shown above, we see that the non-entrepreneurs are mostly of the opinion that they do have sufficient funds to support the kind of research they want to do, but that most of them say they do *not* have freedom to select their research assignments. In other words, we can conclude that most non-entrepreneurs are satisfied to work on research projects assigned by others. Most frustrated entrepreneurs are not. They want to work on projects of their own choosing, but, not being successful entrepreneurs, have not been able to raise sufficient funds to allow them the luxury of choice in research assignments.

Thus these findings do not bear out the generality of Bennis' conclusions from his study of a social science research organization, which indicated that entrepreneurship represents a hindrance, rather than a support, to professional productivity and par-

---

[11] Data for the scientists in the independent research organization are not included here because strictly comparable questions were not asked of them regarding their scientific productivity. However, their responses on comparable questions revealed a similar pattern to the data presented here and in the tabulations that follow.

[12] The finding that scientific productivity is associated with the adequacy of research funding and freedom to select research assignments is substantiated by Leo Meltzer's research on a nation-wide sample of physiologists; see "Scientific Productivity in Organizational Settings," *Journal of Social Issues*, 12, 1956, 33–40.

	Satisfied Entrepreneurs (N = 159)	Reluctant Entrepreneurs (N = 92)	Frustrated Entrepreneurs (N = 60)	Non-Entrepreneurs (N = 67)
Have had sufficient funds to conduct the kind of research preferred by the individual himself	70%	68%	36%	60%
Have had a large degree of freedom in selecting research projects to work on	74%	55%	14%	36%

ticipation. On the contrary, our findings suggest that research entrepreneurship can be a very important adaptation mechanism that insulates research scientists from the kinds of anti-professionalizing pressures that many observers have noted as existing in some organizational contexts where scientists are presently employed.

ENTREPRENEURSHIP IN DIFFERENT ORGANIZATIONAL CONTEXTS

This leads us to the final questions to be discussed in this paper: How does entrepreneurship vary in the different organizational contexts studied? How do such variations affect professional productivity?

It has already been pointed out that it was possible, from interview responses and general observations independent of the questionnaire data, to assess the degree to which each organization generally encouraged or required entrepreneurial activity among its scientist employees. A ranking of organizations studied from the one that encouraged or required it the most to the one that encouraged or required it the least would be as follows: (1) The university research laboratory, (2) the independent research organization, (3) the aerospace research division, (4) the atomic equipment research division, and (5) the

government defense research laboratory. This listing also presents these organizations in what appears to be the reverse order of the degree to which they are bureaucratized in their administrative structure— i.e., the government laboratory could be considered to be the most bureaucratized and the university laboratory to be the least bureaucratized.

The following tabulations of proportions of research scientists in each organizational context who have produced one or more professional publications while in their present context shows consistently that satisfied entrepreneurs were the most likely to have produced publications, although the differences in productivity between satisfied entrepreneurs and those in other categories were quite small in some contexts:

Further examination of the differences between the proportions of publications-producing scientists in the satisfied entrepreneurial category (in which we would generally expect to find the largest proportion of producing scientists) and the proportion of publications-producing scientists in the non-entrepreneurial category (in which we would more often expect to find the smallest proportion of producing scientists) reveals that the differences are largest in those organizations that place more emphasis upon individual research

Those who have produced 1 or more papers in:	(1) Satisfied Entrepreneurs	(2) Reluctant Entrepreneurs	(3) Frustrated Entrepreneurs	(4) Non-entrepreneurs	Diff. (1) − (4)
University research lab.	88% (18)	64% (11)	(Not enough cases)	43% (7)	45%
Independent research org.	51% (68)	39% (79)	23% (44)	25% (48)	26%
Aerospace research div.	72% (46)	66% (30)	50% (16)	64% (14)	8%
Atomic equip. res. div.	69% (16)	56% (9)	64% (11)	50% (8)	19%
Government research lab.	59% (68)	57% (37)	50% (30)	56% (36)	3%

entrepreneurship as an organizational *requirement* (the university research laboratory and, to a somewhat lesser extent, the independent research organization). Conversely, the differences are smallest in the organization that appears to place the least emphasis upon the importance of individual entrepreneurship (the government research laboratory).

These findings lead us to hypothesize that individual entrepreneurial activity can be expected to be associated with markedly increased professional productivity among scientists *only in those organizational contexts that are less bureaucratized* and that place more emphasis upon entrepreneurship as an organizational requirement. One might speculate even further regarding the extent to which industrial and governmental research organizations will become less bureaucratized and more permissive with regard to entrepreneurial activities among scientists, so that industrial and governmental laboratories begin to look somewhat more like university laboratories in the future.

A Concluding Comment

Therefore, it appears that scientists are not necessarily at the mercy of the organizations that employ them, as some literature on this topic might imply. Insofar as scientists can seek out and establish a clientele to support their individual research interests, it appears that they can thereby preserve their professional autonomy and capabilities—whether they be employed in a university, industry, government, or independent research organization. In this regard, "selling one's services" can be a professionally enhancing, rather than degrading, activity. Research entrepreneurship is an important adaptation mechanism that can support productive scientific activities within a variety of organizational environments.

Organizational Adaptation to Professionals

The last paper pointed out that it is in universities that we can expect entrepreneurship to have its most important consequences for professional staff members. This is understandable when one also takes into account the fact that, with regard to organizational structure, universities are generally among the most professionalized employers of professional people. Universities attempt to adapt their organizational structure to the needs of professional staff members, rather than requiring professional staff members to adapt to pre-existing bureaucratic requirements of the employing organization.*

However, in actuality, universities are not completely professionalized in the form of their organization. Instead, as the following paper by Burton Clark points out, their structure might better be described as a form of "federated professionalism," along with "segmentation" and "individualization." Clark's analysis leads us to speculate about the degree to which industrial corporations, government agencies, and other types of organizations which employ increasing numbers of professionals in the future may increasingly adopt the principles and structure of "federated professionalism."

---

* Corwin has found that university-affiliated nursing training hospitals are able to provide greater autonomy for graduate nurses (with attendant minimal role conflict) than are the nursing training hospitals without such affiliation; see Ronald G. Corwin, "The Professional Employee: A Study of Conflict in Nursing Roles," *The American Journal of Sociology,* 66 (May 1961), 604–615.

Burton R. Clark (College Teaching)

As we participate in or study various faculties in American higher education, we observe decisions being made through informal interaction among a group of peers and through collective action of the faculty as a whole. Formal hierarchy plays little part, and we have reason to characterize the faculty as a collegium.[1] At the same time we sense that what we now observe is not a counterpart of the collegiality of the days of old. The modern faculty in the United States is not a body to be likened to the guilds of the medieval European university,[2] or to the self-government of a dozen dons in a residential college at Oxford or Cambridge,[3] or to the meagre self-rule that was allowed the faculty in the small liberal arts college that dominated American higher education until the end of the last century.[4] The old-time collegium has modern reflections, as in the Fellowships of the colleges at Yale, but for the most part it is no longer winningly with us, and the kind of collegiality we now find needs different conceptualization. We also observe on the modern campus that information is communicated through formal

Reprinted from "Faculty Organization and Authority," *The Study of Academic Administration*, Terry F. Lunsford (ed.) (Boulder, Colo.: Western Interstate Commission for Higher Education, 1963), pp. 37–51. Used by permission.

1 A major type of collegiality is that involving collegial decision: "In such cases an administrative act is only legitimate when it has been produced by the cooperation of a plurality of people according to the principle of unanimity or of majority." Max Weber, *The Theory of Social and Economic Organization*, A. M. Henderson and Talcott Parsons, (trans.) (New York: Oxford University Press, 1947), p. 400.

2 Hastings Rashdall, *The Universities in Europe in the Middle Ages*, T. M. Powicke and A. B. Emden (eds.) (Oxford: Clarendon Press, 1936), three vols.

3 C. P. Snow, *The Masters* (New York: The Macmillan Company, 1951).

4 Richard Hofstadter and Walter P. Metzger, *The Development of Academic Freedom in the United States*, (New York: Columbia University Press, 1955); George P. Schmidt, *The Liberal Arts College* (New Brunswick, New Jersey: Rutgers University Press, 1957).

channels, responsibility is fixed in formally-designated positions, interaction is arranged in relations between superiors and subordinates, and decisions are based on written rules. Thus we have reason to characterize the campus as a bureaucracy. But, at the same time, we sense that this characterization overlooks so much that it becomes misleading. Though the elements of bureaucracy are strong, they do not dominate the campus; and though they grow, their growth does not mean future dominance if other forms of organization and authority are expanding more rapidly.

The major form of organization and authority found in the faculties of the larger American colleges and universities, and toward which many small campuses are now moving, is now neither predominantly collegial nor bureaucratic. Difficult to characterize, it may be seen as largely "professional," but professional in a way that is critically different from the authority of professional men in other organizations such as the business corporation, the government agency, and the hospital. To approach this unusual pattern, we will first discuss trends in the organization and culture of the campus as a whole and then turn to the related trends in the organization and authority of the faculty.

We begin with broad changes in the nature of the campus because they condition the structure of authority. Authority is conditioned, for example, by the nature of work, the technology of an organization. The mass assembly of automobiles does not allow much personal discretion on the part of the worker; surgery in the hospital operating room requires on-the-spot judgment and autonomous decision by the surgeon and one or two colleagues. To understand faculty authority, we need some comprehension of what academic work has in common with work in other settings and how it differs from work elsewhere. Authority is also conditioned by patterns of status. Status comes in part from formal assignment, hence men called deans usually have much of it, but status is also derived in academia from one's standing in a discipline, and this important source of status is independent of the official scheme.[5] Authority is also conditioned by traditional sentiments. Legends and ideologies have a force of their own. Conceptions of what should be are formed by what has been or by ideals handed down through the generations. The stirring ideologies of community of scholars and academic freedom are forces to be reckoned with when one is dealing with faculties and in understanding their organization. Thus, the work itself, the status system, the traditional sentiments, all affect authority.

Trends in the Social Organization of the Campus

Four trends in the campus, closely related, are as follows: unitary to composite or federal structure; single to multiple value systems; nonprofessional to professional work; consensus to bureaucratic coordination.

Unitary to Federal Structure

The history of American higher education is a history of movement from unitary liberal arts colleges to multi-structured colleges and universities. The American college of 1840 contained a half dozen professors and fifty to a hundred students;[6] in 1870, average size was still less than 10 faculty and 100 students. All students in a college took the same curriculum, a "program of classical-mathematical studies inherited from Renaissance education."[7] There was no need for subunits such as division and department; this truly was a unitary structure. In comparison, the modern university and college is multi-structured. The University of California at Berkeley in 1962–63, with over 23,000 students and 1,600 "officers of instruction," was divided into some 15 colleges or schools (e.g., College of Engineering, School of Public Health); over 50 institutes, centers,

and laboratories; and some 75 departments (including Poultry Husbandry, Romance Philology, Food Technology, and Naval Architecture). In three departments and three schools, the subunit itself contained over 50 faculty members. Such complexity is not only characteristic of the university: a large California state college contains 40 or so disciplines, grouped in a number of divisions; and even a small liberal arts college today may have 20 departments and three or four divisions.

The multiplication of subunits stems in part from increasing size. The large college cannot remain as unitary as the small one, since authority must be extensively delegated and subsidiary units formed around the many centers of authority. The subunits also stem from plurality of purpose; we have moved from single- to multi-purpose colleges. Goals are not only more numerous but also broadly defined and ambiguous. Those who would define the goals of the modern university speak in such terms as "preserving truth, creating new knowledge, and serving the needs of man through truth and knowledge."[8] The service goal has a serviceable ambiguity that covers anything from home economics for marriage to research and development for space. A tightly integrated structure could not be established around these goals. Organizational structure accommodates to the multiplicity of goals by dividing into segments with different primary functions, such as liberal arts and professional training, scientific research and humanistic education. The structure accommodates to ambiguity of goals with its own ambiguity, overlap, and discontinuity. We find some liberal arts disciplines scattered all over the campus (e.g., satistics, psychology), residing as components of professional schools and of "other" departments as well as in the appropriately-named department. No neat consistent structure is possible; the multiple units form and reform around functions in a catch-as-catch-can fashion. Needless to say, with a multiplicity of ambiguous goals and a variety of subunits, authority is extensively decentralized. The structure

[5] Logan Wilson, *The Academic Man* (New York: Oxford University Press, 1942); Theodore Caplow and Reece J. McGee, *The Academic Marketplace* (New York: Basic Books, Inc., 1958).

[6] Hofstadter and Metzger, *op. cit.*, pp. 222–223.

[7] *Ibid.*, p. 226.

is federal rather than unitary, and even takes on some likeness to a loosely-joined federation.

Single to Multiple Value Systems

Most colleges before the turn of the century and perhaps as late as the 1920's possessed a unified culture that extended across the campus,[9] and this condition still obtains in some small colleges of today. But the number of colleges so characterized continues to decline and the long-run trend is clear: the campus-wide culture splits into subcultures located in a variety of social groups and organizational units. As we opened the doors of American higher education, we admitted more orientations to college—college as fun, college as marriage, college as preparation for graduate school, college as certificate to go to work tomorrow, college as place to rebel against the Establishment, and even college as a place to think. These orientations have diverse social locations on campus, from fraternity house to cafe espresso shop to Mrs. Murphy's desegregated rooming house. The value systems of the students are numerous.

The faculty is equally if not more prone to diversity in orientation, as men cleave to their specialized lines of work and their different perspectives and vocabularies. Faculty orientations differ between those who commit themselves primarily to the local campus and those who commit themselves primarily to their farflung discipline or profession; between those who are scientists and those who are humanists; between those who think of themselves as pure researchers or pure scholars and those who engage in a professional practice and train recruits. The value systems of the faculty particularly cluster around the individual disciplines and hence at one level of analysis there are as many value systems as there are departments.

Nonprofessional to Professional Work

Intense specialization characterizes the modern campus; academic man has moved from general to specific knowledge. The old-time teacher—Mr. Chips—was a generalist. He covered a wide range of subject-matter, with less intensity in any one area than would be true today, and he was engaged in pure transmission of knowledge. In the American college of a century ago, the college teacher had only a bachelor's degree (in the fixed classical curriculum), plus "a modest amount of more advanced training, perhaps in theology..."[10] There was no system of graduate education, no reward for distinction in scholarship, and the professor settled down into the groove of classroom recitation and the monitoring of student conduct. We have moved from this kind of professor, the teacher generalist, to the teacher of physics, of engineering, of microbiology, of abnormal psychology, and to the professor as researcher, as consultant, as professional-school demonstrator. We have moved from transmission of knowledge to innovation in knowledge, which has meant specialization in research. Taking the long view, perhaps *the* great change in the role of academic man is the ascendance of research and scholarship—the rise of the commitment to create knowledge. This change in the academic role interacts with rapid social change: research causes change, as in the case of change in technology and industrial processes; and such changes, in turn, encourage the research attitude, as in the case of competition between industrial firms, competition between nations, competition between universities. In short, the research component of the academic role is intimately related to major modern social trends.

In his specialism, modern academic man is a case of professional man. We define "profession" to mean a specialized competence with a high degree of intellectual content, a specialty heavily based on or involved with knowledge. Specialized competence based on involvement in knowledge is the hallmark of the modern professor. He is pre-eminently an expert. Having special knowledge at his command, the professional worker needs and seeks a large degree of autonomy from lay control and normal organizational control. Who is the best judge of surgical procedure—laymen, hospital administrators, or surgeons? Who

9 Hofstadter and Metzger, *op. cit.*; Schmidt, *op. cit.*

10 Hofstadter and Metzger, *op. cit.*, p. 230.

is the best judge of theories in chemistry—laymen, university administrators, or professors of chemistry? As work becomes professionalized—specialized around esoteric knowledge and technique—the organization of work must create room for expert judgment, and autonomy of decision making and practice becomes a hallmark of the advanced profession.

Not all professional groups need the same degree of autonomy, however. Professionals who largely give advice or follow the guidelines of a received body of knowledge require extensive but not great autonomy for the individual and the group. They need sufficient leeway to give an honest expert opinion or to apply the canons of judgment of their field. Those requiring great autonomy are those who wish to crawl along the frontiers of knowledge, with flashlight or floodlight in hand, searching for the new—the new scientific finding, the new reinterpretation of history, the new criticism in literature or art. Academic man is a special kind of professional man, a type characterized by a particularly high need for autonomy. To be innovative, to be critical of established ways, these are the commitments of the academy and the impulses of scientific and scholarly roles that press for unusual autonomy.

Consensual to Bureaucratic Coordination

As the campus has moved from unitary to composite structure, from single to multiple systems of values, from general to specialized work, it has moved away from the characteristics of community, away from "community of scholars." A faculty member does not interact with most other members of the faculty. In the largest places, he may know less than a fifth, less than a tenth. Paths do not cross. The faculty lounge is no more, but is replaced by coffee pots in dozens of locations. The professor retains a few interests in common with all others, such as higher salaries, but he has an increasing number of interests that diverge. Even salary is a matter on which interests may diverge, as men bargain for themselves, as departments compete for funds, as scientists are paid more, through various devices, than the men of the humanities.

In short, looking at the total faculty, interaction is down, commonality of interest is down, commonality of sentiments is down. With this, coordination of work and policy within the faculty is not so much now as in the past achieved by easy interaction of community members, by the informal give-and-take that characterizes the true community—the community of the small town where everyone knows nearly every one else, or the community of the old small college where the professors saw much of everyone else in the group. The modern campus can no longer be coordinated across its length and breadth by informal interaction and by the coming together of the whole. Informal consulting back and forth is still important; the administration and the faculty still use the lunch table for important business. But campus-wide coordination increasingly moves toward the means normal to the large-scale organization, to bureaucratic means. We appoint specialists to various areas of administration, give them authority, and they write rules to apply across the system. They communicate by correspondence, they attempt to make decisions fairly and impartially by judging the case before them against the criteria of the rulebook. Thus we move toward bureaucratic coordination, as the admissions officer decides on admissions, the registrar decides on the recording of grades, the business officer decides proper purchasing procedures, and various faculty committees decide on a wide range of matters, from tenure to travel funds to the rules of order for meetings of an academic senate.

In sum: the campus tends toward composite structure, toward a multiplicity of subcultures, toward intense professionalism, and toward some bureaucratic coordination.

CHANGE IN FACULTY ORGANIZATION AND AUTHORITY

The organization and authority of the faculty accommodate to these trends in at least three ways: by segmentation, by a federated professionalism, and by the growth of individual power centers.

Segmentation

As campuses increase in size, complexity, and internal specialization, there is less chance that the faculty will be able to operate effectively as a total faculty in college affairs, less as the governmental body we have in mind when we speak of a community of scholars. The decision-making power and influence of the faculty is now more segmented—segmented by sub-college, by division, and particularly by department. Since the interests of the faculty cluster around the departments, faculty participation in government tends to move out to these centers of commitment. Who selects personnel, decides on courses, and judges students? The faculty as a whole cannot, any more than the administration. Indeed, as departments and professional schools grow in size and complexity, even they often do not; it is a wing of the department or a part of the professional school that has most influence. A liberal arts department that numbers 40 to 80 faculty members may contain six or eight or a dozen specialties. The day has arrived when a department chairman may not even know the name, let alone the face and the person, of the new instructors in "his" department.

What happens to the governmental organs designed for the faculty as a whole? They move in form from Town Hall to representative government, with men elected from the various "states" coming together in a federal center to legislate general rules, which are then executed by the administration or the faculty committees that constitute an administrative component of the faculty. With the move to representative government, there is greater differentiation in participation: a few "actives" participate a great deal; a considerably larger group constitutes an alert and informed public and participates a modest amount; the largest group consists of those who are not very interested or informed and who participate very little. The structure of participation parallels that found in the larger democratic society, and

apparently is normal to a representative mass democracy. The situation is, of course, vexing to those who care about faculty government.

Professionalization

The authority of the faculty which flows out toward the departments and other units of the campus becomes located in the hands of highly specialized experts; and, as suggested earlier, takes on some characteristics of professional authority. Almost everywhere in modern large-scale organizations, we find a tug-of-war going on between administrative and professional orientations. In the hospital, the basic conflict in authority lies between the control of the non-medical hospital administrator and the authority of the doctors. In industry, a fascinating clash is occurring between management and the scientist in the research and development laboratory.[11] The fantastic expansion of research and development has brought over 400,000 scientists and engineers into industry, there to be committed to innovation and to the development of new inventions to the point of practical utility. Many of these technologists have a high degree of expertise, a strong interest in research—often "pure" research—and they press for a large degree of freedom. Their fondest wish is to be left alone; they make the point that in scientific work it seems rational to do just that, that basic discoveries stem not from managerial direction but from the scientist following up his own initial hunches and the leads he develops as he proceeds. Management has found such men difficult to deal with; their morale suffers easily from traditional forms of management, and they present unusual demands on management to change and accommodate. In this situation, professional authority and bureaucratic authority are both necessary, for each performs an essential function: professional authority protects the exercise of the special expertise of the technologist, allowing his judgment to

[11] See William Kornhauser, *Scientists in Industry: Conflict and Accommodation* (Berkeley: University of California Press, 1962); and Simon Marcson, *The Scientist in American Industry* (New York: Harper & Row, Publishers, 1960).

be pre-eminent in many matters. Bureaucratic authority functions to provide coordination of the work of the technologists with the other major elements of the firm. Bureaucratic direction is not capable of providing certain expert judgments; professional direction is not capable of providing the over-all coordination. The problem presented by the scientist in industry is how to serve simultaneously the requirements of autonomy and the requirements of coordination, and how to accommodate the authority of the professional man and his group of peers to the authority of management and vice versa.[12]

The professional-in-the-organization presents everywhere this special kind of problem. He gains authority, compared to most employees, by virtue of his special knowledge and skills; he loses authority, compared to a man working on his own, by virtue of the fact that organizations locate much authority in administrative positions. The problem of allocation of authority between professionals and bureaucrats does, however, vary in intensity and form in different kinds of organizations. As mentioned earlier, advisers and practitioners need a modest degree of authority, while scientists and academics have perhaps the highest requirements for autonomy to engage in research, in unfettered teaching, and in scholarship that follows the rules of consistency and proof that develop within a discipline.

The segmentation of the faculty into clusters of experts gives professional authority a special form in academic organizations. In other situations, there usually are one or two major professional groups within the organization who, if they are influential, substitute professional control for administrative control. This occurs in the case of medical personnel in the hospital who often dominate decision making. The internal controls of the medical profession are strong and are substituted for those of the organization. But in the college or university this situation does not obtain; there are 12, 25, or 50 clusters of experts. The experts are prone to identify with their own disciplines,

and the "academic profession" over-all comes off a poor second. We have wheels within wheels, many professions within a profession. No one of the disciplines on a campus is likely to dominate the others; at a minimum, it usually takes an alliance of disciplines, such as "the natural sciences" or "the humanities," to put together a bloc that might dominate others. The point is that with a variety of experts—chemists, educationists, linguists, professors of marketing—the collective control of the professionals over one another will not be strong. The campus is not a closely-knit group of professionals who see the world from one perspective. As a collection of professionals, it is decentralized, loose, and flabby.

The principle is this: where professional influence is high and there is one dominant professional group, the organization will be integrated by the imposition of professional standards. Where professional influence is high and there are a number of professional groups, the organization will be split by professionalism. The university and the large college are fractured by expertness, not unified by it. The sheer variety of the experts supports the tendency for authority to diffuse toward quasi-autonomous clusters. Thus, faculty authority has in common with professional authority in other places the protection of individual and group autonomy. It is different from professional authority in other places in the extremity of the need for autonomy and in the fragmentation of authority around the interests of a large variety of groups of roughly equal status and power. The campus is a holding company for professional groups rather than a single association of professionals.

Individualization

When we speak of professional authority we often lump together the authority that resides with the individual expert and the authority that resides with a collegial group of experts. Both the individual and the group gain influence at the expense of laymen and the general administrator. But what is the division of authority between the individual and the group? Sometimes group controls can be very tight and quite hierarchical, informally if not formally, as young doctors learn in many hospitals, and as assistant professors learn in many departments. The personal authority of the expert varies widely with the kind of establishment, and often with rank and seniority. The campus is a place where strong forces cause the growth of some individuals into centers of power. We will review several of these sources of personal authority.

First, we have noted the expertise of the modern academy. The intense specialization alone makes many a man into king of a sector in which few others are able to exercise much judgment. Thus, *within* a department, men increasingly feel unable to judge the merits of men in specialties they know nothing about. The technical nature of the specialized lines of work of most academic men, then, is a source of personal authority. If we want to provide a course on Thomas Hardy, we are likely to defer on its content to the judgment of the man in the English Department who has been knee-deep in Hardy for a decade. The idea of such a course would really have been his in the first place; Hardy falls within his domain within the English Department, and his judgment on the need for the course will weigh more than the judgment of others.

Second, some professorial experts now have their personal authority greatly enhanced by money. Despite his location within an organization, the professor in our time is becoming an entrepreneur. It used to be that the college president was the only one on campus, other than an enterprising and dedicated member of the board of trustees, who was capable of being an entrepreneur. Many of the great presidents were great because they were great at coming home with the loot—adventurers who conquered the hearts and pocketbooks of captains of industry and then with money in hand raided wholesale the faculties of other institutions. Presidents who can raise money and steal faculty are still with us, but they have been joined by professors. Kerr has suggested that the power of the individual faculty member is going up while the power of the collective faculty is going down because the individual as researcher, as scholar, and as consultant relates increas-

ingly to the grant-giving agencies of the Federal government and to the foundations.[13] He has direct ties to these major sources of funds and influence; indeed, he participates in their awarding of grants and even has problems of conflict of interest. A professor-entrepreneur, by correspondence and telephone and airplane trips, lines up money for projects. He sometimes arranges for the financing of an entire laboratory; occasionally he even brings back a new building. Even when the professor does little of the arranging, it is *his* presence that attracts these resources. He represents competence, and the grant-givers pursue competence.

The entrepreneurial activity and resources-gaining influence of professors, which extends down to assistant professors in the social as well as the natural sciences, has had remarkable growth since World War II, and the personal autonomy and power thus achieved in relation to others in the university is considerable. A professor does not have to beg postage stamps from a departmental secretary nor a two hundred dollar raise from the department chairman nor travel money to go to a meeting from a dean or a committee if he has monies assigned to him to the tune of $37,000, or $175,000, or $400,000. His funds from outside sources may be called "soft" funds, in the jargon of finance, but they are hard enough to hire additional faculty members and assistants, to cover summer salaries, and to provide for travel to distant, delightful places.

The following principle obtains: a *direct* relation of faculty members to external sources of support affects the distribution of influence within the campus, redistributing influence from those who do not have such contacts to those who do, and moving power from the faculty as a whole and as smaller collectivities to individual professors. In the university of old, members of the faculty achieved a high degree of influence by occupying the few professorial positions available in a structure that narrowed at the top. Their source of influence was structural and internal. The source of great

[13] Kerr, *op. cit.*

influence in the modern American university is less internal and less tied to particular positions; it is more external and more tied to national and international prestige in a discipline, and to contact with the sources of support for research and scholarship that are multiplying and growing so rapidly.

The individualization in faculty organization and authority excites impulses in the faculty and the administration to establish some collective control, for much is at stake in the balance of the curriculum, the equality of rewards in the faculty, and even the character of the institution. But the efforts at control do not have easy going. Collective bodies of the faculty and the administration are hardly in a position, or inclined, to tell the faculty member he can have this contract but not that one, since the faculty member will define the projects as part of his pursuit of his own scholarly interests. When the faculty member feels that this sensitive right is infringed, he will run up the banners of academic freedom and inquiry, or he will fret and become a festering sore in the body politic of the campus, or he will retreat to apathy and his country house, or he will make it known in other and greener pastures that he will listen to the siren call of a good offer.

Third, personal authority of the professorial expert is increased in our time by the competitiveness of the job market. The expansion of higher education means a high demand for professors, and the job market runs very much in the professor's favor in bargaining with the administration. His favorable position *in* the market enhances his position *on* campus. He can demand more and get it; he can even become courageous. In the world of work, having another job to go to is perhaps the most important source of courage.

To recapitulate: faculty organization and authority tends in modern times to become more segmented, more professional in character, and somewhat more individualized. We are witnessing a strong trend toward a federated structure in colleges and especially in universities—with the campus more like an United Nations and less like a small town—and this trend affects faculty

authority by weakening the faculty as a whole and strengthening the faculty in its many parts. Faculty authority becomes less of a case of self-government by a total collegium, and more of a case of authority exercised department by department, subcollege by sub-college. The *role* of faculty authority is shifting from protecting the rights of the entire guild, the rights of the collective faculty, to protecting the autonomy of the separate disciplines and the autonomy of the individual faculty member.

Faculty authority in our time tends to become professional authority in a federated form. We have a loose alliance of professional men. The combination of professional authority and loosely-joined structure has the imposing function of protecting the autonomy of the work of experts amidst extensive divergence of interests and commitments. The qualities of federation are important here. The federation is a structure that gives reign to the quasi-autonomous, simultaneous development of the interests of a variety of groups. Within an academic federation, a number of departments, divisions, colleges, professional schools, institutes, and the like can coexist, each pushing its own interests and going its own way to a rather considerable extent. Professional authority structured as a federation is a form of authority particularly adaptive to a need for a high degree of autonomous judgment by individuals and subgroups.

This trend toward a federation of professionals is only part of the story. To hold the separate components of the campus together, we have a superimposed coordination by the administration, and, as Kerr has suggested, this coordination increasingly takes on the attributes of mediation.[14] The administration attempts to keep the peace and to inch the entire enterprise another foot ahead. The faculty, too, in its own organization, also counters this divisive trend with a machinery of coordination. The very fact of a diffusion of authority makes the faculty politician more necessary than ever, for the skills of politics and diplomacy are

14 *Ibid.*

needed. There must be faculty mediators; men who serve on central committees, men with cast iron stomachs for lunch table discussions and cocktail parties, men who know how to get things done that must be done for the faculty as a whole or for part of the faculty. There must be machinery for setting rules and carrying them out impartially across the faculty. The modern campus is, or is becoming, too large and complicated for collegial or professional arrangements to provide the over-all coordination, and coordination is performed largely by bureaucratic arrangements—e.g., the rulebook, and definite administrative domains.

Federated professionalism within an organization, like many other trends, thus promotes counter-trends. Specialization and individualization seriously weaken the integration of the whole. The weakness of collegiality or professionalism in the large organization, as suggested earlier in the case of industry, is that it cannot handle the problem of order, it cannot provide sufficient integration. Thus the above trends in faculty organization and authority open the door to bureaucracy—more bureaucracy in the administration, more within the faculty itself. The modern large faculty, therefore, combines professionalism, federated structure, and bureaucracy—perhaps in a mixture never before evidenced in human history.

This combination of what seem contradictory forms of organization perplexes observers of academia. Is the faculty collegial? Yes, somewhat. Is it split into fragments? Yes, somewhat. It is professional? Yes, somewhat. Is it unitary? Yes, somewhat. Is it bureaucratic? Yes, somewhat. Different features of the faculty strike us according to the occurrences of the week or the events we chance to observe. The ever-mounting paperwork firmly convinces us that the campus is doomed to bureaucratic stagnation. The fact that the president often gets what the president wants convinces us that he really has all the authority. The inability of a campus to change a department that is twenty years behind in its field convinces us that departmental autonomy has run amok and the campus is lacking in leadership and in capacity to keep up with the times. One observer will see the campus as a tight ship, the next will speak of the same campus as a lawless place where power lies around loose. No wonder we are confused and no wonder that outsiders are so often even more confused or more irrelevant in giving advice.

But in the combination of forms of organization and forms of authority that we find today within the campus and within the faculty itself, there are certain trends that are stronger than others and certain features that tend toward dominance. The society at large is tending to become a society of experts, and the campus has already arrived at this state. Expertise is a dominant characteristic of the campus, and organization and authority cluster around it. Because of its expertness, together with its ever-growing size, the faculty moves away from community, moves away from collegiality of the whole. The faculty moves toward decentralized or federated structure, and authority moves toward clusters of experts and the individual expert. Thus professional authority tends to become the dominant form of authority, and collegial and bureaucratic features fall into a subsidiary place. In short, when we say college, we say expert. When we say expert, we say professional authority.

The Interdependence of Professions and Organizations

So far, our emphasis in this chapter has been upon the relations between individual scientists and employing organizations. We have seen how conflicts between bureaucratic and professional roles can arise and can be alleviated. But an important question remains: *need* these conflicts arise and *need* they be alleviated?* Is it possible for professional persons and complex organizations to exist apart from each other in modern society? Some answers to such questions are provided by William Kornhauser in the following conclusions from a study of scientists in industry. He points out that complex organizations and professions are *of necessity interdependent*. Adaptation between the two institutional forms is a basic requirement of our advanced technological society.

* Divergent answers are provided by R. J. Hill, "The Sociologist in the Industrial Position: An Opinion" and D. L. Mills, "The Sociologist in the Industrial Position: Another Opinion," *Sociological Inquiry*, 31, No. 2, 1961, pp. 150–166.

William Kornhauser (Research)

This study has sought to analyze strains and accommodations between professions and organizations. Fundamental problems arise as a result of the transformation of professional work from an activity conducted primarily by separate individuals on a relatively small scale to an activity increasingly carried on by professional groups in large organizations. This change has produced a wide gap between older images and newer forms of the professions, and has raised new problems concerning the effectiveness and consequences of the new forms.

The theme of *autonomy versus integration* of professional activity in organizations recurs throughout this study. It is the central problem posed by the interdependence of professions and organizations. The case of professional scientists in industry reveals the strains between autonomy and integration. Associated with functional autonomy is the emphasis on free inquiry, scientific standards, research creativity, and responsibility to the scientific community. Associated with functional integration is the emphasis on research organization, administrative standards, research utility, and responsibility to the organization. *Professionalism has as its primary function the protection of standards for creative activities; organization has as its primary function the efficient coordination of diverse activities.* Professionalism is a response to

the need for functional autonomy engendered by the special character of social action that places a premium on intellectual judgment. It is embodied in a set of standards governing the training and assimilation of people in roles specialized to creative work. Bureaucracy is a response to the need for rational coordination engendered by the complex interdependence of specialized activities. It is embodied in a set of rules and offices governing communication and control among the diverse participants in a common enterprise.

Problems arise when both needs exist in the same area of activity, as they increasingly do. For the combining of professionalism with bureaucracy entails certain contradictory principles. We have tried to analyze concrete manifestations of the contradictions that arise when scientific research is instituted in complex organizations. In doing so, we have sought to overcome the limitations of two common perspectives in the literature. Students of the professions have tended to treat the need for functional autonomy of professions as the primary requirement; they see only the negative consequences of bureaucracy for professionalism. Thus they generally fail to analyze the profession's need for organizational resources and its contributions to the goals of organizations. On the other side, students of organizations have tended to stress the need for integrating professional groups in organizations.[1] They generally fail

Reprinted from *Scientists in Industry: Conflict and Accommodation*, a publication of the Institute of Industrial Relations, University of California (Berkeley and Los Angeles: University of California Press, 1962), pp. 195–197. Used by permission.

[1] A recent example is Tom Burns and G. M. Stalker, *The Management of Innovation* (London: Tavistock Publications, 1961).

to analyze the negative consequences of organizational pressures for professional values and performance.

In the nature of the case, science has the greater need for autonomy, and industry has the greater need for integration. Therefore, industrial scientists develop mechanisms of autonomy, and industrial managers develop mechanisms for the integration and control of scientists. However, since science is dependent on industry for resources, and industry is dependent on science for innovation, there are strong pressures for the accommodation of their interests.

The scientist's problem is to gain *access* to the organization without becoming *available* for manipulation by the organization. The professional identity and the professional group make the individual scientist unavailable for total participation in the organization. But since the organization requires the services of scientists, it puts pressure on them to participate; for example, it seeks to summon the loyalty of scientists and to entice them into a career in the organization. However, the very dependence of the organization on scientists tends also to make it accessible to scientists, as manifested in their claims on the budget, participation in

the formulation of research policy, and the like. At the same time, the scientist's participation in the organization is *regulated* by the profession; therefore it is *limited* participation. Where participation is mediated by partly autonomous relations, and where at the same time there is access to the organization, the system tends to acquire a *pluralist* character. This means that there are multiple centers of power. The organization does not wholly absorb professionals, nor do professionals wholly absorb the organization. To the extent that a system of relations is pluralist, it tends toward a balance of freedom and power or, in functional terms, between the conditions conducive to creativity and those conducive to control. We are not suggesting that such an equilibrium in fact obtains among research, production, administration, and other functions in industrial (or other) organizations. What we are suggesting is that *the tension between the autonomy and integration of professional groups, production groups, and other participants tends to summon a more effective structure than is attained where they are isolated from one another or where one absorbs the others.*

Questions for Discussion and Further Research

This chapter began with a discussion of conflicts between bureaucratization and professionalization, as related by Scott, and ended with a description by Kornhauser of the functional interdependence of the two processes in modern society. In between these two papers, we saw how some individuals in highly professionalized occupations assume the initiative to express professional interests within the context of bureaucratic organizations (in the Vollmer paper) and how some organizations adapt themselves to the needs of professional personnel (in the Clark paper). Both papers illustrate, in different ways, Kornhauser's conclusion that "the tension between the autonomy and integration of professional groups...and other participants tends to summon a more effective structure than is attained where they are isolated from one another or where one absorbs the others." Both papers also illustrate Everett Hughes' statement in his paper in Chapter 2 that "employing organizations, as well as occupations, can also become more professionalized."

Although we can begin to see why, and how, the professionalization of employing organizations occurs from our readings in this chapter, we need further research and thought to be able to describe systematically how, and in what respects, this process takes place. Certainly, the employment of more professional people—salaried professionals—is not enough; there must be fundamental changes in the structure of the organization itself for us to be able to speak in a meaningful way of professionalization as an organizational attribute.

Current studies by the editors of this volume are suggesting some ways in which employing organizations become more professionalized—developments which may be seen in research organizations, for example, whether they occur in university, government, or industrial contexts. These changes involve at least three main facets: organizational structure, performance evaluation, and the use of incentives for personnel recruitment and retention. Highly professionalized organizations have a characteristically more decentralized decision-making structure with regard both to the initiation and day-to-day conduct of research projects and programs and to the translation of research findings into useful applications within larger institutional contexts. More and more research organizations are adopting techniques for measurement of both the quantity and the quality of research outputs (e.g., through the counting of research publications and subsequent citations and through the calculation of ratios of publications in high stature media to these in low stature media) in ways that attempt to accommodate to professional value systems. In addition, greater numbers of professionalized research organizations are using non-monetary professional incentives—challenge in work and opportunity for independent investigation—to attract and retain highly capable professional personnel. Perhaps most important is a growing tendency toward tailoring jobs to fit individual professional capabilities and interests, rather than hiring personnel in professional categories to fit the pre-specified requirements of job positions.*

It may be noticed that such developments do not represent any drastic reversal in rational bureaucratic elements of organization, but they do represent organizational accommodations to professional interests. There are many studies on how such accommodations also occur in hospitals, teaching institutions, religious institutions, and other organizations that employ large numbers of professional people but, as yet, we do not have an adequate systematic theory of organization to account for the new organizational forms themselves. What are their essential characteristics? Under what conditions are these characteristics likely to emerge? What factors inhibit their emergence?

---

* The development of all these tendencies within one federal government research organization is described in H. M. Vollmer, *Applications of the Behavioral Sciences to Research Management: an Initial Study in the Office of Aerospace Research* (Menlo Park, Calif.: Stanford Research Institute, a report to the Air Force Office of Aerospace Research, 1964).

9

Professionals and the Government

Perhaps the most complex and most significant organizations to which professionals inevitably become related in some way are the various government agencies. This appears to be the case in all modern nation-states. Lewis and Maude have explored certain relationships of six broad categories of "professions" (each classified according to the degree of "State control") to various levels of government in Great Britain. At one extreme are those professional occupations where "public authorities possess a complete monopoly of employment" (e.g., civil servants and the military), and at the other, "a group of callings in which the volume of public employment is very small and which are at the same time comparatively free from direct State control" (e.g., theologians and most journalists). This analysis led to the conclusion that:

> ...the number of professions in which public authorities neither directly regulate practice nor possess a substantial influence as potential employers proves on examination to be startlingly small. Even more startling is the precariousness of the freedom which most of these appear to possess.*

Where are such fundamental social changes leading us? These authors deplore what they see as the trend and point to alleged examples of governments allowing "poor salaries, poor conditions of work and second-rate qualifications in staffs."† Moreover there is overspecialization and even, perhaps, excessive "professionalism." As a further consequence, Lewis and Maude state that"...increased dependence on the State results in a progressive lowering of the social and economic status of a profession."‡ Together, then, they claim that these

---

* Roy Lewis and Angus Maude, *The English Middle Classes* (New York: Alfred A. Knopf, Inc., 1950), p. 183.
† *Ibid.*, p. 187.
‡ *Ibid.*, p. 197.

events have led to a "dilution" of the professions, an undermining of the middle class, and a resultant challenge to traditional ways of life.

But is this all there is to be said about professionals and the government? Not at all. As was pointed out in the readings of Chapters 1 and 2, professional groups tend to perform important functions for the larger society, and it follows that the governing bodies of larger societies always tend to take a special interest in the way professional groups perform these functions. Therefore, it is understandable that community or societal legitimatization and control is ordinarily imposed formally upon professional groups in the advanced stages of professionalization.§ Legal regulation has attendant problems, as it is necessary to balance adequate control with the preservation of sufficient professional autonomy.** True professionals are distinguished from quacks, phonies, and illegitimate practitioners of various trades by means of professional certification, which often takes the form of professional licenses granted and policed by appropriate government agencies.††

Governments not only attempt to control and regulate the activities of professional groups in the public interest, but professionalized groups and individuals also attempt to influence the activities of governments. Professionals may do this, in part, by becoming employees of government agencies,‡‡ and in part, by participation in political movements and parties. In fact, certain leading professional groups sometimes form the most powerful organized pressure groups influencing government decisions and policy in modern societies. The relations of governments, as organized agencies representing public interests, to professional groups and associations, as organized agencies representing certain specialized occupational interests, is certainly a two-way street.§§ And whether this relationship works more to the advantage of the general public or to the advantage of the special occupational group concerned may be a moot question in many societal contexts.

The following readings provide examples of the influence of governmental regulations upon professional activities and the influence of organized professional groups upon governmental decisions and policies. Advantages and disadvantages of both kinds of influence are also discussed.

---

§ The attitudes of one important professional association toward some of these governmental measures may be seen in "The American Medical Association: Power, Purpose and Politics in Organized Medicine," *The Yale Law Journal*, 63, No. 7, 1954, 997–1017. A more recent Canadian example is presented by M. C. Shumiatcher, *Assault on Freedom—Reflections on Saskatchewan's Medical Care Crisis* (Regina: Saskatchewan K.O.D. Association, 1962).

** This process has been termed "closure" by A. M. Carr-Saunders and is discussed in his *Professions; Their Organization and Place in Society* (Oxford: The Clarendon Press, 1928), pp. 21–26. Also see A. M. Carr-Saunders and P. A. Wilson, "Professions," in *The Encyclopaedia of the Social Sciences*, XII, February 1934, p. 479.

†† Some implications of licensure for teaching are explored in articles appearing in the *California Teachers Association Journal*, 56, No. 6, November 1960.

‡‡ See C. Ray Jeffery, *et al.*, "The Legal Profession" in E. J. Davis, *et al.*, *Society and the Law* (Glencoe, Ill.: The Free Press, 1962), pp. 326–327.

§§ Some time ago Carr-Saunders detailed instances where "The State turns to professional associations for advice and assistance." (See A. M. Carr-Saunders, *op. cit.*, pp. 17–18.) Today countless examples exist of such interdependency, and as is noted in some of the selections to follow, professional associations are often delegated quasi-governmental authority.

Licensing of Professionals

Countries vary in the ways in which they grant formal public recognition to different professional groups. This is especially true for newer and emerging professional groups, in contrast with the more traditionally recognized professional categories. The following section of a paper by Alexander King describes differences in licensing and other means of formal recognition of professional engineers in different countries, indicating how such differences affect labor markets in larger, international economic units, such as the European Common Market.

Alexander King (Engineering)

Political and economic trends in Europe are towards larger markets, larger units of production, greater concentration of research and design effort, lower tariff walls between individual countries and greater mobility of labor. These movements are themselves partly the result of scientific and engineering developments which have produced a complex technology offering efficiency and prosperity but demanding operations on a scale unknown in Europe until recently. It is probable that labor mobility within an economically integrated Europe will first become an important flow at the extremes of qualifications—untrained labor from underdeveloped to industrialized countries on the one hand, and skilled professional engineers, scientists and managers on the other. If this is true, it becomes obvious that top managements of large firms and governments will require to know more and more about the levels of education in neighboring countries, criteria for professional recognition and the reputations of various universities and technical colleges. It is for this reason, for example, that F.E.A.N.I. is already concerning itself with the problem of accrediting the schools of engineering of different countries with their very varied standards, methods of both theoretical teaching and practical experiences and lengths of instruction.

The EUSEC report is essentially a factual

Reprinted from "Criteria for Professional Recognition," *De Ingenieur, Algemeen Gedeelte,* 42 (19 October 1962), 557–558. Used by permission.

survey of the various systems of education and training for engineers in operation in the member countries and wisely does not attempt critical appraisal of the systems as such or of quality within the systems. The present meeting does however give an opportunity for a certain amount of discussion of the relevance of particular systems to contemporary conditions. The first part of the present paper seeks to analyze the section of the report concerning criteria for professional recognition, while its second part outlines some of the problems inherent in the present trends.

The information concerning the criteria for professional recognition was collected through a questionnaire sent to member countries and is to be found in Section E of the report (page 71 onwards of Volume II) which calls for the following remarks:

(i) Volume II of the report is intended as a comparative study of engineering education and training in EUSEC and O.E.E.C. member countries. As regards Section E, such comparison has to be drawn by the reader himself since it sets out in succession a summary of the replies received from the various countries. The only basis for comparison is the table on pages 82 and 83 which summarizes the answers to the questionnaire.

(ii) The answers to the first series of questions on the *definition of a professional engineer* show that two countries only have a strictly legal definition of the professional engineer— Spain and the United States, while five countries (Denmark, Germany, Switzerland, the United Kingdom, and the United States) reply that there exist accepted definitions given by the profession itself. It seems therefore that in the majority of countries surveyed, the status of the professional engineer is defined neither rigidly nor very clearly. This contrasts with the strict regulations prevailing in the same countries for some other professions such as law, medicine, etc.

(iii) *Legal regulation of professional practice.* In five countries only—Belgium, Greece, Italy, Spain and the United States—is the practice of engineering regulated by law, whereas in most of them the right to practice legally is conferred only upon receipt of a degree or diploma. Under the same heading an additional question was asked concerning the possibility of practicing engineering without any specific requirement. Most countries, with the exception of four—Greece, Italy, Turkey and the United States—answered affirmatively. However, in the case of two countries—Belgium and Spain— there seems to be some contradiction between their answers to this question and to the two preceding ones: they state that the profession is regulated by law and that the right to practice is legally conferred upon receipt of a diploma and, at the same time, that anyone may legally practice without any specific requirements.

(iv) As regards the practice of engineering by corporations, companies and partnerships, there is an affirmative answer from all countries with the exception of Italy.

(v) In all countries with the exception of Belgium from which there is no reply, the criterion for professional recognition is graduation from an engineering college or the passing of a certain examination. It seems therefore that in the majority of countries the requirement to practice is only professional and not legal. This is the case in Austria, Denmark, Finland, France, Germany, Ireland, the Netherlands, Norway, Sweden, Switzerland, and Turkey.

(vi) As regards practical training required for professional recognition, there are still countries where no such condition seems to exist—Belgium, France, Greece, Norway, Spain and Turkey. It would thus appear that in many countries the obtaining of a degree or the passing of a theoretical examination is deemed sufficient to qualify as a professional engineer and presumably therefore that the experience gained through practice is not officially a credit for qualification as such.

(vii) In countries where a certain amount of practical work is required to qualify as a professional engineer, there is a great variation in the length of the period—from sixteen weeks in the Netherlands to seven years in the United States. In fact, the information as set out in table VI of the report is, at first sight, somewhat misleading, in that the various periods mentioned cannot correspond to the same goal. The seven years in the United States correspond to the practice necessary to be eligible for the higher grades of a professional society (a graduate from an engineering college is eligible straight-away for membership in a society). In contrast, the sixteen weeks in the Netherlands correspond to a compulsory period of practical training in industry and form part and parcel of the curriculum at the Technische Hoge-scholen and there is, in fact, no other practical experience for recognition. Among the various systems described for official recognition of professional engineers, those prevailing in the United Kingdom and the United States are the only ones where both academic degrees and practical experience are fully taken into account. A full member of a British Institution is, for instance, sure to have a recognized engineering degree or equivalent theoretical education and several years of practical experience *as a professional engineer.*

(viii) In all countries recognized professional engineers are awarded a special title. At this stage, a comment should be made which underlies most of the substance of the rest of this paper—namely that the title of professional engineer once awarded, remains valid for life. There is no country reporting the possibility of an engineer being deprived of his title or being required or even encouraged to ensure that his qualifications remain valid. It follows therefore that there is no clearcut official or professional method of assessing whether an engineer who has been recognized as of professional status many years before, has kept his proficiency up to date in terms of evolving technology and user requirements. The EUSEC definition does, however, contain an implicit recognition of the need to maintain qualifications up to date (Volume II, page 71) when it says *inter alia* that "His (the engineer's) education will have been such as to make him capable of closely and continuously following progress in his branch of engineering science by consulting newly published work on a world-wide basis, assimilating such information and applying it independently." The special title which exists in all countries is evidence of full and up-to-date proficiency.

We know of course that the EUSEC definition, as with most definitions, is an ideal one and that all professional engineers do not satisfy every part of it, especially ten or fifteen years after being awarded the title of professional engineer, simply because of the speed of technological change, the pressure of their normal work and the shift of many engineers to positions of managerial responsibility, which, while not necessarily demanding detailed engineering competence, are particularly well fitted by those who have received a good engineering education.

The outcome of these and other circumstances is that in spite of the initial formal professional recognition conferred to some engineers, there are many indications of a certain degree of *de facto* "demotion":

(a) many instances exist where a professional engineer is actually doing less qualified work, especially after a certain age;

(b) the "market value" of young graduates as compared to engineers in their forties is out of proportion to what would normally be the case.

Because young graduates are aware of the latest developments of engineering science and technique, they are offered salaries that not only cannot be justified in terms of their experience, but cannot be followed up as the young men grow in their profession and inevitably possess a more and more tenuous contact with newest developments. This may well lead to frustration. It should be realized, however, that many firms are compelled to put a high preference on young graduates in contrast to the more experienced engineers to be found either on the market or in their own staff, since the latter have not always kept in touch with recent developments in science and technology.

This leads us to ponder on the fragility of the regulations defined by man in his desire to secure stability of status and employment which, in practice, if not in an outspoken way, are being demolished by evolving conditions. We have now entered the era of moving structures and the only realistic way of tackling the problem of professional recognition is to take a dynamic view.

The Politics of Professionals

The following previously unpublished paper by S. M. Lipset and Mildred Schwartz reviews a wide variety of studies in different countries that indicate certain common patterns in the political participation of professional persons. Since they generally tend to represent privileged and satisfied strata in society, professionals are more often conservative than liberal in their political tendencies. There are considerable differences in the political attitudes and behavior of various substrata within the general professional category in many countries, however, as the review indicates. As might be expected, professionals seem to be little different than other men in this regard: where they see their interests to be in accord with the perceived interests of the "establishment" in a society, they tend to support the status quo; where they perceive a divergence of occupational interests from the interests of the ruling classes, professionals are likely to seek ways and means to promote social and political change.

S. M. Lipset and Mildred A. Schwartz (General)

The professional occupations have played a crucial role in political life since the beginning of modern politics. By virtue of

"The Politics of Professionals," a previously unpublished paper. Used by permission.

their skills professional persons have increasingly formed the political elite, both as influential participants and as leaders of political parties.[1] The major role which

[1] Evidence for this has been accumulated from different countries, different types of communities, and periods of time. See for example Harold D. Lasswell, Daniel Lerner, and C.

professionals play in political life would, in itself, justify a systematic examination of the forces which affect political behavior and opinion within this group. In addition to being political leaders and influential persons and constituting a sizeable section of the electorate, professionals are among the best organized occupational groups. As such, they have the capacity to serve as major interest groups which channel political communication and affect political decisions.[2]

Easton Rothwell, *The Comparative Study of Elites, An Introduction and Bibliography* (Stanford: Stanford University Press, Hoover Institute Studies, Series B, No. 1, 1952), p. 30; Donald R. Matthews, *The Social Backgrounds of Political Decision Makers* (New York: Doubleday & Company Inc., 1954); Paul F. Lazarsfeld, Bernard Berelson, Hazel Gaudet, *The People's Choice* (New York: Columbia University Press, 1948), p. 50; Julian L. Woodward and Elmo Roper, "Political Activity of American Citizens" in Heinz Eulau, S. J. Eldersveld, M. Janowitz (eds.), *Political Behavior* (Glencoe: Free Press, 1956), p. 136; Robert E. Agger and Vincent Ostrom, "Political Participation in a Small Community" in Eulau, *et al.* (eds.), *op. cit.*, p. 139; John Meisel, *The Canadian General Election of 1957* (Toronto: University of Toronto Press, 1962), p. 132; Mattei Dogan, "Political Ascent in a Class Society: French Deputies 1870–1958," in Dwaine Marvick (ed.), *Political Decision-Makers* (New York: The Free Press, 1961), pp. 63–82 and "L'Origine sociale du personnel parlementaire francaise en 1951" in Maurice Duverger (ed.), *Parties politiques et classes sociales* (Paris: Librairie Armand Colin, 1955), especially Table A, p. 328; D. E. Butler, *The British General Election of 1959* (London: The Macmillan Company, 1960), p. 127; William Kornhauser, *The Politics of Mass Society* (Glencoe: The Free Press, 1959), pp. 183–185.

[2] For comments on this aspect of the political power of professionals see William J. Goode, "Community Within a Community: The Professions," *American Sociological Review*, 22, 1957, 195. See also Malcolm G. Taylor, "The Role of the Medical Profession in the Formulation and Execution of Public Policy," *Canadian Journal of Economics and Political Science*, 26. 1960, 125; A. M. Carr-Saunders and P. A. Wilson, *The Professions* (Oxford: Clarendon Press, 1928), p. 27; "The American Medical Association, Power, Purpose, and Politics in Organized Medicine," *Yale Law Journal*, 63, 1954, 937–959; V. O. Key, Jr., *Public Opinion and American Democracy* (New York: Alfred A. Knopf, Inc., 1961), pp. 125 and 545.

GENERAL POLITICAL BEHAVIOR

With the exception of the men who own and operate large businesses, professionals as a group are probably the most privileged and satisfied stratum in the society. Their superior position is demonstrated by a variety of indicators:

1. Studies of occupational prestige in a number of countries reveal that, while there are wide variations in prestige within the stratum and even within specific occupations, the professions are accorded more prestige by the general public than any other occupational category.[3]

2. Professionals as a group receive higher pay than any other occupational groups except for the owners and managers of large businesses.[4]

3. It is not surprising, then, that given their high income and occupational prestige, professionals are more likely to place themselves in the middle and upper classes than any other stratum other than owners or top executives of large business.[5]

4. Probably because they provide more autonomy, freedom for personal decision, and creativity than other occupations, those in professional occupations have been found to exhibit a high degree of job satisfaction.[6]

Collectively, these factors contribute to the expectation, upheld by studies in the various stable democracies of western Eu-

---

[3] National Opinion Research Center, "Jobs and Occupations: A Popular Evaluation" in Reinhard Bendix and S. M. Lipset (eds.), *Class, Status and Power* (Glencoe: The Free Press, 1953), pp. 412–414; Alex Inkeles and Peter Rossi, "National Comparisons of Occupational Prestige," *The American Journal of Sociology*, 61, 1956, 329–339.

[4] United States Bureau of the Census, *Statistical Abstract of the United States; 1960* (Washington, D. C.: G.P.O. 1960), p. 325.

[5] Richard Centers, *The Psychology of Social Classes* (Princeton: Princeton University Press, 1950), p. 86; for France, data supplied by Natalie Rogoff from a study conducted by I.N.E.D.

[6] See, for example, Donald Super "Occupational Level and Job Satisfaction," *Journal of Applied Psychology* 23, 1939, 550; Nancy C. Morse and Robert Weiss, "The Function and Meaning of Work," *American Sociological Review*, 20, 1955, 198.

rope and the English-speaking nations, that professionals tend to be among the more conservative elements in society, using conservative in Rossiter's sense of satisfaction with the status quo and opposition to change.[7] The chief exceptions to this generalization occur in nations in which political conservatism is identified with traditionalism or religion and in which certain types of higher education are associated with anti-clericalism or anti-traditionalism, as in some of the Latin countries of Europe or the developing nations of the "third world" and Japan.

Variations Among Professions

The major concern of this paper is not with the general political behavior of professional groups, but with the sources of internal variation. We will consider internal variation as arising from two sources. The first of these stems from social stratification variables and pertains to the rewards associated with a given status. The second deals with professional values as these affect political orientations.

Stratification Variables

The same gross factors which affect political behavior generally can be expected to operate among professionals as well. For example, those professionals who receive higher pay, higher prestige, live in smaller communities and are members of dominant ethnic groups can be expected to be more conservative than their opposites.[8] However, our concern here is more particularly with the causes of differences among pro-

fessionals which are more distinctive of the entire professional class, rather than being characteristic of only the middle and upper class in general. We state these as a number of hypotheses which the data allow us to illustrate, but which still require further research.

I.1. By virtue of the specialized and prolonged training and the high level of commitment associated with professional occupations, professionals are more likely to feel frustrated when faced with limited job opportunities and to express this frustration in political protest. Schumpeter, in fact, has even argued that higher education in itself, particularly when it does not lead to the acquisition of technical skills, may produce political discontent.[9] University students, in that they are aspiring professionals, are especially exposed to constricted opportunities in times of economic depression. They are thus more prone at these periods to support extremist political movements than are other segments of the middle class.[10] But those already established in a profession also suffer from external circumstances—those imposed either by general economic factors or by the demands of their clientele. For example, studies of the Nazi movement in Germany suggest that a disproportionate percentage of the leadership came from professionals who had either been unemployed for long periods of time, or could not find satisfactory employment

---

[7] Clinton Rossiter, *Conservatism in America* (New York: Alfred A. Knopf, Inc., 1955), pp. 4–9. For evidence on voting behavior see John Bonham, *The Middle Class Vote* (London: Faber and Faber, 1954), p. 129; Angus Campbell, Gerald Gurin, and Warren E. Miller, *The Voter Decides* (Evanston Ill.: Row, Peterson & Company, 1954), pp. 72–73.

[8] The most comprehensive effort to isolate stratification differences among the various middle-class occupational groupings in Britain reports a large difference in support for the Labor party between higher and lower professions. The

former are those such as doctor and lawyer which require "long and expensive training," while the latter are those such as nurse, journalist, primary school teacher, and the like. In the three elections studied between 1945 and 1951, about 25 per cent of the lower professionals voted Labor, while about one-half voted Tory. Among the higher professional group, Labor's support dropped from 15 per cent in 1945 to but 6 per cent in 1951, while the Conservatives increased from 58 to 78 per cent. Bonham, *op. cit.*, pp. 134–135, 144–146.

[9] Joseph Schumpeter, *Capitalism, Socialism, and Democracy* (New York: Harper Torchbooks, 1960), pp. 152–153.

[10] Kornhauser, *op. cit.*, pp. 187–188; Karl D. Bracher, *Die Auflösung der Weimarer Republik* (Stuttgart: Ring Verlag, 1955), pp. 146–149; *Monthly Public Opinion Survey* of the Indian Institute of Public Opinion, Aug. 1955.

commensurate with their own self conceptions.[11]

I.2. Those who have been forced to enter a second-choice occupation are more likely to show higher degrees of discontent than those who have reached their original aspirations, and this is revealed in a propensity to back radical parties. In our previous hypothesis, discontent was related to difficulties of achieving a satisfactory position within a profession, while here it is with not being able to enter a preferred profession. Unfortunately most occupational studies do not focus simultaneously on career choice and political orientation. For example, studies of students of dentistry, pharmacy, and physiology indicate that a considerable proportion would have preferred to enter another profession, that of medicine.[12] We have no knowledge, however, of the political orientation of these groups beyond some early data on party registrations of American pharmacists, which indicated that they were the most Democratic of all professional categories with the exception of musicians.[13] More comprehensive data are available on librarians and teachers. For the former, it was found that almost half stated that librarianship was not their first career choice during their last year in college. While no attempt is made to correlate career choice with political choice, the same study also indicates that 17 per cent of the total listed

third party candidates as their choice for president in the 1948 election.[14]

The hypothesis that second-choice professional occupations are disproportionately represented among protest parties has also been advanced with regard to elementary school teachers—in particular among the men in these occupations. This appears to be the case particularly where teachers are young men who have been unable to attend normal school or have failed in other occupations, yet who could not expect to advance beyond their original position without increasing their educational qualifications. This has been found to be the case for Communist school teachers in pre-war Japan.[15] These conditions suggest three empirical consequences: (1) primary school teachers should be more likely to back radical parties than secondary school teachers; (2) primary school teachers should be more likely to back such parties than other professionals; (3) among primary school teachers, male teachers should be more likely to support such parties than women. Since in many European countries men, at any given occupational level, are more radical than women, the difference between the sexes within the primary school groups should be even greater than is found in the population as a whole. While data are far from conclusive, they tend to support these generalizations when the political behavior of teachers is examined in Britain, Germany, France, Belgium, the Netherlands, Norway, Sweden, and to some extent the United States.[16]

In suggesting that those in second-choice professions will reveal a disproportionate degree of occupational frustration and dis-

[11] See Walter M. Kotschnig, *Unemployment in the Learned Professions; an International Study of Occupational and Educational Planning* (London: Oxford University Press, 1937), especially pages 117–119, and 175; Daniel Lerner, *The Nazi Elite* (Stanford: Stanford University Press, 1951), pp. 32–33; Konrad Heiden, *Der Führer* (Boston: Houghton Mifflin, 1944), pp. 28–29.

[12] D. More and Nathan Kahn Jr., "Some Motives for Entering Dentistry," *The American Journal of Sociology,* 66, 1960, 48–53. Howard S. Becker and James Carper, "The Elements of Identification with an Occupation," *American Sociological Review,* 21, 1956, 346; Thelma H. McCormack "The Druggist's Dilemma: Problems of a Marginal Occupation," *The American Journal of Sociology,* 61, 1956, p. 312.

[13] H. D. Anderson and P. E. Davidson, *Ballots and the Democratic Class Struggle* (Stanford: Stanford University Press, 1943), p. 119.

[14] Alice I. Bryan, *The Public Librarian, A Report of the Public Library Inquiry* (New York: Columbia University Press, 1952), p. 119. A report of presidential choice is contained in a mimeographed version of the study.

[15] Nobutaka Ike, *The Beginning of Political Democracy in Japan* (Baltimore: Johns Hopkins Press, 1950), pp. 215–216.

[16] Stein Rokkan, "Party Preferences and Opinion Patterns in Western Europe: A Comparative Analysis," *International Social Science Bulletin,* 7, 1955, 575–596; Ernest Havemann and Patricia S. West, *They Went to College* (New York: Harcourt Brace, 1952), p. 113.

position to back political parties opposed to the status quo, we do not suggest that this will necessarily result in a greater vote for the radical left; the tension may also be reflected in support for the radical right. Thus Rudolfe Heberle explicitly suggested such a source of motivation for Nazi support in Germany.[17]

In discussing second-choice occupations as one of the principal sources of occupational frustration among professionals, several qualifications are in order. Specifically, these concern the feelings of relative deprivation which those in second-choice professions have in evaluating themselves. Thus, a second-choice occupation, which is in itself highly rewarded in terms of income and prestige, may be sufficient to mitigate practitioners' feelings of frustration. This may also be related to the profession's recruitment base. Those professions which recruit disproportionately from such disadvantaged groups as ethnic minorities, lower social classes, and those with rural backgrounds, may represent considerable achievement for such people and thus again allay feelings of discontent.[18]

I.3. The main locales of employment and the circumstances attendant on these appear to affect the professional's political orientation. The popular conception of the professional is that of the self-employed practitioner, although this has never been completely true—currently the self-employed are in a rapidly declining minority. In addition to self-employment, the professional may be found in industry, government, universities and various non-profit organizations. In order to evaluate the political implications of each of these locales of employment we need to consider first of all how they affect recruitment. For example, in the United States, while the profession of law is presumably open to all those with the requisite technical qualifica-

tions, this is not the case of the most highly prestigious and lucrative specialties within the law. Instead of being employed by financially secure large law firms with important business connections, such minority groups as women are more likely to find employment with the government, while Negroes and those of second-generation immigrant background may make a precarious livelihood as their own employers.[19] Other indications of how social characteristics affect employment opportunities come from studies of the American medical profession where, although trend data indicate that physicians have been recruited from a broader social class base over the past fifty years,[20] those medical professionals of lowly evaluated ethnic and class backgrounds are not as likely to practice in the most advantageous hospitals.[21] Other professionals with similar backgrounds are more often recruited by trade unions than by industry.[22] While none of these studies give the political affiliation of the professionals, other sources indicate that the most conservative professionals are those employed by business.[23] For the others, where lack of employment by business presents a limitation of opportunity, this limitation, par-

---

[17] *From Democracy to Nazism* (Baton Rouge: Louisiana State University Press, 1945), pp. 84–85.

[18] See for example Becker and Carper, *op. cit.*, for a discussion of how physiology students, who had often wanted to become doctors originally, saw their present career choice as a notable advancement over their lower or lower-middle class background.

[19] C. Ray Jeffery with the collaboration of E. Eugene Davis and Henry H. Foster, Jr., "The Legal Profession," in F. J. Davis, *et al.* (eds.), *Society and the Law* (New York: The Free Press, 1962), pp. 319–320. Some evidence on the increase of favorable opportunities for Jewish lawyers is continued in Erwin O. Smigel, "The Impact of Recruitment on the Organization of the Large Law Firm," *American Sociological Review*, 25, 1960, p. 51. See also Reports of the Columbia Law School Bureau of Applied Social Research Metropolitan Lawyer Study.

[20] Stuart Adams, "Trends in Occupational Origins of Physicians," *American Sociological Review*, 18, 1953, pp. 404–409.

[21] David N. Solomon, "Ethnic and Class Differences Among Hospitals as Contingencies in Medical Careers," *The American Journal of Sociology*, 66, 1961, pp. 463–471.

[22] Harold L. Wilensky, *Intellectuals in Trade Unions* (Glencoe: Free Press, 1956), especially pp. 266–268.

[23] Havemann and West, *op. cit.*, p. 113. Data derived from secondary analysis of the *Time* magazine study of college graduates revealed that 78 per cent of the social workers voted Democratic in 1944. These data are the same as used by Havemann and West, *op. cit.*

ticularly where it occurs in combination with low prestige class and ethnic backgrounds, might be expected to contribute to opposition to the status quo and thus make for greater support for radical parties.

Where one works will also affect exposure to social problems and hence to political solutions to these problems. The most notable example in this regard is found among social workers. Leftist voting was found to be most pronounced among public assistance workers in France,[24] while in the United States one study found them to be strongly pro-labor.[25] Related to this point is the nature of the professionals' clientele.[26] Dependence on a privileged clientele is likely to lead, as in the case of the professional employed by business or finding the major part of his practice among business men, to take on the political attitudes of his clients. A similar response may occur among other professionals who have, like the social workers, less advantaged clients. An illustrative case history of this phenomenon may be found in the life of Victor Adler, founder of the Austrian Socialist Party, who began his career as a physician working among the poor of Vienna.[27]

Different employers may hold out different kinds of rewards, and in this way contribute to the professional's sense of satisfaction or frustration which may then bear

on his political views. Industry may serve as such a satisfaction-inducing employer by providing very extended channels for mobility even into the upper echelons of management. In other cases, however, any employer, whether industry or government, may foster frustration by offering only limited rewards for the professionally-oriented.[28] Some of this frustration may be overcome where professionals can identify strongly with the objectives of the organization for which they are working. Thus professionals employed by government may become responsive to the extension of governmental activities as a concomitant of their own employment position. For example, a study of the attitudes of British physicians toward various proposals for state provision for medical care completed prior to the introduction of socialized medicine found that medical practitioners employed by the government or other public bodies were much more favorable to the various proposals than were those in private practice.[29] Similar results are indicated in a survey of American college graduates which found that physicians in private practice were much more likely to be Republicans than those who were salaried.[30]

Also related to the kinds of rewards which different types of employers provide are the patterns of authority which result for professionals. Basically, the question is whether the employer permits professional autonomy in relation to training and practice, a condition which has been considered essential in defining an occupation as a profession,[31] or whether the employer him-

24 Report prepared by the Mutual Security Agency.

25 Norman Polansky, William Bowen, Lucille Gordon, Conrad Nathan, "Social Workers in Society: Results of a Sampling Study," *Social Work Journal*, **34**, 1953, pp. 74–80.

26 Angus Campbell, Phillip E. Converse, Warren E. Miller, Donald E. Stokes, *The American Voter* (New York: John Wiley & Sons, Inc., 1960), p. 482.

27 Albert Fuchs, *Geistige Stroemungen in Oesterreich* (Wien: Globus, 1949), p. 99; Jacques Hannak, *Im Sturm eines Jahrhunderts* (Wien: Wiener Volksbuchhandlung, 1952), p. 51. In an account of recent changes in medical training in Latin America, it was stated that the medical schools were first being depoliticized. Yet, because of new concerns with upgrading scientific qualifications and working with economically depressed groups, it is likely that these will have implications for the politics of the doctors. Gabriel Valazquez Palau, "New Generation in Public Health," *World Health*, **14**, September–October 1961), 32–34.

28 See for example, Bernard Goldstein, "Unions and the Professional Employee," *The Journal of Business*, **27**, 1954, 268–275.

29 See for example, Harry H. Eckstein, "The Politics of the British Medical Association," *The Political Quarterly*, **26**, 1959, 345–359. See also *Supplement to the British Medical Journal*, London, August 5, 1944, The British Institute of Public Opinion. "The White Paper and the Questionary."

30 Data from a secondary analysis of material collected by *Time* magazine in a 1947 survey of American college graduates.

31 Ernest Greenwood, "Attributes of a Profession," in Sigmund Nosow and William H. Form (eds.), *Man, Work and Society* (New York: Basic Books, Inc., 1962), pp. 209–210.

self exerts ultimate control over these matters. While presumably these are mainly problems for the employed professional, they may even affect the self-employed. Such would be the case where State licensing agencies attempt to control professional activities in ways not completely to the liking of the profession. This control may also be exerted by the clientele. Ordinarily they do not have the requisite knowledge to do this, but in the case of groups such as engineers, clients often have sufficient experience to influence specific individuals even more strongly than the profession.[32] But more prominently, it is those professions who are employed, particularly when one employer has a monopoly over the use of a particular profession, who are most subject to employer control.[33] Whether subject to this monopoly or not, the professional in a bureaucracy often finds himself in conflict with the standards of his employer.[34] Where these lines of authority are experienced as unsatisfactory, they may result in a desire on the part of professionals to alter these, and this alteration may involve some attraction to political liberalism, or even radicalism.

Thorstein Veblen, in his famous discussion of engineers, argued that a basic cleavage exists between the pecuniary norms of modern capitalism and standards of engineering excellence, which would ultimately push many engineers to support leftist politics.[35] Although this expectation has not been fulfilled, and there is a variety of evidence which indicates that engineers are among the most conservative of professionals in America and France, there are also data which indicate that some engineers do experience the conflict Veblen discussed, and that it does lead some of them to join trade unions.[36] A survey which compared the minority of engineers who favor trade unions with those opposed reveals that men who report themselves working for companies employing over 100 engineers are more likely to be pro-union, as are those who say much of their work is "detail" rather than "creative."[37]

While there is no evidence of any significant leftist tendency among engineers in any industrially developed country, it may be argued that the support given to technocratic and Fascist movements by engineers during the 1930's validates Veblen's assumptions that they are predisposed to oppose private capitalism. The Nazis and other fascist parties distinguished between "predatory" (banking and finance) and "productive" or industrial capital.[38] The available evidence suggests that the Nazi party received disproportionate backing from graduate engineers, and that among university students, it had strongest appeal

[32] Goode, *op. cit.,* p. 197.

[33] See, for example, Roy Lewis and Angus Maude, *The English Middle Classes* (London: Phoenix House Ltd., 1952), pp. 162–164.

[34] For a comprehensive discussion of this point see W. Richard Scott, "Professionals in Bureaucracies—Areas of Conflict," in this volume. See also the sources he cites.

[35] Thorstein Veblen, *The Engineers and the Price System* (New York: B. W. Huebsch, 1921), pp. 70–75; see also James Burnham, *The Managerial Revolution* (New York: The John Day Company, Inc., 1941).

[36] On the politics of American engineers compared to other professions see S. M. Lipset, *Political Man* (New York: Doubleday, 1960), pp. 315–316, and William Kornhauser, *Scientists in Industry* (Berkeley: University of California Press, 1962), pp. 151–152; on the politics of French engineers see Francois Jacquin, *Les Cadres de l'industrie et du commerce en France* (Paris: Armand Colin, 1955), p. 191 and Dogan, *op. cit.,* p. 298; on factors related to unionization of American engineers see Goldstein, *op. cit.,* pp. 268–275. On some of the frustrations of engineers see Opinion Research Corporation, *What is Troubling Industry's Engineers* (Princeton: 1956), *The Conflict Between the Scientific and the Management Mind* (Princeton: 1959).

[37] *Opinion Research Corporation, op. cit.* (1956), p. A-39. However, only 18 per cent of the entire sample were pro-union, so that the large majority in every category were opposed to engineers joining such organizations. Detailed analyses of the strains between organizational requirements and the goals of professionals may be found in Kornhauser, *op. cit.* (1962), pp. 50–82, and Simon Marcson, *The Scientist in American Industry* (New York: Harper & Row, Publishers, 1960), pp. 72–85. See also Anselm Strauss and Lee Rainwater, *The Professional Scientist* (Chicago: Aldine Publishing Company, 1962), pp. 113, 118–123.

[38] On this distiction see Franz Neumann, *Behemoth: The Structure and Practice of National Socialism, 1933–1944* (New York: Oxford University Press), pp. 320–321.

in elections in engineering colleges.[39] It may
be that as members of a very conservative
profession, engineers, when pressed to reject
the status quo, opt for a movement of the
radical right, rather than the radical left.

The foregoing discussion on the political
effects which different sources of employment may have on professionals has been
limited by the lack of empirical evidence in
this area. Obviously, because of the varied
implications which follow from each type
of employment, no simple predictions can
be made on the kind of political behavior
which will follow. However, among the
generalizations we have suggested which
require empirical testing are the following:
when a profession tends to recruit most of
its members from the dominant groups in
the society, the minority members chan-
neled into less desirable fields will be prone
to support political parties opposed to the
status quo. This will also tend to be true of
those professions, who through their activities and the nature of their clientele
come in contact with major social problems.
Support for the status quo will more likely
follow where the employer or the conditions
of professional practice allow accessible rewards and a high degree of autonomy.
Many more propositions could be generated
by an analysis of employment, but these
may serve as examples.

I.4. The greater the ease with which
professional skills can be transferred to
political ones, the more varied that profession's political orientation. This is a function of available political opportunities. The
most obvious example here is that of lawyers, who have tended to dominate the
political party structure and legislatures of
many countries.[40] Not only do their skills

in compromise, debate, and law-making
aptly suit them for these political roles but
also, while fulfilling them, they are even
able to enhance their professional status as
lawyers.[41] While lawyers as a group can,
for many of the reasons already discussed,
be expected to be among the more conservative elements in the society, the high
transferability of their skills to politics has
meant that many leaders of non-conserva-
tive parties are drawn from the ranks of
lawyers.[42] This contrasts rather sharply with
the case of medical doctors whose knowledge and skills appear to have little bearing
on political roles.[43]

Even though, as Max Weber pointed out,
lawyers are more readily available to engage in politics and more skilled in the arts
of persuasion than other occupations, professions other than law would seem to lend
themselves to political roles.[44] At least in
terms of articulateness, this would seem
particularly true of teachers and journalists.[45] Next to members of the legal profession, these two other professions contribute
most candidates elected with professional
background in many countries.[46] While

39 See Hans Speier, *The Salaried Employee
in German Society* (New York: The Department of Social Science, Columbia University,
1939), pp. 43–45; Daniel Lerner, *et al., op. cit.,*
p. 47; and Karl Bracher, *Die Auflösung der
Weimarer Republik* (Stuttgart: Ring Verlag,
1955), pp. 146–149; and Kornhauser, *op. cit.,*
(1959), p. 189.

40 See, for example, Matthews, *op. cit.;*
Dogan, *op. cit.* (1955), pp. 308–311; Meisel,
op. cit., p. 132; Butler, *op. cit.,* p. 127; and G.
Sartori, "Parliamentarians in Italy," *International Social Science Journal,* 13, 1961, 592–595.

41 Walter I. Wardwell and Arthur L. Wood,
"The Extra-Professional Role of the Lawyer,"
The American Journal of Sociology, 61, 1956,
304–307; Joseph A. Schlesinger, "Lawyers and
American Politics," *Midwest Journal of Political
Science,* 1, 1957, pp. 26–39; and Jerome Carlin,
Lawyers on Their Own (New Brunswick: Rutgers
University Press, 1962), pp. 133–135, 152.

42 Previously quoted sources on the participation of lawyers in politics indicate also the spread
of their leadership role in diverse parties. See
notes 1 and 41.

43 William A. Glaser, "Doctors and Politics,"
The American Journal of Sociology, 66, 1960,
231–232. For a discussion of the way in which
aspects of the roles of physicians, engineers, and
scientists limit their participation in politics, see
Harold Lasswell, *Politics: Who Gets What,
When, How* (New York: Meridian Books, 1958),
pp. 98–100.

44 Max Weber, "Politics as Vocation," in H. H.
Gerth and C. W. Mills, *From Max Weber: Essays
in Sociology* (New York: Oxford University
Press, 1946), pp. 85, 94–95; Lasswell, *op. cit.,*
107–109; Dogan, *op. cit.,* (1961) pp. 69–70.

45 Raymond Aron, *The Opium of the Intellectuals* (New York: Norton, 1962), p. 205; Weber,
op. cit., pp. 96–99; Dogan, *op. cit.,* pp. 80–82.

46 Dogan *op. cit.,* (1955) pp. 295; and Dogan,
op. cit., (1961) pp. 65–67; R. B. McCallum and

lawyers are inclined to support conservative parties and teachers and journalists to oppose them, one of the reasons for finding each occupational group among the candidates of the opposing party is that they have such readily marketable political skills which can be attracted wherever opportunities are richer.

Professional Values

One of the major differences between the professions and other occupations is that the professions are assumed to be concerned with the fulfillment of certain intrinsic values, such as disinterested service and universalistic standards based on science or intellect, which are different from and even opposed to the money-making ethic of business.[47] Professional values generally, as well as those specific to a particular field, may then exert some independent influence on political attitudes and variations among political attitudes. Again, we shall suggest a number of hypotheses concerning the impact of values.

II.1. Large-scale discrepancies between professional values and the realities of the work situation lead to generalized social discontent manifested in the support of more liberal or even radical political parties. Theodore Geiger has suggested that one reason for the greater leftism of social scientists in many countries is that of "all groups in the *intelligentsia,* the social scientists are most sensitive to the power dimension in society, and also the most exposed to the attacks on intellectual freedom by those in power."[48] In the United States a study of the impact of McCarthyism on social scientists in colleges and universities found an interrelated cluster of proneness to demand the right of teachers to discuss unpopular ideas, strong professional-orientation, being in the better universities, and propensity to political liberalism.[49]

Another example is that of journalists. As a profession they are concerned with the accurate reporting of news, but many newspapers seek to slant the news in some fashion. The consequence is to make many reporters frustrated and cynical, and politically their leanings are often to the left.[50] Another group, which, like the journalists, often faces a clear conflict between their professional work norms and the requirements inherent in the demands of the market, are creative artists such as writers, painters, musicians and actors.[51] This hostility towards business and the mass market seems to be reflected in the propensity of creative artists to support liberal or left

A. Redman, *The British General Election of 1945* (London: Oxford University Press, 1947), pp. 273–274; D. E. Butler, *The British General Election of 1951* (London: Macmillan, 1952), p. 41; D. E. Butler, *The British General Election of 1955* (London: Macmillan, 1955), p. 43; Butler, *The British General Election of 1959,* p. 127. These two occupations were also prominent among the candidates for office in the Canadian General Election in 1958.

[47] Talcott Parsons, *Essays in Sociological Theory, Pure and Applied* (Glencoe: Free Press, revised edition, 1954), p. 35.

[48] Theodore Geiger, *Aufgabe und Stellung der Intelligenz in der Gesellschaft* (Stuttgart: Ferdinand Enke, 1949), p. 124.

[49] See Paul F. Lazarsfeld and Wagner Thielens, Jr., *The Academic Mind,* (Glencoe: Free Press, 1958), especially page 156.

[50] Leo Rosten, *The Washington Correspondent* (New York: Harcourt, Brace & World, Inc., 1937), p. 348, for a study reflecting depression conditions. For more recent data, Theodore Edward Kruglak, *The Foreign Correspondents: A Study of the Men and Women Reporting for the American Information Media in Western Europe* (Geneva: Librarie E. Droz, Etudes d'Historie Economique Politique et Sociale, 1955), pp. 87–89, 157. For Britain, see Lewis and Maude, *op. cit.,* p. 179. See also Gabriel A. Almond, *The Appeals of Communism* (Princeton: Princeton University Press, 1954), p. 188.

[51] Bertrand de Jouvenal has pointed out that business is institutionally committed to giving the public what it wants, for the customer is always right. See his article, "The Treatment of Capitalism by Continental Historians," in F. A. Hayek (ed.), *Capitalism and the Historian* (Chicago: University of Chicago Press, 1954), pp. 118–120. On the frustrations of creative people in the movies see Leo Rosten, *Hollywood: The Movie Colony, The Movie Makers* (New York: Harcourt, Brace & World, Inc., 1941), pp. 326–327, 352. On the antagonism between the jazz musician and the non-musical public see Howard S. Becker, "The Professional Dance Musician and His Audience," *The American Journal of Sociology,* 57, 1951, 138–139. On writers see Crane Brinton, *Ideas and Men* (Englewood Cliffs: Prentice-Hall, Inc., 1950), p. 449.

politics, and to belong to regular trade unions in many countries. In the United States, such occupational groups have heavily backed the Democrats, thus sharply diverging from other professional and high prestige groups, and have given disproportionate backing to leftist "third parties."[52] There are a number of suggestions that similar patterns occur in other countries.[53] Market demands may not, of course, be determined by business, but by any dominant group, such as government. A case in point is the position of the artist in present-day Russia, even though there the opportunities for political protest are limited.[54]

II.2. The values inherent in different professions predispose the direction of their members' political orientation. This is a thesis suggested by Michels, Durkheim, Mannheim, and Laski.[55] Implied here are the questioning nature of the scientist's mind, the lawyer's concern with the past, and so on. Little empirical evidence on these hypotheses is available, but some studies present evidence that scientists, as opposed to those with technical training and identifications such as engineers, are led to develop a broader perspective generally and more universalistic standards. They are less likely to identify with an

employer such as government or industry and this also has implications for their greater political liberalism.[56] In a Detroit study, clergymen who expressed a political preference were more likely to support the Republicans than might be expected on the basis of their class background alone. The author is led to conclude that they were at least partly influenced in their political choice by the "identification of the Republican Party as the party of personal morality and integrity."[57] Professional values of this sort may contribute to the conservatism of lawyers, (e.g. Laski's suggestion that "lawyer's habits are rooted in precedent and tradition"), and because of their humanistic ethos, to the relatively greater liberalism of medical doctors among the more rewarded professions.[58]

52 Rosten reports Hollywood professionals as five to one for Roosevelt in 1936, *op. cit.*, p. 160; on writers and musicians see Anderson and Davidson, *op. cit.*, p. 119; on support for Communists see John Cogley, *Report on Blacklisting, I, Movies* (New York: The Fund for the Republic, 1956), pp. 24–46; and II, *Radio and Television*, pp. 142–162. Lipset, *op. cit.*, pp. 315–318.

53 See T. C. Truman, *The Pressure Groups, Parties and Politics of the Australian Labor Movement* (M. A. thesis, University of Queensland, 1943), p. 86; Hans Speier, *op. cit.*, p. 77; Kornhauser, *op. cit.*, 1959, p. 185; Sigmund Neumann, *Die deutschen Parteien: Wesen und Wandlung nach dem Kriege* (Berlin: Junker und Dunnhaupt, 1932), p. 31.

54 "Khrushchev and the Arts," *New Statesman*, 64, 1962, 924.

55 Robert Michels, *Political Parties* (New York: Hearst's International Library, 1915), pp. 256–257; Emile Durkheim, *Professional Ethics and Civic Morals* (Glencoe: The Free Press, 1958), p. 5; Karl Mannheim, *Ideology and Utopia* (New York: Harcourt, Brace & World Inc., 1936), pp. 119–122; and Harold Laski, *Democracy in Crisis* (Chapel Hill: University of North Carolina Press, 1933), p. 141.

56 Kornhauser, *op. cit.* (1962), pp. 153–155 and S. M. Lipset, *op. cit.*, pp. 315–316. For an argument that there is "a general connection between the exact sciences and a leaning towards left-wing ideas," see Helmut Plessner, "Ideological Tendencies Among Academic Thinkers," Congress for Cultural Freedom, *Science and Freedom* (London: Secker and Warburg, 1955), p. 178. This notion is also found in Michels, *op. cit.*

57 Gerhard Lenski, *The Religious Factor* (Garden City: Doubleday Anchor, 1963), pp. 305–307.

58 This statement may seem surprising given the image presented by the American Medical Association of a very conservative profession. However, data analyzed from the 1947 *Time* college graduate study cited earlier indicate that free professionals as a group are much more likely to be Democrats than are professionals employed by business, such as engineers, accountants, and the like. And when lawyers, physicians, and dentists are compared, holding income position constant, the lawyers turned out to be consistently more Republican than the doctors; the dentists seemed somewhat less inclined to the Republicans than the physicians. All three professional groups, of course, gave a majority to the Republicans, although about 40 per cent of those outside the South report having voted Democratic in the 1944 Presidential elections. In 1956, a survey of a random sample of American physicians conducted for the American Medical Association which asked respondents to indicate whether the political philosophy of Roosevelt, Eisenhower, or Taft was closest to their own, reported that 33 per cent said Roosevelt; 50 per cent Eisenhower; and only 17 per cent Taft. It is doubtful that a comparable study of another group as high in income and status as physicians would have yielded such a high Roosevelt preference.

In discussing values of different professions and their relation to politics, it is necessary to distinguish between those intrinsic to the profession from those which have arisen outside it.[59] For example, the intellectual battles between science and religion waged in the nineteenth century at various universities shaped the outlook of whole generations and various professions for many decades. The struggle, of course, did not pit all professions against the Church and authority. Lawyers have always given considerable support to the Church and the traditional structure. The conflict against traditional religious interpretations was most violent among the natural scientists—in particular the biological ones, including medicine.[60] Thus the initial fight between science and religion which was associated with the struggle of the bourgeois left against the traditionalist right in Europe, placed a number of professions which are linked to science, such as medicine, on the anti-clerical side, a place where many of them seem to remain today. And being located on the anti-clerical rather than the clerical side has served to increased the possibilities that they would support left anti-clerical parties, even though many, if not most of them, have backed the middle class anti-clerical parties. The one European country for which available data suggest that physicians have been on the right politically is also the country (Germany) in which large sections of the nationalist right waged a *Kulturkampf* against religion.[61] The contrast between Germany and other European countries is also reflected in the political affiliations of school teachers. While anti-clericalism in France, Belgium, and the Netherlands is reflected in a high degree of socialist sympathy among the school teachers in those countries, this is much less pronounced in Germany where it became focused on conservative nationalism.[62] These examples indicate the importance of considering how values which have become associated with a profession through historical circumstances may continue to impinge on political perspectives.

Somewhat similar processes are operative today in a number of the developing nations of Asia, Africa, and Latin America. (The Latin American picture varies between patterns comparable to Latin Europe and to the new states.) The intellectuals of these countries who, as Edward Shils has pointed out, tend to include "all persons with an advanced modern education," that is, all professionals as well as creative artists and scholars, are the leaders of social change.[63] As university graduates, they tend to have a more cosmopolitan outlook than the traditional, usually less educated, land-owning or mercantile elite. They then see the traditional values and structures of a pre-industrial society as the major source of the economic and political inferiority of their nation. The desire to modernize, to develop their country, tends to be associated with progressive or leftist ideologies. And consequently, we find that in many of these countries university students, creative intellectuals, and often most of the professional strata as well, back leftist parties. In a sense, the issue for them is akin to the clericalism-anti-clericalism struggle of much of nineteenth-century Europe. In Japan, in many Moslem countries, in India, and in parts of Africa, the intelligentsia, including the professionals, are involved in a *Kulturkampf* against conservative tradition-

[59] Edward Shils, "The Scientific Community: Thoughts after Hamburg," *Science and Freedom*, No. 1 (November 1954), p. 10.

[60] Robert Michels, *Die Umschichtungen in den herrschunden Klassen nach dem Kriege* (Stuttgart: Kohlhammer, 1934), pp. 68–69; René Rémond, *La Droite en France de 1815 à nos jours* (Paris: Edition Montaigne, 1954), p. 248.

[61] Willy Kremer, *Der Soziale Aufbau der Parteien des deutschen Reichstages von 1871–1928* (Ph.D. thesis, University of Cologne, 1934); and Mildred S. Wertheimer, *The Pan-German League 1890–1914* (New York: Columbia University Press, 1924), pp. 66–70.

[62] Hans Gerth, "The Nazi Party: Its Leadership and Composition," *The American Journal of Sociology*, 45, 1940, pp. 517–541, for data on the membership and leadership of non-Catholic teachers in the Nazi party.

[63] Edward Shils, "The Intellectuals in the Political Development of New States," in John H. Kautsky (ed.), *Political Change in Underdeveloped Countries* (New York: John Wiley & Sons, Inc., 1962), pp. 198–205.

alists.[64] A variety of opinion surveys in Japan point out the way in which antagonism to traditional Japanese values is associated with opposition to the conservative party, and that dislike of traditionalism strongly correlates with increased education, so that the university educated are anti-traditional and pro-Socialist.[65]

To sum up then, our contention has been that features of social stratification and values specific to professions as a group or to specific ones differentially tend to affect their members' political behavior, first in ways often different from the middle class as a whole and second, so as to produce variations both within and between professions. The evidence on which we have based our generalizations and hypotheses has often been sketchy, but it has been at least indicative of the kind of differences which exist. Hopefully, this should influence subsequent research to pay greater attention to political variations among the professions.

[64] See S. M. Lipset, *The First New Nation* (New York: Basic Books, Inc., 1963), pp. 66–74. Harry J. Benda, "Non-Western Intelligentsia As Political Elites," in Kautsky (ed.), *op cit.*, pp. 238–246.

[65] Joji Watanuki, "White-Collar Workers and the Pattern of Politics in Present-Day Japan", in S. M. Lipset and Stein Rokkan (eds.), *Party Systems and Voter Alignments* (New York: The Free Press, forthcoming); see also Z. Suetuna, H. Aoyama, C. Hayashi and K. Matusita, "A Study of Japanese National Character," Part II, *Annals of the Institute of Statistical Mathematics* (Tokyo: 1961), pp. 52–54.

Politicians and Professionals

The degree to which professionals are able to influence politics and, vice versa, the degree to which politicians are able to gain respect and influence in professional circles, depends upon how members of each group perceive members of the other. As in the case of previous examples, major technological breakthroughs can affect these perceptions. The following reading indicates how American politicians tended to view scientists somewhat differently after the first breakthrough in nuclear warfare.

Harry S. Hall (Science)

Until the revelation of Hiroshima, Congressmen, like most laymen, had little reason to be much concerned with either science or scientists. The majority of them undoubtedly shared the popular conception of science as the well from which material benefits flowed in an endless stream symbolized by the familiar picture of the man in a white smock holding up a test tube to the light. As for scientists, most politicians seemed to view them either as useful tools for increasing the productive resources of industry, or as impractical visionaries and eccentric crackpots puttering with complicated equipment in their laboratories. As Senator Tydings candidly admitted to Dr. Szilard in 1945 during the hearings of the Special Senate Committee on Atomic Energy:

Doctor, if in 1939 we had been conducting a hearing like we are conducting today, and men like yourself had come before our committee and projected the possible development of the bomb up to now with reasonable accuracy, I imagine they would have been called a lot of crackpots and...visionaries who were playing with theories. I certainly would not have had the receptivity that I have today to say the least.[1]

[1] *Atomic Energy: Hearings before the Special Committee on Atomic Energy*, U.S. Senate, 79th Congress, 1st Session, (Washington, D.C.; U.S. Government Printing Office, 1945), p. 290.

Reprinted from "Scientists and Politicians," *Bulletin of the Atomic Scientists*, 12 (February 1956), 46–52. Used by permission.

The atomic bomb changed this situation completely, forcibly thrusting science and scientists into the forefront of politicians' focus of attention. It demonstrated as never before the destructive possibilities of science. But, what was far more important, detonation of the bomb drove into peoples' consciousness the realization, hitherto understood by only a few laymen, that science was a major social force. Moreover, their preoccupation with the complex problems brought about by atomic energy necessarily involved Congressmen with scientists, even had the latter not voluntarily entered the arena of political action. For the first time, senators and representatives found themselves in considerable interaction with scientists. Whatever their previous conceptions of scientists might have been, politicians could not afford to ignore them. Whether Congressmen liked it or not, they had to take note of the crucial role of science and scientists in the atomic age.

How did politicians react to their enforced venture into strange new territory inhabited by equally strange men who spoke a foreign language and dealt with matters utterly beyond the experience of most Congressmen? What conceptions and attitudes regarding science and scientists did they form as a consequence of such entry?

Some answers to these questions may be obtained from the transcripts of Congressional hearings on matters in which scientists were interested in the immediate postwar years. Outstanding examples of such hearings were the ones on domestic control of atomic energy and establishment of a National Science Foundation. Most of the illustrative citations have been culled from these hearings,[2] although they are by

no means exhaustive of the material. A few quotations from the 1953 Senate hearings into the Bureau of Standards rejection of the claims made for a battery additive indicate the contemporary nature of some conceptions and attitudes respecting scientists. Finally, it should be pointed out that while scientists were the principal witnesses of these hearings, the testimony of respected laymen, like General Groves and Morris L. Cooke, former head of the Rural Electrification Administration, about science and scientists undoubtedly helped shape Congressional thinking on such matters.

SCIENTISTS AS SUPERIOR BEINGS

After the astonishing news of Hiroshima and Nagasaki, overnight to many people, scientists became charismatic figures of a new era, if not a new world, in which science was the new religion and scientists the new prophets. Like everyone else at that time, politicians, too, looked upon scientists with considerable awe and deference. Scientists appeared to them as superior beings who had gone far ahead of the rest of the human race in knowledge and power. Indeed, politicians seemed to regard scientists in much the same way that primitive men regard their magician-priests. That is to say, Congressmen perceived scientists as being in touch with a supernatural world of mysterious and awesome forces whose terrible power they alone could control. Their exclusive knowledge set scientists apart and made them tower far above other men. As Senator Tydings put it:

There are a few men...or maybe several thousand in the world whose mental develop-

---

[2] *Atomic Energy: Hearings before the Special Committee on Atomic Energy,* U.S. Senate, 79th Congress, 1st Session.

Atomic Energy Act of 1946: Hearings before the Special Committee on Atomic Energy, U.S. Senate, 79th Cong., 2nd Session, (Washington, D.C.: U.S. Government Printing Office, 1946).

Science Legislation: Hearings before the Subcommittee of the Committee on Military Affairs, U.S. Senate, 79th Congress, 1st Session, (Washington, D.C.: U.S. Government Printing Office, 1945, 1946).

National Science Foundation: Hearings before

the *Committee on Interstate and Foreign Commerce, House of Representatives,* 80th Congress, 2nd Session, (Washington, D.C.: U.S. Government Printing Office, 1948).

National Science Foundation: Hearings before a Subcommittee of the Committee on Interstate and Foreign Commerce, House of Representatives, 81st Congress, 1st Session, (Washington, D.C.: U.S. Government Printing Office, 1949).

Battery AD-X2: Hearings before the Select Committee on Small Business, U.S. Senate, 83rd Congress, 1st Session, (Washington, D.C.: U.S. Government Printing Office, 1953).

ment in many lines—and particularly in the scientific line—is like comparing a mountain to a molehill when you compare them to the rest of us. (*Spec. Comm.,* 1945, p. 309)

Senator Russell expressed his feelings by remarking:

My attitude toward scientists is...pretty much like the boy living in the country and going to the country doctor. He thinks the doctor can do anything. (*Spec. Comm.,* 1945, p. 170)

Senator Hickenlooper spontaneously referred to the magical quality of scientists in his comment to Dr. Bush on the release of atomic energy:

We have got to the point where we have rubbed the lamp and the genie has come out and we cannot get him back into the lamp. (*Spec. Comm.,* 1945, p. 183)

The most explicit acknowledgment of scientists' superiority came from Senator Johnson of Colorado. In an exclamation that was both protest and plea, he burst out:

I have one further observation to make, and that is that you scientists have gotten a long way ahead of human conduct, and until human conduct catches up with you, we are in a precarious way unless you scientists slow up a little and let us catch up. (*Spec. Comm.,* 1945, p. 141)

Senator Johnson's outburst also expressed the resentment and fear that ordinary men feel toward superior beings who are considered to be in a position to influence their destinies. Nor was Johnson the only Congressman who felt afraid. When Dr. Rabi complained to Senator Fulbright that the May-Johnson bill made scientists feel that politicians were treating them as a special class of citizens from whom other people had to be protected, Fulbright tacitly agreed, explaining:

The reason for that is that you scientists scared us all to death with your atomic bomb and we are still very frightened about it. (*Sci. Leg.,* 1945, p. 992)

Earlier when Senator Magnuson asked Dr. Karl Compton:

Doctor...After all, the reason that scientific hearings are now not only fashionable but interesting is because of the atomic bomb.

Senator Kilgore remarked:

May I amend that and say we are all scared to death. (*Sci. Leg.,* 1945, p. 635)

An extremely significant dimension of politicians' perception of science as a major social force was the dynamic and progressively expanding character which they ascribed to it. Because of such a nature, science's role and impact would grow even greater with time. In this view, science was likened to some sort of juggernaut rolling inexorably and invincibly forward. Its power and momentum were so irresistible that all obstacles in its path were crushed or swept aside.

SCIENCE AS INTERNATIONAL

Politicians' belief in the juggernaut character of science rested ultimately on two other perceptions: (1) that scientists were an exclusive in-group, a tightly-knit fraternity of dedicated theoreticians and visionaries; (2) that science was international in scope in terms of its jurisdiction, activities, and membership. These two factors were responsible for science's invincible advance and for scientists' independence of control. The zeal with which scientific research was pursued plus its world-wide scope made it impossible to control either science or scientists. For, if repressed in one country, science would be carried on in another by different or even the same devotees.

Senator Hickenlooper expressed his view of the international character of science when he asked Szilard:

Doctor, as a scientist and with what knowledge you have of the history and present activities of international science, do you believe that science or even countries will stop the examination and exploration into the atomic energy field by any treaties or agreements? (*Spec. Comm.,* 1945, p. 272)

Senator Magnuson discussing his ideas on what the National Science Foundation should do, declared to the scientists:

As you gentlemen so well know, science knows no geography. (*Sci. Leg.,* 1945, p. 566)

Their perception of science's international character and their distress, even resentment, of this fact was revealed in politicians' questions about the feasibility of international exchange of scientific information by itself, without an accompanying exchange also of other cultural material. Essentially, politicians were reluctant to admit that science was independent and self-sufficient enough vis-à-vis the rest of social affairs that its knowledge could successfully be exchanged without having at the same time other forms of international communication and interaction. Senator Millikin expressed his reluctance to Harlow Shapley in the question:

Do you believe that the general exchange of scientific information between the nations and the exchange of scientists is feasible unless you have at the same time a general exchange of information and the permission for all kinds of people to cross borders? Do you think it can be confined to scientists? Can you isolate just one department of human knowledge and say, "Now after all this we will exchange information and personnel but we will not exchange anything else." Is it practical to do that? (*Spec. Comm.*, 1946, p. 164)

Senator Tydings, too, was concerned and reluctant to accept the fact that science could effectively be divorced and exist apart from the rest of society and culture. In a discussion with Vannevar Bush, he queried:

Do you think it is possible to accomplish in the world a free exchange of scientific knowledge—in a world that does not permit the free exchange of religious knowledge?

Tydings indicated his unwillingness to accept Bush's affirmative reply by insisting:

If we cannot do it in one field, what hopes may we have that we can do it in another field? If freedom of the mind is interdicted, so to speak, by the government in one of the oldest and strongest traditions, why is it reasonable to believe that the freedom of the mind will not be interdicted in this other field of science?

In return, Bush pointed out:

Science, Senator, has always been more or less free; it has always had a flavor of internationalism, you know.

Tydings retorted,

So has religion. (*Spec. Comm.*, 1945, p. 163)

THE SCIENTIFIC IN-GROUP

Congressional reluctance to admit the independence of science from other areas of social life may be correlated with their perception of scientists as an exclusive little in-group sharply differentiated and set apart from the rest of society. This perception and its implications require more detailed analysis.

To begin with, politicians had a vague, inarticulate understanding that the scientists dealt with abstract symbols. Scientists and others, like General Groves, tried to explain the nature of basic scientific research. Yet, politicians couldn't really understand. Their dim perception of the abstract and symbolic nature of scientific work was expressed in an indirect way by the use of "theoretical," "visionary," etc., to characterize scientists. Thus when Bernard Baruch said:

It has been my experience, having been in touch with the medical end of it, that there are two types of minds, one that will drift over into the applied sciences and another which is the roaming mind, what Edison told me once was the "source mind," the fellow who is interested in a particular subject and no money can get him off it. That fellow will develop that line—almost will make his own demarcation.

Kilgore rejoined:

He is what we sometimes call the more visionary type. (*Sci. Leg.*, 1945, p. 919)

When the scientists tried to explain their orientation to abstract and remote symbols, it was clear that politicians did not understand—not even Senator Fulbright, who had an academic background himself. Thus, Dr. Wilson and Oppenheimer tried to explain the difference between fundamental and applied research as they conceived it. Wilson started off by saying:

Programmatic (research) is when you just envisage research, when you can say that a man should do such-and-such a problem and measure such-and-such a quantity. That is programmatic work. In general when a man is really doing research, he is not able to tell you what he is doing. He is working on the frontier of knowledge. He does an experiment in an entirely exploratory manner, and then on the basis of a hunch he does another experiment. Finally, he sees something. He can't see it, but eventually it comes out. It is entirely creative, as opposed to most workaday physics that is in general done.

Oppenheimer tried to clarify in these words:

Dr. Wilson said that programmatic research consists in the measurement of quantities which are known to exist. That may sound very funny, but half of the work of physics and most of the work of fundamental physics is not to measure the quantities that are known to exist, but to find out what quantities do exist. That is, what kind of language, what kind of concepts correspond to the realities of the world. What Dr. Wilson was saying—and I think quite rightly—was that if you really know what it is you have to do, if you can give it a name and say, "We don't know whether it is 10 or 20, but we would like to measure it," then you are doing something that increases knowledge very much but which doesn't qualitatively increase knowledge. When you try to find out whether it is possible to talk about such things as simultaneity and position...then you are going to make a contribution.

When Wilson tried to continue with "I think we can say that since 1940—" the listening senators interrupted to express their bewilderment and incomprehension. Magnuson said: "Dr. Fulbright would understand that"; but it was clear he did not for when Fulbright started to say: "That was a fine explanation—" he, in turn, was interrupted by Magnuson who commented, "He doesn't understand you either." (*Sci. Leg.,* 1945, p. 332)

Scientists as Dedicated Men

A second characteristic of scientists as an exclusive in-group was their intense commitment to the ideals and pursuit of science. Their devotion seemed to resemble, in some respects, the fervor shown by the members of a religious sect who concentrate almost exclusively on realizing their goals to the neglect of everything else. Thus, Senator Young commented:

Mr. Berne, I think you raised a very important point when you mentioned the salaries of scientists and so on. I have personal knowledge of several scientists who stayed in the work almost entirely because of the love of the work rather than the salary that they received. (*Sci. Leg.,* 1945, p. 845)

Senator Millikin made the same point in asking Compton:

Do you believe this is a correct statement that probably of all the professions in the world, the scientist is less interested in monetary gain —I am speaking of the pure scientist?

Compton replied:

I don't know of any other group that has less interest in monetary gain. (*Spec. Comm.,* 1946, p. 263)

The clearest expression of politicians' image of scientists as a band of dedicated men whose devotion to the ideals and pursuit of science has a religious quality was contained in politicians' conviction that scientists world continue developing the field of atomic energy—regardless of the consequences or attempts to prevent their work.

Senator Connally expressed his belief in the dedication of scientists during a discussion with Dr. Bush on other possible sources of atomic energy. Connally asked:

They will keep on trying, will they not, scientists will keep on experimenting, will they not?

When Bush replied: "Well, even scientists do the things they think can probably be done," Connally persisted in his image, saying:

That is true, but they will be trying other things, they will be working in other fields and among other elements Maybe they think that they will fail but they will keep on trying. (*Spec. Comm.,* 1945, p. 171)

Langmuir strengthened this image of scientists by putting their commitment to scientific ideals and research in an explicitly religious context. To Hickenlooper's question:

Having seen the proof, Doctor, that fission is possible on substantial scales, and having been admitted to this at least first dawning of this great field of energy, is there any reasonable possibility that science the world over could be prevented in any way from dabbling in this thing further and going on? In other words, science is inevitably bound to go forward with further experimentation in this field?

Langmuir's reply was framed in terms of one religious faith trying unsuccessfully to halt the progress of a competing religion; he asserted:

It is just like the Catholic Church trying to stop progress in science. It just can't be done, because the knowledge already is there to be found. It is in nature, and to prevent us discovering the facts of nature is a hopeless job.

Hickenlooper's rejoinder indicated his acceptance of Langmuir's statement on the futility of trying to control scientists in their work when he asked:

And scientists will go on exploring the field despite what politicians or anyone else attempts to do?

Langmuir warned:

If you regiment them here so they cannot do it, they will go elsewhere. (*Spec. Comm.*, 1945, p. 127)

Politicians, then, were given to understand that scientists, like all sectarians, would and did disregard any attempt to obstruct their efforts to achieve the ideals they believed in. Their resistance and defiance extended even to the commands of legitimate authority which had moral justification for its orders. For example, Senator Hickenlooper asked Dr. Oppenheimer:

Doctor, does the history of scientific development in the world at any time show that the scientists have ever discarded something that opens new ground for scientific investigation? In other words, can you by legislation, or even by intent of government, stop scientists from investigating or exploring new fields, especially when they have had success in a field, as is the case, the proven case, with atomic energy?

Oppenheimer's answer was:

Well, enormous discouragements can be proposed and scientific advances can certainly be opposed. It was not easy during the days of the Renaissance for a man to investigate the laws of nature because he was likely to get himself into extreme personal trouble.

Hickenlooper's rejoinder indicated his belief that scientists would succeed in overcoming all obstacles because of their intense commitment to scientific ideals:

But scientific development did go on. (*Spec. Comm.*, 1945, pp. 200–201)

The ethical imperatives of their scientific faith were perceived by politicians to take precedence over all other moral obligations and demands for scientists. Scientists pursued their work in complete indifference to its social and ethical consequences. This view of scientists was expressed by Senator Johnson when he exclaimed:

Dr. Langmuir, how do you compose your two viewpoints? On the one hand you say that this country should appropriate $5,000,000,000 for scientific research; on the other hand, you say that this country should destroy $5,000,-000 worth of the products of science. The scientists, according to your testimony, have made the world extremely insecure. Science has made, according to your statement just now, aggression inevitable and yet, at the same time, you say that we ought to keep pouring money into science.

When Langmuir argued: "Science is not a thing that we make; scientists don't create science in that way," Johnson retorted:

But, you create atomic bombs, and now you want to go and throw them into the middle of the ocean because they have made the world insecure.

Langmuir explained:

In order to get security—in other words, we buy something by that. It is a price. You cannot get security for yourself without giving it to other nations. We have no security now for the future, because we are now in stages one or two. We are now secure but we can foresee the case that this security is only temporary, that the time will come when not only we but no nation is secure, and we must do something about that. We must start now to do something about it, because otherwise disaster lies ahead, probably a worse disaster for us than for anyone else.

Johnson persisted in his conviction that all scientists wanted to do was to go on with their work under the financial support of the government with no concern for the social consequences of their research. He declared again:

It looks to me as though you scientists have made the world extremely insecure, and now you are coming to the politicians and asking us to go about and make the world secure again by some sort of political agreement. At the same time, you are asking that the scientists who made the world insecure be given further appropriations to discover still another and more destructive element than atomic energy. (*Spec. Comm.,* 1945, pp. 120–121)

SCIENTISTS AS "UNCOMMON" MEN

Their orientation to the abstract and remote symbols of science and their devotion to scientific ideals and research set scientists apart from other men in politicians' eyes. Scientists were different. A simple but striking illustration of this view was contained in Congressmen's repeated use of the words, "you scientists," or, "you fellows." Politicians' use of these words is taken here to mean they perceived scientists to be considerably removed from ordinary people. Scientists possessed distinctive attributes which put a wide gap between them and other persons. Hence, when Millikin remarked to Watson Davis, head of Science Service,

I notice in the Orphan Annie strip they now have the atom bomb down to hand size and you can tote your own private demolition. But as a scientific man, you wouldn't know about the Little Orphan Annie strip. (*Spec. Comm.,* 1946, p. 192)

he was expressing his belief that scientists lacked the simple tastes and interests of the common man. Senator Thye's comment seven years later in the hearings on the Bureau of Standard's rejection of the claims made for a battery additive indicated the strength of this view. Thye stated his belief that scientists took very seriously trivial matters that no ordinary person would even worry about.

Dr. Astin, since this question came up and for the sake of an amusing scientific argument, I saw a paper where two scientists had debated at great length on the question of whether boiled water would freeze quicker than unboiled water, and it was amusing to me to read the scientific language used in the debate on the simple question of whether water boiled would freeze more rapidly than water not boiled. (*Bat. AD-X2,* 1953, p. 230)

The image of scientists as a differentiated group that was set apart from other men was closely related to the further perception of its solidarity and exclusive nature. Politicians' resentment of this nature was expressed by Rep. Busbey in his complaint at the treatment one of his friends received:

This friend of mine is, in my opinion, quite a scientist. He has many valuable inventions on the market. While he is a university graduate, he is not a Ph.D. He has one of the most modern laboratories, I think, in the United States. He has tried on numerous occasions to make his services and his ideas available down here to people and constantly he is given form after form to fill out.... He supports his ideas with certain research data and most of the time he cannot get replies to his letters.... Now I do not think that George Washington Carver had a Ph.D. degree, at least in his earlier years of research. I am inclined to agree with this friend of mine that it is possible that a man might have a good idea that does not have a Ph.D. Now, I would like to know why a man like that cannot get consideration.... I thought I had found the proper place for him to present that and they referred it back to the Chicago Office. They sent some young 23-year-old kid out there to look over his laboratory and discuss this thing with him who did not know the difference between the moon and a hunk of green cheese, and he went back and made an unfavorable report. I want to know who the man in authority is that a man of this caliber can discuss things of importance with down here. (*NSF,* 1948, pp. 33–34)

Congressman Beckworth also was concerned that once the scientists were in positions of power and responsibility—as in the National Science Foundation, for example—they would use their position to favor members of their own group, or those who were apprentices on their way to the status of full membership. Beckworth was afraid that men of equal, innate ability who lacked the necessary educational qualifications would be ignored and not even given the chance to try to compete. He also expressed his resentment and concern that, once an alienated group with a monopoly of knowledge such as the scientists possessed, was elevated to positions of power, it would proceed to put its own value system into effect and thereby violate democratic standards.

Politicians' perception of the alienated nature of scientists is considered here in terms of their image of scientists as withdrawn from the usual social relations and indifferent to concerns of ordinary people. The aloof and isolated nature of scientists was graphically presented to politicians by Morris L. Cooke, in his testimony on the National Science Foundation:

The relationship which scientists—and engineers too—bear to the hurly-burly of American life, including its politics, is difficult for those outside these professional fields to understand. The scientists, as a matter of fact, are themselves only dimly aware of how detached they are individually and as a profession from the pulsating world around them. In the days when science was persecuted, the scientist was a recluse living as far as possible from the haunts of men. He still lives a life apart sharing almost not at all in our common activities and assuming no responsibility for the conduct of affairs outside the narrow confines of his own professional interest. Decisions dictated by slide-rule and test-tubes are his daily meat. The settlement of issues by the give and take involved in democratic compromise seems too crude in comparison with determinations reached by the two-plus-two-equals-four method of mathematics. Scientists and engineers, with few exceptions, feel no responsibility whatever for the life of the community—the hospitals, the school system, the boys clubs, the forums for the discussion of public questions, the homes for the aged. (*Sci. Leg.,* 1945, p. 1003)

Politicians' acceptance of this characteristic of scientists, particularly with reference to their isolation from and rejection of political participation, was revealed by Sen. Fulbright's question. He asked Cooke:

Why do you think people have such an aversion to politics? What is the basic reason that scientists and professional people do have such an aversion to it? (*Sci. Leg.,* 1945, p. 1003)

The fact of such isolation and rejection had been stated earlier by Dr. Curtis:

But scientists don't care much, by and large, about political matters. Let somebody else take care of politics—we have our atoms to attend to. But the scientists have felt that they can

and should make whatever contributions they could. (*Sci. Leg.,* 1945, p. 328)

INTERNATIONALIST ORIENTATION OF SCIENTISTS

The obvious corollary to the internationalism of science was the internationalist orientation of scientists. Such an orientation was explicitly affirmed by the scientists themselves, and, seemingly, accepted by politicians as one aspect of their image of scientists. Dr. Bowman gave one example of this orientation in urging governmental sponsorship and support of international scientific meetings. Similarly, Dr. Moulton declared:

I want to assure you that the scientists are high-minded and often simple-minded in terms of political things but in international matters they have been high-minded; they are the ones who have maintained the highest level of international cooperation of any class of people. Dr. Shapley said that in the past few years... over 500 international conferences have been held. I have attended some of them. Scientists meet together with a minimum of friction. They speak the same language; they are interested in the same problems; they are looking forward to the same things. (*Sci. Leg.,* 1945, p. 80)

Even more impressive evidence of scientists' international orientations was presented to politicians by Dr. Meyerhoff. Citing the results of the poll of its membership by the American Association for the Advancement of Science, Meyerhoff stated:

...the dissemination of information, both on a national and international basis, is favored by 76 and 74 per cent respectively.... And then the sort of thing which has been talked about by preceding speakers including Dr. Shapley this morning, that of international collaboration, loomed rather large, to the extent of 64 per cent who felt that much more should be done in a more formal way. Incidentally, there was considerable interest expressed in the acquisition of information about research going on in other countries, so that we might be brought up to date and not lag behind as so commonly is the case.

Politicians indicated their perception and sensitivity to scientists' internationalism when Magnuson asked:

In other words, your 74 per cent for international dissemination ties right into the 64 per cent group that wanted more formal international collaboration?

Meyerhoff confirmed Magnuson's understanding:

That is right. All people who voted for international collaboration voted for the exchange of information between countries. (*Sci. Leg.*, 1945, p. 88)

After having heard a number of scientists testify, Senator Millikin summed up his concept of their orientation in the following words:

The scientist, as I see it and as I get it from the testimony that we have had, is an idealist. He is, in a true sense—and I am not using this in a disparaging sense—an internationalist. He is, because he is accustomed to interchange and meeting people from all over the world. His speciality is science.... (*Spec. Comm.*, 1945, p. 327)

The alienative aspect of scientists' international orientation was its supranational character. Scientists' alienation was perceived by politicians not merely in their withdrawal from affairs and their indifference to human concerns. More positively, it was seen in their adherence to ideals and interests that normally transcended those of the nation, and, under certain circumstances could conceivably be in conflict with them. Inevitably, therefore, politicians were led to the conclusion that scientists had attenuated sentiments of loyalty and attachments to national boundaries.

The ready mobility of scientists to go wherever they could do their work under the kind of conditions they required was seen as one index of such attenuation. Langmuir's statement that any attempt by authority to regiment and control scientists would result in their departure explicitly supported this view. Additional confirmation was found in the emigration of scientists from Italy, Germany, and other countries before the Second World War. The continuing readiness of scientists to leave their countries of origin for more favorable conditions elsewhere was demonstrated to politicians by Dr. Schade's testimony. In a discussion with Schade who had been sent to Germany by the U.S. Navy, Magnuson asked concerning German scientists' attitudes:

Do many of the scientists with whom you have talked feel that they want to stay in Germany and help rebuild Germany or would they rather come to, say, America or Russia, or England, or other countries that might offer them refuge?

Schade answered:

There is an astonishingly prevalent interest among the people of that kind that you talk to in the direction of wanting to come over here and work for us. Many of them feel that the future of Germany is nonexistent, or not very pleasant from their point of view, which is, of course, the truth. I think perhaps that is one of the reasons why such people have been astonishingly cooperative with people such as myself and my organization over there who were over there to find out what we could from the technical point of view as to what went on during the war that might be of interest to the Navy.... The Germans (i.e., scientists) were most cooperative and I suppose it was because many of them hoped to get a job over here some day. (*Sci. Leg.*, 1945, p. 272)

As politicians saw it, the mobility of scientists and the ease with which they could transfer from one country to another were mainly due to their having weaker sentiments of loyalty and citizenship. Scientists lacked that visceral feeling of rootedness, of being part of a land and a kinship group that true citizens had. As a consequence, they were able to leave their native land to go and work elsewhere without much feeling of regret or loss. They were never really citizens in the first place. Furthermore, scientists' mobility and lack of rootedness were intensified by the fact that their important possessions and necessities of life were abstract. Scientists carried them in their heads, hence were not hampered by valuing and owning material things that would make their movement more difficult. The role of scientists was thus inherently international and supranational. Nothing about it bound the scientist to any one country. He could live and work anywhere and would so long as he had the necessary conditions for carrying on his research. Transfer from one country to another could be accomplished without sustaining any significant and serious losses.

Their supranational orientation and attenuated feelings of loyalty and attachment to nation were explicitly affirmed by the scientists themselves. In a statement prepared for the hearings on the National Science Foundation, Shapley declared:

Our American scientists and technologists at the present time have been derived from the adventurous pioneering stock of practically all the nations of the world. We call ourselves American by citizenship, but our blood is cosmopolitan. The scientists should, as rapidly as possible, call themselves citizens of the world and not the citizens of individual countries. (*Sci. Leg.*, 1945, p. 58)

Oppenheimer added his contribution to Shapley's clarion call when he said to Senator Fulbright:

May I be very honest? Most scientists, because they are scientists, were certainly not happy with the absolute national sovereignty that prevailed ten years ago. They were not happy with the war. (*Sci. Leg.*, 1945, p. 313)

That politicians viewed scientists as having weak loyalties and attachments to nation was indicated by Senator Fulbright's observation:

We have been told that they are very internationally minded people, that in peacetime they move back and forth between countries, and they have a great deal of resentment against restrictions on their development.... *I have always had the feeling that scientists did move about and are not so conscious of national sovereignty as lawyers or politicians or others.* (emphasis supplied) (*Sci. Leg.*, 1945, pp. 274–275)

While Fulbright saw no particular cause for alarm in this characteristic of scientists, it should be pointed out that he had come from an academic environment as professor and university president, and therefore could be sympathetic. But it seems hardly probable that most politicians who lacked such a background, shared his toleration. Rather, as Fulbright himself suggested, politicians elevate sentiments of loyalty and citizenship, attachment to nation and respect for the authority of government to the status of pre-eminent virtues. In their

eyes, concern for the national interest and welfare should always be paramount.

Therefore, when Dr. Urey advocated destroying the stockpile of atomic bombs and all fissionable materials if necessary to convince the world of our peaceful intentions, politicians could see in such a proposal a failure on the part of scientists to put the national interest and security over all other concerns. Even more important, such advocacy suggested a lack of faith and trust in the government, since it had said it would not use the bombs aggressively. Thus, Johnson could react to Urey's proposal in the following exclamation:

Dr. Urey, the members of this committee, and insofar as I know, no one else unless it be General Groves and some of the people at the top know exactly the amount of the compound that we have that is ready to go into the development of bombs. It seems to me that your paper displays a lack of faith that others might have in us. Now, how are you going to convince the world, for instance, that we don't have a sizable amount of this compound stored away which can never be detected, never discovered, that we are holding back from the world? You do not seem to think that the other nations will have very much faith in the United States' good intentions.... (*Spec. Comm.*, 1945, p. 107)

The low intensity of scientists' feelings of loyalty and patriotism was also demonstrated to politicians by the fact that under the normal conditions of peacetime, the ideal of basic scientific research was considered by scientists to conflict with work for the government—even though their services were vital—and was given preference. An additional factor in their decision to return to private life was that their work for the government had never been held in high esteem scientifically. It violated their ideals of scientific research. Szilard, Urey, Langmuir, and others made this point in their testimony before Congressional committees.

Politicians, then, were given to understand that only an extraordinary situation such as war could intensify scientists' weak sentiments of loyalty and attachment to nation to the point of giving up temporarily their primary allegiance to the ideals of

320 Professionals and the Government

science and basic scientific research. Politicians' perception of the alienated nature of scientists was perhaps strengthened when they learned that, even under the crisis of war, the loyalties of Japanese scientists were suspect because they had trained abroad for years. The international orientation and sympathy, which they were presumed to have, raised doubts of their attachment to the nation and the government, to the point where their services were hardly used. As Dr. Compton testified:

...The Japanese civilian scientists were apparently greatly distrusted by both the army and the navy, and we didn't find a single case of a university scientist who had been asked to do a war job who was given the information as to what the war job was to be—what was its military use.... The reasons for failure to trust the civilian scientists were several. One was that most of the Japanese top scientists have been trained in Europe or America and had been for four to seven years in residence, with frequent visits, and they were suspected by the Japanese military of having foreign connections or foreign sympathies, and that is one reason they were not trusted....

Kilgore asked:

Did you find this which was asserted 2½ years ago prevailed before the fall of France, that the military forces in France would not accept information or advice from the scientific personnel of their universities or their leading scientists in solving problems? (*Sci. Leg.*, 1945, pp. 638–639)

Senator Magnuson reflected politicians' suspicion that scientists' primary allegiance was normally to the value system of science and scientific research and that such allegiance might conflict with the needs of government. To a witness's comment that every loyal American scientist would gladly join a proposed scientific reserve, Magnuson replied:

And now, during the war we had no such Reserve, but the scientists voluntarily came down here and did the job. Do you think that while the scientists might do that again, the Reserve would probably be an anchor to windward? (*Sci. Leg.*, 1945, p. 176)

Another issue stemming from the same basic source of conflict that reinforced politicians' image of their attentuated

loyalty and attachment to nation was the scientists' insistence on a more full and complete freedom to publish and exchange scientific information than politicians thought desirable. The vigor with which practically every scientist who came before the politicians insisted on their right to this article of their scientific faith was just one more proof of the dedicated nature of the scientific in-group. Politicians' concern was that granting this demand might well jeopardize the national security, since vital secrets, whether inadvertently or deliberately, might be disclosed in the process.

The conflict on this issue was complicated by two factors. On the one hand, politicians feel that they are among the foremost champions and guardians of the national interest and security, especially as regards external sources of danger. As Congressman O'Hara said:

Personally, I am a nationalist; first, last, and always. I think when we get to the point where we are thinking about everybody else in the world and forgetting our own national welfare and our own people, we are in rather bad shape. Maybe that is isolationism. Call it what you will, that is the way I feel. (*NSF*, 1949, p. 90)

On the other hand, they were confronted with the fact that the subject matter with which scientists dealt was, and always would be, a mystery to them. Politicians were permanently barred from gaining access to and knowledge of scientific matters. Consequently, in this one respect, they looked upon scientists as a sort of secret society from which they were excluded.

Politicians' perceptions of scientists as a secret society and their resentment of this barrier in their dealings with scientists was clearly voiced by Senator Tydings. After Alvin Weinberg had told Senator Johnson he was wrong in believing that resistance to forward motion in water increased with the depth of the water, Tydings remarked rather bitterly:

Apparently that is one of those scientific facts we are supposed to accept and not ask why. (*Spec. Comm.*, 1945, p. 337)

Senator Thye indicated that politicians still held the same view of scientists several years later in his comment during the hearings on the Bureau of Standard's rejection of the claims made for a battery additive. After Dr. Astin, the Director, had explained the technical grounds for the Bureau's decision, Thye exclaimed:

That is where you have always got us as a scientist because you can get into that technical field and we are left behind in a daze: we are not sure whether we dare challenge you or not. ...(*Batt. AD-X2,* 1953, p. 304)

Politicians were not only frustrated by their inability to challenge scientists but also by their dependence on scientists in the new

atomic age. Whether Congressmen liked it or not, their survival depended to a large extent upon trusting the scientists and admitting them to the public policymaking process. Senator Thye's outburst points up what is probably the single most important aspect of the relations of politicians and scientists: namely, the ability of men with such wide divergences in training and experience to achieve that degree of common agreement and mutual understanding that is required for cooperative effort in advancing the goals of a democratic society.

Professional Pressure Groups

Organized political lobbies and pressure groups to promote the interests of certain social groupings and strata are normal occupants of legislative halls in any representative form of government. Some professional associations maintain political lobbies and engage in political tactics that are among the most organized and effective in modern societies. Such is certainly the case with the American Medical Association, as is shown in the following *Yale Law Journal* report.

The Editors of the *Yale Law Journal* (Medicine)

THE POLITICAL BASIS OF POWER

Prestige

The political strength of the AMA is to a large degree attributable to the status of the doctor in society. Because of his services to humanity, his learning, and economic position, the physician enjoys prestige and public confidence. The public looks to the doctor for advice and gives great weight to his opinion.[1] This trust, unchallenged in the realm of medical science, extends also into economic and political aspects of health.

Because of the AMA's high percentage of physician membership and its status as spokesman for the doctor, the lawmaker turns to organized medicine to ascertain medical opinion.

Mastery of political tactics

Attempting to influence governmental decision is one of the historic purposes of organized medicine.[2] Without encouraging public action of a regulatory nature, the

Reprinted from "The American Medical Association: Power, Purpose, and Politics in Organized Medicine—The Political Basis of Power," *The Yale Law Journal,* 63, No. 7 (May 1954), 954–959. Used by permission.

[1] "Doctors properly rate high in the social scale and sometimes politically they exercise important influence. The reasons are partly the many varied contacts they have with cases and people and partly the professionally-trained type of personnel they have become. Thereby they qualify to teach of things that relate to the body and that people do not any too well understand and likewise exert over them an influence in political and family matters." Brown, *Organization for Health* 1938, p.15.

[2] One of the principal reasons for the organization of the Medical Society of Virginia was "to memorialize the legislature of Virginia for the passage of a Medical Practice Act." Blanton, *Medicine in Virginia* 1923, p. 110. Reporting in 1854 upon the early accomplishments of AMA, the President cited as highly important the AMA's role in "the enactment of wholesome, laws both by the Federal and State Governments." Fishbein, p. 59.

early medical societies could not have fully realized their objective of raising medical standards. But regulation of the professions is a function of the states, and medical legislation has been, until recently, devoted primarily to policing medical practice rather than providing medical care.[3] So the American Medical Association had few occasions to influence political action on the national level.[4] However, with growing public acknowledgment of governmental responsibilities in furnishing medical care[5] the political activities of the AMA have expanded enormously.[6] This development, most pronounced on the federal level, has also been manifest in the states.[7] But while the public may have confidence in the judgment of individual doctors, it may be suspicious of selfish motivations in an organized group. Therefore organized medicine's new "lobbying" has developed techniques of creating a favorable public opinion to supplement the older techniques of direct contact with lawmakers.

The American Medical Association is considered by some observers the most powerful legislative lobby in Washington.[8] Measures apparently assured of passage have been voted down, buried in committee, or substantially amended upon the announcement of AMA disapproval.[9] In

physical size the AMA's lobbying facilities are not impressive.[10] Yet during 1949 and 1950 the AMA reported the highest expenditures of any group registered under the federal lobbying law.[11] While its financial outlay has since declined,[12] its potential influence remains unimpaired.

Both national and state organizations

---

3 Garceau, p. 14.

4 In 1899 the Committee on National Legislation was first created to represent the AMA. Fishbein, p. 1018. As recently as 25 years ago the AMA's lobby was described as relatively inactive. Herring, *Group Representation before Congress*, 1929, p. 184.

5 Anderson, "Public Health—A Mandate from the People," *Am. J. of Public Health* 42, 1952, 1367, 1369.

6 "The Doctor in Politics," *Consumer Reports*, Feb., 1950, p. 75; Means, "The Doctors' Lobby," *Atlantic Monthly*, Oct., 1950, p. 57.

7 See text at note 28.

8 "Some rather expert observers of the art of lobbying as practiced in Washington assert that the AMA is the only organization in the country that could marshal 140 votes in Congress between sundown Friday night and noon on Monday. Performances of this sort have led some to describe the AMA lobby as the most powerful in the country." Huston, "AMA is Potent Force Among the Lawmakers," *N.Y. Times*, June 15, 1952, § 4, p. 7, col. 6.

9 E.g., in 1950 the AMA Washington office reported that no bill opposed by the AMA had

been passed by Congress and that several favored by the AMA were enacted. *JAMA* 144 1950, 637.

The 1952 social security bill was defeated by a 150 to 140 vote after the AMA had announced its opposition to a single feature of the bill. A few days prior to the AMA's anouncement, proponents had been able to muster a two-thirds vote for a suspension of the rules, apparently ensuring an immediate favorable vote. Huston, note 8.

See also *JAMA* 143 1950, 1264 (federal aid to medical education bill pigeon-holed); *JAMA* 143 1950, 478 (provision in 1950 social security bill dropped).

10 The Washington office, established in 1944, has only three registered lobbyists, although a few state societies also send representatives to Washington.

Measures proposed in Congress are studied and reports on bills of medical interest are made to a committee of the Board of Trustees and a decision is reached on what position, if any, the Association will take. *JAMA* 144 1950, 637; *It's Your AMA*, 21 1953. Once the organization's position has been determined, legislators are informed of it and public pressure is brought to bear on important measures.

Personal contact with legislators is stressed and the personal physician of every Congressman is informed of the stand taken so that he may present the Association's views if the occasion arises. "The Doctor in Politics," *Consumer Reports*, Feb., 1950, pp. 75, 76. At Committee hearings it is customary to have high officials of the AMA and state societies appear to testify.

Those opposing the AMA's stand are frequently labelled "subversive" or accused of selfish motivations. See e.g.: "Nickolay Lenin, one of the Gods of the Marxist party line, laid down this fundamental precept: 'socialized medicine is the keystone to the arch of the Socialist State.' " AMA, *Compulsory Health Insurance—Politically Controlled Medicine* 1949 p. 17. See also Means, "The Doctors' Lobby," *Atlantic Monthly*, Oct. 1950, pp. 57, 58.

11 7 *Cong. Quarterly Almanac* 718 (1951) (the AMA's 1950 lobbying allocation was $1,326,078.)

12 In 1952 the AMA was reported as the second highest spender among registered lobbyists in Washington. The Association reported expenditures of $309,514 for that year. *N.Y. Times*, May 3, 1953, p. 34, col. 1. In 1953 it dropped to sixth place, reporting expenditures of $106,624. *New Haven Register*, Apr. 6, 1954, p. 14, col. 2.

have public relations programs to present the views of organized medicine.[13] Attempts are made to solicit editorial support and societies have purchased advertising in the press and on radio and television.[14] These efforts are generally designed to illustrate the achievements of American medicine; sometimes they may be directed to medico-political issues.[15] Member physicians are urged to participate in these political endeavors by delivering public addresses— the texts of which are often furnished by state or national headquarters,[16] and by distributing literature in waiting rooms[17] and with monthly bills.[18] Doctors' wives, working through medical society auxiliaries, are also active in this type of work.[19]

Organized medicine also attempts to demonstrate numerical support for its position by getting outside groups to "go on record" as allies. Related professions in particular share common political interests

with medicine. The recently formed Inter-Association Committee on Health, consisting of the AMA and the American Dental, Hospital, Public Health, Nursing, and Public Welfare Associations, serves as liaison in this area.[20] During health insurance controversies, medical supply houses, pharmaceutical firms, and insurance companies cooperated closely with the AMA, rendering financial assistance and publishing tie-in advertising furnished by the medical societies.[21]

Some of organized medicine's present political power may be attributable to the increased activity of its members in political affairs. The AMA supports no party or candidate, but in many localities physicians organize separate "healing arts" committees to campaign for candidates favorable to the Association's views.[22] The formation of these committees has been approved and their choice of candidates endorsed in some instances by local medical societies,[23] although the latter practice is not common. The work of these healing arts committees is thought to have been influential in several close congressional contests and primaries.[24]

The medical societies also exert great influence over medical legislation on the state and local levels. The enactment of favored measures and the defeat of those

[13] AMA, *Guide to Services* 1952, p. 68. Many state societies employ full- or part-time public relations officers. *Questionnaire* No. 62.

[14] Several societies purchased, or were given as a "public service," newspaper space and radio or television time for public information and "AMA campaign" purposes. *Questionnaire* No. 64.

[15] See collection of newspaper advertising layouts on file in Yale Law Library.

[16] Thirteen state societies reported the existence of state or county Speakers Bureaus and one society was supplied with speakers by the AMA Councils on Medical Service and Public Relations. *Questionnaire* No. 63. The AMA Department of Public Relations will furnish state and county societies with slides and "sample talks" describing AMA activities. *It's Your AMA* 1953, p. 26.

[17] Almost all societies reported that members displayed pamphlets in their waiting rooms during the AMA's campaign against compulsory health insurance. *Questionnaire* No. 80. Initial shipments from national headquarters to state societies were to be "on the basis of 50 pamphlets per doctor." *A Simplified Blueprint of the Campaign against Compulsory Health Insurance* (1949) hereinafter, cited as *Blueprint*).

[18] Doctors' bills "are covered with stickers reading, 'as your personal physician. . .Please write your U.S. Senators and Representatives. For more information, ask me.'" Mayer, "The Dogged Retreat of the Doctors," *Harper's,* Dec. 1949, p. 25.

[19] AMA, *Putting PR to Work* (1st Public Relations Institute, 1952), p. 64.

[20] See *JAMA* 146 1951, 835.

[21] *Questionnaire* No. 81; "The Doctor in Politics," *Consumer Reports,* Feb., 1950, pp. 75, 76–77.

[22] *Questionnaire* No. 80.

[23] E.g., in Pennsylvania's 26th Congressional District the Healing Arts Committee's candidate was officially endorsed by the Cambria County Medical Society. The Society was also active in the Committee's formation. Cunningham, "Can Political Means Gain Professional Ends?", *Modern Hospitals,* Dec. 1951, p. 51.

[24] In Florida the defeat of Senator Pepper by Congressman Smathers "can be attributed in part to their respective stands" on health insurance. *Florida Questionnaire* No. 83.

The New Hampshire Society takes credit for making greater the already inevitable defeat of a pro-health insurance candidate. *New Hampshire Questionnaire* No. 83.

In Montana a Senatorial incumbent favoring health insurance was re-elected, but the society claims his victory cannot be attributed to his stand on that issue. *Montana Questionnaire* No. 83.

opposed can usually be secured.[25] State societies have a lobbyist or legislative agent, often the executive secretary.[26] The societies also actively encourage their members to run for legislative positions to insure adequate representation of the organization's interests.[27] Personal contact with each legislator, if possible by his own physician, pis stressed.[28] County societies may also endeavor to have prominent local doctors write their legislators and encourage their patients to do likewise.[29] Much state medical legislation originates with the state societies,[30] bills are often drafted with the aid of counsel, and such measures are easily introduced.[31]

While influencing the actions of legislative bodies constitutes the most apparent means of determining governmental action, the continuing relationships of organized medicine with administrative agencies are no less important. It is at this level that much public health legislation originates[32] and is implemented by rules and regulations; here also enforcement takes place. The AMA and its constituent societies have many councils and committees which serve public agencies in an advisory capacity.[33] Such bodies can gather information of a professional nature not readily available to government officials. And by receiving the views of the profession on specific regulations the public agency obtains the opinion of one of the groups vitally affected and whose cooperation is necessary for the success of most programs.

The medical societies have also attempted to increase the profession's influence in administrative decisions by trying to make medical licensure a prerequisite for positions of control over health or medical programs.[34] The influence of medicine upon administrative agencies is probably stronger on the state than on the national level. Many state health officials are appointed on the recommendation of the medical

[25] Almost all societies report that their members have been active in drafting subsequently enacted legislation such as state Basic Science Laws and Medical Practice Acts. *Questionnaire No. 67.*

[26] *Questionnaire Nos. 65–66.*

[27] See, e.g., Iowa State Medical Society, *Handbook for the House of Delegates* 1952, **49**. And it is not uncommon to find society officers serving in the legislatures. See note 32.

[28] "The Doctor in Politics," *Consumer Reports,* Feb., 1950, pp. 75, 76; *N.Y. State J. of Med.* **31**, 1931, 109.

[29] The New York Society's legislative agent suggests the names of legislators to whom prominent local physicians should write and all county members are urged to contact their patients. New York Medical Society Legislative Bull., March 3, 1953.

[30] *Questionnaire No. 67.*

[31] E.g., in 1935 Dr. Marcus Newcomb was majority leader of the New Jersey Assembly and in 1936 served as Speaker. During this period he was also President of the New Jersey State Medical Society and managed all public health bills in its behalf. McKean, *Pressures on the Legislature of New Jersey,* 1938, p. 232.

[32] Anderson, "Public Health—A Mandate from the People," *Am. J. of Public Health* **42**, 1952, 1367.

[33] E.g., the AMA Council on Food and Nutrition works with federal and local health regulatory agencies; the Committee on Federal Medical Services cooperates with governmental groups; and in 1949 the Director of the Bureau of Health Education was loaned by the AMA to military government as a consultant in public health practices. AMA, *Guide to Services* 1952, pp. 39, 58, 65. And in New York the state society's Workmen's Compensation Bureau has worked closely with the state's own Workmen's Compensation Board on matters involving medical practice under state law. *You and the Medical Society of the State of New York* 1952, pp. 35–37. One of the reasons for placing organized medicine in a position of responsibility was the eradication, in industrial accident cases, of fee splitting and "kick-backs" at the state's expense. Governor Herbert Lehman's Special Message to the Legislature (1934), quoted in Greenberg, "Studies of Medical Leadership: The New York County Medical Society and Workmen's Compensation," *Physicians Forum Bull.,* Sept. 1951, p. 11. But the societies' representatives have been severely criticized for having "seemingly closed their eyes to this widespread system, except as to one commercial establishment engaging in x-ray examinations in competition with physicians...." Report to Governor Thomas E. Dewey by Commissioners to Examine and Investigate the Administration of the Workmen's Compensation Law of the State of New York (1944), quoted in Greenberg.

[34] "Public health relies in the last analysis on medical science.... The physician must be a central figure in any successful public health program." Bauer, "The Physician's Place in the Health Program," *JAMA* 107 1936, 485. See also *JAMA* **143** 1950, 560.

society,[35] and it is often through their offices that federal health grants are administered. Health officials, knowing the legislative influence of the medical societies, are not likely to incur their antagonism. Having accused Federal Security Administrator Oscar Ewing of sympathies toward "socialized medicine," the AMA consistently opposed provisions which would grant his agency discretionary authority in administering health programs. But such outright enmity between organized medicine and health agencies is the exception rather than the rule.

Legal Recognition

As a consequence of its monopoly position, financial resources, and political strength,

[35] *Questionnaire* Nos. 36, 38. In over half the states reporting, the societies recommend appointees for heads of the state health departments, while in Alabama the society itself makes the appointment.

organized medicine is able to maintain a quasi-legal status in medical affairs. In many states, laws authorize state and local medical societies to appoint or recommend members of regulatory bodies.[36] AMA standards in medical education, training, and practice are usually adopted by law. In addition, AMA inspection to determine whether its own standards have been satisfied is seldom subject to judicial review. Thus the political authority of the state itself has in effect been delegated to organized medicine.

[36] In half the states reporting the society recommends appointees for the State Board of Medical Examiners, in others the society nominates candidates for this office, and in one state the State Medical Society Board of Censors itself constitutes the State Board of Medical Examiners. *Questionnaire* No. 31. See, e.g., Conn. Gen. Stats. § 4365 (1949) (nominations by society); Mass. Laws Ann. c. 13, §10 (1952) (Governor appoints with consent of society).

Questions for Discussion and Further Research

In the reading in Chapter 2, we obtained a glimpse of Emile Durkheim's vision of professional groups serving as independent sources of political power mediating between the power of a central government and the interests of the masses of the electorate. In the readings in the present chapter, however, we see how some governments impose restrictions on professional groups through licensing (King) and how some professional groups, acting as organized political lobbies, exert strong influences on government policies (Editors of the *Yale Law Journal*). These considerations raise the general question as to the degree to which professional associations represent truly *independent* sources of political power in terms of Durkheim's concept, or the degree to which professional groups integrate their interests and activities with those of governmental agencies to form an *interdependent* power elite in modern societies, more in accord with C. Wright Mills' concept.* More specifically, under what circumstances are modern governments becoming more dependent upon professional contributions and cooperation? Conversely, to what extent, and under what circumstances, are modern professional groups becoming any more or less dependent upon governmental sanction and protection? Moreover, what are the effects of governmental sanction and protection of older professions in relation to the emergence of newer professions with interests in somewhat overlapping and competing areas? Under what conditions may licensing establish professional monopolies that lead to social rigidity and the inability of a society to adapt to technological and social change?

* See C. Wright Mills, *The Power Elite* (New York: Oxford University Press, 1956).

In addition, the writings of C. P. Snow and others might lead us to expect some shifts in the patterns of relations between certain professional groups and government agencies.† As social and technological changes occur, to what extent might changes in the professional backgrounds of elected and appointed government officials be expected? For example, to what extent would scientists and engineers be expected to increase and attorneys to decrease in number and influence in government employment? If scientists and engineers do not actually become government officials themselves, they may exert increasingly strong influences upon government policy through scientific advisory boards connected with administrative agencies and as individual consultants to legislative committees, as may be predicted in part from the material prepared by Hall in this chapter.

The paper by Lipset and Schwartz raises significant questions about the influence of professionalization upon the behavior of the electorate in a democratic society. Professionalization does not necessarily lead to liberalism in political behavior. Indeed, Lipset and Schwartz show that it is more likely to result in commitment to the status quo, except where professional expectations are thwarted by a lack of job opportunities in the national society. While political theorists in the traditions of Thomas Jefferson have seen advances in the educational level of the electorate as a support for liberal democracy, there are indications that advancing the general level of education, coupled with advanced professionalization of key groups in the electorate, may lead to rigidities in political structure and even to authoritarian movements under certain conditions. Therefore, it would appear that a viable democratic society needs more knowledge about the conditions under which authoritarian movements may be associated with professionalization and about how this kind of linkage can be avoided.

† See, for example, C. P. Snow, *Science and Government* (Cambridge, Mass.: Harvard Univ. Press, 1961).

IO

Status Differences and Professionalization

Professionalization is profoundly affected by outside social forces which may appear to be extraneous and irrelevant, but are influential nonetheless. The editors and authors of selections in this volume have alluded to some of these influences previously, but here we wish to concentrate special attention on the effects of certain extraoccupational factors.

What are some of the links between the large social life and occupations? One of the more obvious involves social status and prestige. For example, although occupations may develop in different ways in different societies, the study cited earlier by Alex Inkeles and Peter Rossi indicated that highly professionalized occupations, along with certain leading political and industrial occupations, are consistently ranked highest in social prestige in modern industrial societies.* The authors of this report attributed the consistent high ranking of these occupational categories to a common recognition of fundamental social needs for administrative coordination, health protection, socialization and training of youth, and enhancement of scientific and technical knowledge performed by these occupations. In all of the more complex societies, socio-economic status-conferring characteristics are associated with how men make their living.

Occupations, to a considerable extent, serve to place a man in his society. Occupations which are middle- or high-ranking in socio-economic status may offer a mobility potential. The individual who seeks and attains a prestigious occupation often has bettered his socio-economic status. But how is it that occupations come to have higher or lower prestige associated with them? According to R. M. Thomas, prestige involves a number of subdimensions, and higher prestige is accorded "an occupation which represents greater power or control over larger numbers of people or over sources of greater wealth...";

* Alex Inkeles and Peter Rossi, "National Comparisons of Occupational Prestige," *The American Journal of Sociology*, 61, 1956, 329–339.

one "...which yields higher financial rewards..."; one "which figures crucially in an individual's life at times of crisis (the physician at times of illness, the lawyer when a person is threatened with prison)..."; one "...which demands more formal education..."; one "...which involves primarily mental-verbal activities..."; and, finally, "an occupation which contributes more to the society's pursuit of its ideals...."†

In the context of professionalization, part of the interest in prestige stems from an observation made in the discussion about client-practitioner tensions: the prestige of occupations has a way of influencing relations between clients and practitioners,‡ as well as among practitioners themselves. In his discussion of teamwork among professional people, for example, Eaton says, "The difficulties of integrating different levels of prestige has been a primary stumbling block of many team research efforts."§

It was also remarked in passing in Chapter 3 that socio-economic background, together with ethnicity, tends to affect the recruitment process, particularly in the highly professionalized occupations.** As Hughes clearly recognized, fitness to pursue an occupation is evaluated by colleagues and public alike, not solely in terms of actual competency at work skills, but also in terms of what he called "auxiliary characteristics." When the public comes to recognize and behave in accordance with these auxiliary characteristics, then the characteristics become enshrined in occupational stereotypes—a process discussed in Chapter 4. As Hughes put it, "There tends to grow up about a status, in addition to its specifically determining traits, a complex of auxiliary characteristics which come to be expected of its incumbents."†† A society may select any particular characteristics people associate with an occupation in an evaluative way. For the most part, however, a few characteristics become salient. We have noted socio-economic status, but consideration must also be given to other forms of social differentiation which involve invidious comparisons, such as age, sex, and ethnicity.

For example, what, if any, are the influences exerted by "retired" persons upon the gainful occupations which they follow after they have concluded their major career interest? The effects would be diffuse and unimportant if these persons distributed themselves proportionally throughout the labor force; but such is not the case, for they tend to be attracted to certain occupational sectors. In the instance of retired military officers, they are attracted to administrative positions in business and industry (particularly defense-connected operations), education, and government, where they can exercise some of their past skills. This category of persons is of significance in our society not only because of its size, but because of the early age at which retirement takes place

† R. Murray Thomas, "Reinspecting a Structural Position on Occupational Prestige," *The American Journal of Sociology*, 67, No. 5 (March 1962), 565.
‡ See Chapter 6.
§ Joseph W. Eaton, "Social Processes of Professional Teamwork," *American Sociological Review*, 16, No. 5 (October 1951), 710.
** For detailed examples, see C. Stuart Adams, "Trends in Occupational Origins of Physicians," *American Sociological Review*, 18, No. 4 (August 1953), 404–409, and J. H. Fichter, *Religion as an Occupation* (South Bend: University of Notre Dame Press, 1961), pp. 59–87 *passim*.
†† Everett C. Hughes, "Dilemmas and Contradictions of Status," *The American Journal of Sociology*, 50 (March 1945), 353.

and the consequent possibility for the exerting of long-term influences on the shaping of occupations.‡‡

An intriguing facet of the relationship between social status differences and occupational change is the direct and sometimes deliberate modification of the professionalization process. There is the use of emerging occupations, especially the more professionalized, as vehicles of social mobility. Because some people want to "get ahead" in life, they may engage in vigorous efforts of professionalism in the occupation. If enough occupational members act this way, the status of that occupation may come to be enhanced over time. This is particularly evident with new scientific disciplines, in the entertainment and mass communications industries, and in health and welfare occupations.

In this connection it is interesting to speculate about the possible effects of the Jews as an ethnic group on the development of new occupations. In the fields of entertainment and communication, in which individuals of Jewish background have played prominent parts, there has been considerable professionalization. In the past, there was a time when entertainment was considered a very low-status activity. This has changed; now actors, directors, and production specialists usually undergo formal training and occupational socialization experiences to fit them for their work. The expected level of expertise and quality of production continues to increase. Within the Jewish culture there is a longstanding emphasis on work achievement and intellectual excellence; that is, the Jewish culture has provided fundamental values which tend to support professionalism in newly created or already existing occupations. Where significant proportions of Jews have participated in occupational development, the impact of their cultural heritage is manifest. The same may be said about the influences of other ethnic groups on certain occupations.

Ethnic Status and Occupational Dilemmas

Thus race, religion, and national background have all played their part in the development of occupations and in the way occupations are followed. Often, though, these auxiliary characteristics create occupational dilemmas. Jeffery has discussed differential entrance policies in the occupations of law and medicine.§§ These policies have not always been exercised as blatantly as has been the case with Negro entrants, yet even less noticeable differential treatment has had its effect. Jeffery notes that Jews have experienced significantly different career patterns than have their gentile counterparts. The dominant and ideal professional career pattern that has evolved for the middle-class, white, Protestant male is either in medicine or law; but Jeffery seems to feel that ethnic discriminatory practices have not been as evident in the legal as in the medical profession.

Similarly, Lieberson "...considered some effects of the auxiliary status of

‡‡ See Leonard Reissman, "Life Careers, Power and the Professions: The Retired Army General," *The American Sociological Review,* **21**, No. 2 (April 1956), 215–221.

§§ C. Ray Jeffery, with the collaboration of E. Eugene Davis and Henry H. Foster, Jr., "The Legal Profession," in E. J. Davis, *et al., Society and the Law* (New York: Free Press of Glencoe, Inc., 1962), pp. 320–321.

ethnic membership upon the practice of medicine."*** He compared Anglo-Saxon, Irish, Italian, Jewish, and Polish practitioners and found that

...the data strongly suggest that the ethnic identification of physicians significantly influences their pattern of medical practice. Both the spatial distribution and the functional differentiation [specialization within practice] of physicians reported here suggest that medicine may be viewed as a system resulting from and concordant with the more specialized and segregated services performed by each component of the medical profession.†††

Why status differences have so much to do with medicine and how they come into being must be considered. In the chapter on professional associations and colleague relations we confined most of our remarks to formal kinds of organization. As sociologists and others have recognized for some time, however, the informal organization of any situation may be just as important, or perhaps more important, than the formal. The discussion of these informal factors is undertaken here because status differences may enter so importantly into the informal organization of work, as Oswald Hall learned in his studies of the medical profession.‡‡‡ He found that ethnicity and religion were the most significant variables in the recruitment process. He refers to the dominant group as the "inner fraternity."

The situation which Oswald Hall described for the medical profession is by no means atypical. It is common for highly professionalized occupations to be controlled, to a large extent, by an "inner fraternity" who operate through the control of professional associations such as those discussed previously, and through what Hall calls the "sponsorship process." The latter mechanism is used extensively in all highly professionalized occupations. If, as is usually the case with these occupations, a relatively small group shapes occupational development both formally and informally, then informal means must also be studied. The following selection from Oswald Hall's paper describes concepts of informal organization and lists the conclusions he draws regarding their application to professional development.

*** Stanley Lieberson, "Ethnic Groups and the Practice of Medicine," *American Sociological Review,* **23**, No. 5 (October 1958), 549.
††† *Loc. cit.*
‡‡‡ Oswald Hall, "The Informal Organization of the Medical Profession," *The Canadian Journal of Economics and Political Science,* **22**, 1946, 30–44.

Oswald Hall (Medicine)

The title of this paper calls attention to a neglected feature of professional life and offers a basic concept for the study of professions. It is presumed here that the *established* members of the profession will in the course of time develop a sort of organization which functions to provide

Reprinted from "The Informal Organization of the Medical Profession," *The Canadian Journal of Economics and Political Science,* 12, 1946, pp. 32–33 and 43–44. Used by permission of the author and publisher.

order, to ascribe and maintain status, to control the conduct of the members, and to minimize competition and conflict. In other words they will develop an orderly manner of incorporating new members into their community, of repelling the unwanted and the intruder, of allocating rights and privileges, of distributing clients among colleagues, of applying sanctions and penalties, and preserving their status.

To call such an organization 'informal,' implies that it does not originate by establishing a constitution. Actually it may possess no formal constitution. In this case the activity precedes the recognition of a purpose, and the group may have a well-defined pattern of action without any official apologia. It is an assumption of this paper that the working constitution of any established profession is something that has to be discovered. Moreover it is very likely to deviate significantly from the formal constitution. The latter is likely to present an idealized picture of what the members would like outsiders to believe, and should not be accepted uncritically as a description of the workings of the professional group.

The foregoing discussion has set forth some of the activities of the profession over which the informal organization exercises control. In this paper the informal organization of the medical profession is referred to as the "inner fraternity." The name connotes that the group has some of the characteristics of the secret society, some of the features of the primary group, and that the relationships are closer and more inclusive than those of sheer colleagues.

While the inner fraternity influences the practice of medicine in diverse ways it has one dominant method of functioning. Its basic activity is referred to here as "sponsorship." By sponsorship is meant simply that established members of the inner fraternity actively intervene in the career lines of newcomers to the profession. By so doing they influence the careers of those selected. The intervention may continue over very long spans of time and relate to many features of the professional career. Sponsorship is a dual process. It facilitates the careers of those selected, and relegates those not so selected to a position where they compete under decidedly disadvantageous terms. In this way it tends to keep the inner fraternity a stable, self-perpetuating group, and maintains its control over the profession in general.

Much of the assistance given by the sponsor to his protégé is of an intangible sort. It may be as nebulous as the help of an older person who encourages a younger person to define himself as a potential colleague. Since the professional ambition is, in its early stages, a fragile affair this aid is very important. However, the aid may be much more substantial. It may mean smoothing the path to easy acceptance to the right training school; it may mean appointments to positions within the appropriate institutions; it may mean deflecting clientele from the sponsor to the protégé; it may mean designating the protégé as successor to the sponsor.

Such sponsorship is not necessarily a one-sided process. It permits the newcomer to share in the established system of practicing medicine, but it also imposes responsibilities upon him. It obligates him to fulfil the minor positions in the institutional system. Where he needs expert advice or assistance it obligates him to turn to his sponsor. And if he is designated as a successor to an established member of the profession he necessarily takes over the duties and obligations involved there. Hence the protégé is essential to the continued functioning of the established inner fraternity of the profession.

The assumption of the inner fraternity provides a frame of reference for observing the conduct of the members of the profession. It provides a sort of lens for drawing into focus types of facts which would otherwise escape the notice of the enquirer.

The above materials document the existence of an inner fraternity within the medical profession, a spatially segregated group, homogeneous with respect to ethnic and religious affiliations, involved in the lucrative specialized fields of medicine, occupying the dominant hospital posts, and having preferred claims on the good paying clienteles of the city. It maintains its existence, and controls the practice of medicine, by sponsoring new members.

The interview materials exhibit the ramifications of the sponsorship process. Six distinctive activities are worthy of note. (1) The selection of recruits to the profession. The members of the inner fraternity exercise an indirect control over the selection policies of medical schools by their recommendations of students. No significant studies have been made to date of the manner in which medical schools recruit and select their students. (2) The selection of interns. His internship is one of the most important status badges that the doctor wears. It can never be discarded, and serves immediately to categorize the doctor. It constitutes a persisting judgment on the young doctor, and represents a crucial turning-point in his career. By their institutional positions the inner fraternity control the allocation of the better internships. (3) The appointment of externs. An externship is the legitimate avenue to progress in the hospital system of the community. It obligates the doctor to work in the charity clinics. It involves a heavy tax on time and energy. It is an index that the incumbent is in earnest about his medical career. The inner fraternity controls the allocation of these. (4) Appointment to staff positions. These are an indication that the doctor has "arrived." Externships are both sifting devices and periods of probation. The inner fraternity decides which externs will be selected for staff positions, and how long the periods of probation will be. (5) Incorporation into the office practice. The durable medical practices of the community persist beyond the lives of the founders. The latter can invite younger men to share and inherit such practices. Such an invitation carries with it the prestige associated with the office itself, and with the name of the established doctor. It carries the endorsa-

tion and certification of the established doctor. The members of the inner fraternity have a monopoly over such favors. (6) Incorporation into the system of referrals. The practice of medicine is synonymous with the acquisition of a clientele. The chief vehicle for acquiring patients is the referral of another doctor. There is no speedy route to this goal. One must traverse the designated stages and be vouched for at each stage by an established member of the fraternity. One maintains his position in such a system by remaining personally acceptable to the membership of the inner group.

In conclusion it seems worthwhile calling attention to the type of knowledge that can be obtained concerning a profession by ignoring the techniques of the profession and focusing attention on the social organization. The concepts of the inner fraternity and the sponsoring process seem to offer a particularly fruitful lead to the study of any profession. They are useful tools for tracing the stages in the professional career, for understanding the mechanisms of control within the profession, and for interpreting the milieu within which professional life is carried on.

We have been considering the situation of ethnicity where cultural and religious backgrounds influence the professionalization process. As a consequence, a justifiable concern about occupational standards may lead to social exclusiveness, which in turn leads to occupationally irrelevant and sometimes socially dysfunctional behavior. Moreover, ethnicity affects the way people follow an occupation and the way people avail themselves of the services provided by that occupation. To further the examination of ethnic status, however, we should consider the more complex case of the great and disturbing ethnic problem in our time: the Negro. This is where cultural background is complicated by a racial difference which has high social visibility.

A notable example of an occupation fundamentally affected by the Negro is that of the jazz musician. The influence of the Negro upon other sectors of the work world has generally been less—something attributable not to a lack of talent, but rather to the categorical exclusion of the Negro from these kinds of work. This exclusion has been particularly pronounced in the more highly professionalized occupations where non-Negro occupational incumbents have practiced involved forms of direct and indirect discrimination. The Negro who pursues a highly professionalized occupation often has extraordinary work experiences. The process of professionalization certainly contributes to *ambiguity* in job opportunities for Negroes. On one hand, it enhances discriminatory practices by fostering tendencies toward exclusiveness among groups who control access to colleague relations; on the other hand, professionalization lays greater stress on universalism and achieved status—a man is to be judged upon what he can do, rather than who he is or was. The following selection reports on the situation of the Negro colleges and universities and affords examples of some of the dilemmas that go along with being a Negro college teacher.

Daniel C. Thompson
(College Teaching)

In some respects the study on which this paper is based may be described as the first comprehensive analysis of the career patterns of teachers in colleges for Negroes. This is not to say that no previous inquiries have been made. The truth is, literature dealing with Negro colleges is fairly extensive, yet for the most part attention is focused upon the colleges as a unit, and only incidental consideration is given to the teacher as such.

Nature of the Study

This study makes use of four kinds of material: (1) literature on the occupational culture of teachers in higher education,[1] (2) observations as a former student and graduate of three Negro institutions of higher education, and as a teacher in Negro colleges for ten years, (3) interviews with 50 teachers in 30 different Negro colleges, and (4) a mailed questionnaire consisting of 96 questions which was filled out and returned by 1,110 teachers in 53 of the 72 accredited Negro degree-granting colleges.

The teachers responding to the questionnaire constitute 22 per cent of the estimated 5,000 teachers on the faculties of the 72

Reprinted from "Career Patterns of Teachers in Negro Colleges," *Social Forces*, 36, No. 3 (March 1958), 270–276. Used by permission of The University of North Carolina Press. The original publication bore the following note: "Read before the twentieth annual meeting of the Southern Sociological Society, Atlanta, Georgia, April 12, 1957. Data used in the paper were taken from Daniel C. Thompson, 'Teachers in Negro Colleges: A Sociological Analysis,' an unpublished doctor's thesis, Columbia University."

[1] When data concerning the career patterns of teachers in Negro colleges are treated as if they were unique it is because comparable data for college teachers at large are inadequate or unavailable.

accredited Negro colleges and 31 per cent of the estimated 3,537 teachers in the sample of 53 representative colleges.

Approximately one-third of the teachers in the sample are female, 11 per cent are white,[2] 28 per cent professors, 19 per cent associate professors, 18 per cent assistant professors, 24 per cent instructors, and 11 per cent not ranked. Also 25 per cent hold some "earned" doctorate, 64 per cent hold the master's, and 11 per cent hold the bachelor's degree only.

The Recruits

As background for discussion of the career patterns of teachers in Negro colleges we shall have to remember that Americans commonly attach great value to education, and that college graduates generally enjoy greater prestige and respect than those who have not attended college. This is especially true among Negroes for whom, in addition to the tangible and intangible values which education symbolizes for Americans generally, a "good education" serves to discredit the doctrine of racial inferiority which has usually embarrassed and penalized Negroes. The better educated Negro is often regarded by others as the most persuasive evidence that Negroes are mentally not unlike other persons of different races, because they have, "in one important respect, become equal to the better class of whites."[3]

Despite the high value Negroes place upon education, they lag, on the whole, far behind white people in their academic

[2] Throughout the study white teachers in Negro colleges are used as a rough controlled group.

[3] Gunnar Myrdal, *An American Dilemma* (New York: Harper & Row, Publishers, 1944), p. 879.

attainments, and these considerable differences in the extent of education among white and Negro Americans help to explain two important facts: first, why there is a relative shortage of well-qualified Negro college teachers; and second, why educated Negroes, particularly those who hold the doctorate or some significant academic administrative post, are usually assigned a higher status in Negro society than their counterparts in white society.

Training of Teachers in Negro Colleges

Although it is beyond the scope of this paper to search out the complex sources of the differences in academic attainments of Negroes and whites, if we are to properly understand the career patterns of teachers in Negro colleges, it may be instructive to mention two conspicuous handicaps the majority of Negro teachers have had to overcome in preparation for academic careers. These are poverty and the substandard character of their graded school and college education.

First, as is well known, the average annual income of Negroes is substantially lower than that of whites. Toward the end of the Great Depression—a strategic decade for our purposes, since fully 53 per cent of the teachers in the sample graduated from college between 1930–1940—the median wage and salary income for white individuals and families was $1,324 and for Negroes only $489. And even today the demian income for Negroes is only about half that for whites.[4]

Since it is a matter of general and firmly documented knowledge that the higher the income of parents the greater the proportion of children going on to college, the relative poverty of the majority of Negro families (particularly during the 1930–1940 period) in itself, quite apart from other restrictions, means that higher education is less accessible to Negroes than to whites.

Marked differences in the financial re-sources of Negro and white families require a substantially larger proportion of Negro than white college students to support themselves in part or entirely, during the course of their studies. Thus 87 per cent of the Negro teachers worked their way through college, compared with 68 per cent of their white colleagues, and some 71 per cent of college graduates at large.[5] In fact 41 per cent of the Negro teachers had to earn half to all of their college expenses, in comparison with just 27 per cent of their white colleagues who earned that proportion.

Not only did the vast majority of Negro college teachers work their way through college, but fully 75 per cent of those with advanced degrees earned some of their graduate school expenses, with 46 per cent earning from half to all. Among their white colleagues just 56 per cent earned some part of their graduate school expenses, with only 29 per cent earning from half to all.

In addition to the work the teachers did to defray the expenses of their education, 52 per cent of the Negro teachers (compared with just 25 per cent of their white colleagues and 33 per cent of college graduates at large) received some scholarship aid while in college. Furthermore, 63 per cent of the Negro teachers compared with 52 per cent of their white colleagues depended heavily upon fellowships to pay for their graduate training.

A second major reason why there is a relative shortage of well-qualified Negro college teachers and why they tend to enjoy higher social status in Negro society than do their counterparts in white society is the fact that the great majority of them have had to overcome inadequate high school and college training in preparation for academic careers.

More than two-thirds of Negro teachers in the sample (69 per cent and 67 per cent respectively) graduated from segregated high schools and colleges in the South where academic standards have been shown to be considerably lower than those main-

[4] See *The Economic Almanac,* 1951–1952 (New York: National Industrial Conference Board), p. 162, and *1952 Negro Year Book* (Tuskegee Institute, Alabama: W. M. H. Wise and Co., 1952), pp. 125–130.

[5] See Ernest Havemann and Patricia S. West, *They Went To College: The College Graduate In America Today* (New York: Harcourt, Brace & World, Inc., 1952), p. 208.

tained for white schools in the same area, to say nothing about the degree to which they fall below national norms.

The extent of the handicap of an inadequate high school and college education as received by the majority of Negro college teachers is suggested by the fact that, whereas 77 per cent of all master's degrees held by Negros were awarded by Negro graduate schools, yet only 20 per cent of the Negro college teachers with master's received them from Negro universities. This means that by and large Negro colleges recruit their teachers from among those who have successfully competed with superior-trained white students in the better graduate schools outside the South. This in itself, apart from the worry and strain of financial difficulties, would limit the number of highly trained Negro college teachers. Thus about 13 or 14 of every 100 white students who graduate from college go on to receive the master's degree subsequently, with about two of every 100 going on for the doctorate. However, only 5 or 6 Negro college graduates of every 100 ever receive a master's degree, with only about one in 1,000 Negro college graduates subsequently receiving the doctorate.

The shortage of highly trained Negro college teachers is best illustrated by the fact that even in 1945, after several years of war that interrupted the education of the vast majority of young men, the "median" American college had 35 per cent of its faculty members holding doctorates.[6] Consequently the Negro colleges in our sample with only 16 per cent of their teachers holding doctorates may be regarded as much more poorly staffed than the "median" American college was even in 1945.

PROFESSIONAL DUTIES

Teaching

The primary function of any educational institution is the dissemination of knowledge. Of course, the teaching function is

[6] President's Commission on Higher Education, *Higher Education for American Democracy*, Vol. II, p. 45.

given different emphasis according to the type of institution. As a rule the smaller or more elementary the institution, the more emphasis it places upon teaching in regard to other academic activities. Yet even the major universities or "research centers" require teachers to spend the greater part of their professional time in instruction.

Since the teaching function is the heart of the academic process, let us consider briefly the contents of the teaching role as it is now performed by the teachers in the sample of 53 colleges. The following points may be instructive:

1. About 90 per cent of the teachers in the sample indicated that they are satisfied with their choice of an academic career. At first glance it seems that the vast majority of teachers in the sample of colleges are dedicated to their profession as a "calling." However, 24 per cent of the Negro teachers and 40 per cent of the white teachers in the sample desire to acquire some non-academic position as soon as possible. Upon closer analysis, then, much of what appears to be dedication to teaching as a "calling" turns out to be a more or less realistic appraisal of existing estimable job opportunities. And so we find that the teachers who, because of sex, race, age, and field of specialization, would normally have the greater chances of preparing for and success in some new nonteaching occupation with comparable or greater prestige are precisely those who most frequently would like to change to some other nonteaching occupation sometime in the future.

2. Almost two-thirds of the teachers indicated that they tend to maintain low or, at least, flexible academic standards in their classes.

Unfortunately there are no comparable data about the academic standards maintained by teachers in colleges where all, or practically all, of the students are white. But lacking such information it seems safe to conclude that the proportion of teachers in Negro colleges who are willing to adjust academic standards to some level lower than normally expected for college students is likely to be larger than for college teachers generally. There may be several reasons for this. In the first place Negro colleges recruit about 85 per cent of their students from among the graduates of segregated high schools where, as a rule, academic standards are lower than what are regarded as national norms. Thus, if a majority of teachers in these colleges would impose normally high academic standards in all of their courses the drop-out rate would likely be so high that enrollment would fall below what might be regarded as minimum. Secondly, several teachers expressed strong humanitarian concern for their students and for the Negroes' struggle for advancement. Some, for example, expressed reluctance to accord low or failing grades to students whose parents make great sacrifices to educate them. Others felt that it was professionally justified to accord relatively high grades to students who plan graduate study because Negro professionals are badly needed and low grades in college may prevent their promising students from being accepted for advanced, or graduate, study.

This does not mean that all teachers in Negro colleges—or that all of these colleges—maintain low or flexible standards. The truth is that, even in colleges that are known to adjust standards to some level below what is normally expected of college students at large, there are individual teachers and departments equally well known for high and exacting standards. And for several decades a few Negro colleges have consistently provided the highest quality of education for their students.

3. The median "teaching load" (the actual number of hours which the teacher spends in the classroom each week) for teachers in the sample is 15 hours a week. Fully 57 per cent carry more than 12 hours, and 10 per cent more than 18 hours. Those who carry 12 hours or less are usually professor-administrants. Thus Negro colleges generally require their teachers to carry what rating agencies regard as the maximum teaching load regardless of the size of the classes or the extent of special help the students require.

4. About a third of the teachers in

Negro colleges may be classified as "itinerant teachers"—that is, they change from one college to another frequently. And unlike what seems to be true of American colleges generally, where the highest turnover is among those of the lowest ranks, the highest turnover in Negro colleges is among the professors and those with the doctorate. Perhaps the primary reason for this is the fact that higher education for Negroes is expanding rapidly creating a serious shortage of well qualified teachers so that such teachers have a wide choice in the selection of colleges in which their services are needed. Therefore 84 per cent of the 364 teachers in the sample who had changed colleges within the last five years had voluntarily resigned their previous positions.

Among the most frequently cited reasons for changing colleges are the following:

(a) Forty-one per cent indicated that their present positions afford greater academic freedom than did their previous positions.

(b) Forty-one per cent improved their academic rank by changing colleges.

(c) Whatever other reasons teachers might have for moving from one college to another, salary is the most important. Almost three-fourths (73 per cent) of those who changed colleges increased their earnings.

Practically all of those who changed colleges cite some "fringe" benefit, such as better working conditions, better living arrangements, and better cultural environment along with the major reasons listed above.

RESEARCH

Although 49 per cent of the teachers in the sample indicated that they were engaged in reseach or creative writing at the time of the study, only 18 per cent of the teachers (26 per cent of the white teachers and 17 per cent of the Negro teachers) had actually contributed anything to published literature during the last five-year period. They are considerably less productive than even the teachers in the "lesser" colleges where 32 per cent made some contribution to printed literature over a five-year period.[7]

There are several major reasons for the low productive scholarship of teachers in Negro colleges. Among them are the following:

1. Most of the teachers are isolated from the main stream of academic life in the United States. The vast majority have at best only infrequent contacts, personally or academically, with "top flight" scholars in their fields of specialization. As a result they can hardly get the needed stimulation to engage in significant research and writing.

2. A large number of the teachers are simply unprepared to do worthwhile independent research or creative writing because their formal training was terminated before they reached the level where some proficiency in these areas is required.

3. The heavy academic duties of most of the teachers do not allow sufficient time for extended research.

4. Funds available for research are usually insufficient or lacking altogether.

5. Few Negro colleges seem to expect teachers to engage in research or creative writing. Only 4 per cent of the teachers ever received a leave of absence to do research; and just 14 per cent of those actively engaged in research indicated that their teaching loads had been reduced. Furthermore, only 25 per cent of the department heads and 32 per cent of the academic deans emphasized independent scholarship as an expected part of the teacher's academic duties. The apparent lack of interest which most of the college administrations manifest in creative scholarship is reflected in the fact that though 55 per cent of the teachers had been teaching on a college level for seven years or more and 34 per cent have had that much experience in the same college, only 7 per cent have ever had a sabbatical leave with continued salary.

6. Since, on the whole, Negro colleges are accorded low status in the academic world, publishing houses and scholarly journals may be somewhat more reluctant to publish their works than they would be to accept the works of teachers from the higher status universities or "research centers," even if their merit is equal.

ADMINISTRATION

In the social system of Negro higher education the adminstrative function seems to be more highly valued than either the teaching or the research function.[8] This is true in spite of the fact that practically all decision making in most of these colleges is centered in one office—the presidency. And unlike what is true of rational bureaucracies, authority is not inherent in the subordinate administrative offices as such, but whatever authority a particular professor-administrant may have is likely to be delegated to him personally, and often arbitrarily, by the college president. The truth is that a little more than half of the deans (54 per cent) and only 13 per cent of the department heads feel they play an important part in the policy-making decisions of their colleges.

Practically all teachers indicated that their college president habitually makes relatively small decisions which might be made more intelligently by the professor-administrants themselves. And most agreed that this centralization of authority is largely responsible for the widespread insecurity and low morale among the teachers.

REWARDS

Professional Status

It is generally agreed that professional advancement, or promotion in rank, is of crucial importance for the morale of the teacher. And, as a rule, colleges will have some more or less definite criteria according to which the worth of the teacher is recognized and rewarded. However, this seems not to be so in most Negro colleges because the teachers disagree widely on what they regard as the best way of getting a promotion in rank and increase in salary.

Teachers in the sample mentioned several factors which seem to influence one's promotion or raise in salary in their colleges. Among the determining factors mentioned

[7] Logan Wilson, *The Academic Man* (New York: Oxford University Press, 1942), pp. 107–108.

[8] E. Franklin Frazier, *The Negro in the United States* (New York: The Macmillan Company, 1949) p. 478.

are the following: personal bargaining, "pull" with the president, goodwill of students, and community popularity. However, it is significant that relatively few of them cited proficiency in the three basic academic functions as determining the teacher's welfare. Thus only 14 per cent mentioned good teaching performance; just 8 per cent mentioned research or creative scholarship; and a mere 4 per cent believed that superior administrative ability may be the most important factor in the teacher's welfare. The truth is, the largest majority agreed that their colleges followed no consistent policy in regard to promotion and salary increases.

Analysis of the actual promotion practices in these colleges suggests that a good deal of the criticism is made by teachers who have failed to make satisfactory adjustment professionally, and their criticism may be somewhat unjust. Yet the fact that some degree of uncertainty and criticism of promotion policies was expressed by the great majority of teachers, even those who have been most successful, leads one to conclude that human relations in some Negro colleges are not as good as they might be. Furthermore, it is a fact that according to widely-established criteria for promotion and tenure, some teachers who hold lower ranks with limited or no tenure should be holding higher ranks with permanent tenure, and others who hold the highest ranks with permanent tenure do not qualify for them. In any case much of the low morale among the teachers can be traced to their feeling of insecurity regarding promotion policies. This feeling of insecurity is in turn a major cause for the high rate of faculty turnover noted earlier.

Salary

Money income, or salary, is important to the professional man, first because of what it can buy, and second, because it is a symbol of recognition or degree of professional success. Therefore the truly "successful" man, in the social sense of the term, is one who has attained both economic well-being and social recognition in some chosen occupation.

To what extent can we say that teachers in the higher education of Negroes are successful? Before attempting to answer that question in terms of salary it may be well to remember that rarely does a professor in our society receive acclaim for his work outside the narrow confines of the academic world, and even then this acclaim is likely to be restricted to those in his own field of specialization.

The professor in most Negro colleges is generally ascribed the status of an "outsider" in both the nonacademic world and in the broader academic profession; and his chances of getting recognition and acclaim for his work are even more limited than are those of the average academician. It may well be then that money income is a more independent symbol of success for teachers in Negro colleges than would be true of treachers in colleges generally.

Salary tends to vary according to sex, academic rank, training, and academic duties. The range is quite wide with 8 per cent of the teachers in the sample earning $2,500 or less annually and 10 per cent earning $6,000 a year and over. The median salary for all teachers in the sample was $3,971 in 1952. This means that teachers in Negro colleges have the lowest income of any professional group where graduate training is a prerequisite for entrance.

A comparison of the salaries of teachers in Negro colleges with those of college teachers at large (in colleges of comparable size) shows that the salaries in Negro colleges are uniformly lower, but the over-all differences are not always great or consistent. The major difference between the salaries of teachers in Negro colleges and those of college teachers generally, is the fact that a larger proportion of teachers in Negro colleges are paid the minimum salary, and only rarely does any one of these colleges have professors paid what might be described as a "top" professorial salary.[9]

9 See *American Association of University Professor's Bulletin,* **37,** No. 4, 796, 798; also *Faculty Salaries in Land Grant Colleges and State Universities,* Circular No. 358 (Federal Security Agency, Office of Education), p. 6.

SOCIAL STATUS

Teachers in Negro colleges are recruited from almost every section of the United States (a few also from abroad) and from every type of community. Although all socio-economic classes in the Negro society are represented among them, more than half of the Negro teachers, compared with approximately a third of their white colleagues, come from what might be classified as lower-class homes where the parents are "common laborers" with little or no formal education. Further, 82 per cent of the Negro teachers and 73 per cent of the white teachers in the sample have one or more gainfully employed siblings in a low status, or "common labor" occupation.

Negro Teachers as a Part of the Upper Class

As we have seen Negroes tend to place high value upon education, and as a result we would expect them to accord high status and deference to college teachers. In fact, in the view of Myrdal and other observers of the Negro social class structure, "Practically all Negro college teachers are upper class," and this is one respect in which "the American Negro world is strikingly different from the American white world."[10]

To reinforce the high status of Negro college teachers is the prestige accorded college teachers in the nation as a whole. A well-known study of education found, in American society at large, college teachers "rank seventh in a rating of prestige of 90 occupations, topped only by the United States Supreme Court Justices, physicians, state governors, members of the president's cabinet, diplomats in the U.S. Foreign Service, and mayors of large cities."[11]

As is well known, there are no Negroes in any of the six highest ranking occupations except medicine, and only relatively few even in that profession. Given these facts, if the Negro college teachers had

rated themselves according to the status hierarchy in Negro society only (on the basis of national norms) practically all of them presumably would have assigned themselves to the upper class.

The apparent reluctance of the teachers to regard themselves as upper class may, of course, be only verbal in character. There are not many generally in American society who select the term "upper class" as most appropriate for describing their social position within the class structure.[12] And so, like the vast majority of Americans, 81 per cent of the Negro teachers and 79 per cent of the white teachers selected the middle class (either upper or lower) as the most descriptive of their social status.

The most plausible, though still only suggestive, explanation of the hesitancy of Negro college teachers to describe themselves as upper class (despite the apparent readiness of Negroes generally to accord them that status), is illustrated by the telling comment of one of them: "I belong to the upper class professionally but because of my race I am considered lower class." To the extent that this is symptomatic, it would appear that the self-evaluated class position may be a resultant judgment of both "class" and "caste" factors, and that, for some Negro teachers at least, they are thinking of their position within American society at large and not simply their status in Negro society. In other words, the social class self-rating is for some Negro teachers a reflection of what they take to be prevailing attitudes toward their profession and also toward their race.

Another probable reason why such a small percentage of Negro teachers rated themselves as "upper class" is suggested by the bitter statement of one of them: "Intellectually I am upper class, but economically I am lower class." The truth is, during the period of interviews with teachers in Negro colleges the most frequently expressed complaint made by them was about

---

[10] Gunnar Myrdal, *op. cit.*, p. 694.

[11] President's Commission on Higher Education, *Higher Education for American Democracy*, Vol. IV, *op. cit.*, p. 28.

[12] See Alfred Winslow Jones, "Class Consciousness and Property," in Richard Bendix and Seymore M. Lipset (eds.), *Class, Status and Power* (Glencoe, Ill.: The Free Press, 1953), pp. 340–344.

the low salaries they received. Practically all of them pointed out that their present salary is woefully insufficient to enable them to maintain a style of life commensurate with the high social status accorded them in Negro society. Thus to the extent that the teachers regarded economic factors as basic in determining social status they world find it difficult to regard themselves as upper class.

All of this does not, of course, radically deny the validity of the observation of Myrdal and others regarding the exceptionally high position accorded college teachers by Negroes. But it does raise a question as to whether the discrepancy between Negro and white society is so marked as to justify being described as "strikingly different." For one thing, as we have seen, all college teachers are accorded high status in American society. Another is the fact that 10 per cent of the white teachers in Negro colleges as compared with 11 per cent of their Negro colleagues—a negligible difference—rated themselves as upper class.

Further (and still unavailable) data would be needed to see whether a cross-section of American Negroes would indeed assign different status values to college teaching than those assigned by white people generally. In all likelihood they would because of the difference in occupational structure of American Negro and white societies. But even in the absence of such evidence it can be said that college teachers enjoy very high status in Negro society where they have relatively little status competition from other prestigious occupational groups.

Sex Status and Occupational Dilemmas

There is another arena of status dilemmas which we want to review in its relation to professionalization. We still have fairly rigid notions in our society about what is suitable work for men and women, although these notions now seem to be in transition. The most highly professionalized occupations have been, historically, almost the exclusive province of men. Engineering, for example, has practically no women in its labor force, and medicine and law include few women in Western countries. In contrast, some of the not-so-highly professionalized occupations retain larger proportions of females in them. In fact, some occupations are commonly thought of as "female occupations"; e.g., nursing. In writing about sex role and professionalism among high school teachers Colombotos noted that

...family versus career is a problem familiar in greater or lesser degree to all working women in our society. It is commonly assumed that this conflict blocks the development of the professional orientation, thereby interfering with the professionalization of occupational roles—such as nursing, social work and teaching—filled mainly by women.*

The outline of the problem emerges: Because some occupations have been peopled largely by women the opportunity for professionalization has been retarded. Why is this so? Some have maintained that it is a matter of commitment, that woman's paramount interest in life is to find a suitable mate and produce well-adjusted children; that these are such preoccupying and time-consuming activities that women run into marked conflict when following a career outside the home. As a consequence, women are not likely to commit themselves wholeheartedly to a work career. The longstanding prejudice that "a woman's place is in the home" serves to reinforce these stereotypes.

There are no immutable relationships between sex role and occupational life. Because relatively few North American women work in highly professionalized occupations, we should not assume that this is a social universal. A majority of the physicians in the Soviet Union are women, as are many engineers. In fact, oftentimes the situation is the reverse of that in North America; in consequence, the resultant dilemma of working women is largely our own social creation. What about women in medicine—are the reasons for their scarcity in our society associated only with the conflicting interests of marriage and family and the prejudices of men? Are there any conditions inherent in the field itself that result in limited opportunities for women? These and related questions are explored in the following selection by Williams.

* John Colombotos, "Sex Role and Professionalism: A Study of High School Teachers," *The School Review*, **71**, No. 1, 1963, 27–40.

Josephine J. Williams (Medicine)

Despite the outstanding success of some individual women physicians, it cannot be said that women play a major role in American medicine today. Emigrants from Germany have been surprised to find the New World more conservative in this respect than the Old. As a matter of fact, the number of women physicians in this country actually declined a little between 1910 and 1940, both absolutely and relatively.[1] This makes us wonder whether many women have wanted to practice medicine; whether medical men have discouraged feminine competition, or whether women have somehow failed to win their patients' confidence. Before presenting some research on the role of women in medicine I want to mention two reasons for thinking that the status of women in medicine will soon change more than the stability of the trend from 1910 to 1940 might suggest. In the first place, the effective demand for medical service will doubtless increase as the health insurance movement gains

Reprinted from "The Woman Physician's Dilemma," *The Journal of Social Issues*, 6, No. 3, 1950, 38–44. Used by permission.

[1] In 1910 the 9,015 women physicians, surgeons, and osteopaths were 6.0% of the total number; in 1940 the 8,810 women were only 5.1% of all physicians, surgeons, and osteopaths. Janet M. Hooks, *Women's Occupations through Seven Decades*. U. S. Women's Bureau Bulletin 218. (Washington, D.C.: Government Printing Office, 1947), pp. 172, 173 and 209.

momentum, and the facilities for medical education will doubtless be expanded, with the result that women, among others, will have more opportunity to study medicine than they have had up to the present. In the second place, there is some evidence that the functional division of labor between medical men and women is breaking down. At one time women monopolized midwifery. Even today most surgeons are men, and women tend to specialize in selected fields, notably pediatrics and psychiatry.[2] However when younger physicians are compared with older physicians, the sex difference in field of specialization is found to be smaller in the younger group. This suggests that women are gradually being accepted as specialists in most fields of medicine. We should, however, be cautious about extrapolating this

[2] In 1941, 21% of the women full-time specialists, but only 9% of the men, were pediatricians; 15% of the women but only 6% of the men were psychiatrists and/or neurologists. These data refer to native white physicians only. They are based on an unpublished national census of physicians, undertaken just before the war by the Committee on Medical Preparedness of the American Medical Association, and made available through the courtesy of Dr. Frank G. Dickinson, Director of the Bureau of Medical Economic Research. The statistics for men, unlike those for women, are sample statistics. The sample of some 8000 male physicians (including general practitioners) is approximately equal to the total number of women. Details of this study may be found in Josephine J. Williams, *The Professional Status of Women Physicians*. (Unpublished Ph.D. dissertation, University of Chicago, 1949).

trend; for some medical women challenge the assumption that women should attempt to do everything that men do. In view of the married woman's responsibility to her family, they advise younger women to practice an office specialty with a minimum of night work, such as ophthalmology or dermatology. A new, and more realistic, division of labor between the sexes may develop in medicine, based more on the domestic responsibilities of married women than on traditional conceptions of the woman's role in medicine or theories of women's special gifts and limitations. In any case, women will probably have greater opportunity than ever before both to study medicine and to specialize in the field of their choice.

The reasons for the modest role of women in medicine are controversial. Three kinds of explanation have been offered. Those who emphasize biological or psychogenic sex differences may claim that women are inevitably at a disadvantage in the practice of medicine. Others argue that professional women who want a more or less normal family life cannot devote as much energy to their careers as many medical men do. And the feminists tend to attribute the status of women to discrimination. Most persons who write on the subject are frankly grinding an ax.[3] And even the more objective studies rarely include a control group of medical men, although facts about women physicians mean little without one. The basic difficulty is the dearth of reliable data. To assess the role of discrimination we need to know what medical men, and what various sections of the public, think of women doctors, but attitudes of this sort have never been systematically collected on a large scale. Two small studies will be reported here, bearing on the second and third factors— the marriage-career conflict and discrimination. On the question of inherent sex differences I shall merely note two pitfalls.

On the one hand, sex differences characteristic of the general population may not obtain without qualification for highly selected groups such as professional men and women. On the other, it is fruitless to argue, as feminists sometimes have done, from individual cases.

In feminist circles, it is almost treasonable to discuss the marriage-career conflict frankly, or to suggest that women on the whole are less ambitious professionally than men. One can sympathize with the feminist point of view. The fact that some women make little use of their professional training has undoubtedly served as a convenient rationalization for refusing women medical training, more particularly at the postgraduate level. Nevertheless, there is evidence that married women as a group differ more from men in their professional activity than single women do, and in this sense they have a more distinctively feminine career. For instance, when age, nativity and urban-rural distribution are controlled, married women are less likely to be in active practice than single women, and *a fortiori* than men; similarly those who do practice are less likely to be affiliated with a hospital, and also less likely to be specialists.[4] Again the comparison is with single women, and holds *a fortiori* in comparison with male physicians. The direction of these differences is consistent with the view that marriage tends to limit the woman's professional activity, but does not prove it; for discrimination could also account for the differences if it were directed primarily at married women, as it is in teaching. But the reverse is more likely to be true in medicine. At least in the private practice of pediatrics, obstetrics, gynecology and psychiatry, patients probably have more confidence in a woman if she is married.

Another reason for thinking the marriage-career conflict important is that the

---

[3] The outstanding exception is Marguerite W. Zapoleon's pamphlet, *The Outlook for Women in Occupations in the Medical Services, Women Physicians.* U. S. Women's Bureau Bulletin 203, Number 7. (Washington, D.C.: Government Printing Office, 1945).

[4] One exception to this statement should be noted: it is the young single women rather than the young married women who differ more from men in that they frequently hold salaried positions. The statements in this paragraph are based on the previously mentioned national census of physicians, and refer only to native white physicians.

married woman's dilemma indirectly influences the single women who expect to marry. They plan their careers, and postpone planning them, with the possibility of marriage in mind. A small study of women medical students provides evidence of this.[5] A majority of the single women students said that they definitely planned to marry; and that they would consider marriage even if it meant giving up their careers altogether. A large majority of these women students thought that a married woman should avoid full-time practice if it involved night calls. When asked whether they thought it important for the husband to be abler than his wife if both were physicians, almost half thought it was important. These women students had postponed the decision to study medicine longer than the male students on the average. Even though they came from families with a somewhat stronger tradition of professionalism than the men in the control group, they had received less encouragement to study medicine from their families and friends. Many of the women had had dead-end, semi-professional jobs, as laboratory technicians or nurses, before they seriously considered a medical career. The men were more likely to have made a choice between two learned professions, choosing medicine in preference to engineering or chemistry. It would be interesting to test the generality of these findings at other professional schools. The available evidence suggests that women usually hesitate longer before deciding to study medicine, and that they need stronger motivation than men— in part because they anticipate some discrimination, and in part because they know that a woman's career may be interrupted or terminated by marriage.

The expectation of marriage may also be related to the fact that a relatively large proportion of women hold salaried appoint-

ments instead of practicing privately. This difference between men and women is particularly marked in the younger group. Some women hesitate to take the risk of trying to establish a private practice until they are fairly sure they will not marry. It is also possible that women tend to lack self-confidence, and to want more preliminary experience in a salaried position than men typically do before undertaking the responsibility of private practice. The relative importance of these factors is hard to assess, but any realistic analysis of the status of professional women must recognize the potential conflict between the married woman's responsibility to her family and to her career.

There is also some truth in the theory that the public, and the medical profession, have been slow to accept women as physicians. Any woman doctor can cite cases of discrimination, whether she has personal grievances on that score or not. Incidentally, it is well to remember that some of the stories of "discrimination" that are passed around should be taken with a grain of salt. It is common observation that anyone who expects discrimination will find it, and women doctors are no exception. This can be illustrated by an anecdote. In a conversation between two senior medical students, a man and a woman, the woman complained that a certain instructor deliberately baited the women in his classes. When her classmate challenged this statement, she pointed to the instructor's attempt to embarrass her that very morning in class. The man immediately suspected that she had been late to class, and it turned out that she had. After considerable discussion, she finally conceded that her being a woman had nothing whatever to do with the incident. There is also confusion between discrimination in the non-evaluative sense, and discrimination in the usual, derogatory, sense which refers to behavior that violates generally accepted principles or values. Where values themselves are in conflict, it is sometimes hard to know whether behavior is discriminatory or not. If we do not push the analogy too far, it is probably more fruitful to conceptualize the problem of professional women in terms

[5] The study of medical students' attitudes is based on questionnaires filled out by fifty-seven women, and a control group of 114 men, at a single medical school in 1946. The conclusions are therefore tentative, and in no sense comparable with the factual statements up to this point, which were derived from a national census of physicians.

of minority group theory.[6] However, in at least three important respects, professional women differ from ethnic minorities. One difference, the married woman's status dilemma, has already been mentioned. A second is that women physicians are a greater threat, potentially at least, to established private practitioners than, say, Negro physicians. Women compete for patients of all income groups and are sometimes suspected of cutting prices, whereas the Negro physicians, in general, treat only their own people. A third difference between ethnic minorities and professional women lies in the special consideration that women expect. An extremely aggressive woman doctor gave an amusing example of this. She confessed that she had once stolen a patient from her chief because she wanted more experience operating, and concluded with the comment, "If I had been a man, he would have knocked me down." I am not for a moment suggesting that professional women often take advantage of this particular feminine prerogative, but merely that women expect and are thought to expect, some special consideration. The women students in the study referred to above, thought the men should curtail their sense of humor when women were around. And many of the men students felt obligated to do the heavy work on cadavers for the girls, and also to avoid swearing when girls were around. However, the women claimed to be willing to cope with their own cadavers, and not to mind swearing (unless it was directed *at* women). So the man may exaggerate the special consideration that women demand, unless women actually accept more than they are inclined to admit on a questionnaire. In any case, if professional women are referred to as a minority group, at least three limitations

must be recognized: women marry, they compete for the "best" clientele; and they expect some special consideration.

If these limitations are kept in mind, minority theory is useful in describing attitudes toward medical women. First we may ask what male medical students think of medical women. Students are presumably more liberal than older medical men, but almost two-thirds of the students in the sample referred to above have less confidence in women physicians than in men; and a quarter have *much* less confidence in women. Half the men think women less stable emotionally. It is perhaps surprising that only half the men, and very few of the women, think so, for the best evidence seems to be that they are.[7] Most of the men think that men make better surgeons, but only half think the sexes differ in aptitude for the various fields of medicine proper. Most of the men who think that there is any sex difference, claim that men have greater aptitude, but there are exceptions. A considerable number of men grant women more aptitude than men for pediatrics and anesthesiology. The idea that women are especially good with children needs no comment, but the tendency for men (and also women) to grant women a special gift for anesthesiology is interesting. In general, a dominant group explains the occupational status of a minority in terms of their inherent fitness for whatever work they happen to do. This is particularly true if the minority's occupational status is low. Anesthesiology has been, and still is to a large extent, a nursing specialty. As such it is a woman's job, and for a number of reasons carries little professional prestige.[8] If the status of anesthesiology relative to surgery continues to rise, we shall doubtless hear less of the theory that women are especially good at it.

Only a sixth of the male students approve

[6] Gunnar Myrdal, *An American Dilemma* (New York: Harper & Row, Publishers, 1944), II, 1173–1178.

Bernhard J. Stern, "The Status of Women," in *When Peoples Meet*, Alain Locke and Bernard J. Stern (eds.), (New York: Progressive Education Association, 1942), pp. 280–286.

Viola Klein, *The Feminine Character: History of an Ideology* (London: Kegan, Paul, Trench, Trubner & Co., Ltd., 1946), pp. 171 f.

[7] Georgene H. Seward, *Sex and the Social Order* (New York: McGraw-Hill Book Company, 1946), p. 239.

[8] Cf. Dan C. Lortie, *Doctors Without Patients: The Anesthesiologist—a New Medical Specialist.* (Unpublished M.A. thesis, University of Chicago, 1949).

of the traditional five per cent quota on women students, but a majority of them think that women applicants should be more carefully selected than men, particularly in respect to personal adjustment. Most of these male students are aware of the discrimination against women; that is, they believe that a woman has to be better than a man to get as far in medicine. They do not think that a woman should just resign herself to the discrimination, but advise her to overcome it either by outstanding work, or by personal popularity, rather than by organized effort on behalf of women. This is a typical dominant group attitude. To say that individual members of a minority should overcome discrimination by developing outstanding personal qualities, in effect condones discrimination against the average member of the group.

Although we are primarily concerned with the men's attitudes, it is interesting to compare them with the women students' answers to the same questions; for the differences conform to minority theory. The women think sex differences in aptitude less important than the men think them, and we expect a minority to stress individual rather than group differences. The women tend to accept the complimentary stereotypes about medical women, for instance, that women physicians are more considerate of patients' feelings; but it is the men who are more likely to subscribe to the derogatory stereotypes—for instance, that women claim equal rights without being willing to accept equal responsibility. Finally, women see a need for organized (but not militant) effort to combat discrimination, but the men, as we have seen, think it up to each individual woman to solve her own status problem. Thus, if these limited data are any indication of the attitudes of the next generation of medical men, women will have to expect some prejudice from their male colleagues.

We may now ask how patients feel about medical women. This question is, of course, a large one, in which social class differences are doubtless important. The data to be reported are based on interviews with a hundred women, mostly housewives living in a middle-class neighborhood of Chicago.[9] The first part of the interview was focused on attitudes toward physicians of various ethnic and religious groups, partly because acceptance of these various socially deviant types provided a standard of comparison for acceptance of women, and partly because the ostensible emphasis on racial and religious prejudices served as a red herring that distracted respondents' attention from the fact that they were expressing prejudice against professional women to an interviewer who was herself a professional woman.

Almost all the respondents assumed that there were sex differences in the quality of medical service, but they didn't agree on what the differences were. Their first choice was usually a male physician of their own faith. Respondents found it difficult to choose between a male physician of a different faith and a woman of their own faith. In general, they preferred an experienced woman to very young male physician, and to an experienced Negro male. They sympathized with a male clinic patient who refused to be treated by a woman physician, were divided on a woman patient's right to protest, but agreed that no clinic patient should insist on having a woman doctor. The characteristics most frequently attributed to women were, on the one hand, less emotional control and less strength than men; on the other, less "interest in money" and a more personal interest in the patient. Strength and emotional control were mentioned particularly in connection with surgery and only in connection with women surgeons. (Some persons who preferred women surgeons thought they had greater manual dexterity than men.) Interest in the patient was frequently mentioned in connection with doctors of both sexes. It touches an anxiety felt by many of the respondents. In explaining their reluctance to consult a woman, these patients apparently had a vague sense of the strangeness of such a relationship but no well formu-

[9] Josephine J. Williams, "Patients and Prejudice," *The American Journal of Sociology*, 1 (January 1946), 283–287.

lated rationalizations to support it comparable to the popular stereotypes about ethnic groups. A single contact with a woman physician, whether satisfactory or not, is probably more likely to lead to a generalization about women doctors than a single contact with a member of an ethnic minority which, if it conflicts with the patient's expectations, may be dismissed as "the exception that proves the rule."

Quite aside from the problem of the medical woman's status, the subject of patients' attitudes deserves the attention of research workers in connection with the actual operation of the "free choice of physician." Even intellectuals are often ignorant of their personal physician's professional qualifications, and often judge him by his personality and his popularity with laymen.

In summary, it has been pointed out that while women have played a relatively minor role in medicine up to this time, they are likely to have greater opportunity in the near future. And evidence has been presented that the marriage-career conflict is more important than some feminists admit, and that discrimination is also a factor in the situation in the sense that male medical students and patients lack confidence in medical women.

The authors of the next and final selection focus on the concept of commitment to an occupation and how it may be achieved. This time we look at what has become to be considered a "female occupation." Davis and Olesen observe that where commitment to an occupation appears to be strongest, there is a high degree of occupational professionalization, along with certain extra-occupational characteristics—"maleness" and a "middle class achievement orientation." They studied an occupation which does not involve one of these dominant auxiliary characteristics, an occupation which is in fact currently characterized by "femaleness." How is it possible then to achieve widespread occupational commitment among nurses?

Fred Davis and Virginia L. Olesen (Nursing)

An important consideration for persons electing a vocation, be it an occupation or profession, is how far they are prepared to commit themselves to it as against how far they choose to remain responsive to and preoccupied with the more mundane pleasures and pursuits of the world. Obviously no vocation in the modern world (with the possible exception of the monastic life) can afford to disregard wholly the private interests and passions of its members in the world-at-large. Conversely, there is no vocation that can tolerate so total an absorption in mundane affairs as to preclude some sustained commitment by its members to the work at hand.[1]

It is, however, well within these conceptually polarized extremes that the vast majority of adults must fashion a life balance between occupational and extraoccupational commitments. But this is never solely a matter of individual choice or fortuitous occurrence. Some fields, particularly the liberal professions, are able to draw upon and support in their recruits a fairly high, if far from all-consuming, degree of

Reprinted from "Initiation into a Women's Profession: Identity Problems in the Status Transition of Co-ed to Student Nurse," *Sociometry*, 26, No. 1 (March 1963), 89–101. Used by permission of the American Sociological Association. This paper derives from an investigation supported by a PHS research grant (G-6726) of the Division of Nursing Resources. An earlier version was read at the 56th Annual Meeting of the American Sociological Association, St. Louis, Mo., September 1961. We wish to thank our project colleagues, Anselm Strauss and Elvi Whittaker, and also Sheldon Messinger and Barney Glaser for their helpful comments and criticisms.

[1] For an extended discussion of the relevance and uses of the concept of commitment, particularly in occupational studies, see Howard S. Becker, "Notes on the Concept of Commitment," *The American Journal of Sociology,* 66 (July 1960), pp. 32–40.

personal commitment to the work of the field. By comparison, many low status occupations, like those reported on by Chinoy and Roy, can hardly expect or count on "a sense of personal dedication to the work."[2] In these fields it is generally accepted by all concerned that workers work, not through any deep attachment to the work as such, but to gain the wherewithal to support as comfortable a living standard as possible. That they are on the whole much less successful in securing extraoccupational rewards than those more deeply committed to vocation per se may be ironic. But this in no way alters the fact of their primary absorption with what lies outside of work.

Central among the arrangements in our society that appear to predispose persons to high degrees of vocational commitment are such structural and cultural attributes as maleness, a middle-class achievement orientation, and professional status. Indeed, nearly the whole membership of such fields as medicine, law, and the ministry could be characterized in these terms. The possession of these attributes not only *motivates* persons to make extensive vocational commitments. It also serves as social justification for their right to do so, while simultaneously shielding them from numerous, though certainly not all, omnipresent demands and distractions of the extraoccupational sphere.

These observations are meant to put into proper perspective the important question of what happens when the bulk of recruits to a profession lack one or more of these familiar commitment-generating attributes. Will they experience unusual cross-pressures and strains in making a career commitment to that profession? Will their socialization into the profession be attenuated through an excessive intrusion of extraoccupational interests and attachments? If so, what consequences does this have for the structuring of careers and standards of practice in that profession?

The authors have had an opportunity to weigh these questions in their fieldwork and questionnaire study of the development of professional identities among students in a collegiate school of nursing. In general, we have been concerned with the vicissitudes of the career socialization process in a profession[3] where, given the patterning of adult sex roles in society-at-large, the same degree and quality of commitment as are thought to obtain in male dominated professions cannot so readily be assumed or institutionally underwritten. More specifically, we have sought to assess the influences and effects of extraoccupational roles and identities (both extant and emergent) on the student's identification with and commitment to the occupational role for which she is ostensibly being prepared, that of graduate nurse. While our investigations have not as yet reached a point where we can provide answers to the whole range of questions raised in the previous paragraph, we have been able thus far to document the students' experience of one important phase of the career socialization process, that of initiation. This encompasses, roughly, a period of six months in which the students "live through" a transition of status from co-ed to student nurse. As we shall soon show, much of the "living through" that is activated by this status transition has to do with issues of identity deriving from the impingement of extraoccupational concerns on the student nurse role.

Adult Female Socialization

It is appropriate to begin with the commonplace observation that for girls in our

2 Eli Chinoy, *Automobile Workers and the American Dream* (New York: Random House, 1955); Donald F. Roy, " 'Banana Time': Job Satisfactions and Informal Interaction," *Human Organization,* 18 (Winter 1959–1960), 158–168.

3 We prefer not to digress here into the familiar argument over whether nursing "really is" a profession. That it is recognized as such by significant sectors of the community cannot be doubted; that others are averse to bestowing this encomium upon it must also be granted. Following Becker, we are of the view that it is difficult to differentiate the alleged objective criteria of a profession from the morally evaluative connotations of the label. In reality there always are significant, and even institutionalized, discrepancies between standards set forth publicly by spokesmen for the profession and actual practice therein. Howard S. Becker, "The Nature of a Profession," in the *Sixty-First Yearbook of the National Society for the Study of Education* (Chicago: University of Chicago Press, 1962).

society the identity equation of adulthood is more complex and less monochromatic in its constituent psycho-social elements than it is for boys—this being true in ways far more complex than that alluded to by the apocryphal Frenchman who proclaimed, "Vive la différence!" Unless willing to pay the price of a deviant adaptation to our culture's traditional status norms—and few middle-class girls seem as yet prepared to do so[4]—they must seek to balance out and effect viable combinations among such frequently conflicting roles as: companion, sexual partner, mother, orchestrator of family status symbols, and increasingly, now that better than 30 per cent of married women are engaged in paid employment,[5] as one who enjoys a possibly limited, yet satisfying, involvement in outside work.

Hence, the middle-class girl's identification with and commitment to a career choice, when she makes one, is almost of necessity more ambivalent, conflict-laden and tentative than it is for her male counterpart. Will it mean that she will become a "career woman," as this is said pejoratively? Or, if she marries, will a too deep involvement in a career cause her to chafe under conjugal and familial obligations? Will she then become a "discontented housewife" who, by her discontent, causes her husband and children to feel discontented too?

These are but a few of the identity stresses that affect the young college girl who, even if only tentatively and with much hedging of bets, has chosen a field of work which asks of her a degree of commitment that is something more than partial, easily alterable, and only incidental to her self-concept. Young women in many different fields and with many different vocational interests face essentially this dilemma. There are, however, relatively few career locales in our society where they experience it as a collectivity. One is in schools of social work; another, in schools of nursing.

The former, though, recruit girls who are several years older, most of whom have moved further toward resolving the manifold issues of career and marriage. Moreover, schools of social work have in recent decades attracted an increasing proportion of men at both student and faculty levels, a development which has served to dilute appreciably the "special world-set-apart" ambience of these establishment. No similar development has taken place to any significant extent in schools of nursing. For these reasons, we believe that the identity stresses attendant to the transition from a generalized, rather diffuse, college girl status to that of an occupational neophyte are enacted more graphically in schools of nursing than in schools of social work.

We now turn to a description of the various facets of the status transition: the persons involved, the institutional setting in which it occurred, its social structural framework, and the identity stresses generated by it.

INSTITUTIONAL SETTING AND BACKGROUNDS OF THE STUDENTS

The school itself is located on the grounds of a large metropolitan medical center. The group of some fifty beginning nursing students who are the subject of this report can, by and large, be characterized as: native born, in their late teens and early twenties, of middle and upper-middle socio-economic origins, affiliated predominantly with the major Protestant denominations, and reared in large and medium-sized cities. (These background characteristics, it should be noted, differ markedly from those which still characterize most recruits to non-collegiate hospital schools of nursing, namely, working and lower-middle class, rural and small-town, girls, including many with Fundamentalist-type church affiliations.) All of them had at least two years of liberal arts studies before entering the school of nursing, the majority of them at a university noted for its high academic standards. As a group, their mean grade point average while at college was at least the equal of former classmates who continued in the liberal arts curriculum.

[4] Cf. Rose K. Goldsen, *et al., What College Students Think* (Princeton: D. Van Nostrand Co., Inc., 1960), pp. 46–59.

[5] Women's Bureau, U. S. Department of Labor, *Handbook on Women Workers* (Washington, D.C.: Government Printing Office, 1960).
its constituent psycho-social elements than

From these data we infer that, except possibly for the small number among them whose backgrounds correspond more nearly to that of the traditional recruit to nursing, these girls were not drawn to the field primarily for reasons of social mobility or in response to a sense of religious calling. For example, in response to an item on a questionnaire administered to the class of forty-nine upon their entry into the school, as few as eleven (22%) checked "religious calling and inspiration" as fitting in with their picture of nursing. Rather, the problem for them seems to be more one of reconciling nursing values and demands with an already well-incorporated imagery of middle-class life styles, particularly as the confrontation of the two impinges on their projected concept of the adult female role. This inference is supported by the students' responses to another item on the same questionnaire. Asked to rank four versions of the female role (home and family, work and career, glamor, and community service) according to the relative emphasis they would give each if they could ideally arrange their adult lives, the large majority, forty-two (86%), ranked "home and family" in first place. Only six (12%) accorded first rank to "work and career." While most (thirty, or 61%) assigned "work and career" to the second rank, as many as thirteen (26%) relegated it to either the third or fourth rank.

FRAMEWORK OF THE STATUS TRANSITION

Comparing the college campuses from which these students came to the medical center setting in which their nursing education takes place, we find: a transition from a relatively diffuse and open collegiate youth culture to one much more narrowly age-graded and sexually segregated; a transition from a milieu in which the occupational identities of fellow students are still largely unformed, or at best highly tentative and experimental, to one in which shared activities, round-of-life and student status are articulated almost wholly in terms of membership in a distinct occupational category; a transition from a setting characterized by a diverse multiplicity and overlap of student ties, interests and associations, to one in which there is a single and overruling tie. The tie is that of being a class of occupational novices together, subjected at the same point in time and in near identical sequence to a common set of experiences, pressures, and choices.

In structural terms, this transition can be characterized as one from a kind of pluralistic, heterogenous, society of undergraduates to a guild-like association of colleague apprentices.

IDENTITY STRESSES

The major stresses experienced by the novice during this transition derive from the difficulties in integrating psychologically the identities attendant to her student nurse role with her concurrently emerging identity as an adult female. Typically, this is marked by much inner conflict, highly ambivalent feelings regarding her adequacy, and a certain early disenchantment with her career choice. This can be inferred from much of what we observed and were told by the students during their first months at the school.

For example, though by no means academically disinterested, many of the girls had anticipated that at the medical center they would also enjoy a unique opportunity to meet medical students and other young men training for the health professions. They expected the atmosphere there to differ little from the relatively casual one they had known on their college campuses, save that they would now have entrée to a more select subsample of male eligibles. Almost immediately upon arrival though, they become aware of the cordoned-off, proto-professional orbits in which their male counterparts, much like themselves, exist. Not only do they have nothing to do with medical students in class or in the wards, but they soon realize that in the cafeteria and student lounge as well, associational boundaries are drawn along occupational rather than sociable, heterosexual lines.

To the extent that the student nurse is noticed at all by medical or dental students, the approach of these males is, from her standpoint, fashioned disconcertingly by their "categorization" of her as a nurse, rather than as someone young, pretty, college-educated, intelligent, makable—or whatever might ordinarily attract a boy to a girl. Even when such qualities are appreciated, it is usually against the backdrop of the prior and controlling imagery of "the nurse," as one might, for example, find himself bemused by a *worldly* clergyman or *spendthrift* French peasant. It would take us too far afield to go into the habits of occupational stereotyping that are endemic to such establishments and that re-enforce the boundaries separating the professional groups. Suffice it to say, the beginning student nurse is neither accustomed nor prepared to have her person subsumed under an occupational classification by the young man, especially when his social background is in most instances so similar to her own.

A second source of identity stress for many of the students is the sharp break in developmental continuity represented by immersion in an all-female milieu. Although no longer encumbered by the cloister-like restrictions of the traditional nursing school, and although free to pursue an independent life away from school in off hours, these students, nevertheless, live, work, and study in the constant presence of other women for the better part of every week. In their daily comings-and-goings, therefore, they are constrained situationally to select from life's cumulative repertory of interactive roles those which put a premium on getting on with women. They must relate to a girlish group and modulate their affect in the muted and circuitous styles deemed appropriate for well brought-up, middle-class, girls: viz., to eschew any aggressive posture and always display sensitivity to the other's finest shades of feeling.

While congenial to some, to many this situation is redolent of an earlier maturational stage, that of latency. For these students, the immersion in a seemingly all-pervasive female milieu signifies a kind of regression to this earlier stage of female identity, when boys seemed either enemies or nonentities, never friends. Many complain of the apparent revivification of this state of affairs and give evidence of what is probably only a temporary loss of such poise and assurance in the company of boys as had been acquired so painstakingly by them since early adolescence.

As a corollary to this, we noted within the student group the formation of a considerable number of intensive and interactionally exclusive friendship-pair relationships, a phenomenon analogous to the "chumming" tendencies of advanced latency and early adolescence.[6] Were it not for unfortunate connotations, we would term such relationships "pseudo marriages," since the emotional access which partners grant *each other* is grossly disproportionate to that which they grant other members of the student group. Thus, we have seen the same mutual monopolization, the same outbursts of jealousy at the intrusion of student third parties, the same tortured difficulty in attenuating or breaking off the tie as is evidenced—albeit in different ways—in both the earlier chum relationship and the later conjugal one. But in much the same fashion as the chum relationship seeks to safeguard the juvenile's identity from the approaching traumas of adolescence, we interpret these latter-day pair relationships as a reactive adaptation to the identity stresses occasioned by transfer to the nursing school milieu. Both students and faculty demonstrate an implicit appreciation of this, judging by the concern they show for the student who is "a loner." The absence of a chum, a friendly shoulder to cry on, someone to whom felt inadequacies can be revealed, is seen as undermining of emotional balance in a situation regarded as inherently stressful.

Finally, a third source of identity stress derives from the direct and immediate impact of nursing per se on the student. Unlike the medical or law student who undergoes an extended period of training before being granted access to patients or clients, the student nurse is from the start assigned to and must assume a certain

---

[6] Harry S. Sullivan, *The Interpersonal Theory of Psychiatry* (New York: W. W. Norton & Company, Inc., 1953), pp. 245–262.

measure of responsibility for the care of hospital patients, nearly all of whom are seriously ill, many of them critically so. She is forthwith exposed to a variety of distressing sights, sounds, and smells such as few of her agemates on college campuses or in the world-at-large will ever be called upon to witness, much less to deal with in a skilled and responsible fashion. Much as she may have rehearsed these exigencies in her mind before coming to nursing, their actual occurrence almost inevitably poses a severe test for the ego. And the grappling with it tends to disturb dramatically the carefully-nurtured scheme of talents, interests and involvements that, in popular thought, comprise the middle-class woman's life style.

In short, the workaday world of the student nurse is far removed from that of the finishing school; and to the degree that the undergraduate college also allows students, perhaps necessarily and wisely, to be spared this kind of adult engagement, it is removed significantly from that world as well. This facet of the student's initiation into nursing is experienced as threatening to that complex of gentility, sheltered dependence, and worldly incapacity which still forms so large a part of the concept of femininity in our society. Understandably, many of the students find it difficult to relinquish or revise radically this component image of themselves. Indeed, one of the first complaints we heard from them was that of "not feeling feminine enough around this place."

Manifestations and Adjustments

Manifestations of identity stress, in addition to those already noted in passing, could be observed at different levels and in different contexts of student behavior. Most obvious were the frequent protestations of inadequacy indulged in by them with each other and with members of the research team. It was not uncommon for this to be carried to obsessive, self-flagellating, lengths, as when students would "confess" that they were unworthy of nursing and devoid of either the talent or character ever to master the role. Beyond its immediate cathartic value, such protestations also served an important integrative function for the

group. Students who in the privacy of their own thoughts feared that their reactions were excessive or abnormal were reassured to learn that others reacted in the same way too.

Closely akin to such reactions were the ruminations of several more articulate students to the effect that they could hardly recognize themselves in the new setting; that their historic sense of personae had come somehow to seem remote and illusive. As might be expected, this genre of self-scrutiny was frequently mingled with an exquisite nostalgia for "the life so late we led" on now idealized college campuses.[7] The latter sentiment, however, could and did receive more than abstract embodiment from the students. According to our records of their leisure time activities, during these first months there would occur every weekend, and frequently in mid-week as well, a mass exodus from their residences at the medical center. Most students repaired to former campuses, although a sizable number chose instead the homes of parents or friends as places of refuge. Needless to say, the incidence of weekend flight diminished considerably by their second semester at the school.

Within the class as a whole, we charted the building-up and eventual dissipation of what can be described most simply as a group depression. Evidencing its first signs some six to eight weeks after their arrival at the school and lasting until their return from Christmas vacation,[8] this phenomenon

[7] Similar reactions have been noted for such transitional states as civilian disaster, migration, and industrial retirement. See James S. Tyhurst, "The Role of Transition States—including Disasters—in Mental Illness," in Walter Reed Army Institute of Research, *Symposium on Preventive and Social Psychiatry, 15–17 April 1957* (Washington, D.C.: U. S. Government Printing Office, 1958), pp. 149–167.

[8] That the calendar, too, is a social creation which generates and gives meaning to a myriad of social purposes, is an insight of extensive lineage in sociology, appearing most notably in the writings of such men as Hubert, Mauss, and Durkheim. See Emile Durkheim, *The Elementary Forms of the Religious Life* (Glencoe, Ill.: Free Press, 1947), pp. 10–11, 439–447; and more recently, W. Lloyd Warner, *The Family of God* (New Haven: Yale University Press, 1961), pp.

had all the earmarks of collective unrest, as might under more general conditions mark the initial stages of a social movement.[9] Once it became apparent to the class that six or seven of their number were extremely unhappy and discontented with their situation, the students began to communicate intensively among themselves. They openly questioned their choice of nursing and at least fifteen proclaimed an intention to resign from the school, although in the end a scant few did so. Feeding, doubtlessly, on the conspicuous dissatisfaction of the few who triggered off the depression, the mood proved highly contagious and soon engulfed many of those who at first felt only passive discontent. The favored, most frequent, and consuming topic of discussion became the day-to-day progress of the depression itself; i.e., "who's down in the dumps today?" and "who's getting ready to pack her bags?" In this way, the depression and its labeling as such by the students emerged as a primary focus of group concern. Later, it also served as the event around which the class acquired a certain distinctive group identity.

Whereas it cannot be said that a group depression is the inevitable by-product of the aggregate experience of stress induced

by the status transition,[10] two additional aspects of this collective phenomenon deserve comment. The first is how closely the reactions of the students (e.g., the sense of discontinuity with a former identity, the mourning for a lost self, the pained anticipation of what the future held in store) parallel those feeling states, symbolic representations, and ceremonial sequences that are formally ritualized in sacred rites of initiation throughout the world.[11] We can speculate, therefore, that such rites attest to something more than a purely conventionalized status passage; that much of their content derives, builds upon, and channels the primary emotional reactions evoked by important status passages. (It is only when this kind of subjective experience eludes a significant number of participants that rites

---

10 Interestingly, no similar *collective* preoccupation manifested itself in the class that succeeded the one that is the subject of this report, despite the fact that a number of individuals in the new class evidenced as much discontent and disillusionment as had members of the subject class. As well as we can determine, the chief reason for the failure of such reactions to become a matter for collective focus again is that, upon their arrival at the school, members of the new class were forewarned extravagantly by their predecessors that they would become "depressed and unhappy" with nursing and would want to "pack their bags and forget all about it." It appears that such forewarning functioned as a *self-negating* prophecy. Because of the knowing manner in which the prophecy was made, the new class felt compelled to show faculty, themselves, the sociologists (us), and—most of all—their predecessors that their adjustment would be more salutary than that of the preceding class, who, by this time, had become identified widely as "the depressed bunch" and "the ones who got all shook-up." This raises in passing the interesting question, untreated by Merton in his well known essay, of the different sets of conditions (structural, interactional and psychological) under which behavioral prophecies prove either self-fulfilling, self-negating or merely indeterminate. Robert K. Merton, *Social Theory and Social Structure* (Glencoe, Ill.: Free Press, 1957), pp. 421–436.

11 Arnold van Gennep, *The Rites of Passage* (Chicago: University of Chicago Press, 1960); Audrey I. Richards, *Chisungu, A Girls Initiation Ceremony among the Bemba of Northern Rhodesia* (London: Faber and Faber, 1956); Elliot D. Chapple and Carleton S. Coon, *Principles of Anthropology* (New York: Holt, Rinehart & Winston, Inc., 1942), Chaps. 19–23.

381–407. In the present case, while it is likely that the group depression would have given way of its own burdensome emotional weight in time, the part played by Christmas vacation in dispelling it is manifold. First is the simple fact of the dispersal of the students, thereby reducing the chances for ongoing mood contagion. Second, being a season which chronologically and symbolically brings to a close one unit of social time and inaugurates the next, the period was a "natural" one for stock-taking and the engineering of fresh resolve. Upon their return, many of the students told us that they had in the interim "thought things through" and had resolved "to make the best of it, and not let it get me down the way it has." Third, this was for many their first protracted encounter with "the outside" since their change of status. Whatever incipient, still very shaky, identity they had acquired as nurses was buttressed by family and hometown friends who, much to the students' surprise, now approached them as specially knowledgeable and wise in matters related to health.

9 Herbert Blumer, "Collective Behavior," in Alfred M. Lee, (ed.), *New Outline of the Principles of Sociology* (New York: Barnes and Noble, Inc., 1946), pp. 170–177.

become empty and cease being rites in a significant sense.) Second, because of the absence of appropriately timed rites of initiation, or their equivalent, in the nursing school setting,[12] the students reacted in a more random and confused way than do initiates in a formal rite. Unable to relate their anxiety ceremonially to an institutional framework outside of themselves, the students may have found the anxiety all the more difficult to bear.[13]

This is not to say that compensatory and psychologically restitutive outlets were few or non-existent for the students. Besides those already mentioned (e.g., the chum relationships, the public protestations of inadequacy, the weekend flights) a variety of more commonplace adjustments appeared during this period. Among them were the classic student response of frequent and vociferous griping and the resort to humor and caricature to afford the students a somewhat more balanced, less impassioned view of their situation.

Griping served the dual purpose of letting off steam and of furthering group solidarity by spawning an image of an ubiquitous "they" (faculty) opposed to "we" (students). As for humor, two costume themes dominated a Halloween Party which the students gave some six weeks after their arrival. One caricatured the nurse, as in the case of the student in disheveled uniform who lumbered about with a coarse rope tied to an empty coke bottle, meant to signify a Foley catheter. The other caricatured the 'femme fatale,' many girls appearing in sheer nightgowns or other décolletage set in absurd juxtaposition to such conspicuously desexualized apparel as baggy mumus, old lady bonnets, and oversized oxfords. Thus were the career and glamor versions of womanhood satirized. It is noteworthy that none of the

students saw fit to guy the other readily available model of the woman's role, that of spouse-housewife-mother.

CONCLUSION

In this paper we have described certain of the identity stresses experienced by a group of young initiates in a woman's profession, that of nursing. In particular, we have tried to indicate the important degree to which such stresses are derived, articulated, and coped with in terms of an identity equation (i.e., a projected concept of the adult female role) which transcends and, in numerous respects, conflicts with the specific occupational identities for which the students are being prepared. That in some significant sense the students "adjust" to these stresses is self-evident; the vast majority of them do go on to complete their training and acquire licenses to practice as registered nurses. But whether such institutionally circumscribed adjustments alter fundamentally the balance of their life commitments to nursing, as against other womanly pursuits, is much more problematic. Indeed, one of the most vexing problems in the field of nursing is that of retaining the services of very large numbers of its graduates for a significant portion of their adult lives.

There remains the question of whether student novices in other professions experience similar identity stresses in attempting to reconcile the role demands of the field with their extraoccupational interests and identities. Although the main drift of our analysis has been to suggest that this kind of identity stress is somewhat unique to nursing by virtue of its being a women's profession, it would be premature to conclude that analogous phenomena are not to be found in other professional fields as well.

Quite possibly, because most studies of occupational socialization have dealt thus far with such prestigious, male dominated, professions as medicine and law, there has been a natural tendency to overlook the extraoccupational facets of *adult* socialization that aspirants are exposed to while simultaneously being socialized into a profession. Implicitly, a congruence is assumed

12 The one exception to this statement is a highly vestigial, quasi-religious, capping ceremony held by and for the students themselves within mere days of their arrival at the school. This ceremony, moreover, is frowned upon privately by faculty and receives no official sanction from the school.

13 Everett C. Hughes, *Men and their Work* (Glencoe, Ill.: Free Press, 1958), pp. 14–15.

between the person's emerging occupational role and the other life roles for which he is being prepared. This has led to an unwitting depiction of career socialization as a uni-dimensional, institutionally self-contained process in which the progress, travail, and rewards of the aspirant are analyzed wholly within the context of the occupational role per se.[14]

Convenient as the assumption of identity

14 Two recent studies from this point of view are Robert K. Merton, George G. Reader, and Patricia L. Kendall (eds.), *The Student Physician* (Cambridge: Harvard University Press, 1957); and Howard S. Becker *et al., Boys in White* (Chicago: University of Chicago Press, 1961). The latter does employ a concept of "latent identity" in its analysis of student culture, which in a limited way addresses itself to the question of extraoccupational impingements on the socialization process.

congruence may be for socialization studies in a field such as medicine, the value of our own findings lies in indicating how problematic such an assumption can be for other fields, and in the implications this has for the investigation of career commitments. For example, taking into account a phenomenon like the large numbers of engineering and law school graduates who never practice their respective vocations, one has reason to suspect that extraoccupational impingements have a considerable bearing on socialization in even these male-dominated professions. Irrespective of the line of work, however, it is important to assess the interplay of occupational and extraoccupational identities in career socialization, and not to assume either a congruence among them or a propensity by human actors to keep them neatly distinct and separate.

Questions for Discussion and Further Research

Oswald Hall illustrates that what goes on in the day-to-day activities of an occupation and the general direction it takes over time may be profoundly influenced by the values and status characteristics occupational incumbents bring to it. He is, of course, referring to how extra-work values, such as ethnicity and religion, help shape an occupation. But do only the most professionalized occupations possess an "inner fraternity," an elite group which dominates the profession and is largely responsible for the sponsorship process in launching careers of newcomers to the occupation, or is such sponsorship to be found in other areas of work? On the surface it would seem that there are instances of less professionalized occupations where essentially irrelevant status factors affect the occupation, but perhaps this is indeed most typical in the highly professionalized occupations. Why is this so?

Daniel Thompson's article on career patterns of teachers in Negro colleges indicates how the reward system associated with a highly professionalized occupation may be affected by ethnic status. He also notes the way in which professional duties, including teaching and research administration, may differ in emphasis. This suggests that the variations associated with ethnic status do not develop entirely as a consequence of attitudes of the larger society, but also reflect differences in values within the ethnic group itself. This may in part be a response to the attitudes of the larger society, and in part reflect unique cultural heritages stemming from within. A question arising from these observations has to do with the frequent social visibility of the Negro: Over time has such visibility continued to preclude membership in highly professionalized occupations, or is the pattern gradually changing? If the latter is true, what are some of the effects on productivity and worker satisfaction for all persons in these occupations?

In her discussion of the female medical physician, Josephine Williams records difficulties associated with a woman's undertaking a medical career. Patriarchal notions of an earlier day still persist in the world of work, and are particularly notable in some of the more highly professionalized occupations. We need to gather systematic information on the extent to which occupations commonly recognized as predominantly for women are permanently relegated to lower or intermediate levels of professionalization. For example, there are some instances of male nurses; but nursing has been so overwhelmingly unpopular with males that they may well adopt a different occupational title with a corresponding culture that distinguishes between the kinds of work tasks performed by men and women within the nursing profession. Some social scientists argue that only limited professionalization can occur in such occupations until our general social attitudes on the equality of work opportunity change markedly.

If, as Davis and Olesen maintain, commitment to a highly professionalized occupation is associated with certain characteristics which one brings to the job, namely "maleness" and middle-class achievement orientation, it seems evident that in the so-called female occupations there is only a limited amount that the female can do about the first of these extraoccupational characteristics. The other characteristic, an appropriate value orientation, is something capable of modification. It would be of interest to determine why it is that middle-class achievement orientation has been largely associated with men in Western society; there would seem to be no biological necessity for such an attitudinal monopoly.

In addition, the fact that North American society places great importance on the housewife-mother status configuration prompts another question: Is it inevitable that the female suffer identity stresses if she goes to work outside the home, whether in highly or in less highly professionalized occupations? And if, as seems to be the case, some occupations are less stressful for females, what is there about them that is less stress engendering? For example, where a display of supportive feelings is required in an occupational role, will less stress be experienced by a working woman?

Such questions bring us full-circle in our analysis of professionalization in a matrix of interacting social processes. The directions professionalization takes cannot be understood without such an analysis employing the particulars of time and place. At the same time we must not allow a preoccupation with details to prevent us from being sensitive and alert to discovering new processes of change in the world of work, which may be only dimly visible at present. Thus our thoughts return to a question raised earlier: beyond professionalization, what?

INDEX